Pauline Bonaparte

ALSO BY FLORA FRASER

Princesses

Beloved Emma

The Unruly Queen

Pauline Bonaparte

VENUS OF EMPIRE

Flora Fraser

ALFRED A. KNOPF   NEW YORK   2009

THIS IS A BORZOI BOOK
PUBLISHED BY ALFRED A. KNOPF

Copyright © 2009 by Flora Fraser
All rights reserved. Published in the United States by Alfred A. Knopf,
a division of Random House, Inc., New York.
www.aaknopf.com

Knopf, Borzoi Books, and the colophon are registered trademarks of
Random House, Inc.

Library of Congress Cataloging-in-Publication Data

Fraser, Flora.
Pauline Bonaparte : Venus of Empire / by Flora Fraser.
p. cm.
Includes bibliographical references and index.
ISBN 978-0-307-26544-9
1. Bonaparte, Paolina, 1780–1825.   2. Napoleon I, Emperor of the French,
1769–1821—Family.   3. Princesses—France—Biography.   I. Title.

DC216.87.F73 2009
944.05092—dc22
[B]   2008028639

Manufactured in the United States of America
First Edition

CONTENTS

FAMILY OF PAULINE BONAPARTE,
PRINCESS BORGHESE

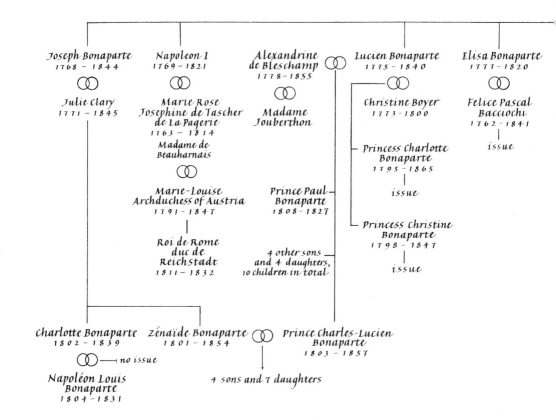

Joseph Bonaparte
1768 – 1844

Julie Clary
1771 – 1845

Napoleon I
1769 – 1821

Marie Rose
Josephine de Tascher
de La Pagerie
1763 – 1814
Madame de
Beauharnais

Marie-Louise
Archduchess of Austria
1791 – 1847

Roi de Rome
duc de
Reichstadt
1811 – 1832

Alexandrine
de Bleschamp
1778 – 1855

Madame
Jouberthon

Prince Paul
Bonaparte
1808 – 1827

4 other sons
and 4 daughters,
10 children in total

Lucien Bonaparte
1775 – 1840

Christine Boyer
1773 – 1800

Princess Charlotte
Bonaparte
1795 – 1865

issue

Princess Christine
Bonaparte
1798 – 1847

issue

Elisa Bonaparte
1777 – 1820

Felice Pascal
Bacciochi
1762 – 1841

issue

Charlotte Bonaparte
1802 – 1839

no issue

Napoléon Louis
Bonaparte
1804 – 1831

Zénaïde Bonaparte
1801 – 1854

4 sons and 7 daughters

Prince Charles-Lucien
Bonaparte
1803 – 1857

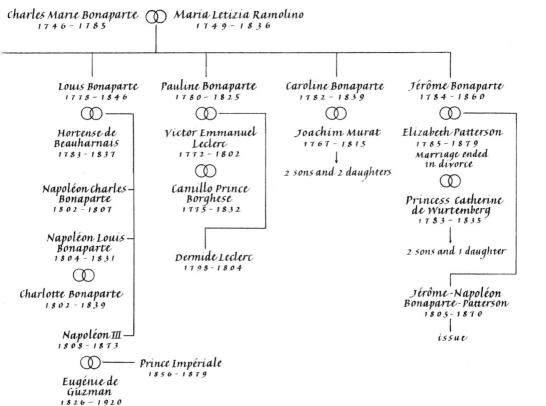

Charles Marie Bonaparte
1746 - 1785
⊕ Maria Letizia Ramolino
1749 - 1836

Louis Bonaparte
1773 - 1846
⊕
Hortense de
Beauharnais
1783 - 1837

Napoléon Charles
Bonaparte
1802 - 1807

Napoléon Louis
Bonaparte
1804 - 1831
⊕
Charlotte Bonaparte
1802 - 1839

Napoléon III
1808 - 1873
⊕ ——— Prince Impériale
1856 - 1879
Eugénie de
Guzman
1826 - 1920

Pauline Bonaparte
1780 - 1825
⊕
Victor Emmanuel
Leclerc
1772 - 1802
⊕
Camillo Prince
Borghese
1775 - 1832

Dermide Leclerc
1798 - 1804

Caroline Bonaparte
1782 - 1839
⊕
Joachim Murat
1767 - 1815
↓
2 sons and 2 daughters

Jérôme Bonaparte
1784 - 1860
⊕
Elizabeth Patterson
1785 - 1879
Marriage ended
in divorce
⊕
Princess Catherine
de Wurtemberg
1783 - 1835
↓
2 sons and 1 daughter

Jérôme-Napoléon
Bonaparte-Patterson
1805 - 1870
↓
issue

ONE EVENING after dark in Rome some time ago I was walking with my husband between the via del Corso and the
Tiber, and we stopped in a little piazza to let a car enter
through the gateway of a massive palazzo. We saw, briefly illuminated
within, a double courtyard with godlike statues surmounting the interior colonnade. Then the palace gates swung shut again, and we were
left in darkness.

The building, I discovered from my map under the light of a street-
lamp, was the Palazzo Borghese. So it was here, I thought, that
Napoleon's outrageous sister Pauline Bonaparte had lived when she was
married to Prince Camillo Borghese, here that she was immortalized by
Antonio Canova in *La Paolina,* the near-naked, near-life-size marble
statue that is now on public view in the Villa (or Museo e Galleria)
Borghese, in the gardens of that name up above the Piazza del Popolo.

Two distinct memories came into my mind as I contemplated the
palazzo's identity. First I remembered standing some years before in
front of a portrait of Pauline Borghese at Apsley House in London. I
was with a friend, Sabina Zanardi Landi, whose mother was a Borghese. And, as we gazed at Pauline's seraphic smile and at her diaphanous
dress exposing rosy nipples, Sabina said, "You know, nobody speaks of
her in my family. But you can see all her letters if you want. They're in
the Vatican." The conjunction of scarlet woman, correspondence, and
cardinals was immediately appealing, but I was busy writing another
scarlet woman's life, that of Emma, Lady Hamilton, and we turned
away from the picture.

And the second memory? While staying with Belgian friends on
Corsica, in the course of writing about George IV's wife, Queen Caro-

line, I visited the Maison Bonaparte, a tenement house in Ajaccio where Pauline and her brother Napoleon, as well as their six other siblings, were born and raised. No double courtyard there. Just a dowdy, flat-fronted house in a side street running down to a small dark church that bears the name "cathedral."

As we walked on that night in Rome, I reflected on Pauline's beauty in her portrait and in her statue, on that tenement house, on the chain of circumstances—insofar as I knew them—that had brought Pauline Bonaparte to the Palazzo Borghese, this acme of wealth and grandeur. And I thought about her unsavory reputation within the family into which she had married—and outside it. I told my husband that I would write about Pauline after completing the book I was then working on, about the six daughters of George III. He nodded, not especially impressed. Biographers have a habit of making such pronouncements.

Time passed. I forgot my declaration and concentrated on writing *Princesses*. When I finished I was resolved to write about a man, and a man with a public career. I went to the British Library and looked through the papers of various worthy candidates. And then one evening on impulse I rang Bob Gottlieb in New York, my editor at Knopf and good friend all my working life. "Can I pitch you an idea?" I said, for some reason using the language of the Hollywood of yesteryear. Bob, it turned out, was about to head off to the ballet, but, responding as a mogul might, he said he could give me three minutes. "Oh well, I'll ring when you've more time," I said, reverting to shy and retiring English type. "No, pitch it," he replied. And I said that I wanted to write the life of Pauline Bonaparte, Napoleon's favorite sister, a legend both for her lovers and for her loyalty to her brother—not least after his exile, first to Elba and then, following Waterloo, to Saint Helena. "Done," came the answer. "And that leaves two minutes to chat. How's your mother doing?"

So I began, in late 2004, and I was immediately engrossed by the background to Pauline's story. For, as Stendhal has shown, the Napoleonic Wars, from the point of view of French historical characters, are quite as colorful and varied in pace as they are when viewed by the British—for instance, in *Vanity Fair*—or when surveyed from the Russian perspective, as in *War and Peace*. In the case of Pauline, she was sometimes at the side of, sometimes a thorn in the side of, but always dearly beloved by the central character of this dramatic period, her brother Napoleon.

She was with him in Milan following his victories with the Army of Italy at Lodi and Rivoli. With her first husband, General Leclerc, she lived modestly in Consular Paris, and visited Napoleon and Josephine at Malmaison. Under the Empire, following her marriage to Prince Borghese, she inhabited the sumptuous Hôtel Charost, which Wellington later bought when he was British ambassador to France, and which is still today the British Embassy in Paris. She lived with Napoleon on Elba and begged to be allowed to go and join him on Saint Helena. Researching Pauline's life, I was examining the reverse of the coin in which I had till now dealt, tracing the lives of eighteenth-century women based in England.

When I wrote about Emma Hamilton, I came across a letter from her lover, Admiral Lord Nelson, in which he holds out to her "the protecting shield of a British admiral." And George IV's wife, Queen Caroline, whom I wrote about next, felt an intense pride in the war record of her father, the soldier Duke of Brunswick. "I am the daughter of a hero," she said, "and married to a zero." To be fair, the six sisters of George IV, whose lives I next considered, were very far from thinking their brother a zero. With some reason they hero-worshiped him and saw him as their protector. But in all cases these women had been menaced ultimately by the same aggressor—the Corsican-born emperor of the French, Napoleon Bonaparte.

Although, in these previous books, I write little directly of the Napoleonic Wars, that prolonged European conflict is always there in the background, as are the suspense and danger and inconveniences that were part and parcel of it. The vagaries of war, furthermore, account quite as much as those of character or of any succession for the course of Emma's, or of Queen Caroline's, or of the princesses' lives. Two of their protectors—Nelson and the Duke of Brunswick—died fighting Napoleon's forces. The other, George IV, triumphed when the

Duke of Wellington's army defeated the French emperor at Waterloo. Napoleon Bonaparte lurks like a dragon to be slain in the shadows of each narrative. But in *Pauline Bonaparte: Venus of Empire* he shares center stage with his sister and is both protector and, arguably, destroyer of his sister's welfare, as well as that of France.

I hope that readers will enjoy this account of the twists and turns in Pauline's career, which reflect her brother's rise and fall from grace. As his power grew, black and white lovers, lesbian affairs, nymphomania, gonorrhea, and even accusations of an incestuous relationship with Napoleon himself featured in the stories that gathered around her. Some were true, some not, but they lost nothing in the telling—by the enemy British press and, later, by the French government itself, after the restoration of Louis XVIII.

Pauline was indifferent when made the subject of scandal. She took lovers without regard for her brother, who wished his court to appear moral, at least, or for the feelings of her second husband, Prince Camillo Borghese. And while she cherished her reputation as the most beautiful woman in Europe, setting and resetting jewels, lavishing hours on her wardrobe, she was also matter-of-fact, speaking of her face and figure, which were commonly likened to those of the Venus de Medici, as "advantages of nature." In fact, whether Pauline was in Rome, where she was regarded as *nonconformista* when she behaved as she liked, or in Paris, where she was more often called *séduisante,* or seductive, she was always practical and as direct, in her way, as her brother. As a result her observations on imperial life are often pithy and frequently witty, none more so than her response to the lady who asked if she had not feared to pose, so lightly veiled, for Canova. Once heard, Pauline's answer, which I give later in the book, is never to be forgotten and only adds to the pleasure I take in making a pilgrimage to the statue whenever I am in Rome.

THERE HAVE BEEN many other pilgrimages to undertake in the course of researching *Pauline Bonaparte,* all of them enjoyable and many of them accomplished owing to the kind offices of family and friends old and new. I wish to thank my uncle Michael Pakenham for introducing me to some of his many Parisian friends, including Ben Newick at the British Embassy. Marie-Eugénie de Portalès shared Bonaparte family lore with me during a most enjoyable stay in Corsica and subsequently in Paris. Penny Holmes, while British ambassadress to France, was a wonderful hostess, and knowledgeable guide to the embassy residence, formerly Pauline's home, in the rue du Faubourg Saint-Honoré. In addition, the Marquis d'Albufera kindly gave me a tour of the Château de Montgobert, which Pauline and her first husband, General Leclerc, owned. To my sister Natasha Fraser-Cavassoni, to Rana Kabbani and Patrick Seale, to Janine di Giovanni, and to Laure de Gramont I am, besides, infinitely grateful for their encouragement and good company.

In Rome, Scipione Borghese and Barbara Massimo made me most welcome at the Palazzo Borghese. Prince Borghese also arranged a very moving visit to the Borghese vault in the Basilica of Santa Maria Maggiore, where Pauline is buried with many of his ancestors. The late Giulia Cornaggia, in addition, was fascinating on the subjects of her Borghese forebears, while Giovanni Aldobrandini has also kindly shared with me information about the family. 1 wish to thank Pierre Morel, who, as French ambassador to the Holy See, showed me the delightful Villa Bonaparte by the Porta Pia—once, as the Villa Paolina, a residence of Pauline's. I am also grateful to Filippo di Robilant, Eduardo Ibáñez López, and Marino Serlupo Crescenzi, who arranged on different occasions for me to see the Circolo della Caccia and the Spanish Chancellery, apartments in the Palazzo Borghese once inhabited by Pauline and Camillo Borghese. Domenico Savini, who introduced me to many of those above, and also Laetitia del Gallo and Zenaïde Giunta, who shared with me their Bonaparte family memories, deserve special thanks. I thank besides Milton and Monica Gendel and all members of the di Robilant family for making every one of my trips to Rome so enjoyable and convivial.

In France again, Peter Hicks, at the Fondation Napoléon in Paris, has been continuously helpful in answering my many inquiries, and I have made much use of the Fondation reading room, the Bibliothèque Lapeyre. I am also grateful to Madame Danuta Monachon and her staff at the Bibliothèque Thiers in Paris, which houses Frédéric Masson's invaluable papers on Napoleon and his family. All at the Archives Nationales in Paris were unfailingly helpful, and I especially wish to thank Madame Martine Boisdeffre of the Archives de France. I also thank Madame Stéphanie Guyot-Nourry of the Archives Départementales de l'Yonne for her help when I was consulting General Leclerc's papers, and I am grateful to Jacques Grimbert of the Société Historique of Pontoise, the general's birthplace.

In Italy, Dottoressa Giulia Gorgone, director of the Museo Napoleonico in Rome, has been unfailingly kind in responding to my many queries. The staff of the Archivio Segreto Vaticano were most helpful, and in addition I thank Monsignor Charles Burns for helpful conversations about the Borghese papers there. To the splendid research of Anna Coliva and her curators at the Museo e Galleria Borghese into Canova's statue of Pauline I am greatly indebted. At the American Academy in Rome I wish to thank Adele Chatfield-Taylor and Christina Huemer for their enthusiasm for this project. In Florence, meanwhile, Niccolò Capponi has been very supportive; and I treasure the memory of a visit to the Marchese di Torrigiani's home in that city, where he showed me a lock of Pauline's hair. Farther south Carlo Knight in Naples was his usual erudite and helpful self, and in Venice I thank Giovanni Volpi. Marco Fasano and Carla Ceresa of the Fondazione Cavour of Santena besides gave me access to valuable correspondence between Pauline and the Comtesse de Cavour.

In BRITAIN I thank the staffs of the Public Record Office at Kew, the National Archives of Scotland, the British Library, and the London Library for their patience with my inquiries. I thank Her Majesty the Queen for permission to read the diary Queen Victoria kept during her visit to Napoleon III's Paris, and am grateful to Pam Clark, registrar of the Royal Archives, for an interesting discussion about that royal journey. I am grateful also to the dukes of Devonshire and of Hamilton for permission to read their family correspondence. In addition I thank Charles Noble, the archivist at Chatsworth, for showing me the statue the sixth duke of Devonshire commissioned of my subject.

With Bernard Chevallier, director of the Château de Malmaison, I had a most helpful and wide-ranging discussion of the sources for Pauline's life. With Professor Jean Tulard, thanks to the kindness of Dr. John Rogister, I had an opportunity to touch on the myth and the reality of Pauline's existence. Meanwhile Béatrice de Plinval, curator of the Chaumet archives, kindly gave me a private tour of the Nitot jewelry commissioned by Napoleon and other members of the Bonaparte family, which was on exhibition in 2004.

Others to whom I am indebted for specific help or indeed inspiration of different kinds are: Laura Chanter, Guy de Selliers, Emilio di Campo, Edmondo and Maya di Robilant, Countess I. G. du Monceau de Bergendal, Jacques and Romy Gelardin, Jill, Duchess of Hamilton, Christopher Huhne, Mark Le Fanu, Jaclyn Lucas, Candia McWilliam, Eliza Pakenham, Clare Pardini, Roberta Martinelli, the Hon. Lady Roberts, Mark Roberts, Sam Stych, and the late Wendy Wasserstein.

I thank my cousin William Stirling for skillfully locating and photocopying references to Pauline in a mass of Napoleonic literature in the British Library. (It has been a feature of writing this book that very few former biographers of Pauline—and in that group I include Frédéric Masson—have seen fit to give references for their anecdotes and stories.) I have been fortunate once more in having Lesley Robertson Allen's assistance with this project, while to Leonora Clarke, as usual, go grateful thanks for typing the manuscript. At Capel and Land I thank Abi Fellows; at Knopf I thank Sarah Rothbard; and at John Murray I thank Rowan Yapp and Helen Hawksfield, all of whom contributed in great measure to its successful production. In addition I thank Helen Smith for the index, an invaluable guide to the Parisian, Roman and even Haitian salons Pauline adorned.

I thank Georgina Capel, my literary agent, for her enthusiastic and professional support of this project, and for reading and commenting on the chapters as fast as I could write them. I also thank Jonathan Lloyd, Alice Lutyens, and all at Curtis Brown for their encouragement and advice.

Meanwhile, Bob Gottlieb at Knopf has continued to be the editor a girl, or even a woman of nearly fifty, can only dream of. I thank Roland Philipps of John Murray, my friend and editor of many years, for his constant support for the project, and for his perceptive comments on the text. And I am happy to report that, following the book's cross-examination by Peter James, line editor supremo, Peter and I are still as good mates as ever. I hope that French speakers and historians will bear with my decision to abandon French Revolutionary dates well before January 1806, when that system of dating was in fact abolished.

I thank Philip Mansel for early and helpful advice about this book. My mother, Antonia Fraser, Professor Munro Price, and Peter Hicks have kindly read and commented on the manuscript at different times. I am grateful to my three children, Stella, Simon, and Tommy, for distracting me intermittently from my task of writing, but also for recognizing its place in the great scheme of things. To them and to my husband, Peter, who I hope is not too busy with schemes of his own to read it, I dedicate *Pauline Bonaparte: Venus of Empire.*

Pauline Bonaparte

CHAPTER ONE

Dinner at Marseille, 1796

T HE STORY OF PAULINE BONAPARTE, legendary beauty
and seductress, begins, appropriately, with a meeting of three
men. At dinner in the port of Marseille in the south of France
were her elder brother General Napoleon Bonaparte, her fiancé, Citizen Stanislas Fréron, and her future husband, Adjutant General Victor
Emmanuel Leclerc. According to the Gregorian calendar it was March
22, 1796. But that annual register had been suppressed, and, according
to the Revolutionary calendar, which the national government had
instituted with effect from September 1792, the day was 2 Germinal,
Year Four.

We have no record of what Pauline Bonaparte herself was doing on
that day in Marseille. Fifteen years old, with her widowed mother,
Letizia, and others of her siblings she had been an inhabitant of the
south of France since dramatic events had caused them to flee their
native Corsica. The island was in the throes of a struggle for independence backed in its early stages by members of the Bonaparte family.
Latterly Napoleon and his brothers had supported the French Revolution, an adherence that had brought them into conflict with Corsican
patriots. The family had settled first at Toulon and then in Marseille
in 1793.

Nor indeed until shortly before this dinner do we have much reliable information about Pauline's individual life. Her birth on October 20, 1780—she was the sixth of eight children—was recorded by her father, Charles, in his *livre de raison,* or commonplace book, which survives him. (He died when she was four.) The date of her baptism the next day in the small cathedral of Ajaccio in Corsica—Archdeacon Luciano Bonaparte, her great-uncle, stood godfather—is recorded in that town's archives. She was christened Maria Paola, and as she grew up was known as Paoletta. With the later fame of her brother Napoleon eclipsing all interest in the stories of his siblings, Pauline's childhood in the Maison Bonaparte in the harbor town of Ajaccio is distinguished by only a few mentions in the correspondence and anecdotes his admirers have so avidly collected.

When she was eleven, in 1792, Napoleon, aged twenty-two, sent her a fashion plate. Writing in the same month about her elder sister, Elisa, who had been educated far from Corsica at Madame de Maintenon's convent school of Saint-Cyr, and doubting the overeducated girl's chances in marriage, Napoleon mused that she was much less knowing than Paoletta. Both references, at once telling of Napoleon's affection for Pauline, of her love of finery, and of her mischievous character, might seem invented did they not come from reputable sources. Years later, while in exile on Elba, the emperor remembered that he and his sister had been caught mimicking their crippled grandmother, who was "bent . . . like an old fairy," and that Letizia punished Pauline rather than him—"it being easier to pull up skirts than undo breeches." If true, the story testifies to the harsh justice that the Bonapartes' mother meted out as well as to the taste this brother and sister displayed all their lives for unkind fun.

In the absence of other details about Pauline, these slivers of family life must represent her childhood years, her squabbles and games with elder brother Louis and younger siblings Maria Annunziata (always known as Caroline) and Jérôme. More generally her mother later spoke of a room in the Maison Bonaparte given over to the children, where they were allowed to play as they pleased, even scribble on the walls. That not much education—at most a dame school or the teaching of nuns—entered the lives of these younger Bonaparte children we know from later references to Pauline's deficiencies in this area. A good deal of healthy living was part of the picture, and through the difficult years when, following the early death of Pauline's father, Charles, the family might have been classed as *pauvre,* or unable to sustain themselves, they still summered at I Milleli, a substantial house in the *maquis,* or mountain scrub, above Ajaccio. It was here that Paoletta, her mother, and other siblings sheltered in the summer of 1793 when fleeing Corsican patriots, who had set fire to their home in Ajaccio following provocative remarks by her elder brother Lucien Bonaparte in a Jacobin club. From the nearby seashore they were sensationally rescued by Napoleon, and a French frigate bore them to the relative safety of the south of France. There Paoletta soon became known as Paulette, a gallicization that gradually gave way to Pauline.

But enough of vague accounts of a childhood we cannot reconstitute. Let us return to the dinner table in Marseille on March 22, 1796, and to the three men at it—Bonaparte, Fréron, and Leclerc. All three had been dedicated to the Revolution since it had first broken out in Paris on July 14, 1789, and all of them had played a distinguished part during its subsequent transformations. The Bourbon king Louis XVI had been executed in January 1793, and France, already steeped in blood at home, was now at war. Its enemies—Great Britain, Austria, Prussia, Spain, and Naples—had banded together to stop the French national government from spreading revolution throughout Europe and to support French royalists in their bid to restore the Bourbon monarchy. Although this struggle, which has since become known as the War of the First Coalition, provided the inescapable backdrop as the men dined that spring evening, we know that two of them at least had Paulette Bonaparte much in mind.

Despite the difference in their ages—he was forty-one to her fifteen—Stanislas Fréron had every intention of marrying Pauline within days, and her elder brother Napoleon favored the match, as well he might: Fréron was a person of consequence. He had been the national government's choice to take up the appointment of proconsul in Marseille the previous year and reestablish order in a city torn by faction and still bruised from the excesses of Robespierre's Revolutionary Terror of two years earlier. He had succeeded wonderfully well in his task, aided by one of the two younger men at the dinner, Adjutant General Leclerc, who had restored discipline to the disorderly troops in the town garrison. The third man at the table, General Bonaparte, had interrupted important preparations at Toulon for the launch of an Italian campaign to come and inspect the Marseille garrison, and this dinner marked the end of his visit and the successful conclusion of Fréron's and Leclerc's mission.

Some criticized the pomp and extravagance in which Fréron had lived at Marseille since his arrival the previous November, likening his behavior to that of a "Persian viceroy." The house he had commandeered was illuminated day and night by lanterns, and he never ventured out without a large suite of attendants. But he ordered theater and bullfights, which pleased the Marseillais. The salons of the city, slowly opening again following the overthrow of Robespierre and the installation of the new government called the Directory, marveled at his wit and address. He had been brought up, before the Revolution, in the household of Louis XVI's aunts, and among his attractions for the young Pauline Bonaparte was the lordly air he had preserved. When, exactly, over the past few months Pauline had come to the attention of this magnificent, decadent Parisian being, and where they had first met, we do not know. But it was almost certainly Lucien, acting as Fréron's aide-de-camp in Marseille, who introduced them. From political life in Paris Fréron knew the three eldest Bonaparte brothers, Napoleon, Joseph, and Lucien—and indeed had singled out for praise in the Convention, the national assembly that preceded the Directory, Napoleon's conduct in a royalist insurrection. Napoleon, meanwhile, noted with approval his brother Lucien's appointment to Fréron's staff.

What is certain is that Pauline and the other Bonaparte females would have known of Fréron long before they encountered him during this pacificatory mission to Marseille. For, after they left their native Corsica in the summer of 1793, they lived between Toulon and Marseille in the south of France. And in the summer of 1794 in the Midi, Fréron's name was synonymous with the Terror, after he had, with Paul Barras, been dispatched by Robespierre and the Committee of Public Safety to oversee in that region the national bloodshed in the Revolution's name that so horrified the rest of Europe. In Marseille he and his fellow commissioner, Barras, punished those who had backed the Girondins, moderate opponents of Robespierre's Jacobins. In Toulon they exacted vengeance on the royalist town for turning to the English. (It was at the siege of Toulon in late 1793 that the twenty-four-year-old Napoleon had first made his name, dispersing the British fleet in his capacity as captain of artillery.)

During this return visit two years later to the scene of his earlier crimes, however, Fréron had now succeeded by wise government in conciliating many. The day after the dinner, on March 23, 1796, General Napoleon Bonaparte reported from Toulon to Barras, now a member of the Directory, "Fréron has behaved well at Marseille. They seem to fear his departure and the renewal of assassinations." And on the thirtieth of that month from Nice he repeated his encomium to the same correspondent: "I found Fréron at Marseille. His departure has been a matter for regret—it seems he has behaved well there."

Fréron had certainly succeeded in attracting the heartfelt passion of Pauline Bonaparte, and already six weeks before Napoleon's visit to Marseille their imminent marriage was the subject of discussion between them. The fifteen-year-old girl was preparing herself to leave her family and follow Fréron, wherever the government might next send him. ". . . I swear, dear Stanislas, ever to love but you alone," Pauline wrote on 19 Ventôse (February 9). "My heart is not for sharing. It's given to you whole. Who could oppose the union of two souls who seek only happiness and who find it in loving each other? No, my love, not Maman, not anyone can refuse you my hand." She went on, "Laura and Petrarch, whom you quote often, were not so happy as us. Petrarch was constant, but Laura . . . No, my dear love, Paulette will love you as much as Petrarch loved Laura."

This rather surprising excursus into the world of Renaissance literature requires some explanation. We know that Fréron admired and translated into French the Italian poet's sonnets. That he shared his knowledge of Petrarch, and of the sonnets dedicated to "Laura"—the woman the poet claims to have first seen in a church in Avignon and who, being married, could never return his passion—with Pauline, an ignorant and more or less unlettered refugee from Corsica, says much for the power of love to transcend all boundaries. It is probable that Pauline had help from someone more literate than herself in framing this and subsequent letters, to her "idol" Fréron. Her brother Lucien and her sister Elisa have been suggested as possible secretaries. But Fréron's teaching left an indelible impression on Pauline. Later in life she was to take pleasure in reciting the lines from Petrarch he had taught her—to other lovers.

Pauline's reference to her mother shows that Fréron had not succeeded in conciliating all at Marseille: "No, my love, not Maman, not anyone can refuse you my hand." Following the early death of her husband, Charles, in 1785, Letizia Bonaparte had shared the duties that would have naturally fallen to him, as father of a family of five boys and three girls, with her two eldest sons, Joseph and Napoleon. Hence resistance from her to the match that Pauline and Fréron contemplated was to be taken seriously, even if Napoleon was in favor. (Within the family Napoleon was a figure of greater authority than his elder brother. In part this was because, unlike Joseph, he had spent months at a time at home in Corsica, helping his mother in her quest to make ends meet. In part he had the more dominant character.) That Madame Bonaparte objected, or at least wished the couple to delay their marriage, is made clear in a letter from Fréron to Napoleon days after his dinner with the young general. His mission concluded, Fréron was on the point of journeying north to Paris, where he had been called by the Directory, and intended taking Pauline with him as Madame Fréron:

Your mother is putting an obstacle in our way. I hold to the idea of marrying in Marseille in four or five days' time. Everything is arranged for that. Independently of possessing this hand that I

burn to unite to mine, it is possible that the Directory will name
me straightaway to some distant post, which will mean an
immediate departure. If I am obliged to come back here, I will
lose precious time. Moreover, the government, which, rightly,
occupies itself little with matters of the heart, might blame an
absence that could retard [the object of] the mission entrusted
to me.

On what ground Madame Bonaparte objected to her daughter's
marriage to Fréron we do not know. The bridegroom's age may have
been a factor—or, indeed, the bride's youth. Or, being endowed with a
remarkable ability to see which way the wind was blowing, Madame
Bonaparte may have had some inkling, either from her links with the
Corsican community in Paris or from information from the merchant
community of Marseille with whom the Bonapartes were friendly, and
indeed into which her son Joseph had recently married, that Fréron's
earlier crimes in the south were about to come back to haunt him. She
may even have known of and objected to the five-year liaison that
Fréron had enjoyed with an actress from the Italian theater. Two children had been born, and the actress was pregnant with a third. But her
objections were certainly not shared at this point by her son Napoleon.
Indeed Pauline later reminded him, "You consented to my marriage to
Fréron," and referred to "the promises you made me to smooth all
obstacles."

It was perhaps surprising that Madame Bonaparte made objections
to her daughter's marriage. When she and her children had fled Ajaccio
for the mainland after the Maison Bonaparte had been burned down,
the modest income they derived from the produce of vineyards and
other smallholdings on their native island had come to an end. Indeed
Corsica was now in British hands. In addition the support of a close-
knit if quarrelsome structure of relations—paternal and maternal—
had been lost to them. In Toulon, where they landed in June 1793, and
afterward in Marseille, they had had to depend on small sums that the
new republican government meted out to refugees from Corsica. Leg-

end even has it that the Bonaparte women resorted to taking in laundry and washed it in the public fountain.

Now, however, in the spring of 1796, Napoleon had been appointed to head the Army of Italy, which had as its mission the expulsion of the Austrians from northern Italy and the introduction of republican government into that region. As a result he was able to supplement his family's income from his salary. Equally Madame Bonaparte's stepbrother, François Fesch, who had escaped with them from Corsica, had recovered some of his Swiss father's patrimony and could also help. Fesch, whose vocation was the priesthood and who had earlier been archdeacon of Ajaccio after Luciano Bonaparte's death, had been living a secular life since religious orders were suppressed under the Revolution.

But the times were still unsure. It was as easy to fall into disgrace as to win a command, as Napoleon had found to his cost two years earlier when he had come under suspicion and been briefly put under house arrest at Nice. Surely any bridegroom, especially one with a position and prospects like Fréron, was preferable to refugee life? But the Bonapartes had what some would call a remarkably inflated idea of what was due their status. A house above Antibes in which the family summered shortly after Napoleon was freed, for instance, was a property of some dignity, with pepperpot turrets. The family disapproved strongly when Lucien, appointed to a commissary post in Saint-Maximin, promptly married the daughter of the innkeeper with whom he lodged and had a daughter by her. Again, Napoleon directed that a "Citizen Billon" at Marseille who wished to marry Pauline in October 1795 should be rejected, as he seemed to have no occupation. And he refused Pauline's hand in marriage to a subaltern, Andoche Junot: "She has no money. He has no money. No money, no match."

Shortly before the dinner in Marseille took place, both of the eldest Bonaparte brothers had committed themselves to marriage. Joseph made what all agreed to be an excellent match—to Julie Clary, the plain and slightly backward but very rich daughter of a merchant family based in Marseille who had interests as far afield as Smyrna.

Napoleon was for a time engaged to her sister, Désirée, but broke it off. (Désirée later married another officer, Jean-Baptiste Bernadotte.) There were to be no further worries about Joseph's career, as he entered the Clary house of business. But Napoleon's subsequent marriage in March 1796 to Josephine, the beautiful widow of an aristocrat called de Beauharnais who had been guillotined in Paris during the Reign of Terror, did not please his mother. As part of his mission to Marseille later that month, Napoleon hoped to persuade Madame Bonaparte to acknowledge his bride.

General Bonaparte did not doubt, on parting from Fréron, that the proconsul's marriage to Pauline would take place within days, or that she would then accompany Fréron to Paris as his wife. During his brief visit to Marseille he therefore promised the proconsul a letter of introduction for Pauline to his new bride, Josephine, whom he had left with her two de Beauharnais children in Paris. When the letter did not materialize, Fréron sent a courier after Napoleon to Toulon, to try to extract it from the busy general. Fréron wanted it, he wrote, "so that she [Josephine] will not be astonished by the sudden apparition of Paulette when I present her." Fréron needed no introduction to Josephine as he knew her well already, not least because she had between the end of one marriage and the beginning of the next had an affair in Paris with his southern fellow commissioner Barras. Josephine de Beauharnais was, with Madame Tallien and Madame Récamier, an extremely fashionable member of Paris society. Pauline's life, despite her mother's objections, seemed set to take a dazzling, metropolitan path that would remove her all at once from the uncertainties of refugee existence in Marseille.

AND THEN EVERYTHING CHANGED. But before we follow the very different course that Pauline's life took over the next few months, let us look at the man who made a third at the dinner in Marseille on March 22—Adjutant General Victor Emmanuel Leclerc. This young man was awaiting a fellow adjutant general, Alexis Grillon, whom

Napoleon had ordered to take over as garrison commander at Marseille. Once his transfer into a suitable regiment had been effected, Leclerc was to join the Italian campaign that Pauline's brother had been chosen to head.

Blond, slight, and with a bony face, Victor Emmanuel Leclerc was certainly known to Pauline, as he had worked in concert with her fiancé, Fréron, to subdue the town over the preceding months. Moreover Leclerc, a merchant's son from Pontoise near Paris, had another claim to Fréron's attention. He was a protégé of Fréron's brother-in-law, the Marquis de la Poype, who was a landowner in the Pontoise region. Patriotism had led nineteen-year-old Victor Emmanuel to join up within days of the French Revolutionary Army's formation in September 1792. In so doing he abandoned his life as the promising scion of a prominent burgher family in Pontoise, an important town on the Seine, and in the Val-d'Oise near Paris, where his father had held the grain concession up to his death.

Victor Emmanuel's widowed mother, Madame Musquinet Leclerc, like his father from a prominent Pontoise family, no doubt had a hand in arranging his entry into the regiment commanded by the Marquis de la Poype. However, it was Victor Emmanuel's own military talents and flair for organization that led to his rise through the ranks. As early as 1793 he distinguished himself (like Napoleon) at the siege of Toulon, the following year he served in the Ardennes, and finally he came to Fréron's attention, perhaps after a commendation from de la Poype. His powers of organization and the confidence with which he had subdued the unruly garrison in Marseille now won him greater rewards— the attention of General Bonaparte.

Neither Leclerc nor Pauline dreamed in the spring of 1796 that within a year they would be publishing their banns in Milan with a view to marriage. Pauline, of course, was preparing for marriage to Fréron and a life as the wife of an administrator in some part of the expanding French republic. And in the coming months Leclerc was to be entirely occupied with the campaign in Italy, which began in April with successes in Piedmont and which he joined a month later in Lombardy. In June, commending a young cavalry general, Joachim Murat, under whose command the cavalry had performed "prodigies of valor," Napoleon also singled out the brigade chief of the tenth Regiment of Hussars, Leclerc, who had "equally distinguished himself." Later that month Napoleon sent Leclerc as a special envoy on a reconnaissance mission, masquerading as a diplomatic visit, to the Swiss canton of Grisons on the Tyrolean frontier, to see if that republic chose to acknowledge the government of France. His envoy Leclerc, announced Napoleon, "joins to excellent conduct a pure patriotism."

Meanwhile, in Marseille, Pauline's life had taken a very different turn, and one could say that thanks to Napoleon she had been saved from a marriage that would have brought her not grandeur but penury and disgrace. Fréron, delay as he might in Marseille, could not succeed in overcoming Letizia Bonaparte's objections to his marriage to her daughter, and willy-nilly set off for Paris—still affianced but without his bride-to-be. On arrival in the capital he learned that he had been denounced on March 30, the very day Napoleon had written his second encomium of the man he confidently expected to be his brother-in-law. The charges were of peculation and embezzlement during the proconsul's first mission to Marseille. And despite immediately penning a memorial in which he skillfully answered the charges, opinion in these volatile times swung against him. Fréron was disgraced. To add to his troubles, his Parisian mistress, Mademoiselle Masson, heard that he was about to marry and, on the point of giving birth to their third child, informed the Bonaparte family of her situation.

Not surprisingly, then, Napoleon changed his tune when he wrote to his wife, Josephine, in May following success at the Battle of Lodi. "Let Fréron know the intention of my family is for him NOT to marry Pauline, and that I am prepared to take whatever part is necessary to achieve this. Tell my brother." The next day he wrote to Barras, of the Directory, "Do me a favor, persuade Fréron not to marry my sister. This marriage suits no one in my family. He is too reasonable to persist in marrying a child of sixteen [in fact she was still fifteen]. He could be her father. And one doesn't look for another woman when one has two children by another woman already." And in a letter to Joseph on the fourteenth of that same month, Napoleon came down firmly against the match: "All goes well. I beg you, arrange Pauline's affair. I have no intention of letting Fréron marry her. Tell her that, and tell him to tell her. We are masters of all Lombardy."

But Pauline was not concerned with her brother's victories, or with anyone's disapproval of her love for Fréron. On 30 Floréal (May 19), ill in bed, she replied to a letter her lover had written to her after "a silence" and in which he addressed the subject of "that woman." Pauline told him that she was very anxious to hear of "the outcome for that woman," and added, "I put myself in her place and feel for her"— she referred to the impending birth of Mademoiselle Masson's third child. She added that a portrait of Fréron that he had given her was the greatest consolation to her. "I pass days with it, and talk to it as though you were here." She promised him her own, as soon as she was better able to support the fatigue of sittings.

Lucien, who remained attached to Fréron despite the commissioner's disgrace, tried to plead the lovers' cause when he joined his brother at headquarters in Milan in June. But Napoleon, the conquering hero of Rivoli and Lodi, Mantua and Bologna, was too busy to discuss anything but his plans for an assault on Rome. Lucien reported: "No family news could be discussed between us. His object occupies him so exclusively that it is impossible to make him take an interest in anything else." Meanwhile Pauline continued to write to Fréron, apparently reconciling herself to his relationship with Mademoiselle Masson and making little mention of his political disgrace.

On 14 Messidor (July 2) she told him that she had been to the country, where she had fallen into a river while trying to jump into a boat. "You nearly lost your Paulette," she wrote. She was still hopeful that a way would be found to unite her with Fréron and relied on Lucien, who was leaving for Paris, to promote their interests. "I don't talk more about your mistress," she wrote. "All that you say reassures me. I know your honest heart, and approve the arrangements you are making in that respect. The water I drank in the river has not cooled the warmth of my heart for you. It was more likely nectar I swallowed."

Breaking into Italian, she added, "Addio, anima mia, ti amo sempre, mia vita" (Adieu, my soul, I will love you always, my life), and ended by copying the words to a popular aria, written to be sung with a guitar accompaniment:

> *Non so dir se sono amante;*
> *Ma so ben che al tuo sembiante*
> *Tutto ardor pressa il mio cuore,*
> *E gli è caro il tuo pressar.*

> [I don't know if I am in love
> But I know when I see you
> My heart burns with ardor
> And your embrace is sweet.]

Pauline's cheerful mood did not last long. Only four days later, on July 6, she wrote again to Fréron:

All the world conspires against us. I see by your letter that your friends are ingrates—including Napoleon's wife, who I thought was for you. She writes to her husband that I would be dishonored if I were to marry you, so she hopes it can be stopped. What have we done to her? I can't bear it, everything is against us! We are wretched indeed! But what am I saying . . . no, while we love, we are not unhappy. We may experience setbacks, we have troubles, it's true, but a letter, a word, "I love you," consoles us for the tears we shed.

The girl went on determinedly:

All these difficulties, far from diminishing my love, only increase it. Courage, my beloved, our constancy will see a time when all these obstacles are swept away, I hope. I advise you to write to Napoleon, I would like to write to him. What do you think? It seems to me my letter wasn't strong enough to persuade him fully of my feelings for you. Maybe he will be moved by the tears of a sister and the prayers of a friend. You know that he is capable of much. I will do my best to send you my portrait. You can send your letters to Maman's address. Adieu, my love, for life your faithful lover.

Her letter ended again with sentences in Italian, the language she had spoken growing up in Corsica: "Il mio coraggio cominciava ad abbandonarmi, non ch'io dubitassi dei tuoi sentimenti, ma tante contradizioni m'impazientavano. . . . Sta di buon cuore, malgrado le tue disgrazie, mi sei sempre più caro; forse le cose camberanno; amami sempre, anima mia . . . mio tenero amico, non respiro se non per te; ti amo." (My courage began to abandon me, not because I doubted your faith, but so many obstacles made me impatient. . . . Be of good heart, despite your misfortunes, you are ever more dear. Maybe things will change. Love me ever, my soul . . . my dear love. I live only for you.)

Only one letter from Pauline to Napoleon survives from this period, during which, as she writes, he was "in the middle of brilliant victories." Without a date, it cannot be assigned a secure place in the developing drama of love blighted and marriage denied that forms this first chapter of her life. Nevertheless it is worth reading carefully, not least for the acknowledgment that Pauline first makes here of her obligation to her brother, as the head of the Bonaparte clan:

I have received your letter. It caused me the greatest pain. I didn't expect this change on your part. You had consented for me to marry Fréron. After the promises you had made me to smooth all obstacles, my heart was given to this sweet hope, and I regarded him as the one who would fulfill my destiny. I send you his last letter; you will see that all the calumnies that have been heaped on him are not true.

As for me, I prefer by far to be unhappy all my life than to marry without your consent and to draw down on me your malediction. You, my dear Napoleon, for whom I have always had a most tender love, if you were witness to the tears your letter made me shed, you would be touched, I am sure. You, from whom I expected my happiness, you want me to renounce the only person I can ever love. Although young, I have a firm character; I feel it is impossible to renounce Fréron, after all the promises I have made to love only him. Yes, I will honor them. No one in the world can stop me keeping my heart for him, receiving his letters, replying, repeating that I love him. I know too well my duty to deny it. . . . Goodbye, this is what I have to say to you. Be happy, and in the middle of these brilliant victories, of all this good fortune, remember sometimes the life full of bitterness and tears that is P.B.'s every day.

Whether Napoleon accepted Pauline's rather unusual promise that she would not marry Fréron but would continue to love him and correspond with him, we cannot know. The last letter extant from her to Fréron she wrote on July 6, following more days spent in bed, and when she was on the point of changing residence at Marseille. "You must have been worried not to receive my letters, but I suffered also not to be able to chat with you. . . . You know that I idolize you. And to see that we are so sinned against and so unhappy. No, it is not possible for Paulette to live at a distance from her dear friend Stanislas," she declared.

She had had the comfort of opening her heart to her elder sister, Elisa, on the matter of her lover. However, the seriousness of Fréron's disgrace appears to have penetrated Pauline's consciousness at last, three months after he had been denounced. "Lucien showed me your letter," she told him. "I see that your situation is still the same. . . . I would like to be with you, I would console you for all the injustices that have happened to you."

In Italian she concluded:

Che soffranza d'essere separati così molto tempo! Ma conservo la speranza che saremo presto riuniti; addio dunque, cara mia

speme, idol mio, credo che alla fine la sorte si stancherà persegui-
tarci. . . . Ti amo, sempre, e passionatissimamente, per sempre ti
amo, ti amo . . . sei cuore mio, tenero amico. [What suffering to
be separated for so long a time! But I keep up my hopes that we
will soon be reunited. So adieu, my dear, my idol, I believe that
in the end fate will tire of persecuting us. . . . I love you, always,
and so passionately, for ever I love you. I love you . . . my heart,
my dear love.] Ti amo, amo, amo, amo, si amatissimo amante.

But Napoleon, whose star continued to rise, had other plans for his
beautiful younger sister, and Pauline turned sixteen at Marseille in
October 1796, still a spinster, still without having set eyes on Fréron
since he had been called north that March. Two months later
Napoleon gave orders for Pauline, escorted by their uncle Fesch, to
meet him and Josephine at his Italian headquarters at Milan. Pauline
Bonaparte's adolescence at Marseille, marked by financial uncertainty
and emotional turbulence, was at an end—as was her vow of constancy
to Stanislas Fréron. Napoleon had plans for her in Italy, and they
involved Adjutant General, now Brigade General, Victor Emmanuel
Leclerc.

Meanwhile Fréron's career and prospects slipped away from him,
and even an attempt to gain a salary as a deputy for New Guinea failed.
Of his former life he was left only with Mademoiselle Masson, whom
he seems to have married and with whom he lived in slowly increasing
poverty. Strange to think that this woman's fate would have been
Pauline Bonaparte's had not the will of her mother intervened.

CHAPTER TWO

Garrison Bride, 1797–1798

Toward the end of April 1797 there was cannon fire in Paris in the middle of the day. "It's probably a new victory for the Army of Italy," someone said. Since Jean Victor Moreau, Napoleon's contemporary and commander of the French Army of the Rhine, had retreated back across that river, General Bonaparte's campaigns were being followed all the more eagerly in the French capital. It was indeed news from the Italian front. On April 16 Napoleon had signed at Leoben in Austria the preliminaries of peace with the Austrians, the overlords of northern Italy, and the general officer who now brought the resulting treaty to the Directory was Brigade General Victor Emmanuel Leclerc.

As the Directors had not authorized peace negotiations, they were privately not pleased with Bonaparte or his emissary. But, as all Paris was delighted at the prospect of an end to the war with Austria, they had to affect enthusiasm. In addition Leclerc had inspected the different movements of the enemy troops as he passed through Germany en route to France, while he bonhomously shared with them the news that the peace treaty had been signed. The enemy consequently relaxed its guard, and, on Leclerc's arrival at the Rhine and at his suggestion, the French general Moreau recrossed the river with four thousand men and twenty cannons, and gave the Austrians a bloody nose. This was all in accordance with General Bonaparte's instructions to Leclerc, and he had once again proved himself an able second-in-command—in recognition of which he was promoted to brigade general. Six months later, under the Treaty of Campo Formio, France would acquire former Austrian territories in northern Italy and in the Netherlands. The War of the First Coalition had thus ended in triumph for the Revolutionary forces, and only Britain now remained in the field against them.

"I beg you to send [Leclerc] back to me straightaway," Napoleon wrote on April 19 from Leoben to the Directory. "All the officers I send to Paris stay there too long. They spend their money and lose themselves in pleasure." That evening Leclerc appeared, as if in echo of Napoleon's words, at a ball in Paris to celebrate the marriage of two persons of fashion. There two of his friends, the poet Antoine Arnault and another intimate, the actor Lenoir, congratulated him on following their advice the previous year when he had chosen to enlist in the Army of Italy rather than serve with the Army of the Interior, where he would have been confined to the antechambers of the Directory in Paris. Now Leclerc was the toast of the town. He was a brigade general at twenty-five, he represented that evening the most illustrious army in Europe, and he could indeed have lingered and enjoyed being feted, as his superior had feared.

However, Leclerc was not one to disobey Bonaparte, and he made haste to return to headquarters in Italy. But he had some private business to attend to before he left France, as his superior was well aware. The day after he left Napoleon at Leoben, Leclerc had appeared before General Louis Alexandre Berthier, chief of staff at the French army headquarters in Milan, armed with a copy of his baptismal entry from the Church of Notre-Dame in his native Pontoise. At his side was Pauline Bonaparte, and on that day, April 20, 1797, they gave notice of their intention to marry. The banns were duly read and posted, with their names, dates, and places of birth for all to read, before Leclerc resumed his journey to Paris as the envoy of Pauline's brother.

At the Parisian ball Leclerc declared to his friends that this honor, to have won the hand of his general's sister, outdid all the others lavished on him. And his friends agreed with him. Not only had word of the beauty of sixteen-year-old Pauline Bonaparte by now spread to Paris, but her brother's renown gave Leclerc's bride additional cachet. Leclerc's mother, Madame Musquinet Leclerc, no doubt agreed and had an opportunity to tell him so when he visited her and his younger sister, Aimée, at their house in the town of Pontoise before returning to Italy. Leclerc's mother was not especially literate, unlike her sophisticated son, but she was an experienced businesswoman, having now managed the family business for five years since her husband's death. The details of the dowry that Pauline Bonaparte would bring to the family—an unimpressive forty thousand francs—were no doubt discussed. But what was most remarkable was that General Bonaparte's plans for his sister and Leclerc's feelings for her should dovetail. For according to Leclerc's friend Arnault, who now traveled with him to Milan to be present at the couple's marriage, Leclerc had loved Pauline for three years, even before her brother's rise to power had added to her attractions.

WHAT OF PAULINE in all this? We last saw her in Marseille, mourning the end of her relationship with Fréron. Was she content with her new life at her brother's Italian headquarters? Was the match with Leclerc an arrangement made by her brother in which she had no part to play but to acquiesce? And did the love affair with Fréron of the previous year cast no shadow over this marriage that she now contemplated? The answer seems to be that she embraced the coming marriage with delight.

There exists a terse letter from Napoleon to his uncle Fesch, who was at Marseille in early December 1796 and whom he had appointed a commissary, or victualler, to the Army of Italy. In it he writes: "I beg you to come as soon as possible to Milan with Paoletta, whom my wife wants to have with her. . . . You can go to Nice by land and then embark for Genoa." Two days later he called on his brother Joseph, who was in Ajaccio taking the first steps toward restoring the Maison

Bonaparte following the British evacuation of the island, to join the family party in Italy. Napoleon wrote: "I think my wife is pregnant. I expect Fesch and Paoletta at Milan in a fortnight."

Josephine, after much prevarication, had reluctantly left Paris and joined Napoleon in Italy the previous summer. Accordingly, after the sea voyage from France with Fesch, it was under this fashionable Parisienne's chaperonage that Pauline, in the last days of December, made acquaintance with her brother's headquarters at Milan—the Palazzo Serbelloni, all shimmering pink granite and classical proportions. Here General Bonaparte held court. His recent victories—at Rivoli, at the bridge of Arcola—had guaranteed him a reputation for invincibility, and all at headquarters shone in his reflected glory.

Officers of the Italian campaigns—giants like André Masséna and Auguste de Marmont, lumbering provincials like Pierre Augereau—dined in the marble and porphyry salons and the colonnaded galleries opening onto terraces and gardens at the Serbelloni. Their companions were Josephine and the ladies she had prevailed on to follow her from Paris, all of "immodest behaviour," with their arms, bosoms, and shoulders uncovered, as the Milanese noted. The Milanese disapproved of the very arrangement of the Parisiennes' hair, adorned with flowers and feathers and crowned with little military helmets from which untidy locks escaped. The ladies' fashionable tunics, revealing their legs and even their thighs, clad in flesh-colored tights, were another matter for scandal, and finally their manners matched their clothes. It was all arrogant talk, provocative looks, and meat eaten on Fridays. Needless to say Napoleon was delighted by the arrival of Josephine and the sophisticated troupe she brought with her.

In addition there were the staff officers, led by round, fat Berthier, who had been brought up at Versailles and was Napoleon's trusted chief of staff. There were Henri Clarke, the Directory's representative; Karl Ludwig von Haller, the financier; Jean-Pierre Collot, the munitioner. And envoys and ambassadors crowded in from all over Italy—Tuscany, Naples, the Papal States, and the Republic of Venice. Over them all presided Napoleon, a slight, even scrawny figure whose gray gaze was glacial and whose reserve in the midst of the assembly seemed bound-less. Berthier, Charles Kilmaine, Clarke, Jacques-Pierre de Villemanzy, Augereau, noted an observer, all waited in silence till he addressed them. Never, in short, had a headquarters so resembled a court; it was like the Tuileries in its heyday, the royal palace in Paris that Louis XVI and Marie Antoinette had inhabited before the abolition of the French monarchy and their own execution.

Now that Pauline Bonaparte had joined the party, she would sit before dinner with her sister-in-law Josephine and her intimates Madame Visconti and Madame Berthier in the gallery that resembled, a Parisian said, "the foyer of the Opéra" in the French capital. In Milan the via degli Orefici, or Street of Goldsmiths, afforded her opportuni-ties to bedeck herself, the Scala opera house opportunities to display herself. In Marseille, Pauline had had the attention of individuals. Now an entire headquarters admired her, and Victor Emmanuel Leclerc most of all. What did she look like? One has to turn to later portraits, to surviving dresses with court trains, even to slippers that belonged to her, but most of all to a famous later statue for evidence of the sixteen-year-old's appearance.

Simply put, Pauline Bonaparte was exquisitely lovely—dark haired, with pale skin, dark eyes, and a well-cut, mobile mouth. Her counte-nance, it was sometimes said, bore a strong resemblance to that of her brother Napoleon. At other times, it was said, she looked like her mother, who had been a beauty in her day. She was always inordinately proud of her feet and hands, milk white, like the rest of her. Whether or not her figure had by now gained the perfect proportions later cele-brated in Canova's statue, we cannot say. She was about five feet five, or at most five feet six—the same height as her brother Napoleon and as her sister-in-law Josephine. As with Napoleon, what Pauline lacked in stature she made up in personality.

Napoleon still had work to do before he could follow the Direc-tory's standing instructions to invade Austria from the south in order to meet up with the other French generals who commanded the French armies on the Rhine. Accordingly Pauline accompanied Josephine to campaign quarters in Bologna and Modena, until Mantua fell to the French in February 1797, and Napoleon departed for Austria. It would seem very likely that by this time the marriage between Pauline and Leclerc had been agreed, as a copy of that officer's baptismal certificate, a necessary document for marriage, was obtained from Pontoise on February 22. Thereafter there was little time to dwell on personal matters. Leclerc was sent by Napoleon to urge the French generals on the Rhine to halt their offensive, and by the end of March, Napoleon himself was just outside Vienna, with the Austrian court packing up to flee. In April he and Leclerc were both, as we have seen, in Leoben in Austria, and for the bridal couple events then moved swiftly.

At the beginning of May, with the brigade general's return to headquarters, Leclerc and Pauline were reunited. "Pretty Paulette," whom Leclerc's friend Arnault pronounced "eager to become Mme. Leclerc," did not, however, behave with the decorum that might have been expected either from her venerable brother's sister or from the fiancée of her distinguished young husband-to-be. Shortly after Leclerc's return to Milan, Napoleon set up a summer headquarters a few leagues outside the city at the Château of Mombello, and there Arnault was placed next to Pauline at dinner. General conversation being impossible, as a medley of military marches and Italian patriotic airs was played throughout the meal, the poet had ample opportunity to study the character of the young beauty, who treated him with disarming familiarity. Although she had seen him before only at Marseille, she knew him to be in her fiancé's confidence.

"Singular mix of all that was most complete in physical perfection, and most bizarre in moral qualities," wrote Arnault, long years later.

> Although she was the most beautiful person one could imagine, she was also the most unreasonable. No more deportment than a schoolgirl, talking inconsequentially, laughing at nothing and at everything, she contradicted the most serious people and put out her tongue at her sister-in-law when Josephine wasn't looking. She nudged my knee when I didn't pay enough attention to

her rattling on and attracted to herself from time to time those ferocious glances with which her brother recalled the most intractable men to order. But this didn't work with her. A minute later she would start again. To have the authority of the general of the Army of Italy checked thus by the giddiness of a little girl! A good child, besides, by nature rather than by effort, since she had no principles and was likely to do the right thing only by caprice.

One wonders who was more glad, the sorely tried Arnault or saucy, show-off Pauline, to rise from the table and take coffee and ice cream out on the terraces after dinner. Did the malice she displayed toward her sister-in-law arise from Josephine's earlier opposition to her match with Fréron? Or was it simply jealousy of her sister-in-law's primacy at headquarters?

Either way, the time of Pauline's marriage drew near, while Napoleon and his officers came and went, exacting terms from the Venetians and negotiating the final clauses of the peace with Austria to be signed at Campo Formio. Napoleon's stepson, Eugène de Beauharnais, and Jérôme, the youngest Bonaparte, who were at the Macdermott School in Paris together, joined the Mombello party. At the beginning of June, Pauline's mother arrived from Marseille with her elder sister, Elisa. Elisa was regarded as ill favored, with "those things we call arms and legs . . . haphazardly stuck on to her body," as a contemporary, the Duchesse d'Abrantès, put it. However, she had found a husband, a Corsican named Felice Bacciochi. (The match was blighted only by his unfortunate fondness, given his lack of talent, for playing the violin.) And so it was decided that, following Pauline's civil marriage to Leclerc, which took place on the morning of June 14 at Mombello, the two couples should go through a religious ceremony that same evening in the Chapel of San Francesco. Archbishop Visconti, from Milan, gave his dispensation—the banns had been posted for the civil marriage but not read in church—the priest of a neighboring parish was hauled in to officiate, and Uncle Fesch and Leclerc's brother Nicolas stood witness while the nuptial benediction was given. Leclerc, we know, was religious in an irreligious age, and though it was Napoleon who requested the dispensation for this ceremony, it may have been at the urging of his new brother-in-law. Pauline was no doubt more occupied with her appearance than with spiritual affairs.

The double marriage was a focal point of a summer whose "unique spell" was felt by all, as General Marmont observed. It had "a character of its own which no later circumstances could re-create. There was grandeur, hope and joy. We were all very young, from the supreme commander down to the most junior officers; all bright with strength and health and consumed by love of glory . . . we felt unlimited confidence in our destinies." There were those who found the tendency of Napoleon's officers, Marmont and Leclerc among them, to imitate his mannerisms, his way of walking, his gravity, his silences—they even copied his practice of wearing a simple gray riding coat—laughable or even irritating. But Leclerc took the appellation "the blond Bonaparte" as a compliment.

Napoleon, meanwhile, unbent in the presence of his trusted fellow officers. He told ghost stories, "stories that frightened the imagination," improvising and using actors' tricks with the inflections of his voice. He even showed a sense of humor. Walking in the garden at Mombello, he noticed one of the cooks jump out of his way and inquired as to the cause of the man's alarm. It transpired that the cook's dog had fatally bitten Fortuny, a lapdog precious to Josephine and her children, Eugène and Hortense. Josephine had since acquired a new dog, and Napoleon asked the cook: "Where is your dog now? Don't you have him anymore?" "I keep him in," came the reply. "Well, let him out," said the general. "Maybe he'll get rid of this one too."

There was another important matter in the affair of Pauline's marriage that required attention—the signing of the marriage contracts before a notary in Milan, whereby Pauline's brother settled forty thousand francs on her, to be conveyed to Leclerc. In return she gave up all claim on the Bonaparte family property. In monetary and household matters she was later to have what the French call a good head on her shoulders. However, at this point she was probably more interested in the honeymoon journey to Lake Como that took place a few days after the marriage ceremonies, and in which most of the staff joined. While Napoleon parleyed with the Neapolitan ambassador to Vienna, the Marchese di Gallo, Pauline and Leclerc voyaged on the lake, rode in carriages flanked by Polish officers, and attended meals prepared in the lakeside villas.

The golden holiday atmosphere slowly dissipated. Napoleon was recalled to Paris, and with his departure and that of Josephine most of the assembly dispersed, and Milan resumed its workaday northern aspect. From Pauline's point of view, if Milan was not Paris, at least Leclerc took over Napoleon's duties as commander in chief of the Army of Italy, which gave her a position of importance as the general's lady. Meanwhile General Berthier was in due course replaced as chief of staff by General Guillaume-Marie-Anne Brune.

Pauline's brother Joseph had already left for Rome, where he had been appointed French ambassador, and had taken her younger sister, Caroline, with him. Letizia Bonaparte returned to Ajaccio with Elisa and Bacciochi, where they intended, as a matter of family piety, to further the work of restoration on the Maison Bonaparte that Joseph had begun the previous autumn. Pauline and Leclerc settled down to a life at headquarters in the Palazzo Serbelloni, and she soon performed the first duty of the wife of a republican officer: She became pregnant.

In October, Leclerc's friend the waspish Arnault, who had been on a tour of Italy, returned to Milan and visited the Leclercs at home. *He* was bathed in domestic happiness, he reported. *She* struck him as very happy too—not only to be married to Leclerc but to be married at all. Her new state had certainly not imbued Madame Leclerc with as much gravity as her husband, whom Arnault found even more serious than usual. "As for her, it was still the same folly. 'Isn't that a diamond you have there?' she asked me, pointing at a brilliant of the most modest nature that I wore as a pin. 'I think mine still better.' And she started comparing with some vanity these two stones, of which the better was not much bigger than a lentil."

Pauline remained pleased with her husband, with her jewel box, and in due course with her child, a boy who was born on April 20, 1798, at the couple's home in the Palazzo Graziani. As a measure of the respect Leclerc felt for his brother-in-law, he left it to Napoleon, who was appointed one of the godparents (Leclerc's mother would be the other), to name the child. The baby was not only an heir to the Pontoise family fortune; at this point this Leclerc child was the only heir Napoleon acknowledged, as he regarded his brother Lucien's marriage to the innkeeper's daughter Christine Boyer as a misalliance and the birth of their child, Charlotte, in 1795 as a further outrage. The birth of another niece, Christine, later that year, he would simply ignore. Unaccountably, although a mother of two by her first marriage and despite numerous false hopes during two years of marriage, Napoleon's own wife, Josephine, had not become pregnant. On the point of setting out for Toulon and the expedition to Egypt which was to blaze his name still more boldly in the journals of Europe, Napoleon therefore gave the matter of his small nephew's name some thought and replied: "Thank you, my dear brother-in-law, for the agreeable news you have given me. I am sending my proxy to General Brune [who was to stand in his place at the baptism]. I name my little nephew Dermide."

This unusual name was that of a hero in the poems of Ossian, supposedly translations from a Gaelic epic, which had been published thirty years earlier and which Napoleon, among others, greatly admired. "I beg you to give this little fan to my sister while a small jewel that I am having made for her is being finished," the godfather went on. Then, looking ahead, he wrote, "When my sister is better, General Brune could allow you to spend a month at Paris. Then, depending on circumstances, you could either join me or return to Italy. You cannot doubt the pleasure I would have to have you with me."

While Napoleon and his Army of Egypt, accompanied by archaeologists and botanists, embarked at Toulon, Leclerc arranged for his child to be baptized, and on the evening of May 29, 1798, at the Capuchin Church in Milan the six-week-old infant duly received the names of Dermide Louis Napoléon Leclerc. The garrison marked the event with every attention, cannons were fired and Milan rejoiced—for all the world as though an Austrian archduke had been born. The proud father celebrated further by buying an estate at Novellara, between Parma and Guastalla, for 160,000 francs.

If Leclerc intended Novellara as a residence rather than as a speculative purchase, he was to be disappointed. Ill health led to his resignation as commander in chief of the Army of Italy, which General Brune accepted on 5 Fructidor (October 14), and he was transferred to Paris. While Pauline Leclerc certainly did not wish ill health on her husband, there can be little doubt that she looked forward with immense excitement to the move to the French capital. A visit that she had made "in search of diversion" to Florence that August found her, according to Madame Reinhardt, the French minister's wife there, "keen . . . to talk fashion. The new vogues are of the utmost importance to her." Madame Reinhardt noted further of her "young and pretty" guest that she was "very natural, gay, a good child." When they went out sightseeing, Pauline's "elegant appearance, the animation with which she speaks," attracted attention. "A small circle gathered around us wherever we went."

Pauline was no doubt delighted with the attention. Victor Emmanuel Leclerc, on the other hand, was later to express some disappointment that, despite his efforts in Italy, both administrative and in the field, and despite public approval for those efforts, he had no great gains to show for them. He could, with some justice, deplore the ill luck that had left him languishing in Milan when so many less able had joined Bonaparte on the Egyptian adventure and were to return to Paris having gained greater rewards and renown. It remained to be seen if his fortunes would alter with the move to Paris. For Pauline, young and confident, the only fly in the ointment appears to have been worries about her health, as well as that of her husband. The birth of Dermide, though a welcome event, had apparently not been without its problems, and she would be plagued for years to come by troubles arising from it.

CHAPTER THREE

Madame Leclerc in Paris, 1798–1799

ARRISON LIFE IN MILAN had had its advantages for Pauline Leclerc—there she had easily carried off the palm for beauty. The foray to Florence and the attention she had attracted had also been delightful. It had been enough in Italy, in short, to be the wife of an ambitious officer, a young mother, and the admired sister of General Bonaparte. But in Paris she faced challenges of a different kind.

First of all, within a month of their reaching the capital, Leclerc was dispatched on October 14, 1798, to Rennes in Brittany, to serve under General Kilmaine, who commanded the Army of England. This was a force of ships and troops that had been drawn up on the French littoral facing the Channel some months before Bonaparte left for Egypt in May that year. It had been hoped by the Directory that the French fleet accompanying the general south would inflict such a defeat on the British navy in Mediterranean waters that its home fleet would be unable to patrol the Channel. In consequence an invasion of England could be attempted.

In the event, Nelson had destroyed the French fleet at the Battle of the Nile that August, and it was now plain to all that the invasion of England would never take place. The Army of England, however, had still not been disbanded, and Leclerc, as ever not in good health but in demand as a noted administrator, was sent to northern France to keep order. He went without much hope of improving his financial position—or, indeed, the morale of the troops.

Pauline meanwhile had to make what she could of the unknown capital without her husband, who knew the city well from his university days. She stayed at the house in Paris that Leclerc had taken in the rue Ville-l'Évêque. It belonged to an army contractor friend of Leclerc's, Monsieur Michelot, who lived next door, and Pauline soon became intimate with her landlord and his wife, calling them "Poulot" and "Poulotte." She relied on them, as seasoned Parisians, to help her navigate her new life in the capital and her obligations to her husband's family. Besides her mother-in-law, or "Mama," as she called her, and two Leclerc daughters still unmarried, there was another brother-in-law to encounter—Jean Louis, bachelor partner with his mother in the milling business in Pontoise and, in Paris, member of the Corps Législatif (legislative body). Nicolas, who had stood witness to Victor Emmanuel's marriage to Pauline in Milan, was meanwhile absent with the Army of Egypt.

"My dear friend, Leclerc has just told me," writes Pauline to Madame Michelot during one of her husband's leaves of absence from the army, "that we are engaged at Mama's . . . for tomorrow. This really puts me out as I had counted on the pleasure of dining with you and Madame Alcan. But all can be saved if you can put off the party till six." Pauline could take satisfaction from the fact that Leclerc was usually not particularly anxious to see much of his mother, much less spend time in his native Pontoise. Indeed, when he bought a country house, as he did shortly before leaving for Rennes, it was to the north of Paris, near Senlis, while Pontoise lies to the capital's west. Montgobert, as the imposing property set in parkland high above church and fields was named, bordered the land of a friend of his, Montbreton, rather than that of any Leclerc family member. (It was, however, close to a house at Plessis-Chamant that Leclerc had bought and then sold to Pauline's brother Lucien.) Montgobert was to occupy Leclerc's imagination as he did his unpalatable duty in Rennes and elsewhere in the bleak northwestern winter. Plantations, woods, allées, gardens—all were planned to bear fruit when he would retire from his soldiering and live there with Pauline, Dermide, and children to come. Pauline too took an active interest, but it was limited to the house's interior. Meanwhile there were more practical matters to consider.

Dermide's wet nurse, having completed her term, had to be dispatched to Milan in the *diligence,* the public coach service. A visit from Pauline to Leclerc at Rennes in February 1799 occasioned a demand for a wool shawl to be sent to her from Paris as a shield against the cold. A month later she wrote again from Rennes to Madame Michelot: "I cannot tell you if I will be away long. It depends entirely on where Leclerc is sent. I see here several officers' wives, and go sometimes to the theater, which is passable for a provincial theater." Pauline reveals herself as an equestrienne. She wanted her amazons, or riding habits, from her wardrobe sent, as well as her linen chemises, for going on horseback.

Whether Madame Michelot performed these errands out of friendship, or whether she was already employed by Pauline at this point, these notes are the first examples of a long correspondence between the two women. Perfectionist Pauline Bonaparte relied on Madame Michelot as a woman of taste and with a good eye, who could be trusted to act as an agent in the important matter of clothes and linens. In addition, Madame Ducluzel, who was to be a stalwart member of Pauline's household, joined the establishment at the rue Ville-l'Évêque as Dermide's nursery nurse. From the beginning of her employment she appears also to have acted as a secretary who took dictation. All her life Pauline liked to dispatch letters in number and at speed but did not always care to write herself. She was to tell one correspondent that the act of writing fatigued her, while promising that every word had been dictated by herself. The truth may have been that she did not wish to expose her poor spelling and grammar.

Pauline had, besides the Michelots and Madame Ducluzel, the occasional company of her sister-in-law Aimée, who was two years younger than she and living at Madame Campan's celebrated school in

Saint-Germain-en-Laye outside Paris. Jeanne Campan had in her time educated the sisters of Louis XV and served Queen Marie Antoinette. Now she had among her pupils, apart from Aimée Leclerc, Josephine Bonaparte's daughter, Hortense, and the daughter of the American Republic's ambassador to France (future U.S. president James Monroe). Although education was the focus of the establishment, cavaliers and followers were not wholly discouraged, and in years to come the distinguished preceptress would boast that among her former pupils were the wives of eight marshals of France—including Aimée Leclerc.

Leclerc had removed Aimée from his mother's care in Pontoise on their arrival in Paris, and Madame Campan wrote to Joseph Bonaparte on January 20, 1799: "Citizen Leclerc entered my establishment six months ago. Her progress in all has been astonishing, and she did not know how to read or write." Impressed by this, Joseph in due course placed his younger sister Caroline among the scholars of the school. For in December 1798 Joseph's embassy to Rome came to an abrupt end when feeling against French occupation resulted in the assassination of one of his colleagues. Joseph, in whose care sixteen-year-old Caroline had been living, headed for Paris, where he established himself in the rue Rocher and Caroline at Madame Campan's school.

The name "Citizen Leclerc" has been taken to refer to Pauline, and it has been proposed that she spent six months, when a wife and mother, at Madame Campan's. But Leclerc's correspondence with Aimée over the next three years shows that she was the pupil in question, and one whose progress Leclerc encouraged. "I am glad to see from your letters . . . that your style in composition is improving," he wrote in 1801. Pauline Bonaparte, wartime bride, was to make her way in the world without a formal education, unlike her sisters, Elisa and Caroline, and her sister-in-law Aimée. Leclerc might have wished it otherwise, but, as with so many other aspects of Pauline's personality, he accepted it.

Pauline Leclerc was nevertheless at a disadvantage in Paris, where the salon was the meeting place of society and that meeting place traditionally a forum of ideas. In the drawing rooms of Madame Necker and of Madame de Geoffrin the *philosophes* of the Enlightenment had exchanged ideas, and the nature of the Revolution itself had been forged. The salons of the Directory—those of Madame Récamier, Madame Tallien, Madame de Staël, and Josephine, Pauline's own sister-in-law—were less numinous affairs, the conversation centering on the republic's army movements and the diaphanous fashions of the day. But the *incroyables,* as these sophisticated women were known, were admired for the elegance of their conversation as much as for that of their dress, for their interest in the arts as much as for their looks. Indeed, in the case of Madame de Staël, her conversation was said to be so intoxicating that men forgot that she was plain and happily fell into bed with her. For a feature of Directory society in general, most vividly seen in the lives of the *incroyables,* was that women began to seize the lead and initiate sexual relationships, taking the Revolutionary watch-words "Liberty, Equality, Fraternity" rather literally. And, of course, while these women knew how to be alluring and seductive to the men they desired, they knew also how to be cruel to other women. Pauline Leclerc, ignorant, young, and vibrantly beautiful, was meat for these cats.

Fortunately she had a protector in the shape of Madame Permon, a wealthy widow of Corsican origin who kept a salon in her house in the rue Sainte-Croix in Paris. Here Madame Permon seamlessly enter-tained both the members of *ancien régime* society who inhabited the Faubourg Saint-Germain and the men and women who had made their names since the Revolution.

Madame Permon, who had been brought up on Corsica as part of the Greek community at Cargèse, had known the Bonaparte parents well. When living in Montpellier she had nursed Pauline's father, Charles, when he fell ill while visiting doctors before his death there of liver cancer in 1785. She felt warmly toward all the Bonaparte children and made a pet of Pauline upon the latter's arrival in Paris. "My mother, who put herself out for no one," remarks Madame Permon's daughter, Laure, in the highly colored memoirs she later wrote as the Duchesse d'Abrantès, "loved Paulette with as much tenderness as if she had been my sister." Perhaps significantly, Madame Permon's other daughter had recently died at the age of eighteen, Pauline's current age. Madame Permon was indulgent to Pauline in all her butterfly moods, and encouraged the young wife and mother to come to the house as often as she wished, not just on salon days.

As we have seen on her trip to Florence, Pauline was enthusiastic about fashion, indeed preoccupied by it. Nothing had occurred to change her disposition following her journey to Paris and establishment there with Leclerc and Dermide. In the French capital, as a newcomer, she "still felt the need to make great efforts to please," as Laure d'Abrantès put it in her memoirs. But Pauline quickly grew ambitious, too, and a ball planned by Madame Permon gave her the opportunity to show her mettle.

Culture, letters, and musical knowledge Madame Leclerc could not supply. But Pauline had another claim on people's attention. In Egypt her brother Napoleon, in command of a massive force en route to do battle with the British for the riches of India, was winning glory for France and making illustrious the name of Bonaparte. At the Battle of the Pyramids in July 1798 he had routed the fearsome Mamelukes. Though balked—by Nelson's victory at the Battle of the Nile—in one objective, to pry the wealth of India from the British, Napoleon went on to march on Palestine, sacking Jaffa and besieging Acre. Meanwhile the archaeologists and naturalists on the expedition claimed the sites of Thebes and Karnak in Egypt. Pauline, enjoying her brother's renown, was resolved to have her day in the sun too, and told the Permons she would prepare a toilette for their ball that would "immortalize her." Not only did Pauline turn this toilette into "the serious affair of an entire week, according to her custom," but she insisted that her couturier Madame Germon and her coiffeur, Charbonnier, keep it the darkest secret. In addition she asked permission to dress at Madame Permon's, as she had several times before, so that her ensemble would appear as dazzling as possible.

Pauline chose the best possible moment to appear. There was plenty of company in the salon, but the room was not too crowded to allow her to be seen and appreciated. She was dressed as a bacchante, with golden grapes and bands of panther skin in her hair. A Greek tunic, clasped at the shoulders with cameos and under the bosom with an ancient intaglio, fell over a dress of fine Indian muslin, hemmed with vine leaves of gold thread. "As Madame Leclerc had dressed in the house, she had not put on gloves," Laure d'Abrantès recorded, "but had left her lovely round, white arms on display, decorated with gold bracelets and more cameos. . . . Nothing can give an idea of this ravishing figure. She truly lit up the salon when she entered." And a crowd of the young men who frequented the Permons' house and who had been bent over other ladies' chairs, murmuring praises, drew away and followed Pauline as she took her place by Madame Permon.

Now that Pauline's week of work had had its effect, she was content. But her hostess now had her own work to do, as the other women, deserted at their stations, recovered themselves and began to mutter jealously. Such brazen display—and from a Corsican who had had to beg for her dinner three years before—stuck in the gullet, they said. Madame Permon moved about to quell this envious friction. But one woman, the aristocratic Madame de Contades, escaped her. Seizing the arm of an unfortunate gentleman, Madame de Contades propelled him toward Pauline, who had established herself in a graceful attitude on a sofa in Madame Permon's boudoir.

This room was small and brightly lit. Madame de Contades, a statuesque beauty with the gaze of a goddess, bent her stare on her diminutive and recumbent rival. She admired it all—toilette, figure, face, hairstyle. And then she exclaimed to her companion: "Oh God, God. What misfortune! And such a pretty woman. But how has this defect never been noticed? God, how unfortunate!"

Pauline went bright red, so that she looked almost ugly, while someone asked, as Madame de Contades had intended, "What do you mean?"

"What?" she replied with relish. "Why, those two enormous ears planted on either side of her head. If they were mine, I would have them cut off. In fact, I will advise her that's what she should do." All eyes were now trained on Pauline, this time not on her many charms but on two parts of her anatomy that, Laure d'Abrantès happily tells us, were indeed slightly less than perfect. Pauline's ears, although not enormous, in Laure's opinion lacked the elegant curl of real beauty, being flat and shapeless. Madame de Contades had triumphed, and the evening ended with a crumpled Pauline in tears and home before midnight.

The next day, however, Pauline was prepared to do battle, although it was a battle she conducted lying in bed and with her ears hidden under a cap thick with lace. Receiving a concerned Madame Permon, she spoke indignantly of Madame de Contades as a great long stick of a woman and declared she had no idea what any man could see in her. Madame Permon was patient with her, but then Pauline went on to laud the appearance of a woman at the ball who was famously ill favored, tempering her praise only with the reflection that she was not fair enough to wear silver. The older woman ended her visit, saying genially, "You are quite deluded."

Madame Permon was an invaluable and frank guide for Pauline in these early days. There were traps galore for the incautious in Directory society, and it is impossible to know how many others Pauline fell into. There were temptations too, but one titillating note written by a certain Guillaume in February 1799, shortly before Pauline left to visit Leclerc in Rennes, suggests that at this date she was still a virtuous wife and mother: "To the beautiful dancer, to the amiable Madame Leclerc, to the woman uncaring of all one writes. . . . If you want me to amuse you, to sing to you while waiting as another beautifies you, employ your moments of leisure to reply to me . . . I will not be amorous toward you. That cannot be. If I love you, it will be only with an affection tender but chaste."

While Pauline's admirers, whether chaste or not so chaste, swelled in number, Leclerc was promoted to general of division and transferred at the end of August 1799 to a command in Lyon. There he had the charge of troops who had been the Austrians' prisoners of war at Mantua and elsewhere and who now required clothing, arming, and redeploying. Pauline meanwhile was occupied with the arrival in Paris of her mother, whose ill health had prompted her to leave Ajaccio and settle with her son Joseph and his wife, Julie, in the rue Rocher.

In the unfamiliar city Letizia Bonaparte made the acquaintance of her one-year-old grandson Dermide, and was glad to become reacquainted with her old friend Madame Permon, with whom she could speak in Italian. Madame Bonaparte's French, explained Laure d'Abrantès, was incomprehensible, despite her years in the south of France. Besides, Laure adds, Madame Bonaparte had an absolute ignorance of literature in her own language, as well as that of France, and she assumed a stately manner and forbidding air in Parisian society so as to ward off exposure of her ignorance. Madame Permon was someone to whom Madame Bonaparte could speak freely of her home in Ajaccio and of her network of relations in Corsica. "And everyone who knows Madame Bonaparte knows that, once on that subject, she did not get off it very easily," Laure remarks.

While the two older women conversed, Pauline Leclerc did her own kind of filial duty at the Permons' house, seating herself on her favorite sofa and admiring herself in a mirror. Playing with the folds of her dress and shawl, she reminisced with her mother about their escape from Ajaccio after the patriots had set fire to their house. They spoke of the treacherous path along the coast in the darkness, the appearance of her brother Napoleon wading ashore from the boat that had come in search of them, the vagaries of the weather as they voyaged north to Toulon. Now, six years later, Pauline and Madame Bonaparte could recite the details with tranquil pleasure.

While Napoleon and the Army of Egypt penetrated Palestine and the kingdoms of the Upper Nile, the Bonaparte family was gathering in Paris in force, but not necessarily in amity, as Laure d'Abrantès records. Pauline's sister Elisa and her husband, Felice Bacciochi, and her brothers Louis and Jérôme joined their siblings over the course of the year. They found that Pauline was learning to be cruel, as befitted a beauty of the time. Entering and seating herself on the sofa next to her hostess at the Permons' one day, she said, "So where's Joseph? I saw his carriage at the door. And is Julie here? Poor Julie, she is so ugly. Don't you agree, Laure?" She appeared stupefied to receive a negative. "No? What! Julie isn't ugly? Do you hear your sister, Albert?" she said to the son of the house, apparently at the top of her voice. At that moment Joseph and Julie entered. To someone desperately making signs, Pauline merely said, "Oh pooh, Joseph knows perfectly well his poor wife is plug-ugly."

On another occasion, Laure reports, Pauline appeared in great elegance, with Aimée her foil, at a soirée at the Permons'. In attendance hovered a Monsieur Auguste de Montaigu, alive to every wish that Madame Leclerc could express, her willing slave. And then Pauline's mother entered, bringing with her Caroline, the youngest Bonaparte sister, who was at school with Aimée. Caroline, all golden curls, white shoulders, and rosy skin, displayed a general air of pleasure at being out in the world and particular excitement at seeing her sister. She fell on Madame Leclerc to embrace her. But Pauline had noticed Auguste de Montaigu admiring the pretty picture Caroline made. "My God, Maman," said Madame Leclerc, ruthlessly repulsing her sister's advance, "she is as clumsy as a peasant from Fiumorbo," naming a savage part of Corsica. Now Caroline was the one to weep and retire from Madame Permon's salon, as Pauline herself had done not so long before.

Laure d'Abrantès relates a curious conversation between her brother, Albert, and her mother, in which Madame Permon asked her son if a certain notorious thief was targeting passersby in the rue Ville-l'Évêque. Albert answered innocently that he did not believe so. In which case, asked his mother, why had he escorted Madame Leclerc to her home in that street every evening for the last eight days? When Albert had the grace to blush, his mother warned him, "Paulette is a madcap, a pretty madcap." And she exhorted him to leave the business of escorting her to a certain "Ajax." Monsieur de Montaigu, she suggested, could meanwhile serve as her page. A private exchange in Greek followed, after which mother and son burst out laughing.

So runs Laure d'Abrantès's narrative. The implication is that "Ajax" was Pauline's lover and de Montaigu an aspiring admirer. As Laure offers an identity for "Ajax"—General Pierre de Ruel, later Marquis de

Beurnonville—we can add from army records and other sources that this soldier was in his late forties and had, after a distinguished appearance at the Battle of Valmy and a spell as an Austrian hostage, recently been inspector of infantry with Leclerc in the Army of England. But Laure does not stop there. She declares that Pauline was dividing her favors between Beurnonville and General Moreau—who had been in Paris for some time without occupation, following the Peace of Leoben and the end of his leadership of the French army in Germany. To the reader's gratification, there is more. The Duchesse d'Abrantès declares General Étienne-Jacques Macdonald, who had fought against the Russians under Suvarov and was now governor of Versailles, to be a third lover. And all three generals were great friends with one another. It was a comic opera indeed.

According to Laure d'Abrantès, Pauline successfully kept all three generals in the dark about her relations with the other two, until she made the mistake of repeating to each of them hostile comments the others were supposed to have made. She "put them at each other's throats." At that point, unfortunately for Pauline, one of the generals, wishing to preserve his friendships, made overtures to the others. They compared notes, discovered the source of their disagreements, and resolved one and all to break with their troublemaking mistress. To this end Beurnonville handed over to Pauline letters in which his friends repudiated her, and in person announced his own resignation as her lover. Pauline apparently admired Beurnonville for his candor and persuaded him to continue their relationship.

How far we can trust this story is unclear. Laure d'Abrantès tells us she had the story from General Lannes, who was told it by Pauline herself long after the trio of generals had ceased to be her satellites. We can say only that the twenty-five volumes of d'Abrantès's memoirs are an entertaining source for stories about Pauline Bonaparte in Paris at this period, when we have few of Pauline's letters preserved, and when Madame Leclerc of the rue Ville-l'Évêque was not of sufficient importance to attract more distinguished attention. Laure's mother's house in the rue Sainte-Croix did offer the Bonaparte family an asylum in the early days in Paris, when they were still nostalgic for their Corsican heritage. But those days were about to end, and Pauline Bonaparte Leclerc's position in Parisian society was about to alter.

To RETURN TO THE HISTORICAL RECORD, Napoleon had left Egypt unexpectedly in August 1799 and landed on the French mainland in October. During his absence his wife, Josephine, had been conducting an affair with Hippolyte Charles, formerly one of Leclerc's aides-de-camp. Napoleon learned of this affair while in Egypt and swore that he would divorce his wife, but Josephine managed to placate him. He was anyway otherwise occupied immediately upon his return to Paris, planning a coup d'état to overthrow the unpopular Directory government and browbeat the Conseil des Anciens (Council of Elders) and the Conseil des Cinq-Cents (Council of Five Hundred), the upper and lower chambers of the Corps Législatif established in 1795, into framing a new constitution, giving him draconian powers.

The 18 Brumaire (November 9) saw the first upheaval. Of the five members of the Directory, three resigned voluntarily and two resisted to no effect. Meanwhile the two councils, falsely warned that they were in danger from a Jacobin rebellion, had removed to the Château of Saint-Cloud, west of Paris, where General Bonaparte assured them they would be safe with the troops he commanded. With him went not only Joachim Murat, the cavalry officer who had distinguished himself at the Battle of Abukir and then accompanied Napoleon from Egypt to France, but Victor Emmanuel Leclerc, who had been recalled from Lyon to Paris a few days earlier.

The following day both councils were in an uproar. Napoleon Bonaparte dealt with the Council of Elders himself, marching into the chamber with an escort of grenadiers and accusing the deputies of destroying the republic's constitution. He then proceeded with his grenadiers to the château's Orangery, where the Council of Five Hundred was meeting, and met with a stormy reception. He was assaulted by Jacobin deputies, and a motion was raised, after he had fled the chamber, to declare him an outlaw. At this point Lucien Bonaparte, who was president of the council, left the chamber and called on Leclerc and Murat to enter and restore order. He declared that a group of deputies brandishing daggers were holding the assembly hostage inside and motioned to Napoleon's bloody face as proof. If his brother was a traitor, said Lucien, seizing a sword, he would himself plunge it through the traitor's heart.

Leclerc and Murat duly entered the chamber and, between them, successfully expelled the disputatious deputies. Characteristic of the two men were their orders. Murat, the flamboyant Gascon, cried: "Foutez-moi tout ce monde dehors" (Get this mob out of here). Victor Emmanuel Leclerc was more restrained: "Représentants, retirez-vous, c'est l'ordre du général." They were obeyed, the council dispersed, and the Directory years, in which General Bonaparte, Murat, and Leclerc had served as comrades, were at an end. Under the new constitution that was soon approved, Napoleon Bonaparte became first consul of the French republic, the other two being the Abbé Sieyès and Pierre Roger-Ducos.

For an account of these stirring events, as viewed from the perspective of Pauline and the other denizens of the Permons' salon, we turn once more to the gossipy *jeune fille* of the maison Permon.

The 18 Brumaire was a highly charged day in Paris, during which rumor was rife, without substantiation being possible, to the irritation of all. The Permon ladies, paying a visit on Madame Letizia Bonaparte, found her superbly calm. Madame Leclerc, on the other hand, they found dictating a letter every quarter of an hour to General Moreau to solicit news of developments. Whether her lover or not, he was closely involved in the coup and had charge of the Directory members at the Luxembourg Palace. (She was not to be deterred, Laure informs us, even when told that Moreau was not at home and was not necessarily expected back that night.)

The next day, Saint-Cloud being remote from Paris and Fouché, chief of police, exercising a remarkable control of information issuing from that quarter, the Bonaparte women knew nothing of what had passed there until halfway through the evening. Pauline and her mother were at the Théâtre Feydeau with Madame Permon and Laure when the performance was interrupted by a dramatic announcement: "Citizens, General Bonaparte has narrowly missed being assassinated at Saint-Cloud by enemies of the republic."

A general hubbub erupted, Pauline reeled backward, then burst into tears. Her mother, tight-mouthed, urged her to compose herself. Setting about organizing an exit from the theater, the Permons had their carriage brought around. For once in her life Madame Bonaparte chose to make her first port of call her daughter-in-law Josephine's house in the rue Chantereine, where the most news was to be had. They found the road outside packed with horses, carriages, and curious onlookers. But a comedy developed, as Madame Permon, who did not know Josephine, swore that, whatever the circumstances, etiquette was etiquette and she could not accompany the Bonapartes into the house.

While they were arguing the point, an opponent of the coup leaders pulled down the carriage window and said to Laure, "Your friend Lucien has made his brother the general a king." The Bonaparte women hurried inside to find that Fouché had brought to Josephine a more sober account of the proceedings at Saint-Cloud. All were safe, Leclerc included, and Napoleon, they learned, was to be sworn in within hours as first consul.

In reward for Murat's part in the Brumaire coup, Napoleon consented to his marriage to the eighteen-year-old Caroline Bonaparte, which took place in January 1800. Murat had hurried to her with an account of events late in the evening of 19 Brumaire, alarming all at Madame Campan's with his ferocious knocking on the door. But there were rewards for others who had played their part. To Moreau was assigned the command of the Army of the Rhine, and, in the campaign against the Austrians that now opened in Germany, Leclerc was appointed head of a division. Pauline and Leclerc could hope for advantages from his service there, and Napoleon gave every indication that he intended to honor not only his mother but his seven siblings too at his Consular court. These were heady days.

CHAPTER FOUR

Sister to the First Consul, 1800–1802

FIRST CONSUL BONAPARTE DECLARED that, with the coup d'état of 18 Brumaire, the Revolution was "perfected," although those visiting the splendid Tuileries Palace, formerly the residence of Louis XVI and Marie Antoinette, where he made his home in February 1800, might have begged to differ. Caustic as ever, Napoleon said to his valet Benjamin Constant, with reference to the Tuileries' previous occupants, that the art lay not in obtaining entry but in staying there. But some were in no doubt that Napoleon possessed the black arts necessary for dominion. Madame Permon had said on 19 Brumaire, "He is a monster fish who will swallow whole the other consuls." Pauline continued to exhibit the lively pride in her brother that she had always displayed. She also maintained her animosity toward her sister-in-law Josephine.

Josephine Bonaparte had a strange existence now that her husband was first consul. She had no official status as consort, and indeed to a degree preferred it that way. Napoleon had the architect Fontaine draw up plans to adapt for him the royal château of Saint-Cloud, where the events of 18 Brumaire had taken place. But Josephine refused to abandon Malmaison, her small country retreat west of Paris at Rueil, and, busy with her garden and greenhouses there, and with her daughter

Hortense's upbringing, did not always appear in what now became known as Consular society. Nevertheless both she and Hortense attended the ball that followed Laure Permon's wedding in October 1800 to General Andoche Junot—a bridegroom, now commander of Paris, whom Napoleon had once spurned for his sister Pauline.

In the memoirs she wrote as Duchesse d'Abrantès, Laure Junot gives no details of Pauline's toilette for an event at which most of the Bonaparte family was present. But she indicates that Madame Leclerc was "as ever charming, as ever elegant"—until naughty Pauline chose to comment on her sister-in-law's appearance. Josephine's dress was embellished with poppies and golden wheat sheaves, and she wore a garland in her hair to match. "Really," said the twenty-year-old Pauline. "I can't believe someone of forty putting flowers in her hair." (Josephine was thirty-seven.) Embarrassed, Laure Junot pointed out the bunches of jonquils that adorned the turban and dress of her own mother, Madame Permon. Pauline looked astonished at this intervention. "That's quite different," she said firmly. "Quite different."

First Consul Bonaparte did not himself always appear at the balls and parties that marked Consular society. There was a new constitution to establish, a central administration, the Bank of France, and a legal system, the Code Napoléon, to initiate. Meanwhile a lasting peace between the state and the Catholic Church was being engineered, which was to be formalized in the Concordat of 1801. But some things did not change. Officials and military officers continued to be appointed to posts and commands, and Napoleon's family benefited from his exaltation. Lucien became minister of the interior, Caroline's husband, Murat, became chief of the Consular Guard, and Louis Bonaparte, aged twenty-two, took charge of a cavalry brigade. Even sixteen-year-old Jérôme left school and became a naval lieutenant. And Pauline in Paris awaited news of her husband's fortunes in the Rhine campaign, where he had been serving since December 5, 1799, as commander of the Second Division of the center. (Moreau was commander of the entire force.)

The Allies had taken advantage of the absence of Napoleon in

Egypt to open a further offensive—the War of the Second Coalition. In June 1800 Leclerc's division received the order to take the Bavarian town of Landshut, which was in the hands of the archduke Ferdinand. The Austrians had about 120,000 men in all, deployed in the Black Forest north of the Alps, under the command of General Paul Kray, to obstruct any French advance along the Rhine and Danube rivers to Vienna. Although the town, on the river Isar, appeared impregnable, such was the verve of Leclerc's attack that in short order much of the enemy had been put to flight and of those remaining, four hundred were dead and six hundred taken prisoner.

Despite this success Leclerc had received a wound in the leg and had to retire to the rear, so he saw no more action on the Rhine. Furthermore Moreau's Army of the Rhine, although ultimately successful in December 1800 at the Battle of Hohenlinden, was quite outshone by the Army of Reserve that Napoleon led that summer over the Alps and into northern Italy. In a journey that piqued the imagination of Consular artists, who depicted Napoleon on horseback amid frozen masses, this force crossed the Alps by the Great Saint Bernard pass, which was still snowbound in May. By a mixture of luck and vigor Bonaparte and his troops then defeated the Austrian force mustered south of the Alps, at the Battle of Marengo in June 1800, and threw the enemy out of Italy. Once again Leclerc had, by bad luck, been attached to the less glorious fighting force.

However, in consolation for his troubles, if it was no sop to his ambition, Leclerc was to spend much of the summer of 1800 with his wife, to whom he remained devoted. The faults Laure Junot and others were quick to note in Pauline, Leclerc seems to have easily overlooked. He was, a friend wrote, hard on himself and indulgent toward others. Laure Junot had her own view of this "singular" marriage: "Madame Leclerc treated her husband despotically, and yet she went in fear, not that her husband would rebuke her but that the first consul would."

The Leclercs were to have as their rendezvous the watering resort of Plombières-les-Bains in the Vosges, where Pauline arrived in June, some weeks before her husband. She struck a General Jean Hardy, who was there taking the cure, as "a fine little woman, very sweet and very kind." She begged the general to visit her, and he told his wife that Madame Leclerc was there to reestablish her health, and tend to her pelvis, "which had been weakened by childbirth. . . . She knows no one at Plombières and seems very happy to have as a neighbor a comrade of her husband's." (Hardy had served under Leclerc in Italy.) "I owe her the care that I would wish for you, were you in her place. Besides, without reading the future, one cannot foresee what will result by chance of a meeting; good intentions are not always fruitless." And indeed when Leclerc arrived, weeks later, Hardy's solicitude for Pauline may have been a factor in stirring the senior officer to promote the other's career. "I will write to Bonaparte myself," Leclerc was to declare. But privately he was beginning to despair, and to doubt that he had any influence with his brother-in-law. Although Bonaparte had anxiously asked after Leclerc's health each time he had corresponded with Moreau after the Landshut action, he seemed to wish to do nothing for him now.

This was the first of many visits that Pauline was to make for her health to fashionable watering resorts or bathing stations. As on future visits, she now made a habit of living retired, and, as now, on future occasions there would always be those who sought to develop an acquaintance with her. But late as she might dance into the night in Paris, as a valetudinarian in Plombières she was dedicated to a regime of waters, exercise, and rest. Besides, the society available in the town was not designed to please her. At a dismal ball that General Hardy attended, there were sixty women—but no more than a dozen men, and only four among them young and fit enough to dance.

Pauline's sister-in-law Josephine had earlier sought at Plombières a cure for the continuing infertility that beset her relationship with Napoleon. Hardy's claim that Pauline's visit to the resort was occasioned by her need to recover following childbirth is somewhat surprising, given that Dermide was now two years old. But Dermide's birth appears to have presented his mother with long-lasting complications. Certainly in the autumn of 1801 and again some years later Pauline was to order a girdle to support her pelvis. (Today women faced with sacroiliac pain and pelvic instability following childbirth wear a special belt.) She added to that order two bidets, and there is evidence to suggest that later in life she suffered from salpingitis, or inflammation of the fallopian tubes. This can occur after childbirth, although multiple sexual partners and gonorrhea are other causes, and possibly she was already affected when she was at Plombières. Symptoms of salpingitis include lower abdominal pain, which can cause difficulty in walking. In other words Pauline's apparently capricious desire to be carried everywhere may have had its root in either sacroiliac or abdominal pain, or perhaps both.

Content with her cure for the moment, Pauline wrote to Madame Michelot on July 11, "I am well. I have benefited enormously from the waters and still more from the exercise that I take here. I have seen Brulière, whom my husband sent to tell me to stay here longer. I hope you are happy about my health." Leclerc duly arrived himself later in the month, much worn by his fatigues on the Rhine, and pursued, like his wife, a regime of baths, exercise, and rest. But in this letter to Madame Michelot, Pauline added, "How are you coping with your big stomach?" Madame Michelot was to have a baby later that summer. Although Pauline was full of concern for her friend as the day neared, she appears, with this question, to feel the distaste of one who had regretted seeing her own stomach grow big with child, her fashionable silhouette distended.

Although Dermide was now more than two years old, there is no suggestion that Pauline was at Plombières to improve her fertility. As we shall shortly see, she was not above claiming that she was pregnant to try to avoid unwelcome duties. But there is no speculation in Leclerc's correspondence with his family, or in that of the Bonapartes—both of which refer freely to pregnancies and childbirths—about another pregnancy for Pauline. If she was indeed suffering from salpingitis, then she would have been most unlikely to fall pregnant again. And her doctors would have known that, and have made her and Leclerc aware of it. But for want of firm evidence on the matter we cannot say whether her first pregnancy had left her unable or unwilling to reproduce again.

A few weeks later the Leclercs settled at their estate, Montgobert—an invalid couple with a small son, enjoying themselves in the Picardy landscape with visits from Leclerc and Bonaparte relations and friends. The couple amicably planned decoration inside the château and renovation of the garden and lands without. Leclerc changed the parterre garden *à la française* that summer into a landscaped English garden and to that end planted thousands of trees and bushes. Pauline appears to have remained in charge of the interior decor for the rooms they occupied, but her husband had ambitious plans to add another floor to the house and had already consulted Fontaine, the architect from Pontoise who, with his associate Percier, was making a name for himself in Paris. (Fontaine, meanwhile, was relying on Leclerc to protect him at the Ministry of the Interior, where Napoleon's plans for him to alter Saint-Cloud were calling down on the alien architect from Pontoise the wrath of the ministry's architects.)

At Montgobert, Leclerc made "improvements" as though he were a returning general who had amassed a considerable war chest during campaigns. In fact, it would seem from his papers, he had amassed considerable debt, and that year, when sending him three thousand francs for decoration that Pauline had instigated, he told his brother Jean Louis, who was overseeing the works, that he could do no more. One wonders what his mother, living modestly at Pontoise, made of his extravagance. But Leclerc was in the grip of an obsession, and the expenditures continued.

There were visits to be made to neighboring properties. Leclerc's friend Montbreton owned the property that bordered Montgobert. Joseph and Julie Bonaparte had meanwhile bought and embellished the Château of Mortefontaine, which lay close to the forest of d'Ermenonville between Montgobert and Paris, where they made all the family welcome. And Pauline's brother Lucien was nearby at Plessis. Although Lucien's wife, Christine, died in May, he put off mourning that summer to play host to amateur theatricals, in which the Bonapartes' eldest sister, Elisa, played an active role. Pauline informed Madame Michelot in late August that she was to take part in a comedy that was being staged at Plessis. "I am very happy with my role as a servant girl," she wrote.

The legend runs that, upon his return from Marengo, Napoleon was outraged by the lascivious gestures and diaphanous costumes that were a feature of his siblings' theatricals and banned Lucien and Elisa from performing Voltaire's *Alzire*. If so, he seems to have taken his time, as he had returned from Italy to Paris by early July, and this performance of which Pauline writes was scheduled for late summer. Moreover, if Napoleon felt distaste for his family's amateur theatricals, he relished the professional stage. A young actor from the Midi, Rapenouille, took the name of Lafon and dazzled audiences on his debut that May in Racine's *Iphigénie* at the Comédie Française. Napoleon told the star of the troupe, the great Talma, that he should welcome the advent of the younger actor. "It's a stimulant you needed. You were acting in your sleep, now you must wake up."

Lafon is said separately to have been taken under the protection of Lucien Bonaparte and may have been involved at Plessis in tutoring the Bonaparte family in their theatrical roles. Pauline, moreover, is credited with having embarked on an affair with the handsome young southerner, all flashing black eyes and deep seductive voice. But Leclerc's correspondence with his family contains no hint that summer of marital discord. "Paulette has left this morning for Paris and won't return here this year," he records placidly from Montgobert, on September 23. "I follow her once they have finished planting." And he goes on to write of harvests and donkeys, of mares to be sold and carpenters to be paid. If a cuckold, he was a remarkably complacent—if not an unwitting—one.

In Paris the Leclercs, with Dermide and his nurse, had been occupying apartments in the house of Victor Emmanuel's brother Nicolas, as they had left the Michelots'. But now they signed a contract to buy for 20,500 francs an elegant house in the rue de Courcelles, close to the Faubourg Saint-Honoré and next to the Church of Saint-Philippe-du-Roule. The house, although not large, was commodious, with a salon, a boudoir, a dining room, a billiard room, and a library, as well as an upper floor of bedrooms, with a "grotto" and a swing in the garden.

Pauline had indicated that they would wait for the general to receive command of an army before they purchased a house. But perhaps it had proved too galling to see the other Bonapartes in the smart Parisian houses they now occupied. Pauline's mother enjoyed the hospitality of her half brother Fesch in a luxurious *hôtel,* as these large town mansions were known, in the rue Mont Blanc. Joseph and Julie were now in the Hôtel Marboeuf in the rue du Faubourg Saint-Honoré, which had belonged to the governor of Corsica. (On that island at least, the Marquis de Marboeuf was popularly believed to have been Letizia Bonaparte's lover.) Caroline and Murat were installed in the Hôtel de Brienne, to the north of the Tuileries. And Lucien, with Elisa and Felice Bacciochi as lodgers, occupied the Hôtel de Brissac in the rue de Grenelle.

While Pauline decorated her boudoir to her satisfaction, Leclerc was at last given a command, but it was not one to please him. He was dispatched in December 1800 to Dijon, to command the Army of Reserve, which had now returned from northern Italy and was in winter quarters. If there is any doubt that Leclerc was unhappy with this stagnant posting, a letter exists from his former commander, General Berthier, written shortly after his departure for Dijon: "I have seen your wife, and I have tried, with her, to persuade the First Consul to let you come to Paris." Pauline's efforts to obtain her husband's return to Paris, where he might himself press the War Ministry for a more advantageous posting, do not preclude her simultaneously conducting one or even more than one affair. It does show, however, that she was still ambitious for him and eager to see him singled out. Leclerc himself later recorded, "I was vexed that I was forgotten during the war. . . . Although I was full of admiration for Bonaparte, who sacrifices himself all day long to assure France's well-being, I was indignant to see these wretches who, by the worthlessness of their resources, ought never to have had a role to play, not content with the fine place he had assigned them, try to put themselves at his side and even in his place." Leclerc had in mind General Bernadotte, Désirée Clary's husband, and other officers who had earlier curried favor with Bonaparte before attempting to stage a coup during his absence in the east.

Between them Berthier and Pauline were successful, and Leclerc was agreeably surprised with the new post assigned him in March 1801, after the War of the Second Coalition had been brought to an end by the Peace of Lunéville. He was made lieutenant general of the Army of Observation of the Gironde that was assembling in Bordeaux, preparatory to going to Spain. Once there the French corps would support Spain in the so-called War of the Oranges that it was conducting against Portugal, Britain's oldest ally. On arrival at Bordeaux, Leclerc wrote to his sister, Aimée, at Madame Campan's school: "The roads getting here were terrible, but the beauty of the town and the affability of the inhabitants are compensation enough." When Pauline joined him there, attending balls and concerts with him, he was more than content.

But once Pauline had returned to Paris, and the Army of Observation set off for Spain, Leclerc was grumpy. He wrote to Aimée in mid-June from Ciudad Rodrigo, in western Spain, "I have been constantly on the road for a month, and always in the most frightful rush. This is a horrible country, five centuries behind France." Furthermore, for all his exertions, once more the campaign to which Leclerc was assigned failed to provide him with a proper theater of war. Once more a great destiny was denied him, for Spain and Portugal rapidly signed a peace. And, no doubt mindful of his expenditure on the new house in Paris, of the building works at Montgobert, he appealed on August 7 from Salamanca to Lucien Bonaparte, who had recently become ambassador to Spain: "If you find an opportunity at Madrid to help me increase my fortune, I will be obliged to you."

While Leclerc labored in Spain, Pauline spent most of the summer at Mortefontaine, at her brother Joseph's house, with some excursions to Montgobert, where her brother-in-law Jean Louis Leclerc was still overseeing the improvements. "You see, my dear brother," wrote Leclerc from Spain, "that I have more and more ambitious plans for the property." And again he wrote, "This year we should begin to have a little fruit from the vines we planted."

What made her husband's stymied campaign all the more galling for Pauline was the successful career of her younger sister Caroline's husband, Murat. A description of the two pretty sisters tormenting an elderly Italian poet by repeatedly seizing his wig when he was sitting out in the sunshine shows that Pauline and Caroline could be the best of friends. But they were also all their lives jealous of each other, and now Caroline had a small baby, Achille Louis Napoléon Murat, and was pregnant with another. Murat, moreover, had been named commander in chief of the French forces in Italy, while Leclerc battled against fatigue and loss of morale in Spain and fell prey to anxiety about his loved ones in France. "I see with pain that you do not speak to me of Paulette," he wrote from Ciudad Rodrigo on July 28 to his sister, Aimée. "Has there been some coldness between you? I would see with pain a rift between two people who are so dear to me."

And then in early October, just as Leclerc had taken his men into winter quarters in Bro, near Valladolid, Napoleon addressed the following momentous dispatch to General Berthier, the minister of war: "Send an order by special courier to General Leclerc to come to Paris with all speed. He should bring his aides-de-camp, two adjutants-commandant, and five artillery and reconnaissance officers of quality to serve under him in an overseas expedition. . . . He can leave the command of the observation corps to the most senior general." Leclerc left Spain the moment he received the dispatch. At last his chance had come.

Napoleon went on to outline, in this and further dispatches to Berthier, the details of the vast overseas expedition that Leclerc was to head. It was to comprise a fighting force of more than twenty thousand men, with an equal number of sailors supplied by the Admiralty—and commanded by Admiral Louis Thomas Villaret de Joyeuse—to man the seventy-one vessels, including twenty-five ships of the line, that would transport the army. One squadron was to set sail from Brest, another from Rochefort, and others from Lorient, Toulon, Cádiz, and even Vlissinden in Holland. The force also included Spanish and Dutch contingents. And the object of this powerful expedition? To recover for France the formerly profitable sugar colony of Saint-Domingue, known as the Pearl of the Antilles and now in the hands of rebel slaves led by Toussaint Louverture. Saint-Domingue, present-day Haiti, forms the western part of the Caribbean island, which, with its much larger eastern part, Santo Domingo—the present-day Dominican Republic— was originally claimed for Spain by Columbus in the fifteenth century as Hispaniola. Spain ceded Saint-Domingue to France in 1697.

A recent endeavor of Toussaint's, to frame a new constitution according to which he would be governor-general for life, had incensed his former masters. The National Convention of 1794 had granted the slaves of Saint-Domingue, as well as those of other French colonies, their freedom, and by degrees Toussaint had won control of the country, as well as of Spanish Santo Domingo. Now that the preliminaries of the Peace of Amiens, which would tie up the loose ends left dangling by the War of the Second Coalition, had been settled, and now, indeed, that the protracted expedition to Egypt had ended in defeat—the French surrendered Alexandria to Sir Ralph Abercromby in March— Napoleon had troops and ships at his disposal, and was eager to bring the unruly former colony to heel. In particular he meant to recover the enormous revenues of Saint-Domingue for France—and, to that end, he planned to reestablish slavery.

In Toussaint, however, Napoleon had an opponent of extraordinary charisma and intellect, who was in addition a proven warrior. Over the years the former slave had won the loyalty of local chiefs and trained a large army in guerrilla warfare against the Spanish and the British. Now he was expecting an attempt by the French to regain control, and he was ready.

As Leclerc learned when he arrived in Paris, it was the express wish of the first consul that he should take his wife and small son with him to Saint-Domingue. For this was no short military campaign that awaited the commander, as Napoleon's instructions made clear. Once Leclerc had subdued Toussaint and the other island commanders, he was, as captain general of the colony, to introduce and oversee the implementation of a series of legal, administrative, and fiscal reforms. He might be away for some years in this latter capacity, and in the circumstances it was deemed by the first consul only proper that Leclerc's family go with him. Nevertheless there were those who were startled by the proposition that Pauline and Dermide Leclerc were to accompany the expeditionary force.

In the first place Toussaint, the chiefs who served him, and their guerrilla forces would almost certainly resist the French expeditionary force. But in addition the history of Saint-Domingue was a violent one, checkered with rebellions by the slave population of five hundred thousand and with massacres they perpetrated among the thirty thousand plantation owners who farmed coffee, sugarcane, and indigo. Toussaint had subdued most of the country, but news of battles between his forces and the mulattoes under General Rigaud, who occupied the south of the colony—of voodoo crimes, of atrocities—continued to percolate back to France. And then there was the ever-present threat in the Americas of yellow (or, as it was then called, Siamese) fever, with hemorrhage, high temperature, and black vomit preceding death. It would, in short, have been hardly surprising if Pauline had not felt some dread at the idea of leaving her settled life in Paris for unknown, fearsome Saint-Domingue. But diminishing all other concerns, there was always the prospect of glory and fortune to be won, debts to be eliminated, in the distant Caribbean.

According to one account, Pauline was positively ebullient the evening after Leclerc arrived in Paris from Spain. Their neighbor from Montgobert, Montbreton, called at the rue de Courcelles with his brother, Jacques de Norvins, to congratulate the couple. (There had been rumors since the peace with England had been signed that an expedition to Saint-Domingue would take place, but it had been thought that the command would be given to General Bernadotte.) "Leclerc and his wife received us with the greatest friendship," Norvins tells us. "I was astonished to learn that she, so young, so delicate, so happy in Paris, would follow her husband to Saint-Domingue with her son, aged about three. The first consul had decided it, and she spoke with frank pleasure of this great adventure." Norvins explains that everyone in Paris had been somewhat thrown by the news of the expedition. "I said, 'My God, madame, I would go with you too, if Leclerc wants me to come.' 'Yes, yes, you must come with us!' And she called her husband who was talking to General Davout: 'Listen, Norvins says he wants to come with us.' 'You're joking,' replied Leclerc. 'Norvins is not a man to leave Paris, where he is so well off. Aren't I right, Norvins?' 'No, you're quite wrong, and if you want, I'll be of your number.' Leclerc looked at my brother, Montbreton. 'What do you say?' 'I say, in my brother's place, I'd do the same.' 'Then shake on it,' said Leclerc, extending his hand."

The general was not usually so cavalier in choosing his regular staff. "I only take notice of good conduct and talent," he had written from Spain to his sister, Aimée, when she asked him to advance a protégé's military career out there. Now General Charles-François-Joseph Dugua, who had served in Egypt, was co-opted for the Saint-Domingue expedition, as was General Hardy, with whom Pauline had dined in Plombières. "I hope to acquire legally and honestly funds to assure your well-being and educate our children," Hardy wrote optimistically to his wife. Despite Leclerc's love of order, everything now took place in the most tremendous hurry. "It is just as you would expect," he grumbled to Davout, "when the commander is appointed at the last minute." He was kept constantly busy, answering requests from those who wished a son or a godson or a protégé to form part of the army and share in its glory. Nor were his own and Pauline's families unrepresented. Leclerc's elderly uncle General Jean-Charles Musquinet de Beaupré joined the force, and Pauline's younger brother Jérôme was to accompany the expedition as a naval lieutenant.

Madame Campan's nephew Pannellier won a place as secretary to the general, even as the schoolmistress lost Aimée Leclerc, with Hortense de Beauharnais one of her prize pupils, to matrimony. Leclerc wanted to see Aimée married to his friend and colleague General Davout before he left France, and the ceremony was duly performed on November 9, 1801. But it could have been set for a month later. The date of the expeditionary force's departure was constantly postponed, as preparations were not complete, and arms, clothing, hospital supplies lacking. In the meantime, according to legend, Pauline began to fret and told her brother she could not accompany her husband as she was pregnant. The first consul promptly sent around his physician to examine and declare her mistaken. Laure Junot gives this account of visiting the general's lady in the rue de Courcelles:

"Oh, little Laure," said Pauline, throwing herself in the other's arms. "Lucky you! To stay in Paris. Good God, I am going to be so bored. How can my brother have so hard a heart, so mean a soul as to exile me in the middle of savages and snakes. . . . And I am ill too. Oh, I'll die before I even get there."

Laure Junot talked to the disconsolate beauty "as one would to a child, of toys and pom-poms." Pauline would be queen in Saint-Domingue, said Laure, she would be carried in a litter. A slave would be attentive to her every wish, and she would walk through arbors of orange trees and flowers. There were, besides, no snakes in the Antilles, and the people weren't savages. Getting nowhere with these arguments, Madame Junot had the canniness to suggest that Pauline would look very pretty in Creole dress.

Pauline's tears dried instantly, and she set to imagining the costume. "Oh, it would be pretty. A madras handkerchief, tied Creole fashion, a little corset, a skirt of pleated muslin?" Immediately she rang for her maid and had her entire stock of Indian cotton, a present from Madame Permon, brought out. As that lady had habitually worn a madras handkerchief at home in bed, her daughter, Laure, proved adept at knotting the four corners of the cloth selected and fitting it to Pauline's head. And Madame Leclerc was thrilled with her coiffure *à la créole.* "'Laurette,' she said, arranging herself on her sofa, 'do you know how I love you? You prefer Caroline to me, but let's see if we can't change that. Here's a proof of my love for you. . . . Come to Saint-Domingue. You will be the first lady of the island after me. I'll be queen, as you say. Well, you'll be vicereine. I'll talk to my brother about it.' 'Me, go to Saint-Domingue,' I cried. 'What are you thinking of?' 'Don't worry, I'll talk to Bonaparte, and as he likes Junot, he'll let him come.'"

Pauline then enumerated the balls she would give, the parties in the mountains—"something every day." And she ticked off on her fingers the couturiers, milliners, and jewelers that Laure must patronize before she would be fit to travel—"Mademoiselle Despaux, Madame Germon, Le Roi, Copp, Mesdames Roux . . . no, Nattier is better." In the end, as she would not take no for an answer, according to Laure, Junot himself intervened to ask how his wife could possibly travel, given that she was vastly pregnant "Oh," said Pauline. "So you are."

Frivolities aside, Pauline and Leclerc had sober legal action to take before they left Paris. Such were the risks of the journey to come that they each signed a bond leaving to the other their property on death. It is said that Leclerc even picked out at Montgobert the site of a grave, should the need for burial arise. In any event he gave his brother Jean Louis a proxy so that works at Montgobert could continue, and received a proxy from Josephine Bonaparte, who, by coincidence, and although a Martinique Creole by birth, had property in Saint-Domingue.

"Don't bother me about money anymore," Napoleon is said to have told Leclerc, on bestowing on his brother-in-law this prime command. And when Leclerc and Pauline embarked with Dermide on the flagship L'Océan, at Brest, and set sail for the Caribbean on December 14, 1801, the general had every hope that he would return a rich man. At the last minute, and it seems to have been a matter of regret for Pauline, their house in the rue Courcelles, which she had so recently decorated, was sold. But, although she sighed for Paris and for her boudoir there, she had what Norvins describes as sumptuous quarters on L'Océan, and at Le Cap, the former capital of Saint-Domingue, she would inhabit the governor's palace. On board the ship, as the bad weather off the French coast gave way to balmy breezes in the Canary Islands and farther west, Pauline played with Dermide on deck.

It was a picture that Norvins, for one, appreciated, but another member of the expedition had preferred to wait and find a separate passage at Brest. Stanislas Fréron, down on his luck now for years, had obtained a post as subprefect at Les Cayes in Saint-Domingue, but on finding that his berth was booked on *L'Océan,* chose not to travel on the same vessel as his former fiancée and her husband. He had to wait four months for another berth.

There were others who found the sight of *L'Océan* and the rest of the fleet from Brest more than off-putting. As the ships sailed into the Bay of Samana in eastern Hispaniola at the end of January 1802, Toussaint Louverture was on the lookout. "Friends," he addressed his lieutenants, "we are doomed. All France is come to Saint-Domingue." And he sent a message to the vassal chief General Henri Christophe, who occupied Le Cap, ordering him to set fire to the town when the French troops threatened it.

CHAPTER FIVE

Expedition to Haiti, 1802

U NAWARE OF TOUSSAINT LOUVERTURE'S grim words, the combined fleets that had set out from Brest, Rochefort, and Lorient the previous year made their way slowly south from the Bay of Samana and sailed in a westerly direction along the southern shore of Hispaniola, a tropical landmass of thirty thousand square miles. Soon they left behind the eastern two-thirds of the island known as Santo Domingo. Although it was still nominally in Spanish hands, it was in fact now under Toussaint's control. At last they entered the waters of Saint-Domingue, the mountainous and fertile western third of the island, humid and forested, rich in minerals, flora, and fauna— and their destination.

Not for nothing was this colony, French since the late seventeenth century, known as the Pearl of the Antilles. Adam Smith had called it in his 1767 *Wealth of Nations* "the most important of the sugar colonies of the West Indies," but Saint-Domingue's indigo, coffee, and cotton plantations were nearly as lucrative. It was hardly surprising that the French regretted losing control of its income, and indeed Toussaint had long expected a challenge to his hegemony. When warned by the British in neighboring Jamaica that an expedition was forming against him in France, he had placed his generals and troops in a state of readiness to do battle, as Leclerc and his forces would all too soon discover.

Now, sailing westward, the French expeditionary force passed Les Cayes, the small town where Pauline's former lover Fréron was to be subprefect. Proceeding up the western coast, they sailed past the wooded island of La Gonâve and entered the harbor at Port-au-Prince, capital of the colony since 1770. There the black Jacobin, General Jean-Jacques Dessalines, occupied the governor's palace and commanded twelve thousand troops. Now Admiral Louis-René Levassor de Latouche-Tréville's squadron, carrying General Jean Boudet's division, anchored here, while General Jean-Baptiste Rochambeau with two thousand men was dispatched to Fort Dauphin. Pauline and Leclerc continued northward on *L'Océan* with the rest of the fleet that had set out from Brest under Admiral Villaret de Joyeuse's command, all the time watched by Toussaint's lookouts. Finally, proceeding along the northern shore of the colony toward the east and passing the small island of Tortue, once a base for French pirates, they anchored on February 3, 1802, in the Bay of Le Cap.

This opulent French colonial town, founded in 1711 and capital of Saint-Domingue for much of the eighteenth century, had been dubbed "the Paris of the West," in allusion to the fashionable shops, theater, and concerts that the Creole merchant and plantation families enjoyed there. Besides eight or nine hundred substantial houses of stone and brick, fine churches, and two hospitals, there were two handsome squares with public fountains and a governor's palace. This elegant residence, which successive governors had occupied, however, was not as yet to house the Leclerc ménage. For, at Le Cap, the former slave General Christophe commanded a total of five thousand troops and flatly refused Leclerc's request to surrender the town. Deputations came and went in canoes between Leclerc and the black general, but in vain.

In consultation with General Dugua, his chief of staff, Leclerc therefore resolved to disembark in the night some nine leagues to the west and, with his brother Nicolas, General Hardy, and six thousand troops, cross mountains and plains in order to lead an attack on the rebel town, under cover of cannon from the fleet. Meanwhile, according to Jacques de Norvins, her husband's amanuensis, Pauline reclined gracefully on an ottoman in the great cabin of the flagship *L'Océan*. He found her "beautiful as any angel, suffering"—the seas had risen high—"and caressing her son, a stalwart child of nearly three." (Dermide was actually nearly four.) Norvins remarked that the boy exhibited "a singular strength which made one fear as much as hope for his well-being."

But that very night, while Leclerc and Hardy were making their way painfully through the darkness, Christophe set fire to Le Cap, as he had threatened to do. From *L'Océan* Pauline and her fellow voyagers had a clear view of what Norvins described as "immense clouds of red and black smoke billowing above the town, shedding horrible shadows and shafts of light. At the will of the winds they illumined by turn rocks, woods, and sea. The sinister clouds ventured even as far as the fleet, and so every ship became palpably aware of the destruction." What Toussaint had ordered, Christophe had enacted, and the inferno was to rage for three days.

Meanwhile Leclerc and Hardy, ignorant of what lay ahead, traversed unknown plain and mountain. As Hardy wrote to his wife, their minds were not eased by the intermittent appearance of the inhabitants of the interior, who loomed threateningly out of the night. Two leagues from Le Cap a disparate force actually attacked Hardy's men but was dispatched without too much difficulty. And then they too saw the ominous red clouds. When they arrived in the town of Le Cap, the gracious buildings that they had seen from the ships and that had ringed the bay like an amphitheater were charred and burned, the inhabitants homeless in the high hills that lay behind.

Leclerc's courage did not desert him, although with Le Cap in ruins it would be more difficult to implement Napoleon's instructions to restore order to the colony. He and his troops did battle with Christophe and his men and, at a cost of five hundred casualties, gained the advantage. Leclerc then announced to the inhabitants of Le Cap that reconstruction would begin as soon as he had suppressed insurgency elsewhere. He published proclamations—of his own, of Napoleon's, in French and in Creole, the bastard French that was spo-

ken in the colony—all of which declared that he and his forces represented legitimate government but emphasized that the inhabitants of
Saint-Domingue were free Frenchmen and would remain so.

"Blancs, nègues, tout cé zenfant de la Répiblique" (Black, white, all
are children of the Republic), declared Bonaparte in Creole. "Zabitans
de Saint-Domingue," ran Leclerc's text:

> Lire proclamation Primié Consul Bonaparte. Voyez pour zote,
> Zote à voir que li vélé nègues resté libre. Li pas vélé ôté liberté à
> yo que yo gagné en combattant, et que li va mainteni li de tout
> pouvoir à li. [Inhabitants of Saint-Domingue, please read First
> Consul Bonaparte's proclamation; see for yourselves that he
> wishes all blacks to stay free. He does not wish to take away that
> liberty for which you have fought so hard, and he will do all in
> his power to maintain it.]

And Leclerc proclaimed that the first consul's promises would be faithfully fulfilled. To think otherwise would be a crime.

Finally Leclerc dispatched to Toussaint Louverture, who had
retreated to his home at Ennery on the west coast, the black leader's
two sons, who had been educated in France. They took with them their
tutor and a letter begging their father to submit to Leclerc's gover-
nance, but Toussaint gave the French general no reply.

While her husband moved rapidly about the former colony, Pauline
was left on board *L'Océan* at Le Cap with Dermide. The heat at this
season of the year, according to Hardy, was no worse than on a June
day in France. But Pauline had no previous experience of a climate in
which heavy skies, thunderstorms, and showers followed brilliant sunshine twice or three times a day. She did not like the motion of the sea
at the best of times. And there was the anxiety she felt about the outcome of each of Leclerc's successive forays against Toussaint's generals.

"Madame Leclerc is at the moment at Le Cap," wrote Leclerc to
Napoleon on March 5. "She is fairly well. The disastrous events in the
midst of which she found herself wore her down to the point of making

her ill. Today, now that all that is over, she has recovered her spirits."
(Pauline had indeed made herself popular with the officers who formed
her guard, distributing wine among them. On hearing that one of them
was the son of a notary and from Paris, she said, gesturing with her fan
to his shoulder, "When we leave this island, I will have you enter my
brother's private guard.") As for Dermide, Leclerc assured Napoleon,
he was well and had survived the crossing from France better than anyone. Even of young Jérôme, Pauline's naval lieutenant brother, Leclerc
had good reports: "He has the makings of an excellent officer."

Leclerc was writing to Napoleon from Port-au-Prince, where he had
given thanks to God for their successes. "Confidence returns," he said.
"Yesterday I had a Te Deum sung, which I attended with all my staff.
All the inhabitants of the town, who could not get into the church,
pressed about my path, and everywhere I received the strongest proofs
of their satisfaction."

A month later he wrote to the first consul that he was sending his
brother Nicolas to Paris with an account of his situation at Saint-
Domingue. "I have made one of the most exhausting campaigns possible and I owe my position to the rapidity with which I moved." He
spoke of his altered health (he had been pulled down by bouts of fever):
"Once I have reestablished order, I will ask to return to France."

He wrote to the minister of marine and colonies on March 26 from
Saint-Marc giving details of that campaign. They had besieged a
stronghold at Crête-à-Pierrot, "an extremely important position" in the
interior occupied by Dessalines, one of Toussaint's most feared generals, who had formerly held Port-au-Prince. "I didn't know of its existence or its importance," Leclerc rebuked the minister. He had three
generals attack it from different points, but Dessalines and his men
within the fort fought fiercely. One day saw six hundred of the attack-
ers killed or wounded, among them fifty officers. Leclerc wrote, "It was
the hottest affair I have seen in my life." There was no alternative but to
besiege the position and hope to starve out the inhabitants. But at
night the French officers in their tents were discomfited by the sound
of the "Marseillaise" and other French Revolutionary songs floating

out from within the stronghold's walls. Dessalines had convinced his men that they were the true heirs of the Revolution and that the first consul and the expeditionary force he had sent to Saint-Domingue had perverted its cause.

When at last Leclerc took the stronghold, he found within, besides bodies of those killed during the prolonged siege, and cannon and gunpowder, "all of Dessalines' music"—the orchestral instruments that had so disturbed his soldiers' peace of mind—"and many crates of tambours." "You can have no idea of the atrocities committed here," he told the minister of marine and colonies. "More than 10,000 white and black or mulatto inhabitants have had their throats cut on the orders of Toussaint or Dessalines and Christophe. In our expeditions we found more than 6,000 men, women, and children whom they had led into the woods and whom they intended to kill."

The tide turned when Leclerc took Crête-à-Pierrot. Soon all the black generals, with the exception of Toussaint, had surrendered. As Napoleon's instructions allowed, Leclerc enrolled them and their troops in his army with due honor and with a rank equivalent to the one they had held in Toussaint's. Meanwhile Pauline and Dermide joined Leclerc at Port-au-Prince, and husband and wife could exchange news of their experiences in this demanding colonial habitat while the heat of the day grew more onerous as March gave way to April.

DURING THE DAY small boys chased away flies and fanned the Leclercs with long feathers, while butterflies fluttered around the governor's palace and plumes of smoke rose from the hills behind the town, denoting the manufacture of sugar. To drink there was fresh lemonade, made from cane sugar, lemons, and red apples; to eat, apricots, sapodillas, and fig-bananas. The smell of jasmine and of orange flowers pervaded the town. But sleep was difficult, the night air pernicious. Even with mosquito nets it was difficult not to feel dread of the spiders, scorpions, and bloodsucking creatures native to the colony.

Leclerc's work took him, after this short respite with his family, to

Le Cap in mid-April to oversee the work of reconstruction in the town. Norvins, who accompanied him, gives an idea of how quickly the town had been reerected. "Nine weeks earlier we had left a town in ashes; imagine our astonishment when we saw a totally new town rising above the bay. The white wooden roofs of a thousand houses glistened there, forming an elegant amphitheater, and the crowded quays spoke to the town's renaissance."

Leclerc wrote to Napoleon, "My situation is fine and brilliant." In only forty days he had subdued the whole island, and, once he had completed his preparations, Pauline could look forward to reigning at Le Cap as her consort's queen just as long ago in Paris with Laure Junot she had imagined she would. Moreover, Leclerc had conceived the idea of asking for the forested island of La Gonâve, which lay off Port-au-Prince, as a gift from the first consul in recompense for his efforts. The Leclercs would thus have a colonial property and an annual income of as much as two hundred thousand francs from the timber.

At Le Cap, Leclerc waited for a response from Paris, while framing judiciary reforms and penal law. In addition he called for skilled botanists and mineralogists to be sent to the colony—"the richness in medicinal plants here is incalculable"—as well as mechanics to conduct mining experiments. He dispatched to France for the Museum of Natural History in Paris an example of an exotic animal—"which Buffon calls the 'little *lamantin* [manatee] of the Antilles.'" It was ten feet long, and its flesh, which he had tasted, he informed the minister of the interior in Paris, was like beef.

There is no doubt that the "blond Bonaparte," Leclerc, hoped that the fruits of his expedition to the Pearl of the Antilles would fascinate the French, just as Napoleon's expedition to Egypt had awakened interest in the ancient and modern civilizations of that country. With the naturalist Descourtilz, who had visited the colony three years earlier, he might have asked, "Oh, why is Saint-Domingue, made for its climate, by the fertility of its soil, by the beauty of its sites, to be an enchanted isle, inhabited only by lovers of money and not those of nature?"

But Leclerc's desire to showcase the flora and fauna of Saint-

Domingue ran parallel with, not contrary to, his colonial ambitions, and, despite his words to Napoleon, he had reservations about his position that he felt he had to express to the government in Paris. It was essential that they dispatch, he wrote, besides money, food, and hospital supplies, a further twelve thousand men from France. With five thousand men in hospital and another thousand dead, he had only six thousand fit for action of those who had voyaged out with him. He could not count, he said, on the loyalty of the black troops who had come over to him. Without these reinforcements, he believed, he must lose control of the colony within two months. "Once I have lost it, imagine what it would take to regain it," he warned.

General Hardy reported to his wife in France that, at Port-au-Prince, Madame Leclerc was bored to death, and he was content to have left Madame Hardy at home. However, in the years following the expedition to Saint-Domingue, exotic rumors circulated about the six weeks that Pauline had spent in the capital without her husband, and, as her fame spread, so did the tales of her infamous doings during this period. She succumbed to the "island vice," runs one account, and indulged in lesbian affairs with two women at a time, then passed from their arms to those of General Jean-François Debelle, known as the "Apollo of the French army." Another lascivious report asserts: "The tropical sun was, they say, astonished by the ardor of her passions." A third source claims that she experimented with white and black lovers to see which she preferred. Finally there is the accusation that she conducted an affair with General Jean Robert Humbert, a notoriously cruel French administrator. Her later employment in France of a large black page to carry her to her bath and act as outrider on her carriage did nothing to dispel the rumors.

Few of those who attacked her reputation were with Pauline or Leclerc in Saint-Domingue. Many of the allegations formed part of a later mudslinging campaign by the British in which Napoleon's family was condemned for a multitude of vices. Alternatively they were written after Napoleon's fall from power and the restoration of the Bourbons to the throne of France. However, Pauline received two letters from her brother Napoleon, one written in mid-March, the other in July 1802. The first was mild and encouraging:

> I have received your letter, my good little Paulette. Remember that fatigue and suffering are nothing when one shares them with one's husband and when one is useful to one's country . . . make yourself beloved by . . . your affability, and behave prudently, never thoughtlessly. They are making you the outfits, which the captain of the *Sirène* will bring out to you. I love you very much. Make sure all the world is pleased with you, and be worthy of your position.

The second letter began well: "I have learned with pleasure that you have bravely withstood the ardors of the campaign." However, a stern note follows: "Take care of your husband, who, from what they tell me, is a little ill, and don't give him any ground for jealousy. For a serious man, all flirtatious ways are insupportable. A wife must be good and seek to pleasure, not demand. Your husband is now truly worthy of the title of my brother, given the glory he is amassing. . . . Unite with him in love and tender friendship."

Napoleon's information about the state of affairs in Saint-Domingue was necessarily not current, given that it took six weeks for a ship to reach France from the West Indies. But if he alludes in this second letter to specific misdeeds on Pauline's part, his admonitions hardly amount to a condemnation of much more than flirtation. Lesbian relationships, sex with the natives of the island, affairs with his officers, orgies—transgressions of this magnitude would have called forth a different response. In fact there is no real reason to think this July letter anything other than a general lecture of the kind that Napoleon thought it necessary periodically to deliver to his younger sister. And as Napoleon's harangues to Pauline on the subject of her behavior usually proved unavailing, if she was indeed not behaving with circumspection at Port-au-Prince, his letter was unlikely to have had much effect. Nevertheless, if the embers of sexual fire that gave rise to the clouds of smoky rumor that later wreathed Pauline are anywhere to be found, they are at Port-au-Prince, where she lived in the palace that Toussaint Louverture had so recently vacated.

At any rate Pauline's husband was looking forward to her arrival at Le Cap in early May. "I left her for six weeks in Port-au-Prince, not wanting her to live in the middle of ruins. She is coming here in a few days," he told his brother-in-law Davout on May 8. In addition Leclerc had the news to impart that Toussaint had come to parley with him. After the black general had protested his loyalty to France, he had refused to join the French army, pleading age—he was nearly sixty— and the wish to live retired with his wife and children at his home in Ennery. All the while his cavalry guard in fine uniforms had waited outside in the courtyard, leaning on their swords. Neither side trusted the other, and when they sat down to eat together Toussaint accepted only a piece of Gruyère, fearing poison. Leclerc agreed, however, to the other's plan of retirement, while he counseled Toussaint to use his influence with the inhabitants of the colony wisely.

On leaving, Toussaint said, "Providence will save us," a remark that infuriated and alarmed the French. Providence was the name of the hospital in Le Cap, and the season when yellow fever could sweep the West Indies was near. It was believed that Europeans were particularly at risk. At any rate Leclerc considered that this was a good time to establish a hospital free of "an air poisoned by fire, massacre and battlefields," as Norvins put it. The general chose the island of Tortue, northwest of Le Cap, and, settling there with Pauline and Dermide on a former plantation owner's estate, the Habitation Labattut, set about staffing a hospital of four hundred beds.

Army headquarters were established in outlying houses and former slave quarters in the village, while the Leclercs and a guard detachment occupied the main house on the estate. A small population of farmers, who had lived on the plantation since their former masters left, "philosophically set about serving us and provided vegetables, fruits, and fish," Norvins tells us. He adds that the chief duty of the general's guard on what he called the "enchanted isle" was to protect his wife from the adoration of the inhabitants of Tortue. They appear to have mistaken Pauline for some deity when she first arrived. "Their admiration on setting eyes on her was so energetic that, despite us and also her who was the cause of it, they all tumultuously followed us into the house, from which we had some trouble in evicting them. During our stay," Norvins continues, "they stationed themselves constantly before the door, peering in at the windows in hopes of catching sight of the goddess; it needed a cordon sanitaire to stop them from entering. But nothing could prevent them from following us on the promenade too, although the guards kept them at a safe distance."

The problem was how to acknowledge the homage that the people wished to pay to Madame Leclerc. Norvins reports that "knowing the passion negroes feel for dance, we conceived the idea of hosting a chica for them all." A great clearing in a neighboring wood was chosen as the site of the spectacle—a *chica,* the French understood, was a traditional dance—and some of the old West Indies hands among the French sailors were told to arrange the event.

Old, young, children of both sexes—the whole population of the Habitation Labattut estate went on ahead, and, when the Leclerc party set out, they heard cries coming from the clearing, indicating that the dancers had not waited to begin. Upon arrival, writes Norvins, it became evident that "we had surprised the strange pantomime of the chica at its climax, a point of exaltation cheered on lustily by our soldiers and sailors." The dancers' costumes were scanty, their movements suggestive. "We were really very embarrassed, for our ravishing *madame la générale,* and then for ourselves."

Whether Madame Leclerc was so embarrassed is not clear. As the guest of honor, she took her place on a big seat of banana leaves, under an arbor of frangipani and scented roses, that the sailors had placed at a distance from the "pandemonium." She watched from that place of safety what Norvins termed the "infernal bacchanal" in her honor, all "wild chants and barbaric cries." Tom-toms and tambourines beat out an infectious rhythm, while couples fell exhausted to the floor and then rose to writhe together again in their unbridled dance. The Leclercs retreated back home, but the dancers continued their "abominable orgy" till daybreak. In Norvins' opinion, "A month earlier or several months later, these same blacks who knelt when Mme. Leclerc passed by, would have cut her throat with the same fervor, she and her child both, fine as he was. We knew it when we had them dance."

TORTUE AND ADULATION at the Habitation Labattut soon became a distant memory for Madame Leclerc, when, with the hospital there functional, she, her husband, and her son returned to Le Cap in early June. As the heat was still sweltering, they settled in a summer residence in the hills, the Habitation L'Estaing, while officers instructed by Leclerc performed an unpleasant duty. Only a month earlier Leclerc had guaranteed Toussaint his safety, but now he had grown suspicious of the black general. Around his estate at Ennery more and more of his supporters had gathered, and Leclerc feared an insurrection. He decided, with fateful consequences, that the security of the colony made it imperative that he break his word to Toussaint.

Following Leclerc's orders, General Jean-Baptiste Brunet asked Toussaint to meet near the town of Les Gonâves, under the pretext of military discussions. The French then disarmed his guard, and Leclerc's aide-de-camp Ferrari demanded Toussaint's sword. Under arrest, the black leader was then embarked with his wife and two sons for France, where he was to be imprisoned. On leaving his native land, with whose destiny his own had been so closely tied, Toussaint pronounced, "You have axed the trunk of the tree of liberty, but it will grow again, for its roots are numerous and deep." Meanwhile Leclerc warned the minister of marine and colonies, "You must make sure his prison is both secure and as far from the sea as possible. This man has fanaticized this country to a point that his presence would put it once more in combustion." His directions were followed, and, on his arrival in France, Toussaint was separated from his wife and children and imprisoned in a cold stronghold in the Jura. Alone and forgotten except in his native land, he died there of cold and malnutrition the following April.

Toussaint had gone, but his prediction that yellow fever rather than his troops would lay low the French command might yet come true. Leclerc wrote to his brother Jean Louis in early June, "We have here a terrible sickness. Men die in twenty-four hours. Few are exempt. I have lost four generals and five of my aides-de-camp." Among the officers who succumbed early on was General Hardy, who had dined two years before at Plombières with Pauline. The symptoms of the dread disease, borne by mosquitoes, were paralysis of the nervous system accompanied by vomiting, high fever, and delirium, and all too often it had a fatal outcome.

"Soon every day the yellow fever filled our hospitals, and every day death emptied them," wrote Norvins. Nevertheless Leclerc, expecting reinforcements, was content. The colony was tranquil. He was still optimistic, and proud of his campaign and of those who had served in it. "This brave army," he wrote to the first consul, ". . . has undergone a campaign that would astonish Europe in its energy, despite suffering deprivations of all kinds. Today it withstands the ravages of a hideous disease and still isn't discouraged." When his uncle Beaupré, who had accompanied the expedition as an adjutant commandant, returned to France to take the waters for a wound in his leg, Leclerc wrote begging his brothers-in-law Davout and the first consul to recognize the old soldier as "one of the warriors of the army of Saint-Domingue."

Leclerc received his own encomium, and promise of riches, in the form of a letter Napoleon wrote in early July, shortly before he was confirmed first consul for life:

Great national rewards are being marked out for you, and for the principal officers and soldiers who have distinguished themselves. Act in the best interest of the Republic, and it will be grateful and take care of your private interests. . . . Defeat for us these gilded Africans, and we have nothing left to ask of you. . . . You are en route to acquiring great glory. The Republic will enable you to enjoy a suitable fortune, and the friendship I have for you is unalterable.

Leclerc had, to all appearances, fulfilled the task that Napoleon had set him, and, as the first consul knew, he was driven by a desire for recognition as well as for pecuniary reward. Those days in Rennes, in Landshut, in Spain, where Leclerc had lamented the lack of opportunity to shine were now mercifully over. At Le Cap the victorious captain general of Saint-Domingue awaited the reinforcements promised him, as well as sugar and coffee traders, from France. "Commerce is activating and heading for Saint-Domingue," Napoleon told him.

Leclerc wrote to Davout of his hopes of handing over to a successor at Saint-Domingue, and of returning to France in the spring. "The arrival of Toussaint in France will give pleasure," he continued, and emphasized the tranquillity of the colony. "Those in Paris who laughed at my chances here will have to change their tune." Thinking ahead, Leclerc purchased hunting dogs from Norvins's brother Montbreton, his neighbor at Montgobert, to await his return with Pauline and Dermide to France. In addition he issued a series of letters to his brother Jean Louis with instructions for embellishing Montgobert at considerable expense. The fashionable architect Fontaine was to add two wings to the main house, but the floors were not to be laid. "I will bring with me exotic woods to panel and parquet Montgobert and my house in Paris," Leclerc announced. Moreover he wished a hothouse to be built near the château. "I want to bring back all the trees and flowers of this island. I think they will do very well," he declared ambitiously. In the park a lake was to be dug, and the English garden embellished, as well as a dairy and milking parlor constructed at a picturesque spot.

Leclerc, as a good servant of the republic, continued also to attempt to interest the authorities in France in the remarkable flora and fauna of the region. In July he sent a stuffed cayman and from Caracas a live "American tiger" (ocelot) just a few months old, with the remark that the latter hated cold. If it died, it would still make a fine exhibit at the Museum of Natural History, stuffed with straw. In addition, as he informed the minister of the interior, he had dispatched an officer— Norvins—to South America to search out llamas, vicuñas, and other exotic species. "Let me know if there are any items—mineral, vegetable, or animal—native to Saint-Domingue that the museum of natural history lacks," he urged, "and I will send them." He believed that mineralogists would find supplies of gold, silver, iron, copper, and even platinum in the interior. As for the botanical garden he envisaged, he advised that its staff—he thought of a director, two deputy directors, and four gardeners—should arrive no sooner than September. "Then they will have nothing to fear from this climate, which is no longer fatal in that season."

Leclerc's request to his brother in July to send out a waiting woman for Pauline and a "good nurse" for Dermide, as well as a cook, indicates that the previous incumbents of these posts had fallen victim to yellow fever. But Pauline and Dermide, as well as Leclerc, remained healthy in their summer residence, the Habitation L'Estaing, on a "wooded eminence" above Le Cap, while a miasma of heat hung over the island. Leclerc wrote in his wife's praise to Napoleon: "Considering how cruel it has been for her to stay in a country where she has had before her eyes only the spectacle of those dead or dying, I have often pressed her to go to France. She has never agreed to do so, saying that she will share my misfortunes and my successes. Her stay here is indeed agreeable for me."

Loyalty was always to be Pauline's strongest suit. She had stood by her husband through all the vicissitudes of his earlier career. Now that Leclerc had defeated the "gilded Africans" of whom her brother had written, she could look forward, beyond her time in Saint-Domingue, to a life in Paris and at Montgobert, enriched by the fruits of her husband's success. But not for long. For, as quickly as Leclerc had won control of the colony, he was to lose it.

CHAPTER SIX

Pestilential Climate, 1802–1803

L ECLERC WROTE CONFIDENTLY to Napoleon in early July
1802 of his intention—at the celebrations he planned for the
tenth anniversary of the republic in September—to declare
Saint-Domingue formally restored to France. Three elements, however, now conspired to loosen the captain general's control of the
colony. First, isolated insurgencies followed the arrest and dispatch of
Toussaint to France, and in addition, as Leclerc wrote to Decrès, the
minister of marine and colonies, "some of the colonial troops have had
the air about them of insurrection . . . at the moment they hide their
discontent, but licentiousness operates." The chilling end of the insur-
rections, he suspected, would be the massacre of all the Europeans.

In early August, however, Leclerc believed that he had dealt with
this threat, informing the first consul that he had hanged thirty chiefs
who had led risings in different parts of the island, and that he had
given orders for any disaffected colonial troops to be shot. The colony
was disarmed and once again tranquil. He was battling, however, more
than ever to maintain a fighting force as well as an administrative staff
that were being ravaged by yellow fever. Pauline was ill, although not
dangerously so, but he had lost five thousand men in the last few weeks
alone. The hospitals were in crisis, and most of the medical staff were
dead, while the fever had also swept through the French ships, leaving
devastation and yellow corpses in its wake.

No one was immune. Men who had survived the ardors of Moreau's campaigns in Germany, the desert heat in Egypt, and Alpine bivouacks now succumbed. All of Leclerc's generals of division were abed, as he wrote, and most of his generals of brigade. Many of these were to die, including fat General Dugua, Napoleon's chief of staff during the Egyptian campaign; and Debelle, the "Apollo of the army" with whose name Pauline's was to be linked, was already dead. Among those who died elsewhere in the colony was Pauline's former lover Stanislas Fréron, only weeks after he had at last arrived to take up a post as underprefect at Les Cayes. (In Paris, Lucien Bonaparte was to solicit a pension for his widow and children.) All they could do was wait till this murderous phase of the epidemic subsided, as it was expected to do in September, when the extreme heat of summer would be over and the heavy, pestilential atmosphere that hung over the colony dissipated.

The third cross Leclerc had to bear was the hardest of all. "All the blacks here," he wrote to Decrès, "are persuaded by letters coming from France, by the law reestablishing the slave trade, and by General Richepanse's orders reestablishing slavery in Guadeloupe, that we mean to make them slaves once more." A law had indeed been passed in France in May sanctioning the slave trade, and slavery had been reintroduced in Guadeloupe in July as part of the peace treaty signed with the British. Leclerc wrote bitterly, "On the eve of ending every-thing here, these political circumstances . . . have all but ruined my work. I cannot any longer count on my moral authority here, it is destroyed. . . . Now I can only manage the blacks by the force of arms. For that, I need an army and funds."

Of the twelve thousand men he had requested months before, three thousand only had come, and half of them were already in hospital. Moreover, none of the funds he had asked for had been forthcoming. To Napoleon, Leclerc wrote, "If you abandon us, as you have done till now, this colony is lost, and, once lost, you will never get it back." The black inhabitants of Saint-Domingue, who prized their liberty above pearls, began once more to arm against the French. The insurgencies, which had been sporadic, became more organized, and by mid-August the rebel forces had set a date a month thence to combine and attack Leclerc and his forces at Le Cap.

Norvins, who, with Leclerc's old comrade Lenoir, acted as the captain general's secretary, has left us a description of those dog days of August up at the Habitation L'Estaing, while Leclerc tried desperately to combat the rising tide of destruction. To fend off the "thousands of bloodsucking insects" that threatened them, they removed the general's bed from his room, replaced it with a table, and, seated there together beneath a mosquito net, dealt with business as best they could, while the sweat streamed from their every pore down onto the dispatches over which they bent.

Miraculously, while so many of his staff and household had died of yellow fever, Leclerc himself—and Pauline and Dermide—had suffered only passing episodes. It was possible to survive the fever, and indeed Norvins had a severe bout of it at this time, complete with vertigo, loss of consciousness, paralysis, and fearsome sweating. But sickness, the climate, and the scenes of death and destruction all around seem not to have shaken Pauline's resolve to remain at her husband's side—until a letter arrived from her younger sister, Caroline, in Paris.

Caroline, with her husband, Joachim Murat, had been *en poste* in Italy when Pauline set out for Saint-Domingue. Now that Murat was commandant of Paris, Caroline was enjoying both Consular society and, in her more beautiful sister's absence, the compliments she received there. Pauline shared the contents of Caroline's letter, outlining her successes, with Norvins, whom she invited during his convalescence to a tête-à-tête dinner. "Imagine, my sister Murat has a carriage. She has written it to me to enrage me, talking of parties and balls and all that Bonaparte does for her."

Norvins tells us that he had been sure she would ask something impossible of him that Leclerc had already refused her. He was right. "You know Leclerc wants me to leave for Paris," Pauline went on tempestuously. "I consent on one condition. He must give me a hundred thousand francs." This enormous sum, it transpired, was to fund a carriage to trump her sister's and a *parure* of jewelry to put any baubles

Madame Murat might be wearing at the Tuileries court quite in the shade. Pauline repeated, "Get the hundred thousand from my husband . . . and I'll go."

Norvins duly learned from Leclerc that there was no such sum available, and indeed that there was no question of Pauline's departure. With a heavy heart he went to give Madame Leclerc this unwelcome news but found her in a sunny mood. "The ravishing creature, utterly sanguine, said, 'My sister Murat has a carriage like all the bourgeoisie of Paris. She's just one of them, while I reign here like Josephine, I am the first lady. . . . Anyway, I'm perfectly happy. . . . I don't want to go anymore.'" And indeed, according to Norvins, Pauline had constructed her little court to be as gay as possible. She dressed her band of musicians in brilliant uniforms and, surrounding herself with officers' pretty wives, entertained her husband and his general staff as well as could be managed in the ominous circumstances, when the absence of habitual attendants from Pauline's soirees often presaged their death.

There were still moments for the shrinking French colony to enjoy. Before his death Dugua, coiffed in a madras turban and wearing a white chemise, had pursued the various butterflies of the island with a net. Now Leclerc proposed making a tour of the entire island to find items for the natural history museum. In addition, he told the interior minister, he proposed working on an edition of the flora of the colony. "This work could be finished within five years, with the plants drawn exactly from nature—not from the dried state in which they appear in herbals. I have noticed here how far the engravings in the *Encyclopédie* are from the reality." He also wrote to his brother Jean Louis, instructing him to add to the other buildings at Montgobert an aviary for the birds he was acquiring in Saint-Domingue: "It must be made so that it can be easily heated in winter."

The most bizarre moment came when the governor of Cartagena in Colombia, responding to Leclerc's efforts to recruit animals for the menagerie at the Jardin des Plantes in Paris, sent to Saint-Domingue a vast collection of beasts. Cages of lions, tigers, panthers, and bears were duly unloaded, to be admired at Le Cap before continuing their journey to France. Sailors bore monkeys and parrots on their arms, and tambourines and music preceded the noisy menagerie as it wound its way through the streets. Mongrel dogs came running, as well as the town's inhabitants, attracted by the hullabaloo. While the wild animals stayed in the palace stables in Le Cap, Leclerc arranged a courtyard planted with trees and roofed over with sailcloth, where they let loose the parrots and monkeys.

Against the cries of these new companions, Pauline wrote to her friend and former landlady, Madame Michelot, in early September:

> It has been impossible to write more often. This climate is so hot and humid that I suffer nearly all the time. . . . This is a truly sad country. . . . Disease has accounted for many deaths, but thankfully Leclerc and Dermide and I have survived several passing illnesses. I hope, my dear, good friend, that in seven months I will be back in Paris, never to leave it again. I have suffered too much, and I suffer still. Leclerc is fearfully busy, and works day and night. . . . In a few days I will go down to Le Cap.

As we have seen, Leclerc had proposed to make 1 Vendémiaire (September 22) the occasion of a grand fete at Le Cap. But all thoughts of that were driven out by the news that the mass insurrection that Leclerc had long feared was appointed for the sixteenth of the month. Mulatto and black troops deserted Leclerc's army in the days before and reverted to their former generals' command. Meanwhile some of the white inhabitants of Le Cap, providing themselves with a sword and a horse, declared themselves ready to help Leclerc and save the colony. Others, fearing massacre, pressed about the government palace, where Leclerc and Pauline had their quarters. The women, in particular, begged to be embarked with their children rather than face the rape and death they feared.

The odds appeared hopeless. There were thousands in the hospitals. At most Leclerc had two thousand troops to deploy, and the black generals headed a force estimated at nine or ten thousand men. But, mounting his horse and preparing to lead his army out to do battle, Leclerc was coolly in command. Pauline, bidding him adieu, was no less composed. "Her charming face," Norvins tells us, "was suffused by a supernatural beauty, where dignity and courage mingled." But uppermost in everyone's minds was the conviction that the black generals and their troops would rape Pauline and cut her throat and that of Dermide without compunction if they gained the town. Leclerc therefore put Norvins and his other secretary, Lenoir, in charge of his wife and son. "I leave you these four sergeants," he said, "and this piece of cannon. If I am defeated, you will receive the order to embark my wife and son, and their attendants."

Norvins followed Pauline inside the palace to her apartments, but they were pursued by a crowd of supplicant officers' wives and townswomen. Pauline in reply was magnificent. With an energy in her gestures and her voice of which Norvins had not believed her capable, she said, "You may be afraid to die, but I am the sister of Bonaparte. I am afraid of nothing." "Oh madame, if you knew what those monsters are capable of," the women responded. "They will find me dead—and my son, too," said Pauline with "an inflexible sangfroid." Then, turning to Norvins, she said, "You promise to kill us both?" Norvins replied grimly that he had confidence in God and in her husband. "But if the order comes to embark you, I will execute it," he warned her.

The order duly came, brought by an aide-de-camp, but Pauline refused to cooperate. A long hour passed, the echoes of cannon and gunfire from the battlefield of Haut Le Cap above the town audible below. Then another aide appeared at the palace and, without even getting off his horse, told Norvins, "The general orders you to embark Madame Leclerc—by force if necessary." And off he galloped back to Haut Le Cap.

Norvins called the four sergeants Leclerc had left him and ordered them to carry Pauline, just as she was, in her armchair, down to the port. Dermide was apportioned to a grenadier, and the child played with the plume of his porter's helmet. Meanwhile Norvins and Lenoir and a few others, sabers in hand, formed an escort, but during the journey from palace to sea Pauline repeated, "I don't care. I'm still not leaving." Then, mockingly, she said, "Do look, Norvins, we're like a masquerade at an Opéra ball in Mardi Gras. If your brother Montbreton could see us, how ridiculous he would think us." And she laughed and pointed at Lenoir, who had tucked his sword under his arm like an umbrella.

Just at the point when Lenoir was going to force Pauline aboard the waiting ship, a third aide arrived. "Victory!" he cried. "The general has routed the blacks. Madame, he begs you to return to the palace, where he will join you shortly." Pauline, so happy she would willingly have kissed the messenger, said only, "I said I wouldn't leave." Back up to the palace she was carried, and when Leclerc arrived, covered in dust and glory, Pauline told him after a thousand embraces, "I swore I wouldn't go back to France without you." That day, said Norvins, who when she was on board *L'Océan* had likened Madame Leclerc to the nymph Galatea, and during subsequent days in Saint-Domingue to the enchantress Armide, she showed the courage and determination of a Spartan woman.

But Leclerc's victory was short lived. Every day the rebels launched some new guerrilla initiative. "The men I am against are fanatically brave," wrote Leclerc to Davout. "Richepanse's orders reestablishing slavery at Guadeloupe have launched this general unrest. They would rather be killed than surrender, and they kill those of my men whom the yellow fever spares." He had given up attempting to control the interior, concentrating on maintaining in French hands Le Cap, Port-au-Prince, and Port-de-Paix, and awaited anxiously the reinforcements without which he had no hope of restoring order.

How altered was the general's opinion since he had boasted to Napoleon in July of his hold on the colony, when he had been proud of his good government! Now he wrote in September to the minister of marine and colonies, "I have not had one day's satisfaction since I have been in this country." A month later, on October 7, he wrote to the first consul, "Here is my opinion about this country. All the blacks in the mountains, men and women, need to be destroyed, and children older than twelve. Half of those in the plains must also be killed, and not a single black who has worn rebel uniform should be left alive. Otherwise every year, especially after the murderous fever season, you risk civil war." Already, in pursuit of this policy, he was employing Dessalines, the black general who had previously led attacks against the French, as "the butcher of the blacks. I get him to perform all the odious measures necessary."

In a bitter, private letter addressed to Napoleon the same day, Leclerc wrote: "Since I have been here, I have had only the spectacle of fires, of insurgencies, of assassinations, of deaths, of the dying. My soul is wounded, nothing can make me forget these hideous scenes. I struggle here against the blacks, the whites, the misery and lack of money, against my army which is discouraged, against yellow fever." For Pauline, however, he had nothing but praise: "Madame Leclerc is . . . a model of courage. She is well worthy to be your sister." Napoleon's opinion of Pauline was similarly high: "I am very content with my sister's behavior. She need not fear death, because she would go to her death with glory in dying with an army and in being useful to her husband. All passes swiftly on earth, except the opinion we leave imprinted on history."

Both Leclercs had now abandoned hope of glory from Saint-Domingue. They were looking ahead to a time when he would be succeeded on the island by some other unfortunate, and, turning his mind to life in Paris, Leclerc asked his brother to rent a house there—somewhere between the Tuileries and the Italian theater. It should be on a quiet street, with a courtyard and garden, and needed to be of a certain size, to accommodate five or six officers, as well as Pauline and Dermide and their immediate entourage. Pauline began to think of the styles that next spring would bring into fashion in the French capital, Leclerc of future postings.

Conditions, meanwhile, had not altered in the colony. The yellow fever season was abnormally prolonged that year, and fifty to sixty men a day were still dying at Le Cap. But Pauline continued to host her little receptions, summoning her band of musicians to play each evening.

A welcome energy was injected into these assemblies when the young General François Watrin, with a pretty wife, arrived with a small detachment from France and with promises of further reinforcements. But then disaster struck.

Leclerc was about to get into his carriage early on the morning of October 22, when he suddenly found himself unable to move, and he was carried to his bed. The director of the army hospital at Le Cap, Peyre, was summoned, and diagnosed the ailment as a slow, nervous fever, "caused by the bodily and mental hardships the general had suffered." But the symptoms were those of yellow fever.

Five days after he had taken to his bed—and despite the entreaties of his wife and doctor that he should stay there—Leclerc insisted on showing himself to the inhabitants of the town, fearing that there would be a general loss of morale if his condition was suspected to be serious. Then he collapsed. Two days later he revived. But he spoke strangely to Norvins, saying that he intended to leave Saint-Domingue in secret and return with Pauline and Dermide to his forest retreat of Montgobert.

In the evening the general attended his wife's assembly, entering the salon with Pauline at his side and with General Watrin supporting him on the other. But, as he walked over to the window to inspect his beloved menagerie, he fainted. The fever was back with a vengeance, and it seemed very unlikely that the general would survive this bout. Certainly Leclerc, between bouts of sweating and vomiting, now made arrangements for what should happen after his death—not least detailing General Boyer to oversee Pauline and Dermide's passage to France. In the event of Leclerc's death the administration of the island was to pass, following Napoleon's instructions, to General Rochambeau—a succession that no one relished, as that officer's cruelty and irascibility were notorious, and the threat of which added to the sense of gloom as Leclerc's condition grew worse. But no one dared to counter the first consul's orders.

Two nights after the assembly, Leclerc said he longed to die, such was his agony. The next day he was delirious, his spirits as high as his fever. And then the delirium passed, leaving him once more conscious of his suffering. At eleven o'clock in the evening of November 1, his purgatory ended. Peyre pronounced the "blond Bonaparte" dead at thirty years and seven months. It seems that Pauline and four-year-old Dermide were at Leclerc's bedside at that moment, for Norvins, waiting with other staff and officers outside the private apartments, heard a high-pitched cry: "My father is dead!"

Almost before she could absorb the shock of the death of the husband she had called "mon joli petit gamin," Pauline was embarking for France on November 8 with Dermide. On board the *Swiftsure* frigate with them was Leclerc's corpse, embalmed and in a lead coffin placed within another of rich cedar. Separately his heart and brain made the voyage in a lead box, later to be enclosed in a gilded urn bearing this inscription: "Paulette Bonaparte, married to General Leclerc on 20 Prairial, Year V, has enclosed in this urn her love with the heart of the husband with whom she shared dangers and glory. With this sad and dear inheritance of his father her son will inherit his virtues."

Nor did this inscription alone bear testament to Pauline's distress. In the hours succeeding her husband's death, when Peyre and other surgeons were embalming the body, she had cut her hair and had them place a cushion of it under the bandages on Leclerc's face impregnated with embalming ointment—"as a gauge of her conjugal love." In return she had asked for Leclerc's own blond hair. And so it was with her hair cropped close and dressed in black that the widow Leclerc returned to France. On New Year's Day 1803 she wrote to Napoleon from the Bay of Toulon, having anchored at the isle of Hyères two days earlier: "I am arrived . . . after a dreadful crossing and am in abysmal health, but this is still the least of my sorrows. I have brought with me the remains of my poor Leclerc. Pity poor Pauline, who is truly unhappy."

Whatever the truth of Pauline's relationships with other men during her marriage to Leclerc, she had never expressed the least dissatisfaction with him as a husband and father. Their ties had been very strong, for they shared an ambition to shine (with a love of domestic comfort and with a love of their son) in which Leclerc had led and Pauline, imperious though she was, had followed. Now Pauline was left to fashion a life for herself and Dermide without Leclerc.

Leclerc's mother at Pontoise received an official letter from the minister of marine and colonies: "It is with great regret, madame, that I inform you of the death of your son, General Leclerc. . . . He was taken from a glorious career on 11 Brumaire last by a sickness of ten days, during which the last moments were given to the care of his army." Decrès wrote of Leclerc's "noble and courageous spouse" and of the arrangements for burial at Montgobert—arrangements that may not have pleased Leclerc's mother. But first there was a period of state mourning to observe. General Rochambeau and Hector d'Aure, the prefect of Le Cap, had been anxious that no news of Leclerc's calamitous death should become public before the first consul knew it and could decide how the matter should be handled. In the event Napoleon decided that this death in his Consular family should form a first occasion for official mourning at his court at the Tuileries, and so his minister Talleyrand informed the foreign ambassadors in Paris.

While Pauline completed fifteen days of quarantine off Toulon, Leclerc's coffin was transferred from the *Swiftsure* to another frigate, the *Cornélie,* and landed at Marseille to be greeted by a guard of honor and conveyed to a resting place overnight in the cathedral there. Stage by stage, church by church, the coffin progressed northward, toward Villers-Cotterêts, where it would lie in the church before committal to the earth at nearby Montgobert. At Lyon the officiating archbishop was Pauline's uncle Fesch, who had been present only six years earlier in Milan at the wedding of Leclerc to his niece. The clergy everywhere, rejoicing in Napoleon's new Concordat, which had reestablished the Catholic faith in France, seized the opportunity to deliver sermons extolling the virtues of the consul and his brother-in-law, whom more than one likened to David and Jonathan. Alternatively they praised Napoleon as a new Constantine. Leclerc's aide-de-camp Bruyères oversaw the troops who accompanied the cortege and guarded it with pomp and ceremony at each staging place. Finally, at the end of February, the coffin reached Villers-Cotterêts, and for twelve days Leclerc's embalmed body was exposed to view in the church there, before he was privately buried in a tomb at the end of one of the allées he had laid out with such enthusiasm.

But the honors Napoleon was determined to heap on his brother-in-law after his death were not concluded. The first consul commissioned not one but two statues of Leclerc. One, sculpted in Italy, in which the general appeared heroically nude and more than life size, was destined for Versailles. The other, where Leclerc wore his general's uniform, was destined for the Panthéon, the Church of Saint Geneviève, which since the Revolution had acquired a new role as a mausoleum. These attentions were only just. Much later, Napoleon, reflecting on all those who had served him over a long career, was to single out Leclerc as the man above all those he had commanded who had combined administrative and military skills. But, more than that, Leclerc had, through thick and thin in Saint-Domingue and elsewhere, never questioned the decisions or orders of Napoleon. His sense of duty to the republic, his admiration for the first consul, had been absolute. Had he returned alive to France from Saint-Domingue, as he had hoped to do, and joined the theater of war elsewhere, a bright future would no doubt have lain ahead of him. Had he become, as one may posit, a marshal of France, Pauline would have made a charming *madame la maréchale.* But the destiny of this talented young member of the petty bourgeoisie turned revolutionary officer had been otherwise, and so Pauline Bonaparte's own path now took a new turn.

PAULINE COMMISSIONED from Fontaine a stele, nearly ten feet high, to stand sentinel over her husband's burial chamber in the park at Montgobert. At a cost of 850 francs a retired officer then worked for six months, under the architect's direction, to embellish it with a Roman helmet, a laurel wreath, and a sword on each face. She was not present, however, when the coffin lay open in Villers-Cotterêts or when Leclerc was buried at Montgobert. From Saint-Cloud Napoleon had written to her while she was still in quarantine in January at Toulon, giving notice that he was sending his equerry Lauriston to Toulon to bring her to Paris: "You have been worthy of Leclerc and of me. Return here soon. You will find in the friendship of your family consolation for your unhappiness."

At the end of January, Pauline and Dermide duly arrived in Paris and, with no home in Paris to go to—it would appear that Jean Louis Leclerc had not rented the house that his brother had requested—they became the guests of Pauline's brother Joseph and his wife, Julie, in the Hôtel Marboeuf in the rue du Faubourg Saint-Honoré. Here and elsewhere in Paris there were additions to the Bonaparte family for Pauline and Dermide to encounter. In the first place, in a most incestuous court alliance her elder brother Louis had taken as his bride Josephine's daughter, Hortense de Beauharnais, and they had had a son, Napoléon Charles. (The child was at once Napoleon's nephew and his stepgrandson.) Then, while Pauline was away, her sister Caroline Murat had given birth to two children, Achille and Letizia. At the Hôtel Marboeuf, moreover, Dermide had the company of two further cousins, Charlotte and Zenaïde. But still the union of Napoleon and Josephine proved frustratingly barren. Pauline did not hesitate to express her dissatisfaction with her sister-in-law, and Josephine was blamed within the Bonaparte family for this sorry situation. Despite the self-evident proof that Josephine had once been fertile, in the shape of her children, Eugène and Hortense de Beauharnais, she was now in her late thirties. It was easier for all to suggest she was no longer fertile than to hint that the first consul was sterile.

At the Hôtel Marboeuf, Pauline slowly recovered her health, which had been badly affected during the voyage from Saint-Domingue, and set about reclaiming a place in Parisian society. Her mother was, as ever, a source of comfort to her, and Pauline's spirits were restored sufficiently by April to make a visit from Norvins, her husband's former secretary, an entertaining occasion.

Norvins had brought disastrous news to the first consul and to Decrès, the minister of marine and colonies, from Saint-Domingue. Of the fourteen thousand men who had been sent out to General Rochambeau since Leclerc's death, most were now dead. (Together, black troops in revolt and the arrival of British regiments were to force the evacuation of the island in November. In 1804 Toussaint Louverture's lieutenant Henri Christophe anointed his fellow general Dessalines, who had once carried out Leclerc's butchery, emperor of Haiti, as the new independent state was named.) But in his interview with Decrès, Norvins had been so infuriated by the other's lack of interest in his tale that he had ended by abusing the minister. Jumping onto a silk-upholstered armchair, above which hung a large map of Saint-Domingue, he indicated the extent of the rebels' hold on the island and said angrily: "We wrote to you of this, Leclerc and d'Aure and I, day after day."

Pauline laughed at Norvins's anxieties about the outcome of his interview with Decrès. "I will calm him down," she said. "He is madly in love with me and pursues me night and day. He wants to marry me." Now it was Norvins's turn to laugh, along with Pauline. "He disgusts me, that great rough sailor," she went on. "But, as he is so enamored, I listen to his declarations." Norvins replied, "He wouldn't be so keen if you weren't the first consul's sister." "Oh, he wouldn't look at me," replied Pauline, not a whit disconcerted, and promised to put all right for Norvins with her suitor.

"By the way," Norvins added, "did you get a better carriage than your sister Murat?" "Oh yes, indeed," said Pauline and smiled, remembering the dinner at the Habitation d'Estaing. "Imagine, Norvins, I asked my brother for money, and he sent me eighty thousand francs." "That's not bad," the other replied, no doubt remembering that Pauline had asked her husband in vain for one hundred thousand francs. "Yes. Well, I sent it back and got what I wanted, which was three hundred thousand francs." Thus, early in her widowhood, Pauline Bonaparte Leclerc had established a supply of suitors for her hand, as well as a direct line to the coffers of her brother Napoleon. It remained to be seen whether she preferred the independent life of a rich widow or whether she would once more seek the commitment of marriage.

CHAPTER SEVEN

Union with a Roman Prince, 1803

IF PAULINE HAD NOT BEEN THE MODEL of a republican general's wife, she had loved Victor Emmanuel Leclerc and had respected his principles. But now, upon returning to Paris, she was quick to see how changed the capital was since she and Leclerc had left for Saint-Domingue, and how changed was her status and that of her other brothers and sisters since her brother Napoleon had become consul for life in 1802. The Bonapartes, who had grown up in that modest street running down to the port in Ajaccio, now had all but the status of a royal family.

Being practical as well as independent by nature, Pauline Leclerc made it her business, while staying at her brother Joseph's *hôtel* in the rue du Faubourg Saint-Honoré, to find a suitable home for herself and Dermide and their household. Before his death Leclerc had written of acquiring a house between the Tuileries Palace, where Napoleon and Josephine held Consular court, and the Italian theater. But now the stakes were higher. Pauline's sister Caroline, with Murat, was about to move into the Élysée Palace, which had belonged to the Bourbon kings. Close by, Joseph's house on the rue du Faubourg Saint-Honoré, in which she was staying, had formerly been home to the Marquis de Marboeuf, governor of Corsica and Letizia Bonaparte's protector. Pauline, widow though she might be, wanted a residence as splendid as those of her siblings.

Guided as ever by the spirit of emulation, Pauline's choice fell in the summer of 1803 on the Hôtel Charost, a delightful mansion two doors down from Joseph's *hôtel,* close to Caroline's, and quite as large as either of theirs. Two pretty pavilions framed the main entrance to the property on the rue du Faubourg Saint-Honoré. Across the courtyard inside, the ground floor and first floor of the *hôtel* were connected by a splendid staircase. Meanwhile, on the garden front, three principal salons gave onto expansive gardens running down to the Champs-Élysées. Much of the original early-eighteenth-century decoration was intact, and the house was all long mirrors and glittering enfilades of gilding, glass, and light.

Pauline was quick to see the advantages of acquiring a house that preserved its original character and had a ducal pedigree but had been recently renovated. (The owner, widow of the Duc de Charost, who lived elsewhere, had rented the *hôtel* a year earlier to the diplomat Lord Whitworth, who had repaired and restored it and filled it with furniture to serve as the British Embassy. With the Peace of Amiens foundering, however, he was recalled to London in May 1803, his furniture dispatched after him, and the property lay once again empty.) The only problem was that the Duchesse de Charost had no wish to sell the property. Pauline was not a woman to let such objections defeat her, and with three hundred thousand francs supplied by Napoleon, she wore the reluctant vendor down. But the negotiations took most of the summer of 1803, and the purchase was not effected until November.

In the meantime news of the negotiations circulated in Paris, as did rumors that Pauline had brought home with her from Saint-Domingue untold treasure, with which she proposed to purchase the *hôtel.* Some even said these ill-gotten gains had been hidden on the voyage home in Leclerc's coffin and had made their way to Paris in that sad cortege that passed through France, en route for Montgobert, in January. Pauline was, at any rate, popularly imagined to be now the richest of Napoleon's siblings. In fact she had inherited from Leclerc only seven hundred thousand francs in capital, and Lucien, who inhabited the Hôtel Brienne in the rue de Grenelle and who had made a fortune as ambassador to Madrid, was many times richer. But around the widow Leclerc, secluded in the Hôtel Marboeuf, and "veiled in black, as beautiful as any angel," these and other myths now began to wreathe. Indeed, when Laure Junot visited and noticed an unsightly abscess on Pauline's hand, souvenir of a tropical infection, she had no hesitation in assuming it to be the legacy of a venereal disease.

Officers returning to Paris from the bloody mess that had become the French position in Saint-Domingue contributed to the legend. Some hailed Pauline's devotion to her husband, her patriotism, and her courage. Others added their mite to rumors of her licentious behavior with the natives of the island. Meanwhile Pauline tired of the regulations governing mourning in the Civil Code that her brother had so recently and inconveniently produced. She told Laure Junot, when she visited, "I am so bored. I will die here, and if my brother wants to forbid me seeing company for ever, I will kill myself." Pauline was twenty-two years old, and she had done for the moment with mourning Leclerc. Her brother was the ruler of France, and she was acknowledged to be the most beautiful woman in Paris. Like a caged tigress, she waited to take her place in society, while those about her grew nervous at the thought of it.

Among those who thought to remove Pauline from Consular society altogether was her brother Napoleon. He wrote to Francesco Melzi d'Eril, a Milanese nobleman with estates in Spain and a fine villa on Lake Como, suggesting that he and Madame Leclerc should wed. Melzi had recently and reluctantly agreed to become vice president of the Italian republic, comprising Lombardy and other parts of northern Italy, which Napoleon had founded during Pauline's absence in Saint-Domingue. (Napoleon had reserved the title of president for himself.) This further request, however, Melzi declined, protesting that he was a fifty-year-old bachelor and set in his ways. (These, incidentally, included a mistress of long standing.)

If Napoleon had thought that Pauline's marriage to Melzi would consolidate French Consular ties with the Italian peninsula, so badly ruptured during the Revolution when the republic had first cast off religion and then employed its army to occupy the Papal States and make new republics elsewhere, he was disappointed. Nevertheless he still had useful channels at his disposal, including that of Uncle Fesch, who had recently become cardinal and whom Napoleon had dispatched from Lyon to Rome to serve as ambassador to the Holy See. Through Fesch and through Cardinal Consalvi, the papal secretary of state, honeyed words passed between the first consul and Pope Pius VII. (On all sides there was tacit agreement not to refer to the death of the pope's predecessor, Pius VI, while in French captivity.)

In Paris, meanwhile, Napoleon cultivated the company of Cardinal Caprara, Pius VII's legate. It was Caprara who presented to the first consul in April 1803 Prince Camillo Borghese, a Roman citizen of high birth and great wealth, whose arrival in the French capital had already made a great stir the previous month. Although he was not tall, Prince Borghese had a neat figure, a handsome face, and exotic Mediterranean looks. "This head with coal black eyes and mane of jet black hair, it seemed to me, must contain not only passionate but great and noble ideas," Laure Junot wrote soulfully of her first encounter with the prince. To add to his attractions, Prince Borghese paid great attention to his dress, and still more to his horses, eclipsing with his coach and four even the equipage of the Russian count Demidov, which had till then been the showiest in Paris. But then Camillo Borghese had the advantage, as excited Parisians turned accountants estimated, of possessing a rent roll of two million francs a year.

He also had most distinguished ancestors. Paul V, the Borghese pope, had been patron of the Baroque sculptor Bernini, and His Holiness's nephew Cardinal Scipione Borghese had filled the sumptuous Villa Borghese on the Pincio hill in Rome with paintings, objects, and ancient art. Since those exalted seventeenth-century days Borghese intermarriage with the Aldobrandini family, among others in Rome, had brought estates at Frascati, lands in the Roman Campagna, and further wealth. With Camillo's own mother, Donna Anna, came the Palazzo Borghese in Florence and lands in Tuscany. In Rome, while the Villa Borghese showcased the family art collection, the family resided in the vast Palazzo Borghese, which backed onto the Tiber and was known as the *cembalo,* or keyboard, from its trapezoidal shape resembling that of a harpsichord.

The twenty-eight-year-old prince had impeccable, if unusual, revolutionary credentials too. For when the French forces took control of Rome in 1798, Camillo and his younger brother, Prince Francesco Aldobrandini, despite their family's papal associations, embraced the republican cause. They pulled the vast Borghese family crest off the facade of the Palazzo Borghese in that city and added it to a bonfire of cardinals' hats and Inquisition decrees burning in the Piazza di Spagna. Then they danced wildly around the blaze before compounding their sins, in the eyes of their father and of the pope, by fighting briefly for General Championnet and his French forces and against the papal army. This was the stuff of heroes, or of revolutionaries anyway.

But the first consul does not appear to have taken any interest in Camillo Borghese, despite his wealth, papal connections, and revolutionary exploits. Indeed there was a fatal flaw, evident to anyone upon closer acquaintance with the prince and not overawed by his antecedents. He was, to put it plainly, a booby, if a harmless one. It was this quality that had enabled his father to get him pardoned by the pope for his acts of rebellion. (For penance, it was decided, he must live in exile from Rome for a number of years, upon which Camillo settled in the very comfortable Palazzo Borghese in Florence.) After a time the Parisians noticed this and disillusion set in. "He had nothing to say, although a lively manner of saying it" and "No one was more capable than he of driving a four-in-hand, but no one was less capable of carrying on a conversation" were among their comments. Indeed Camillo could barely write Italian correctly, let alone speak or write French, and it was said that he preferred the company of the concierge at the Hôtel d'Oigny, in the rue de la Grange-Batelière in Paris, which he was renting, to that of anyone more demanding in Paris.

Camillo's father, Prince Marcantonio Borghese, a noted patron of the arts and a man of culture, had, it was said, deliberately neglected his sons' education, believing that, as vassals of the pope, they would do better to remain ignorant than chafe, as educated men, at the restrictions of Roman life. Or then again, it was suggested, he believed that an "incomplete" education would spare his sons, whose spectacular wealth and titles would inevitably attract envy, further resentment. Whatever the explanation, Don Cecco—as Camillo's younger brother was known—if ill educated, was no booby. It was Camillo Borghese's misfortune to be both ignorant and lacking in intellect—and an innocent abroad, who fell into the traps laid by men far more sophisticated than he. For, while the first consul took no interest in the Roman prince's presence in Paris, this was not true of his brothers Joseph and Lucien. It was with Joseph Bonaparte, who had served in Rome as ambassador in 1798, and with Lucien that an Italian diplomat and friend of Cardinal Caprara, the Chevalier Luigi Angiolini, concerted a "great project"—namely, Camillo Borghese's marriage to Pauline Bonaparte Leclerc.

As Pauline emerged from the confines of widowhood in the late spring of 1803, there was occasion for her and Camillo Borghese to meet, even to flirt, no more. But then in June, fatefully for the house of Borghese, Camillo accepted an invitation from Joseph Bonaparte to spend a few days at Mortefontaine, the latter's country house twenty miles north of Paris. The company, with whom the Roman prince innocently drove and walked about the gardens and grounds of the château, included, besides his hosts, the Bonapartes' mother, Letizia; Louis's wife, Hortense; the matchmaker Angiolini; and Cardinal Caprara. Unaware that most of the above were, or became during these few days, resolved that he should marry Pauline—Angiolini having numerous conversations with Letizia on the subject—Borghese returned contentedly to Paris. It was not long, however, before he received a late-night visit from Angiolini at the Hôtel d'Oigny. The Italian diplomat, come on Joseph's urging, to unveil to Borghese the glorious prospect they had in mind, utterly destroyed the Roman prince's peace of mind.

Borghese was "as much frightened as astonished at the prospect, so great did it seem to him," Angiolini wrote to Joseph. "It didn't seem possible to him that it could be achieved." Angiolini said he had let Camillo think the idea was only his own, but he hinted at "favorable circumstances that authorize me to hope for a happy outcome"—in other words, the approval of the Bonaparte family. Their conference was long, but did not suffice to "decide" Borghese. Nevertheless the Italian diplomat did not lose heart. "I have discovered the essential object exists," he wrote coyly. "The person [Pauline] pleases him. We have promised to speak of it more."

By the following day Camillo had ceased to flounder and had been safely landed. Angiolini wrote to Joseph, "The affair is concluded. Prince Borghese would believe himself too happy if the First Consul would accord him the honor of having as his wife our very amiable sister Madame Paulette." Angiolini hoped, however, that they could accommodate Camillo in his plea to keep the news private for the moment—"until he has informed the Princess Dowager, his mother, for whom he feels both tenderness and respect." An answer from Rome should be forthcoming in three weeks, and then the prince "would be happy to share in public his satisfaction in an event which, for all his titles, will be the happiest of his life."

The plea was duly granted, and letters containing the unlooked-for news sent to the princess dowager and to Cardinal Consalvi on June 27. At no point does the question of Pauline's ability to produce an heir seem to have been canvassed, although the fact that she had borne only one child in five years of marriage might have sent warning signals to the prince. Meanwhile, as Pauline later recorded, her brothers Joseph and Lucien urged on her marriage to Camillo as her best course of action. She seems to have been easy to persuade. At any rate, or so Josephine Bonaparte told her daughter, Hortense, she informed Napoleon that "she wanted him [Borghese] for her husband, and that she felt she would be happy with him. She asks Bonaparte's permission for Prince Borghese to write to him to ask for her hand."

Napoleon's reaction to the proposed marriage of his sister and Camillo Borghese seems to have been complex. On the one hand he told his sister that what dazzled her now might seem modest in years to come, and she might repent of remarrying so quickly. On the other hand he was, and remained, to some degree mesmerized by the splendor of Pauline's match. Much later he said, "My origins made me regarded by all the Italians as a compatriot. . . . When there was question of the marriage of my sister Pauline with Prince Borghese, there was only one voice at Rome and in Tuscany, in this family and in all their allied families—'It's good,' they all said. 'It's *entre nous,* it's one of our families.'"

Although the Borgheses would have been startled to hear the Bonapartes claim kinship, the first consul was correct in saying that Camillo's family in Rome approved the match. In mid-July, Don Cecco arrived in Paris to embrace his brother. Cardinal Fesch, moreover, wrote to Napoleon from Rome: "His Holiness is enchanted, the Roman nobility have marked their satisfaction." He called the princess dowager, his niece's future mother-in-law, "an excellent woman who will make life happy for Pauline. It is a family that has a revenue of 100,000 piastres." And the ambitious cleric ended by crowing: "You see me related now to the first family in Rome."

Even the old aristocracy of Paris, which traditionally inhabited the Faubourg Saint-Germain and which had now been assimilated into Consular society, was impressed. In the heat of the moment, when Camillo appeared at the Consular court in his new guise as Pauline's fiancé, the first consul declared, "Prince, my sister Pauline seems destined to marry a Roman, for from her head to her toes she is all Roman." Angiolini told Prince Vincenzo Giustiniani, "The fiancés are already very amorous, and by God, they are right to be so. I am convinced they will be happy." His information from Pauline's mother at the end of July was that the marriage would be celebrated "in the intimacy of Mortefontaine," where the couple would stay for about two months, "to wait out the mourning period of Madame Leclerc." The marriage would then be officially celebrated in Paris.

Matters proceeded apace, with Joseph and Borghese between them managing the details of the marriage contract, in which Pauline brought her husband a dowry of five hundred thousand francs, supplied by Napoleon, while Camillo undertook to buy for her three hundred thousand francs' worth of diamonds. She would also have the use of the celebrated Borghese jewels. She was to keep her Leclerc inheritance, while, in the event of Camillo's death, she would receive a jointure of fifty thousand francs a year, and the right to apartments in the different Borghese residences, as well as two carriages. The contract was duly signed on August 25 at the Hôtel Charost, by which time the banns had been read twice in the parish of Mortefontaine. But an impediment to the marriage itself had arisen: "I cannot tell you when the marriage will take place," Angiolini wrote to Prince Giustiniani, the day before the contract was signed. "The First Consul has decided that he wishes it to be put off until the end of Madame Leclerc's mourning, which is perfectly reasonable. The fiancés must suffer a little longer."

According to the Civil Code, under which a widow could remarry within ten months of her husband's death, Pauline was free to marry from early September. Napoleon, however, ignoring his own code, wished Pauline to defer her marriage until November, when she would have completed a full year of mourning, more in line with French tradition. But Pauline and Camillo had no intention of obeying any such edict. Three days after the contract was signed, early in the morning of August 28 and before Pauline had completed even ten months of mourning, she went through a cloak-and-dagger marriage with Borghese in the chapel at Mortefontaine. Her brothers were present, as was the ubiquitous Angiolini, and the ceremony, conducted by a priest put forward by Cardinal Caprara, apparently had the blessing of Pauline's mother as well as of the cardinal himself. Although the civil marriage was not due to take place until November, from now on Pauline could consider herself Princess Borghese.

And the motive for the early marriage, which was kept hidden from Napoleon as well as the rest of society? Pauline was not known for her patience, and she had a history of disobeying her brother. Furthermore, she and Borghese had already been "amorous" in July, and had certainly not grown less so since. Her mother and brothers, as well as the cardinal, probably endorsed the early marriage in order to bestow a measure of respectability on the couple's unbridled appetites. The only mystery is that Napoleon's army of spies, headed by chief of police Joseph Fouché, learned nothing of the matter. At any rate the couple honeymooned at Mortefontaine, apparently completely content, driving about the pretty estate with its Chinese pavilions, obelisks, and streams, until the demands of the autumn season and of their coming journey to Rome brought them back to Paris.

At the Hôtel Charost, of which she now took possession, Pauline set aside indolence and instructed Monsieur Michelot, whom she appointed steward of the house, in all the improvements she wished to have made. (Another woman might have thought of selling the *hôtel,* though she had so recently acquired it, on going to live in another country and in still greater splendor there. But Pauline was not such a woman.) There were, besides, arrangements to be made for the upkeep of Montgobert, which would one day belong to Dermide. And there was a deed to be signed—by Pauline and her new husband and by members of the Leclerc family—the day before the civil marriage, making the Borghese couple joint guardians to the child. Meanwhile, with Madame Michelot and her other amanuenses, Pauline began a welter of appointments, fittings, and correspondence with dressmakers and haberdashers, with jewelers whom she commissioned to set her new diamonds, and with others whom she ordered to reset the Borghese jewels, which she had had brought from Rome.

BUT IT REMAINED to tell Napoleon that she had disobeyed his wishes. Apparently all unknowing of his sister's marriage, Napoleon ordered Pauline—without Borghese—in September to stay at Saint-Cloud, and there he toasted her coming glory. This passed without incident. But in October, at a gala dinner that he gave at the Tuileries to celebrate the couple's engagement, shortly before they went through the brief civil marriage in the *mairie* in Mortefontaine on November 6, he learned the truth and was furious at having been duped. He showed his displeasure to brilliant effect when Pauline made one of her last appearances at the Tuileries before she left with her new husband for Rome.

Her toilette was "most remarkable," one Jenny Saint-Maur, a new attendant of the princess's, records. Pauline had had her Paris dressmaker sew onto "a dress of green velvet" a great quantity of "white diamonds." Bodice, skirt, bandeau, neckline, belt were all ablaze with jewels, and Jenny Saint-Maur tells us that Pauline "had contributed to the effect all the jewels of the Borghese house." (It is more likely that these were the new diamonds that Borghese had bought for her.) The effect was tremendous, and Pauline was delighted with herself and with the other Bonaparte women's chagrin. Seating herself by Laure Junot, she said, "Look at them, Laurette, do look. They are dying of jealousy, for I am a princess, a real princess."

But, unfortunately for the success of the soiree, Pauline had had herself announced as "Princess Borghese." And now the first consul seized his opportunity. Going up to his sister, he rebuked her in these words: "Please understand, Madame, that there is no princess where I am. Have more modesty and do not take a title that your sisters do not possess." All the women of the family, according to Jenny Saint-Maur, were "charmed by the Consul's egalitarianism, and each one enjoyed maliciously the lesson doled out to pretty Paulette." To drive the lesson further home that evening, and noticing that a general's lady had the words "Liberté, egalité, république ou la mort" embroidered on the train of her dress, Napoleon read and reread aloud the words. "Republic or death. Yes, Madame, you are right," he asserted, while Pauline tried to control her tears. "The Republic. Without it, life is not worth living." Enchanted with the first consul's endorsement, the general's lady looked proudly at the assembly and indeed named the couturier who had created the design that had attracted such attention.

Napoleon's displeasure with Pauline never lasted long, whatever she did to offend him. In a softened mood he wrote to her in early November from Brussels, where he was inspecting troops. "I shall be away for a few more days," he told her. "However, the bad season is approaching

and the Alps will be covered with ice. So start on your journey to
Rome. Be sure to show sweetness and kindness to everyone, and great
consideration for the ladies of your husband's family. More will be
expected from you than from anyone. Above all, see that you conform
to the customs of Rome. Never criticize anything or say, 'We do this or
that better in Paris,'" he instructed her. "Show respect and devotion
toward the Holy Father. . . . What I would most like to hear about you
is that you are well behaved." With the admonition that Pauline should
never receive any English visitors, enemies of the French, at the Palazzo
Borghese, he ended, "Love your husband, make your household happy,
and above all do not be frivolous or capricious. You are twenty-four
years old and ought to be mature and sensible by now. I love you."

PAULINE MIGHT NOT have brought treasure home from Saint-
Domingue, but when she set out on the journey from Paris to Rome on
November 14, 1803, with her went incontestable treasure. Besides her
dowry of five hundred thousand francs—converted into gold and
transported in little boxes of white iron, each containing a thousand
louis—went her new diamonds and the Borghese jewels, as well as a
vast wardrobe of costly dresses, lace, and shawls. On the long journey,
which included an ascent over the Alps, Camillo, still "very amorous,"
and Pauline traveled tête-à-tête. Meanwhile, six-year-old Dermide followed at a slower pace, in a berlin drawn by six horses, with his governess, Madame Ducluzel, and with the young Jenny Saint-Maur, who
had recently been appointed *lectrice* (reader) to Pauline. When they
entered one of the many French and Italian cities through which they
passed en route to Rome, one of the gendarmes asked who they were.
"Messieurs," replied Dermide, "it is the son of General Leclerc traveling with his suite." Saint-Maur corrected Dermide and said that, as at
his age he had only protectors, this expression was ridiculous coming
from him. But she had to admire his spirit.

It was not a spirit that Camillo Borghese liked, however, and his
view that the child was an inconvenient legacy from Pauline's first mar-

riage was to have a disastrous outcome. For the moment, however, everyone was relieved to reach Rome, which they did in early December 1803. And though Pauline told Madame Michelot, "I find myself so isolated," she was sufficiently herself to keep the pope waiting several days after he had offered her an audience at the Quirinale, until the dress she required had arrived from Paris. At the deferred audience, however, Pius VII and Princess Borghese greatly took to each other, as Cardinal Consalvi was happy to report to Napoleon. But Pauline did not endear herself to her mother-in-law when she failed to show at a *cercle,* or assembly, at the Palazzo Borghese held in her honor, to which half Rome had been bidden. Pauline had dined amicably and in apparent good health earlier in the day with the dowager princess, before going off to dress. Her excuse that she had a violent headache—forthcoming only after two times of asking—was in consequence ill received.

Such sins were magnified and reverberated in the small aristocratic society of Rome. But the dowager princess forgave Pauline, took great interest in her daughter-in-law's dress, and even had her seamstress make copies of Pauline's Parisian trousseau (though the flimsy, low-cut creations hung oddly on the dowager's shrunken, elderly frame). Still, Pauline would not "conform to the customs of Rome," as her brother had ordered her to do. On the grounds of economy, she even found fault with her mother-in-law's housekeeping of thirty years' standing. The gatehouse of the Palazzo Borghese was in some measure open to the public, who went there to drink coffee or liqueurs or eat an ice as in a café. Camillo and his mother were mortified and confused by Pauline's edict that this bounty must cease, and the habitués of the gatehouse were not less put out. Her brother-in-law Prince Aldobrandini said nothing but contrived to spend little time with his brother and his new wife.

Soon not only was Pauline turning the established practices in the Borghese household on their head, but she was failing to love and respect, as her brother had instructed her to do, the head of that household. Camillo remained in thrall to Pauline, was still "amorous" toward her, and feared her, in his timid way. But now that she had his titles and money, his jewels, his carriages, and his palaces, she had tired of the prince and saw all the defects that others had noted in Paris. Worse, she had to live with the man, and, among new traits that her husband displayed and that annoyed her, Camillo was maddeningly jealous of other men's attentions to her. He, in return, was "almost continually discontented with [her]," as he told Angiolini in March 1804.

Irritable, regretful, Pauline harked back to her marriage with Leclerc as a great loss. Writing to her brother-in-law Murat in February, she sighed for Paris: "I don't know, but I think the air in Rome may not be good for me. I always have a cold. . . . I hope we may all meet again soon in France." And, married to a great and wealthy prince of the south, she took as a lover a very poor "Prince of the North"—the hereditary prince of Mecklenburg-Strelitz, who was a man as unlike Camillo as possible, being highly educated, cultivated, and the son of an Enlightenment German duke. When her husband went to Naples, Pauline seized her opportunity. By day she picnicked with the prince out in the Borghese houses that dotted the Roman Campagna. At night she had her black servant, Paul, escort the hereditary prince, in disguise, into the palazzo and up a secret stair to her apartments.

Camillo was beside himself with jealousy and rage when he discovered the truth, catching Pauline red-handed with a letter he would have "given the world not to have seen." He wanted all her attendants, conspirators in the affair, to be dispatched back to Paris. Pauline refused, and when Borghese appealed to her uncle Fesch it was clear that the cardinal had no influence with his headstrong niece. Angiolini, when consulted, counseled tolerance: "Women, my friend, especially before they reach a certain age, are determined to have what they want, and neither force nor a show of authority will deter them." Napoleon, however, was not of this opinion. When informed by Cardinal Fesch in April of the Borgheses' quarrels, he wrote to Pauline with the clear intention of frightening her into obedience:

Madame and dear Sister, I learn to my sorrow that you have not had the good sense to conform to the manners and customs of the city of Rome, that you have shown disdain for its people, and that your eyes are constantly turned towards Paris. . . . Do not count on me to help, if at your age you let yourself be governed by bad advice. As for Paris, be assured you will find no support here, for I shall never receive you without your husband. If you fall out with him, it will be entirely your own fault, and then France will be forbidden you. You will lose your happiness and my friendship.

The departure northward of the hereditary prince coincided with the arrival of Napoleon's letter. Pauline had often defied her brother's rule, but his letter—this "show of authority," with its threat that Paris would be closed to her—was enough to make anyone reconsider. In a private letter to Fesch, Napoleon showed himself more understanding of Pauline's behavior than he had been in his official reprimand. He recommended that Camillo remember that women in Paris lived differently.

Meanwhile Pauline's mother, who had been known to reason with her daughter, had arrived in Rome in Holy Week, to be feted by the pope. Letizia Bonaparte was also hoping to broker a peace between Napoleon and her younger son Lucien, who—against Napoleon's wishes—had married Madame Alexandrine Jouberthon, a French merchant's widow, the previous year and had now settled with her in Rome. Declaring that he would henceforward live as a private citizen, Lucien refused to countenance divorcing Alexandrine and abandoning the children whom the union soon produced—they were to number ten in all—in favor of the dynastic marriage his brother sought for him. Letizia now took Lucien's part, estranging her, too, from Napoleon.

Would the first consul's sister be more tractable? Would the Borghese couple now settle down, would Camillo follow the advice provided by Angiolini and "give Paulette a child"—a half sibling for Dermide, a cousin for Lucien's children, and an heir to the great fortunes of the Roman family? Or was a child in fact out of the question and Pauline all but infertile owing to salpingitis? Did the ability to have sex without danger of pregnancy mean that Pauline was all the more hell-bent on trying out different partners? At any rate hers was a *non-conformista* life that appalled the Romans. They were used to discretion and propriety in the affairs that many of them—including, for many years, Pauline's own mother-in-law—conducted. It was Pauline's Parisian openness about her liaison with the hereditary prince as much as the liaison itself that had so tormented Camillo.

As Camillo anxiously waited in Rome to see if there would be more liaisons, as Angiolini counseled him to be "less the lover, more a loving husband," momentous news came from Paris in May. Napoleon had been declared by the Senate emperor of the French, a plebiscite had approved the title as a hereditary one, and his brothers Joseph and Louis and their wives, Julie and Hortense, were made imperial highnesses. Lucien, who remained in his Roman retreat, received no title. Nor did Jérôme, who had married, while in Baltimore, Maryland, the previous year, an American girl, Elizabeth Patterson, to the outrage of his brother Napoleon. The emperor was no better pleased when a nephew, Jérôme-Napoléon Bonaparte-Patterson, appeared.

Days later, following angry representations from Elisa and Caroline in Paris, came a further announcement: All three of the emperor's sisters were to have the rank of imperial highness. At the Palazzo Borghese, where quarrels continued between Camillo and Pauline, the prince, who had not received the rank of imperial highness, received the news of his wife's elevation in silence, "not knowing whether to laugh or cry." Prince Aldobrandini offered his congratulations coldly. And Pauline was not entirely pleased that her sisters now shared the rank of princess and imperial highness with her. (Their mother was to become known as Madame Mère.) But she had further thoughts to offer. Upon reading letters from her family full of pride and joy, she said, "I may be wrong, but I think my brother might have done better to remain First Consul. How astonished, how angry my poor Leclerc would have been to see it. He had such democratic ideas, he so hated despots and grand airs. I promise you, there would have been harsh words between him and my brother."

Pauline had no expectation that Camillo would make any such

protest. Although some in Rome might scoff at her brother's titles, on one point she and Camillo were in accord: They both had the highest admiration and respect for Napoleon. And together, in the summer of 1804, and with the sculptor Antonio Canova, they embarked upon a commission that was both to mark that love and respect and to become one of the most potent emblems of Napoleon's Empire—the *Venus Victrix.*

CHAPTER EIGHT

Bitter Summer, 1804

SO FAMOUS IS THE VERY TILT OF PAULINE'S HEAD, to
say nothing of the tilt of her breasts and of her haunch in the
near-life-size reclining statue that now adorns the gallery of the
Villa Borghese in Rome, it is astonishing to think that this pink and
pearly emblem of the Napoleonic Empire might never have existed. It
was not that Pauline was reluctant to be portrayed in marble—and
"nearly naked"—as Venus Victorious. Napoleon had written of Pauline
to Uncle Fesch in April 1804, "Tell her from me she is no longer beautiful, and she will be still less so in a few years, and it is more important
to be good and esteemed." To have herself represented with her torso,
arms, and abdomen unclothed might not bring her esteem, but Pauline
was, as ever, unconcerned for her reputation. And, whatever Napoleon
might say, she knew she was beautiful and likely to remain so, evoking
admiration in all who looked upon her.

Even the writer Chateaubriand, who was acting as Fesch's secretary
in Rome, fell under the spell of "la diva Paolina" when he was deputed
to bring her some slippers that had arrived in the diplomatic bag from
Paris. Chateaubriand did not generally relish the menial duties Fesch
assigned him, but, on being shown into the apartment at the Palazzo
Borghese where the princess was at her toilette, the bagman forgot his
resentment. His description of their meeting was lyrical: "The virgin

shoe that she put on her foot grazed only for an instant this tired old earth." Later he recalled that "she shone with all the glory of her brother. . . . If she had lived in the time of Raphael, he would have painted her as one of those amours who lie so voluptuously on lions at the Farnesina." Extravagant as Chateaubriand's language is, it may have been the case that a modern Raphael was required to paint Pauline. None of the portraits we have of her by artists of the day, with the possible exception of a beguiling half-length by Lefebvre, captures the mix of classic beauty and allure that so seduced those who saw the princess.

Pauline prized her supple, milk white body, her bosom and hips, her exquisite hands and feet, as much as Chateaubriand and everyone else admired them. They were, as she well knew, perfectly to the taste of her time, and she spoke of them matter-of-factly as "advantages of nature." In Paris the earlier rosy and lusty images of Fragonard and Boucher had now been succeeded in popularity by languorous, long-limbed bodies—on show clothed in David's paintings and unclothed in those of Girodet. In Rome, Pauline's slim figure and small breasts recalled those of the nymphs and naiads of antiquity in the Borghese collection, even those of the *Sleeping Hermaphrodite,* which aroused the admiration of papal subjects and tourists alike. She could have been a model for the sculptures of the seventeenth-century master Bernini, who had reinterpreted in marble for Cardinal Scipione Borghese's collection to erotic effect the stories of Ovid: Persephone, being borne off by Pluto; Daphne, under Apollo's touch, metamorphosing into a laurel tree.

What more suitable, given the wonders of Pauline's body and of the Borghese inheritance, than for Prince Camillo to commission Canova, the internationally celebrated sculptor resident in Rome since the 1780s, and incorporate her image into the family collection? Canova had already depicted Psyche being awakened with a kiss by Cupid, a sculpture group that Murat had bought and that showed the artist's skill in handling mythological subject matter and lissome bodies alike. Later Pauline stressed, in a letter to Camillo, that "the statue was created for your pleasure." It was a commission on which they were both agreed, to which they were both committed, and for which Camillo was happy to pay.

But there was a hitch. Canova was initially reluctant to oblige the couple, as he had been similarly reluctant to go to Paris two years earlier to sculpt the colossal nude statue of Napoleon as Mars the Peacemaker. (Canova came from the Veneto and deplored the French pillage of artifacts from Venice and other Italian cities.) According to Pauline's attendant Jenny Saint-Maur, Canova protested at first that he had a long list of commissions he must honor. But upon seeing Pauline, she attests, he was so excited by her appearance that he agreed to begin work after only a month. And so, just as he had obeyed Napoleon's orders, now Canova bowed to Pauline's commanding beauty.

Once the commission was agreed, Pauline apparently declared that she wished to be depicted as Venus, the goddess of love. Canova demurred and suggested as model Diana, virgin huntress and goddess of the moon. But Pauline laughed and said, "Nobody would believe in my chastity." Besides, the Borgheses, like many still more ancient families in Rome, claimed descent from Romulus, founder of Rome and son of Mars, and hence kinship with Venus, the god of war's sister. (In eighteenth-century Rome such genealogical leaps of faith were not uncommon.) Accordingly it was decided that Pauline should be depicted as Venus. Furthermore the sculpture should bear an apple in one hand in allusion to the famous judgment of Paris in antiquity, when that Trojan eschewed the charms of Hera and Athena and awarded to Aphrodite or Venus the golden fruit, inscribed "to the fairest one of all."

Aphrodite's sister goddesses Athena and Hera, who failed to win the prize for beauty in ancient times, had been suitably disconsolate and had subsequently sided with the Greeks in the Trojan War. Did it occur to Pauline that her own sisters, Elisa and Caroline, would be no better pleased now by this statue in which her beauty was celebrated for eternity? The idea that she had again eclipsed the rest of her family can only have added to her mischievous pleasure in a work of art that scandalized those who in the summer of 1804 saw its plaster model in

Canova's studio. (The full-size version was not to be finished and dispatched to Camillo Borghese until 1808.) For *La Paolina,* as the statue was to become known in Rome, showed Princess Borghese reclining against pillows heaped in lifelike fashion on a divan, naked to the waist. There were only loose draperies around her pelvis and hips, and her lower legs and feet were on display. With one hand the princess supported her head on the pillows behind her; the other, on her thigh, curled around the apple, and drew attention to the drapery plunging to her lower abdomen.

Pauline's reported remarks on the sittings for this celebrated statue are entertaining if not informative. To enquiries about how she had borne posing so lightly clothed for the artist, she variously—but always contemptuously—replied, "Oh, Canova is not a real man," "There was a good fire in the room so I did not take cold," and "Every veil must fall before Canova." A grand saloon in the Palazzo Borghese, with coffered ceiling, blue and gilded walls, and a vast fireplace is today pointed out as the site of the sessions. But Jenny Saint-Maur tells us that the sessions took place both in the Palazzo Borghese and in the artist's studio, which lay close by, behind the Hospital for Incurables. Canova habitually first made sketches at his client's home and worked with clay and plaster at his studio when working on marble portrait statues, and one may assume this was his method here. The sessions were finished by June, and the plaster model in Canova's studio by July 1804. Pauline's brother Lucien, who had recently come to live in the city, apparently took pleasure in visiting the studio and conversing with Canova about the ancient statues of Rome and the environs, in which he was beginning to interest himself. Standing between the models for portrait statues of his sister and of his brother Napoleon as Mars the Peacemaker, Lucien observed, "He looks more belligerent than pacific." His remarks on his sister's near-naked body are not recorded, nor are those of Napoleon, who would have heard of his sister's latest exploit from his spies.

The arrival in Rome of Lucien and his family in February had pleased Pauline, not least because, with her brother and his second wife, Alexandrine, came Lucien's children by Christine—ten-year-old Charlotte and six-year-old Christine—as well as Lucien and Alexandrine's two-year-old son Charles. Pauline, being family minded like all the Bonapartes, welcomed her nieces and nephew but especially valued them as playmates for their cousin Dermide. Lucien had not yet made up his quarrel with Napoleon, but Pauline was expert at remaining friends with her more quarrelsome siblings and did not take sides. When Lucien settled on a country house, the Villa Rufinella, close to the Borghese and Aldobrandini villas at Frascati, she was delighted that Dermide, Charlotte, and Christine would see one another there. Meanwhile, between bouts of illness that kept her in her bed during March, she was arranging for the decoration of a new apartment in the Palazzo Borghese in Rome, which she believed would be very pretty. But she reassured her friend Madame Michelot, "Don't worry, my dear Poulotte, the Rome season doesn't please me enough to make me forget Paris, or the friends I have left there." Nor did the fashions in Rome satisfy her. She continued to requisition them from Madame Michelot—even ribbons and accessories—in Paris. "Dermide is very well and talks often of your dear children." With her letter she sent miniatures to be mounted on a little mother-of-pearl box for Dermide's grandmother in Pontoise. "It's an age since I promised them to Madame Leclerc."

PAULINE, IT SEEMED, was adjusting to life in Rome as Princess Borghese. At her husband's request she had received communion at Easter in the ornate Borghese chapel, beneath which lay the tombs of Pope Paul V and Cardinal Scipione, in the basilica of Santa Maria Maggiore. Pauline, baptized in the small cathedral of Ajaccio, with an archdeacon for a great-uncle and now a cardinal for an uncle, found nothing odd in maintaining a religious belief while disregarding many of the provisions of the Catholic creed. For her additional pleasure, Madame Mère, as we have seen, arrived to stay with Cardinal Fesch in Holy Week. "You know my fondness for her," Pauline wrote to

Madame Michelot and claimed to have won Letizia's approval. "My mother, who is quite severe," she wrote triumphantly to Napoleon, "both praises my conduct and repeats often that I have changed to my advantage."

Pauline was responding to rumors that had reached Napoleon's ears that she and Camillo were on the point of separating, and that such fission would already have occurred if her brother had not forbidden France to her. "Since I have lived in Rome," she replied, "despite the difference in customs, and, I will say frankly, despite the difficult and disputatious character of Prince Camillo, our household is the picture of peace and happiness. For I have made sacrifices you would not have believed me capable of." She surmised, "People jealous of advantages that I have received by nature and fearing my return to Paris invent these black words to encourage you to abandon me. But write to Prince Camillo and his family, for their responses will convince you that my accusers play false."

There was a measure of truth in what Pauline wrote. Although she and Camillo were prone to quarreling—she flustered him with her demands and angered him by flouting his wishes—they shared an aesthetic sensibility and a love of good living, so that the detail of their domestic life was not without its pleasures. Camillo continued to admire his wife's beauty, and she appears to have been content to allow him the privileges of a husband, once the Mecklenburg prince had left for Germany.

By the early summer, at any rate, Pauline's divine body was in need of rest and a cure, and she and Camillo had formed a plan. "We leave," she wrote to Madame Michelot in May, "for Florence in two months, and from there we go to the waters." She had taken the waters at Frascati already with her mother, but to little avail. "I suffer all the time in this climate," she complained. It was hoped that the baths at Pisa would have a better effect. "Please, my dear Poulotte," Pauline added, "have the goodness to send me four or five summer hats, in pale colors, and another straw one." They were to be well made and in the latest fashion, and she required them to be sent to the Palazzo Borghese in

Florence, where they would stop first. "I will be happy to abide by your taste," she ended as usual.

According to Jenny Saint-Maur, "At the moment of arranging the departure, an altercation arose between husband and wife." Pauline wished her son to come with them. But the prince advised leaving young Dermide at Rome. "If you fear the fetid summer air, send him to Frascati," he said. "My brother . . . can supervise him." The boy's uncle Lucien would be nearby, at the Villa Rufinella. "Think too that your entourage is already very considerable," said the prince, who was not overfond of Dermide, "that the lodgings at the waters are very small, and that the fatigue of the road could well hurt his health." Pauline, as she later explained to Napoleon, was swayed by her husband's arguments. "I thought of him surrounded by his little cousins whom he loved, under the care of my brother-in-law, who behaved very well, and of Madame Ducluzel, who loved him and paid the greatest attention to him." She was therefore "without worry" when Dermide, his governess, and his tutor, Monsieur de la Ronde, were installed at the Villa Mondragone in Frascati under the aegis of Camillo's brother, Don Cecco. She and Camillo, meanwhile, took the road for Florence with a caravan of attendants.

"Mon Dieu, what a journey," remembered Jenny Saint-Maur:

> You might say that caprice traveled with us. Every instant some real or imaginary suffering of the Princess's stopped the carriages. Two maids then had to get down into a ditch, or crouch behind a hedge, or just stand in the middle of the road with Her Highness to make some adjustment or other. Her corset needed unlacing, or her hair restyling. . . . Out came all the packages, they opened all the traveling cases and necessaires to find some eau de cologne. . . . The Prince fumed, the suite grew irritable . . . and the postilions did what they could to see the Princess undressed.

But Pauline was all smiles at their first port of call. "I am very content with the town of Pisa," she wrote in Napoleonic fashion to her brother-in-law Murat, now a marshal of the Empire and governor of Paris. With Don Cecco, her brother-in-law, she and Camillo attended the annual regatta held on the feast day of San Ranieri, when night-lights floated on the Arno and candles burned in every window of the town. The widowed Queen of Etruria, Maria Luisa di Borbone, was present and singled Pauline out, paying her attentions in public and making her private visits. Pauline took these favors from the King of Spain's daughter as her right. (When they had first met in Florence the previous year, she had scoffed at the queen's appearance, disfigured by smallpox, but politics now fostered the Bourbon-Bonaparte alliance.) The baths at Pisa did not suit Pauline, however, or her mother, who joined them, and soon they were off to Florence, to mark the feast of Saint John the Baptist on June 24. At nightfall, as fireworks lit up the river, and grandees of the town, bearing candles, proceeded on horse-back from the Piazza Signoria to the Duomo, Pauline sat with her friend the queen, resplendent in the royal box.

In early July the Prussian minister at Rome informed his wife, "Princess Borghese is still at Florence and enjoys the greatest honors possible." But as suddenly as she had appeared in the city, Pauline left it, for the baths of Lucca. On the night of July 7 Signor Raffaello Mansi, a rich merchant in that walled town, was unceremoniously awakened and asked to provide dinner for Pauline and Camillo, who had that moment arrived. Admittedly, while in Florence, he had offered the Borgheses hospitality—both when they were to break their journey in Lucca and at the baths themselves, where he owned a house. But he had not expected his invitation to be taken up at such an hour and without any notice. Following an impromptu midnight feast, the next day Mansi prepared a more orderly dinner and invited a select company. But the Borgheses, it turned out, had already left for his house in Bagni di Lucca, as the bathing station high in the hills above the town was known, and the Lucchese nobility sat down in their fin-ery without the promised guests of honor.

Bagni di Lucca was in great vogue, both for the supposed efficacy of its curative waters and for the beauty of its location, a gorge several miles long. Sulfuric springs, bathhouses, and vertiginous residences with balconies occupied three different levels on one steep side of the gorge. Below, meanwhile, rushed the Lima river, whose eddies visitors could inspect from the safety of a wide path cut along its bank for promenades.

The noise of the torrent and the picturesque form of the mountains above, the fresh air that circulated and was cooled by the river, pleased most invalids. Pauline, however, immediately found fault with the bathhouse facilities, and a new bath had to be made for her. That settled, she and her mother, who now joined her, bathed, douched, and drank glass after glass of acrid water. But then there were the lodgings to consider. Pauline felt that Mansi's house, although large, was poorly laid out and too simply furnished, and its owner was summoned to be rebuked and ordered to remedy the matter.

It was not that Pauline sought to entertain at the Casa Mansi, although such was the general practice in the resort. "There is an enormous crowd of people there, practicing luxury without restraint," wrote one observer, Conte Averardo Serristori, of the scene this summer. "They game all the time, give dinners continually, and often balls." Pauline, her mother, and Camillo, however, appeared rarely in public and they received only a few, if regular, visitors. A local priest said mass every morning, and later in the day came Dr. Rossi, director of the baths. Whether Pauline had a cure for particular ailments in mind or whether she hoped that her visit to this bathing station would act as a general tonic is not known. In addition to the long-lasting problems Dermide's birth had caused, her health had been weakened by bouts of yellow fever in Saint-Domingue. And there was always the possibility, increasing with every lover she took, that she was suffering from one or more venereal infections. At Bagni di Lucca a wide range of cures was offered.

Not only were Pauline and her mother eager to rest and restore their health. There was also the troubling matter of Letizia Bonaparte's status. While Napoleon had made his brothers and sisters imperial highnesses, he had not yet settled on a title for his mother, and, no one knowing quite what to call her, some settled on "Empress Mother," others on "Imperial Highness." As Cardinal Fesch wrote to his nephew the emperor, this caused Letizia great distress, and she wished the matter to be settled before she went about in society. Ultimately, the title of Madame Mère was settled on.

In part, too, it is plain that Pauline and Letizia adopted at Bagni di Lucca, in the shady depths of the Casa Mansi, an almost peasant and penny-pinching existence. It resembled, in a way, the life they had known when they had lived hand-to-mouth, following Pauline's father's death, in the Strada Malerba in Ajaccio, and in I Milleli, their summer house in the hills above that Corsican harbor town. Letizia apparently got the village baker to agree that, of each day's order, she could trade a quantity of stale leftover bread for fresh bread the following morning. Meanwhile Pauline was relentless in the daily tally with her cook of provisions and preserves, demanding that leftovers be recycled the following day and giving orders that dinner should consist of no more than seven or, at most, nine dishes.

Letizia was, by nature, parsimonious to an obsessive degree. In Rome she had forbidden her suite to drink tea or coffee on grounds of expense, and they had had to buy it themselves and brew it in secret. Now Pauline's commands to Madame Michelot betray her mother's influence: "Madame Verdière, who leaves at the end of the month for Paris, will give you my embroidered tunics. I add to them three bonnets of lace. Please have the two dresses embroidered with all economy possible." But Pauline had anyway, with her brother Napoleon, inherited from her mother a belief that the devil was in the detail. Secluded with Madame Mère at Bagni in the months of July and August, adding up her accounts, and with Camillo in attendance, she was not unhappy. From Frascati, Madame Ducluzel sent cheerful accounts of Dermide's health, and at the end of August, Pauline would be reunited with him in Rome. Even with Camillo she could indulge in a "more or less sweet tête-à-tête." She wrote to Madame Michelot, "I am certain I must have some secret enemy who harms me about my brother. None of my conduct merits the least reproach, and their hate must be active and their character truly false to invent all the absurdities they lay at my door. All Italy must be aware that my dear Prince adores me and that I cannot live without him." If this was not entirely true, it was a narrative that could at least pass muster with those at a distance from her.

But while Pauline was recovering her health in Tuscany—Conte Serristori maintained on August 18 that her douches had had a good effect—in Frascati events were unfolding that were to drive a near-indissoluble wedge between husband and wife. In the third week of August, Jenny Saint-Maur was at Pauline's bedside, reading a historical romance to her mistress, when Camillo came in and, out of sight of his wife, made frantic signs to the attendant. "A gesture that he made gave me to understand," Jenny writes, "that a terrible secret weighed on his heart and that he wished me to know it." The princess, however, would not allow the reading to be interrupted.

The prince wriggled around on an armchair, ever more imploring, his wife's calm contrasting with his distress. It was four long hours before the implacable Pauline would let Jenny stop, and the attendant was no sooner in her own quarters and preparing to make her toilette for dinner than the prince entered and threw himself into a chair, his face wet with tears.

"You see me in despair," he said. "Dermide, my wife's son, is dead." A lightning strike could not have convulsed Jenny more. "Dead!" she cried. "It's impossible. We had news yesterday, he is wonderfully well." "That letter was delayed," sighed Camillo. "My brother arrived two hours ago with this cruel news."

Apparently, a few days earlier at the Villa Mondragone in Frascati, Dermide had taken a fever. The doctors had been called in and to begin with had not considered that there was cause for alarm. However, the climate of Frascati, usually so beneficial, had that summer been perni-cious. Lucien Bonaparte and the boy's cousins had had bouts of fever and had recovered. But despite the doctors' best efforts, Dermide did not. (His mother was later to believe that his blood had been thinned by the months he had spent in Saint-Domingue and by the bouts of yellow fever he had suffered there.) At the Villa Mondragone, despite the anxious care of his attendants, the little boy's fever worsened, and on August 14 Dermide died.

Jenny burst into tears on hearing this account, but Camillo was focused on his own unfortunate position. "You alone can be the comforter," he told the weeping woman. "Pauline will regard me with horror. Wasn't it I who wanted her to leave her son in Rome? No doubt he would have died anyway, but she is bound to accuse me of his death. For I have given her the right to be unjust." With these words the prince crushed Jenny to his heart, while begging her not to abandon him. "Certainly never was embrace so pure as that," she recorded.

They decided at length to conceal the fact of Dermide's death until Pauline's health should be better established, and resolved that Don Cecco, who had brought the fateful news, should not appear at the house. He was to return to Frascati to deal with the sad obsequies, but before he left he was to write three letters. The first should announce the onset of Dermide's illness, the second its crescendo, and the third the sad and fatal truth. The dinner hour approached, and Madame Pauline had already asked for Jenny twice. The prince, seeing the attendant's pinched and pale face, said, "She will see something is wrong. Find some cause to justify it."

"Be calm," replied Jenny. "I will have received some news from France that a member of my family is very ill." And she adopted a somber crepe redingote to lend credence to a lie, which the princess accepted. She merely observed that Jenny's family was thoughtless in worrying her when she was so far from home, and when her relative might well by now be recovered. Dinner was nevertheless a tense affair. Jenny had given orders that no one was to approach the princess without talking to the prince or to her first, in case they let slip the awful news. But at one point Jenny was called out to receive a courier, dressed in the livery of mourning, who came with a note of condolence from the Queen of Etruria for the princess. Jenny immediately dispatched the messenger back with a message of acknowledgment, before his presence could come to the attention of her mistress.

The next day Jenny went early to Madame Bonaparte, who received her, although she was still in bed. Thanking the girl for her attentions to her daughter, Letizia approved the plan to keep the news of Dermide's death a secret for some days. But when Jenny declared that the princess's "active imagination" would no doubt force them soon to tell her the truth, Letizia refused to agree that the task should fall to her. When Jenny said that "a mother would, better than anyone, use words to soften such a rude blow," Letizia said "very forcefully" that she would not be drawn into any such arrangement. She had no wish to charge herself, she said, with such a sad commission. She knew her daughter's mercurial personality and did not wish to expose herself to it. She was, besides, careful, she said, to ward off painful emotions and in short refused to reveal the truth.

Over the next few days, knowing nothing of her son's death, Pauline displayed an almost eerie "softness and calm. She had even a kind of gaiety that confounded us," wrote Jenny, who was obliged to hide half of the letters that arrived for the princess, as they expressed regret for her loss. "She talked of her approaching recovery, of the pleasure that the latest news of her son had given her, reproached the Prince for his preoccupied air and Jenny for her sadness." Pauline, while continuing to blame Jenny's relations for worrying her with bad news, even complained that her attendant's melancholy bored her mortally. Jenny would have had her mistress "chagrined, capricious, even unjust; I would have pardoned all, except this calm which tore at my heart."

One day Pauline called on Jenny to take up her pen, saying she had decided to hire a governor, or male preceptor, for Dermide. "Dermide now being six years old, it is no longer suitable that his education is in the hands of a woman. . . . I want him to receive early on the education that befits the son of General Leclerc. Come on, Jenny, sit down and write what I want you to say." Jenny was overcome and wished to excuse herself, but her mistress would brook no argument. The letter, listing the manly virtues this paragon must exhibit, was three pages long, as Jenny had no presence of mind to edit Pauline's thoughts, and the princess, never doubting her powers of dictation, repeated her ideas a dozen times at least.

More than ten days had elapsed since Don Cecco had brought the dreadful news, and since Pauline had had reports from Madame Ducluzel of Dermide's well-being. The governess's silence suddenly seemed inconceivable to Pauline. It was no longer possible to put off the moment when she should learn the truth, and Dermide's tutor was summoned from Frascati so that he could give the princess an account of her son's last days. Jenny meanwhile took Pauline the first letter from Don Cecco, announcing that Dermide was ill.

Pauline's first reaction appears to have been to set out for Frascati immediately. She wrote to Madame Michelot, "My little angel Dermide is ill. I fly to Rome. My baths are not finished, but my heart suffers so much that nothing in the world could hold me here." Jenny added a postscript: "You see by this letter, which your unhappy friend has just dictated, that we have told her half. We leave tomorrow at ten for Rome, she will find there her family who will do all to sustain her in this terrible blow."

However, before they could depart, what the attendant had foreseen occurred. Pauline's "devouring imagination" led her swiftly to review Jenny's earlier tears and other incidents. She called in her attendant for questioning, and the prince, entering at that moment, was similarly interrogated. He lost himself in vague excuses, while Jenny said that Monsieur de la Ronde, Dermide's tutor, who had arrived from Rome that instant, could best tell the truth.

On seeing her son's tutor, Pauline said, "Be truthful, Monsieur de la Ronde, my son is dead." He bowed his head and said nothing. "Oh, I understand this silence," she said. "I have been deceived for a long time . . . my son is dead far from me." After the tutor, under Pauline's questioning, had narrated the painful facts of his pupil's death and had been allowed to withdraw, the princess immediately turned on Camillo. "It's you, Monsieur, who has been the cause of my son's death. Without you I would never have been separated from him, and he would still be alive." As he cowered, Pauline continued: "What will the Emperor have to say? And my family? Leave, Monsieur, I cannot bear the sight of you. You, the butcher of my son!"

The wretched Camillo left, and, alone with Jenny and her women, Pauline said that the death of her son had destroyed all her happiness. While all about her wept, she maintained dry eyes and a calm born of desolation. Of Rome and of Italy, she said, she now had a horror, and nothing on earth would make her stay there. She spoke of the unhappiness that pursued her and of her poignant feelings for General Leclerc. The death of their son now doubled her sorrow, she lamented, and, taking a big pair of scissors that lay to hand, she sheared off her hair. Having cut it in Saint-Domingue for the father, she said, she must pay the same homage to her son. Then, gathering up the tresses, she gave them to Jenny, whom she instructed to leave next day for Rome and see that they were placed in Dermide's coffin, which was to be transported to Montgobert in due course.

As for Pauline herself, on the understanding that Camillo would take her to France, so that she could attend the burial of Dermide beside his father, she agreed to a rapprochement with her husband. Camillo "conducted himself in the most touching manner," Jenny tells us, "and made no objection except to say that the Emperor seemed to want her to stay in Italy." Pauline's reply was magnificent: "What do his wishes matter? It's not Paris I wish to go to, it's Montgobert, where the general lies, and where my son will join him. Is my brother God? Does he have the right to decide my fate? I care no more for the trappings of his court than for his crown. And as you will be accompanying me, there is no more to be said." Camillo, "to have peace, to be pardoned, to have this pretty face that he still loved accord him again a smile," agreed to everything.

Jenny was instructed, therefore, while at Rome, to pack up all the princess's effects at the Palazzo Borghese and dispatch them to Montgobert. While Pauline and Camillo awaited Napoleon's permission to travel, they settled at a villa outside Florence, and, to console the princess, her friend the Queen of Etruria came every evening to dine with her. When Napoleon sent no word, Pauline took matters into her own hands. The Michelots were alerted in early September to her plans: "We will go to Montgobert and not return to Paris until after the coronation." Pauline then wrote to the emperor, toward the end of September:

> This blow has been so severe. Despite summoning all my courage, I find no strength to withstand it. My health is altered visibly, and my husband is so alarmed he wants to take me to France, hoping that the change of air, and the pleasure of being near you, will be beneficial. . . . We leave in four or five days. And I dare to hope that my dear brother will receive me with his usual kindness. We go to Montgobert. . . . Paris at this moment, where all is rejoicing, is not the place for a soul as sad as mine. In all other circumstances it would have been a great pleasure for me to witness your coronation, but fate pursues me in too cruel a manner to allow me such enjoyment.

Pauline's letter was bound to irritate her brother. First, he had not given her permission for her journey to France. Second, if he were to overlook that lèse-majesté, she was now refusing in advance to appear at the December ceremony to which he had devoted much thought and time, and at which he expected all his family, except the recalcitrant Lucien, to play a supporting role. But Pauline was not only grief-stricken and thinking ahead to the inhumation of her son in the tomb with his father at Montgobert. She was also revolted by the role Napoleon's sisters were destined to play at the coronation. They were to be their sister-in-law Josephine's trainbearers, as she bowed her head to be crowned—by her husband, it had been decreed.

As THE BORGHESES and their suite journeyed north to Montgobert, Pauline had much to say, according to her faithful attendant, on the subject of the coronation: "Believe me, dear Jenny, all these grandeurs do not touch me. I have suffered too much. I am determined to live out of the way and cultivate my brother's friendship, but only so that I can be left alone in France, where I am truly better than anywhere else. I leave it to my sisters to shine. I have no ambition, except for a comfortable existence, a small number of good friends, and freedom of action." Pauline persisted with her disapproval of her brother's coronation even after arriving at Montgobert and receiving orders from Napoleon to appear at the ceremony. When her brother Joseph came to remonstrate with her, she told him dramatically and without sparing Camillo's feelings that she wished to bury herself at Montgobert to mourn the deaths of Leclerc and Dermide. She was still awaiting the arrival of Dermide's body, which had been embalmed, like his father's, and was traveling by slow stages from Rome. Dermide's heart, she had determined, was to join that of his father in the gilded urn she guarded so jealously.

Disdaining Joseph's compliance with his brother's imperial wishes, Pauline said angrily, "What do I care for his coronation? Do I have to be there to swell his wife's court? . . . Oh, honorable indeed, Bonapartes in the suite of a Beauharnais. Truly, my sisters make me sick with their submission. We ought to detest her, for the Emperor would betray us all for his dear Josephine." Joseph attempted reason: "But, my dear Paulette, why did you come back at this moment, since you didn't wish to take part in the coronation?" "Why?" Pauline was swift in her reply. "To escape the tyranny of my husband. Because, since my son's death, Italy is insupportable for me. Besides, I needed to breathe the air of France. Every time I leave it, I suffer."

On went the diatribe: "What I suffered in America! And it was the Emperor who forced me to go there. It was the cause of my poor general's death and in consequence the cause of my marriage to the most insupportable of men. Don't talk to me more of going to Paris. I want to stay here. And if I am persecuted further, I declare," she ended, "I will receive my family no more, not even you, Joseph, whom I love dearly."

Pauline had instructed Jenny exactly how to proceed when the corpse of her child should arrive, and on the morning after the cortege had entered the park at nightfall, Jenny, dressed in mourning, approached her mistress's bed in silence. Pauline took her hand, keeping silent too. She rose, dressed herself, and added a hat with a great veil. Leaning on Jenny's arm, she descended to the vestibule, where the small coffin was laid. Members of the suite shouldered it and began the long walk to the tomb in the allée that Fontaine had designed and where Dermide's father had been laid less than two years earlier. Pauline and Jenny walked, too, the princess saying not a word, but Jenny heard her weep. When they arrived at the door of the tomb, Pauline had the coffin set down inside beside the larger one, and she sent away her people. Then she prostrated herself before the two tombs, watering them with her tears and addressing to her husband's and son's shades the most bitter regrets. Later that day, abandoning her usual carefulness with money, she ordered twenty-five louis to be distributed to each of a hundred poor families in the area.

The inhumation of Dermide proved a cathartic event, and the renaissance of Pauline's feeling for Leclerc, and her wish to live secluded, seemed to die. More adroit courtiers than Prince Joseph appeared at Montgobert and talked of the fashions in Paris and of the pleasures that would follow the coronation. In the middle of a very scientific discussion of the form court dress would now take, a lady appeared—an emissary from one of Pauline's imperial sisters. She had a hat and gown made in the latest mode to present to the princess, and Pauline pronounced them delicious. "You know, Jenny," she said pensively to her attendant, when they were alone once more, "I must conciliate the Emperor. He is my protector, he will defend me against the evil designs of my husband. I am determined, in short, to attend his coronation."

And Pauline began to consider her choice of robe for the ceremony. "I need to know first what my sisters have chosen. I don't want to copy them or choose a color they are wearing." On leaving the princess that night, Jenny took with her orders to write to the many couturiers, milliners, haberdashers, and other merchants of Paris who were to help embellish Princess Pauline's appearance in Notre-Dame in the first week of December.

CHAPTER NINE

The Borgheses at War, 1804–1807

PAULINE'S RETURN TO PARIS came at a tense family moment. With the approaching coronation had resurfaced the emperor's resentment that his wife had borne him no children. According to the rather histrionic memoirs of her lady-in-waiting Claire de Rémusat, Josephine wailed: "It is a great misfortune for me, not to have given a son to Bonaparte. It will always be a means by which vicious tongues can trouble my peace of mind." Certainly Pauline was among those who urged on her brother divorce and remarriage to a younger woman. "His family takes advantage of his weaknesses to make him break off little by little his intimacy with me, and abandon all relations with me," Josephine lamented.

Meanwhile, in default of a son and heir of his own, Napoleon had done what he could to secure his legacy, and, in so doing, had managed to aggrieve all four of his brothers. Originally he had thought that the succession should follow the so-called Salic law, which forbade female inheritance. However, given that Napoleon had quarreled with Lucien and Jérôme over their marriages, he wished to exclude those brothers— and Lucien's son, Charles—from the succession. And even should Joseph, Napoleon's natural heir, survive the emperor, the eldest of the Bonapartes had as heirs himself only daughters. So, following Salic law, the imperial mantle must fall next on Lucien, and then on his son,

Charles. To this the emperor was unconditionally opposed, and indeed Lucien, increasingly absorbed in excavations of republican and imperial Rome, disdained his brother Napoleon's modern pursuit of imperium.

The emperor meditated declaring as his heir his brother Louis's elder child, the two-year-old Napoléon Charles Bonaparte. (In Bonaparte birth order, Louis came after Joseph, Napoleon, Lucien, and Elisa and before Pauline, Caroline, and Jérôme.) He even thought of adopting the child in due course, leaving to Louis and his wife, Hortense—Josephine's daughter—their second son, Napoléon Louis, who had been born in October. The question of the imperial succession would then be resolved, even if Joseph was affronted at being passed over, Lucien scornful, and Jérôme no better pleased than Joseph.

But the matter was not to be so easily concluded, so serpentine were the relationships of the Bonapartes and the de Beauharnais, who seem to have been designed by nature to feed off each other's suspicions. Josephine supposedly told Claire de Rémusat that grumbling, reclusive Louis was not happy with the glorious future envisaged for his son and that he doubted the child's paternity. Louis believed, Hortense's mother added, not only that his wife had been adulterous but, to twist the knife further, that she had been so with Napoleon himself. His own family, confided Josephine further, had brought these rumors to Louis's attention. As a result, the empress said, her son-in-law—who was also her brother-in-law—was furious with Napoleon and Hortense, and was resisting the proposed elevation of his elder son as imperial heir.

Josephine's candor, when in private with her women, was renowned and was thought to be a legacy of her colonial upbringing in Martinique. But Claire declared herself amazed by this foray into the interior of the Bonaparte family, and she had been no less astonished by some earlier remarks. The empress, Claire said, had given full rein to her feelings about her husband: "He has no moral principle, he hides his vicious leanings . . . but, if one left him alone to pursue them . . . bit by bit he would give himself up to the most shameful passions. Has he not seduced his own sisters?" Josephine concluded bitterly that her husband believed himself, as emperor, licensed to satisfy "every fantasy."

Even allowing for the empress's anguish—the coronation was drawing nearer, and her husband had as yet assigned her no firm role—these were extraordinary claims that de Rémusat recounts. But other, more trustworthy sources agree that the indolence and tolerance that generally distinguished Josephine in her dealings with her husband had deserted her. For once she did not turn a blind eye to the sexual appetite for her ladies that periodically beset Napoleon. She followed him and one unlucky quarry of the moment into the bedroom to which they had absconded. There she was hot in her denunciation of their conduct. Her husband was predictably furious, and Josephine more miserable than ever.

Are de Rémusat's claims to be believed? She burned her memoirs once, and reconstituted them with the aid of Chateaubriand, no supporter of the Bonapartes. But stories that different members of the close-knit Corsican family were incestuous—Lucien with Caroline, Lucien with Elisa—circulated in Paris. And, rather than being a serious accusation, the empress's denunciation of her husband appears more to have provided an opportunity for her to fulminate against the whole Bonaparte tribe. Other sources would in due course attribute to Josephine more precise allegations of incest, centered on the relations between Napoleon and Pauline, who, according to Count Metternich, Austrian ambassador in Paris from 1806, was "as beautiful as it is possible to be." Opponents of Napoleon's regime and enemy pamphleteers would adopt the accusations wholesale and add, for good measure, that Pauline had been a prostitute at the age of fourteen in a brothel her mother kept in Marseille. For the time being, however, this was invective aired, nothing more—a part of the hubbub and commotion and emotion that marked the approach to the coronation.

In the days before this event, which was to take place on December 2, 1804, Louis Bonaparte agreed to his elder son being named the imperial heir presumptive. But Napoleon and Josephine came nearly to the point of divorce once more over the detail of the coronation ceremony itself. Josephine wanted to be crowned as empress, but Napoleon was reluctant to allow her this dignity. They were both aware that, once she was crowned, the road to divorce would be, though not impassable, less easy. The French people would be reluctant to see a crowned empress cast aside, and the pope, who was coming from Rome to attend the ceremony, less willing to grant the divorce. Pauline, of course, argued fervently that her sister-in-law should not be crowned.

The arguments shifted back and forth in the private apartments of the Tuileries. Napoleon could be objective about the pursuit of rank and title around him, as during the hysterics exhibited by his sisters Elisa and Caroline earlier in the year, after their brothers Joseph and Louis had been elevated to imperial rank. While their sisters-in-law Julie and Hortense were henceforth to be addressed as "Altesse," they remained Mesdames Bacciochi and Murat. Napoleon gave way, as we have seen, and bestowed imperial rank on all his sisters, but he was sardonic: "One would think I was sharing out the patrimony of our father the king."

Now, however, Napoleon was endeavoring to create a coronation ceremony based on that of the Frankish emperor Charlemagne and to add substance to the appearance of empire by appeal to the Julio-Claudian precedents of ancient Rome—prompting Foreign Minister Talleyrand to grumble in private, "The combination of Charlemagne and the Roman empire has quite turned his head." (Napoleon linked his empire to that of Rome by adopting Jupiter's bird, the eagle, as an emblem of military might. Likewise, he revived the use of Merovingian golden bees to link his reign to that of earlier rulers of France.) The emperor was riled that Josephine insisted on being crowned, and the Bonaparte women—Pauline adding her voice to those of Elisa and Caroline—when not seeing to the details of their costume for coronation day, fanned the flames of his discontent. (Napoleon had decided that the court dress of the Renaissance French king François I should be the model, and the painters David and Isabey designed the individual dresses.)

But Pauline went too far. Intercepting a triumphant look that his sister shot at Josephine during one particular battle, Napoleon was seized by remorse for his treatment of his wife. Gathering the empress in his arms, he said tenderly, "Indeed you shall be crowned." Pauline and the other Bonaparte women, he decreed, should bear her imperial train—yards of heavy crimson velvet embroidered with golden bees and lined with ermine. And although Napoleon and Josephine had to go through a hurried nuptial mass, because the pope refused point-blank to consecrate a couple who, owing to the rigors of revolutionary times, had only ever gone through a civil marriage, crowned she was.

THE MOMENT THAT CHILLY DAY in Notre-Dame when Napoleon crowned himself emperor was for many surpassed in felicity by what came next. Josephine knelt at her husband's feet, bowed her head, and clasped her hands together. The emperor raised her up and placed her crown lightly on her head while they exchanged radiant glances. This moment David later captured when he produced a vast painting of the coronation, at Napoleon's request. The graceful incline of Josephine's neck beneath her stiff lace collar and the puffed sleeves of her dress are no doubt perfectly true to life. (Less true to life is his inclusion of Madame Mère in the picture. She had remained with Lucien in Rome and, when asked her opinion of her son's exalted position, said, "Let's hope it lasts.")

But Pauline and her sisters were not going to endure the central part their sister-in-law played at the coronation without complaint. Napoleon's injunction that his sisters bear Josephine's train had already been the subject of argument. The Bonaparte sisters had demanded that the trains of their own dresses be carried, if they must bear that of the empress. Julie and Hortense were also to walk behind Josephine with the three sisters. When Napoleon deputed Gérard Duroc, grand marshal of the Tuileries Palace, to find five chamberlains to carry out this task, Pauline's choice fell on Montbreton, her neighbor at Mont-gobert, brother of Leclerc's secretary and long-standing friend Norvins and, it was said, her lover when no one else offered. He and the other

Above: Pauline's parents, Charles and Letizia Bonaparte

Below: Pauline's childhood home in the Strada Malerba, Ajaccio, Corsica

Above: Pauline's love of cameo jewelry is on show in these portraits by Robert Lefèvre

Below: A drawing by Jean-Baptiste Wicar of an older Pauline

Pauline, immortalized in
Antonio Canova's marble statue,
in a gold "breast cup" by Paris
goldsmith Jean-Baptiste Odiot,
and on a bronze medal

Napoleon as revolutionary general and as first consul

A portrait by Anne-Louis Girodet de Roussy-Trioson of Napoleon
as Emperor of the French, in his coronation robes

The Hand-Writing upon the Wall.

A British cartoon showing Pauline and her sisters bare-breasted and with face patches, denoting blemished reputations

A French cartoon showing Pauline and her brother Napoleon surprised in bed together. Pauline paid little attention to such accusations of incest—or to those who branded her a modern Messalina. See the banner above the bed.

Pauline, with emerald *parure,* to the left of her sisters at their brother's coronation in Notre-Dame, 1804, as shown in a detail from Jacques-Louis David's painting

The Empress Josephine, by Pierre-Paul Prud'hon. Napoleon divorced his
wife reluctantly when she failed to give him an heir.

Above: Pauline's first and second husbands,
General Victor Emmanuel Leclerc and Prince Camillo Borghese

Below: An idealized portrait of Dermide, her son by Leclerc, who died young

Forbin

Blangini

Tchernycheff

Poniatowski

Canouville

Talma

Six of Pauline's many reputed lovers, among them soldiers, a musician, an artist,
and the great actor Talma

While Pauline is buried in a Borghese vault elsewhere in Rome,
it is her marble image housed in this room in the Villa Borghese
that attracts thousands of visitors every year.

chamberlains carrying the Bonaparte women's trains were brought to an abrupt halt as Napoleon and Josephine moved from the altar where their unconventional crowning had taken place and up the flight of twenty-odd steps to the thrones awaiting them. For Pauline and her sisters had simply pulled back on Josephine's train—all twenty-five yards of heavy velvet—and the empress was unable to move forward.

Napoleon fixed his sisters with a look that, for once, quelled even Pauline. They slackened their hold on the train, and the rest of the coronation continued without incident. "What a mummery" was one general's opinion of the long ceremony. "Nothing is missing but the 100,000 men who sacrificed themselves to do away with all this." At the banquet that followed a triumphant Napoleon whispered to his brother Joseph, "If our father could see us now"—a sentiment with which Pauline, with her distrust of her brother's imperial pretensions, might not have wholly concurred. It would certainly have made her furious to know that at supper much later that night her brother asked his wife to keep on her crown while they ate. In his opinion no woman had ever worn a crown with more grace, and he forgot her failure to provide him with an heir. Indeed, for all his lust for a son, there were moments when the emperor accepted that it was his destiny to shine alone, rather than father a dynasty, and leave "a name that should have no equal and glory that would not be surpassed." Reviewing the day's events, he confided to his wife, "I believe I am destined to change the face of the world."

THE CORONATION CONCLUDED, arrangements were made in the new year for the imperial family to sustain Napoleon's dignity by their attendance at numerous court functions, both in Paris and at Saint-Cloud. At the latter country residence, once decorated by Marie Antoinette and now preferred by the emperor, Pauline found her husband no less irksome than before—and showed it. From Saint-Cloud, displaying a sagacity beyond his normal range, Camillo Borghese wrote to his confidant, the Chevalier Angiolini, that he found a morning bath essential, so that he could preserve his equanimity. "It has the gift of calming me and permits me to bear with patience all the rest of the day which passes always in the same manner." Like many, he found the atmosphere of the emperor's court enervating, and indeed, when taxed with the criticism that life at the Tuileries was melancholy, Napoleon agreed. "Yes, so is greatness," he replied. "My mistress is power, but it is as an artist that I love it, as a musician loves his violin."

Pauline apparently punctured the numinous atmosphere when she burst out laughing one evening while the imperial family, including Cardinal Fesch and the pope, were gathered together. When asked what was the cause of her hilarity, the princess replied: "I was just thinking how it would edify our contemporaries, and astonish posterity, had the Holy Father, who sits there so grave, been so fortunate as to convert me to Christianity, or if I possessed the wiles to pervert him into infidelity." When Fesch responded intemperately, Napoleon condemned both his uncle and his sister. Only the pope was calm, pardoning Fesch and Pauline, and telling the latter that he was certain of one thing, that "you, before your death, will become one of my flock." "Then, Holy Father," retorted Pauline, "you must live to a great age."

Discontented, blaming her husband for her continued ill health— his presence preyed on her nerves—Pauline determined that the Borghese ménage should shift to Le Petit Trianon at Versailles, memorably another haunt of the executed queen, which the emperor now made available. While at Versailles, Camillo had an interview with Madame Mère, who had returned to Paris and had healed the breach in her relations with Napoleon that Lucien's second marriage had brought about. She counseled further patience. Her daughter's health continued precarious, she warned, and for the prince to act other than generously would be to put himself in the wrong. Camillo, who though not clever was certainly not unkind, accepted for the moment the supporting role allotted him at the imperial court.

Pauline was instructed by Duroc, the grand marshal of the Tuileries, that she should host a weekly reception at the Hôtel Charost every Wednesday. Other days were allotted to her brothers and sisters. This enforced entertaining Pauline found less to her taste than life at Saint-Cloud or at Versailles, where, as her brother's guest, she could spend all day, should she wish it, in bed or attending to her wardrobe in order to outshine all at night. (Claire de Rémusat tells us that Pauline and her sister Caroline spent hundreds of louis on their court dress and then covered the costly material with a further layer of jewelry.) According to Laure Junot, when Duroc furnished Pauline with a list of guests the emperor wished her to invite to the Hôtel Charost, she crossed out the names of all the pretty women.

Laure added that, although Pauline appeared every Wednesday evening in a concoction of finery that had given infinite trouble for days to her milliner and silk merchant, her haberdasher and jeweler, she had made no effort to prepare her house for the weekly deluge of guests. Their comfort gave her pause for thought, according to Laure, only on the Wednesday morning. The lack of forethought showed in the slapdash nature of the entertainment, the hasty arrangements of flowers, and the insufficient food and drink. The distracted expressions of the sorely tried household and the inadequate service were further evidence that Pauline disliked the role of official hostess. Despite remonstrance from her brother, this was not a way in which she would serve him.

Napoleon was soon gone again. "In Paris nothing is remembered for long," he remarked. "If I remain doing nothing for long, I am lost." In April 1805, Russia, Austria, and England formed what became known as the Third Coalition against France. They had very different aims. The czar Alexander wanted to obtain Constantinople and the Dardanelles and Poland, Austria wanted to reoccupy its former territories in Italy, and Britain wanted to defeat France and recover the colonies that it had lost since entering the War of the First Coalition in 1793. Napoleon was occupied massing an invasion force at Boulogne, which he intended to transport to Dover once his admirals had wrested command of the English Channel. He planned to move against Russia and Austria thereafter, and was transferring further regiments to positions close to the Rhine. The doings of Pauline in Paris, as a result, escaped his notice, although his chief of police, Fouché, kept detailed reports on the activities of the emperor's brothers and sisters.

A vignette of this period shows Pauline in a familiar role, seducing with her beauty and allure a famous mulatto officer from Saint-Domingue. General Thomas Dumas, the officer in question, had been born on the island, and had served with Napoleon in Italy and Egypt. He was now an inhabitant of Villers-Cotterêts and husband of the innkeeper's daughter there. With his small son, Alexandre, the handsome general paid Princess Borghese a visit at Montgobert in the course of 1805, and much later that son, Alexandre Dumas *père* the writer, noted his impressions of that visit, a "luminous" memory of his childhood in which we see the scene through the child's "astonished" eyes.

Father and son were first ushered upstairs by servants in green livery, then led through a long sequence of apartments to a boudoir lined with cashmere. Their hostess was there, lying on a sofa. "It was a charming creature who offered herself to our sight," remembered Alexandre Dumas, "a petite and graceful being who wore little embroidered slippers, such as Cinderella's fairy godmother might have given her." The princess was so young and beautiful, he added, that, though only a child, he was quite dumbfounded.

Pauline didn't get up when they entered, only extended a hand to Dumas's father and lifted her head. Burly General Dumas wanted to take a chair at the princess's side, but she made him rather sit on the sofa at her feet. These she then placed on the officer's knees, toying with the buttons of his coat with the toe of one slipper.

"This foot, this hand, this delicious little woman, milk white and shapely, next to this mulatto Hercules . . . it was the most marvelous picture," enthused Alexandre. The child's sense of wonder only increased when Pauline called him over and gave him a tortoiseshell bonbon box, encrusted with gold. (To his dismay, however, she first emptied out the bonbons.) Pauline then leaned forward to whisper in the general's ear. "Her pink and white cheek grazed my father's dark skin," recorded Alexandre. "Maybe I saw them with the eyes of a child—an astonished child—but if I were a painter, I could make a fine portrait of those two."

The sound of a horn interrupted matters. It was the princess's chamberlain and neighbor Montbreton, out hunting in the park. Over to the window went the general, full of enthusiasm: "Look, here comes the hunt. And the quarry is going to come right down this allée. Come and see, Altesse."

"No, no," replied Pauline. "I am very well where I am, and it tires me to walk. You can carry me, if you like."

And so the general picked up the princess in his big hands, "as a nurse might a child," and took her over to the window that commanded a view of the allées and lawns that Leclerc had so painstakingly laid out before his death. There they waited, for the animal did not break cover for some minutes. At length appeared a stag that flashed across the allée. In hot pursuit came hounds, huntsmen, and gentlemen riders. From above the princess signaled with a handkerchief, and the riders responded, touching their hats, before she allowed the general to carry her back to her sofa.

"I do not know what went on behind me," wrote Alexandre, who remained at the window. "I was so absorbed in the stag . . . the hounds, the hunt. All this was more interesting for me than the princess. My memory of her stops entirely with that signal she made with her white hand and that white handkerchief. . . . Did we stay at Montgobert or did we return to Villers-Cotterêts that same day? I don't recall."

Pauline did not feel constrained in her relationships with other men by her ties to Camillo. Nevertheless she was gratified when her brother the emperor returned in the summer of 1805 from Milan, where he had been crowned King of Italy, and addressed her complaints against the prince. There was also Camillo's list of injuries done him by Pauline for the emperor to consider. Napoleon had already deflected Camillo's threat the previous year to return to Rome unless he was suitably honored and decorated, like his brother-in-law Murat. Knowing that Pauline would refuse to accompany her husband back to Rome, and determined not to have his volatile sister resident in Paris without her husband, Napoleon had conferred on his brother-in-law the Grand Cordon of the Légion d'Honneur. (This honor, created in 1802, conveniently resembled in shape and color the aristocratic Order of Saint Louis.) Waiving the usual law requiring ten years' residence in France before an alien could take French citizenship, Napoleon had also created Prince Borghese a French citizen and a prince of the imperial house.

Satisfied, Camillo had remained, but now he and Pauline were at each other's throats. Providing the makings of a peace with honor for the Borghese couple, Napoleon named Camillo head of his squadrons of mounted grenadiers, a formation of heavy cavalry then encamped at Boulogne and primed to invade Britain. From Munich, en route to survey the troops drawn up against the Austrians in Germany, Napoleon gave orders for Camillo to join his men. The prince was delighted with himself, Pauline could breathe freely in the Hôtel Charost, and only the grenadiers were the losers. Not for nothing did Napoleon say, "It is because the nation believes I possess the civil qualities for a ruler that I govern."

Napoleon was not happy when, after his Channel fleet suffered a reverse at the beginning of August, his plans for an invasion of England foundered. Pauline was delighted, however, by her brother's decision to remove from Boulogne the forces constituting the Army of England and send them to reinforce the Army of the Rhine and combat the Austrian threat. For to Strasbourg went Camillo, now a colonel of carabiniers—another heavy cavalry formation. "I could have come to Paris and not accompanied my troops," Camillo told Angiolini, "but I prefer to go with them, which I'm sure you would agree is the right thing to do. I can tell you," he wrote with a flourish, "that I don't care how much powder flies, I'm not going to make for my carriage. If I'd wanted to be in my carriage, I would have come to Paris." (Fortunately for the honor of the Borghese family, Camillo's brother, Don Cecco, was a gifted soldier and, after Napoleon offered him a command in a cuirassier regiment, ultimately became a general of brigade.) Pauline meanwhile was minded to be gracious. She wrote to her brother-in-law

Murat in August 1805, "Camillo works hard, the Emperor is content, and I am charmed. I never doubted his aptitude." And her health improved—she did not so much eat her dinner, wrote the ever-assiduous Angiolini in October, as "devour" it.

THE BATTLE OF TRAFALGAR, which the French and Spanish fleets fought against the British in October 1805 and which the latter won so convincingly that it effectively ended Napoleon's dream of "colonies, ships, commerce," meant that the emperor had to confine his imperial ambitions to Continental Europe. But the details of her brother's campaigns did not interest Pauline, so long as the emperor was safe and well and her husband was a long way away. "I am charmed by the Emperor's arrangements for Camillo," she wrote, on hearing that her husband had been posted to distant Poland. "I have just received letters from him." News in mid-November that the emperor had entered Vienna and, in December, that he had crushed Austrian and Russian forces at the Battle of Austerlitz were for his sister harbingers of his return to Paris, an event to which she looked forward, even though her health had again deteriorated. "For some days," Angiolini wrote to Camillo in November, "the doctor has forbidden any visits. Her nerves are so feeble that her door has been shut, even to her mother." Her condition was only marginally better in December. Pauline wrote to Murat, "What will contribute to my complete recovery is the presence of those I love, for I do not fear to tell you I lead a sad and monotonous life that doesn't suit me."

The peace between France and Austria that was signed at Pressburg and that greatly enlarged French territories in Europe unfortunately brought back to Paris Pauline's husband as well as the emperor. But before the princess could sulk or upbraid him, Camillo, ever obliging, paid a diplomatic visit to his mother in Rome. Pauline, meanwhile, with her brother's triumphant return to Paris, came back to life. Although she was no more inclined than ever to bow to imperial etiquette, and when the order of the day was for court dresses was likely to appear in a negligee that revealed her figure, she dazzled Paris during the official imperial celebrations to mark the new enlarged empire. Only when Napoleon tried to bend her to his will did she revolt.

The emperor wished his family to act as trustworthy suzerains or satraps, who would, in exchange for the grant of territories and titles, execute only his bidding. A year earlier, in an exchange of territories with Spanish Bourbons, Elisa and Felice Bacciochi had departed for the newly created principality of Lucca and Piombino. At that time Pauline had said, "Our brother loves only Elisa, and forgets us all." Now Napoleon's notable victories over the Austrians and Russians at Austerlitz in the winter of 1805 had brought France as prizes not only Austrian territories in northern Italy but also Naples. The emperor might once have thought of appointing as overseer of the first his Borghese sister and brother-in-law, but Pauline's disinclination for court life as much as Borghese's lack of intellect and their marital discord deterred him. In the event he appointed his stepson Eugène de Beauharnais Viceroy of Italy.

Paris, recently so full of the Bonaparte tribe, was emptying fast. Upon Joseph, Napoleon bestowed the Kingdom of Naples, and off he went southward with his wife, Julie, and two daughters. Meanwhile the Holy Roman Empire, over which Francis II had reigned as emperor, was dissolved, and that ruler became Emperor Francis I of Austria. Of a conglomeration of German states named the Confederation of the Rhine, Napoleon became protector. Caroline departed with Murat and their four children for Düsseldorf in Germany, where they were invested as Grand Duke and Duchess of Berg, a part of the new confederation. With Louis, to whom was apportioned the Kingdom of Holland, northward went Hortense and their two sons, Napoléon Charles and Napoléon Louis.

There remained, therefore, Pauline to consider, in the general apportioning of honors and lands. The Grand Empire was conceived of as a kind of federation of "brother kingdoms." And in addition to the Confederation of the Rhine, a Saxon Duchy of Warsaw sprang into being. In March 1806 Napoleon informed Pauline that she was to be

Duchess of Guastalla. By the Peace of Pressburg this small principality, barely four miles square, had been ceded to France, with the Duchies of Parma and Piacenza, while the Bourbons of Parma had received Tuscany under the name of Etruria.

Pauline was apparently at first delighted with the idea of being joint sovereign, with Camillo, of this new French territory, but then thought to enquire further. "What is Guastalla, dear brother?" she asked. "Is it a fine great town, with a palace and subjects?"

"Guastalla is a village, a borough," replied Napoleon incautiously. "In the states of Parma and Piacenza."

"A village, a borough!" spat Pauline. "What do you expect me to do with that?"

"Whatever you like," came the answer.

"What I like!" And Pauline began to cry. "'Nunziata [Caroline] is a grand duchess and she's younger than me. Why should I have less than her? She has a government and ministers. Napoleon, I warn you I will scratch out your eyes if I'm not better treated. And my poor Camillo, how can you do nothing for him?"

"He's an imbecile," her brother responded.

"True, but so what?" answered Pauline, who had apparently taken to styling her husband "His Serene Idiot."

The emperor shrugged, the spitfire princess wept. And the result of this scene? The principality of Guastalla was ceded to the Kingdom of Italy (a collection of northern states, including Piedmont, Lombardy, the Emilia and the Veneto, that was a dependency of the French Empire), and Pauline, who kept the title of duchess, received six million francs as a sale price. This sum she invested in French government bonds, which gave her an annual income of 400,000 francs. Moreover she kept the feudal lands that went with the duchy, which gave her a revenue of 150,000 francs. With this arrangement Pauline was extremely satisfied. Her inheritance from Leclerc was still the subject of dispute with his family. (Following Dermide's death, the child's share had reverted to them.) Nevertheless, the Hôtel Charost and Montgobert were her own property. Pauline had, besides, by virtue of her second marriage contract, rights to apartments in the Palazzo Borghese in Rome and elsewhere, carriages, and jewels. With the addition of the Guastalla rents she had become, by any standards, a wealthy woman and an independent one. In celebration she extended her house in the rue du Faubourg Saint-Honoré on the garden front and required Camillo to bring paintings from the Borghese collection in Rome to adorn one of the wings she created, while the other she designed to be a banqueting room.

Titles and lands she did not crave, but for the power of money Pauline always had considerable respect. Napoleon, from whom all patronage flowed, continued to give proof of his strong affection for her. (By contrast, his other sisters annoyed him. Elisa he regarded as a shrew. With Caroline, he said, "I have always had to fight a pitched battle.") So Pauline could count herself in one respect a happy woman. But there is no doubt that, in these years following her disenchantment with Camillo and the death of Dermide, she was not at her best. She was querulous, in poor health, and, though as lovely as ever, inclined to quarrel with those around her. A contemporary but anonymous account of Napoleon's court published in England, *The Secret History of the Cabinet of Bonaparte,* had these sly remarks to make: "She is very witty; and very frequently, in her sallies, tells her imperial family some bold truths, and very often mocks them. She thinks, I suppose, that, as she is married to a genuine prince, such liberties are permitted." When Camillo was about to set off for Germany following the resumption of war, this time with Prussia, Pauline supposedly begged her brother, in full hearing of fifty people assembled in Josephine's drawing room, to procure her husband, "after a useless life, a glorious death." "You always go too far," Napoleon replied.

Pauline being Pauline, there were of course lovers, and the frequent visits of a Comte de L———, for instance, vexed Prince Borghese. Defying Pauline's cruel declaration that "to give oneself to Camillo was to give oneself to no one," and despite his alleged impotence, the prince attempted to begin a liaison with one of his wife's ladies in revenge. What was particularly galling to Camillo was Pauline's flaunting of her affairs. She "gave herself carte blanche with her favorites and took a kind of pride in making her preferences public property," wrote a lady at court. "People talked of nothing but Pauline's intrigues," the Polish countess Anna Potocka recorded in her memoirs, "and they certainly did provide material for lengthy discussion." But there is no evidence that Pauline felt much for the lovers she took. That was soon to change, however, as she embarked in the summer of 1806 on a journey to Plombières, the bathing station in the Vosges where she had recovered her health while married to Leclerc, and where she now hoped to do so again. There, in most unseasonable rainstorms that rendered her journeys to and from the baths hazardous, Princess Borghese was to begin a whirlwind romance.

CHAPTER TEN

Messalina of the Empire, 1807

As Madame Leclerc, Pauline had traveled to Plombières with few attendants. Matters were very different now when Princess Borghese undertook one of her imperial journeys. She sent runners ahead to secure her board and lodging in houses of distinction along the route. In addition she chose to make at least part of the journey to Plombières in a litter, borne by porters in the imperial green-and-gold livery. And finally she took with her what was becoming a fixture on these journeys—a bathtub.

When the need to stop at Bar-le-Duc in Lorraine arose, Pauline's former brother-in-law, Jean Louis Leclerc, who was prefect of the Meuse, was selected to be her host. He was informed that his guest required for her health to bathe in milk, and he accordingly sent detachments into the neighboring villages, armed with milk cans and with orders to bring them back full. Well content with his arrangements, the prefect welcomed Pauline. "Carry me as you used to do," she demanded, and Jean Louis Leclerc obliged, bearing her into the principal salon.

When she asked if her bath was ready, he was able to respond in the affirmative.

"And my shower? I take a shower after my bath," she informed him.

"Ah, that I cannot arrange. I have no equipment," he replied.

"My dear man, don't concern yourself. Nothing so easy," came the answer. "Just make a hole in the ceiling above my bath, and have your servants pour the milk through when I am ready. It's a slight inconvenience to you, I know, but think of the consequences to my health."

Jean Louis Leclerc had, like so many before and after him, no answer to Pauline's airy confidence that her every wish was his command. He had his servants follow the princess's directions, and Pauline, well bathed and showered, went on her way. She left the disconsolate prefect to make good his wrecked rooms in a house pervaded by the smell of sour milk for months to come.

The milk bath and shower on which Pauline insisted may have been intended primarily to whiten her skin. Her journey to Plombières, deep in the Vosges country westward of the Black Forest, however, was in search of a cure for deeper-seated ills. The hot springs had had the reputation since antiquity of being particularly beneficial for women. Indeed, they enjoyed the specific renown of curing sterility, and Pauline's sister-in-law Josephine had visited the spa on numerous occasions since her marriage to Bonaparte, in hopes, destined to be dashed, that the waters would promote a fruit of their union. Even now that the empress, aged forty-four, was apparently undergoing erratic menstrual cycles, Napoleon hoped that a visit to Plombières would bring on a "little red sea."

As Madame Leclerc, Pauline might have been happy to have become pregnant with a sibling for Dermide. But now she was not interested in providing an heir for Camillo Borghese, and, as we have speculated, she may have been unable to give him one, if her fallopian tubes were severely infected. Indeed, it was about this time that it suited her to announce to Laure Junot that to "give oneself" to the prince was to give oneself to no one, meaning that he was impotent. (She had evidently forgotten the two months the couple had spent at Mortefontaine enraptured with each other following their church marriage and before she had tired of him.) At any rate, her visit to Plombières appears to have been occasioned by gynecological worries. She was, as so often before, suffering from lower abdominal pain and inter-

mittent lower back pain. There is frequent mention of days spent prostrated, her family was in a state of anxiety about her health, and her
expressions of distress when traveling over rough roads suggest that she
was almost permanently in this invalid state at this time. As noted earlier, even her coquettish demands to be carried from place to place may
have had their source in suffering, with a weakened pelvis the cause.
Certainly she gave detailed instructions for the manufacture of a girdle
or belt for her pelvis around this time, no fashion accessory but a practical aid to living. But Dr. Peyre, the army surgeon who had attended
Leclerc during his last illness in Saint-Domingue and who had now
been Pauline's personal physician for five years, was convinced that at
least some of her current troubles stemmed from inflammation and
infection of her reproductive organs, specifically her fallopian tubes.
The hot springs at Plombières were a logical remedy for such trouble.

As already mentioned, this putative infection may have dated from
1798, when Pauline gave birth to Dermide. During the process of
childbirth, bacteria, entering via the vagina and womb, can penetrate
the upper genital tract and cause disease. In that case the problems
associated with Dermide's birth that had sent Pauline to Plombières
five years earlier still lingered. But it is at least conceivable that she had
contracted chlamydia, gonorrhea, or another sexually transmitted disease, which can also give rise to infected and inflamed fallopian tubes.
An abscess on her hand that took time to heal on her return to Paris
from Saint-Domingue had already led Laure Junot to surmise as much.
And then there were the reports of her uninhibited displays of sexuality
in the former colony. Josephine's former lover Barras, who encountered
Pauline shortly after a visit that she made to Gréoux, another bathing
station about this time, was forthright in his diagnosis: "Excessive sexual activity, in consequence of *furor uterinus*"—Latin for nymphomania—"had given her an incurable ill. Too weak to walk, she was in such
a state she had to be carried everywhere."

Nymphomania, or an obsession with sex and an insatiable appetite
for genital stimulation, was not the only infirmity of which Pauline was
to be accused in these years. Josephine apparently continued to maintain, when distressed, that her husband, Napoleon, was "too intimate"

with Pauline. One Sunday evening at Malmaison during this winter of 1805–6, Volney, one of Josephine's confidants, had been chatting by the fire to Hochet, secretary of the Council of State. The empress suddenly appeared, haggard and in tears, and rushed over to them. "Oh dear, oh Volney, I am wretched indeed!" she cried. Philosopher Volney was used to the empress's laments when she was upset by some new infidelity of her husband's: "Be calm, Madame, it is you the Emperor loves. I am sure you are mistaken. . . . Very well, I believe you, but this is a mere fancy, an enchantment of an hour." Josephine replied grimly: "You don't know what I've just seen. The Emperor is a scoundrel. I have just caught him in Pauline's arms. Do you hear! In his sister Pauline's arms!" And, apparently feeling better for sharing this astonishing confidence, she rushed again from the room.

The rumor that Napoleon was incestuous with Pauline was certainly in circulation around this time. Gouverneur Morris, earlier American minister to France, heard a year later in New York from General Moreau that Josephine had made the latter her confidant in Paris. "Madame Leclerc, as all the world knows, the present Princess Borghese," Morris recorded in his journal, "is a Messalina." This Roman empress, the wife of the Emperor Claudius, had been notably cruel, avaricious, and hungry for power. But she had also had an insatiable sexual appetite and kept a brothel under an assumed name where she competed with prostitutes to see who could satisfy more lovers in a night. Josephine had, according to Moreau, alleged that Pauline had been "too intimate" with Napoleon. When Moreau repeated this to Pauline herself, Morris goes on, the princess denied it at first, "saying the Empress was no better than she should be herself. At length she acknowledged it."

It is a good story that Moreau told Morris, and possibly one that he himself believed. However, having been put on trial and banished by the emperor, Morris was probably willing to smear Napoleon. And both ladies had reason to lie to the general—Josephine to express her distress, Pauline to emphasize her power over her brother. Is Hochet's story any more credible? The truth is, it seems almost inevitable, given the strong sex drive for which Pauline and Napoleon were both renowned, given, too, their mutual affection, their clannish affinity, that they should have experimented sexually together. Perhaps neither of them considered such sexual congress, if it took place, of great importance. Growing up in Corsica, they had been surrounded by examples of intermarriage among relations, even of technically incestuous unions such as those between uncles and nieces prohibited by the church. Marrying within the immediate community thus remained the norm on the island well into the nineteenth century.

The Bonapartes imported these customs into France, Napoleon giving careful consideration at one point, when contemplating divorce from Josephine, to the project of marrying a niece. And of course Louis Bonaparte married Josephine's daughter, Hortense, who was also his stepniece. Not for nothing did Bernadotte say in disgust that the couplings of the Bonaparte clan resembled those in a *chiennerie,* or kennel. In Paris, Pauline plainly liked to shock—and titillate—her contemporaries by alluding to a supposed incestuous relationship with her brother. But much of the time she played to an audience who expected nothing less from Corsicans, regarding them as bandits and as scarcely French. It was a sophisticated riddle that Pauline posed, and one to which only she and her brother knew the answer.

If Pauline had indeed been "too intimate" with Napoleon, if she indeed did have venereal disease, he was at first sight as good a candidate as any for the distasteful role of having supplied it. Indeed, it has been argued, from traces of arsenic in his hair and from his documented use of a "blue pill" containing mercury, that Napoleon suffered from gonorrhea or syphilis, in the treatment of which both were used. But these are deep waters. Arsenic and mercury were also used to treat stomach problems. And besides Napoleon, there were, as we have seen, many other candidates who could have infected Pauline with venereal disease, including of course Moreau himself when he formed part of that trio of generals who first romanced and then renounced Pauline in 1799.

WHATEVER PAULINE'S MALAISE, she and her doctor judged the small spa of Plombières, situated above the rushing Augronne River, ideal for the treatment of her condition. The mountain air gave patients "the color of health," the river trout made for an excellent dinner, and the views of rock, forest, and meadow were picturesque. The lodgings were admittedly rudimentary, rough wooden houses with balconies overhanging riverside promenades below, but, according to one contemporary visitor, the atmosphere in the little spa community was companionable: "No one thinks of anything but their health, and so no one talks of anything but illness."

Every morning two imposing lackeys, dressed in the imperial livery of gold and green, carried Pauline in her litter or in her chair to and from the baths. She then spent the rest of the day in seclusion—or she intended to, as she had done at other spas. When in pursuit of a cure, she was as tireless a huntress as when at other times seeking pleasure. But at Plombières the princess's eye was caught by a fellow patient at the spa, and her languor gave way to animation. The Comte de Forbin was the object of her attention—the handsome scion of a seigneurial family from the south, whose ancestral residence was the Château La Barben outside Aix-en-Provence. While unseasonable tempests swept the Vosges, Pauline and Auguste de Forbin began a passionate relationship, the strength of which appears to have disconcerted and delighted her. With him she lingered at Plombierès, writing to the empress, "Forgive me, Madame, I have had to sacrifice for my health the pleasure of being near you at Saint-Cloud. I am most conscious of your regard for me, and I hear that Camillo is very happy. My regret at being separated from him increases greatly my chagrin." With such duplicitous sentiments, credited neither by writer nor by addressee, did the imperial couriers hasten from Bonaparte to Beauharnais and back again.

Forbin was by inclination an artist who had taken lessons as a boy at the famous school of drawing in Aix-en-Provence and thereafter watercolor lessons while living with his parents in Lyon. Although he had no pronounced aptitude for his chosen career, he pursued it even after his father, Gaspard, was guillotined and his mother settled in Grasse. Auguste, adapting to changing times, moved to Paris and entered the atelier of the revolutionary artist David, exhibiting in 1796. Thereafter, following a year's conscription in the chasseurs and dragoons and a marriage that did not endure, he traveled to Rome to expand his artistic horizons, and dabbled in poetry and architecture as well as painting. Possibly he encountered Pauline during her few months of residence in the Eternal City. It was, however, at Plombières, when Forbin was aged thirty and in his physical prime, that he took the invalid princess's fancy.

The French novelist Stendhal, who served in the Napoleonic army, said of Pauline's brother, "Napoleon made the mistake of all parvenus—that of estimating too highly the class into which he had risen." The same could have been said of her. As we have seen, Pauline had admired the aristocratic airs of Fréron in Marseille. The hereditary prince of Mecklenburg-Strelitz in Rome had attracted her with his brand of Enlightenment culture. And even Camillo Borghese, whose taste in outfits and equipages could not be faulted, had appealed to her before his other failings outweighed his lineage. Auguste de Forbin was the current head of a family that had been of note since they traded at Marseille in coral, corn, and slaves in the fourteenth century. The Forbins of Provence had contributed grand seneschals, cardinals, and ambassadors to the annals of France. Even their home, the Château La Barben, on its rocky eminence, had been the gift of the illustrious King René to a fifteenth-century forebear. Pauline felt the glamour of this accomplished *gentilhomme* and ignored for the moment his lack of income and considerable expenditure.

Princess Borghese was not always so forgiving. In the suite that had followed her to Plombières and that had been assembled prior to the coronation were a number of ladies and gentlemen of the Faubourg Saint-Germain, where the former nobility of France resided in a state of grand disrepair. The Duc de Clermont-Tonnerre, Pauline's chamberlain, had once been famous for his witty epigrams. Now he was grateful for his salary. Madame de Chambaudoin and Madame de Bréhan, Pauline's ladies-in-waiting, were also denizens of the Faubourg Saint-Germain. But Pauline made few friends among these aristocrats, who had been visited upon her by Napoleon. (He sought, by arranging grand households for all his siblings, to make of his imperial court something rich and fine.) Knowing that these noble employees felt little loyalty to her, with her brother Napoleon she might have said, "A prince who in the first year of his reign is considered to be kind is mocked in his second year." Montbreton, alone of her household, was someone she could rely upon—as did her mother, to whom this chamberlain forwarded reports of the princess's health.

Pauline could claim that her salon in Paris was not as brilliant as it might have been, given that the caliber of her upper household was not superior. She therefore asked her brother if Auguste might join her household as an additional chamberlain. Napoleon, preoccupied, failed to suspect that his sister had an ulterior motive and agreed. Forbin duly traveled back to Paris in September with the Borghese suite—including the litter, the chair, and the bathtub—and was formally appointed her chamberlain in early October. Of Pauline's health we hear no more this year, and we may conclude that her Provençal *gentilhomme* had succeeded in sating her "*furor uterinus,*" with no anatomical ill effects.

In Paris to plague Pauline was, of course, her husband, but Camillo was not at the Hôtel Charost long to disturb her or indeed remonstrate with her about the clear partiality she showed for her new chamberlain. For Napoleon was going to war again, and Camillo at the head of his carabiniers was going with him. During negotiations in the summer of 1806 with Britain and Russia, Napoleon had secretly offered to return to Britain the Electorate of Hanover, which had fallen to France during the Peace of Pressburg earlier that year and which Napoleon had at that time bestowed on Prussia. Upon discovering that Napoleon had this betrayal in mind, Prussia had rashly issued an ultimatum to France.

Napoleon, seizing his moment, took his forces, Borghese's regiment among them, into Germany, where he crushed the Prussians first at the Battle of Jena and then at Auerstadt in October 1806. Later that month he entered Berlin, and in November, flushed with victory, he declared a Continental blockade, closing French ports to British ships and forbidding his allies and conquered powers from trading with the enemy kingdom. With Forbin, meanwhile, Pauline had spent an idyllic autumn at Saint-Leu, her brother Louis's country residence in the Val-d'Oise, which had previously belonged to the princes de Condé.

Napoleon's ambitions were not ended. Pressing eastward across the Vistula, he headed toward a confrontation with Russia. As autumn progressed into winter, Borghese and his regiment moved into Poland. Pauline's husband might not be Napoleon's most distinguished soldier, but at least he was absent from France. "The good news we received from the army contributes not a little to the improvement in my health," she wrote.

In the winter, upon Pauline's return to Paris, her devotion to Forbin was obvious. People could not fail to note "the elegant equipage of the chamberlain and his pretty white horses." In addition Pauline had paid Forbin's debts. He was, in consequence, no longer vacillating among the métiers of poet, writer, and artist, but was assiduous in her service, as Laure d'Abrantès reveals.

During Josephine's absence at Mainz, where the empress took up residence during Napoleon's German campaign, it had been decreed that Princess Borghese should receive on a Monday. For the first time Pauline appears to have taken these duties seriously and, having now spent a good deal on the house, wished to make effective display of her taste. Guests at the Hôtel Charost admired in succession the yellow salon, the *salon d'honneur,* which was decorated in a vivid red velvet, and a grand dining room, lit by two chandeliers draped with gossamer fabrics. A state bedroom, decorated in pale blue satin—bed hangings included—lay beyond a violet antechamber. Where Pauline had previously been a lax hostess, now she was fastidious. Every Monday before the guests arrived, she made her rounds "with an implacable eye, noting all the faults, the apprentices who dare to cross from the kitchen, the dogs whom the concierge has let enter the courtyard." Flowers, candelabra, her members of household and their dress, the servants and their livery—all came in for careful scrutiny.

On one of these Mondays, Laure d'Abrantès tells us that "the princess was astonishing, she was so beautiful." Pauline wore a dress of pink tulle, lined with pink satin; diamond brooches nestled amid downy marabou feathers at her neckline, and pink satin ribbons floated at her waist. Her bodice was satin "strewn with diamonds of the first water . . . her headdress consisted of marabou feathers fixed with dazzling diamonds."

Although, like everyone else, Laure admired the princess's appearance, she was not displeased with her own. She had on a dress of yellow tulle, lined with yellow satin and embellished with double violets that were infused with a Florentine concoction, powder of iris. In consequence they gave off a heady perfume when she danced. But her hostess was not happy and dispatched Forbin to call Madame Junot, as Laure then was, to her.

The chamberlain approached Laure with a serious face. "The princess wants to talk to you immediately."

Laure replied, "Well, you're very serious. What is it?"

"It's a serious matter. Come quickly," he replied.

Laure made sure to take her time going over to Pauline, and was vexed when she reached her.

"My dear Laurette, how could you have chosen so ill the flowers of your headdress?" her hostess asked.

"Madame, they match the ones on my dress," Laure replied.

"I can see that," was Pauline's uncompromising reply. "But you must never do that. Use scabious [another violet-hued flower], for instance, instead. For artificial violets in black hair like yours make your curls look triple the size. That gives you a hard air. Now please, promise me to change those flowers."

"Yes, madame," said Laure, highly amused at Pauline's air of gravity. "What she told me, however, was true," she recorded. "Violets look terrible in black hair."

With this perfectionist eye for detail and Forbin her willing assistant, with the aid of Paris couturiers and milliners and of her Borghese jewel box, Pauline made her person as exquisite as her salons. She was moreover as energetic and lively a hostess as she had previously been reluctant, and her reputation for beauty and taste redoubled as fashionable society flocked to her assemblies. Camillo Borghese, whose presence might have sullied her mood, was happily still absent with Napoleon on the Polish campaign that ended temporarily with the inconclusive Battle of Eylau in East Prussia against the Russians in February 1807. (She had dedicated to him and his suite rooms on the first floor of the Hôtel Charost, while she occupied the ground floor.)

The gates of the Hôtel Charost were not always open to guests on Mondays. At times the concierge turned guests away, claiming that the princess was in poor health. Although this may not always have been the case, in April 1807 she twice consulted the imperial doctor, Halle, who examined her internally. Pauline's doctor, Peyre, was present on both occasions. Halle's findings, which he wrote up on the twentieth of that month for Peyre, make interesting reading, although a gloss is naturally often necessary, given the delicate subject matter of his letter:

"I have continued to reflect upon the spasmodic state in which I found Her Highness, and in which we saw her yesterday. The womb was less sensitive yesterday, but was still so in some measure. The ligaments still showed that irritation for which we recommended her to bathe last Thursday. The spasms I saw while she was in the bath were hysterical in origin, her headache also." (It is unclear whether these were uterine or other spasms.) "The general picture is one of weakness and exhaustion. It's not an ordinary inflammation [of the ligaments]. The inflammatory state we saw is temporary. The underlying condition is an overstimulated uterus. If this continues, I can't answer for the consequences." In other words, Pauline's sexual activity was, in his opinion, proving her undoing.

Halle had skirted round this matter when he examined the princess the previous week, choosing his words carefully when he gave her his opinion of her case. He had attributed the aroused state of her uterus to "internal douches," and had spoken "in a general manner" of all that could "irritate the womb." He thought that his admonitions had been heard—"but, I fear, not enough."

He went on, in his letter to Peyre, "I know nothing, I can only conjecture. What I have said of the nature of the symptoms that you and I have seen, and that you have seen more often than me, is more than sufficient to give us the key to the enigma. The douche and the hose cannot be held responsible for everything. One must suppose that there is a more substantial cause for the exhaustion this young and pretty woman, who is so susceptible, so alone, displays." (Indeed, Auguste de Forbin was a very substantial presence in the Hôtel Charost.) "It is high time to forbid the cause, for it is evident that, if we do not make haste, we will be too late. I cannot say anything more than this, because I know nothing," Halle claimed once more, "but I must all the same save this woman from destruction. And if there is someone who has preyed on her weakness and is complicit, this person, whoever he may be, could accuse not himself . . . but us—of having seen nothing, or having permitted everything.

"I am not ready," the doctor concluded, "to be treated as an imbecile, nor to be accused of being lax and complaisant. But more than that, we must save this excellent and unhappy woman, whose fate affects me. Hurry, my dear colleague, for there is no time to lose. Make of my letter any use you like, and be open with me when you reply."

Halle had insisted as vigorously as was consonant with delicacy that Pauline's health required a period of medicinal baths and sexual abstinence. Her chamberlain Montbreton appears now to have been instrumental in securing that period, for she was to write to Forbin in June from the bathing station where she was pursuing a cure, "You know better than anyone how he has behaved. He has been the cause of our separation and of many evils besides. He has betrayed my confidence."

Pauline formed the plan to visit Aix-les-Bains in the Haute Savoie—and without Forbin. Grudging approval came from Napoleon in Poland, in a letter to Archchancellor Cambacérès: "I am not opposed to the plan, only that I see that all the doctors recommend waters to their patients when they want to get rid of them, and I thought it preferable that she tend her health in Paris without running off in all directions to seek a cure." It was a permission of sorts, and Pauline took it, making arrangements to embark with a limited household at Neuilly and travel down the Seine to Auxerre, from where she would travel to her uncle Fesch's archbishopric of Lyon and on to Aix-les-Bains.

But she also made arrangements, which she did not share with the rest of her household, for Forbin to follow her down to the south of France and join her in his native Provence. She had privately determined not to linger long in the fashionable watering hole of Aix-les-Bains but to base herself rather in the Southwest, at Aix-en-Provence. There the Forbin town mansion would be available to her, and from there she could visit his ancestral home, the Château La Barben.

Madame Mère wrote to her brother Fesch in advance of Pauline's journey: "Her departure made me sad. To see her distanced from all the family, in a chronic state of suffering, tears my soul. I see in her suite only one person who merits my confidence, M. Montbreton, and I have recommended him to give me his news with the greatest exactitude and leave me in ignorance of nothing that passes. I must tell you, I am anxious about her situation, and I hear various reports I don't like."

When Pauline arrived at Lyon in mid-May, from these "reports" ensued tremendous scenes. Dr. Peyre, "through fear and stupidity," in Pauline's words, shared his belief with Fesch that Forbin was to join Pauline. "Maman, my uncle, know all," she wrote angrily to Forbin at the beginning of June. "You have no idea how I suffered at Lyon, the tears I shed to discover we were found out." Madame de Bréhan, one of Pauline's ladies, stoked the fire further when she burst out that "it was disgusting how I behaved in front of her, how we forgot ourselves in front of her in Paris." Pauline was outraged, but with tears and caresses she persuaded her uncle that she was penitent. Soothed, he accompanied her for several days down the Rhône and even bestowed upon her as a—not especially welcome—avuncular gift, when they parted, one of his clerics, Monsignor d'Isoard, as traveling confessor.

There was to be much to confess, not that Pauline showed any inclination to do so, merely an appetite to hoodwink and outwit. At Aix-les-Bains she paused only long enough to persuade a council of eminent doctors, some from Lyon, others from Geneva, that her case would be best answered by a sojourn at the little-known spa of Gréoux-les-Bains, some way from Aix-en-Provence. On the other hand, she assured Montbreton and Madame de Bréhan that they would most benefit from the waters of Aix-les-Bains and she could not think of taking them with her. Space was anyway at a premium in the only house inhabitable at Gréoux-les-Bains. It belonged to Monsieur Gravier, the proprietor of the spring, and adjoined the source. Otherwise Gréoux was a sunbaked rocky eminence devoid of trees and with village houses winding up toward a Templar castle.

In high spirits Pauline wrote at the end of May to Madame Michelot from Aix-en-Provence, where she broke her journey to Gréoux: "I have been a little tired by the journey, as you thought I would be, but for the four days I have been here, I am much better than since leaving Paris. I have no more fever. . . . I am lodged at the sister-in-law of M. Forbin in the most beautiful *hôtel*." Two days later she wrote: "Please buy me a pretty gauze muslin to your taste." The summer heat of Provence was proving to Pauline's taste.

The sudden appearance of the emperor's sister at the Forbin mansion in the main thoroughfare, the Cours Mirabeau, had delighted the Aixois. The princess charged herself with the expenses of the Fête-Dieu (Corpus Christi) celebrations on May 22 and watched as revelers followed tradition and threw oranges at one another below her balcony, and troubadours and knights on chargers paraded by. One student was so overcome by her beauty that he spent four thousand francs on a court dress and asked to be allowed to present a bouquet to the object of his admiration. But Princess Borghese, he was told, was indisposed, and his expenditure was for nothing.

Monsieur Thibaudeau, the prefect of Marseille, and his wife, she did receive, however. Pauline had a healthy respect for the power of the prefects in whose territory she traveled, not least because they were responsible for the upkeep and repair of the roads she took. In fact, showing her usual indifference to the needs of others, she proposed that Madame Thibaudeau accompany her to Gréoux. The prefect protesting that he needed his wife at his side in Marseille, Pauline turned to another matter and said that she wanted the road to remote and arid Gréoux to be smoothed and cleared of stones.

"Princess and pretty woman," wrote Thibaudeau in his memoirs, "she believed that she had only to wish for something and that nothing was easier than to satisfy her wishes." There were no funds available for such an extraordinary expense. However, "so as not to disappoint the princess," Thibaudeau had engineers labor "to hastily fill some holes and above all to clear the rolling stones that were all too common. Luckily it was the fine season, but there remained the great hazard for travelers—dust. "He reflected that perhaps a courtier of Louis XIV or Louis XV would have found "a way to water the route." He, however, gave up the challenge at that point and left Pauline to take her chances.

In mid-June she wrote to Madame Michelot from Gréoux, content with her cure: "I am taking the waters and am on my sixth bath. The waters suit me fairly well, they heat me and agitate me a little." But what heated and agitated her much more was the proposed arrival of Forbin. She had sent an express to Paris, bidding him join her. At the same time she enjoined upon him: "Those who surround us must be persuaded that all is at an end between us, so that we can be undisturbed." With Montbreton and Madame de Bréhan at Aix-les-Bains, there were now only Dr. Peyre and Monsignor Isoard and the lower servants to tell tales on them, and she held them of no account. "How this solitude will please me when you are here," she had written on June 10. "If only it could last forever, but we will never, never be separated. With prudence, we can always be happy. . . . Bring what you need for painting, you can make delightful things for me. My modest house"— the Gravier property—"begins to take shape. I am filling it with flowers and furnishing it as quickly as possible so that all is to my well-beloved's satisfaction."

PRINCESS BORGHESE had hidden away in this remote spot. She was awaiting her cavalier. News from the outer world hardly penetrated her cocoon of infatuation: "By the way, I forgot to mention that my husband has been made a general." Napoleon also appointed Borghese his messenger with news of a June victory over the Russians. Unfortunately the prince proved too slow, and Paris heard the glad tidings from

Napoleon's courier Moustache. "He writes me charming letters full of sentiments of love. I can't think what he's up to," Pauline continued. "But I must end because I am tired from writing so much."

Was she destined to break completely with Borghese and live in the south a Provençal idyll with her handsome troubadour, the Chevalier Forbin, as in some medieval romance? There was no doubt that Pauline was thrilled by her love affair. "You are my real husband," she told Forbin. "Mine [Camillo] doesn't merit so sweet, so sacred a title." She called her chamberlain "dear idol," as she had once called Fréron. "I send you flowers that have been at my breast, I have covered them with kisses. I love you, you alone."

But would the emperor permit this loose living? For, however Pauline might pull the wool over her suite's eyes, Forbin's movements did not evade the watchful eyes of Fouché and his army of spies. Upon being informed from Paris by Archchancellor Cambacérès that his sister's chamberlain had headed south to Aix, Napoleon replied: "I am very cross that you didn't tell me that there was disagreement about the good that the journey to Provence would do the Princess Pauline. You know that I was at first opposed to it, but when I was told the whole of the [medical] faculty wished it, I consented. If I had received this letter sooner, I would never have authorized it."

CHAPTER ELEVEN

Southern Belle, 1807–1808

DESPITE ALL OF PAULINE'S amorous preparations, Forbin had still not reached Gréoux when she decided to leave in September 1807. "The princess is tired, fed up with it here," one of her suite informed Prefect Thibaudeau, who had just toiled up the long hot road from Marseille with his wife to pay his respects. Her Royal Highness was done with her cure, whether cured or not. "She can't put up with it anymore," Thibaudeau now heard. "She is going to go to La Mignarde, the prince is expected there."

La Mignarde was an elegant stuccoed château built in the previous century by an Aixois confectioner as a summer home outside the town. With its spacious gardens, ornamented with statues and basins, it was a residence in complete contrast to the Gravier property at Gréoux, where there was not a scrap of shade. La Mignarde had the additional virtue of being extremely close to Forbin's home, the medieval Château La Barben, and within the latter stronghold charming apartments had been prepared for Pauline's use. For, though illness apparently delayed Forbin's departure from Paris, in the meantime his Aixois friend and fellow artist François Marius Granet had been at work. Images of the Four Seasons adorned bathroom walls. A boudoir commanding views of the gardens laid out by Le Nôtre in the previous century had been fitted out with a dressing table and other necessaries, and in the bedroom the violet wallpaper was hand-painted. All that was lacking was the count himself to play host to Her Royal Highness.

Although the princess had determined to leave Gréoux, as her suite had told the Thibaudeaus, no one was expecting her to leave the very evening they arrived. But after dinner, as the newcomers were walking in the garden with Montbreton, who had at last been allowed to join the party, a screen door opened, and out came Pauline in a white peignoir, her hair undressed. Her air was animated, her step quick. "Ladies, I leave tonight," she said. "Make haste, Montbreton, and arrange it." When her chamberlain objected that nothing was ready, that there were no horses available, she said, "I'll take the Thibaudeaus'." And she vanished back into her apartments, "like an actor, who has played her part, and retires into the wings." Behind her the suite exclaimed, "It's caprice, it's madness. . . . She will go alone. . . . Let her arrange it herself." But go the princess did, and everyone became involved in her complicated arrangements, although she reached a compromise with the prefect. He kept his horses but promised to go ahead to La Mignarde to warn them of the princess's imminent arrival.

One can only assume that a letter from Forbin announcing his imminent arrival in Aix-en-Provence was the catalyst for the princess's sudden haste. Certainly the proposed arrival of the prince at La Mignarde was unlikely to have made her hurry. But for her haste she paid a price. She "took nothing and found nothing" at the miserable house en route to Aix where she passed the night. When her path crossed with that of the Thibaudeaus in the forest of Cadarache next morning, she told them she was the "unhappiest woman alive, and had been eaten by every kind of insect."

The prefect was already, despite himself, bewitched by Pauline. During a short airing at Gréoux the evening before, she had wished to be carried over the dry bed of a stream, and he had discovered that she weighed no more than a feather. Now, in the dappled light of the forest, as Her Royal Highness lay back in her open calèche and enjoyed the shade of the trees and the cool breeze, he considered that a "voluptuous languor animated her gaze." Thibaudeau found her charming—

and, notwithstanding his wife's presence in the carriage beside him, told the princess so. "Are you being gallant?" Pauline teased him. Thibaudeau replied that she had only one defect in his eyes—that she was the emperor's sister. "A smile showed that she had understood."

At La Mignarde, where gaiety prevailed, and where the Aixois and the Marseillais gathered in circles, at assemblies, and at fetes in the grounds, Camillo Borghese took a different view of Pauline's relationship to Napoleon. "His Borghese blood revolted in secret against the supremacy of this Bonaparte female," Thibaudeau declares. All homage, all attention was reserved for the princess, and Camillo was "on the footing of a consort of a queen of England, or even less than that." Moreover, the presence of Forbin, who at last arrived, was a daily irritant to the prince. Walking early one morning beneath the windows of his wife's apartments, and knowing that she was "in the arms of another than Morpheus," Camillo said that his wife was indeed lucky to be the emperor's sister. Had she not been, he would have administered a punishment she would remember.

BUT CAMILLO BORGHESE had only to wait. For, as Pauline had tired of Gréoux, so she tired of the Comte de Forbin. Never one to resist a sudden impulse, one day she threw a book at his head. The count apparently bore the public insult with equanimity, but the love affair was over. In October 1807 we find Forbin at Fontainebleau offering his military services to Napoleon. Later that month he was named lieutenant adjutant in the Army of the Gironde under Junot, which was being sent to invade Portugal. (Following French victories over the Russians, Napoleon and Czar Alexander had met at Tilsit to settle the terms of an alliance between the two empires. As part of those terms, and in pursuance of the Continental blockade of British trade, the Russians agreed to secure the Baltic coast, while the French secured the Iberian coast.) The invasion was in response to the refusal of Prince John, regent of Portugal, to join the blockade. The regent's court fled to Brazil, while Spain helped the French occupy his country, on the understanding that it would receive a share of Portuguese territories. Junot duly took Lisbon in late 1807 and was created Duc d'Abrantès.

Passionate lover though she had been earlier, Pauline was not especially disturbed by the break with Forbin. While he headed north, she traveled farther south to Marseille, with the aim of spending the winter in the Midi for her health, and installed herself in La Capelette, at the country house of the military commander General Jean-Baptiste Cervoni. In the harbor town of Marseille she and her sisters and Madame Mère had sheltered as refugees, following their escape from Corsica in 1793. Just behind the port was the house in the rue Royale where she and her sister Caroline had perhaps acted as maids to the Clary family. Up the hill was the house where the Bonaparte women had lodged. Did curiosity drive Pauline to seek out these places, to recall her earlier passion for Fréron, who had occupied the mansion that was now the prefecture, outside whose gates had flamed torches as he and his fellow commissioner Barras partied inside? Even to recall her first meetings with Victor Emmanuel Leclerc, her brother Napoleon's close friend and fellow officer?

So much had passed since Madame Mère and her daughters had made an exiguous living there, accepting the town's charity and even taking in washing. Perhaps Princess Borghese preferred not to recall these scenes of ignominy but to remain the haughty lady at La Capelette, whose wish was the command of an entire household— besides that of the many hapless authorities whom she ordered to make available their homes, repair roads, furnish banquets, and much else. (En route to Marseille she had not only had her household lay down their cloaks and coats on the ground when she wished to rest in a meadow, she had had a subprefect from Grasse provide his back for her to lean against, while an unfortunate general was told to lie down and proffer his stomach as a footrest.) But we shall see that being near these scenes of her youth awakened in Pauline at least once the desire to revisit a past that had been at once stirring and trepidatious.

The princess continued to dazzle and to disappoint when in mid-October 1807 she reached the harbor town of Nice, which had been annexed by France from the house of Savoy and marked the southeastern extreme of French territory. Her arrival caused great excitement, and the ladies and gentlemen who represented the upper tier of society prepared for a season of festivities. "They say that, since the Phoenicians founded Nice, they have not sold so many dresses," wrote the Duchesse d'Escars, a resident of the town.

Apparently Pauline's first act upon arrival was to call for all the dogs in the neighborhood of the *hôtel* where she lodged to be shut up, as their barking disturbed her rest. She further distressed the Niçois by departing for Grasse on a day that had been fixed for the ladies of the town—splendidly attired—to be presented to her. Her object in traveling to Grasse was to visit the Comtesse de Forbin, her discarded lover's mother, who lived there. Pauline was not one to hold a grudge, and in fact she took the countess a quantity of dresses as presents. But it was not the season to admire the roses, jasmine, and other fragrant flowers of which the town's renowned perfume factories made use. Indeed, during Pauline's return to Nice, it rained such torrents that she had to take refuge in the upper story of a mill and wait for the owner to rescue her. Smitten, he immediately offered her the use of his nearby château, which she naturally accepted.

Upon Pauline's return to Nice in mid-November, she settled down to winter in a sumptuous villa belonging to a Monsieur Vinaille, with vast tropical gardens extending to the beach. Views from the villa looked westward to crenellated fortifications; eastward, the coast stretched away to Monaco. With the prefect of Nice, the Duchesse d'Escars visited Pauline at the Villa Vinaille in December and found her "dressed with extreme elegance." But the princess's dress was less remarkable than the pose she had adopted. Her lady in waiting, Madame de Chambaudoin, was lying spread-eagled on the floor, and the princess had placed both feet on the good lady's throat. In the duchess's opinion, the woman seemed "so visibly born for this ignominious situation that she felt no shame in it." But the prefect expostulated, "Madame, surely this position is tiring for you." "Oh no, monsieur, I am well used to it," came the strangled answer.

The duchess was meanwhile mesmerized by the sight of her hostess's restless feet perambulating her victim's exposed gorge. Furthermore, during an exchange of civilities, Pauline asked if her visitor liked the theater, and, if so, whether she preferred tragedy or comedy. The duchess replied in the affirmative, adding, "I prefer tragedy." "Me too," piped up Madame de Chambaudoin from the floor. "Her voice, altered by the pressure of Princess Borghese's foot, made the sentence infinitely ridiculous," the duchess tells us, and, stifling her strong urge to laugh, she cut short her visit and hurried away. But she returned several times to visit the princess, for Pauline had offered to intercede with Napoleon, who had exiled the duchess to Nice, disliking the royalist sympathies she publicly expressed. On those occasions the princess had "other women under her feet."

Away from Paris, living separately from Camillo, Pauline was becoming distinctly eccentric. There was no precedent in the history of French court etiquette for such behavior, let alone in ordinary social intercourse. But over and over again she persuaded her entourage and others to yield to her outrageous demands. Although she was not one to invoke such language, it is plain that Pauline believed that, as she was the sister of the emperor of the French, for them to do otherwise would be lèse-majesté. There were few who were prepared, in those years in which Napoleon dominated Europe, to argue with her.

During her stay at Nice, Pauline took as her lover a young musician from Turin, Felice Blangini, who played violin in an orchestra in Paris, and who was almost more supine than Madame de Chambaudoin and the other ladies. Blangini had originally attracted the attention of Pauline's sister Caroline Murat with some Italian nocturnes and romances that he composed while in Paris. Pauline then offered him the post of *chef d'orchestre* at 750 francs a month, although she had no orchestra. Now she called him to Nice, ostensibly so that she could study duets with him. (The Bonapartes were renowned for having corncrake voices, but they did not on this account renounce musical endeavor.) And indeed study they did. "The princess liked so much to sing duets," Blangini writes, "and I to accompany her, that the hours flew by. . . . Not every throat is made of iron, however, and sometimes I had no voice left at all."

There were other encounters—"hidden within the interior of the house"—between Blangini and Pauline, where no vocal talent was required. But Blangini took fright when the princess wanted him to go out on an airing with her in her open calèche. "I knew the history of M. de Forbin, the chamberlain of whom the princess made a favorite," Blangini writes. "I knew that the Emperor was kept informed of what his sister did, the names of her intimates." Pauline took malicious pleasure in confirming to him that, wherever she went, there followed spies who dispatched detailed reports to Fouché, her brother's chief of police in Paris. Blangini begged again to be spared the public outing. "I had no wish to go and sing my nocturnes in Spain, to a chorus of cannonballs and gunfire." (On Napoleon's orders French troops in Portugal had filtered into Spain, abandoning the pretense of an alliance with that country, and seized key fortresses and cities.) But Pauline's will, of course, prevailed, and the musician cowered throughout the carriage ride.

There were times, however, that winter when Princess Borghese exerted the magical power that kept men willingly in thrall to her. Daily life at the villa was, on the whole, regular and unexceptionable, comprising luncheon, visits from notables, a cruise at sea or an outing in a carriage, music, dinner, and more music. Upon occasion, however, in the evening, Blangini tells us, "the instruments and voices were stilled. Then the princess alone spoke. . . . She passed in review, not without malice, all the living gallery of the imperial court."

On one occasion a member of that exalted congregation—the grand almoner or chaplain assigned to Pauline, Cardinal Spina—was announced at the Villa Vinaille. He was passing through Nice on his way to the Vatican. Pauline, in mid-duet with Blangini, gave orders for the prelate to return at a time more convenient to her. In general Pauline's casual attitude toward the Catholic faith into which she had been baptized was enough to make her devotee mother and uncle Cardinal Fesch despair. Nevertheless she was at heart a believer and had made a good impression on Pope Pius VII when part of his flock in Rome. In Nice—in her own way—she observed the imperial decree that mass be said on a Sunday. "A table was dressed as an altar in the salon," Blangini relates, "as one sets a table in the dining room."

One can detect in some of Princess Borghese's habits remnants of customs that she and her mother and sisters had observed during their penurious years in Corsica and then in Marseille and elsewhere in the south of France, before Napoleon made the family's name and fortune. Proof that that past was still vivid to Pauline in her prosperity comes from a pilgrimage she made by water from Nice to Antibes. Her objective was to revisit the Château-Sallé, a "bourgeois house, quite pretty, but modest," above Antibes, which Napoleon had rented for his mother and sisters in the summer of 1794, when they were living at Marseille and he was based with the army at Nice.

Blangini accompanied the princess on her odyssey, and states, "I do not know how to give an idea of the joy the princess manifested in finding herself once more there. She ran around like a child and explained the division of rooms. 'That was my mother's room. I slept in this little cabinet next to her. My sisters were on the other side. That was the room my brother Napoleon occupied when he came to surprise us and spent two days with us.'" Although Pauline did not mention it, the months at the Château-Sallé had not been without tension. It was at Nice, during the time of the Terror, that Napoleon had fallen under suspicion and had been kept under house arrest, before exculpating himself and being released.

The Midi was to yield up no more souvenirs of Pauline's youth, and Blangini's days as her favorite were numbered. Forbin might have preempted disgrace by volunteering for the army, but Napoleon had determined to put an end to his sister's irregular liaisons. One project, to assign to her and Camillo a portion of Portugal under a secret treaty agreed with Charles IV of Spain, had foundered when France's relations with Spain deteriorated. But Pauline's plea that she must winter in southern climes was no longer acceptable to her brother, when his agents reported that basking in the sunshine with her at Nice was her young music master from Turin. And when Napoleon passed rapidly through Milan, Venice, and Turin, it occurred to him that he could bring order to what he saw as a fragmented northern Italy, and at the same time reunite the Borghese couple.

NOT LONG AFTER Pauline returned from her visit to Antibes word came that Camillo had been made governor-general of the Transalpine Department of the French Empire, embodying the five Piedmontese regions that had previously belonged to the Kingdom of Savoy. (Louis Bonaparte had previously been the region's titular head.) Turin was the seat of government, and to Turin, Pauline received orders, she should proceed with her husband, to act there as governor's lady. She was forced to give credence to these unpalatable instructions when Camillo arrived in Nice, accompanied by a secretary, Maxime de Villemarest, who was in no way inclined to allow Pauline's caprices to stand in the way of his own task, to act as guide and counselor to the inexperienced prince.

A vast gubernatorial household was assembling to swell the Borgheses' dignity in Turin, where the Palazzo Chiablese, a wing of the enormous former Savoy palace, was to be their residence. Camillo was "enchanted" with the splendor of the arrangements, de Villemarest writes. To the new governor-general were assigned six chamberlains, four equerries, and four aides-de-camp. Pauline, meanwhile, was to enjoy the attentions of twelve ladies-in-waiting, besides a mistress of the robes, six chamberlains, and four equerries. And while the catalog of attendants on the imperial payroll allowed for a director of music, Blangini's was not the name there inscribed.

But Pauline had tired of her songbird and his nocturnes, and now in Nice she gave her attention to assembling a wardrobe to fit her new dignity. She might not relish the prospect of official life at her husband's side in a provincial backwater, but she would not compromise the honor of France by appearing in anything less than the most fashionable finery. Madame Michelot in Paris had a slew of instructions for the couturiers of the capital: toilettes in shiny satin for galas, light tulle robes for less formal receptions, gowns in embroidered cotton *à la cosaque* for airings. Hats, gloves, artificial feathers: The princess believed herself in dire need of everything.

Among the truly useful items that were dispatched to Nice was the splendid berlin, or large traveling carriage, in which Pauline was to travel. The saddler Braidy, de Villemarest reports, had made it "as soft as possible, expressly for this journey." But when, in April 1808, it was judged that the worst of the winter weather was over, when the princess at last pronounced herself ready to depart and the Borghese caravan set out, the luxurious vehicle was found wanting. Every time they encountered a steep incline, Pauline insisted on dismounting and being carried in her litter. "The prince could hardly contain his irritation and impatience," writes de Villemarest.

Even when Pauline remained in the berlin, she sometimes complained of the cold, though there were four or five pillows placed in the carriage for her comfort. The indignity Madame de Chambaudoin had suffered when the princess had used her throat as a footrest was as nothing compared to the poor woman's plight now. For when the princess's feet grew chilled, seeking a place of warmth, she would thrust them indecently under the skirts of her lady-in-waiting seated opposite. At other times the princess felt too warm, and then she piled all the pillows in the coach on the Duc de Clermont-Tonnerre's knees. Not being very tall, he was obliged to sit stiffly upright, so as to be able to breathe over the rampart of feathers.

In short Pauline was at her most tyrannical, and, during the journey over the Alps and down into the plain of Piedmont, she developed her grudge against Camillo into an argument. First she reminded him that, following a recent Senate ruling, not only her brothers but also her sisters' husbands, by virtue of being French-born, took precedence over him. Hence, she asserted, she too, being a French-born princess, took precedence over him. That being the case, she concluded triumphantly, it was for her to reply to the harangues and other addresses they would receive from the authorities upon their arrival in their new domain.

In vain the prince objected that it was he who was the governor-general, not she. "She did not wish to give up her point," de Ville-marest recounts, "and told him in a not very amiable fashion that he was only governor-general by virtue of being her husband, and that he would be nothing if he had not married the Emperor's sister. Which," the governor's secretary admitted, "had some truth in it." Then the prince cried, "Paulette! Paulette!" in what de Villemarest describes as "the most piteous manner." But the princess was intractable, and she was undeterred by the vicious weather that swirled around them as they passed over the heights of the Col de Tende. The snow fell densely around them, and the carriage wheels sank into deep drifts. At the very first village they reached in Piedmont, the princess made good her threats. And the mayor's cordial expressions of welcome were suc-ceeded by an unseemly altercation between husband and wife as they both attempted to reply to his address.

When they arrived at the next port of call, de Villemarest took the liberty of approaching the princess and observing that, should the emperor hear of these doings, His Majesty would be very displeased. "The invocation of the Emperor's name could sometimes have its effect, although not always," the secretary had already learned. Cer-tainly there was no other recourse available to those who wished to deflect Pauline from a proposed course of action. On this occasion the "invocation" had its effect. Next day the prince alone replied to the rep-resentations of the bishop of Coni, on behalf of the Stura region. He and de Villemarest could only hope that Pauline would prove equally biddable in Turin.

Upon arrival in Turin the princess took a surprising liking to two of the ladies appointed to serve her. Philippine de Sales, Comtesse de Cavour, was a worldly-wise French aristocrat who had come from Savoy to Turin on marriage twenty years before, and so escaped the guillotine. Her son acted as lord-in-waiting to Camillo. The Baronne de Mathis, on the other hand, was young, pretty, and fashionable. "I am pleased that you like your Piedmontese suite," Napoleon addressed Pauline from Bayonne, a month after she had arrived in the city. "Make yourself beloved, be affable to the world, try to be good-humored, and please the prince," he instructed her, in language similar to that he had employed when Pauline left Paris for Rome as Camillo's bride.

One evening, just a few days after the Borgheses' arrival in Turin, Pauline did indeed make herself beloved—with careful coaching beforehand from de Villemarest. The authorities of the city had resolved to hold a ball at the opera house, the Teatro Carignano, in honor of the new governor and his lady. Pauline was to open the ball. "Madame," said de Villemarest to the princess, "as you know, little attentions can sometimes reap dividends. . . . The Piedmontese take great pride in their traditions . . . why not have the ball begin with a monferrine?" This was a country dance—originally from Monferrina in Piedmont—that had become popular in the ballrooms of Europe. "It's a childish device, I agree, but it will undoubtedly give pleasure."

Pauline was delighted with the plan and followed directions admirably, rising from her chair in the opera house with a blaze of diamonds to take her place in the dance. To produce the maximum effect, suggested the secretary, the orchestra should first strike up the refrain of a French country dance. This was duly initiated. The princess then theatrically commanded silence and made known her preference for a monferrine. As the musicians broached the lively air and the princess began to dance, the opera house exploded with huzzahs and acclamations: "A monferrine! Vive l'empereur, vive le prince, vive la princesse!"

But Pauline tired quickly of a routine that included a small party every Sunday, reviews of troops, and gala dinners. She found relief from these duties in the sylvan setting of Stupinigi, a sumptuous hunting lodge outside the city that she first visited when her brother Lucien came calling at Turin. She was reluctant for Napoleon to know that she had seen their brother, as he surely would if she received him at the Palazzo Chiablese. (The emperor had still not resumed relations with Lucien.) "There is no order that can stop me giving you my news," Pauline had written to Lucien from Gréoux. "But you must know that I owe much to the head of our family and must respect his intentions in all other things." Napoleon might have been surprised to hear this description of Pauline's relationship with him, especially as Lucien's visit was succeeded by the visit to Stupinigi of a young violinist, Niccolò Paganini. According to local legend Pauline and Paganini, who was in the employ of the princess's sister Elisa in Tuscany, enjoyed a forest idyll together at Stupinigi.

But Pauline was more concerned to leave Turin than to tarry with another musician, however talented. Her health was bad, and the damp climate affected her, she told Napoleon. He wrote back, "I suppose you are being good, and that none of this is your fault." She wrote lyrically of the baths in the Alpine valley of Aosta, which lay between Piedmont and the French Alps: "The doctors of Turin speak of marvels at the thermal waters." Napoleon answered in early June: "What you are experiencing are the vagaries of spring weather. Stupinigi can be a bit humid, I admit. . . . I don't see why you don't go to Bagni di Lucca. Alternatively there can be no difficulty about your going to Saint-Didier"—a Piedmont spa—"as it is within the department." But he was firm: "You must not leave the department without my approval."

Napoleon, preoccupied by his Iberian campaigns, wrote too late. For in the meantime Joseph Bonaparte, whom Napoleon had called from Naples to join him in Spain, had stopped at Turin to visit Pauline and had been shocked by what he saw. "I have found Paulette here in a deplorable state of health," he informed Napoleon. "She has not eaten for eight days and can only take thin soup. The doctors have told me she must leave the humid air of Turin as soon as possible and go to the baths of Aix-les-Bains." Camillo had wanted Pauline to wait for Napoleon's permission to depart, but Joseph had overridden the prince's fears. "I have not hesitated, but told her to go, and that I would answer for it to Your Majesty who must want above all to see his sister live."

Three days after Napoleon wrote of Saint-Didier and Bagni di Lucca, Pauline was already at Chambéry. The next day she had reached Aix-les-Bains. Her mother and her uncle Fesch had hurried to join her there, alarmed by Joseph's reports of her health. But the breezes that wafted over the deep waters of Lake Bourget soon revived Pauline, and the French soil beneath her elegant feet had its effect. A little over a month after she had arrived, in mid-July 1808 she embarked for Lyon and from there continued to Paris. Her sister Elisa wrote to Lucien in Rome: "Paulette has tricked us. I said that she would trap the emperor, for her illness is nothing other than the wish for Paris."

It was a wish soon realized, and upon arrival at the Hôtel Charost, Pauline sent to Turin for her wardrobe—and for the Comtesse de Cavour and Baronne de Mathis, who had so pleased her during her brief stay in the Piedmontese capital. She had no intention of ever returning to Camillo's side there. It remained to be seen if her return to the French capital would bring her the satisfaction she anticipated. Certainly pleasure and heady power lay ahead—but, in Spain, there were indications that Napoleon's army might prove less than invincible. As Pauline said, she owed much to her brother. But her prosperity also depended on his, and, should his founder, she too would be vulnerable. What then for the princess?

CHAPTER TWELVE

Agent for Divorce, 1808–1812

OR THE MOMENT Pauline was content. Not only was she in her beloved Paris, but when Napoleon returned from overseeing the Spanish campaign in August 1808, far from reprimanding his sister for disobeying his command to remain in Piedmont, he loaded her with largesse. "The Emperor has been charming to me," Pauline wrote blithely. "I stay in France and he is going to arrange my finances. But only after his return from Germany." Guerrilla forces were devastating the French army in Spain. However, before Napoleon committed more troops westward, he wanted Russia to help protect France's eastern frontiers from attack by Austria. He had therefore arranged to meet Czar Alexander in September at Erfurt in Germany to discuss an alliance.

Napoleon's unexpected goodwill toward his insubordinate sister that summer had a simple explanation. His thoughts had turned once more to divorce—and this was a project that had Pauline's whole-hearted support and encouragement. Already in 1807 there had been signs that Napoleon still dreamed of remarriage and of fathering a son and heir. In the summer of that year, Louis and Hortense's firstborn son, Napoléon Charles, who had been declared the imperial heir, died unexpectedly at the age of eight. The emperor went to some trouble to arrange a sumptuous burial chamber where his nephew's small coffin was laid. The vault would be, he decreed, the place of interment for all members of the imperial family. However, he refused point-blank to declare the child's younger brother, Napoléon Louis, his heir.

The imperial succession was still in abeyance when Napoleon went to meet Czar Alexander at Erfurt in September 1808. In the course of that conference he secretly asked the czar for the hand in marriage of his sister, Grand Duchess Catherine. He promised that his childless union with Josephine could be swiftly terminated. The pope, who might have obstructed such a measure, was conveniently under house arrest in Rome, after refusing to block the ports of the Papal States to English trade. The emperor of the French waited anxiously in hope of an answer in the affirmative. "It will be a proof to me that Alexander is an ally," he wrote to Caulaincourt, his ambassador in St. Petersburg. "It would be a real sacrifice for me. I love Josephine. I will never be happier with anyone else, but," Napoleon, servant of the state, affirmed, "my family and Talleyrand and Fouché and all the politicians insist upon it in the name of France."

Pauline was ready to jeer at *"la vieille"* and the *"Beauharnaille,"* or the "old hag" and the "Beauharnais rabble," and gloat over a displaced Josephine. But the Russian czar foiled her brother's plans, acceding neither to a full alliance nor to the proposed marriage. The French foreign minister, Talleyrand, who had in fact reached the conclusion that Napoleon was acting against the nation's interest, was now secretly in Austria's pay and had coached Czar Alexander in his responses. Thwarted, Napoleon returned to Paris, but his desire to take a new bride only increased. Nothing that Josephine did pleased him, and the "elegant equality" of their relationship, which had struck so many in the early days of the Empire, dissolved in acrimony and recrimination.

The emperor was inclined to turn to his family for company, for comfort. But Madame Mère, although no friend to Josephine, was still opposed to divorce on religious grounds. And the other members of the extended Bonaparte family on whom he had previously relied—Caroline and Murat, Hortense and Louis, Joseph and Julie—he had dispatched to govern distant European realms. For, while Murat had forced the abdication of the Bourbon rulers of Spain in May, he had then been sent to replace Joseph Bonaparte as king of the Two Sicilies, whose capital was Naples. And Joseph, when in Turin in the spring and anxious about Pauline's health, had been en route from southern Italy to Madrid to appropriate the Spanish crown. The crowning of these brothers-in-law in Paris in October 1808 was somewhat farcical. As Chateaubriand later wrote, the emperor "rammed these crowns onto the new kings' heads, and off they went like a couple of conscripts who had exchanged caps by order of the commander." However, both Joseph and Murat considered that they were constitutional monarchs, bringing the benefits of the Revolution and abolishing feudalism.

Thus it fell to Pauline, blandishing and seductive, to play confidante to Napoleon in Paris—an asp in Josephine's bosom. The rewards for Princess Borghese's attentions to her brother were considerable. Napoleon was not long in Paris before he was off again to oversee the Spanish campaign, but in that time he bestowed upon her the Château of Neuilly, a league from Paris, which had been built by the Comte d'Argenson, Louis XV's war minister, and had formerly belonged to the Murats. They had bought it and the adjoining estate of Villiers while Joachim was governor of Paris, but, upon becoming king and queen of Naples, they had had to renounce all French property.

The emperor also resolved to increase his sister's annual income by the sum of six hundred thousand francs. This was to be hers alone, "separate property" on which Camillo could have no call, as Napoleon established in a side letter. In return he required of her that, instead of acting a lackadaisical part, as she had done in the early days of the Empire, she would continue to bring luster and style to the imperial calendar and preside over *cercles* and balls, as she had done more recently. It was a bargain that Pauline was to keep on the whole faithfully, and one that would establish her reputation, in these years when Josephine was distracted by fears about her future, as the presiding deity at the imperial court.

"Pauline Bonaparte was as beautiful as it was possible to be," the Austrian ambassador Count Metternich, who first romanced Laure

Junot and afterward Caroline Murat, later reminisced. "She was in love with herself alone, and her sole occupation was pleasure." (There appears to be no substance to claims that Metternich, who wore Caroline's hair plaited in a bracelet, was also intimate with Pauline herself.) The princess's neighbor at Montgobert, Stanislas de Girardin, confirms the Austrian diplomat's account: "Pauline Borghese was then in the full brilliance of her beauty. Men pressed about her to admire her, to pay court. And she enjoyed this homage as her due. In the glances she exchanged with some of them, indeed, there was a recognition of past favors granted or hints of romance to come. Few women," he concluded, "have savored more the pleasure of being beautiful."

At Neuilly, in the middle of a ball, Pauline would call for a basin of milk, and, when her black page brought it, she would sip from it, languishing—white and appetizing as the milk itself—on a sofa. "When she waltzes, all the other dancers stop," we are told by another Austrian observer, "so as not to hurt this delicate and gentle imperial highness. She is very pretty and says very amusing things." Consolidating this reputation as a fragile fairy princess, at her house in Paris, Pauline slept—when alone—in a little pink bed, hung with embroidered muslin and so small and low it seemed out of a dollhouse.

But of course Pauline was not always alone. "She had a habit of falling into a reverie when contemplating an affair," noted an Austrian, the diplomat Prince Clary. At Neuilly, following a *cercle,* there were generally card games till ten or eleven in the evening. But then, when the assembly dispersed, Pauline kept with her "some few elect" for the rest of the evening. "And then there was dancing, gaming, and all the pleasures of the golden age. Moreover, sometimes among these elect there was one further favored," Clary slyly adds.

One such was a young German lieutenant named Conrad Friedrich, who had formed part of the army of occupation that Napoleon sent to Rome to arrest the pope and annex the Papal States to France. The lieutenant, in Paris to beg reinforcements and the rank of marshal for his commanding officer in Rome, went to Neuilly to inquire if the princess would use her influence with her brother to secure his objectives, and he caught Pauline's fancy. Though she smiled and said she had no influence with the emperor, she asked Friedrich to walk a little with her in the gardens, and murmured to her lady that "for a German" the lieutenant had a good air. It finished with her making a rendezvous with him for the following afternoon at a grotto on the grounds.

Friedrich recites in his florid memoirs a remarkable afternoon that followed next day. When he passed into the interior of the grotto, rooms and galleries opened up to his astonished gaze, among them a magnificent salon with a large bathtub. "The adventure seemed to me out of a novel or even a fairy tale." As he wondered what would be its outcome, the princess appeared, smiling and asking him how he liked the place. As she advanced toward him, Friedrich saw that "the opulent and perfectly molded curves of her body" were only thinly veiled, and were perfectly visible with her every movement. "She gave me her hand to kiss, wished me welcome and had me sit next to her on a yielding daybed," recalls the soldier. "I was certainly not the seducer, but the one seduced, for in the cavernous twilight Pauline employed all her charms to bring my blood to boiling point and my senses to a point of frenzy. Soon the nameless emissions which marked our mutual passions were imprinted on the velvet cushions. In which Pauline revealed herself still more experienced a lover than I, having greater staying power." Afterward, "clothed in fine linen wrappers," he records, they bathed together. "We stayed nearly an hour in the azure water, after which we ate in a neighboring room an exquisite meal, and there we stayed till dusk."

Friedrich, however, disliked being prey rather than hunter: "I had to promise to come back soon, and I spent more than one afternoon like that. All the same, I never felt very proud of my conquest, for Pauline had granted the last favors to more than one before me, and was later to grant them to many more. Moreover, she was almost too routine in seeking her own pleasure, and before long, it was more aversion than anticipation that I felt in going there, despite her beauty."

Pauline might be on pleasure bent in public at her balls and in the cool privacy of the grotto at Neuilly with Friedrich and others, but she was not unaware of the ugly mood in France spawned by the unpopular war in Spain and Portugal. When Napoleon left for the front in November 1808, the princess said that she and all the Bonapartes would be assassinated if he were killed in battle. Not only were decisive victories needed to quell disaffection in France, but the war was proving increasingly costly in men as well as weaponry. When the British came to the aid of the Iberian patriots in August 1808, the French became engaged in a punishing battle for control of the peninsula. After losing the battle of Vimeiro that month, under the terms of the Cintra Convention, Junot and his army evacuated Portugal. The British, meanwhile, advanced from Portugal into Spain, where they would prove a potent foe. By 1809 more than a quarter of a million Frenchmen were under arms in the region, tens of thousands had already died in guerrilla warfare, and conscripts were deserting in quantity.

In the meantime Napoleon not only survived but took Madrid in December 1808. He had to return posthaste to Paris in the new year, however, as Austria, advised by Talleyrand, had made good its threat to arm against France. Although the French emperor was victorious in the battles that ensued, notably at Wagram in July 1809, the death toll was heavy. "This year is an inopportune time to shock public opinion by repudiating a popular Empress," Napoleon declared. Josephine had apparently won a reprieve—and Pauline, disappointed, went off with her mother to Aix-la-Chapelle that summer to take the cure, where the old lady, as usual, disputed the cost of the lodgings and food and demanded an imperial discount on the staff of life itself.

Metternich had observed of Napoleon in the autumn of 1807 that he had ceased to be "moderate." That summer, upon being dispossessed of his Vatican realm and imprisoned in northern Italy, Pope Pius VII issued a bull that, by implication, excommunicated the French emperor. But Napoleon was heedless of such disapprobation. For in September, to his great joy, the Polish Marie Walewska announced that she was pregnant and that he was beyond doubt the father. This changed everything, in Napoleon's mind. For now he had proved he could father a child, and Josephine's vaunted popularity could not be allowed to stand in the way of his clear imperial duty. Divorce and remarriage—not to the beautiful Marie but to a nubile princess of great rank—must follow.

The empress did not need her husband, all protestations and regret, to speak her fate. "I know I will be shamefully dismissed from the bed of the man who crowned me," she said, "but God is my witness that I love him more than my life and much more than the throne." An autumn of humiliation for Josephine, spent mostly at Fontainebleau, ensued. "The divorce was ordered in his head," observed Hortense of her stepfather later. "My family was a charge; his own, now important to him. He went to his sister Borghese nearly every evening, he went out without the Empress in his carriage." From her apartments the lonely empress saw the lights of late-night soirees that her sister-in-law held in her rooms and that the emperor attended. "They say a Piedmontese woman was the cause [of the estrangement]—I think," wrote Hortense accurately, "a distraction from the divorce he meditated."

Pauline, in buoyant spirits, wrote to Murat in Naples, requesting him to send her some of the fans for which the south Italian city was noted. She declared that she was plump and in good health and attended all the *cercles*. She did not mention any Piedmontese woman, but we may name her—Cristina, Baronne de Mathis, one of the ladies assigned to Pauline in Turin and for whom the princess had sent on her return to Paris. As we have seen before, when Napoleon was going through a period of emotional strain, he had invariably started a liaison with one of the ladies in Josephine's suite. The difference now was that Pauline's suite supplied the female in question.

The diarist Stanislas de Girardin gives us the details: "One of those ferrets at Court who detect the latest scandals has told me of a new La Vallière who has taken the eye of the monarch." (Louise, Duchesse de La Vallière, had been one of Louis XIV's mistresses.) "It is an Italian woman attached to Princess Borghese. She is, they tell me, petite, blond, round as a ball, and fresh as a daisy. Like Louis XIV, the lover enters by a window. And the princess, like a good little sister, arranges the rendezvous for His Majesty." Notes from Napoleon to Pauline that survive detail the pander part that the princess played this autumn. "Monday morning," wrote the emperor. "What's the news? Is she amiable or capricious this morning?" Again: "She is very lovely but quite severe. Sometimes I doubt if she loves me." Another reads: "I would be charmed if she were to come to the review, which will be very fine, with top-rate troops." And there is this too: "Tonight I'll come by the garden. Tell Madame de M. to await me."

Dalliance with a Piedmontese daisy notwithstanding, the moment of truth between Napoleon and Josephine had to come, and after dinner on November 30, 1809, he gave orders that they were to be left alone. When he had broken the news that Josephine had expected—they were to divorce—and told her that the ceremony of divorce was to take place two weeks thence, the empress lay on the floor, weeping. The confusion in the emperor's mind is best shown in his remark to Hortense, who, entering, told Josephine that she and Eugène would go away with their mother and live quietly as a family together. "You too would betray me?" Napoleon said to his stepdaughter and sister-in-law.

A few days later, on the fifth anniversary of the coronation in Notre-Dame, it was Jérôme, and not Josephine, who traveled with the emperor to the cathedral, and there was no place of honor for the empress at the banquet that followed. The divorce was pronounced by the Senate ten days later, and in the throne room, as though for a celebration, the court assembled. "The Bonapartes gloated," observed Hortense. "Try as they might not to show it, they betrayed their joy by their air of satisfaction and triumph." Josephine pronounced the words that had been assigned her, and then Napoleon led her back to her apartments. When she collapsed on her arrival there, her courage spent, Hortense came and urged the empress to remember that Marie Antoinette before her had left the Tuileries for prison and the scaffold. Josephine, on the other hand, was to go to her beloved Malmaison.

It was scant comfort, but next day the empress did indeed leave with her dogs and parrots for Malmaison, where she would live a life of retirement. Napoleon departed for Versailles and issued orders for Pauline to join him there, instructing her to bring Madame de Mathis. "I'll be with you in the garden by 9," he wrote to Pauline. "I won't come to you unless you think she will be amenable. I have need of sweetness and contentment, not headaches." But the Baronne de Mathis was not destined to occupy Napoleon's attention long, once the friction of the divorce was past. His thoughts were leaping ahead to remarriage, a project that—astonishingly—had Josephine's support. When Napoleon begged the hand in marriage of the Austrian arch-duchess Marie Louise, the empress Josephine told Metternich that she hoped he would be successful. She did not want, she said, to have made the sacrifice of her happiness for nothing. Marie Louise's father, Emperor Francis I, appears not to have considered his daughter's hap-piness, though she had been earlier taught to view Napoleon, who had occupied Vienna, as a tyrant and an ogre. The Austrian emperor's let-ter, accepting the proposal, arrived in Paris simultaneously with that of the Russian emperor, declining on his sister's behalf the separate over-tures that Napoleon had made to St. Petersburg.

Paris was ready to celebrate the arrival of Marie Louise in March 1810. Plain, ungainly, and red faced she might be, according to reports, but, at nineteen, her age was generally regarded as a delightful attribute. Pauline, however, was less sure and would have preferred her niece Charlotte—Joseph's daughter—to have become the emperor's bride. Princess Borghese did not relish the fact of the Austrian arch-duchess's high birth—and, now that Josephine's hegemony at court was over, there was the possibility, unlikely though it might seem, that Napoleon might feel affection for Marie Louise.

In the newcomer's favor right away was her appetite for sex. The emperor's report was as follows: "I took her straight to bed when she arrived at Fontainebleau, and as soon as we finished, she asked me to do it to her again." But Napoleon Bonaparte and his teenage Hapsburg bride did not otherwise prove especially congenial to each other. Pauline settled for joining her sisters, who came to Paris for the imper-ial wedding at Saint-Cloud in sulks mirroring those in which they had indulged at the coronation of Josephine six years earlier, and centering once more on a reluctance to bear their sister-in-law's train. "Tears, prayers, fainting fits, absolute refusals. . . . One made a moue, the other, her smelling salts under her nose, threatened illness, the third let the mantle fall and that was worst of all, for then she had to pick it up again."

The only one who apparently acted with any dignity was Josephine's daughter, Hortense, whom Napoleon, with his usual tactlessness, had appointed Marie Louise's mistress of the robes. But then, he had sent to meet Marie Louise at the French border Caroline Murat, who had appropriated the crown of the Austrian princess's great-aunt, Queen Maria Carolina of Naples. (More thoughtfully he had provided for Josephine the distant Château of Navarre, to which the slighted empress retired for the course of these nuptial celebrations.)

PAULINE'S ENERGY in these years was prodigious, and the tales of her conquests legion, featuring, among others, the wasp-waisted Russian general Prince Alexander Tchernitcheff, emissary of the czar, and the Polish veteran general Josef Anton Poniatowski, who wore the Grand Eagle of the Légion d'Honneur and was still a spry lover at fifty. The accounts of the balls and fetes that Pauline held in Paris and at Neuilly, and where the celebrated mulatto conductor Julien officiated, are likewise numerous. One fete at the latter place, however, which she planned in honor of Napoleon and his new bride and gave in June 1810, stands out. "Tell the designer, M. Bernard, that it must cost no more than 80,000 francs," she instructed Monsieur Michelot from Compiègne, where the court had taken up residence following the imperial nuptials, that April. "But I want everyone to think it cost 120,000 francs, so economize on the details." Bernard fulfilled this difficult brief, and on the evening of June 14, seven hundred guests enjoyed the gardens of Neuilly, strung with colored lights.

Sixty-five members of the corps de ballet from the Paris Opéra performed allegorical dances on the lawn. Temples of Love, Hope, and

Glory featured costumed pilgrims from the Holy Land, while guards in Austrian livery and Tyrolean dress patrolled in front of a transparency showing the Viennese palace of Schönbrunn. (To a more select audience, sitting in boxes garlanded with flowers in the little theater up at the house, actors from the Théâtre Feydeau had earlier performed a comic opera, *Le Concert Interrompu*.) As the climax to the outdoor festivities Napoleon put a match to a fire-breathing dragon and fireworks burst out on the Seine beyond the lawns, while overhead a tightrope dancer, Signora Saqui, with a torch in each hand, performed acrobatic wonders.

Three days later, at Napoleon's insistence, Pauline illumined the gardens again—this time, for the bourgeois of Neuilly and the surrounding area. Five thousand tickets were issued, and the gardens soon filled. But the visitors were discontented, despite the six dancing orchestras provided. The house, which they had hoped to see inside, was firmly closed, and Pauline was nowhere in evidence—although Napoleon and Marie Louise were there, incognito. "The court sends us its leavings" was the general complaint. "Everything seemed to suggest, 'It is good enough for the rabble,'" wrote de Girardin.

Pauline was unperturbed by the criticism. She was en route to Aix-la-Chapelle for the summer once more, and keen only to ensure that everything necessary for daily life at the Hôtel Charost in Paris was put away or removed so that Camillo could not enjoy the amenities of the place during her absence. When he had come to Paris from Turin, where he was proving a popular governor, for Napoleon's marriage to Marie Louise, Pauline had first read him the document that Napoleon had drawn up, establishing their "separate property," then refused to speak to him, though they shared the same house for days at a time. Nor would she open letters that, in desperation, he addressed to her. Last, she would not feed him and his suite and suggested they eat at a restaurant. Only upon the insistence of Napoleon, to whom her intransigence became known, did she relent.

Upon Pauline's return from her sojourn in Aix-la-Chapelle, she was to feel the weight once more of her brother's disapproval. For she was now intimate with a young hussar, Jules de Canouville, who was on General Berthier's staff, and whom she had first noticed during the carnival season earlier that year. With his close friend Achille de Septeuil, who was himself romantically involved with Princess Borghese's lady Madame de Barral, Jules had taken part in a masque that Count Ferdinando Marescalchi, representative of the Kingdom of Italy in Paris, mounted. He caracoled in a Battle of Chessmen, while his friend played a Fool in a uniform of red and gold. Shut up at Neuilly that autumn with de Canouville, Pauline lavished presents on the handsome, brash officer. He responded with ardor, and the affair appears to have been the first to trouble her mind, not just to represent the pleasures of the flesh, since her liaison with Forbin.

De Canouville's devotion was fierce, sometimes nonsensical. During a ball given by Prince Eugène, the officer approached his host, viceroy of Italy and the Empress Josephine's son. Not a whit abashed by the rank of this great personage, he demanded that the contra dance that was in progress be halted. "The princess wishes to waltz with me." Eugène, ever elegant, demurred. "A waltz, a waltz," de Canouville insisted. Eugène had his way, but Pauline was no doubt entertained by her cavalier's championing of her desires.

A comical scene ensued when the princess had toothache and the imperial dentist, Bousquet, was called to Neuilly. While he inspected the princess's mouth, de Canouville, whom he did not know, lay on another sofa in a dressing gown and gave anxious instructions: "Take good care not to harm her, monsieur. I am very fond of Her Highness's teeth, and I shall hold you responsible for any accident." Understandably Bousquet took the gentleman to be the princess's husband, and, when he had concluded his ministrations and returned to the antechamber, he said to the ladies and chamberlains assembled there: "It is sweet to see such an example of conjugal love in a couple of such great rank." The snickers and broad smiles that met his remark informed the dentist of his error.

Pauline herself now made a mistake in her dealings with de Canouville. Following the court's removal to Fontainebleau in the autumn of

1810, she had made herself agreeable to Marie Louise, entertaining the young empress with a troupe of dancing dogs on one occasion, with a magic lantern show on another. Napoleon had responded suitably and indeed had made de Canouville an imperial baron, at his sister's request. But then Pauline went too far. The Russian czar had sent Napoleon three sable pelisses, one of which the emperor had given his sister. Now she had the fur cut into wide bands and sewn on a dolman, or hussar's jacket, with diamond buttons for her lover. De Canouville wore the gift proudly at the next review in the place du Carrousel. But Napoleon had noted his sister's transgression and, when the officer's horse proved difficult to control, told him, "That hot blood will get you sent to Russia." In the event the emperor ordered Berthier to send de Canouville instead to Portugal. He was to search for Marshal André Masséna, who had now been there several weeks with a large force without sending back any dispatches.

Even in the midst of this duty, de Canouville thought only of Pauline. Knowing that, with her, to be absent was to be soon forgotten, he covered 170 relays at a gallop, a distance of over seven hundred miles, and arrived a few days later, covered in mud, at headquarters in Salamanca. There he learned that the supply lines to Portugal were cut and resolved to return the next day to Paris with the news, rather than pursue his quarry further. An hour without Pauline, he said, was a desert, and he whiled the evening away telling all who would listen that Napoleon had charged him with his mission only by way of vengeance. Reciting the details of his romance with Pauline from the first meeting at the ball on the final day of the carnival, he punctuated his narrative with sighs to make the candles gutter.

They say that when de Canouville reached Paris he was not admitted to the Hôtel Charost and that, as he had feared, the princess had already found another. But reconciliation followed, although he was not to be allowed to remain long in Paris. Berthier sent him back to Spain—and there, soon enough, came his friend and fellow officer Achille de Septeuil. His story was a different one. Following de Canouville's departure, Pauline had courted and been rejected by Septeuil.

"You are a flirt, madame," he said, for he was true to Pauline's lady Madame de Barral. Pauline's answer had been to go to Napoleon and engineer Septeuil's removal to Spain. In her appetite for revenge she was a true Corsican, and her brother was understanding of her need.

Together both de Canouville and Septeuil eventually beat a path to Masséna in Portugal, and in due course both, serving on his staff, took part in May 1811 in the Battle of Fuentes de Onoro, when the French marshal tried to relieve the besieged fortress of Almeida. In that battle de Canouville was wounded; Septeuil, upon charging Wellington's forces at the head of his dragoons, had his horse killed under him and his arm blown off by a shell. Pauline's reaction was cool: "He can still dance."

The princess had a new source of anxiety. On March 20, 1811, at nine in the morning, a hundred cannons had been fired to mark the birth of Marie Louise's son by Napoleon. He was christened that same morning Napoléon François Charles Joseph Bonaparte and given the title King of Rome. Napoleon was beside himself with joy, Pauline less happy, for her brother seemed to transfer the warm feelings he had for her to his baby son—and even to extend them to the mother of his child. That summer, continuing the theme of revenge, Pauline embarked at Aix-la-Chapelle on an affair with "le beau Montrond," the fashionable diplomat and confidant of Talleyrand of whom Napoleon had said, "There will never be morals in France as long as Montrond lives there."

Montrond had been banished from Paris for repeating in public criticisms of Napoleon's imperial strategy that his intimate Talleyrand had made in confidence. (Talleyrand had resigned as foreign secretary in 1807 in protest at the Franco-Russian alliance.) Montrond was living at Spa, and Pauline followed him there with a few of her suite in September. A Colonel Vladimir Kabloukoff, attached to the Russian embassy in Paris, who was convalescing at Aix, escorted her. "There is no one here. I ride and rise early," she wrote mendaciously to Cambacérès, the archchancellor of the Empire, in a letter meant for Napoleon's eyes. But the police spies were aware of both Kabloukoff's role as escort and Montrond's presence in the fine house Princess Borghese rented, and dubbed both of them Pauline's lovers. How much she cared for Montrond is unclear. But when he showed a *tendresse* for Mlle Jenny Millo, her waiting woman, who had married in Turin and was now Madame Saluzzo, the princess was furious. She sent Jenny off to her husband in Turin and demanded she repay the dowry she had given her. Meanwhile Montrond was arrested and imprisoned by French police at Antwerp. Although he escaped to England, Pauline had once again shown that it was unwise to cross her.

In Paris once more, Pauline found, to her dismay, that de Canouville was not available to dance attention on her for long. For in November, on Napoleon's orders, he ceased to be on Berthier's staff and was sent to join the Second Regiment of Cavalry in Danzig as squadron commander. At no point, his instructions ran, was he to venture to Paris. Pauline had not tired of de Canouville, but she submitted to the dictat. For, as the new year of 1812 dawned, it brought fresh troubles in its wake. Pauline's health was in decline once more, and she was thinking of heading south to a warmer climate. Meanwhile Czar Alexander, who had opened his ports to the English in defiance of the pacts made at Tilsit and Erfurt, gave the French emperor an ultimatum in April: If Napoleon did not withdraw to the west of the river Elbe, Russia would mobilize against France.

Napoleon began to amass a Grande Armée, 650,000 troops in all, while he asked for negotiations rather than war. But his hope that the show of arms would frighten the czar into backing down was misplaced. It became evident that Napoleon must indeed lead the Grande Armée in an attack on Russia, and in June, on the point of departure, he visited Josephine at Malmaison, when the empress entreated his valet Constant to keep her former husband safe. By contrast, in May, before heading south to Aix-les-Bains, Pauline had successfully begged Murat, who was to head the cavalry bound for Russia, to allow de Canouville to serve on his staff. Death or glory was a concept that appealed to Pauline.

As the French war machine rumbled into action, and as Pauline headed south to Aix-les-Bains with the intention of spending a year in the south, a ball that she and Caroline Murat had jointly held at the Tuileries during the February carnival seemed a distant memory, of a golden age before debt, loss of men, and nascent nationalism had afflicted the French Empire. At the ball Pauline, carrying a golden lance and shod in purple-laced sandals, had shone in the character of "Rome." Elegant in a golden helmet with a cloud of ostrich feathers and a golden breastplate over a tunic of Indian muslin, she looked into a mirror to see the fate of the Eternal City and discovered, behind her, the reflected face of "France."

To stern critics Caroline Murat—"France"—seemed encumbered by her helmet, and in addition her plumpness detracted from the whiteness of her hands and arms, considered her best feature. But the little drama, in which "Rome" and "France" embraced each other, pleased most of the court. Not so Napoleon. "It's a farce. Everyone knows the Romans hate being yoked to France," he complained. "These young women are more difficult to control than a regiment. I'm not a grizzly bear. They could ask me. But oh no, these women are too confident to do anything of the kind." It would perhaps prove fortunate that Pauline was indeed so confident, because during the next few years, she would have only herself on whom to rely.

CHAPTER THIRTEEN

Survival, 1812–1814

THE ALPINE BATHING RESORT of Aix-les-Bains, near Chambéry, where Pauline took up residence in June 1812, attracted that summer, among a numerous Parisian clientele, several female members of the extended Bonaparte clan and some of their intimates, among them Laure d'Abrantès. The emigration eastward of Napoleon and his enormous staff of marshals, generals, and officers had left their womenfolk in a state of anxiety and uncertainty. In consequence many of them chose, rather than go to their country estates for the summer, to gather where they could more easily glean news of the advance on Russia. Madame Mère came south in July to be with her daughter. They were joined the following month by Joseph's wife, Julie, queen of Spain, who had been suffering from an outbreak of erisypelas, and by her sister Désirée, who had once, as Désirée Clary, been courted by Napoleon Bonaparte. Her husband, Marshal Bernadotte, was now newly crown prince and regent of Sweden.

The latter royal latecomers lodged in a house in the main square, opposite that rented by Laure. Madame Mère occupied, as usual, modest rooms. But Pauline had secured the best house in the spa, the Maison Chevaley. Situated in pastureland up on the alp, it commanded views of Lake Bourget and, beyond, of the jagged mountain range dominated by the Dent du Chat. There Pauline entertained, among other suitors for her pretty hand, the great actor Talma, who had for twenty years dominated the theater in Paris and whom Napoleon had often honored with summonses to come and read from Voltaire and Molière at the Tuileries.

What had drawn together Pauline and Talma, now of a certain age and jowly, when they had been known to each other for so many years, is a mystery. It is said, however, that, for some weeks before Pauline went south, she lived secluded with the actor, and that at Aix they resumed an existing relationship. But, if so, Talma's duties were not confined to the bedroom. Just as Felice Blangini had once feared he would lose his voice, given Pauline's wish to partner him in evening duets, now the great thespian told Laure d'Abrantès that he was condemned, soiree after soiree, to read Molière scenes and did not dare to refuse. "I will have to leave Aix, which I like exceedingly," he lamented. "But I have to perform every evening. For, you know, she wants to learn the roles of Agnès [from *The School for Wives*] and Angélique [from *Le Malade imaginaire*]."

If Talma believed that he had misled Laure into thinking that his role at the spa was merely that of elocution teacher, he was himself deceived. However, he could draw comfort from the fact that he was not the only male drawn into Pauline's orbit up at the Maison Chevaley around whom rumors of a sexual relationship with the princess hung. Princess Borghese's former admirer and chamberlain the Comte de Forbin had left her impetuously five years earlier to be a soldier in Spain. But he had abandoned that career, following imprisonment in Cintra and subsequent involvement in the Austrian campaigns of 1809. Now he stopped off in Aix en route to Paris from Naples, where he had occupied his time producing Spanish history paintings. Still handsome, cultured, and in every way agreeable company, if no richer, Forbin had turned novelist as well as history painter, and gave readings in the Aix salons that summer of his novel, *The Quaker of Philadelphia*. But, although assiduous in his attentions to Pauline, he made no attempt to become intimate with her again. Once bitten, twice shy.

At the Maison Chevaley, Princess Borghese was kept informed of her brother's advance across the Neman River into Russian territory on June 23 and of Alexander's consequent declaration of a patriotic war. Her sisters wrote too—Caroline from Naples, where she was managing the kingdom's affairs during Murat's absence at the head of the cavalry in Russia. The Queen of Naples asked her sister in Aix for "a little chemise like the one I saw you wear next to your skin, with short sleeves." Thus valetudinarian Pauline in her diaphanous dresses warded off the cold. Elisa wrote from her Tuscan grand duchy, sending straw bonnets from Florence and patent remedies, and wishing Pauline and Madame Mère would join her on a visit she projected to the baths of Lucca. Even Jérôme's wife, Catherine, contributed to the family budget, writing in July from Kassel, capital of the Westphalian kingdom. She wanted new fashions, new headdresses, and she was fretting for her husband during his absence with the emperor. "If I thought my letters could charm the hours of so delightful an anchorite, I would write more often," she told Pauline. "But I would have to be gay—the danger Jérôme runs checks all levity in me. . . . From what I understand, from letters of the fourth [July], the Emperor was then at Vilna [in Russia, formerly Polish territory]. I know no more. It's precisely this uncertainty that destroys me." Catherine was by birth a princess of Württemburg. Her marriage to Jérôme in 1808 had been a dynastic alliance—quite unlike his earlier marriage to the American, Elizabeth Patterson, whom he had, without compunction, divorced in order to marry again and please Napoleon.

Pauline accepted the flood of correspondence, and contributed to it too. Her brother Jérôme, with seventy thousand men under his command, wrote to her from Warsaw, acknowledging a letter that their brother-in-law Murat had forwarded to him there, and anticipating the campaign to come: "You would be wrong to doubt my tender and constant love. But you know that being far off and very busy . . . one writes less often. I hope, my dear Pauline, that the Emperor, who is not maladroit, and who knows at least as much as another, will do great things, as is his wont."

Jérôme spoke too soon. For the emperor had not reckoned with a late summer. As July succeeded June, the grain on which he had counted to feed his troops and horses as he progressed eastward had not been forthcoming. Second, heavy rain had turned fields and roads into quagmires. And then a blistering-hot summer struck, creating new and difficult conditions; men grew parched and horses dehydrated, and thousands of both were dying daily. But Jérôme was constitutionally cheerful and wrote from Bielitz (now Bielsko-Biala, Poland) on the Neman: "We are chasing the enemy, and we are, as you see, far away. The emperor is in the best of health and forty leagues to my left. It is very hot, but everything is going well. . . . I am in good health, although on horseback from two or three in the morning till nightfall."

Pauline, in her own way, followed the action in Russia as closely as any other of the imperial women—as well she might. For Napoleon's personal safety as well as his glory and national prestige were all at risk. That her brother Jérôme and her brother-in-law Murat held crucial commands in the mighty war machine progressing eastward toward Moscow made her still more attentive. And then again—of Princess Borghese's former lovers heading for Moscow, one could indeed say, "Their name is Legion." Among them were Marshal Macdonald, General Beurnonville, General Poniatowski, who commanded the Polish army, and Lieutenant Friedrich, with whom the princess had lingered in the grotto at Neuilly. She could even claim a bedfellow among the enemy, for General Moreau had followed Talleyrand in changing sides and was even now furnishing Alexander with advice and military support. But of course, of all the soldiers in the field it was for Jules de Canouville, on Murat's staff, that Pauline retained special feeling—feeling that was given tangible form in the magnificent, jewel-encrusted sword she now commissioned from Paris for the ardent officer.

Archchancellor Cambacérès in Paris kept Pauline closely informed of the emperor's movements. For news of de Canouville's movements, however, she was indebted to his commander, Murat, who wrote to her in August, boasting of victory over the Russians two days earlier. "The Emperor has ordered me to chase them all the way to Moscow. . . . I am seizing a moment when we are rebuilding a bridge they burned to reply to you. My dear sister, it is impossible to love you more than I do. All my thoughts and those of those who love you"—by this he meant her lover—"are with you. I am saddling up, the bridge is back, and some Cossacks ahead of us need a good drubbing."

Neither Pauline's concern for Jules de Canouville, her fondness for Forbin, nor her current relationship with Talma precluded her finding a new admirer at the baths. Auguste Duchand, an oversize artillery officer who had served in Spain under Suchet and Sebastiani, was convalescing at Aix-les-Bains following wounds incurred at the Battle of Valencia. With Pauline's encouragement he became a devoted visitor to the Maison Chevaley. But for some time he remained in awe of the tiny princess and her autocratic ways. One day Laure d'Abrantès found him among the company gathered at the Maison Chevaley. As Laure tells us, the short climb from the spa to the house was steep and some of it not negotiable by horse. In consequence her footwear and hose and those of other guests were irksomely dirty upon arrival, in contrast to those of their elegant hostess—and, mysteriously, those of Lieutenant Captain Duchand. He was something of a dandy, and his unsullied knee boots were gleaming with wax.

Irritably Laure taxed the captain with this anomaly. He showed her his old servant soldier and said he made him carry him up the slope on his back. Laure looked at the large captain and at the shrunken little man and imagined the awkward journey. Such were the lengths to which men would go to please the fastidious princess, when she had not as yet done more than smile sweetly upon them.

On another occasion, after Laure had climbed up to the house, she saw to her dismay that Pauline was arrayed in a manner that boded ill. For when Princess Borghese received wearing a demi-negligée and seated in a bergère, she was ready to entertain and be entertained. There were other outfits she wore to recline on a chaise longue, and then animated conversation was still permitted. But when, as on this occasion, she languished on a sofa in a peignoir, all ribbons and ruffles, it was forbidden to remark even upon her appearance—and she was as pretty as an angel under her lace-trimmed English bonnet. The sole subject allowed was her health.

The doctors, Pauline informed the company that day, had just prescribed a miserable diet for her to follow. In the last eight hours she had taken nothing but soup. "And that without salt," she added. "Without salt," echoed one of the gentlemen present. "Without salt," confirmed Pauline tragically, then glared at Laure d'Abrantès as the latter let out an involuntary peal of laughter. Even Forbin raised a satirical eyebrow. Nevertheless Laure repented of her hardness when Pauline sent her a bouquet tied with a beautiful rope of pearls to which was affixed a note, "From your oldest friend at Aix."

Pauline's health remained a matter of prime concern to herself, if not to others. In August she addressed Baron Vivant Denon, master of the Mint in Paris and director of the Louvre, on this subject. (He stood high in her favor, as he had a cast of her hand by Canova in his cabinet of treasures.) "I am still extremely frail and live on asses' milk and chicken consommé," she informed him. "Eight days ago I began the waters, and although they tire me, I hope they will have a favorable outcome."

But Pauline was also always concerned to burnish her image. She was delighted with a medal featuring her classical profile that Denon had had struck from dies cut by the engraver Andrieu, as part of a series marking alleged visits by women of the imperial family to the Mint. (It was not, in fact, judged necessary for the visits to take place, nor did they.) The medal commemorating Pauline bore, on one side, her celebrated profile *à l'antique* and the inscription in Greek, "Pauline, Sister of the Emperor." On the reverse a naked group of the Three Graces was depicted, with the inscription in Greek, "Beauty, be our Queen." "They are charming," wrote the original. "I am in your debt for the trouble you have taken. You have only to undertake something to be successful, and I have asked Mme. Cavour to beg you for more." In due course Pauline sent a medal to her sister Elisa, who pronounced the likeness exact, and indeed Canova himself could have modeled the neat and regular neoclassical features that aroused so much admiration and desire in Pauline's contemporaries.

Pauline had already that summer had a bust of herself by the sculptor Bosio sent from Carrara to the emperor's doctor, Corvisart, to reward him for medical advice. (He might have preferred payment in coin.) As the summer wore on, she consulted more medics—eminent doctors from Geneva as well as the spa doctor, Desmaisons, and, of course, Dr. Peyre, who had been at her side since they left Saint-Domingue together. It seems clear that by now the princess had a chronic—and painful—inflammation of her fallopian tubes. But, in addition to other remedies for her persistent problems with her reproductive organs, they advised the application of leeches to her genital area. (Enemas, as well as bleedings, douches, purgatives, decoctions of herbs, and extracts of minerals, featured as a matter of course.) Whether her original problems had been occasioned by childbirth, this new and horrific remedy suggests that she was suffering from a venereal disease, probably gonorrhea, in whose treatment leeches were widely used. Pauline appears to have accepted the diagnosis and the medicine. The advice that she would have been given, however—that she should abstain from further sexual intercourse, for fear of infecting others and being reinfected—she showed no signs of heeding, as we shall see. But, to be fair, nor did most of the other men and women of her time who suffered from the *chaude-pisse,* or "a dose of the clap." Unmentioned and unmentionable in polite society, it was nevertheless ubiquitous.

SLOWLY PAULINE APPEARS to have recovered her spirits and her health. At any rate, at the beginning of September she was well enough to propose a boating expedition to the romantically situated Abbey of Hautecombe on the far shore of Lake Bourget. Founded by Cistercian monks in the Middle Ages, it was also the burial place of the counts and, latterly, the dukes of Savoy. By 1812, however, following the French occupation of Savoy, the monks were gone and the abbey buildings lay mostly in ruins, only in part in secular use as a china manufactory. The arrangement was for the party—which included Laure d'Abrantès, Forbin, Duchand, and Talma—to meet midmorning at the dock and set off at ten. The oarsmen were at the ready, the day was fair, but tempers frayed as the princess failed to appear. At last, nearer eleven than ten, Pauline arrived, borne on a palanquin and quite unperturbed by the ruffled feelings of those she had kept waiting.

Laure d'Abrantès tells us that Pauline sported a singular costume for an excursion to the ruins. Over an embroidered skirt, embellished with Valenciennes lace, she wore a shorter, matching dress, a polonaise. Adding a dash of vibrant color to the frilly ensemble, three great red plumes and satin ribbons were secured to a little Italian straw hat that perched on her sleek head. It was hardly surprising that, with such an outfit to concoct, Princess Borghese had run a little late. "She looked like a fine lady from Málaga," recorded Laure, who had accompanied her husband, Junot, on his campaigns in the Iberian Peninsula.

Pauline had a purpose that day, it would seem. Until now she had accepted handsome Captain Duchand's admiration as her due but had contented herself with Talma's embraces alone. However, with Talma about to leave for Geneva, where he was to begin a season of performances, she had grown restive. Captain Duchand, moreover, was resplendent in the white dress uniform with which he had honored the expedition. (His more sophisticated male companions were wearing redingotes, which was the accepted day dress in the spa.)

To Talma's growing dismay, as the boat progressed across the deep waters of the lake, Pauline "declared herself for M. Duchand" in very histrionic fashion. The tragedian's eyes grew round and fearful as the princess, at the helm of the craft, recited lines from Petrarch's sonnets to Laura that Fréron had taught her years before in Marseille:

> *Che fai? che pensi? che pur dietro guardi*
> *nel tempo che tornar non pote omai,*
> *anima sconsolata? che pur vai*
> *giugnendo legno al foco ove tu ardi?*

> [What are you thinking of, looking back
> To days that can never come again?
> Miserable creature, why go on
> Stoking a fire that already consumes you?]

Not only Duchand, at whom the verses were aimed, but all members of the company held their breath on the bright September day as the princess's voice sounded over the lapping of the oars:

> *Levommi il mio penser in parte ov'era*
> *quella ch'io cerco e non ritrovo in terra . . .*

> [My thoughts led me up to where
> She was, whom I seek and find no more on earth . . .]

The picture Pauline presented was so heavenly that it was no surprise Duchand was entranced.

As Pauline continued to declaim the whole way across the lake—the crossing took an hour—Laure d'Abrantès declared herself very glad to reach the farther shore and have the opportunity to wander over the stones of the ruined abbey with erudite Forbin her guide, his strong arm her support. Meanwhile, venturing less far, Pauline continued to weave her spell over the hapless Duchand, and Talma sulked in vain, until the sun set above the chestnut groves that overhung the abbey and its reflection in the water beckoned the party back across the lake to Aix.

Pauline was, as ever, pitiless when she had done with a lover. From Geneva late in September, Talma wrote wretchedly: "A hundred times I have decided to go to Aix just to stare from afar at your windows, to offer you the sighs and sorrows of my heart, without seeing you and troubling with my presence the calm which you need. But I fear I would not be able to be so near, and not press myself on you. I dread displeasing you, and losing perhaps all your favor by an unconsidered move. So I have restrained myself." But the actor need not have held himself in check, for he had already lost all favor in Pauline's eyes. His successor, Duchand, whose convalescence still had some months to run, was at her side as the princess planned a journey to the Midi, where her doctors, hastily consulted after her health took a turn for the worse, had advised she should winter.

Pauline's latest bout of ill health had been brought on by devastating news from the Russian campaign. Her lover Jules de Canouville had fallen at the bloody Battle of Borodino, which had been fought on September 7—the very day she had led her expedition over to the Abbey of Hautecombe and entertained the ship's company with her recitation of Petrarch's sonnets. Murat and his cavalry divisions, as we have seen, had had orders in August from Napoleon to pursue "the Cossacks," who were fleeing before them, to Moscow. For some time the Russian troops adopted a policy of scorched earth as they retreated eastward, burning fields and destroying anything that might be of use to the Grande Armée that followed in their wake. But in early September, at the village of Borodino, 120 miles west of Moscow, the Russian General Kutusov stood and gave fight. Napoleon launched into the fray all the troops available to him, hoping to devastate the Russian forces in one single battle.

The day proved, rather, one of attrition, in which Russian counterattack succeeded French assault and in which an important redoubt was captured by the latter, then regained by the former. At nightfall seventy thousand combatants—marginally fewer French than Russians—lay dead on the battlefield. Among the corpses was that of Jules de Canouville, for whom Pauline had so recently commissioned a new sword. It was later adduced that the bullet that had killed him had been fired by a fellow officer, rather than by any Russian. Some said the French marksman was jealous of de Canouville's relationship with Princess Borghese, others that Napoleon, wishing to put an immediate end to his sister's liaison, had given the order to fire. In the general carnage, it was impossible to substantiate such claims. What is certain is that the Conte di Saluzzo, who formed part of the Borghese suite in Turin and who was at Borodino, discreetly removed from around de Canouville's neck the miniature, set with brilliants, that depicted the princess.

Jules de Canouville's boasting of his liaison with his imperial lover, those headlong gallops to return to her pliant arms, were over, and the news of his death was communicated to the princess at Aix toward the end of September. The blow was severe. Apparently this braggart cavalier, with his joie de vivre and optimism, had touched in Pauline some chord that her other, more sophisticated lovers had not. Weeks later Pauline's librarian and confidant Ferrand wrote: "She does nothing but cry, she doesn't eat, and her health is altered." A journey to the Midi, toward the end of October, was planned, he added, in the hope that it would bring relief. Pauline was evidently suffering in body as well as mind and may even have gone through an operation in the south of France, as she ordered two liters of sulfuric ether—an anesthetic— from Paris at this time. However, the operation that one might think could have cured some of her troubles, a hysterectomy, was at this time so dangerous as to be very often fatal. It is unlikely that her doctors would have suggested it.

Further accounts of the ill-starred Russian campaign reached the French spa community in the course of that month. A week after the Battle of Borodino, Napoleon, with a reduced force of one hundred thousand men, entered Moscow, a city in flames. Its retreating governor, Prince Rostopchin, had given orders for it to be torched, and the fires burned for four days. Meanwhile Pauline recovered her spirits enough to address her steward on the subjects of her projected journey to the Midi and of her jewels: "Send me the amethyst parure, since Friese has finished it. With the carnelian earrings and parure I ordered from Nicolas. Also some bracelets, which must be finished by now. Send them by Lavalette. Tell Nicolas to finish, as we agreed, the turquoise parure, using the stones I bought from Picot." Were these pieces of jewelry intended purely for Pauline's adornment? Or did she see clouds gathering about her brother's Empire and mean to gather about her portable items she could dispose of easily? At the very least, she wished them in her possession and not in the hands of jewelers, who might prove fickle in uncertain times.

After visiting Archbishop Fesch in his diocese of Lyon, Pauline traveled on to Marseille, where Dr. Peyre awaited her. From Paris, Madame Mère rebuked Pauline in mid-November: "Yesterday I got a letter from you at last. I don't expect you to give yourself the trouble of writing when you are not in good health, but it seems to me you could easily give orders . . . for me to be informed of your health at least once a week. . . . Not doing so shows an indifference that has to affect me." But of course what Pauline wanted from her mother was reports of the emperor, reports that were not forthcoming, despite Madame Mère's privileged access to the Empress Marie Louise and—incidentally—to Napoleon's one-year-old heir, the King of Rome. "The Empress and King, whom I've seen this morning at Saint-Cloud," wrote Madame Mère, "are in the best of health. . . . We have no news of the army beyond what you've read in the *Moniteur*."

THE REALITY WAS HARSH and hardly comforting. After occupying the ruined city of Moscow some weeks, while failing signally to win from Alexander his agreement to capitulate, Napoleon had taken the decision in October to retreat back across the Dnieper to Europe, rather than face a winter cut off from supply lines. This time it was the Russian general, Kutusov, who forced the pace, attacking the retreating and demoralized French army where it was weakest and forcing it, in the weeks that succeeded, along the Smolensk road, which had already been stripped bare of supplies by both armies.

Following the disastrous Battle of Berezina in late November, where the pursuing enemy savaged the remnants of the Grande Armée trying to cross the river, Napoleon abandoned his troops to the Russian snow. Even the cavalry was now on foot, as the horses, without fodder, had died or been killed for meat by starving soldiers. While the survivors tramped westward, in early December the emperor made for Paris in a sleigh, accompanied only by his former ambassador to St. Petersburg, Caulaincourt. His decision was hastened by the news that, in Paris, one General Malet had nearly staged a successful coup d'état when he had announced that Napoleon had been killed in combat in Russia. But, before he left, Napoleon prepared a bulletin, dated December 3, to be sent ahead to Paris. "I shall tell everything," he told Caulaincourt. "Full details now will mitigate the effect of the disasters that have to be announced later to the nation."

That same day Pauline settled at Hyères near Toulon, where she declared she would spend the winter. In this pretty town, three miles from the sea, she had the novel idea that she could take the air best on a swing in the garden of the villa she rented. Her suite—the Duc de Clermont-Tonnerre, Madame de Cavour, and Madame de Turbie—were now inured to their mistress's caprices, some selfish, some kind. She sent "productions of the Midi"—hams and salami—to her uncle Fesch at Lyon. "I will eat them in good company," he promised her, "at the feast I give to the authorities after the Te Deum to commemorate the emperor's coronation."

Authorities might have celebrated the coronation of eight years earlier in early December, but there appeared little to celebrate when, ten days later, the Twenty-ninth Bulletin of the Grande Armée was published in the *Moniteur,* giving details of the disastrous losses suffered during the Russian campaign. Nevertheless, when the emperor reached Paris, he was optimistic. "Fortune dazzled me. . . . I thought to gain in a year what only two campaigns [Alexander's capitulation and a peace treaty] could achieve," he said with a frankness that astonished his listeners. "I made a great blunder, but I shall yet recoup." On Christmas Day, Gaudin, the finance minister, wrote loyally to Pauline: "We have enjoyed now for eight days the Emperor's presence. He is arrived from Russia, as he came back from Egypt, when it seemed least permissible to expect him. . . . His Majesty's health is admirable. Since the first day, there has not been the least trace of fatigue on his face."

Did Pauline believe these cheerful words? Although Napoleon called for festivities to greet his return to Paris, the effect of the Twenty-ninth Bulletin, the first in twenty years to acknowledge defeat, lingered on. Private letters began to filter through to Paris, too, detailing the fates of those hundreds of thousands of French soldiers, including many officers of high rank, who had gone with the Grande Armée to Russia and not returned. Comte Montesquiou-Fezensac, who had, like Napoleon, survived the Russian campaign, later reflected on the *cercles* and parties at the Tuileries, those affairs of silk and lace: "I shall always remember one of those dismal balls, at which I felt as if I were dancing on the graves of those who had died in Russia."

Meanwhile Murat, claiming jaundice, had deserted the Grande Armée soon after Napoleon left it, to return to his Kingdom of Naples and forge ties with the Allied powers. It was left to Marshal Ney and to Eugène, Josephine's son, to bring the tattered forces of the Grande Armée—now numbering barely ten thousand men—to France, while King Frederick William of Prussia made a secret alliance with Alexander. Talleyrand felt certain: "It is the beginning of the end."

But if Pauline mourned her brother's failure in Russia as well as de Canouville's death in Russia, she did not intend to show it. In January 1813 she received at Hyères—a gift from the emperor—a Sèvres *cabaret,* or tea and coffee service, embellished with the portraits of celebrated women from history. Pauline returned it with the request that the empress go to the manufactory and select instead portraits of her brother to adorn the china. Significantly, however, early that same month, she commissioned the imperial cabinetmakers Jacob to produce a repository that would hold all her jewels—those she had bought, those Napoleon had given her, those Camillo had lavished on her on their marriage, and those that were, in fact, Borghese heirlooms that she treated as her own. It was thus to be of a substantial size, and, with bronze decoration by the imperial goldsmith Thomire, it was to cost fourteen thousand francs.

Pauline was thinking ahead. Although her jewelry collection in this cabinet would not be portable, it could be kept in a safe place, and pieces released for sale should her brother's rule end abruptly. Her mother, who had still a lively remembrance of being a refugee with a family to support twenty years earlier, appears to have supported Pauline's project. She wrote from Paris: "Monsieur Decazes [Madame Mère's secretary] will have informed you of the fine necklace of pearls you have been offered. Four rows of them, and the owner wants 100,000 francs." Mere cupidity was not at stake here, but future survival.

But none of these plans did Pauline confide to her suite, and when she left Hyères for the sea breezes of Nice in February, she continued an imperious mistress. Her *lectrice,* Mademoiselle de Quincy, complained,

"We don't see a living soul, we spend our time watching Her Royal Highness move from bed to bed, and we only dream of attending the Carnival entertainments." Pauline's household has been well dubbed "the Ministry of Caprices," and Dr. Peyre was dismissed after ten years of service, a handsome though inexperienced physician, Dr. Espiaud, taking his place. Captain Duchand, who had traveled with Pauline to Marseille and Hyères, had been declared fit for military duty and had left to join an army that Napoleon was amassing to fight Prussia, which, as had been expected, declared war on the emperor in March. "Never have the French shown more zeal and attachment to their sovereign and their country," wrote Archchancellor Cambacérès to Pauline, informing her of Napoleon's departure for the theater of war.

But there was some point to Pauline's caprices now. More often than not they involved economy. Her financial prudence began when she reduced the salary of her steward, Monsieur Michelot, while informing him in the same letter that he was to dismiss most of the staff of the Hôtel Charost in Paris and sell the horses. Often her caprices involved arrangements for the disposal of assets, as when she offered Montgobert to the Leclerc family, or calculated the value of Neuilly or of the house in Paris. But although she fretted about her health, about her wardrobe—thinking nothing of sending urgently for cashmere shawls to Constantinople—and about her finances, Pauline was curiously cavalier about her personal safety. She resisted all requests from her mother to leave Nice—"I am very worried to think you are so close to the enemy, in the event of an invasion," Madame Mère wrote—and departed for her old haunt, Gréoux-les-Bains, in May only when the heat in Nice became oppressive.

While taking the waters at Gréoux, Pauline had, at least, the consolation of knowing, if she cared, that Duchand had survived the battles of May 1813 at Lützen and at Bautzen, from which Napoleon had emerged victorious. Indeed, in the latter bloody combat, despite having had two horses shot from under him, Duchand had captured a battery. Madame Mère wrote to Pauline in high spirits of the effect on the public mood of the victories: "May a solid and stable peace ensue." But the armistice and peace congress that followed did not result in terms that Napoleon accepted. By August France was back at war with the Allies, whose armies in the field totaled eight hundred thousand. Meanwhile Wellington's June victory over French troops at Vitória, if it had released troops for combat elsewhere, had signaled the end of the Napoleonic Empire in Spain.

Flitting between Gréoux and another former residence, La Mignarde, at Aix-en-Provence, Pauline was back at Gréoux in August when news of fresh losses in Germany reached her. At the Battle of Grossbeeren on August 23, Bernadotte, Désirée Clary's husband, former marshal of France and now, as Crown Prince of Sweden, on the Allied side, defeated Marshal Nicholas Charles Oudinot. The following day the Austrian field marshal Blücher defeated Marshal Macdonald, Pauline's former lover, at Katzbach. Two days later at the Battle of Dresden, a partial victory for Napoleon, the turncoat Moreau was in conference with the czar when his legs were blown off. He died, his last words being "Calm yourselves, gentlemen, it is my destiny."

Pauline, as usual, evinced only confidence in her brother, as the carnage being wreaked in Germany continued. "Thank you for the dress you had embroidered for me," she wrote calmly to Madame Michelot in September from Gréoux. "I leave in a month for Nice, where I will spend the winter." But everything changed when she received news of the disastrous Battle of the Nations, which took place at Leipzig over three days in October, where the French imperial forces suffered losses of at least forty-five thousand. Among them was one of Pauline's most distinguished lovers, General Poniatowski, who had become a marshal of France the day before and was now leading the Polish contingent. Covered with wounds, while retreating over a bridge he fell backward and drowned, or was killed by friendly fire. At Leipzig the Allies had not only inflicted a great defeat on the French emperor, but they thereafter dissolved the Confederation of the Rhine.

"The latest news has affected me badly," wrote Pauline from Nice to her mother's secretary, Decazes. She had enjoined silence, she said, on all her suite in relation to all political affairs. But, besides this censorship, she had a more practical project: "I am sending with this to Paris my valet, Merlin, whom you may trust. Talk openly to him. I need to know the state of my account, for I have offered 300,000 francs to the Emperor." A necklace—a diamond one—that she had recently bought was to be sold, she instructed, to meet this demand on her purse. In addition she required him to have all her remaining jewels placed with Madame Mère. Pauline was preparing herself for all eventualities.

Eight days later, writing from Gotha on October 25, Napoleon conditionally accepted his sister's remarkable offer. "My expenses have been considerable this year," he wrote euphemistically and envisaged that the campaigns of 1814 and 1815 would be similarly expensive. "The will of my people is such that I think I will have the means necessary for campaigns, if the coalition of Europe against France continues. If I don't meet with success [with the Senate], then I'll use your money."

Pauline remained at Nice, her health declining, as the news grew steadily less encouraging. The nature of Pauline's sufferings is unclear, and they may have been nervous in origin, but there was no doubting her weakness. "She has got pitiably thin, and crisis follows crisis," wrote the Comtesse de Cavour in early 1814, adding that the librarian Ferrand guarded Her Imperial Highness's door—"as an Angel bars the door to paradise"—and, with Dr. Espiaud, conspired to keep from the princess all bad news. There was certainly enough of it. The Dutch had ejected the French in November 1813; in December the Austrians occupied Switzerland. "When the Emperor's soldiers report some small victory," the countess continued, "he has the governor fire cannons to please her."

The members of Pauline's suite were anxious for her safety, and for their own. The princess spoke of going to Paris in the spring, and of her eagerness to see her family there. But her household did not think that, in her state of health, she could be moved farther than Lyon, even if an Allied invasion threatened. Meanwhile Pauline appeared impervious to danger, refusing calls from her mother to hurry immediately to Paris. Instead, from her bed she continued to make economies, erasing at a stroke from her different households secretaries, surgeons, valets, lackeys, and sending Mademoiselle de Quincy to gather all liquid cash and other portable valuables in Paris and deposit them with Madame Mère.

Then, in January 1814, the Allies announced that they were fighting against the French emperor alone, as he had rejected terms that, in their stated view, the French people would have accepted. This declaration on the part of the Allies did at last fire up the emperor in Paris to exert himself. "Invaders?" he questioned one doubting Thomas at the Tuileries. "Do you see Cossacks in Paris? They're not here yet, and I haven't lost all my skills." To prove it, as the English advanced northward on France over the Pyrenees from Spain, as other Allied forces moved into the northern and eastern French territories, Napoleon defended his capital in a brilliant "Six Days' Campaign."

Pauline's spirits revived, her health improved, and she rose from her bed to scold Monsieur Michelot and countermand all the orders she had so recently sent him. She was coming to Paris and would be there in six weeks. Her jewels were all to be returned to the Hôtel Charost. "I am sure you acted from good intentions," she wrote graciously, "but you needed to have a little more confidence in the Emperor, and less haste. If the victories continue"—and Pauline appears to have had no doubt that they would—"everything is to be put back just as it was. I don't want any confusion."

But confusion was, regrettably, to be the order of the day. Despite the individual victories of Champaubert, of Montmirail, of Vauchamps, and of Château-Thierry, Napoleon failed to withstand the Allied invasion. In late March the French capital fell to the Allies, and, for the first time since the Hundred Years' War, a foreign army marched down its streets. The Parisians had earlier watched silently as Marie Louise, the three-year-old King of Rome, Hortense, and other members of the Bonaparte clan had departed the city. Napoleon, who had fought his way as far as Fontainebleau, was forced to abdicate on April 11 and accept in lieu the Kingdom of Elba, a small island off the coast of Tuscany. The emperor betrayed no immediate emotion, but five days later he wrote to Josephine, who was at Navarre, to say that he felt a great burden lifted from him. He intended, he said, to write the history of his reign. It would "prove most curious, for till now I have been perceived in profile only. But I shall not tell the whole. I have heaped benefits on thousands of ungrateful wretches, and what have they done? They have betrayed me." Meanwhile, to the throne of France ascended Louis XVIII, an elderly gentleman who had been living elsewhere on the Continent and in England since his brother Louis XVI had been executed in the Revolution twenty years before. "What is a throne?—a bit of wood gilded and covered in velvet. I am the state," Napoleon had said. No longer, and at Fontainebleau on April 20 he said his adieux to the former Imperial Guard, who had served his every wish.

His adieux were not concluded, however. At the Château Bouillidiou, a gloomy country house in the Var near Saint-Raphaël and Fréjus, where Napoleon would in due course embark for Elba, Pauline waited. Others who had been a part of the imperial adventure and who were now fleeing France offered to take her with them. She refused, and the pope's former delegate to Paris, Cardinal Pacca, found her "pale as death but full of spirit." To her sister Elisa's husband, Bacciochi, she was obdurate: "I have not always loved the Emperor as I should, but as my brother he has a claim on my allegiance. The Emperor is passing by here. I must offer him my condolences and, if he wishes it, follow him to Elba."

Was Pauline serious in this? Such were the Allied governments' suspicions of Napoleon's intentions, and of his sister's, following his abdication that they had provided two regiments of Liechtensteiner guards to patrol the park of the château where Pauline waited. Austrian troops, meanwhile, bivouacked close by. One possibility envisaged was that, with his family's help, the former emperor might reignite loyalties in France and return to scotch the restoration of the monarchy. As a result the interview between brother and sister, when it occurred, was closely monitored by the Austrian and British officers who had Napoleon in their keeping.

Nobody was prepared for the cry of outrage that the princess emitted on seeing her brother. On the journey south the former emperor had lost all presence of mind. Sweating and moaning, he had been convulsed by nameless terrors, as well as by palpable fear of the populace who crowded around the carriage. At different times he had changed coats with one of his companions, in an effort to escape the mob's attention, and he appeared before his sister, still flustered, and dressed in the greatcoat of an Austrian general.

"How can I embrace you when you wear the enemy uniform?" Pauline asked, refusing to hold any further dialogue until her brother had changed into his familiar gray redingote. Then she tenderly caressed him. Her actions, the enemy officers observed, had a most marked effect on the former emperor. Losing his fear, he descended into the courtyard of the château and spoke to the local people gathered there. Some of the menfolk had previously been in imperial service, and one of them he recognized.

Upon his return to the princess, brother and sister, who had not met since the spring of 1812, spoke long and intimately of what had passed, and he accepted without demur the offer of her company on Elba. Naturally—Pauline being Pauline—she could not travel there immediately, for she meant first to take the waters on Ischia. That the island of Ischia was part of the Kingdom of Naples and her brother-in-law Murat one of the Allied leaders did not weigh with her. Nor does it appear to have troubled Napoleon. The Allied governments, however, were perplexed to know what sort of plot might be being hatched.

As evidence of her devotion to her brother, that night Pauline—not known for giving up her creature comforts lightly—offered her quarters at the Château Bouillidiou to the emperor and stayed at a less commodious house nearby. While Napoleon set sail next day for Elba, she bent her attention to the interesting question: Which transport should she gratify with her custom? It had been arranged that the English frigate *Undaunted* would return for her after it had taken Napoleon to Elba. But Murat had sent *Laetitia* from Naples, and a Royal Navy officer, Captain John Tower, was offering the use of his frigate, *Curaçao*, which lay at Nice.

In the end Princess Borghese chose to board the Neapolitan frigate at Saint-Raphaël, while the *Curaçao* sailed alongside to await further commands. France and Pauline Bonaparte had looked their last on each other, but in Naples she was her usual *exigeante* self, writing to Madame Michelot, "Please make sure that the bonnets and dresses you send are better packed than the last ones . . . don't forget to send me some new books. . . . Address them to the Neapolitan Minister at Paris. . . . I have arrived, extremely tired and in need of everything."

CHAPTER FOURTEEN

Diamonds on the Battlefield, 1814–1815

ALTHOUGH SHE HAD TRUMPETED her intention of joining the emperor in exile, Princess Borghese delayed at Naples for some months after her arrival there in June 1814. This did not, however, prevent her from lambasting her brother Joseph and sister Elisa, who showed no sign of proceeding to Elba at all. "One should not leave the Emperor all alone," she wrote. (Napoleon had kept his title, under the terms of the Treaty of Fontainebleau, though he had lost the Empire that gave it substance.) "It's now, when he is miserable, that one should show him affection. Or that's how I see it," she wrote to her mother at the end of the month, urging Madame Mère to precede her to the island.

To compound Napoleon's unhappiness, he had suffered a serious loss. His ex-wife, the Empress Josephine, who had been much feted by the Allied sovereigns upon their arrival in Paris in May, had subsequently caught a chill and died. Meanwhile Hortense, who had for some time lived separately from her husband, Louis Bonaparte, and had remained in Paris on her mother's account, did not thereafter leave the capital. This breached Napoleon's directive, the emperor having declared, according to Pauline, that "none of our family could establish themselves in France without it being an act of gross treachery." An exception was apparently made for the empress Marie Louise, who was following a cure at Aix-les-Bains, and whom the emperor affected to believe would soon join him on Elba. But Hortense, upon whom the attractions of Restoration Paris were not lost, chose to believe that her brother-in-law and former stepfather's reign was firmly over. (There were others who had marked his words at Fontainebleau in April: "I shall return when the violets bloom again.") Pauline saw herself, on the other hand, as triumphantly *sans peur et sans reproche* (without fear and without reproach). For not only was she, in due course, going to winter on Elba, but, at the beginning of June, en route from France to Naples, she had stopped overnight to inspect the emperor's new island domain.

VERY DIFFERENT from the Tuileries was I Mulini, the modest house with a garden that surmounted Portoferraio, Elba's harbor, now capital of Napoleon's kingdom. Moreover, there was no glittering throng or splendid officers to adorn receptions in the poorly frescoed rooms. For company—and as, respectively, grand marshal, governor, and military governor—Napoleon had just three generals, Bertrand, Drouot, and Cambronne—all three more loyal than brilliant. The mood could have been somber, after Napoleon's guard had welcomed the princess with salutes and cannon fire. But the Bonapartes proved now as ever adaptable. In the course of twenty-four hours Pauline dined one day with her brother and the next with his generals. She made a tour of inspection of the island, driving out with the emperor, and above all she made energetic arrangements to obtain the disparate elements that, in her opinion, were required to make life palatable upon her return to Elba. Furniture from Paris, a band of musicians, and orange trees for the garden from Naples—there was nothing the princess did not think of or plan for. Up at I Mulini she handed Grand Marshal Bertrand a necklace. It was to be sold, she told him, and a tract of land purchased to provide a country house for her and her brother, away from the humid air of Portoferraio.

Instructions too went to Madame Michelot in Paris, who had so ably and for so many years interpreted Pauline's demands. Madame was not to leave to her husband the important business of selecting the belongings that were to be sent to Elba. "You know better than he what will be useful to me," Pauline wrote. (Twenty packing cases full of mirrors, clocks, and candelabra in due course arrived on the island.) Then she departed the island fiefdom, so hurriedly that it was believed that she and her brother had quarreled. In fact Pauline had interests of her own to address before she could return to Elba and adopt the guise of "comforting angel."

From Naples in June she told her brother Lucien that she had plans to visit Rome: "I count on you to present my homage to His Holiness the Pope and remind him that I hope he will consider me still as one of the most faithful of his flock." Given that the pope had so long been their brother the emperor's prisoner, these remarks warrant some explanation. In May, Allied forces had returned the pope to Rome and restored to the Vatican the territories that had been ruled by the French since 1808. Meanwhile Lucien Bonaparte had been under house arrest in England, though he had played no part in the imperial drama, having quarreled with Napoleon long before. Now the English exile returned to Rome and to his large family. The pope, recognizing Lucien's neutral status, gave him the title of Prince of Canino. As for Pauline, it would seem that, during the pope's imprisonment at Fontainebleau, she had taken pains to preserve her courteous relationship with him from Roman days. At any rate she was now, not unnaturally, keeping her options open on the question of a permanent residence. Not only Lucien but her brother Louis, her mother, and her uncle Fesch had all been accepted by the pope as residents of Rome. If Paris was denied her, Rome, much as she had disliked it when living with Camillo, was now an acceptable alternative.

Relations with Camillo were also on Pauline's mind. "Tell me a little of Borghese," she instructed Lucien in Rome. "He has given no sign of life." In the general and sudden dismemberment of the Napoleonic Empire that had followed after the Allies took Paris in April, Camillo had left Turin and headed south—but not before he had packed up the numerous family treasures he had imported from Rome and displayed in the northern Italian city during his period there as French governor-general. By a curious twist of fate the ship carrying some of his possessions—among them the famous statue of Pauline, reclining, as Venus Victorious—made landfall at Elba in July. Napoleon, while awaiting his sister's return, attempted to claim her marble image. But to no avail. The statue proceeded to Rome, where it was installed in the Palazzo Borghese.

Camillo, however, was not so fortunate. The pope, though ready to forgive Bonaparte sins, had been poorly treated as a prisoner in Savona, part of Governor-General Borghese's fiefdom. Now he refused to allow the prince to return to Rome, on the ground that he was living an immoral life. It was true that the prince had, while in Turin, formed an attachment to a widowed cousin, the Duchessa Lante. Her company and that of her three daughters had proved congenial after the fireworks of life with Pauline. Now Camillo was forced, with the duchess and her daughters, to take up residence in his palace in Florence. But there too he found life agreeable—until Pauline intervened to bedevil his existence once more.

Camillo had heard that the princess had the Hôtel Charost up for sale, so he arranged to have the Borghese collection that adorned the walls of the Paris house returned to Rome. Pauline was immediately up in arms. "Don't give any picture up, whoever he sends," she instructed Michelot in mid-July. "Take twenty-five of the best paintings out of their frames and hide them somewhere safe. If they ask for them, say you sent them to me." The missing works would, the princess noted with satisfaction, be useful as bargaining tools in the financial arrangements she expected to make with the prince, now that the Empire was at an end. As an afterthought, she instructed Michelot to send, with the twenty cases that were en route to Elba, the Borghese silver that had graced her dining room in Paris.

Pauline's principal concern, when not arranging for her residence on Elba, was to rid herself of her properties in France. Although the Treaty of Fontainebleau had allowed her an income from the French government—never to be paid—of three hundred thousand francs, she was not convinced that the Bourbons would long allow her to own the Hôtel Charost, Neuilly, and Montgobert. To avoid sequestration her intention was to sell them one by one, and, by the end of April, she had let it be known that she wished to dispose of her town house. During the Allied sovereigns' May balls to celebrate Louis XVIII's accession to the throne, the Austrian emperor Francis I occupied the house. But it was quite a different power who expressed an interest in the house later in the summer of 1814. And it was no sovereign who wrote, "I have come into her house," on August 29, but Arthur Wellesley, newly created Duke of Wellington, who had earlier trounced Napoleon's forces in Spain.

But for a disagreement between his brother and the British prime minister, Lord Liverpool, the new duke would have been given a position in the London government. As it was, Wellington had been appointed British ambassador to the court of Louis XVIII, and, casting about for a Paris residence, he settled on the Hôtel Charost. (Meanwhile the Prussians bought for their Paris residence Eugène's *hôtel* on the rue de Lille.) After negotiation with Pauline's notary, Edon, the British government agreed to pay "by installments" a sum of 863,000 francs for the house, its sumptuous contents—valued at 300,000 francs and listed in a detailed inventory—and stables.

For some weeks, before his mousy wife, Kitty, arrived to cramp his style, Wellington could revel in Pauline's grand bed, examine his reflection in the princess's mirrors, and entertain in her dining room and grand saloons. Now it was his turn to pay for the candles—in candelabra on tables and on mantelpieces, in chandeliers above, four tiers deep—that illumined the poppy red silk, the bronzes, and bright gold of the *hôtel*'s Empire decor. Honoring the previous enemy occupation, the duke hung Princess Borghese's portrait on one side of a likeness of Pius VII. On the pope's other side, he placed a portrait of La Grassini, the singer who had once granted the "last favors" to Napoleon, and was now energetically lavishing them on the Iron Duke. "Exactly like Our Lord between the two thieves," exclaimed the Comte d'Artois on seeing the trio of portraits. As for the duke's opinion of Pauline, whom he was destined never to meet, he described her to a niece as a "heartless little devil." But on his return to London, when he hung a certain Waterloo chamber, the only portrait of a woman among a mass of field marshals and scenes of battle was that of—Pauline Borghese.

Meanwhile Madame Mère had answered Pauline's call to arms and, leaving Rome for Elba at the beginning of August, settled in unassuming apartments close to I Mulini. Her presence was believed by the Bonaparte family to bring her son comfort. But, as the old lady was increasingly absorbed by the mysticism to which the Abbé Buonavita, a Corsican in her suite, had introduced her, and as Napoleon disliked anything but the most orthodox faith, that comfort was necessarily circumscribed. Nevertheless Sir Neil Campbell, the British commissioner whose responsibilities were now limited to reporting on the emperor's movements, wrote to Castlereagh, the British foreign secretary, in mid-September: "I begin to think he is quite resigned to his retreat." And Madame Ducluzel, once Dermide's governess and now Pauline's attendant, who spent some time quarantined offshore, said, "I would be happy to live at Portoferraio. The town seems to me a little Paris. There are fine grenadiers and handsome Poles on horseback. One would think one hadn't left France."

Following the melancholy into which he had plunged on hearing news of Josephine's death, Napoleon had been cheered by a secret visit from Marie Walewska. She brought with her to a mountain rendezvous in the Elban hinterland their young son, Alexandre, and promised to return. But no such promises were forthcoming from Marie Louise, who had been given the Duchy of Parma by the Allied powers. And the three-year-old King of Rome, now known as the Prince of Parma, remained with his mother. Napoleon was, in consequence, delighted to welcome Pauline when she finally left Naples at the end of October and arrived in Portoferraio on November 1. Though she had delayed, the princess was magnificent when she appeared. At the ball that Napoleon gave to welcome her—and where the orchestra played, as well as the "Marseillaise," the popular air "Où peut-on être mieux qu'au sein de sa famille?" ("Where can one better be than in the midst of one's family?")—her gaiety and beauty greatly enlivened the proceedings. To Pons de l'Hérault, governor of the lucrative island iron mines, whom Napoleon had co-opted to form part of his household, she was Napoleon's "good angel . . . the treasure of the palace." Further, he declared that, such was the princess's obvious attachment to her brother, if the emperor had struck her she would have said, "Let him do it, if it gives him pleasure."

When Pauline appeared in a dress of black velvet that displeased Napoleon, she went to take it off. Her appearance in a white dress caused him to ask if she was dressed *à la victime*. Again she retired to change. And finally, when the emperor directed the princess to put away her fine jewelry, as she outshone the other women, who had none, she complied. In short, while Pauline had not revered her brother as he would have wished when he was emperor of the French, she now paid him full homage—and, leading by example others at the court in exile, she never crossed his path in the dingy drawing room at I Mulini without making a deep curtsey.

An enemy press would later seize upon these examples of Pauline's self-abnegation in Elba to claim that she and Napoleon enjoyed an incestuous relationship at I Mulini. There was certainly the opportunity. Once indeed Pons de l'Hérault saw Napoleon plant a kiss on his sister's mouth. "It is the custom in Corsica," said the emperor. But Pauline was used flagrantly to exercise power over the men whom she was currently bedding, and Pons de l'Hérault and other witnesses noted no such displays. One may conclude that, while the relationship between Pauline and her brother had at different times earlier been sexually charged, on Elba she provided succor rather than sex.

Indeed Princess Borghese found after some weeks that the emperor was growing morose, disenchanted with his island kingdom and with the few entertainments to be had, which, upon his first arrival, he had pursued with energy. Pauline set to and established a small coterie of attractive women—wives of the officers serving on Elba and a Greek interpreter's wife—who could be counted on to coax her brother out of the doldrums. And Napoleon, who had no interest in isolation unless it was to plan military and strategic maneuvers, brightened and acceded to his sister's wishes for parties and picnics—the weather was still clement—and airings and balls.

Although Pauline was pleased with the success of her plans, her health remained an issue, and one that she and her mother took seriously. They were right to be concerned, as her ailments at different times included sacroiliac pain, salpingitis, and even anemia and jaundice, remnants of the bouts of yellow fever she had endured in Saint-Domingue. To this we can probably add gonorrhea, unless the application of leeches in Aix-les-Bains or other medication had cured her. But Napoleon would have no truck with his sister's valetudinarianism. He recommended instead fresh air, as the princess informed Pons de l'Hérault in tragic tones when the governor met her in the lower part of the town. She was being bumped down the steep steps on a litter, and de l'Hérault did wonder if her brother had not just intended her to stand at an open window. But de l'Hérault had grown to understand, as had others who spent time in the princess's company, that she required to be thought of, first and foremost, as an invalid. Indeed, the princess was furious when de l'Hérault said, on New Year's Day 1815, that she looked "as fresh and healthy" as the roses he had seen in the garden that morning.

One of Napoleon's servants, the mameluke Ali, was censorious of Pauline and of her caprices. She dressed like a girl of eighteen, he declared, and yet, under her makeup, she was plainly a woman in her thirties. (Pauline had turned thirty-four in October.) She pleaded illness, then danced vigorously at the balls she gave in her apartments. And she would have gone on till late into the night, he claimed, only her brother intervened to draw the proceedings to a halt. Indeed, for want of any on-island lover Pauline seized upon her brother's generals for partners. But, after an energetic dance, Cambronne declared he would rather risk gunfire again than accompany her once more into the fray, and Drouot was similarly unpromising material who preferred his Bible to the dance floor.

Pauline does not appear to have borne any grudge against the generals who spurned her. But, perhaps contemplating the revival of a former romance, she wrote to Madame Michelot for news of Duchand, who had last visited her just before she left for Naples. Meanwhile she saw to the construction of a theater on the site of a demolished church, below I Mulini, and arranged a program of plays. She drove out with the emperor to inspect San Martino, the country house that was being prepared for their occupancy. And she wrote tranquilly enough: "There are great winds here, the weather is very changeable. I enjoy being with my brother, but I am anxious for the future."

Pauline's anxiety was, in part, inspired by her brother's restlessness, although the failure of Montgobert and Neuilly to find buyers disturbed her too. Napoleon had news that the Allied powers at the Congress of Vienna were quarreling. In Paris, moreover, Louis XVIII had not proved popular, and a kind of quiet anarchy obtained, in which hopes that Napoleon would return and overthrow the Bourbons were openly and covertly expressed. On the Paris boulevards violets, as a symbol of that hope, were to be seen in hats alongside the Bourbon white cockade. When Napoleon's supporters met, to the question "Do you believe in Jesus Christ?" the required response was "Yes, and in his resurrection." The English were detested, and Pauline's house in Paris lay empty after the British government thought it politic to remove Wellington from the capital and send him to Vienna.

Napoleon began to think that a bid for power might yet prove successful, and Pauline, as she told Pons de l'Hérault, found her brother more inclined to solitude and reverie. Nevertheless, she continued to plan entertainments in the emperor's honor. She persisted in her guise, to use Pons de l'Hérault's words, as "the princess, so gay, so sweet, and whose every word was an expression of grace and pleasure. Whose lively face and animated regards, whose enchanting smile gave life and spirit to all who approached her." And among the fetes she planned was a ball to be held on February 26.

Rarely can the refusal of an invitation to a party have had such an effect upon the destiny of Europe. For when the British resident, Sir Neil Campbell, received—on February 16—Pauline's request that he attend her ball ten days later, he wrote that he was unable to accept. He was bound for Florence, where he intended to consult a doctor, and would not return to Elba until the ball was over. (Campbell suffered from deafness as a result of head wounds incurred in the Spanish campaign. But he was also being economical with the truth, as he had a mistress in Livorno, whom he intended to visit.) Pauline showed this note to her brother, and, so the story goes, once Sir Neil was safely gone, the emperor asked her to bring the ball forward by several days. But he told neither her nor his mother the reason why, until after the ball was over, on the evening of the twenty-fifth. Taking first Madame Mère and then Pauline into the garden of I Mulini, Napoleon explained that the following day he planned to take ship for the southern coast of France. A few hundred men would accompany him, and, from there, gathering support, he would advance on Paris. In his opinion, and according to information he had received, many of the regiments stationed on his route north would declare for his cause. Meanwhile, in Naples, Murat—who had turned his coat once in favor of the Allies—had once more pledged his support, and a substantial number of troops, for the emperor.

Pauline, mournful but practical, offered her brother a diamond necklace worth five hundred thousand francs that could be sold should money be scarce. The stones, upon being accepted, were entrusted to Marchand, Napoleon's valet, but the latter was shocked by the princess's wretched appearance. "Don't abandon him, Marchand. Take care of him," she said. Kissing her hand, the valet thought to encourage her by saying she would be soon reunited with her brother. But Pauline answered that she did not believe she would ever see Napoleon again.

The inhabitants of Elba were hardly less perturbed than Pauline when they learned of the emperor's plans from Napoleon's chamberlain, General Lapi: "Inhabitants of Elba, our august sovereign, recalled by Providence to his glorious career, is about to quit our island. He has left me in charge and, says that, as a proof of his confidence in you, he leaves his mother and sister to your protection." The renown that the small island had enjoyed during Napoleon's stay would now be a thing of the past. But the emperor's arrangements for a swift departure were unstoppable. He shut the gates of the harbor before Lapi made his announcement, so that no shipping could carry the news abroad. And by eight in the evening on February 26, when Napoleon went on board the brig *L'Inconstant* that was to carry him over to France, all his officers, troops, horses, and supplies were embarked and ready to depart on that and other transports.

That afternoon Bertrand, Drouot, Cambronne, and Pons de l'Hérault, who were all to accompany the emperor, had come to say their adieux to the princess. According to de l'Hérault, she was pale, her eyes were bathed in tears, and her lips were without color. He hardly recognized this doleful woman as the gay hostess who had charmed him all winter. "Good-bye, my friends," she said, and kissed each of them in turn. "May success attend you. Take care of my brother. Send me news." And then, after saying a last good-bye to Napoleon, Pauline waited to hear the outcome of his bid for power in France. At the same time she prepared herself for the return of Sir Neil Campbell, and the consequences to herself of her brother's departure from Elba.

It was two days later that the *Partridge* brought a mildly apprehensive Sir Neil back to Portoferraio from Livorno. Campbell had heard, while in Tuscany, that the Polish cavalrymen on Elba were mending their saddles, and that cases of plate belonging to Pauline had been transported to the Tuscan coast. In consequence he wished to assure himself that the emperor was not meditating leaving Elba. But he was not seriously concerned and had recently told Castlereagh that their prisoner appeared to have lost all ambition and had grown fat and idle.

Upon his arrival in Portoferraio, Campbell learned that he had been deceived and that Napoleon "with all his generals, and all his French, Polish and Corsican troops" had evacuated the island. "Your brother has broken his parole," he said to Pauline, "for he promised not to leave the island, but the Mediterranean is full of shipping, and"—predicted Campbell—"he is now a prisoner."

Pauline replied that that was no way to speak to a woman. And in fact news soon came that Napoleon and his six hundred men had landed in the Gulf of Saint-Juan near Antibes on March 1 and were gathering support as they marched north. But, to torment the anguished Campbell, Pauline declared that she was very disturbed by her brother's departure. She "laid hold of my hand and pressed it to her heart," wrote the British resident, "so that I might feel how much she was agitated. However, she did not appear to be so, and there was rather a smile upon her face."

Pauline had apparently shaken off her earlier presentiments that her brother's mission would fail. But in fact, while Campbell left the island in search of Napoleon, and while, in France, increasing numbers of soldiers mustered around Napoleon's standard as he headed for Paris, Pauline organized her own departure from Elba—for Italy. Although the intention had been for her and her mother to join Napoleon in Paris, once he was secure there, she was worried, following threats that Campbell had made in their interview, that she would be interned by the Allied powers. And so she took the decision to strike out on her own and seek sanctuary with Lucien in Rome—whether temporary or permanent remained to be seen. But from that base she intended to negotiate with Camillo.

Leaving Madame Mère at Portoferraio, Pauline and Madame Ducluzel embarked with another attendant, Madame Molo, and her mother, Madame Lebel, in an open felucca on the night of March 4. Lieutenant Monier, one of Napoleon's officers who had been on the dependent island of Pianosa when the emperor left Elba, was their guide, and, after an uncomfortable journey, they landed at Viareggio on the Tuscan coast. Hearing that Signor Raffaello Mansi, who had been such an affable host in Lucca and in Bagni di Lucca, was in residence at his villa in Viareggio, Pauline sent to ask for accommodation. But Mansi had no wish, now that an Austrian grand duke ruled Tuscany, to be associated with Princess Borghese and her Bonaparte clan. He begged off, claiming that his family was in residence at the villa, so there was no room.

Balked, Pauline applied to take up residence in her sister Elisa's former villa at Compignano, which lay between Viareggio and Lucca. In this she was successful. But unfortunately Elisa was disputing with Austria its claim to Lucca and its territories, which included Compignano. (She asserted that the city, anciently a republic, had made an autonomous decision in 1805 to declare her and her husband, Felice Bacciochi, their sovereigns.) Elisa had been interned at Brünn (now Brno, Czech Republic) by the Austrians and could hardly lay claim to her villa at Compignano in person. Nevertheless the Austrian governor at Lucca, Colonel Wercklein, sent a detachment of cavalry to occupy the park, and Princess Borghese was permitted very restricted access to the outside world. One of those allowed through was the priest whom she had asked to come from Lucca. As she took her bath behind a curtain while he said mass on the other side of it, it could be argued that their contact was minimal.

The news that Louis XVIII had fled and that Napoleon had been carried into the Tuileries on March 20, that he was once more emperor of the French, gave Pauline fresh energy. She dictated urgent directives: "She does not wish her household to be named before she arrives, above all she refuses to have back anyone who left her." But it was not only the composition of her household in Paris that occupied her. Although her correspondence was restricted, letters and couriers appeared often enough during April and May for the princess to grasp the salient details of the situation in France.

Once back in Paris, Napoleon was having to present himself as a constitutional monarch to a people who had bad memories of his dictatorship. It was no easy task, but upon it depended his domestic security and that of his family. "I am growing old. The repose of a constitutional king may suit me," he said. "It will more surely suit my son." Moreover, upon hearing the news of Napoleon's advance on Paris, the Allied powers in Vienna had disbanded the congress and each had pledged 150,000 troops to put into the field against the emperor, whom they declared an outlaw. Napoleon could therefore count on fighting an invasion force before he could fully count on the loyalty of his people.

In the circumstances Pauline had no great hope of a long reign in

France for her brother but was eager for him to bring pressure on the Austrian authorities to free her, while he was still in government. Monier, who had remained with her following the flight from Elba, managed to evade the Austrian guards at Compignano in May and bring Pauline's plight to the emperor's attention in Paris. Upon Napoleon's orders the French chargé d'affaires then pleaded in Florence with the Austrian grand duke: "The arrest of a woman is against all received usage. There can be no interest in holding her."

In addition, Napoleon ordered Decrès, now once again minister of marine and colonies, to send a frigate to wait off Viareggio for the princess, should she be freed. But the frigate was never sent, and in the meantime Pauline's health had deteriorated. After doctors from Lucca, from Pisa, and from Viareggio had been summoned to give their opinions of her case, it was judged urgently necessary by all that she take the waters at Bagni di Lucca. Reluctantly Colonel Wercklein let her go, and at the beginning of June, Princess Borghese took up residence in the bathing station where she had last stayed when the news of Dermide's death was broken to her.

Meanwhile, in Paris, growing discontent with Napoleon's "reforms" had culminated in a liberal politician who opposed the emperor being elected president of the Chamber of Deputies at the gaudy Champ de Mai—a ceremonial to ratify the new constitution, in fact deferred till the beginning of June. But the emperor had no time to brood on such setbacks and indeed said that it was not the time to engage in subtle discussions when the enemy ram was at the gates. On June 12 he set off with fewer than two hundred thousand men to do battle for the northeastern frontier of France, where the Allied forces had massed.

Pauline was at Bagni to receive news of the fatal outcome of this battle at Waterloo on June 18, which ended Napoleon's hundred days of power. Napoleon, pale and sluggish in his slate-colored greatcoat, left Marshal Ney to direct operations for much of the encounter. Even when he roused himself to take command, however, he was undone by his belief that the Prussians, under Marshal Blücher, could not come in time to the aid of the British forces commanded by the Duke of

Wellington. The Prussians duly proved him wrong, fighting their way to the battlefield through rain and mud. The Allies triumphed, and Napoleon made for Paris, in hopes that he could organize national resistance. But he soon saw that that was a task beyond even him. "Dare to do it," urged his brother Lucien, who had, those last months, been in Paris, putting aside quarrels with Napoleon to support his brother's bid for power. "I have dared too much already" was the answer. And the emperor abdicated for the second time, paving the way for Louis XVIII to return to Paris in July.

Colonel Wercklein took pleasure in coming in person to inform Princess Borghese of the details of Napoleon's defeat, his abdication, and even his attempted flight to America as they emerged. Although her attendant Madame Molo declared, "Death would be a boon in these circumstances," Pauline remained energetic. Believing, after the emperor had surrendered at Rochefort to an English naval captain, that he would be placed under house arrest somewhere in the United Kingdom, she sent to Metternich, now Austria's foreign minister, imploring him to intervene and arrange that she could live with the emperor. But it became clear that instead the Allied powers intended to embark him for Saint Helena, a rocky outcrop in the Atlantic, where it was decreed he should spend the remainder of his days. Only then did Pauline write to the pope, begging him to give her a refuge in Rome—a request that received a favorable answer.

After remaining a period of months at Bagni di Lucca, in October 1815 Pauline made the journey to Rome, where she at first took up residence in the Palazzo Falconieri in the via Giulia with her uncle and mother. She had yet to come to an accommodation with her husband about the apartments in the Palazzo Borghese, which she declared to be hers as of right, and a struggle lay ahead of her in the Roman law courts. But there was another matter unresolved. One detail of the epic struggle at Waterloo that Wercklein had not known to confide to Pauline was that Napoleon had left his carriage on the field. It contained, besides a sword, its hilt set with diamonds, and a traveling case, all the items in it of gold, the Borghese diamond necklace, which

Marchand had hidden in the lining of the coach before the battle. The valet had then not had time to extract it before he and his master fled for Paris. Accounts of the necklace's fate differ. On the one hand it is said it disappeared from the carriage before the vehicle, captured by the enemy, went on show in London. According to another legend, however, the emperor's trusted companion, Las Cases, took the jewelry and, when he embarked with Napoleon on the *Northumberland,* bound for Saint Helena, had it with him. No reference to the necklace, however, is made by Napoleon or any of his comrades in their accounts of life on Saint Helena.

Schemes and conspiracies now swirled in Europe and in America around the absent but still potent figure of the emperor of the French. Would he yet be persuaded to convert the Borghese necklace—if he had it with him—or other valuables into hard currency and once more, like an eagle, take wing for France? Or would he, as he claimed, be content at Longwood House on Saint Helena to write a memoir of his "distinguished career"? The Allied powers were aware of Princess Borghese's devotion to her brother and were eager to counter any plots and plans in which she might become involved. Though the princess declared herself relieved to have found asylum with her mother and brothers in Rome, they placed her under the most stringent surveillance—a surveillance that Pauline, naturally, delighted in evading.

CHAPTER FIFTEEN

Plots and Plans, 1815–1821

M Y FIRST THOUGHT is to thank Your Holiness," Princess Borghese wrote, upon her arrival in Rome in October 1815, to Pius VII. And indeed the pope's clemency, despite his earlier treatment at the hands of Napoleon, in affording a refuge to Pauline and certain other members of the Bonaparte family was worthy of acknowledgment. The Allied powers had decreed Austrian exile for Elisa Bacciochi, Jérôme, and the widowed Caroline Murat, who could potentially muster support for Napoleon in their former principalities and kingdoms. (Murat had been executed, following his support for Napoleon in the Hundred Days, at Pizzo in Italy.) Metternich's police, it was judged, would best keep these Bonaparte siblings under observation. And Pauline had very nearly been added to their number in Graz and Trieste, because she was still viewed as having been a channel of communication between Napoleon and the Murats before the emperor's departure from Elba. But her brother Louis, resident at Rome, had entered upon an adroit correspondence, replete with references to Pauline's status as a Roman princess, with the Austrian and papal authorities. As a result she received the permission of the Allied powers, and that of the pope, to return to Rome.

Henceforward Pauline's conduct would come under scrutiny not only from the Roman police but from Louis XVIII's ambassador to

Rome, the Comte de Blacas, as well as from the Prussian, Russian, and Austrian ministers in that city. Furthermore, should she secure permission to visit Bagni di Lucca or other bathing stations in Tuscany, she would be the subject of Austrian and British police reports. Blacas, for one, was by no means the most impartial of judges. Indeed, upon Napoleon's return to Paris in 1815, the emperor found, among the papers that the count, foreign minister in Louis XVIII's first brief reign, had left behind, a disgruntled letter that one of Pauline's maidservants on Elba had written. Interpolated with accounts of Napoleon's fondness for his sister and of his furnishing apartments for her was, in another hand, the allegation that the brother and sister had slept together. "Good, to print," a royalist minion had written in the margin. But Pauline had never altered her behavior one jot for private or public consumption, not even when Napoleon's creature Fouché had reported on her daily doings in Paris. The knowledge that her activities—as well as those of her other relations in Rome—Madame Mère, Cardinal Fesch, Louis, and Lucien—would now be canvassed by two or more government agencies did not cause her to lose her composure.

Something else, however, greatly distressed Pauline, and she lost no time in informing the pope himself of her anxiety—namely, Camillo's "extraordinary and inexcusable behavior." During the Hundred Days, Prince Borghese had remained at the Palazzo Borghese in Florence, the Duchessa Lante at his side, and there he now appeared to have every intention of remaining. But hostilities had broken out while Pauline was still in Bagni di Lucca and making arrangements for her residence in Rome. Camillo had expressly forbidden her to take up residence in her apartments in the Palazzo Borghese there. "Extraordinary" as Pauline claimed to find her husband's order, when she received word to this effect from Gozzani, the Borghese steward in Rome, she had, in fact, expected nothing less. For, as she knew well, Camillo had long wished to secure a separation, then a divorce, and marry the Duchessa Lante. Denying Pauline a home, following her brother's fall from power, was a first step in this direction.

While she had no wish to live with Camillo, Pauline was determined, following the loss of her imperial titles and estate, to remain married and keep the rank of "true" Roman princess—and the Borghese residences, carriages, and jewels as well. "I am ready to accede to whatever Your Holiness should decide," Pauline wrote winningly to the pope, begging him to intervene. "As proof, I ask you to choose one or more judges to settle in private and without appeal all the differences between the prince and me."

So illustrious in Rome was the Borghese name—though its current holders might not lend it distinction—that several cardinals were directed to break their heads upon the divisions between Pauline and Camillo. Lucien Bonaparte had tried without success to broker a settlement in 1814 while Napoleon was confined at Elba. But Camillo had then insisted upon the return of the Borghese jewels, which he had given into Pauline's eager grasp in 1803 upon their marriage. Lucien, without dwelling upon the presence of the Duchessa Lante in Camillo's house, had replied that, as there was no official separation, there was no reason for his sister to return the stones. Now it was Louis Bonaparte's turn to champion his sister. While Pauline presented herself as a much injured wife, taking up residence in an underheated villa on the via Nomentana, Louis weighed in with some judicious remarks on Camillo's morals, which he addressed to one of the pope's cardinals.

"A wife is not a friend," wrote Louis, whose own wife, Hortense, had for some years elected to live separately from him. "No matter how cool the relations between the spouses, in all Christian countries, legal judgment must precede a formal separation. A husband cannot refuse to receive his wife without doing her great injury." And he wrote again, now specifically attacking Camillo's cohabitation with the Duchessa Lante in Florence: "It is not enough for him to live publicly with another woman in his wife's apartments. . . . He causes even greater scandal in the Capital of Christianity [Rome]." It was outrageous that Pauline, Camillo's wedded wife, should be "obliged to ask for judges to secure her entry to her husband's house."

Such indeed was the cardinals' conclusion, and it was of no avail for Camillo to write a memorandum detailing Pauline's neglect of almost every wifely duty. (Adulterous behavior was not an offense with which he could directly tax her, given his relationship with the duchessa.) Pauline had wished, wrote Camillo, throughout their marriage to live "separate and independently." Indeed, only the previous year, when electing to join the emperor on Elba rather than meet him in Italy, she had written, "Adieu, Camillo, I have known for a long time that our personalities are not compatible, so it is better to live separately and not make each other unhappy." But Pauline was proof against such truths, and now she wrote a beguiling letter to Camillo, hoping that they could put aside the differences that had so cruelly divided them and live together once more. The prospect of this so alarmed the prince— as was the princess's intention—that he gave up his objections to an unofficial separation. Thereby all his hopes for a judicial separation, from which divorce and remarriage could follow, dissolved.

By June 1816 terms had been agreed. Apartments in the Palazzo Borghese were ceded to Pauline, two carriages apportioned to her, and besides the twenty thousand francs a year she already received from Camillo, fourteen thousand scudi were to be hers annually. (Scudi, Roman currency, were worth five francs each.) In addition she was to have the wherewithal to buy a villa removed from the mephitic air of the Tiber, the river that lay beneath the windows of her palace. Then there was the use of the Casino Don Francesco at Frascati to be mentioned—and finally the Borghese jewels. These Camillo did ask to be separated from the other jewels in Pauline's collection and to be kept in a safe-deposit box—as was the custom in Rome—from which she could remove individual pieces upon submitting a request. Pauline tossed her head, refused to surrender any stones to such a repository, and called the Parisian jeweler Devoix to Rome. He was to witness that no one could now tell which were Borghese and which had been acquired from other sources, as she had had them all set and reset so many times. Her victory was complete, although characteristically she told Monsieur Michelot in Paris that she had made "great sacrifices" in coming to an arrangement with the prince.

Pauline had spurned Rome as a residence when she lived there with

Camillo in 1804 and had made little effort to charm its inhabitants. But now Paris, for which she sighed, was the domain of Louis XVIII, Neuilly was French crown property, and a new British ambassador, Sir Charles Stewart, occupied the Hôtel Charost. Accordingly Princess Borghese, having won from her husband all that she had wanted and more, set about, with an energy that would have bewildered those who had known her as a languorous invalid in the south of France, establishing herself as a "little queen" in Roman society. She made her receptions, soirees, and concerts the most sought-after invitations in town, though, as George Ticknor, a young American scholar touring Europe, noted, the Roman nobility was at a loss to know how to treat the Bonapartes: "for they belong, now at least, to no nation, and live at home as among strangers. Their acquaintance, however, is more sought after than that of any persons in Rome, and, as for myself, I found no societies so pleasant." As for Pauline herself, said Ticknor, she was "the most consummate coquette I ever saw . . . she has an uncommonly beautiful form and a face still striking, if not beautiful. When to this is added the preservation of a youthful gaiety, uncommon talent, and a practical address . . . it will be apparent she is . . . a most uncommon woman."

Pauline's apartments in the Palazzo Borghese were described by the Irish novelist Lady Morgan as "beyond beyond" when she attended a concert that the princess gave there. On another day, when Lady Morgan dined with Pauline, the princess invited the company to see her jewels, among them the emerald tiara set with diamonds that she had worn at Napoleon's coronation in Notre-Dame. "We passed through eight rooms en suite to get to her bedroom," the visitor reported. "The bed was white and gold, the quilt point lace and the sheets French cambric, embroidered." We know that Camillo installed a bathroom in Pauline's quarters, and, as she found no fault with it, we may assume it was appropriately luxurious.

Pauline's jewels were, of course, magnificent, but the princess was also happy, upon occasion, to show the Canova statue of herself as Venus, which now resided in Camillo's apartments. During its years in

Turin a mechanism had been installed within a painted base that allowed the statue to revolve before the spectator. Seen at night, illuminated by the light of small torches, the life-size portrait of Pauline on her marble mattress took on a fleshy tone, and, from the grave head to the cocked toes, by way of a titillating display of derriere, became one of the sights of Rome. There was no shortage of tourists, now that the long European wars were over and the borders open. Indeed, not being one to hold a grudge, Pauline told Camillo in the autumn of 1816 that "all the foreigners" agreed with her that the Villa Borghese, his property set in a capacious parkland, incorporating a lake and temples, and extending over the Pincio hill, was "the finest in Rome."

Pauline had herself bought and had fitted out over the summer of 1816 a charming small villa with a garden close to Porta Pia in the shadow of the Aurelian Wall. She liked to drive to it from the Palazzo Borghese through the grounds of the Villa Borghese—not least because those strolling or driving on the Pincio hill could admire her appearance. Apparently she thought of naming her new property, previously the Villa Sciarra, Villa Bonaparte, but her mother complained that the house was not of an order to bear the family name. (Despite Napoleon's fall from grace, Madame Mère's servants wore imperial livery and, in general, the Bonaparte residences in Rome boasted a splendor and sophistication not found elsewhere in the city and included such items as abundant fires and carpets throughout.)

Princess Borghese named her new plaything Villa Paolina instead, and soon appreciative guests came to dine, to attend concerts, or simply to walk in the gardens and take refreshments. Lady Morgan records a spring morning there, enjoying a *déjeuner* with an assortment of Roman and German princes, English milords and ladies, and American businessmen. "We were served pastries, ices, light wines, and coffee. . . . The principal entertainment was to walk in the elegant apartments and wander through the gardens, admiring the ancient walls that surrounded it, and where once the praetorian guard had done sentry duty."

Lady Morgan, noting the cardinals and bishops among the

princess's habitual guests, observed that "not since the time of Pope Joan had a woman been so surrounded by cardinals as la belle Pauline." But it was rather the presence of Englishmen and Englishwomen at Pauline's table, at her *cercles* and receptions, as well as the pretty attentions she paid them, that others noticed. Napoleon, informed in Saint Helena of the situation, merely smiled: "Then I will have a few enemies the less." But Lucien Bonaparte's intimate the painter Charles de Chatillon remonstrated with the princess, having been present while she entertained a Scottish peer, the Marquess of Douglas, who was heir to the Duke of Hamilton: "Do you forget Saint Helena?"

For reply de Chatillon received a flea in his ear. "Forget Saint Helena?" said Pauline. "Didn't you see how the Marquess of Douglas suffers all morning, standing more than an hour, for all his rheumatism, assisting at my toilette, and handing pins to my maid like a clown? . . . As for the evening—I employ him as my footstool. Imagine the joy I feel to have under my feet one of the grandest milords of Great Britain, one of the first peers of the land. So I, the sister of an unhappy prisoner, treat his assassins."

But Pauline was being disingenuous, and Prince Metternich in Vienna understood the situation better, when he noted in December 1816: "Members of the British opposition are frequenting the Bonapartes in Rome." For it was not all the English—or Scots—whom Pauline welcomed, but members of the British Whig Party, many of whom were at Rome in the winter of 1816–17 with their wives and families. According to Lady Frances Shelley, a correspondent of the Duke of Wellington, "The immaculate Pauline Borghese, and the Bonaparte family . . . receive the homage of the Jerseys, the Lansdownes, the Cowpers, the Kings, in short the regular Opposition. They have made Pauline Borghese their bosom friend. This causes surprise to the foreigners generally," added Lady Frances, herself of the Tory persuasion, "who do not understand that, with us, politics play a grand role, in cementing or destroying friendships."

Pauline had found common cause with the Whigs because both she and they wished to protest against the conditions of Napoleon's existence on Saint Helena. The Tory government in London, led by Lord Liverpool, resisted any such demands. In this they were supported by the Prince of Wales, who had been prince regent ever since his father, George III, was declared unfit to rule in 1812. (George III was never to recover and was still inhabiting a twilit world of delirium when he died in 1820. The regent then succeeded as King George IV.) In Rome, Pauline concentrated on charming the Whig tourists, and in this she succeeded admirably. Lord Gower, his sister-in-law, Lady Granville, in Paris heard, was "dying" for her. Pauline, Lady Granville was told, was "as pretty as a princess in a fairy tale, but fiendish, truly fiendish. She asks if her hair is as well styled as the day before, or whether it was better some other day. Then says no, that day some braid, some plait was less successful."

Lord Jersey became quite besotted with Pauline, to the indignation of his wife, one of the "Queens" of Whig society. In raptures he said that she was "clever and delightful." Exclaiming over her habitually elegant pose on a sofa, he said, "her foot looks as if it never had a shoe on." But in England, Lord Holland, the Whig leader in the upper house, was the great hope of Pauline and her relations. Although there was little hope that Lord Liverpool's Tory government would fall on this or any other issue, Holland commanded sufficient respect that a remonstrance on the subject of Napoleon's treatment that he submitted to the House of Lords in March 1817 was the occasion of feverish interest in the British and foreign press.

When Napoleon had hoped for asylum in England following Waterloo, he invoked the example of an Athenian leader who had first warded off a Persian invasion, then, when ostracized, found asylum with Artaxerxes, the Persian king. "I have terminated my political career," Napoleon wrote from Rochefort to the new prince regent, "and come, like Themistocles, to share the hospitality of the British people. I place myself under the protection of their laws, and I claim that from Your Royal Highness as the most powerful, the most constant, and the most generous of my enemies." But the prince and his Tory government, headed by Lord Liverpool, were not inclined to clemency.

Instead "General Bonaparte"—for so the Allied powers now dubbed the emperor—was dispatched to the basalt rock of Saint Helena out in the South Atlantic, to be guarded by patrolling British ships and a host of troops.

When Sir Hudson Lowe, the British commissioner entrusted with Napoleon's custody, arrived on the island in 1816, he bore with him instructions from Lord Bathurst, the British colonial secretary, which the former emperor viewed as sadistic. Among them was the requirement that, to confirm his presence on the island, "General Bonaparte" should show himself twice a day at Longwood House, the dingy bungalow he shared with the officers and their families who had accompanied him from Europe to this remote—but not unpopulated or unvisited—location. (Saint Helena had previously belonged to the East India Company and continued, as British Crown property, to serve the watering needs of ships traveling between Western Europe and India and farther east. Besides, the island's location in the South Atlantic, with Brazil to its west and the Cape of Good Hope to the southeast, made it a convenient stopping place for traffic between the Americas and the East.) Both residents and travelers in transit heard that Lowe's treatment of Napoleon was demeaning.

Even the Austrian and Russian commissioners who visited the island to see the conditions in which the prisoner of state was held were appalled by the manner in which Lowe followed Bathurst's instructions to the letter. Napoleon was denied access to newspapers. Books he had requested from Europe were not forthcoming. His exercise ground was curtailed, and the budget for his household was slashed, while, it was alleged, his family's correspondence was withheld from him. Slowly, these ignominious conditions of Napoleon's exile became known in England. But when Lord Holland addressed these grievances in the House of Lords, Lord Bathurst belittled them. And, in particular, he declared that no letters had been received in government quarters from any members of his family for "General Bonaparte"—except one from his brother Joseph, which had been forwarded to him.

The Bonaparte family was immediately up in arms. Madame Mère

requested that letters for her son that she had, through the medium of
an English peer, Lord Lucan, sent to England, be located. In the meantime Pauline dispatched to Lord Holland another letter for Napoleon
and a list of items that she wished to have sent out to her brother in
Saint Helena. Holland's reply came in May 1817. He was pleased to
learn that his "feeble efforts" had met with the approval of Napoleon's
relations. As for Pauline's letter to Napoleon, Lord Bathurst had assured
him that this and any subsequent communications would be sent out.
Should she write "Private" on the envelope, none but the colonial secretary would read the enclosure. Regarding the objects she had
requested, however, Bathurst had said: "Napoleon cannot need so
many things." Holland enclosed a list of what the colonial secretary had
sent out to Saint Helena the previous year. "Lady Holland has compared that with the list of items you wish me to send. We will send first
those items that are not on Lord Bathurst's list." As for the other items,
"if you think them necessary, you have only to let me know." And
there, in a very British manner, the Opposition remonstrance ended.

But Pauline did not confine herself to wooing the English—according to police authorities in Rome, at least. In those early years following
Napoleon's imprisonment on Saint Helena, there were plots aplenty to
free him—not only in Europe, but in North and even South America,
where many French "malcontents" had gone to live, following the
Bourbon restoration. It was believed that, should Napoleon only be
freed and take up residence in the Americas, he could, from there, once
more build support in France.

Every project of the Bonapartes' devising was suspect. When Lucien
Bonaparte asked permission to go with his son, Charles, to his brother
Joseph, who was living in style in Philadelphia—there was a plan afoot
to marry the boy to Joseph's daughter Zenaïde—it was refused. The
voyage was viewed as a pretext for Lucien to rouse support in America
for his brother. In Rome, Pauline and Lucien were carefully watched,
every visit to their palazzi noted by the papal, French, and Austrian
secret police. It was thought that Lucien, long a resident in Rome, performed introductions of "disaffected elements" to his sister, and that

she then supplied these dissidents with money. A visit to the Palazzo Borghese, for instance, from one Casamarte—a Corsican sailor whose mother had been the Bonapartes' wet nurse—occasioned a flood of reports. Meanwhile a Polish officer, Charles Piontkowski, who had served Napoleon in Elba, then in Saint Helena, feared to carry reports of the former emperor to his relations in Rome, believing that he would be arrested there as a spy. Pauline's annual requests to take the waters at Bagni di Lucca, although ultimately approved, resulted each summer in a flurry of speculation and conjecture about her intentions there.

In short, rumor and myth swirled about Pauline and the other Bonapartes in Rome, although on Saint Helena Napoleon himself stoutly denied that he would ever agree to leave the island, except with the concordance of the Allied powers. As a fugitive in America, he said, he would be an easy prey for a hireling's bullet that the French government would be only too glad to pay for. For her part Pauline neither encouraged nor discouraged the rumors. Her focus was still Napoleon, although her appearance, her toilette, and her health naturally continued to be matters for concern. At Bagni di Lucca, where she summered in 1818, the French foreign minister, the Duc de Richelieu, heard, "She has succeeded with the English without exception." At a ball she gave in the bathing station, wrote the duke's agent, she performed her duties as hostess with "the address of a classic courtesan." And although every winter she succumbed to bouts of ill health, in the spring she reemerged, phoenixlike, to fascinate Roman society once more. An English invalid, Henry Matthews, felt his heart beat more strongly when he saw her promenading on the Pincio hill "with a bevy of admirers; as smart and pretty a little bantam figure as can be imagined. The symmetry of her figure is very striking." Sometimes Pauline's outfit was pink, sometimes a becoming pearl gray taffeta or satin, set off by a matching bonnet trimmed with blond lace. The politics of Restoration France were not to her taste, but the Parisian dressmakers continued to supply her wants.

· · ·

As TIME PASSED it was Napoleon's health, rather than the restrictions on his liberty, that preoccupied Pauline. Reports came that he was suffering in the damp climate of Saint Helena, where liver complaints, dysentery, and inflammation of the bowel were widespread among the population and often proved fatal to Europeans. When news came that O'Meara, the surgeon on Saint Helena, had found a swelling on Napoleon's right side and diagnosed hepatitis, Madame Mère wrote— as "an afflicted mother"—to the Allied powers who were gathered at the Congress of Aix-la-Chapelle of 1818, begging them to sanction the removal of Napoleon to a healthier environment. Others, including the pope, wrote too, but the British government was adamant. Napoleon must remain where he was, and reports that the former emperor's legs were swollen and his digestion was shot to pieces did not alter that determination.

Anxious and frustrated, Pauline lost that sublime confidence in her looks that had till now distinguished her. "I confess I do not see that exquisite beauty she was so celebrated for," Lady Morgan wrote in 1819. "She is, she says, much altered, and grown thin fretting about her brother." Laure d'Abrantès, visiting Rome the previous year, observed that, beneath a necklace of large pearls, the princess's once lovely neck was grown thin. And when Laure wished to see the Canova of Pauline as Venus, the princess was impatient. Indeed, now that she had lost the perfect curves that had won her such admiration, which she had loved to display in silhouette, Pauline took against the statue that revealed them, and wrote to Camillo asking him not to allow it to be shown anymore. "The nudity of the statue approaches indecency. It was created for your pleasure. Now it no longer serves that purpose and it is right that it remains hidden from the gaze of others," she insisted. She ignored the fact that she herself had happily exhibited it to the curious until recently. The truth may have been, as she expressed it to Laure, that she suspected the motives of those who viewed the statue, then came calling on her "to inspect the ravages that sorrow has inflicted on me. . . . They are not content to poison my poor brother with suffering on Saint Helena. They wish to see me here exhibit the same symptoms."

Pauline did not come off entirely victorious in her battle with her husband. For, although the statue was put under lock and key, Camillo's steward, Gozzani, could still be persuaded to show it. And in 1820 no less a personage than the vicar-general of Rome, Cardinal Litta, addressed the prince at Pauline's behest. She was "very saddened and aggrieved," wrote Litta, that this statue was shown to foreigners, and "she was willing to do anything she could to stop the scandal." So reluctant, indeed, was the princess now to have others see her flesh made marble, Litta added, that she was even willing to reimburse the prince for its purchase price, if the offending item could be locked away. Indeed she offered to sit to Canova for another, more "respectable" statue. Camillo continued to protest that no one had access to the statue, Pauline to counterclaim that Gozzani, his steward, was open to bribery. And meanwhile every year Pauline's own flesh grew a little more lined, a little more yellow, as bilious and "putrid" fevers first contracted in Saint-Domingue, and from which she had since suffered increasingly in Europe, took their toll.

More significantly Pauline had been recently vanquished in another combat—this time with her mother and uncle. In a concession to the Bonaparte family in 1819, the Allied powers had agreed to allow a doctor, selected by Madame Mère and Cardinal Fesch, to proceed to Saint Helena. Grand Marshal Bertrand had written to Madame Mère, painting a pitiful picture of his master's health and asking for medical aid in the wake of surgeon O'Meara's departure from the island. Following numerous deaths on the island, Bertrand also asked for a cook and a steward, as well as priests to act as secretaries. To Napoleon's chagrin, however, when these gentlemen eventually arrived on the island, it transpired that the doctor, Francesco Antommarchi, was a student of anatomy and useless as a physician. Meanwhile, of the priests, Buonavita was an ignorant fellow who also suffered from palsy and whose diction, in consequence, was badly affected. The other, Vigani, was a youth and was barely trained.

In an extraordinary twist of events, under the influence of an Austrian mystic, the elderly duo, Madame Mère and Fesch, had come to believe that Napoleon was no longer on Saint Helena but had been transported to a nameless elsewhere. According to them the choice of doctor and of priest was therefore of no importance, and they blindly ignored the offer made by Foucault de Beauregard, Napoleon's former physician at the Tuileries and on Elba, to travel out to Saint Helena. Indeed Madame Mère and Fesch believed that, before Antommarchi, Buonavita, and Vigani reached Saint Helena, they would be miraculously diverted to that nameless other place where Napoleon now was.

Pauline and Louis attempted to make their mother and uncle see reason. "You cannot believe what scenes and quarrels there were," wrote Pauline, reflecting later upon the schism that developed between the older and younger generations. But it was Madame Mère and Cardinal Fesch whom the Allied powers had authorized to respond to Bertrand. Pauline and Louis had no redress. And although Napoleon, in dismal spirits, asked that companions for his exile be sought, after all, in Paris rather than in Rome, the British government considered that no further correspondence on the subject was necessary.

At least the new arrivals on Saint Helena could bring Napoleon news of his family. When Antommarchi told the former emperor that, the moment he sent word, Princess Borghese was ready to leave Rome and come to him, he replied: "Let her remain where she is. I would not have her see me insulted like this." He asked if she was still young and beautiful, and Antommarchi, to whom Pauline had given audiences at Rome, replied, "Still." "Ah, she has only ever cared for her toilette and for pleasure," said her brother.

In Rome, as if in response to the conversation on Saint Helena, Pauline had recovered her beauty. A young musician, Giovanni Pacini, encountered in the winter season at the Teatro della Valle, had reawakened in her the lust that had lain dormant during these years of exile. To the Palazzo Borghese came other musicians, among them Rossini. Pacini, in his memoirs, described the scene in fanciful prose: "Her palace was a new Olympus, where Venus did the honors." Pauline now was once more confident of her power to charm and fascinate—supremely confident, as Madame Hocheneck, a German lady, discovered when she was bidden with a Roman lady, Princess Ruspoli, to attend the princess's toilette. Upon entering, they found Pauline "in a delicious boudoir . . . casually lying on a chaise longue, with her little feet on show. . . . A page as pretty as a cupid, and dressed in a tabard, came in," records Madame Hocheneck. He "bore a silver basin, linen, perfumes, and cosmetics," and set a velvet stool beside the sofa on which the princess then placed one of her feet. While the page, kneeling, pulled down the princess's stocking—"even her garter too"—she chatted to her visitors. And as the page washed and dried and perfumed each foot, Madame Hocheneck and Princess Ruspoli—not to mention Pauline herself—admired the "truly incomparable" extremity.

But although Napoleon had declared that her toilette and pleasure were Pauline's only concerns, she was increasingly worried about his well-being. At the end of June 1821 she wrote to Lady Holland: "I have heard from Lord Gower that you are in Paris. Have you heard anything about my brother's health?" Pauline had hoped to hear, she said, from the priest who had traveled out to Saint Helena, but no reports had as yet been forthcoming. Less than two weeks later, on July 11, Pauline was paying her mother a visit in the latter's apartments that overlooked the Piazza Venezia, when she became convinced that Madame Mère was suppressing some news or information. Under questioning, her mother revealed that the Abbé Buonavita, in ill health, had returned from Saint Helena and was actually elsewhere in Madame Mère's apartments. Upon his being brought forward, Pauline found that Comte Montholon, one of Napoleon's companions, had entrusted to Buonavita, when the abbot left the island in March, a letter addressed to her. It made sad reading:

Madame, Napoleon charges me to tell you the deplorable state of his health. The liver complaint from which he has been suffering for several years, and which is endemic and fatal on the island, has made frightening progress these past six months. . . . He is extremely weak, he can barely endure a drive of half an hour, he cannot walk without help. And then his intestines are also under threat. . . . His stomach rejects all food . . . he lives on jelly. . . . He is dying without aid on a frightful rock, his agony is terrible.

For Pauline it was a clarion call to action. The same day that she extracted from Buonavita the letter that Montholon had written on March 17, she sent a copy of it to the British prime minister, Lord Liverpool. And she wrote:

In the name of all the members of his family, I beg the English government that he [Napoleon] be moved to a different climate. If that request is refused, it's a death sentence for him, and I ask permission to go and join him, and be there when he breathes his last.

Please have the goodness, milord, to authorize this, so that I can leave as soon as possible. The state of my health does not allow me to travel by land. Hence it's my intention to embark at Civitavecchia and go from there to England, where I will take the first ship for Saint Helena. However, I will need to come in to London, to procure what I will need for such a long voyage.

Pauline added: "I know Napoleon has not long to live, and I would reproach myself for ever if I had not tried by every means in my power to soften his last hours, and prove to him my devotion."

This letter was most unwelcome to Lord Liverpool and his government, who were busily combating the claims of George IV's estranged wife, Queen Caroline, to attend that monarch's coronation. (It was to take place on July 19.) They wanted nothing less than to have to combat this new potential source of disorder and disaffection. And Pauline begged Liverpool to send a copy of her letter and of the enclosure to Lady Holland, "who had always shown such an interest in Napoleon's fate." Pauline in London, en route to Saint Helena, with the backing of her Whiggish friends, could easily inflame a populace whose radical sensibilities had been whipped to fever pitch the previous year during the trial of Queen Caroline for adultery.

In the event Pauline never did go to London, and Liverpool was saved a reply. For only a few days after Pauline had written to the British prime minister news came that "General Bonaparte" had died in his bed at Saint Helena on May 5, Montholon and Antommarchi at his side, Grand Marshal Bertrand closing his eyes. At the end the former emperor's mind had roamed, and he had spoken of Josephine, of France, and of his beloved son the King of Rome, known since 1815 as the Duc de Reichstadt. Writing to her sister-in-law Hortense from Frascati in August 1821, Pauline echoed her brother, who had named in his will the "English oligarchy," or Tory government headed by Lord Liverpool, as his "assassins." "I have made a vow to receive no more of the English," she declared. "Without exception they are all butchers." Pauline was now waiting to hear with the rest of the family whether their mother's application to Lord Liverpool for Napoleon's remains to be brought back to Europe would be successful. While she was vengeful, she was also in great distress. "Dear Hortense," she wrote. "I cannot accustom myself to the idea that I will never see him again. I am in despair. Adieu. For me life has no more charm, all is finished. I embrace you." It remained to be seen how Pauline, who had for so long regarded the interests of her brother as paramount, would fare in a world without him.

CHAPTER SIXTEEN

"Great Remains of Beauty,"
1821–1825

PAULINE'S EFFORTS on her brother's behalf during the last few months of his life and before the news of his death in May reached Rome had already taxed her strength. In particular, Montholon's letter of March that the Abbé Buonavita had given her in July, deploring Napoleon's health and begging her intercession with the British government, had seen her screw her courage to the sticking point, determined not to fail the ailing ex-emperor.

The same day that she wrote to Lord Liverpool, she started writing an account of her mother's and uncle's dependence on the Austrian mystic, and of their insistence that Napoleon was no longer on Saint Helena. This was for Planat de la Faye, one of her brother's former officers, who had received permission to go out to Saint Helena and—knowing nothing of Napoleon's death—was in England readying himself for his journey. Pauline stayed up four nights in a row to complete the letter that she meant de la Faye to carry out to Napoleon, and ended with a flourish that she would see her correspondent when she herself reached Saint Helena. "In taking these steps," she wrote to Montholon, "I have consulted only my heart. . . . I trust my strength will sustain me so that I can prove to the Emperor that no one loves him so much as I do."

The shock of learning, days after she finished her missives to Planat de la Faye and to Montholon, that Napoleon was dead, confounded the princess's health and destroyed her boldness. While she had assailed the British government, had contemplated with equanimity the test of nerve that would be the journey to Saint Helena and a residence there, now she shrank from action and shunned company. When Leclerc had died, when her son Dermide had died, Pauline—the young widow and mother—had sheared her hair, prostrated herself before their graves. But after their deaths, though she carried with her that gilded funerary urn, her life had resumed its butterfly quality. She was older now, and her bereavement following Napoleon's death was of a different order. There was no rending of hair or garments. Remaining at Frascati throughout the summer months of 1821, Pauline offered to contribute to the costs of transport, should her mother's campaign to have Napoleon's body returned to Europe succeed. "Milord," wrote Letizia Bonaparte to Lord Castlereagh, "the mother of the Emperor Napoleon begs to claim from his enemies the ashes of her son." The petition went unheeded, for, following instructions received from Lord Bathurst, the colonial secretary, Governor Lowe had buried the imperial captive on Saint Helena. On this issue Pauline corresponded with her mother, but she did not visit Letizia or any others of her family in Rome. Preferring to remain alone in her desolation at Frascati, she wrote to Hortense in August of spending the winter by the sea in Genoa: "The sea air will do me good. My spirits are so oppressed, I am in need of travel."

There was now nothing to stop members of the Bonaparte clan moving freely about Europe. With the death of the great man, their surveillance by the secret police of the European powers was at an end. Now Napoleon's brothers and sisters, who had once been kings and queens, who had been suspected many times over the previous five years of playing a part in plots to rescue the deposed emperor and restore Napoleonic rule in France, were declared "sans importance," or irrelevant. Their children too, some now in their late teens and early twenties, were free to travel. Lacking either firm homeland or roots, they headed for America, where Joseph lived in style as the Comte de Survilliers. In due course marriages there were arranged for his daughters—heiresses both to the gold that Joseph had acquired when king of Spain. Zenaïde was married to Lucien's eldest son, Charles, and Charlotte to Louis's elder son, Napoléon Louis—unions that had long been contemplated by their elders and that were in keeping with the Corsican tradition of intermarriage between cousins.

Princess Borghese, however, showed no interest in joining her brother and younger members of the family in America. And indeed she did not, after all, spend the winter of 1821 in Genoa. Instead she received in Rome the companions of her late brother, who, in accordance with the instructions that Napoleon had issued before his death, came bringing news of his last moments, bearing his will, and carrying items that had been bequeathed to her in that testament and in its codicils. In August, Pauline had begged Hortense to send her any details of Napoleon's last days that she might hear from his companions who now returned to Europe, promising that she would perform the same service for her sister-in-law. That autumn she interrogated Dr. Antommarchi minutely when he reached Rome and gave an account of his imperial patient's last days, of his death, of the autopsy. "Although suffering, she still admitted me," wrote the doctor, "and wanted to know everything, understand everything. She showed the most vivid regret when she heard the outrages and agonies that Napoleon had endured."

Pauline herself later recalled just how agitated she was during this period of bereavement: "When they read his [Napoleon's] will and I heard the passage concerning me, I fell back, on the floor, as if dead." Coursot, Napoleon's valet on Saint Helena, brought her the smaller items mentioned in the will—a lock of hair, Chinese chains and necklaces, some medals made from iron ore mined on Elba. The villa of San Martino on Elba, on the other hand—complete with provincial frescoes of the emperor's Egyptian campaigns—which had been purchased with the princess's money and which Napoleon had now bequeathed her, was not a legacy of which she could expect to make much use. Nevertheless the bequest was to provide Pauline with an idea for a memorial to her life with her brother.

Slowly Pauline returned to health, and her interest in those around her quickened. Her brother on Saint Helena, barred the company of the great and grand, had amused himself with the children on the island, playing blindman's buff with one family and giving General Bertrand's daughter a bonbon box that had once been Pauline's. The princess had always been kind to children, especially, of course, members of her family. Lucien's elder daughters, who had once been playmates of Dermide, were now married, and she welcomed them with their husbands at the Villa Paolina in Rome, which continued to offer, as one visitor put it, "English neatness, French elegance and Italian taste." Lucien's teenage son Paul was something of a favorite, as was Louis and Hortense's second son, Napoléon Louis, who had been born some months after Dermide's death. By virtue of his brother's death in Holland in 1807 he was now his parents' elder son, Charles-Louis-Napoléon, the future Napoleon III, having been born in 1808.

In general, the princess's relations with all her family were good, and, with Bonaparte migration now allowed, her Murat nephews and nieces visited from Trieste, where the widowed Caroline had made her home. So there was all the more reason for the Bonaparte clan to be outraged in the winter of 1821 when Princess Borghese made a pet of a newcomer to Rome, the sixteen-year-old Jerome Bonaparte-Patterson. This young American, who had the Bonaparte "classical profile," was her brother Jérôme's son by his first marriage to the American Elizabeth Patterson—a woman whom Jérôme had divorced long before, at Napoleon's insistence, so that he could marry Princess Catherine of Württemberg. But now mother and son had traveled to Rome, following assurances from the American fur king, John Jacob Astor, who had visited the city a year earlier, that the princess would receive them.

Meanwhile Jérôme and Catherine, who had married in 1808, were still living in Trieste but had plans to move to Rome with their three young children—Jérôme, Napoléon, and Mathilde. In the circumstances Jérôme viewed his sister's reception of his son by his first marriage as an insult—to his wife, Catherine, and to himself. Indeed, as Pauline was fond of Catherine, her championing of young Jerome seems at first sight a contrary act. On the other hand Napoleon's death and his will had made a great impression on Pauline. We have the evidence of Elizabeth Patterson that, while she and her son were in Rome, the princess was engaged in making her own will. And Pauline spoke of arranging a marriage between the young man and one of her brother Lucien's daughters. Pauline, now having no use for the considerable sums of money that she had kept in reserve for Napoleon, was casting about for an heir. Just as Joseph's daughters were promised in marriage to their first cousins, thus ensuring that Lucien's and Louis's stock would share in Joseph's inheritance, so Pauline herself thought of dividing her considerable wealth and property between two branches of the family by leaving it to a Bonaparte husband and wife.

For some time in pursuit of this plan Elizabeth Patterson, a handsome brunette, and her son were to be seen everywhere with the princess—at the Palazzo Borghese, at the Villa Paolina, out in her carriage in the Pincio gardens. And then the relationship soured, and Elizabeth Patterson, returning empty-handed to America, spat venom on the subject of her erstwhile benefactor: "Every day she [Pauline] makes a new will and will end by leaving her property to complete strangers. She has quarreled with all the world, and, even to win her inheritance, no one can put up with her caprices which are so bizarre it's impossible not to think her touched with madness. All I was told about her was not a half of the truth."

Pauline was to remember her nephew Jerome in her will, but not to the tune his mother, Elizabeth, would have liked. Meanwhile, the breach apparently healed, Jérôme and Catherine concluded their move to Rome, swelling the Bonaparte numbers in the city and settling with their children into the Palazzo Núñes, close to the Pincio gardens. But from now on Pauline's relations began to wonder and speculate who would be her heir, as in Paris—before the birth of the King of Rome—they had once speculated who would inherit Napoleon's throne.

As if wishing to sharpen her relations' lust, in the new year of 1822 Pauline acquired two properties in Tuscany that, with the Villa Paolina in Rome, she would be free to leave to whomever she wished. (The apartments in the Palazzo Borghese and her residence in Frascati would, at her death, revert to the Borghese family.) The princess's relationship with Giovanni Pacini, the young singer whom she called "Nino," which had continued by fits and starts during her year of mourning her brother, prompted both purchases. Pacini had taken up a position as chapel master to Maria Luisa, the former Queen of Eturia now restored as Duchess of Lucca, in September 1821. The following summer Pauline bought from the Arnolfini family a villa on the San Quirico hill above Lucca, which she renamed Villa Paolina.

This purchase allowed her to be nearby when Pacini was occupied with his duties at the Lucca court. At the same time she began the process of having built on the shoreline at Viareggio a villa that would be shaded by a plantation of pines on the eastern front but whose loggia to the west would be open to the beach and to the sun and sea breezes. "Every week she changes residence, rents and leaves houses at Bagni di Lucca or at Viareggio," gossiped an elderly Tuscan diplomat, "while she waits for her pavilion there to rise from the ground and offer a comfortable home for next winter. . . . Her health," he added, "gives the prince great hopes that he will soon need to go into mourning."

Pacini himself had a villa at Viareggio, which explains, in part, the choice of location for this residence, which Pauline yet again named Villa Paolina. But it was also here at Viareggio that the princess had landed when she left Elba, where she had last seen Napoleon before the Hundred Days began. From her villa, when completed, she would be able to gaze across the sea at the distant bulk of Elba. Moreover, the decoration of her villa she modeled after that of the villa on Elba that her brother had left her, while adding to the Egyptian and trompe l'oeil elements of the frescoes in that villa Chinese and pastoral scenes.

At Viareggio, Pauline, bathing herself in the rays of the noonday sun she so unfashionably loved, constructed a residence where, should she so wish, she could pass her mind over her days on Elba with Napoleon and further back, to those days in the south of France with Forbin, even as far back as those childhood days in Corsica, which had ended in flight from a burning home in Ajaccio. It was, in a sense, a memorial to a past that had been always illuminated by the existence of her brother Napoleon. Few visitors came to the Villa Paolina at Viareggio to distract Pauline from her memories or from the disturbing truth that, where all had been sumptuous and gorgeous, now there were only shadows.

Pauline could, alternatively, live in the moment with Pacini—but as the months progressed the affair with him grew less satisfactory. The truth was that Pacini was not enamored of the princess, as had been her previous lovers. He was happy to stage his opera *The Slave of Baghdad* in her home, or set verses by Tasso to music for her, compose pieces for her to play on the piano or the harp. But he was the one rather to accept homage from the princess. Pauline, once the most beautiful woman of her generation, was growing older, and years of illness had marked her face. Moreover, her public bathing arrangements, her determination to dress in the latest fashion, as she had for the last twenty years, were beginning to mark her out, elegant though she still was, as odd, eccentric, even a remnant from another age. A description of her during the winter of 1822, when she inhabited apartments in the Palazzo Lanfranchi on the Arno in Pisa, bears this out. She wore, according to a young girl later to become Princess Corsini, "a white dress embroidered with gold. Her hair was curled on her forehead, a little bonnet on her head. Pale and transparent, she was like a fluttering sylphide [forest nymph], excelling in little attentions, compliments, and blandishments."

Jean-Jacques Coulmann, a young Frenchman and Bonaparte enthusiast who brought to Pauline at Pisa, at the author's request, a copy of Las Cases's *Memorial of Saint Helena,* an account of conversations with Napoleon there, was embarrassed to find Pauline still behind a screen, bathing, when he was shown in. Other gentlemen were conversing in the room, and when the princess emerged he was struck by her appearance. He wrote: "Events and emotions seemed to have used and desiccated her. Her features were still noble and regular, her eyes expressed benevolence but determination too. And her figure was still refined and symmetrical. But—her skin had yellowed and the blood seemed to have drained from her veins." Was Pauline aware that her looks had withered? She told her visitor that it was since her brother's death that she had been ill. Coulmann was nevertheless keen to converse with her and show her those passages that concerned her in the book he bore. He regarded the dialogue that followed as "a page of history."

Pauline was delighted with Napoleon's assertion, in the *Memorial,* that all the artists agreed her to be "another Venus de Medici." "Oh, as for that," she said, "I never would have claimed that. Before, I was better, it's true." Still she showed the reference with great joy to the other gentlemen present. She repudiated the story that a whole post wagon had traveled daily from Paris to Nice, when she was in the south of France, to bring her new toilettes and alterations. ("My sister is the queen of trinkets," Napoleon declared, according to Las Cases.) But she spoke with more sincerity when she declared that she had read neither the verses of Pierre-Antoine Lebrun on her brother's death nor any others. "Anything that recalls my brother upsets me," she said. Coulmann was fascinated by her and by her scorn for the Bourbon restoration. When Napoleon entered the Tuileries in March 1815, said Princess Borghese, there were "beds not made, tables not cleared. It was a stable. . . . Now we were so clean, there was order and regularity throughout, even flowers on our travels. . . . The Emperor was right to call cleanliness next to virtue. Well, the French will see the difference. Do they regret us?" she ended suddenly.

For, all the time, while Coulmann was attempting to remember her conversation for posterity, Princess Borghese had been busy on other accounts: "Bring me another bonnet. I don't want that one . . . a cashmere shawl for my shoulders. . . . I'll need a warming pan. . . . Doctor, I have a fever. . . . You're going to the Opéra, what's on this evening?" Then the page of history turned, and she swept off to bed.

Later in 1823, when Pauline was back in Rome, there appeared every chance that Prince Borghese in Florence would have the opportunity to wear mourning. Following severe and repeated bilious attacks, she was barred from going out. Her condition worsened, she took communion at Christmas—and it was not expected that she would survive into the new year. And yet she rallied again, so much so that she felt more than able to conduct a flirtation in the spring with the Duke of Devonshire. This grand bachelor Whig was in Rome with the laudable aim of commissioning pieces for a sculpture gallery he had built at Chatsworth, his Derbyshire home. He wrote in his diary after their first meeting: ". . . she is curious to see, great remains of beauty, very civil and gracious to me." Now at last was Pauline's opportunity to appear in a "respectable" pose, and well covered. After lunch in the garden of the Villa Paolina, watched by the duke and by her brother Jérôme, Thomas Campbell, sculptor, took plaster casts of the princess's hand, foot, and nose.

Eventually a reclining statue would emerge, and again much later the duke would record in his *Handbook to Chatsworth:* "She was no longer young, but retained the beauty and charm that made her brother strike the [Andrieu] medal in honour of the Sister of the Graces." At the time of his visit to Rome in 1824, however, the duke was less measured in his admiration for Pauline. His sister Lady Granville heard that he was infatuated, and remarked, "It's *assez de son genre* [quite his style] to squiddle [waste time] with a princess, and he was sure to be taken with all those little clap-traps of embroidered cushions, satin slippers, dressing-gowns of cachemire, morsels of Petrarch with which this one assails our nobility."

Pauline enjoyed the attention and entertained her noble admirer with stories of the imperial court she had once inhabited. After he escorted her to a masked ball at the house of the Russian count Demidov, she was "full of whims and childishness, but now and then very entertaining about her family, and *bellissima,*" he wrote in his diary. He ended, like all visitors to Rome, by relishing Pauline's soirees above all others on offer: ". . . party at Pss Borghese. I was presented to Jerome and his wife. . . . I waltzed with Mme de St Leu—*la reine* Hortense—a very nice person. Pauline danced opposite her in a quadrille, and I thought myself in Paris in the last reign." Upon his return to England the duke took with him as a gift a mourning bracelet that Pauline had had made when Napoleon died, and which now hid a repair to the arm of a Venus that Devonshire had bought in Rome.

But it was the Calabrian, Pacini, not the English duke, who occupied Pauline's heart. And he was proving false. While she was at the Villa Paolina at Viareggio in the summer of 1824, she heard that the composer had been nearby but had never made his presence known to her. Moreover her brother Jérôme wrote from Trieste, where Pacini had professional commitments, to say that the composer had engaged in "gallantries" there. The lies, omissions, and commissions were multiplying, and Pauline was helpless to stop them, though she had laid out considerable sums on Pacini's behalf and had even appointed his sister, Claudia, and her husband, Giorgio, as members of her household, at his request.

"Caro Nino, I write two lines to tell you I am tired and suffering," she began one of many letters in which she expostulated with her lover. "Today I have not slept . . . then Giacomo Belluomini [her Viareggio agent] told me you wanted him not to say you passed by Pescia. Why do you always lie? I don't want to hear any more lies from you, big or small. They cost you my respect. I am ill and sad to think my Nino doesn't speak the truth." But she relented: "Beloved Nino, you are on your travels, you are far from me, but it is so you can win fame and admiration. I am content with what makes you happy. . . . May God make you see that I merit from you a true proof of your affection. This is the moment to prove to me how dear I am to you. Adieu, dear Nino."

But Nino was not destined to prove his affection for the princess. His lies continued, and Pauline knew better, in the end, than to continue the flawed relationship. "I told him at the beginning that the first lie would end it all," she wrote to Belluomini, who was a friend of Pacini's:

I have pardoned him since, so many times. I am tired of being deceived by a man that I have heaped with benefits. I have taken the firm resolution to break with him and leave him to his lies and falsehoods. . . . My health is in a dangerous state, and I don't want to endure waiting two months perhaps and then risk being disappointed in my plans. In short I feel wounded to my heart, I did not expect such coldness. It is an insult he'll regret one day. Then he'll understand what he's lost. . . . I will not reply to his letters, which will be returned to him unopened. There is the decision that will let me at last be at peace.

And from now on Princess Borghese, having shed Pacini—and indeed his sister and brother-in-law—was indeed at peace, although she was not well. She had spent some time, following Pope Pius VII's death in 1823, pursuing the idea of a new settlement with Camillo in the Vatican courts, for she declared she had submitted to papal jurisdiction in 1816 only from a disinclination to trouble that benevolent churchman. Now that Leo X was pope, it occurred to her that she might wrest some extra scudi from her husband, on the ground that the 1816 settlement did not reflect adequately the arrangements for a jointure in her nuptial contact of 1803. But when Camillo declared himself ready to do battle with her before the Sacra Rota, the Vatican law court, Pauline formed a new plan. She told Camillo that she would halt her action if he increased her annual income from fourteen thousand scudi to twenty thousand.

Far from agreeing to this amiable compromise, Camillo submitted to the Rota a number of documents, including a sixty-page pro memoria in which he wrote feelingly of having been spurned, humiliated, and ignored by the princess. The auditors, or judges, of the Sacra Rota viewed with dread the prospect of intervening in the altercation but judged that the 1816 settlement should stand. At that point Pauline took to her bed and wrote a charming letter to her husband in May 1824, expressing her hope that she and he could forget their differences and once more live together. To Camillo's dismay, this was followed by a letter from the pope declaring that Princess Borghese was a sick woman and that it was a sad matter for a good Catholic, and especially for a Roman prince, to live separately from his wife. Pauline's health had indeed deteriorated, and it would seem likely that she was now suffering from liver cancer.

Camillo, knowing when he was beaten, made only one condition.

He would take in his wife, but he would have none of her "band of comedians"—by which he meant Pacini and his relations. As she had already parted with those characters, Pauline happily acceded to his condition and prepared for the journey to Florence. A disconsolate Camillo made arrangements for the Duchessa Lante and her daughters, who had moved with him from Turin into apartments in the Palazzo Borghese at Florence, to live elsewhere.

Initially Pauline and Camillo dealt extremely well together, once they had recovered from the surprise of cohabitation after so many years apart. The Palazzo Borghese, a fifteenth-century stronghold close to the Duomo, had recently been redecorated by Camillo, and its costly interiors were thick with gold—which met with Pauline's approval. Camillo's appearance was rather less appealing. If Pauline's beauty was now paper thin, the prince's good looks were almost lost under flesh and jowls so that, in profile, he resembled one of the more decadent Roman emperors on a coin. But he remained kind as ever and took his wife out on airings in his carriage. They walked arm in arm in the Cascine, the fashionable Florentine park. He invited Florentine society to receptions, concerts, and balls, and they flocked to the palace. Indeed, the reunion of the Borghese couple—so unexpected, so miraculous an event—inspired a local poet to write an ode on the subject of their matrimonial felicity.

Pauline's health, however, took a turn for the worse in the spring of 1825, and she began to fret. She grumbled that her apartments let in no noonday sun, the Prussian minister heard. But in fact the princess was at last relinquishing the tenacious hold on life that had seen her survive so many crises. Her sufferings did not abate, and she wrote to Louis in May 1825: "I am in pain and I suffer, I am reduced to a shadow. They are mending the cobbles in the street outside and the noise is frightful. I can't stay here, so the Prince is renting me a villa a mile away, where I'll spend May." In her state of health, she added, she could not think of traveling to her villa at Lucca.

The prince rented the Villa Fabbricotti up on the Montughi hill above Florence, and there Pauline was moved during the month of

May. With her went Sylvie d'Hautmesnil, a bedchamber woman who
had been with her for some years. But the princess's ailments were not
such as could respond to a change of air, or to quiet. Camillo kept an
anxious watch over her. Pauline's brothers were sent for. Jérôme arrived
at the beginning of June. Louis had not yet arrived when, in the night
of June 8, the doctors reported that the end was at hand and she should
be given the last rites. But Pauline, ill though she was, said, "I'll tell you
when I am ready. I still have some hours to live." Not until eleven the
following morning did she agree to receive the priest who had been
hovering outside. And even at the moment of communion, when the
priest wished to speak a few words, Pauline, on easy terms with the
Church to the last, stopped him and spoke herself. It was a discourse,
wrote Sylvie d'Hautmesnil, who was present, most touching in its
piety.

Matters spiritual having been so admirably and concisely dispatched, Pauline was free to attend to the material in her last precious
hours of life. Out went the priest and in came a Florentine notary and
companions, who had been summoned to take down and witness her
last earthly wishes. "These were all strangers," Sylvie d'Hautmesnil
informs us, "but the princess put them at their ease, spoke to them
charmingly and apologized for disturbing them. One would have
thought her a person in perfect health."

From her bed, dressed "as ever" with elegance, Pauline dictated the
terms of her will. It was a lengthy document, for there were many family members of whom to make mention. To Zenaïde and Charles
Bonaparte fell the Villa Paolina at Lucca. Napoléon Louis and Charlotte won the villa at Rome, and sister Caroline was left the seaside residence at Viareggio. (In addition, to Caroline passed the gilt urn
containing the embalmed hearts of Leclerc and of Dermide.) The
American Jerome gained by Pauline's will, and her nephew Paul, too,
although not his father Lucien—"for reasons," she wrote, as a child
might. But Princess Borghese was not finished. She left sums of money
to the children of her wet nurse in Ajaccio—"should they still be
living." Meanwhile Camillo's brother, Don Francesco, received the

Gérard portrait of the princess's husband. To a Luccan neighbor, the Marchesa Torrigiani, went a travel toilet mirror. And her British admirers were not forgotten. She left the Elban medals that Napoleon had bequeathed her to the Duke of Devonshire and to the Duke of Hamilton, whom she had used, when he was Marquess of Douglas, as a footstool, a magnificent traveling case filled with gold implements.

IT WAS THE CHRONICLE of a life that had ranged near and far, a life that was now nearly over. "I die in the middle of cruel and horrible sufferings," she declared, and indeed her bedchamber woman wrote that Pauline had not been free from pain for over eighty days, her liver, lungs, and stomach all causing her torment. At the end, as Napoleon had done before her, Pauline asserted that she was a good Catholic. "I die without any feelings of hatred or animosity against anyone, in the principles of the faith and doctrine of the apostolic Church, and in piety and resignation."

Having signed the will, Pauline handed the pen to Sylvie to place back on her *écritoire,* or writing desk, and the notary exited, leaving the princess to say a punctilious good-bye to the members of the household. To Sylvie, Pauline gave cool instructions about the toilette and the *parure* in which her embalmed corpse was to be attired. Apparently she called for a mirror to inspect her appearance. More certainly Pauline Borghese's last act before she died was to hand her keys—the keys securing the jewels and coffers and apartments over which they had fought so long—to the prince. Her affairs were in order, and she died at one in the afternoon on June 9, 1825. The cause of her death, like that of her father years before in Montpellier, was given as a *scirro*—or tumor—on the stomach.

A lock of hair cut from the princess's head an hour after death and preserved in Florence—in a drawer of that toilet mirror bequeathed to the Marchesa Torrigiani—is still a rich, dark chestnut color. Pauline's body, after embalming, was taken, as she had wished, to Rome and laid in its coffin in the Borghese family vault in the Basilica of Santa Maria

Maggiore. It had been a remarkable journey from the tenement house in Ajaccio, where the Bonapartes' sixth child was born in October 1780, and from the small font in the dark cathedral there, where she was baptized Maria Paoletta, to this opulent resting place. There her coffin lies to this day, in the company of the Borghese pope, Paul V, and of Cardinal Scipione Borghese, who laid out the Villa Borghese. Famous men in their day, today their renown is eclipsed by that of the parvenu princess, the Corsican cuckoo in their midst.

For many Pauline's true memorial lies in the titillating pink perfection of the Canova figure, lying seductively on that marble mattress in the Villa Borghese. Even copies of this statue can arouse admiration, and two Quaker ladies in Philadelphia were once embarrassed to stand by while Pauline's brother Joseph extolled his sister's beauties. He "stood some time perfectly enraptured before it [his copy of the statue], pointing out to us what a beautiful head Pauline had; what hair; what eyes, nose, mouth, chin, what a throat; what a neck; what arms; what a magnificent bust; what a foot—enumerating all her charms one after another, and demanding our opinion of them. Necessity made us philosophers, and we were obliged to show as much sangfroid on the subject as himself; for it was impossible to turn away without our prudery's exciting more attention than would be pleasant." How Pauline would have enjoyed both her brother's praise and the ladies' discomfiture! One can almost hear her laugh echo through the halls of Joseph's lavish mansion.

NOTES

ALL TRANSLATIONS are the author's own, unless otherwise indicated. All original text is in the language of source, whether archive or publication, unless otherwise indicated. Some of Napoleon's many bons mots come from the *New Cambridge Modern History*, vol. 9, edited by C. W. Crawley (1961), others from the great variety of biographies attached to his name.

ABBREVIATIONS

Arch. Borghese   Archivio Borghese
ASV   Archivio Segreto Vaticano, Rome
Segr. Stato   Segretaria di Stato

Chapter One / Dinner at Marseille, 1796

3   Victor Emmanuel Leclerc: Champion, *Général Leclerc*, 8; Arnault, *Souvenirs*, vol. 2, 219.

4   commonplace book, which survives him: Versini, *M. de Buonaparte*, 155.

4   in that town's archives: Saint-Maur, *Pauline Borghèse*, vol. 2, document 1.

4   less knowing than Paoletta: Napoleon, *Correspondance générale*, vol. 1, 112–13.

4   "pull up skirts than undo breeches": Marchand, *Mémoires*, 134.

4   even scribble on the walls: Larrey, *Madame Mère*, vol. 2, 529.

6   in the town garrison: Champion, *Général Leclerc*, 8.

6   that of a "Persian viceroy": Arnaud, *Fils de Fréron*, 332.

7   "he has behaved well there": Napoleon, *Correspondance générale*, vol. 1, 270; 300; 309.

7   "as Petrarch loved Laura": *Revue Rétrospective*, vol. 3, 99–100.

8   taught her—to other lovers: d'Abrantès, *Mémoires*, vol. 14, 311–12.

9   "to smooth all obstacles": *Revue Rétrospective*, vol. 3, 101; 108–9.

10   to have no occupation: Napoleon, *Correspondance générale*, vol. 1, 272.

10   "No money, no match": d'Abrantès, *Mémoires*, vol. 1, 251.

11   "when I present her": *Revue Rétrospective*, vol. 3, 101.

12   garrison commander at Marseille: Napoleon, *Correspondance générale*, vol. 1, 299.

12 commendation from de la Poype: Champion, *Général Leclerc,* 3–8.

13 "Tell my brother": Napoleon, *Correspondance générale,* vol. 1, 423; 465; 397.

14 "masters of all Lombardy": Napoleon, *Correspondance générale,* vol. 1, 397–98; 400.

17 "P.B.'s every day": *Revue Rétrospective,* vol. 3, 102–9.

18 "amo, si amatissimo amante": Ibid., 106–7.

18 Italian headquarters at Milan: Napoleon, *Correspondance générale,* vol. 1, 698.

Chapter Two / Garrison Bride, 1797–1798

19 "the Army of Italy": someone said. Arnault, *Souvenirs,* vol. 2, 334.

20 "lose themselves in pleasure": Napoleon, *Correspondance générale,* vol. 1, 914.

20 The envoy of Pauline's brother: Champion, *Général Leclerc,* 9; Fonds Masson, box 67, 3.

21 had added to her attractions: Arnault, *Souvenirs,* vol. 2, 335.

22 "at Milan in a fortnight": Napoleon, *Correspondance générale,* vol. 1, 698–99; 705.

23 their own execution: Arnault, *Souvenirs,* vol. 3, 12.

24 from Pontoise on February 22: Fonds Masson, box 67, 3.

25 "the right thing only by caprice": Arnault, *Souvenirs,* vol. 3, 30; 34–35.

25 a contemporary, the Duchesse d'Abrantès, put it: d'Abrantès, *Mémoires,* vol. 9, 106.

26 the nuptial benediction was given: Fonds Masson, box 67, 4–5 (Italian).

26 "unlimited confidence in our destinies": Marmont, *Mémoires,* vol. 1, 296.

26 "the blond Bonaparte" as a compliment: Thiébault, *Mémoires,* vol. 3, 201.

26 "get rid of this one too": Arnault, *Souvenirs,* vol. 3, 33–34.

26 the Bonaparte family property: Champion, *Général Leclerc,* 9.

27 "not much bigger than a lentil": Arnault, *Souvenirs,* vol. 3, 338–39.

28 in the Palazzo Graziani: Fonds Masson, box 67, 6–9.

28 "I would have to have you with me": Champion, *Général Leclerc,* 10, n. 40.

29 an Austrian archduke had been born: Frédéric Masson, in Masson, *Napoléon et Sa Famille,* vol. 1, 230.

29 and Guastalla, for 160,000 francs: Fonds Masson, box 67, 205–52.

29 he was transferred to Paris: Fonds de Blocqueville, album C, 429.

29 "around us wherever we went": Reinhard, *Une Femme de diplomate,* 13.

Chapter Three / Madame Leclerc in Paris, 1798–1799

30 who commanded the Army of England: Champion, *Général Leclerc,* 9.

31 calling them "Poulot" and "Poulotte": Cornuau, *Correspondance,* 28.

31 "put off the party till six": Ibid.; 42.

32 the *diligence,* the public coach service: Fonds de Blocqueville, album A, 173 ff.; 139.

32 had been dictated by herself: Cornuau, *Correspondance*, 43–45.

33 "did not know how to read or write": Fleuriot de l'Angle, *La Paolina*, 52.

33 "improving," he wrote in 1801: Fonds de Blocqueville, album A, 115.

37 "You are quite deluded": d'Abrantès, *Mémoires:* vol. 2, 215; 211–20.

37 "an affection tender but chaste": Cornuau, *Correspondance*, 28.

39 not so long before: d'Abrantès, *Mémoires*, vol. 2, 333; 314–15; 261.

40 to continue their relationship: Ibid., 319, 325, n. 1; vol. 19, 282.

42 "c'est l'ordre du général": Furet and Richet, *La Révolution*, 332.

43 within hours as first consul: d'Abrantès, *Mémoires,* vol. 2, 338.

Chapter Four / Sister to the First Consul, 1800–1802

45 she said firmly. "Quite different": d'Abrantès, *Mémoires,* vol. 3, 333–34.

46 four hundred were dead and six hundred taken prisoner: Forges, *Général Leclerc*, 13–14.

46 and indulgent toward others: Fonds de Blocqueville, album C, 1.

46 "but that the first consul would": d'Abrantès, *Mémoires,* vol. 6, 82.

47 Leclerc was to declare: Hardy, *Correspondance*, 205–10

47 to support her pelvis: Fonds de Blocqueville, album A, 225.

48 "with your big stomach?": Cornuau, *Correspondance*, 42.

49 a name for himself in Paris: Fonds de Blocqueville, album A, 189, 193, 197, 179.

49 that he could do no more: Ibid., 177.

50 "as a servant girl," she wrote: Cornuau, *Correspondance*, 43.

50 "now you must wake up": George, *Mémoires*, 17.

50 "once they have finished planting": Fonds Masson, box 67, 20.

50 a swing in the garden: Fleuriot de L'Angle, *La Paolina*, 57.

51 "let you come to Paris": Fonds de Blocqueville, album C, 69.

51 "even in his place": Champion, *Général Leclerc*, 13

52 "five centuries behind France": Fonds de Blocqueville, album A, 105; 115.

52 "I will be obliged to you": Masson, *Napoléon et Sa Famille*, vol. 2, 33–34.

52 "the vines we planted": Fonds de Blocqueville, album A, 213; 179.

53 "who are so dear to me": Ibid., 123.

53 "to the most senior general": Napoleon, *Correspondance générale*, vol. 3, 802–3.

56 "said Leclerc, extending his hand": Norvins, *Souvenirs*, vol. 2, 305–6.

56 military career out there: Fonds de Blocqueville, album A, 97.

56 Hardy wrote optimistically to his wife: Hardy, *Correspondance*, 259.

56 "appointed at the last minute": Hohl, "Papiers du Général Leclerc," 179.

58 "Oh," said Pauline. "So you are": d'Abrantès, *Mémoires*, vol. 6, 64ff.

58 their property on death: Fonds de Blocqueville, album A, 147.

58 had property in Saint-Domingue: Saint-Maur, *Pauline Bonaparte*, vol. 2, document 12.

58 this prime command: Nabonne, *Pauline Bonaparte*, 70.

59 "All France is come to Saint-Domingue": Hardy, *Correspondance*, 266, n. 1.

Chapter Five / Expedition to Haiti, 1802

60 were nearly as lucrative: Smith, *Wealth of Nations,* 450.

62 "aware of the destruction": Norvins, *Souvenirs,* vol. 2, 348–49.

62 the ominous red clouds: Hardy, *Correspondance,* 268ff.

63 would be a crime: Tulard, "Général Leclerc," 147.

63 a June day in France: Hardy, *Correspondance,* 271.

64 "recovered her spirits": Roussier, *Lettres du Général Leclerc,* 116.

64 "my brother's private guard": Bro, *Mémoires,* 10.

64 "to return to France": Roussier, *Lettres du Général Leclerc,* 114; 116–17.

64 "I have seen in my life": Champion, *Général Leclerc,* 30.

65 had perverted its cause: James, *Black Jacobins,* 257–58.

65 "whom they intended to kill": Champion, *Général Leclerc,* 33–34.

65 native to the colony: Descourtilz, *Voyage d'un naturaliste,* 31ff.

66 "to the town's renaissance": Norvins, *Souvenirs,* vol. 2, 387

66 "fine and brilliant": Roussier, *Lettres du Général Leclerc,* 145.

66 was like beef: Ibid., 148.

66 "not those of nature?": Descourtilz, *Voyage d'un naturaliste,* 40.

67 "to regain it," he warned: Champion, *Général Leclerc,* 34.

67 Madame Hardy at home: Hardy, *Correspondance,* 288.

67 "Apollo of the French army": Blond, *Pauline Bonaparte,* 82.

67 "the ardor of her passions": Pasquier, *Histoire de mon temps,* vol. 1, 403.

67 to see which she preferred: Barras, *Mémoires,* vol. 4, 191.

68 "in love and tender friendship": Napoleon, *Correspondance générale,* vol. 3, 934; 1012.

69 Davout on May 8: Champion, *Général Leclerc,* 45.

69 infuriated and alarmed the French: Norvins, *Souvenirs,* vol. 2, 398.

71 "when we had them dance": Ibid., 389–92.

71 "its roots are numerous and deep": James, *Black Jacobins,* 271.

71 "once more in combustion": Roussier, *Lettres du Général Leclerc,* 183.

72 "five of my aides-de-camp": Hohl, "Papiers du Général Leclerc," 183.

72 "death emptied them," wrote Norvins: Norvins, *Souvenirs,* vol. 2, 398.

72 "and still isn't discouraged": Roussier, *Lettres du Général Leclerc,* 181.

72 "warriors of the army of Saint-Domingue": Hohl, "Papiers du Général Leclerc," 180.

73 "heading for Saint-Domingue,": Napoleon told him: Roussier, *Lettres du Général Leclerc,* 305–6.

73 "have to change their tune": Hohl, "Papiers du Général Leclerc," 180.

73 at a picturesque spot: Fonds de Blocqueville, album A, 243; 247; 239.

74 "no longer fatal in that season": Champion, *Général Leclerc,* 38–39.

74 victim to yellow fever: Hohl, "Papiers du Général Leclerc," 183.

74 "indeed agreeable for me": Roussier, *Lettres du Général Leclerc,* 190–91.

Chapter Six / Pestilential Climate, 1802–1803

75 "but licentiousness operates": Roussier, *Lettres du Général Leclerc*, 190; 182.

75 massacre of all the Europeans: Tulard, "Général Leclerc," 151.

76 linked, was already dead: Champion, *Général Leclerc*, 39–40.

76 "you will never get it back": Tulard, "Général Leclerc," 152.

77 over which they bent: Norvins, *Souvenirs*, vol. 3, 7.

78 " 'I don't want to go anymore' ": Norvins, *Souvenirs*, vol. 3, 22ff.

78 butterflies of the island with a net: Ibid., vol. 3, 10.

78 "from the reality": Champion, *Général Leclerc*, 41–42.

78 "easily heated in winter": Hohl, "Papiers du Général Leclerc," 183.

79 the parrots and monkeys: Norvins, *Souvenirs*, vol. 3, 25.

79 "I will go down to Le Cap": Cornuau, *Correspondance*, 44.

81 determination of a Spartan woman: Norvins, *Souvenirs*, vol. 3, 36ff.

81 "my men whom the yellow fever spares": Hohl, "Papiers du Général Leclerc," 181.

81 "since I have been in this country": Roussier, *Lettres du Général Leclerc*, 239.

82 "well worthy to be your sister": Ibid., 256; 230; 260.

82 "imprinted on history": Napoleon, *Correspondance générale*, vol. 3, 1168–69.

82 their immediate entourage: Fonds de Blocqueville, album A, 259.

83 "the general had suffered": Roussier, *Lettres du Général Leclerc*, 36.

84 "My father is dead!": Norvins, *Souvenirs*, vol. 3, 43.

84 "her son will inherit his virtues": Dupâquier, "Pauline Bonaparte," 172.

84 "gauge of her conjugal love": Fonds de Blocqueville, album C, 371.

84 "Pauline, who is truly unhappy": Masson, *Napoléon et Sa Famille*, vol. 2, 231.

85 may not have pleased Leclerc's mother: Fonds de Blocqueville, album C, 374.

85 David and Jonathan: Champion, *Général Leclerc*, 24, n. 98.

87 "consolation for your unhappiness": Napoleon, *Correspondance générale*, vol. 4, 22.

88 "what I wanted, which was three hundred thousand francs": Norvins, *Souvenirs*, vol. 3, 67; 69–70.

Chapter Seven / Union with a Roman Prince, 1803

91 "I will kill myself": d'Abrantès, *Mémoires*, vol. 7, 207.

91 (. . . of long standing): Masson, *Napoléon et Sa Famille*, vol. 2, 241.

92 her first encounter with the prince: d'Abrantès, *Mémoires*, vol. 7, 208.

93 anyone more demanding in Paris: Masson, *Napoléon et Sa Famille*, vol. 2, 245

95 "the happiest of his life": Angiolini, *Correspondance*, 50–51.

95 "to ask for her hand": Masson, *Napoléon et Sa Famille*, vol. 2, 251–52.

96 remarrying so quickly: Saint-Maur, *Pauline Borghèse*, vol. 1, 21.

96 "the first family in Rome": Angiolini, *Correspondance*, 75, n. 1.

96   "from her head to her toes she is all Roman": Larrey, *Madame Mère*, vol. 1, 335.

97   "suffer a little longer": Angiolini, *Correspondance*, 67; 81; 85.

98   joint guardians to the child: Fonds Masson, box 67, 12–18.

99   "all the jewels of the Borghese house": Saint-Maur, *Pauline Borghèse*, vol. 1, 20ff.

99   "I am a princess, a real princess": d'Abrantès, *Mémoires*, vol. 7, 209–210.

99   the design that had attracted such attention: Saint-Maur, *Pauline Borghèse*, vol. 1, 20ff.

100   "I love you": Napoleon, *Correspondance générale*, vol. 4, 439.

100   But she had to admire his spirit: Saint-Maur, *Pauline Borghèse*, vol. 1, 23–25.

101   until the dress she required had arrived from Paris: Cornuau, *Correspondance*, 44.

101   his brother and his new wife: Saint-Maur, *Pauline Borghèse*, vol. 1, 46–48.

102   as he told Angiolini in March 1804: Angiolini, *Correspondance*, 92.

102   "meet again soon in France": Masson, *Napoléon et Sa Famille*, vol. 2, 406.

102   "neither force nor a show of authority will deter them": Angiolini, *Correspondance*, 93; 95.

103   women in Paris lived differently: Napoleon, *Correspondance générale*, vol. 4: 666; 668.

104   momentous news came from Paris in May: Angiolini, *Correspondance*, 96.

104   "harsh words between him and my brother": Saint-Maur, *Pauline Borghèse*, vol. 1, 80–81.

Chapter Eight / Bitter Summer, 1804

106   "it is more important to be good and esteemed": Napoleon, *Correspondance générale*, vol. 4, 668.

107   "on lions at the Farnesina": Chateaubriand, *Mémoires d'Outre-Tombe*, vol. 1, 856; vol. 2, 1990–91.

107   "advantages of nature": Saint-Maur, *Pauline Borghèse*, vol. 1, 44.

107   "created for your pleasure": *Venere Vincitrice*, 125.

109   "Every veil must fall before Canova": Chastenet, *Pauline Bonaparte*, 109.

109   "He looks more belligerent than pacific": Angeli, *I Bonaparte a Roma*, 90.

111   claimed to have won Letizia's approval: Cornuau, *Correspondance*, 45.

111   "my accusers play false": Saint-Maur, *Pauline Borghèse*, vol. 1, 43–44.

112   she ended as usual: Fonds Masson, box 68, 33–34.

112   "to see the princess undressed": Saint-Maur, *Pauline Borghèse*, vol. 1, 93; 126; 93–94.

113   marshal of the Empire and governor of Paris: Murat, *Lettres*, vol. 3, 142.

113   "the greatest honors possible": Kühn, *Pauline Bonaparte*, 95, n. 1.

114   "give dinners continually, and often balls": Angiolini, *Correspondance*, 105–6.

115   "with all economy possible": Cornuau, *Correspondance*, 46

115 a "more or less sweet tête-à-tête": Saint-Maur, *Pauline Borghèse,* vol. 1, 94.

116 "I cannot live without him": Cornuau, *Correspondance,* 46.

119 her son's last days: Saint-Maur, *Pauline Borghèse,* vol. 1, 96–101.

119 "this terrible blow": Cornuau, *Correspondance,* 46.

120 agreed to everything: Saint-Maur, *Pauline Borghèse,* vol. 1, 102–4.

120 "until after the coronation": Cornuau, *Correspondance,* 46–47.

123 in the first week of December: Saint-Maur, *Pauline Borghèse,* vol. 1, 127; 137–40; 143.

Chapter Nine / The Borgheses at War, 1804–1807

126 licensed to satisfy "every fantasy": Rémusat, *Mémoires,* vol. 1, 203–5.

126 "as it is possible to be": Metternich, *Mémoires,* vol. 1, 312.

127 "the patrimony of our father the king": d'Abrantès, *Mémoires,* vol. 9, 99.

129 might not have wholly concurred: Larrey, *Madame Mère,* vol. 2, 364.

130 "always in the same manner": Angiolini, *Correspondance,* 124.

130 "you must live to a great age": [Stewarton?], *Female Revolutionary Plutarch,* vol. 3, 200–201.

131 (. . . a further layer of jewelry): Rémusat, *Mémoires,* vol. 2, 347–48.

131 the insufficient food and drink: d'Abrantès, *Histoire des Salons,* vol. 6, 281.

133 "I don't recall": Dumas, *Mes Mémoires,* vol. 1, 152–54.

134 "I would have come to Paris": Angiolini, *Correspondance,* 146.

135 "I never doubted his aptitude": Murat, *Lettres,* vol. 4, 2.

135 "devour" it: Angiolini, *Correspondance,* 155.

135 "I have just received letters from him": Kühn, *Pauline Bonaparte,* 109.

135 "shut, even to her mother": Angiolini, *Correspondance,* 159.

135 "monotonous life that doesn't suit me": Murat, *Lettres,* vol. 4, 164.

136 "and forgets us all": Hortense, *Mémoires,* vol. 1, 237.

137 styling her husband "His Serene Idiot": [Goldsmith?], *Court of St. Cloud,* vol. 2, 131.

138 "such liberties are permitted": [Goldsmith?], *Secret History, Cabinet of Bonaparte,* 494.

138 "You always go too far," Napoleon replied: [Goldsmith?], *Court of St. Cloud,* vol. 2, 131–132.

138 one of his wife's ladies in revenge: Masson, "La Princesse Pauline," 799.

139 wrote a lady at court: Ducrest, *Mémoires,* vol. 2, 26.

139 "material for lengthy discussion": Potocka, *Mémoires,* 209.

Chapter Ten / Messalina of the Empire, 1807

141 pervaded by the smell of sour milk for months to come: Stiegler, *Récits de guerre,* 77–78.

141 a "little red sea": Napoleon, *Lettres à Josephine*, 279–80.

142 specifically her fallopian tubes: Parlange, *Étude médico-psychologique*, 67.

142 "she had to be carried everywhere": Barras, *Mémoires*, vol. 4, 191–92.

143 she rushed again from the room: Favre, *Les confidences d'un vieux palais*, 215–17.

143 "At length she acknowledged it": Morris, *Diary and Letters*, vol. 2, 491–92.

145 "increases greatly my chagrin": Masson, "La Princesse Pauline," 803.

146 "the class into which he had risen": Crawley, *New Cambridge History*, vol. 9, 321.

148 "his pretty white horses": Masson, *Napoléon et Sa Famille*, vol. 3, 343.

149 "Violets look terrible in black hair": d'Abrantès, *Histoire des Salons*, vol. 6, 285–88.

151 "be open with me when you reply": Kühn, *Pauline Bonaparte*, 117–18.

152 "in front of her in Paris": Masson, *Napoléon et Sa Famille*, vol. 4, 429–33.

153 "a pretty gauze muslin to your taste": Cornuau, *Correspondance*, 48.

153 his expenditure was for nothing: Laflandre-Linden, *Les Bonaparte en Provence*, 147–48.

154 "a way to water the route": Thibaudeau, *Mémoires*, 223–24.

154 "and agitate me a little": Cornuau, *Correspondance*, 48.

155 "I would never have authorized it": Masson, *Napoléon et Sa Famille*, vol. 4, 430–35.

Chapter Eleven / Southern Belle, 1807–1808

158 a punishment she would remember: Thibaudeau, *Mémoires*, 224–27.

159 (. . . his stomach as a footrest): Barras, *Mémoires*, vol. 4, 192.

161 "other women under her feet": Nadaillac, *Mémoires*, 305; 199–201.

163 "'spent two days with us'": Blangini, *Souvenirs*, 138–50.

164 and four equerries: Fonds Masson, box 68, 61ff.

165 *à la cosaque* for airings: Masson, *Napoléon et Sa Famille*, vol. 4, 443.

166 prove equally biddable in Turin: Constant, *Mémoires sur la vie de Napoléon*, vol. 6, 245–59.

167 for Rome as Camillo's bride: Masson, *Napoléon et Sa Famille*, vol. 4, 444.

167 "vive le prince, vive la princesse!": Constant, *Mémoires sur la vie de Napoléon*, vol. 6, 280–85.

169 "nothing other than the wish for Paris": Masson, *Napoléon et Sa Famille*, vol. 4, 444–46.

Chapter Twelve / Agent for Divorce, 1808–1812

170 "after his return from Germany": Masson, *Napoléon et Sa Famille*, vol. 4, 447.

171 "in the name of France": Caulaincourt, *Mémoires*, vol. 1, 274.

173 "her sole occupation was pleasure": Metternich, *Mémoires*, vol. 1, 312.

173 "the pleasure of being beautiful": de Girardin, *Journal et souvenirs*, vol. 4, 383.

173 Clary slyly adds: Clary, *Trois mois à Paris*, 301; 222

174 "in going there, despite her beauty": Kühn, *Pauline Bonaparte*, 159–61, quoting Friedrich, *40 Jahren aus dem Leben eines Toten*, 3 vols. (Tübingen, 1848–49).

176 "a distraction from the divorce": Hortense, *Mémoires*, vol. 2, 42–43.

176 attended all the *cercles*: Murat, *Lettres*, vol. 6, 514.

177 "arranges the rendezvous for His Majesty": de Girardin, *Journal et Souvenirs*, vol. 4, 339.

177 "Tell Madame de M. to await me": Cornuau, *Correspondance*, 30–41.

177 her beloved Malmaison: Hortense, *Mémoires*, vol. 2, 43–55.

178 "sweetness and contentment, not headaches": Cornuau, *Correspondance*, 38.

179 "had to pick it up again": Clary, *Trois Mois à Paris*, 78–80.

179 "economize on the details": Kühn, *Pauline Bonaparte*, 159.

180 "' . . . for the rabble,'" wrote de Girardin: de Girardin, *Journal et Souvenirs*, vol. 4, 390–91.

182 "sent to Russia": Ducrest, *Mémoires*, vol. 2, 23–26.

182 sighs to make the candles gutter: Thiébault, *Mémoires*, vol. 4, 443.

183 "He can still dance": Kühn, *Pauline Bonaparte*, 169–70.

183 a letter meant for Napoleon's eyes: Ibid., 180.

185 the reflected face of "France": d'Abrantès, *Mémoires*, vol. 14, 186.

185 "to do anything of the kind": Hortense, *Mémoires*, vol. 2, 139–40.

Chapter Thirteen / Survival, 1812–1814

187 "and Angélique [from *Le Malade imaginaire*]: d'Abrantès, *Mémoires*, xiv, 262.

188 "uncertainty that destroys me": Cornuau, *Correspondance*, 17; 13.

190 "a good drubbing": Cornuau, *Correspondance*, 12; 19.

191 "From your oldest friend at Aix": d'Abrantès, *Mémoires*, vol. 14, 293–301.

191 "to beg you for more": Fleuriot de l'Angle, *La Paolina*, 204, quoting original letter then in possession of Comte de Meribel.

192 (. . . featured as a matter of course): Parlange, *Étude médico-psychologique*, 70.

193 in very histrionic fashion: d'Abrantès, *Mémoires*, vol. 14, 310–11.

194 "find no more on earth . . .": Petrarca, *Rime, Trionfi e Poesie Latine*, 359; 388.

194 "So I have restrained myself": *Lettres d'Amour de Talma*, 69–70.

195 brilliants, that depicted the princess: Ducrest, *Mémoires*, vol. 2, 26–27.

196 "and her health is altered": Masson, *Napoléon et Sa Famille*, vol. 7, 381–82.

196 "the stones I bought from Picot": Fonds Masson, box 69, 493.

197 "what you've read in the *Moniteur*": Cornuau, *Correspondance*, 5.

197 "announced later to the nation": Caulaincourt, *Mémoires*, vol. 2, 193.

198 "to commemorate the emperor's coronation": Cornuau, *Correspondance*, 21.

198 "but I shall yet recoup": Caulaincourt, *Mémoires*, vol. 2, 373.

198 "trace of fatigue on his face": Cornuau, *Correspondance*, 26.

198 "those who had died in Russia": Fezensac, *Souvenirs Militaires*, 356.

199 "It is the beginning of the end": Harris, *Talleyrand: Betrayer and Saviour*, 387, n. 10.

199 "the owner wants 100,200 francs": Cornuau, *Correspondance*, 9.

200 "attending the Carnival entertainments": Masson, *Napoléon et Sa Famille*, vol. 8, 335.

200 departure for the theater of war: Cornuau, *Correspondance*, 25.

200 of the house in Paris: Masson, *Napoléon et Sa Famille*, vol. 8, 330–31.

200 "solid and stable peace ensue": Cornuau, *Correspondance*, 9.

201 "I will spend the winter": Ibid., 49.

202 "offered 300,000 francs to the Emperor": Kühn, *Pauline Bonaparte*, 205.

202 "fire cannons to please her": Masson, *Napoléon et Sa Famille*, vol. 8, 350; 354; 359.

203 "I don't want any confusion": Ibid., vol. 10, 72.

204 "They have betrayed me": Napoleon, *Lettres à Josephine*, 400–401.

204 "follow him to Elba": Masson, *Napoléon et Sa Famille*, vol. 10, 76; 78.

205 she tenderly caressed him: d'Abrantès, *Mémoires*, vol. 18, 246.

206 "in need of everything": Cornuau, *Correspondance*, 49.

Chapter Fourteen / Diamonds on the Battlefield, 1814–1815

207 to precede her to the island: Masson, *Napoléon et Sa Famille*, vol. 10, 328.

207 "an act of gross treachery": Kühn, *Pauline Bonaparte*, 215.

209 "useful to me," Pauline wrote: Cornuau, *Correspondance*, 50.

209 adopt the guise of "comforting angel": Pons de l'Hérault, *Souvenirs*, 238.

209 "given no sign of life": Masson, *Napoléon et Sa Famille*, vol. 10, 316–17.

210 installed in the Palazzo Borghese: Corsini, *I Bonaparte a Firenze*, 214.

210 graced her dining room in Paris: Masson, *Napoléon et Sa Famille*, vol. 10, 318–19.

211 trounced Napoleon's forces in Spain: Longford, *Wellington: Years of the Sword*, 369.

211 a detailed inventory—and stables: Ronfort and Augarde, *À l'ombre de Pauline*, 21.

212 "heartless little devil": Longford, *Wellington: Years of the Sword*, 383.

212 "resigned to his retreat": Campbell, *Diary*, 130.

212 "one hadn't left France": Cornuau, *Correspondance*, 51.

213 "if it gives him pleasure": Pons de l'Hérault, *Souvenirs*, 238.

214 in the garden that morning: Ibid., 241–42.

214 a woman in her thirties: Mameluck Ali, *Souvenirs*, 64–65.

215 "anxious for the future": Kühn, *Pauline Bonaparte*, 226.

215 "and in his resurrection": Longford, *Wellington: Years of the Sword*, 378.

215 "all who approached her": Pons de l'Hérault, *Souvenirs*, 238.

216 ever see Napoleon again: Marchand, *Mémoires*, 155–56.

216 "and sister to your protection": Campbell, *Diary*, 183, n. 89.

217 "Send me news": Pons de l'Hérault, *Mémoire*, 118–19.

218 "a smile upon her face": Campbell, *Diary*, 184–85.

219 their contact was minimal: Sforza, "Pauline Bonaparte a Compignano," 150.

219 "she refuses to have back anyone who left her": Masson, *Napoléon et Sa Famille*, vol. 12, 78.

221 Pauline remained energetic: Ibid., 81.

222 life on Saint Helena: Constant, *Mémoires intimes*, vol. 1, 206–08; Marchand, *Mémoires*, 225.

Chapter Fifteen / Plots and Plans, 1815–1821

223 in October 1815, to Pius VII: ASV, Segr. Stato, Interni, packet 565, bundle 9, letter of Oct. 18, 1815, "Beatissimo Padre."

224 a royalist minion had written in the margin: O'Meara, *Napoleon in Exile*, vol. 1, 225.

225 "differences between the prince and me": ASV, Segr. Stato, Interni, packet 565, bundle 9, letter of Oct. 18, 1815, "Beatissimo Padre."

225 "doing her great injury": Borghetti, "Davanti alla Sacra Rota," 103.

225 "entry to her husband's house": ASV, Segr. Stato, Interni, packet 565, bundle 9, letter of Jan. 10, 1816, "Monsignor, la position pénible."

226 "not make each other unhappy": ASV, Segr. Stato, Interni, packet 565, bundle 9, "Pro Memoria per il Principe Borghese."

226 and live together once more: Kühn, *Pauline Bonaparte*, 243.

226 an arrangement with the prince: Fonds Masson, box 70, 227.

227 "a most uncommon woman": Ticknor, *Life, Letters, Journals*, vol. 1, 181–82.

227 "the sheets French cambric, embroidered": Morgan, *Memoirs*, vol. 2, 122–23, 129–30.

228 "the finest in Rome": Guerrini, *Paolina*, 526–27.

229 "by cardinals as la belle Pauline": Morgan, *Italy*, vol. 2, 418, n.; vol. 3, 51.

229 "a few enemies the less": Masson, *Napoléon et Sa Famille*, vol. 13, 266.

229 "treat his assassins": Kühn, *Pauline Bonaparte*, 247.

229 "frequenting the Bonapartes in Rome": Masson, *Napoléon et Sa Famille*, vol. 12, 286.

229 "cementing or destroying friendships": Shelley, *Diary*, vol. 1, 359.

230 "it never had a shoe on": Granville, *Letters*, vol. 1, 111–13.

230 "most generous of my enemies": Napoleon, *Correspondance publié par ordre de Napoléon III*, vol. 28, 348.

232 "you have only to let me know": ASV, Segr. Stato, Interni, packet 565, bundle 9, letter of May 19, 1817, "Je suis extrémement flatté."

233 her intentions there: Ibid., bundle 1; police report, Apr. 30, 1817; bundle 9, passim.

233 "a classic courtesan": Fleuriot de l'Angle, *La Paolina*, 271.

233 "her figure is very striking": Matthews, *Diary of an Invalid,* 127–28.

234 a healthier environment: Larrey, *Madame Mère,* vol. 2, 183.

234 "fretting about her brother": Morgan, *Memoirs,* vol. 2, 252.

234 "from the gaze of others," she insisted: *Venere Vincitrice,* 125, n. 13.

234 "exhibit the same symptoms": Kühn, *Pauline Bonaparte,* 249.

235 another, more "respectable" statue: ASV, Arch. Borghese, packet 346, "1820. Posizione concernente la statua fatta da Canova,"; letter of Jan. 17, 1820, "Eccellenza, da qualche tempo."

236 the older and younger generations: Planat de la Faye, *Rome et Sainte-Hélène,* 21.

236 "for pleasure," said her brother: Antommarchi, *Derniers Moments,* vol. 1, 70.

236 "where Venus did the honors": Pacini, *Memorie,* 23.

237 the "truly incomparable" extremity: Montet, *Souvenirs,* 400–401.

237 "anything about my brother's health?": Holland, *Foreign Reminiscences,* 340–41 (French).

238 "his agony is terrible": Antommarchi, *Derniers Moments,* vol. 2, 205–6.

238 "prove to him my devotion": Ibid., vol. 2, 207–8.

239 "all is finished. I embrace you": Guerrini, *Paolina,* 542–43 (French).

Chapter Sixteen / *"Great Remains of Beauty," 1821–1825*

240 "no one loves him so much as I do": Montholon, Comtesse de, *Souvenirs,* 222–23.

241 "the ashes of her son": Larrey, *Madame Mère,* vol. 2, 266.

241 "I am in need of travel": Guerrini, *Paolina,* 542 (French).

242 "agonies that Napoleon had endured": Antommarchi, *Derniers Moments,* vol. 2, 148.

242 "on the floor, as if dead": Coulmann, *Réminiscences,* vol. 2, 200.

243 "French elegance and Italian taste": Morgan, *Italy,* vol. 2, 418.

245 "to go into mourning": Kühn, *Pauline Bonaparte,* 261–64.

246 "compliments, and blandishments": Silvagni, *La corte e la società romana,* vol. 3, 65–66.

247 she swept off to bed: Coulmann, *Réminiscences,* vol. 2, 198ff.

248 "very civil and gracious to me": Devonshire Collection, Sixth Duke's Papers, Diary transcript, Feb. 15, 1824.

248 "the Sister of the Graces": Devonshire, *Handbook to Chatsworth,* 92–93.

248 "this one assails our nobility": Granville, *Letters,* vol. 1, 267.

248 "in Paris in the last reign": Devonshire Collection, Sixth Duke's Papers, Diary transcript, Feb. 26, 1824; Feb. 19, 1824.

249 "Adieu, dear Nino": Lazzareschi, *Paolina,* 241–43.

250 "at last be at peace": Campetti, "Lettere di Paolina Bonaparte," 74–75 (French).

250 ignored by the princess: Lumbroso, *Miscellanea Napoleonica,* vol. 5, lxxiv–lxxxiv.

251 Pacini and his relations: Chastenet, *Pauline Bonaparte,* vol. 5, 234.

251 their matrimonial felicity: Gorgone, "Paolina Bonaparte, principessa inquieta," 22.

251 the Prussian minister heard: Kühn, *Pauline Bonaparte,* 277.

251 traveling to her villa at Lucca: Guerrini, *Paolina,* 544 (French).

252 dictated the terms of her will: Fonds Masson, box 70, 285–87.

252 (. . . of Leclerc and of Dermide): Fonds de Blocqueville, Campan Correspondence, letters of 1834.

253 "in piety and resignation": Guerrini, *Paolina,* 548–64.

253 so long—to the prince: Fonds Masson, Box 70, 285–88.

253 a *scirro*—or tumor—on the stomach: Gorgone, "Paolina Bonaparte, principessa inquieta," 24.

253 rich, dark chestnut color: Author visit to Palazzo Torrigiani, Florence, 2006.

254 "than would be pleasant": "A Sketch of Joseph Bonaparte," *Godey's Lady's Book* (Apr. 1845), 187.

SOURCES

I AM GREATLY INDEBTED throughout my narrative to the thirteen volumes of Frédéric Masson's *Napoléon et Sa Famille,* for which he drew on his massive collection of Bonaparte papers. Many of those are now conserved in the Fonds Masson, Bibliothèque Thiers, in Paris. Joachim Kühn's *Pauline Bonaparte* has much to recommend it, but, as readers wishing to locate quotations in the text and turning to the Notes will see, many other biographies have individual merits.

MANUSCRIPT SOURCES

Archivio Borghese, Archivio Segreto Vaticano, Rome
Cavour Papers, Fondazione Cavour, Santena, Turin
Devonshire Collection, Chatsworth, Derbyshire
Fondo Borghese, Archivio Segreto Vaticano, Rome
Fonds de Blocqueville, Archives Départementales de l'Yonne, Auxerre
Fonds Masson, Bibliothèque Thiers, Paris
Fonds Napoléon, Archives Nationales, Paris
Hamilton Papers, Lennoxlove, Scotland
Leveson-Gower Papers, Staffordshire County Record Office
Royal Archives, Windsor
Segretaria di Stato, Interni, Archivio Segreto Vaticano, Rome

PUBLISHED SOURCES

Angeli, Diego. *I Bonaparte a Roma.* Rome, 1938.

Angiolini, Luigi, Chevalier. *Correspondance: Angiolini et le Prince Camille Borghèse; Le Mariage de Pauline Bonaparte.* Edited by B. Sancholle-Henraux. Paris, 1913.

Antommarchi, Francesco. *Les Derniers Moments de Napoléon, 1819–1821.* 2 vols. Edited by Désiré Lacroix. Paris, 1898.

Arnaud, Raoul. *"Fils de Fréron, 1754–1802": Journaliste, Sans-Culotte et Thermidorien.* Paris, 1909.

Arnault, Antoine Vincent. *Souvenirs d'un Sexagénaire.* 4 vols. Paris, 1833.

Barras, Paul-François-Jean-Nicolas, Vicomte de. *Mémoires.* edited by George Duruy. 4 vols. Paris, 1895–96.

Beal, Mary, and John Cornforth. *British Embassy, Paris: The House and Its Works of Art.* London, 1992.

Blangini, Felice. *Souvenirs . . . 1797–1834.* Edited by Charles-Maxime-Catherinet de Villemarest. Paris, 1834.

Blond, Georges. *Pauline Bonaparte: La nymphomane au coeur fidèle.* Paris, 1986.

Bonaparte, Napoleon.. *Correspondance générale, 1784–1804.* vols. 1–4. Edited by Thierry Lentz, Henry Laurens, Gabriel Madec, Jean Tulard, and François Houdecek. Paris, 2004–7.

———. *Correspondance de Napoleon 1er publié par ordre de l'Empereur Napoléon III.* 32 vols. Paris, 1858–70.

———. *Lettres d'Amour à Joséphine.* Edited by Chantal de Tourtier-Bonazzi and Jean Tulard. Paris, 1981.

Borghetti, Giuseppe. "Paolina Borghese davanti alla Sacra Rota." *Nuova Antologia: rivista di lettere, scienze ed arti* (1932, Sept. 1): 102–13.

Bro, Général. *Mémoires, 1796–1844.* Edited by Baron Henri Bro de Comères. Paris, 1914.

Bruce, Evangeline. *Napoleon and Josephine: An Improbable Marriage.* London, 1995.

Campbell, Sir Neil. *Napoleon on Elba: Diary of an Eyewitness to Exile.* London, 2004.

Campetti, P. "Lettere di Paolina Borghese." *Bollettino Storico Lucchese* 10 (Oct. 1932), 72–75.

Canova e la Venere Vincitrice. Edited by Anna Coliva and Fernando Mazzocca. Exhibition catalog. Rome, 2007.

Carrington, Dorothy. *Portrait de Charles Bonaparte, d'après ses écrits de jeunesse et ses mémoires.* Ajaccio, 2002.

Caulaincourt, Général de, Duc de Vicence. *Mémoires.* 3 vols. Edited by Jean Hanoteau. Paris, 1933.

Champion, Jean-Marcel. *Le Général de Division Victoire-Emmanuel Leclerc (1772–1802): Éléments pour une biographie.* Pontoise, 1979.

Chastenet, Geneviève. *Pauline Bonaparte: La fidèle infidèle.* Paris, 1986.

Chateaubriand, François-René de. *Mémoires d'Outre-Tombe.* Edited by Jean-Paul Clément. 2 vols. Paris, 1997.

Chevallier, Bernard. *La douce et incomparable Joséphine.* Paris, 1999.

Clary et Aldringen, Prince Charles de. *Trois mois à Paris lors du marriage de l'Empereur Napoléon 1er et de l'Archiduchesse Marie-Louise.* Edited by Baron de Mitis and Comte de Pimodan. Paris, 1914.

Constant [Wairy], Louis. *Mémoires intimes de Napoléon 1er.* Edited by Maurice Dernelle. 2 vols. Paris, 1967.

———. *Mémoires sur la vie de Napoléon.* 6 vols. Paris, 1830.

Cornuau, Pierre. *Correspondance Inédite de Napoléon 1er, de la Famille Impériale et de divers Personnages avec Pauline Borghèse, provenant de la succession de M. Lacipière, Hôtel Drouot, Vente du 20 juin 1939.* Paris, 1939.

Corsini, Andrea. *I Bonaparte a Firenze.* Florence, 1961.

Coulmann, Jean-Jacques. *Réminiscences.* 3 vols. Paris, 1862–69.

Crawley, C. W., ed. *The New Cambridge Modern History.* Vol. 9, *War and Peace in an Age of Upheaval, 1793–1830.* Cambridge, 1965.

d'Abrantès, Duchesse. *Histoire des Salons.* 6 vols. Paris, 1837–38.

———. *Mémoires.* 25 vols. The Hague/Brussels, 1831–37.

de Girardin, Louis-Stanislas-Cécile-Xavier, Comte. *Discours et opinions, journal et souvenirs.* 4 vols. Paris, 1828.

Descourtilz, Michel Étienne. *Voyage d'un naturaliste en Haiti, 1799–1803.* Edited by Jacques Boulenger. Paris, 1935.

Devonshire, William, Sixth Duke of. *Handbook to Chatsworth and Hardwick.* Privately printed, 1844.

Ducrest, Georgette. *Mémoires sur l'Impératrice Joséphine, ses contemporains, la cour de Navarre et de la Malmaison.* 3 vols. Paris, 1828.

Dumas, Alexandre. *Mes Mémoires, 1802–1833.* Edited by Pierre Josserand. 2 vols. Paris, 1989.

Dupâquier, Jacques. "Pauline Bonaparte, Femme Leclerc," *Mémoires de la Société historique et archéologique de Pontoise, du Val d'Oise et du Vexin* 86 (2005): 165–181.

Favre, Louis. *Le Luxembourg 1300–1882: Récits et confidences sur un vieux palais.* Paris, 1882.

Fezensac, Duc de. *Souvenirs Militaires de 1804 à 1814.* Paris, 1863.

Fleuriot de l'Angle, Paul. *La Paolina, Soeur de Napoléon.* Paris, 1946.

Forges, M. A.-P. de. *Le Général Leclerc . . . notice historique et biographique d'après les documents officiels.* Paris, 1869.

Furet, François, and Denis Richet. *La Révolution du 9-Thermidor au 18-Brumaire.* Paris, 1966.

George, Mademoiselle. *Mémoires inédits.* Edited by Paul Arthur Cheramy. Paris, 1908.

Godey's Lady's Book and Ladies' American Magazine, 127 vols. Philadelphia, 1830–93.

[Goldsmith, Lewis?]. *The Secret History of the Cabinet of Bonaparte, Including His Private Life, Character, Domestic Administration, and His Conduct to Foreign Powers.* London, 1810.

———. *The Secret History of the Court and Cabinet of St. Cloud.* 2 vols. London, 1845.

Gorgone, Giulia. "Paolina Bonaparte, principessa inquieta." In *Il rifugio di Venere: La villa di Paolina Bonaparte a Viareggio.* Edited by Glauco Borella and Roberta Martinelli. Exhibition catalog pages 13–25. Lucca, 2005.

Granville, Harriet, Countess. *Letters, 1810–1845.* Edited by Hon. Edward Frederick Leveson-Gower. 2 vols. London, 1894.

Guerrini, Teresa Luzzatto. *Paolina.* Florence, 1932.

Hardy, Jean, Général. *Correspondance intime de 1797 à 1802.* Edited by Général Hardy de Perini. Paris, 1901.

Harris, Robin. *Talleyrand: Betrayer and Saviour of France.* London, 2008.

Hohl, Claude. "Les Papiers du Général Leclerc au Musée d'Eckmühl." *Bulletin de la Société des Sciences historiques et naturelles de l'Yonne* 107 (1975): 173–88.

Holland, Henry Richard, Lord. *Foreign Reminiscences.* Edited by Henry Edward, Lord Holland. London, 1851.

Hortense, Reine. *Mémoires de la Reine Hortense.* Edited by Prince Napoléon and Jean Hanoteau. 3 vols. Paris, 1928.

James, C. L. R. *The Black Jacobins: Toussaint L'Ouverture and the San Domingo Revolution.* London, 1980.

Kühn, Joachim. *Pauline Bonaparte (1780–1825).* Translated from the German by G. Daubié. Paris, 1937.

Laflandre-Linden, Louise. *Les Bonaparte en Provence.* Nice, 1987.

Larrey, Baron Hippolyte. *Madame Mère (Napoleonis Mater).* 2 vols. Paris, 1892.

Lazzareschi, Eugenio. *Le sorelle di Napoleone: Paolina.* Florence, 1932.

Lettres d'amour inédits de Talma à la Princesse Pauline Bonaparte. Edited by Hector Fleischmann. Paris, 1911.

Longford, Elizabeth. *Wellington: The Years of the Sword.* London, 1969.

Lumbroso, Alberto. *Miscellanea Napoleonica.* 6 vols. Rome, 1895–98.

Mameluck Ali [Louis-Étienne Saint-Denis]. *Souvenirs sur l'Empereur Napoléon.* Edited by Gustave Michaut. Paris, 1926.

Marchand, Louis-Joseph. *Mémoires de Marchand, premier valet de chambre et exécuteur testamentaire de l'Empereur.* Edited by Jean Bourguignon. Paris, 1985.

Marmont, Maréchal, duc de Raguse. *Mémoires de 1792 à 1841.* Edited by Auguste Frédéric Viesse de Marmont, duc de Raguse. 9 vols. Paris, 1857.

Masson, Frédéric. *Napoléon et sa Famille, 1769–1821.* 13 vols. Paris, 1897–1919.

———. "La Princesse Pauline, 1805–1809." *La Revue de Paris* 7, no. 2 (Feb. 15, 1900): 791–823.

Matthews, Henry. *The Diary of an Invalid . . . in the Years 1817, 1818 and 1819.* London, 1820.

Metternich, Clément, Prince. *Mémoires, documents et écrits . . .* Edited by Prince Richard de Metternich and Alphons von Klinkowstroem. 8 vols. Paris, 1880–84.

Montet, Marie-Henriette-Radegoude-Alexandrine Fisson, Baronne du. *Souvenirs, 1785–1866.* Paris, 1904.

Montholon, Comtesse de. *Souvenirs de Sainte-Hélène, 1815–16.* Edited by Comte de Fleury. Paris, 1901.

Morgan, Sydney, Lady. *Italy.* 3 vols. 1820–21.

———. *Memoirs: Autobiography, Diaries and Correspondence.* Edited by William Hepworth Dixon. 2 vols. London, 1862.

Morris, Gouverneur. *Diary and Letters.* Edited by Anne Cary Morris. 2 vols. London, 1889.

Murat, Joachim. *Lettres et documents, 1767–1815.* Edited by Prince Joachim-Napoléon Murat and Paul Le Brethon. 8 vols. Paris, 1908–14.

Nabonne, Bernard. *Pauline Bonaparte: La Vénus Impériale: 1780–1825.* Paris, 1948.

Nadaillac, Marquise de, Duchesse d'Escars. *Mémoires.* Edited by Marquis de Nadaillac. Paris, 1912.

Norvins, Jacques de. *Souvenirs d'un historien de Napoléon: Mémorial.* Edited by L. de Lanzac de Laborie. 3 vols. Paris, 1896–97.

O'Meara, Barry Edward. *Napoleon in Exile: Or, a Voice from St. Helena.* 2 vols. London, 1822.

Pacini, Giovanni. *Le mie memorie artistiche.* Edited by Luciano Nicolosi and Salvatore Pinnavia. Lucca, 1981.

Parlange, Henri. *Étude médico-psychologique sur Pauline Bonaparte.* Lyon, 1938.

Pasquier, Étienne Denis, Chancelier. *Histoire de mon temps: Mémoires.* Edited by Edme Armand Gaston, duc d'Audiffret-Pasquier. 6 vols. Paris, 1893–95.

Petrarca, Francesco. *Rime, Trionfi e Poesie Latine.* Edited by F. Neri, G. Martelloti, E. Bianchi, and N. Sapegno. Milan, 1951.

Planat de la Faye, Nicolas-Louis. *Rome et Sainte-Hélène de 1815 à 1821.* Paris, 1862.

Pons de l'Hérault, André. *Mémoire aux Puissances Alliées.* Edited by Léon-G. Pelissier. Paris, 1899.

———. *Souvenirs et Anecdotes de l'Île d'Elba.* Edited by Léon-G. Pelissier. Paris, 1897.

Potocka, Comtesse de. *Mémoires (1794–1820).* Edited by Casimir Stryienski. Paris, 2005.

Reinhard, Madame. *Une Femme de diplomate: Lettres à sa mère, 1798–1815.* Edited by Baronne de Wimpffen. Paris, 1900.

Rémusat, Claire Elisabeth Jeanne Gvavia de Vergennes, Comtesse de. *Mémoires, 1802–08.* Edited by Paul de Rémusat. 3 vols. Paris, 1880–81.

Revue Rétrospective, ou bibliothèque historique, contenant des mémoires et des documents authentiques, etc. 5 vols. Paris, 1833–34.

Ronfort, Jean Nerée, and Jean-Dominique Augarde. *À l'ombre de Pauline: La Résidence de l'ambassadeur de Grande-Bretagne à Paris.* Paris, 2001.

Roussier, Paul. *Lettres du Général Leclerc, commandant en chef de l'armée de Saint-Domingue en 1802.* Paris, 1937.

Saint-Maur, Madame de. *Pauline Bonaparte jugée par une femme: Mémoires.* Edited by René Hinzelin. 2 vols. Paris, 1948.

Sforza, Giovanni. "Paolina Bonaparte a Compignano e ai Bagni di Lucca nel 1815." *Revue Napoléonienne* 2, no. 1 (Oct.–Nov. 1902): 144–83.

Shelley, Lady Frances. *Diary, 1787–1873.* Edited by Richard Edgcumbe. 2 vols. London, 1912–13.

Silvagni, David. *La corte e la società romana nei secoli XVIII e XIX.* 3 vols. Naples, 1967.

Smith, Adam. *An Inquiry into the Nature and Causes of the Wealth of Nations.* London, 1870. First published 1776.

[Stewarton?]. *The Female Revolutionary Plutarch: Containing Biographical, Historical and Revolutionary Sketches.* 3 vols. London, 1806.

Stiegler, Gaston, *Récits de guerre et de foyer: Le Maréchal Oudinot, duc de Reggio, d'après les souvenirs inédits de la maréchale.* Paris, 1894.

Thibaudeau, Antoine Claire, Comte. *Mémoires, 1799–1815.* Paris, 1913.

Thiébault, Général Baron. *Mémoires.* Edited by Fernand Calmettes. 5 vols. Paris, 1893–95.

Ticknor, George. *Life, Letters and Journals.* Edited by G. S. Hillard. 2 vols. London, 1876.

Tulard, Jean. "Général Leclerc." *Mémoires de la Société historique et archéologique de Pontoise, du Val d'Oise et du Vexin* 86 (2005): 137–62.

———. *Nouvelle bibliographie critique de mémoires sur l'époque napoléonienne.* Geneva, 1991.

Venere Vincitrice: La sala di Paolina Bonaparte alla Galleria Borghese. Edited by Claudio Strinati. Exhibition catalog. Rome, 1997.

Versini, Xavier. *M. de Buonaparte, ou le livre inachevé.* Paris, 1977.

INDEX

The Urban Explosion
in Latin America

▨ ▨ A CONTINENT IN PROCESS
OF MODERNIZATION

GLENN H. BEYER, *Editor*

Cornell University Press

ITHACA, NEW YORK

First published 1967

Library of Congress Catalog Card Number: 67–23759

PRINTED IN THE UNITED STATES OF AMERICA
BY THE COLONIAL PRESS INC.

All through the developing world, we face an increasing crisis of accelerated and uncontrolled urbanization. Men and women and children are streaming into the great cities, generally the capital cities, from the monotony and all too often the misery of rural life, and they are moving, bag and baggage, long before farming can afford to lose their labor or the city is ready to put them to work and accommodate them properly.

Can we lessen or redirect this flow? Can we prepare the urban world better to receive it? Or improve the rural world enough to diminish the flood? We don't know, because we have not sought seriously to find out.

We lack adequate policies, because we have so few facts and so few people trained to develop and implement programs. For too long we have proceeded on the false assumption that people would really rather live in villages than anywhere and that it is better for society if they did. The trouble is they don't—even when the village is modernized and sanitized and electrified, people move into larger towns and cities.

Some countries have in fact recognized that the problem is not less urbanization but more urban areas—not just one or two in each country. Some are experimenting with regional development programs . . . in an effort to create new urban centers which will not only deflect migration headed for already over-crowded capital cities but will have an impact on the surrounding countryside and improve rural living in a wide area around the new cities. But the process of decentralization is difficult and complex and failures—temporary or permanent—are as common as successes.

From Adlai Stevenson's last speech to the Economic and Social Council of the United Nations, quoted by James A. Moore in opening a session of the conference, "The Role of the City in the Modernization of Latin America."

Preface

"The Role of the City in the Modernization of Latin America," the conference that served as the basis for this volume, was a feature of the Cornell Latin American Year, 1965–1966. The organizers of the conference decided that the focus would be on the positive functions performed by the city in the modernization process, instead of on the usual "urban problems." Their aim was to identify the components of urbanization that could be accelerated without unduly exacerbating those problems normally (perhaps even necessarily) associated with rapid urban growth.

The outstanding characteristic of the discussion was its multidisciplinary nature. When the program was being planned, it was felt that the desired focus on the positive functions of the city could best be achieved by concentrating on the basic disciplinary areas of history, economics, sociology, demography, and politics. The integration of the disciplines and the application of any bodies of theory from them to the role of the city in the modernization process required participation by city planners and architects as well as by specialists from the basic disciplines.

A principal achievement of the conference was the establishment of communication among the different disciplines. While this constituted a new type of experience for many participants, all of whom were specialists, it also created problems. Outstanding among these was the time limitation for discussion, which often prevented additional desirable depth. To correct this deficiency at least partially in this volume, we have frequently utilized outside materials and quoted extensively from writings especially pertinent to the subjects under discussion.

The papers and discussions of the conference covered a broad area, but frequently the same issues were found to be recurring. One of these was the importance of the relation of people to the economy and the relation of the economy to urban problems. It was emphasized that we needed a better basis of knowledge to make the relationships work. Another issue seemed to be the need for guidance on alternatives for urban growth in terms of such factors as organization, cost of providing facilities, and social integration. Should the growth of large primate cities be encouraged at the cost of secondary and tertiary cities? What are the economic, social, and political implications of this choice? Related to such questions is that of the ideal size of a city. Also related is the location of cities, especially as it concerns economic integration. Another issue which emerged quite regularly during the conference was urbanization as a development different from that of industrialization. Still another was the need to establish national guidelines for growth and change —the need for national urbanization policies as against local planning. The importance of relating economic, social, and physical planning was emphasized, as was the importance of understanding the values and needs of immigrants to the city. It was felt that standards and solutions needed to be related to the practical situation in Latin America, involving limitations of both economic and human resources, rather than to different North American and European situations. Finally, a positive approach to the modernization process of the city was felt to rely heavily on interdisciplinary research, since so many factors are always simultaneously at work in the same situation.

The first chapter of this volume is comprised of one of the public lectures given during the conference. Chapters II through VI begin with formal papers delivered at conference sessions and conclude with a synthesis and elaboration of the discussion of the topic at the conference. Chapter VII begins with parts of the keynote address for the conference and concludes with a general discussion of planning. The final chapter is a résumé of the main themes and issues of the conference.

The conference on which this volume was based was made possible in part by funds granted by the Carnegie Corporation, the Ford Foundation, and the Agency for International Development.

I want to thank the participants in the conference—twenty from Latin American countries and twenty-five from the United States—for their contribution to the conference and to this volume. Their names are listed separately later. Several exerted the extraordinary effort of submitting detailed supplementary comments after the conference. I also want to thank Professors Tom E. Davis and J. Mayone Stycos of Cornell University and Professor Walter Harris of Yale University for their considerable assistance in arranging the conference. Gerald Breese, former Director of Princeton University's Bureau of Urban Research, reviewed the manuscript and made many helpful suggestions. Mrs. Irene Hernandez not only served as my principal aide in handling details of arrangement and in typing the tapes of the discussion sessions but was indispensable on the many occasions when she served as translator. Mrs. Phyllis B. Brodhead and Mrs. Marjorie W. Knox are thanked for their labors in typing the various drafts of the manuscript.

Finally, it was Miss Margaret E. Woods who made it possible to prepare this volume within a reasonable period of time after the conference. She had the primary responsibility for screening the voluminous typed copy from the tapes, and suggested where various remarks appropriately fitted into the topics that emerged from the meetings. She also pursued additional sources to fill gaps in the discussion in order to have a more detailed development of the theme of the conference; and she assisted in innumerable other ways.

Responsibility for the development of the volume, as well as for its shortcomings, remains, of course, with the editor. While extreme care has been taken to ensure proper quotations and credits in the chapter summaries where participants are cited, if in any instance it is found that a quotation is credited to the wrong participant or if any remark is placed in a faulty context, the editor expresses his sincere apologies.

GLENN H. BEYER

Ithaca, New York
March 1967

Principal Contributors

GLENN H. BEYER has been Professor of Housing and Design at Cornell University since 1947 and Director of its Center for Housing and Environmental Studies since 1950. Previously he served as economist and administrator in U.S. government housing agencies. He has directed research on a number of problems related to housing and urbanization and is currently codirector of a multidisciplinary research program on the social, economic, political, and health aspects of urbanization in Latin America. He is the author of a number of books, the most widely recognized being *Housing and Society*. In 1960, he received the Centennial Award from Augustana College (South Dakota) in recognition of his distinguished service to his profession and higher education.

HARLEY L. BROWNING is Director of the Population Research Center of the University of Texas and Associate Professor in the Department of Sociology. He is also currently directing a program in research in Middle American demography. An important part of this project is a survey of Monterrey, Mexico, and the interrelations between migration and occupational mobility. Previously, he has been a research sociologist at the International Urban Research Project, University of California at Berkeley, where he specialized in urbanization and internal migration in Latin America. He holds a Ph.D. from the University of California.

RALPH A. GAKENHEIMER is Associate Professor of City and Regional Planning at the University of North Carolina and Editor of the *Journal of the American Institute of Planners*. In 1960–1961, he was Fulbright scholar to the Institute of Urbanism, National Engineering University of Peru, the first of several professional associations in Latin America. He holds a Ph.D. in planning from the University of Pennsylvania. His doctoral dissertation was on the determinants of physical structure in the colonial Peruvian town.

GINO GERMANI, Monroe Gutman Professor of Latin American Affairs at Harvard University, is a well-known sociologist. He was recently Director of the Institute of Sociology, University of Buenos Aires, and of the Center for Comparative Sociology, Instituto Torcuato Di Tella, Buenos Aires. He has been a Visiting Professor of Sociology at prominent universities in the United States. He has served as Vice President of the International Sociological Association, President of the Asociación Sociológica of Argentina, and on the board of directors of various Latin American professional organizations. He is the author of a number of books and articles on social and political science. Many of his articles have been published in North American and European journals. He holds degrees from Harvard and the universities of Rome and Buenos Aires.

JORGE E. HARDOY is Director of the Center for Urban and Regional Studies, Instituto Torcuato Di Tella, Buenos Aires, and President of the Interamerican Planning Society. Previously, he was Director of the Institute of City and Regional Planning at the University of Buenos Aires. He has also been Director of the Institute of City and Regional Planning, and Professor of Planning, at the Universidad del Litoral, Rosario, Argentina. He has directed several Latin American regional development programs, served as vice president of international planning congresses, and acted as consultant to national and international organizations. He is coeditor of *Ediciónes infinito*. Besides numerous articles, he has written *Ciudades precolombinas*. He holds a Ph.D. from Harvard University.

BENJAMIN HIGGINS is Ashbel Smith Professor of Economics and Director of Research on Economic Development at the University of Texas. He has served in advisory, consulting, and directing capacities on numerous commissions and committees and as a member of expert groups. He has been visiting professor at a number of universities and institutes, including Instituto Torcuato Di Tella in Buenos Aires, the Centro de Estudios Monetarios Latinoamericano, and the Getúlio Vargas Foundation in Rio de Janeiro. He is the author of a number of books and articles on economic development and economic theory. He holds a Ph.D. from the University of Minnesota.

IRVING LOUIS HOROWITZ is Professor of Sociology and Director of Studies in Comparative International Development at Washington University. He has served as chairman of the Sociology-Anthropology Department at Hobart and William Smith Colleges, and has been a visiting professor at major universities in the United States, Europe, and Latin America, among them the University of Buenos Aires, National University of Mexico, London School of Economics and Political Science, and the universities of California and Wisconsin. His writings on Latin America cover a broad range. He is Senior Editor of *Trans-Action* and serves as Advisory Editor for the *Journal of Conflict Resolution* and *Journal of International Studies*.

BERT F. HOSELITZ is Professor of Economics and Social Science and Director of the Research Center in Economic Development and Cultural Change at the University of Chicago. In 1955–1956, he was a Fellow at the Center for Advanced Study in the Behavioral Sciences at Stanford. He has served as a consultant on industrial economy in El Salvador and as a member of an expert group on metropolitan planning on a Ford Foundation project for the government of India. He has published many articles and books in the field of economic development. He holds an LL.D. degree from the University of Vienna and an M.A. degree from the University of Chicago.

TOMÁS JOSÉ SANABRIA is an architect in Caracas and an Associate Professor of Architecture and Urbanism at the Universidad Central de Venezuela, where he is a member of the Faculty Council of the School of Architecture and Urbanism. He is also on the Advisory Council of the Office of Urban Planning of Caracas. He has been a delegate to national and international commissions, Principal Director of the School of Architecture and Urbanism in Caracas, President of the Second National Convention of Architects, President of the Executive Council of Parks and Gardens of Caracas, and has received several national awards. His writings on architectural subjects have been published internationally. He holds degrees from the Universidad Central de Venezuela and Harvard University.

LUIS ALBERTO SÁNCHEZ is a Senator of the Republic of Peru and President of the Senate. He is also Rector of the Universidad Nacional Mayor de San Marcos de Lima, and, in addition, a writer and literary critic. His writings include *Don Manuel, La Perricholi, ¿Existe America Latína?, Aladíno o vida y obra de José Santos Chócano,* and *Literatura Peruana.* He has served as a sub-director of the National Library of Peru, and has lectured at numerous cultural centers in Europe and at various universities throughout the world. He is a graduate of the Universidad Nacional Mayor de San Marcos de Lima.

Contents

CONTENTS

V

Tables

TABLES

The Urban Explosion in Latin America

🏛 🏛 A Continent in Process of Modernization

I | *Introduction*

Urban Growth and the Latin American Heritage
Luis Alberto Sánchez

The problem of urban growth in Latin America, that is to say, the demographic growth that turned into the sudden formation of great cities, is one that architects and urbanists consider from one point of view, while sociologists and politicians look at it from another. To the former it represents a problem of rationalizing and ordering; to the latter it represents a complex and confused situation. The disequilibrium produced by the agglomeration of population in great urban centers (great by reason of size but not always by reason of quality) creates problems of a diverse character. Among them are centralization, from the administrative point of view; restlessness, from the psychological viewpoint; and the awareness of social differences, from the economic point of view; all of which result in great divergences among the different population groups. From this arise motives and pretexts for actions that are helping to precipitate the social, economic, and political crisis that shakes Latin America today.

Looked at from another angle, this phenomenon of rapid urbanization signifies a serious break with traditional habits in our America, whose history is fundamentally rural, agricultural. It is being changed in appearance—though basically it remains as it was—into what is called a culture of great cities.

1

A LEAP INTO THE VOID

Developments have taken place with amazing speed. Buenos Aires, which had a population of 1,200,000 in 1910, has become a metropolis of approximately six million inhabitants, while the country has grown in the proportion of some ten to twenty-eight million; Santiago de Chile is near the three-million mark but thirty years ago it was not even one million. Lima's change has been more violent—in 1920 it had a population of less than 300,000; today it is over two million. Mexico City's population is today over five million. São Paulo's growth is even more impressive.

It is often suggested that the population growth in Latin America will be 3 per cent a year, and in the large cities 5 per cent a year. Capital cities are expected to grow even faster; some "educated guesses" would indicate that they may grow at rates reaching 7 per cent, 10 per cent, and in some instances even 12 per cent.

THE BIRTH RATE IS NOT THE PROBLEM

Birth control will not solve the problem of urban growth—for social reasons. Latin America, whose density index now represents less than ten inhabitants per square kilometer, has the productivity and the space for a much bigger population. Individuals most interested in birth control are the large landowners and proprietors, and the most backward capitalists. They see a threat to their profits in population growth, which, although the greater number of consumers would create greater demand, would provide a greater number of participants for distribution of economic and social benefits.

The urban problem requires, therefore, an *ad hoc* policy, for it will not be solved by a law for urban reform, just as the land problem was not solved by a law for agrarian reform. Rather, it requires a total replanning of our structural situation.

INTRODUCTION

Latin America has been essentially agrarian. For this reason, it has been in large part communitarian. The most profound and intense tradition in Latin America has dealt with community property, the cooperative, call it "Ayllus," "Milpas," and so forth. This tradition is being broken by the absorbing attraction of the large cities that bewitches countrymen, drawing them out of their natural environment without offering the compensations that industry creates. Such historical development is taking place before everyone's eyes and is meeting with everyone's indifference. In reality, the pre-eminence given to agrarian reform is justified, inasmuch as it tackles a permanent condition, an endemia; but nonetheless, the crisis of urban growth must be given higher priority because it constitutes a mortal growth, an epidemic. Following medical terms and procedures, we must attack the epidemics aggressively and at the same time treat the endemias systematically.

It is true that, parallel to the indigenous agrarian community, historically there developed religious and imperial cities such as Tenochtitlan, Cuzco, Chichen-Itza, Cajamarca, Huamanga, Oaxaca, and so forth. But they were cities closely linked to the rural process, large agricultural centers, and, in a way, as in the case of Machu Picchu, an autochthonous American form of feudalism.

CITY-LABYRINTHS

All the autochthonous cities, like the ones named, have always had a rural character, as shown by the *ejidos*, which existed before the coming of the Europeans. What occurred with the Spanish, and to some extent the Portuguese, conquest is that the founders took advantage of the indigenous foundations and combined, in the cities, the *ejido* with the Spanish *cercado*. The city of Quito still has its *ejido*, though only in name. Lima had outside the walls its *cercado*, which was a huge enclosure for Indians, where they were forced to follow a way of life that the poor provincials, in freedom, follow in the big cities today. It was characteristic of towns of the sixteenth and early seventeenth centuries, without exception, to grow in accordance with the immediate requirements of the environment. As a result, cities are whimsical, twisted, tangled, shaped solely by everyday needs, which is what gives them character and beauty, even though they irritate the planners and urbanists of today. Guanajuato is the most beautiful, with its ever-present alleys and lanes so much like those of Cuzco, Toledo, Algiers, old Lisbon, old San Juan, Bahia del Salvador, and even downtown New York—all those cities created by the magical variety of everyday need, or, like Huancavelica, Cerro, and Potosi, the fruit of greed and haste.

GREED AND HASTE

It is possible that greed, need, and haste cannot be considered proper motivation by a planner, nor can they be taken into account in the curricula of schools of engineering and architecture. Nature and passion have their own architecture and their own engineering; otherwise, Veracruz and Acapulco and La Paz would not exist. The whimsical features of our old cities are not very different from those of old European cities, which were formed as a consequence of the same elements. Geneva and old Marseilles have similar appearances and were formed by similar forces.

The anxiety and need of today's planning, coming at the same time as the sudden materialization of the *barrios* or *favelas*, has brought an unanticipated discord between *feeling* and *thinking*, between *anarchy* and *rationality*, between *expediency* and *planning*, between the *inevitable* and the *desirable*. Though perhaps excessive to call it a dilemma, the duality was built into our cities at their founding and has remained with them throughout their subsequent growth.

INTRODUCTION

Duality is now being presented in the form of a conflict between the *inevitable* (the design imposed on our cities by historical forces) and the *desirable* (the design we want them to have).

Inevitable cities, the most picturesque, the least functional at their time of origin, can be exemplified by La Paz. La Paz was in 1548 a simple stop for muleteers, called Chuquiabo. It was the uniting point between Lower and Upper Peru. After crossing Lake Titicaca from one direction or another, always for the transportation of minerals, the muleteers needed inns and lodgings. Juliaca, Puno, Juli, Copacabana, and La Paz originated from this need. The cities were formed without regard to roughness or unevenness, and today, although they are picturesque, they are difficult to adapt to present-day needs and beyond the scope of modern planning to redesign. Something similar could be said of San Francisco, started by the horde of gold-seekers, whimsically, which gives it the character that contemporary urbanists have no desire to destroy.

By the seventeenth century La Paz was already a town. When Upper Peru, by then Bolivia, declared its independence from the government of Lima, even though the capital was Chuquisaca (later Sucre), where the executive, legislative, and judicial powers resided, all three around the old university, La Paz started gaining in activity and size. It was the natural connection with Peru, the point where almost all goods went through, until routes were laid to Bolivia's own port, which at that time was Antofagasta, separated from the heart of the country by the desert of Atacama. The *inevitable* growth of La Paz led to the transfer of executive and legislative power to it around the middle of the nineteenth century, leaving the peace of colonial Sucre to the judicial power, the archbishopric, and the university. Later, the University of San Simon was established in

La Paz. And so around old Chuquiabo, the muleteer's post, a modern city has grown up, not subject to urban norms, that is, to what is "desirable."

Lima's growth has been different. In the Rimac valley nothing that could properly be called cities existed: only temples and small towns, probably ruled by petty kings, vestiges of which remain in the present ruins of places like Pachacamac, Puruchuco, and Cajamarquilla. When the Spaniards arrived, they decided to build a city to serve as a link between the sea and the hinterland. The city was designed according to the practice of that time, in other words, in the same way that almost all the Spanish cities in America were planned. The main square was designed first; around it the buildings for the governor, the town council, the Archbishop, and the Cathedral were placed in such a way that the branches of government were functionally arranged together. Concessions around the square were later given to merchants. Further, the adjacent area was divided into blocks of 10,000 square meters, called *manzanas;* each *manzana* was subdivided into four parts, each of which constituted the lot of a founder. Later a blockade was raised, forming a closed redoubt where the Indians lived and which offered immediate access to roads that led to the Sierra. Lastly, a road was opened to the port of Callao (so called because of the many stones around there). An analogous arrangement can be observed in one of the oldest cities in Europe: Athens, with its port of Piraeus. Paris, also, in a way resembles it, since it is connected to Le Havre by the Seine.

Lima was originally a planned city, as it is today, its central perimeter almost geometric. It is similar to that part of New York, principally between Fourth and Fourteenth streets, that was built between 1800 and 1900. The Republican avalanche, with its innumerable war emergencies, destroyed the symmetry of Lima and broke through the original walls erected to protect the city from pirates. Lima started to grow, following an irregular development or, at least, a development less regular than its early growth had shown.

Mexico City and Cuzco, on the other hand, had a different evolution, inasmuch as they emerged into colonial life from the remains of old native cities. Narrow streets that never knew a horse or carriage were a common urban arrangement and one of the legacies of native cities is streets so narrow that a modern vehicle can hardly pass through them.

Consequently, when one focuses on the urban problem in Latin America (whose historical roots reach to such a depth that modern scientists assign to the man of the Peruvian Pacific coast an antiquity of not less than 7,000 years B.C.), it is necessary to consider at the same time not only the contemporary necessities of planning and urbanism but also the traditional roots, the quasi-legendary and mystical past with an antiquity of not less than a thousand years. Achieving harmony between this ancient tradition and modern urbanism constitutes one of the greatest worries of our development.

But, as we said before, in the last twenty-five years a veritable madness that provokes urban concentration has surged up. The growth of industry, the negligence or decline in agricultural production, the irresistible attractions of the great city, and the myth of urban wealth are producing a phenomenon whose social and political reverberations exceed every estimate: I am referring to the slum.

It is a fact that the function of planning has very strong exponents, especially in the case of Brasilia, a city created by the decisions of men rather than by the pressure of environment. Something similar happened with the city of La Plata, near Buenos Aires, and the same could be said of the remodeling of Santiago de Chile and of the modern sectors of all of our large cities. Each of them is reminiscent of European cities (Paris, in the case of Buenos Aires; Seville, with respect to Lima) or of North American metropolises (like almost all the others). But the deliberate, systematic effort of men, with a view toward extensive, professional development, with an ambition to overcome the archaic, has been suddenly halted by the phenomenon of the *barriada*, a reflection not of demographic outburst alone, but above all of the desire for a better life. The ambitious regulatory plan has suffered a sharp distortion in the slums.

All the cities in Latin America find themselves facing a dramatic problem, that of suddenly arising and haphazardly built settlements that grow like mushrooms (in Chile they are called *Poblaciones Callampas*, which means mushrooms). In these veritable labyrinths of straw, wood, and tin, without water or light, along random lanes, lives a diverse multitude, eager to leave poverty, but only exchanging the humble province for the illusion of the Great City. As a matter of fact, of the population of two million or more in Lima, no less than 400,000 live in zones which form the belt of misery and filth called *barriadas*. These constitute a real challenge not only to urban specialists but also to sociologists, economists, and modern politicians.

GLORY AND PASSION OF THE SLUM

Perhaps because of an inevitable professional bias, I refuse to pay attention to any social phenomenon that does not have a direct or indirect reflection in literature and that, at the same time, does not show a plausible relation to history. In fact, I contend that nothing absolutely technical or autonomous exists in any activity that jeopardizes man individually or collectively, because even personal passions may have vast resonance. Writers are like antennae of society. If they do not perceive the flow of an event, it is because this event is no more than an episode, lacking significance and loftiness.

When the "literature of slums" began in Peru, in 1953, I realized that this phenomenon was not only significant but also uncontainable. It was a young writer, Enrique Congrains, who made literary use of the new subject in his book, *Lima hora cero*. This was followed by numerous stories, novels, essays, and reports: *El lider,* by Mario Castro Arenas, *En el cielo no hay ventanas,* by Armando Robles Godoy, *La tierra prometida,* by Luis Felipe Angell, *Comunidad San Gabriel* and *Gallinazos sin plumas,* by Julio Ramon Ribeyro, among others. Bernardo Verbitzky, author of *Es dificil empezar a vivir,* anxious to portray the afflictions of his generation, undertook the subject of the slum from his point of view as an Argentinian in his novel *Villa Miseria.* In general, writers substituted for the old themes of Indians, revolutions, and immigrants this subject of the suburban and infrahuman plague called *la barriada.*

This subject was not something new. In Argentina, around 1930, an event arose which was made famous through tangos, movies, and popular poems: that of Puerto Nuevo. The well-known actor Pepe Arias made a cinematographic version of that first assault from the land and despair against the rich metropolis. In Chile, chronicles of this kind began with the writings of Joaquín Edwards Bello (*La cuna de esmeraldo, El roto,* 1918 and 1920), Eduardo Barrios (*Un perdido*), and much later, the spate of writing of Carlos Sepúlveda Leyton (*Hijuna,* 1934), Nicomedes Guzmán (*Vidas oscuras,* and others), Alberto Romero, and even the exquisite José Santos Gonzáles Vera.

These references are enough to make us aware that the problem of the abandonment of the land has been with us since the end of World War I, resulting in the decrease of cultivated land and a consequent rise in the cost of living and the illusion of affluence in the great city. The arguments of the politicians jumped from the political to the social aspect. Although the Mexican Revolution was mobilized in the beginning with the constitutionalist slogan of "Effective suffrage, no re-election," in other countries (such as Chile with the first candidacy of Arturo Alessandri; Peru, with the second candidacy of Augusto B. Leguía; and Brazil, later on, with the opposition between Washington Luis and Getúlio Vargas), the political campaigns were built on the basis of lowering the cost of living and housing, which implied raising the pressure of the rural disinherited for better living to the category of systematic and national aspiration.

To diminish class strife, the politicians thought of creating a middle class or strengthening the existing one. In fact, the middle class was thought of as some kind of buffer between the rich and the poor, between the landowner separated from the land and the industrial or fiscal entrepreneur, on one side, and, on the other, the impoverished masses of the city and the country, who in this case could make common cause. Where the evolution of the middle class had been more accelerated, it was possible in some measure to diminish the shock of the impact between the "haves" and "have-nots"; such was the case in Mexico, Costa Rica, and, in part, Venezuela, Argentina, and Chile. But in those places where the middle class did not receive any support or stimulus, as in Peru, Bolivia, a great part of Central America, including Panama, the problem of class strife assumes a character of undeniable seriousness.

THE METROPOLIS AND THE MIDDLE CLASS

The policy of buffering was a kind of urban and fiscal application of the diplomatic principles of the Congress of Vienna in 1815, from which emerged so many small countries that were destined to serve as cushions between rival nations. Here it was translated into a more or less dynamic planning of *Cajas de Provision* for salaried employees and small proprietors, in the form of subsidized housing projects, long-term credit to build with the government's backing, and municipalization of certain urban services. Or, in other words, dissatisfaction and protest, rather than being opposed, were channelized by the wealthy, and a human buffer zone was created by arousing the interests of a class which until then had been as proletarian as the worst-paid workmen and laborers.

Of course, this policy of containment, which has had magnificent results in Puerto Rico, is applied with more or less celerity and success in different countries. As might be expected, it arouses opposition and criticism, because of typical differences between the middle class and the upper class, and because the whole society is organized to function on a basis of only two classes. It is a fact that the owners of sumptuous mansions in the Avenida Salaverry of Lima do not conceal their disgust because in the old adjacent zone of Santa Beatriz, location of the former Hipodromo (race track), tall multidwelling buildings are being constructed for middle-class tenants. The satisfaction these people will receive from obtaining low-cost and healthful housing is not a convincing argument to those who want their properties to increase in value at a vertiginous rate from year to year, indifferent to the direct or indirect consequences such inequality generates.

Here is an aspect to which we do not pay enough attention. The old cities were really concentrations of four well-differentiated social classes, which could be distinguished, among other means, by their housing. (1) The big house (in this respect let us remember the study made by Gilberto Freyre) in the cities of Spanish America was a huge manor house with several patios, almost always with a decorated portal, lattices, porches, balconies, and ample windows. Streets or even entire districts were named after the owners of many of these big houses, palaces, or manor houses, as, for example, those of Baquijano and Villalta in Lima and that of Conde in Caracas. (2) The uniform houses of the middle class, exactly like those of Spain, generally only one story high, had one or more windows at the front, doorways less imposing than those of the manor houses, and tiled or flat roofs, according to the climate. (3) Outside-the-walls areas or enclosures were where Indians and foreigners were "converted" or kept together. (4) The courtyards and inner corrals were intended for slaves. Monasteries and their dependencies constituted a special section in the cities. They occupied huge areas, almost never less than an entire *manzana*, and frequently stretched out into several nearby or distant blocks, as in the case of the real estate property of the Jesuits.

The accumulation of great fortunes subsequent to the discovery of sources of wealth, such as fertilizers, nitrates, minerals, sugar, coffee, cotton, petroleum, rice, tobacco, cattle raising, wheat, and so forth, promoted a deep change in the physiognomy of the cities, and especially the capital cities. The principal owners and managers, of necessity, concentrated in the capitals, to maintain their advantages and to keep themselves near the government.

The urban sectors of the middle class do not improve, but the ostentation of the rich increases, and, unfortunately, the indigence of the poor gets worse. The cities reflect this fact with greater eloquence than do conventional statistics. New gorgeous suburbs are being born: it is the hour of new sections in each of the Latin American cities, crowned by Las Lomas of Chapultepec and The Angelin, in Mexico; old Chapinero, in Bogota; the suburb Oriente of Caracas; San Isidro, Orrantia, and Miraflores, in Lima; old Ejido, in Quito; Condes and El Golf, in Santiago. It can be affirmed that between the years 1920 and 1960 the politics of the so-called "urbanizations" did nothing but increase the distance between rich and poor, abolishing completely, at least in terms of urban life, the diverse shades of the middle class.

The reaction, we might almost say the *revenge*, represented by *barriadas*, *favelas*, *villas miserias*, makes perceptible suddenly, in a sharp, almost irrevocable way, the social dichotomy characteristic of Latin America, where is exhibited the historic paradox of democratic regimes that have existed without the support of a vigorous middle class. To emphasize the division between classes even more, it happens that the public powers invariably, when they construct buildings for their offices, appeal to ostentation rather than to functionalism. They in fact affiliate themselves with the rich, in open combat with the needy. A rational and democratic policy that interprets at city level the needs and aspirations (the what-to-do and the ought-to-be) of all classes would inexorably lead to a fruitful urbanistic policy that would diminish or eliminate the tremendous distance existing between the munificence of the newly rich person (by reason of inheritance or of fiscal operations) and the displaced countryman that incessantly creates the terrific slums.

On this possible solution, much could be said, since it would not be a matter only of building, but of localizing, of shutting out, and preventing; and in all of this, unfortunately, almost always is found the black, hairy demon of sectarian politics, the mortal enemy of true politics.

THE DREAM OF A "VERY NEW CITY"

Students of history know very well that one of the most serious and edifying treatises on Greek and Roman social organization is that by Fustel de Coulanges, *The Ancient City.* Those who toil to bring out the significance of the new metropolises use as their main reference the voluminous work of Lewis Mumford, *The Culture of Cities.* With regard to the colonial city, the work of José Agustín García, *La Ciudad Indiana,* is often referred to, as well as *El Cabildo Colonial* of Julio Alemparte. Without any pretensions of erudition we wish to state that in all these studies social evolution is identified with the structure and evolution of cities and of their representative organizations, the municipal councils or town halls.

But in Latin America, the predominance of the land continues and 80 per cent of our population and our commercial exchange still depend on the fields. At the same time, poverty in the rural areas sends the people more and more to the cities and creates the urgency to industrialize our economic life. The urban population grows phenomenally, a growth that starts and develops in an irregular way, arbitrarily, around the large metropolis, where elements of dissatisfaction, rebellion, illiteracy, and improvidence are introduced, which the state has to alleviate.

Consequently, the urban problem cannot remain solely in the hands of urbanists, architects, and planning experts if among them a marked influence is not exerted by sociologists, anthropologists, psychologists, economists, jurists, and poets. This last nomination will surely excite smiles. They are foreseen and justifiable, but a poet's work in order to be fruitful does not admit of predetermined channels or inflexible rules. But the modern city, like the old city, is the reflection, the receptacle, and the synthesis of our contemporary life. In it are joined together the reality and the dream, dissatisfaction and hope, riches and misery, local spirit and universal longing. There are no specialists in "everything"; as a result, the participation of everyone is required in order to attain goals. When Walt Whitman prophesied in the unforgettable poems of *Leaves of Grass* the era of the "electric body," of the "multitudes," and of the "skyscrapers," and then, in an impulse of fierce realism, defined love as a "poem of breasts and hips in action," he foreshadowed what was to come. He was foreseeing the epoch of the functionalism of Le Corbusier and of the great architects of Brasilia. He was foreseeing a world necessarily diversified, but with a new civilization, ruled by a logos that, however unattractive and selfish it might appear, was by its own nature obliged to be altruistic and serviceable.

The Latin American city faces at this moment a challenge more pressing than the one that confronted the era of Walt Whitman. Heir to a legacy, native and Spanish, made up of old empires and sumptuous viceroyships, it must now answer to the challenge of its rapid growth and the even more demanding challenge of its necessities and its goals. A union of old nations incorporated into new states, democratic organizations that have proclaimed democracy for over a century and a half but that until thirty years ago had not started to practice it seriously and methodically, Latin America has to solve the problem of its concentration as much as that of its demographic expansion. One is worthless without the other. We must develop our cities in a functional way, and at the same time, disseminate them. That means that we will find ourselves having to strengthen and at the same time weaken them; the one by means of functional organization and the other by means of a planned and likewise functional decentralization.

This duty is clear and does not need further comment. But what demands major attention, almost, we might say, passion, is the procedure by which to adapt ourselves to the future without losing our personality; to erase or diminish the apparent disparity between tradition and planning; between industrialization and a rich or self-sufficient agriculture; between unification and decentralization; between the metropolis and the province; between privilege and misery. All of these require the undertaking of a deep and broad political program, whose synthesis could be tried out in cities as they exist today, forcing us to discover in these apparently circumscribed problems the fundamental ingredients of our national problems and our continental problems.

JUDICIAL REVERBERATION

Through this briefly outlined process, we can arrive at a main conclusion: it is not only an urban reform in the strict technical sense we are dealing with, but a profound social transformation. Human groups moving from one point to another in a country is not extraordinary. Neither would it be unusual if they settled in the place of their choice and built their homes. But what does constitute a serious conflict is that those migratory groups *take possession of* (or invade) lands that have duly registered owners, or government lands also legally recorded, stubbornly stay there and build their houses without considering either the right of property or municipal and fiscal regulations. They do not respect urban plans. They do not submit to sanitary provisions (lighting, water and drainage, and others), nor do they comply with any of the legal requirements for taking possession of land or for transferring real estate property. Since this invasion is treated as a "consummated fact," a *fait accompli*, and since "social interest" should be respected above that of "the individual" (according to formulas not very well defined or acceptable and in contradiction of a basic principle in our jurisprudence, namely, that our laws are not retroactive), we are facing an abrupt alteration of the usages and rights acknowledged by our constitutions. That is, we are facing, in a spirit of compliance and benevolence, a deliberate, public, systematic, and noisy uprising against the established order.

What are we to do? What is being done? What should not be done?

To these three questions logical answers cannot be given, much less legal ones. They remain beyond the field of law or even of economics; they fall, by default, somewhere in the area of sociology and politics. And so, the problem that we have before us, of conciliation or rupture between the traditional practice of the population and the imperious urban reality, compels us to revise all our concepts and to adopt an effective and cautious policy in order to find a plausible solution for a conflict that can surpass the agrarian problem itself in its capacity for seriousness and violence. Or, perhaps, to be more accurate, this problem that confronts us, being sequel to the agrarian problem, extends and goes beyond it, and transfers into daily ambit, without any attenuation, the oppressing questions of rural injustice, of all types of past discriminations, and of educational backwardness from which cities had been spared.

Here is one of the major challenges that arises in our time, a challenge that must be approached with a strong spirit and without demagogism.

II | *The Role of the City in Historical Perspective*

Editor's Introduction

Some aspects of the history of Latin American cities were touched upon in the preceding chapter. This chapter will elaborate on that subject, which is so important to an understanding of those cities today. In order to establish the broadest possible perspective, the chapter begins with a concise but important review of the history of cities in general. This discussion will not only provide background for the more specific discussion of Latin American cities, but will put into focus one very important element, that is, the significance of the change in the size of cities, both in area and population, in relation to technology and to their function. It also will show the increase in complexity and importance of cities, especially their effectiveness as an organ in articulating culture.

Then the focus moves to urban development of a large and interesting region of the South American continent—the urbanized region of the Viceroyalty of Peru which, in the sixteenth and seventeenth centuries, covered an area that today includes not only Peru but parts of several other nations as well. This discussion will emphasize particular characteristics of Latin American cities; it will show how many cities were planted by political designation rather than having grown primarily out of economic needs. It will show the lack of a frontier (at least in

17

the sense of the North American "West"), and the provisional nature of cities. The result: centralization. This centralization had several bases. One was the focus of bureaucracy and service operations. Related was the matter of the frequent overdevelopment (relatively) of the capital city. The industrial complex had not emerged; and cities were not stimuli for national growth and development.

A History of the Long-Term Development of the City
BERT F. HOSELITZ

EARLIEST HISTORY

Although human beings have lived on earth for perhaps 200,000 years, it is certain that for the greatest part of this time no cities existed. As a matter of fact, the first cities were built in the neolithic age; they did not come into existence before 6000 to 4000 B.C. The agricultural revolution was primarily responsible for the building of cities. The cultivation of crops had gradually developed in the lower Middle East—the "Fertile Crescent"—and from there slowly spread over the whole world. By 1000 B.C., that is, three or four thousand years after the inception of the agricultural revolution, the entire world population practiced cultivation of crops, except in those few areas, such as parts of Africa, where enough land was sufficiently productive in the wild state to allow the population to survive on mere food-gathering.

Apart from China (with which I am not familiar in respect to size of cities), the first cities were established in the lower part of Mesopotamia and India. Recent work by Robert McCormick Adams[1] and various previous studies by V. Gordon Childe[2] give a few indications of the size of the oldest cities. Childe

[1] *Land Behind Baghdad* (Chicago: The University of Chicago Press, 1965).
[2] *Social Evolution* (London: Watts, 1951).

estimates that the size of a city can be determined either by the area covered with houses or by the size of its cemetery. He states, for example, "The typical settlement sites throughout North Syria and Assyria are now marked by oval mounds varying in size from 400 m. × 300 m. (435 × 330 yards) to 230 m. × 150 m. (250 × 164 yards). None has been so completely excavated or published that the total built-up area can be accurately estimated at any given period." [3]

In any event, Childe's data indicate that the earliest cities were no larger than approximately thirty acres. In later times, Khafaje on the Diyala covered 100 acres, Ur 220 acres, and Erech perhaps two square miles, which suggests that Ur's famous population could not have included more than 5,000 inhabitants, nor Erech's more than 25,000. The two city mounds in India, Mohenjo-Daro and Harappa, were respectively 1 and 2½ square miles in their destroyed states, indicating that these walled cities had no more than 5,000 to 15,000 inhabitants. [4] Adams gives various measures of some of the Diyala regions from about 2500 B.C. to 100 A.D., and the majority of these urban settlements were no more than sixty to one hundred hectares.

Finally, with reference to the old cities of Crete and Greece, Childe says that "with a cluster of hamlets outside their walls [they] belong to a different order of magnitude from the Bronze Age cities of Mesopotamia or India with a walled area of over one hundred acres. For all their specialized craftsmen and merchants they are not cities." [5] There are some grounds for suspecting that modern towns—e.g., of Argos and Thebes—occupy the sites of Mycenaean towns larger and more "urban" than Mycenae or Tiryns but yet small in comparison with Ur or Assur.

What does all this suggest? Except for a few very large cities,

---

[3] *Ibid.*, pp. 154–155.
[4] Kingsley Davis, "The Origin and Growth of Urbanization in the World," *The American Journal of Sociology*, LX, 5 (March, 1955), 431.
[5] Childe, *op. cit.*, p. 52.

such as Persepolis, Babylon, and Athens, whose actual size cannot be estimated for periods before 500 B.C. because so much has happened since that time on the same sites, we must assume that most larger cities covered about one hundred hectares, that is, 250 acres, and many were smaller, probably only sixty or seventy hectares. These cities were capitals or principal cities of various empires, and their small size must be viewed as a reflection of the small proportion of their populations that were urbanized. Perhaps 99 per cent of mankind lived in small villages.

As indicated before, what made possible the invention of cities was the invention of agriculture. Between 6000 and 4000 B.C., the cultivation of crops had called into being a minimum technology, which both created enough surplus to release a tiny portion of the population from the sole concern of growing food, and at the same time required their release to maintain that technology. It included the ox-drawn plow, the wheeled cart, the sailboat, the elementary control of water and irrigation, and the domestication of wild plants. Of course, each of these advances took place in different parts of the world at different times, but by 3000 B.C. they had been adopted in every area of the Near East. When this technology was utilized in places where climate, soil, and water were the most favorable, the result was a sufficiently productive economy to make possible the concentration in one place of people who did not grow their own food, but imported it from the regions around them. Such developments were especially possible in areas where there were broad river valleys that had alluvial soil, not exhausted by excessive cropping, with a dry climate and plenty of sunshine, and with little sediment borne away by the river itself, for example, the valleys of the Tigris and the Euphrates and the Nile, as well as several places in India and China. Therefore, nonindustrial towns grew up in these regions before they did in others.

The people in towns were not only dependent upon organized agriculture, but also upon religion, commerce, and a meager amount of industry. Of course, these occupations were extremely marginal, because only a limited number of the townspeople worked at them. When we read, for example, of the Greek tribes who fought against Troy, we must remember that even then the majority of people were occupied most of the year in agriculture and only at certain times could be employed in the service of the army. It is at periods when relatively large numbers of the peasantry could afford to be away from the fields that the main scenes of the *Iliad* occur.

The most important profession in these cities was undoubtedly that provided by religion. Some individuals were entirely occupied in it, but most of them held religious and administrative jobs simultaneously. Only four or five great empires existed at that time, and usually for no longer than the lifetime of one or two emperors—for instance, the empire of Sargon, the conquest of western Asia by Seti and Ramses II of Egypt in the thirteenth century B.C., or the Hittite Empire at the height of its power.

The first really great empire was the Persian in the sixth century B.C., which maintained its greatness through several dynasties. Our knowledge of its administrative structure is still limited. It is probably the result of administrative difficulties that the preceding empires were relatively short-lived.

Finally, the task of trade and industry also fell to the lot of the cities. Even though sails had been developed, large sailboats still often had to be rowed in the sixth century B.C. As a result, widespread distribution of goods by large ships was confined to products which were of relatively high value and small bulk, that is, products for the elite, and not those necessary for the maintenance of a large urban population. Over land, the oxcart, with its solid wheels, and human bearers were the only means of transportation. Thus, the size even of Greek cities of a later period, not to mention that of the early cities of Mesopotamia, Egypt, and India, was severely limited by the amount of easily transportable, nearby food, fibers, and other bulk goods. Lack of medical services, of adequate widespread communication and transportation, of large-scale machinery, of a bureaucracy with firm control over the peasantry, as well as the traditionalism and religiosity of all classes, hampered society's technological and economic advance. These limitations explain why cities in existence up to and including the period of the early British Empire remained relatively small in size.

FROM 500 B.C. TO THE MIDDLE AGES

In late antiquity, roughly from 500 B.C. to 400 A.D., we find two or three definite changes from the earlier period. First, it became possible to establish a world empire that lasted for several centuries, instead of only for fifty or one hundred years at best—the Roman Empire. Second, technological advancements in agriculture made possible the release of a greater number of individuals to cities. Although it is difficult to say what portion of the population lived in cities during this period, probably 2 per cent, or twice the portion of the previous period, lived in places that could be designated as urban. Third, as is well known from Roman history, many previously unknown secondary and tertiary occupations developed in cities—for example, those of actors and gladiators—and a general increase in luxury took place, especially in feasting, including imported exotic goods. We see the introduction of opulent dress and ornaments, extravagant urban palaces, villas, and gardens, the service of slaves, and last but not least, luxurious funerals. Further, society could for the first time afford the luxury of fine architecture, sculpture, painting, music, literature, philosophy, and education, and with it all, the rising belief in a unique deity.

These many developments were made possible by advancing technology, by increases in the production of agricultural raw materials, and above all by the more numerous exchanges of agricultural raw materials and the increasing production of other commercial products on a large scale. The emperor, for example, was able to have brought to Rome every year several thousand tons of food from Egypt, to ensure the populace adequate food supplies. Thus, the growth in size and comfort of cities in this era is reflected in (a) the greater amount produced; (b) the heavier reliance on shipping and land transportation; (c) more control of the populace by the bureaucracy; and (d) stronger desire of the upper classes to control the lower classes on a world-wide scale.

With regard to city size, the figures on Rome are somewhat questionable. On the one hand, we have the traditional estimate by Jérôme Carcopino,[6] which gives between 1,165,000 and 1,677,000 inhabitants in the second century A.D., supposedly its greatest number in this era. Since Italy had at that time a population of about six million, his estimate puts one fourth of the Italian population in Rome, which appears excessively high. A second estimate, which interprets the word *insulae* to mean houses, rather than apartment houses, results in a figure of 300,000 or 400,000. In the opinion of this writer, the latter gives a much more accurate picture of the Roman population than Carcopino's estimate. The later interpretations of the meaning of *insula* as a one- or two-storied building, in which three to seven people lived, are supported by other data.[7] In the third century A.D., the total surface area of Rome was 1,380 hectares, or roughly two or three times as big as other Italian cities and the other large cities of the empire. In Spain, for example, the biggest city was Cadiz, which had an area of 384 hectares and only 65,000 inhabitants. Similarly, the town of Carthage had an area of 288 to 325 hectares and 33,000 to 50,000 inhabitants. In Greece, Athens had 245 hectares and a population of 28,000 in the second century A.D., and Byzantium had about 1,200 hectares and 150,000 inhabitants in the fourth and fifth centuries A.D. (when its population was much greater than at any previous period). In Egypt, the largest city was Alexandria, which in the

---

[6] *Daily Life in Ancient Rome* (London: Penguin Books, 1962), pp. 29–31.

[7] J. C. Russell, *Late Ancient and Medieval Population* (Philadelphia: The American Philosophical Society, 1958). A discussion of Rome's population is on pp. 64 and 65. Populations of other cities in the Roman Empire are shown on pp. 66 ff.

first century A.D. had an area of 920 hectares and 216,000 inhabitants. By the fourth century A.D. these figures had declined to 640 hectares and 122,000 inhabitants. These data suggest that 300,000 to 400,000 is a more reasonable figure for the population of Rome.

But the most important aspect of Rome's development was its capacity to administer a relatively large territory. By the sixth century A.D. Rome had evolved a legal system of which certain elements exist even today. There is no need here to detail the rights of the Roman citizen, yet it should not be forgotten that in 212 A.D. any male adult who was not a slave was given citizenship. Therefore, in an empire including probably fifty to seventy million people, every male had the same status. If the administrative structure of the Roman Empire is compared with that of any other ancient empire, we begin to understand its fundamental contribution to the development of society. In every new country they conquered the Romans immediately imposed their administrative patterns, and by the second century A.D. the entire Western world was under the same form of government. In island Britain and in semitropical Egypt the same sorts of public officers governed. All were dependent on Rome, which possessed the large administrative structure necessary to maintain order throughout the empire, and there the policies were set. The result was three to five centuries of lasting security of government.

Agriculture and commerce were also much more highly developed than in the centuries before 500 B.C. In the four or five centuries following the second century B.C. agricultural surpluses combined with improvements in the means of transportation, primarily bigger and more reliable sailboats, to enable Egypt to become a breadbasket for the empire's city dwellers.

In the second and third centuries A.D., however, piracy increased to such an extent that only the official fleets protected by a detachment of soldiers could be sure of making voyages safely. Private shippers were more often than not the victims of pirates. The inability of the transportation system to withstand this attack resulted in the weakening of the interrelations of the various parts of the empire by the fifth century A.D. In addition, the shift of the capital to Constantinople undermined the administrative structure of the western part of the empire. By 476 Rome was nothing; the East had become more powerful and unified and was no longer very strongly connected with the West. We see, therefore, that Rome's magnificence in the first and second centuries A.D. was based upon a complicated set of factors, and when they began to fail, Rome fell from glory.

THE MIDDLE AGES TO A.D. 1500

Before turning to the Middle Ages, from the eighth or ninth century to the fourteenth century A.D. (which together with late antiquity holds many lessons for the understanding of the path of development and the accomplishments of the larger concentration of human beings), we must consider the decrease in population experienced by European cities from their maximum populations in the first and second centuries A.D. until some time between the ninth and twelfth centuries. The main cause was the impact of the tribes that overran them. The Goths and Franks were the most notable, and their power reached its zenith by about A.D. 800. Charlemagne was perhaps the most outstanding ruler in Germany and France; according to some historians of these countries, a power so centralized and so united never recurred. The Goths had taken Italy. Other Christian groups had taken Spain and the island of Britain. With the exception of Spain, these countries saw the gradual unification of their empires in the following five hundred years; even Spain experienced its great national unification in 1492. The year 800, therefore, might be considered the nadir of European cities; after 800 they again began to grow.

The growth pattern of cities elsewhere was different, especially in the Eastern Roman Empire. First, their decline was not so great as in western Europe. Constantinople did not decline at all but in fact grew somewhat up to the fifth or sixth century

A.D. Although the Egyptian, Syrian, and Babylonian cities experienced some decline, it was not extreme. In 700 or 800 another power became dominant—Islam. It set off a new period of city growth, and by the ninth century Baghdad covered, according to one historian (whose figures I consider unreliable, however), 6,400 hectares and Sumarra 6,800 hectares.[8] This would suggest populations of one million each or above. According to Russell,[9] however, the walled portion of Baghdad covered only 453 hectares, with an additional 110 hectares, approximately, across the river. The addition of the various settlements around Baghdad brings the figure up to 2,000 hectares, suggesting that the population may have been as high as 300,000. Because in both the walled city and the suburbs most of the houses had large gardens, it is especially difficult to accept the larger figure, which was never reached in the West.

But what happened in western Europe also happened eventually in eastern Europe. In the course of the following centuries, the population decreased, the empire was conquered by the Turks and Ottomans, and in 1300 the great and magnificent empire of Baghdad was mixed with the ashes of its forefathers. If, therefore, we are interested in the growth of cities since A.D. 800, we may well confine ourselves to western Europe.

In 800, when settlements were as yet relatively small, the only "city" inhabitants were a few royal families—the actual administrators were the large landowners—a few church administrators, and a few highly skilled tradesmen. This was the base upon which urban population began to expand, although there was little real growth for some time. During the plague of Black Death of 1348, European countries, and especially their cities, lost somewhere between one fourth and one third of their total inhabitants. There were many other periods of diminution, at different times in different countries. Fairly reliable figures are available for the fourteenth century, when on the whole the

[8] Adams, *op. cit.*, p. 98, and discussion on pp. 89–90.
[9] *Op. cit.*, p. 89.

European countries had restored their population losses. At that time most cities covered an area of less than 175 hectares, although the best known were larger.

In Italy, for example, Bologna had 420 hectares, Florence 512 hectares, Milan 314 hectares, and Venice 324 hectares. In France and Belgium, Antwerp had an area of 352, Bruges 430, Brussels 449, Ghent 640, and Louvain 410 hectares. In 1377 London had a population of 34,971, and in 1292 Paris had 59,200 inhabitants; they covered 288 and 378 hectares, respectively. In Germany only two walled cities larger than 175 hectares existed—Hamburg covered 204 hectares in 1250, and Cologne 397 hectares in the thirteenth century.[10]

By 1450 to 1500, the end of this period, three or four European cities evidently had populations of 100,000 or more—Paris, Naples, and Venice are fairly certainly in this category; London possibly; while in Germany no city attained this size, and very few in Spain. In actual numbers of people, these centers were no bigger than those of the Roman Empire; perhaps the more central location of France and Germany in northwestern Europe attracted a greater concentration of people than there had been in Roman times. Perhaps, also, many of the smaller cities, those with 5,000 to 10,000 inhabitants, of which there were a large number in Germany and France, formed the real historical base for European urbanization. Berlin, for example, had an area of 87 hectares and only 4,000 inhabitants before 1400 and only 6,000 after 1450. It would have been hard to anticipate that five hundred years later Berlin would have over four million inhabitants and be by far the leading city in Germany. Thus, around 1450 to 1500, European cities were developing as focal points for the surrounding territory.

An outstanding feature of the newly growing cities was that the population they attracted was free. Whether they had been accused of crimes and now wished to begin anew, or were for other reasons not well off in their original rural occupations and

[10] *Ibid.*, pp. 60–63.

wished to become traders or merchants or ordinary city in-habitants, they came to the cities. The most important thing was that they were no longer responsible for prior commitments to masters, but could follow their daily occupations and serve only themselves.

Up to the twelfth century the military commitments of cities were not very great; most battles were carried out with swords and other very cumbersome armament. From the thirteenth century on, however, methods of fighting became more efficient and by the fifteenth century no longer involved large bodies of knights in heavy armor, but relatively much more expensive armies of soldiers bearing firearms and the various inventions of modern warfare. In 1529, for example, the Turkish siege of Vienna was much more serious, even though it ended in the defeat of Turkey, than it would have been had it taken place three hundred years earlier.

In addition, European cities began to produce art. After the thirteenth century, or the beginning of Giotto's time, art be-came rapidly more prominent in cities, and the number of artists grew. The eleventh century marked an expanding construction of cathedrals and churches, and the support of artists by imperial and noble families began about the same time. Of course, man-kind has had art from the most ancient times, but the extensive participation in art—for example, the church building stimu-lated by mass church-going and the growing popularity of portraiture—resulted in a growth of art, particularly in the urban centers, unparalleled since the great Greek pottery-making pe-riod.

But the primary development was the growing importance of commerce and industry in the cities. When we think of the changes of the Middle Ages, we often remember first the de-velopment of small industries; though they remained small, they became one of the most important of city activities. In Italy, for instance, there were gold works and valuable textile manufactur-ing, while France developed an extensive metals industry. Germany provided food and objects procured by its trade with eastern Europe. From the thirteenth to the fifteenth centuries came the famous expansion of the Flemish and Dutch textile centers.

In the thirteenth century, commercial representatives from all European states were established in London. Many European geographers traveled over all of Europe; sooner or later they were accompanied by commercial travelers who worked in the interest of their countries wherever they went. Even complete mercantile companies were founded. The Hansa at its height, for example, combined most of the trading centers in northern Germany; its one great privilege was the right to pass through the Oresund Canal between Denmark and Sweden. Thus, the industrial growth of cities by the fifteenth century prepared them for their role as the main industrial and commercial links with the developments of the industrial revolution of the eighteenth and nineteenth centuries.

Two points remain to be noted. First, cities by themselves were sufficiently powerful to make unnecessary the creation of large states around them. Almost all the German cities established only a small sphere of influence in the surrounding countryside. The German emperor's power was based on his family's position, rather than on the support of the large cities. Such "unified" countries as existed, Italy and Spain, for example, were organized very loosely. It is true that France and England were centrally ruled, but they did not dominate Europe as they would dominate it in the late eighteenth century or the nineteenth century. Second, the gradual growth of cities during this period permitted their architectural unity as "Gothic" towns, and their beauty was noted by the architects and the historians of the day. Even now, the relatively few surviving areas of such towns are greatly admired for their beauty—for example, the city of Carcassonne, the medieval sections of Rome, Florence, and Venice, and parts of Cambridge and Oxford in England. The desire to have beautiful cities never deserted mankind, and the rapid growth of industrial cities in the nineteenth century without consideration for the aesthetics of building is to be much regretted. Only since the beginning of the twentieth century has a general feeling arisen that industrial cities can be places of permanent beauty in addition to serving the needs of industry. This is the reason why so many large cities are now in the process of being at least partially rebuilt.

THE CITY IN MODERN TIMES

The first, second, and third periods of city development—in ancient times before 500 B.C., in late antiquity between 500 B.C. and 400 A.D., and in the Middle Ages to 1500—were basically responses to the first great change which was to affect all mankind, the agricultural revolution, and resulted in only limited progress in industry and trade. The fantastic growth of cities in modern times has been the direct result of the industrial revolution, spurred by the new industrial development which began around the sixteenth and seventeenth centuries. This second great change started in England and spread first to northwestern Europe, then to all of Europe, and later to parts of America; it is today in the process of encompassing the whole world. Only a small proportion of the populations in many of the countries of Africa, Asia, and Latin America have been affected by industrialization as yet, but we can foresee that in one hundred or two hundred years the entire population of the world will have the kind of society the industrialized countries possess today.

Urbanization has risen to previously unimagined dimensions. In 1800 only 2.4 per cent of all people lived in cities of 20,000 or over. By 1950 this figure had risen to 20.9 per cent, and by 1960 to 23 or 24 per cent—nearly a quarter of the world's population. In 1800 about 15.6 million people lived in cities of 100,000 or more; by 1950, 313.7 million, or more than twenty times as many, did. In 1800 fewer than fifty cities had 100,000 or more inhabitants; today there are more cities with a million or more inhabitants than there were with 100,000 in 1800. By 1950 almost nine hundred cities had 100,000 or more inhabitants; this is more than the number of cities with 5,000 and more population in 1800. Yet we have seen no indications of any slackening in the pace of urbanization. If the present rate of growth continues, a quarter of the world's population will live in cities of 100,000 or more in the year 2000, and half of the population will be in cities of 100,000 or more by 2050.

How rapidly urban growth is advancing can be seen by the projections for Latin America up to 1975. In 1950 only 39 per cent of the total population lived in cities of more than 2,000. By 1964 about half of the people made their homes in cities. By 1975, 57 per cent of Latin America's population may be urban.[11] Yet this is a part of the world we think of as being highly rural. Of course, the urban population is employed largely in service occupations because of their economic backwardness, and much unemployment exists, but even so the people continue to migrate to cities in search of better jobs.

Cities and their innumerable influences on the lives of their inhabitants have become the subject of a separate science in the last twenty years. While we cannot go into the details here, a few points are worthy of mention. Public employment has lost some importance in recent times, and industrial and service organizations provide the majority of jobs for urban populations. The earnings of city people are, of course, substantially higher than those of people remaining in the countryside. *There is no doubt that the great concentration of people in the cities has been extremely advantageous for them: people are able to enjoy better incomes, higher standards of living, better educational facilities, better health facilities, and more cultural advantages and public benefits.*

[11] Carmen A. Miró, "The Population of Latin America," *Demography*, I, 1 (1964), 21–24, and Table 9. It should be noted that while the projected estimate indicated is quite precise, frequently other sources (and sometimes the same source) will give a different estimate for the same period. More important than the precise figure is the level of the estimate in the trend which is shown.

At the same time, we are becoming alarmed by the problems that increased urbanization has brought: higher crime rates, unemployment, juvenile delinquency, mechanization of human resources, and concentrations of poverty-stricken persons. Many of these problems result from the rapidity with which cities have grown. The efforts which have been made and continue to be made to solve them will probably succeed to a large extent, but the solutions will not come easily.

The great cities will need extensive renovation. For London and Paris, this will require two or three generations. For the new cities in Asia, the process will be slower, because the poor are so poor that their lack of money for new houses will make it difficult to resettle them. The poor sections of large cities will remain with us for a long time, but eventually, it is my hope, earnings will increase sufficiently so that even slum areas will disappear. It should be kept in mind that two hundred years ago most of the people in the world lived in abject poverty and had no voice in their government. Only in the last fifty years has gradual improvement taken place, and that mostly in North America and Europe. It is slowly beginning to occur in some of the marginal countries of the underdeveloped world—Japan and Israel are two outstanding examples—and even in Latin America, the population is on the frontier of a better standard of living for all, particularly in countries like Mexico, Chile, and Venezuela.

We have seen that until about 1750 cities, although of considerable historical importance in a predominantly agrarian world, grew slowly, probably less than 2 per cent of the world's population living in cities with 20,000 or more inhabitants by then. Their rapid growth after 1750 was primarily the result of the industrial revolution and modern technology. Just as the agricultural revolution ultimately brought about the highly compact and beautiful medieval cities, so will the industrial revolution in the future result in modern cities on a world scale. We may go through some very difficult years, but my belief is that half of the world's population will live in urban places by 2050 and that this urbanization will be the prelude to increased happiness for all mankind.

The Peruvian City of the Sixteenth Century[12]

Ralph A. Gakenheimer

When a new city is established, many determinations are made about relations between the new occupants of the land and their sociophysical environment. Relations among groups of people in the city are also determined. These determinations, whether adaptations to the apparent demands of the environment or rationalized decisions about the role of the city, are closely controlled by the founders' cultural framework. In the normal course of development long-term physical and institutional factors become established in a regional setting. Before one sets out strategies for the "modernization" of Latin America it would seem useful to examine its early cities for the extent of the conceptions by which relations were established, to check the rationalized pattern created against our own biases, and to understand how management of the future was understood in the tradition.

The urban colonization of western South America was part of the largest town-building movement in history. Systematic exploration, colonization, and urbanization began with the arrival of Francisco Pizarro's expedition on the northern coast of Peru in 1532. The following half-century was the formative period of the urban ecology of the region as well as of the Viceroyalty.

[12] This paper is based on research for a dissertation, "Determinants of Physical Structure in the Peruvian Town of the Sixteenth Century," Department of City Planning, University of Pennsylvania, 1964. The research was supported by a Fulbright Scholarship and a Fels Foundation Fellowship. Another paper which contains some interesting historical highlights with regard to a different but important Latin American city appears in the Appendix. See Tomás José Sanabria, "Urbanization on an *Ad Hoc* Basis: A Case Study of Caracas."

By 1582 a pattern of cities and hinterlands, an almost complete framework of human habitation, covered the arable and otherwise useful areas of Peru, Ecuador, and Bolivia, with parts of Chile, Argentina and Colombia—what was then the urbanized region of the Viceroyalty of Peru.

Urban growth during that period can be examined through certain elements of the economic, political, and social pattern of the region. Although the stimuli for expansion, the constraints on development, and the particular morphology of city growth that took place were in some ways typical of other regions and periods, they were in many ways peculiar to the nature of this great urban movement and the culture of those who accomplished it. The events and decisions of this period set a format which was to guide and control urban growth for a long time to follow. The format was in large measure set by understandings of scarcity and the particular attitudes that these imposed.

The organized nature of urban colonization in the Viceroyalty was fundamental to the incipient urban pattern. The conquerors did not consolidate fronts close to the shores against the alien environment, pushing cautiously inland and stabilizing their achievements behind—with the knowledge that much more land lay beyond than behind. Instead they advanced immediately to the loci of indigenous habitation in the central mountains and expanded from these points back to the coast and in other promising directions, gaining a fairly full perspective on the potentialities of the entire region in a short time. Thus, mineral wealth and arable land were soon made *scarce*—scarce in the sense that they were finite, that the quantities of them were known to be limited. There was no frontier.

Significance is added to the concept of scarcity when it is related to the purposes of colonization. Though it is overly simplified to claim that the only motive of the Spanish monarchs was profit from the collection of taxes and extraction of minerals, this was surely a dominant purpose. Colonial administrators were responsible for its accomplishment, and it set the tone for personal objectives in the new continent. Most immigrants who arrived in America were destined to remain there and doubtless knew it. Only a few returned wealthy to Spain. Still there was an uneasy aggressiveness; the colonists were eager to hear of opportunities for fortune beyond the limitations of their immediate situation. They hastily abandoned the older towns in hope of better success in newer ones, even contrary to rigid prohibitions set against this by colonial authority. The towns and their inhabitants were not as "temporary" as asserted by some writers, founded casually and occupied as way stations. Yet they were pervaded in this period by a *feeling* of provisionality, increased by political unrest and threat of attack from remnants of the indigenous people. This was reflected by a hesitation to construct substantial buildings. Despite these factors the focus was on opportunities for wealth and the advancement in prestige available from it in a formative society. This relative unity of intention was necessarily directed rather narrowly toward a limited number of high-yield resources, namely farmland, mineral deposits, and Indians who could be pressed into the service of working them. Arable land in western South America is in short supply anyway, but in this perspective the opportunities were definitely limited and competition for them was keen.

There is evidence that arriving Spaniards expected to be, and insisted upon being, city dwellers. Even a person of rural origin in Spain had dealings in a city, probably Seville, before proceeding to the colonies and on arrival normally made connections in one of the ports of entry before passing on to the front of colonization. This contact was probably sufficient to alter whatever peasant outlook he may have had at the outset. No doubt an extraordinary proportion of the immigrants actually originated in cities, since the reports of the conquests must have been most current in them and opportunities for enlistment the greatest. In any case, a person attracted to America by the promise of great opportunity was not apt to isolate himself, by becoming a country dweller, from reports that would guide him to it. The effect is reflected by the absence of traditional European farm communities in America.[13] The peasant village rarely appeared except as inhabited by Indians or Negroes.

This attitude of the Spanish population was complemented by that of the Indians, for a special aspect of Inca culture was its amenability to urban living. Though it is unlikely that many of the Indians could have been classified as city dwellers before the conquest, the complex social and economic organization which characterized the Inca Empire and the rigid social controls exerted on the population made adjustments to urban life fairly easy for the Indians. Many had highly specialized occupations, and they were accustomed to the kind of discipline necessary to live in a city, even in an essentially alien city. Thus, though normally regarded by the Spaniards as a supporting agricultural peasantry, the Indians soon began to filter into the cities, having come perhaps to sell products or deliver tribute to their absentee landlords, or wandering in search of livelihood after the truncation of their rigid political and economic order. The colonial city was not organized for their participation and did not afford them the best opportunities, but it gradually adjusted to make their contributions viable.

OBJECTIVES IN THE ESTABLISHMENT OF TOWNS

The reasons for the founding of cities clarify the intent of this urban thrust of colonization and its way of organizing the environment. Since it was forbidden to build a town without specific directions to do so by the viceregal officer—a regulation only infrequently broken—we are able to categorize the objectives according to administrative reasons for designating the creation of new cities. The provisional or continuing nature of the reasons, and of the resources on which the reasons depended, is often a key to the later growth patterns of the towns.

Interest of the Crown in urbanization. Charles V and Philip

[13] Richard M. Morse, "Some Characteristics of Latin American Urban History," *American Historical Review*, LXVII, 2 (January, 1962), 317.

II, who ruled Spain during the sixteenth-century colonization of Peru, showed constant interest in the founding of towns, and it is suggested that their special favor was to be conferred on those who were successful at this aspect of the enterprise. Both gave considerable attention to means of direction in town-building. Their letters, like Francisco Pizarro's, to discoverers of new regions directed that the regions conquered were to be populated and jurisdiction over the towns conferred to the leader. Letters addressed to the king by expedition leaders invariably emphasized the number and substantiality of the towns they had founded, obviously considering this a good measure of their achievement. Thus, there was an impetus to take advantage of any opportunity that presented itself.

Urban nature of the people. The urban tendencies of colonists were intensified in a strange land among alien peoples. In fact, American settlement was sharply dichotomized in this period between the Indian hinterland and the Spanish city, causing the arriving immigrant to be a city dweller almost by definition. Cities were therefore necessary merely for the satisfactory housing of people.

Religious indoctrination. The purpose of collective worship has been a cause for the aggregation of people in various periods of history, and religious leaders have occasionally encouraged urbanism as a means of keeping people within the reach of doctrine and discipline.[14] The teaching of Catholicism or "that God be better served" was the reason most frequently found in the directives to establish individual cities. Only rarely was it omitted in even the briefest of them, and the missionary ardor of the time suggests that it was more than conventional rhetoric. In connection with the founding of Chachapoyas, Pizarro wrote: "Since there is a good disposition of land and Indians in the region, a city ought to be founded for the service of God and

---

[14] In North America, Cotton Mather was to object to people leaving towns to live away in the wilderness like "beasts" in defiance of their church.

His Majesty for teaching of the Catholic Faith. . . ." [15] The founding of *reducciónes* for Indians, mostly after this period, was another example of this conviction.

Military occupation. In the midst of an only partially subjected Indian population, the town was an obvious and necessary establishment for defense of the settlers and control of possible uprisings among the Indians. It also served the need for defense in the civil wars among the Spaniards themselves. A letter to the king from Bishop Vicente de Valverde of Cuzco in 1539 mentions that the city was founded in part for the "security of the land and so that damage not be done in it." [16] The garrison established at Piura by Pizarro upon his arrival in Peru served as nucleus for a city. Chachapoyas was founded in part to control the quarrelsome tribes in its locality. [17] This function was occasionally recalled in answers to the *Interogatorio de Indias,* a geographical questionnaire circulated by the Crown. The report for Loja (1571) stated that the road between Quito and Cuzco had been very dangerous, and that for this reason the city was founded. [18] The Huamanga (Ayacucho) report (1586) recalled that the city was originally used for the storage of weapons. [19]

Cities founded for specifically military purposes frequently disintegrated after the need for them disappeared, unless they found themselves later in the path of other fortune.

Opening agricultural land. Towns were sometimes founded for the express purpose of providing access to agricultural land and Indians to supply labor. Not only was more taxable wealth

[15] "Libro primero de cabildos de la Ciudad de San Juan de la Frontera de Chachapoyas," Raúl Rivera Serna, ed., in *Fénix*, XI (September 5, 1538), 295–296.

[16] Raúl Porras Barrenechea, *Cartas del Perú* (Lima: Sociedad de Bibliófilós Peruanos, 1959), p. 327.

[17] "Libro primero de cabildos de la Ciudad de San Juan de la Frontera de Chachapoyas," p. 292.

[18] Marcos Jiménez de la Espada, *Relaciones geográficas de Indias* (4 vols.; Madrid: Ministerio de Fomento, 1879–1897), III, 197.

[19] *Ibid.,* I, 105.

created but also administrators were enabled to convey awards of land to people who had assisted in the conquests or performed other meritorious services. One of many examples is the founding of Huanuco by Francisco Pizarro in 1539. He assigned lands there to a number of the minor personalities of the conquest who were becoming impatient for not having received such award.[20] He thereby ensured their loyalty to him rather than risk their defection to the rival faction of Diego de Almagro.

Cities which exist as centers for agricultural activity are, of course, typical the world over. The unique characteristic of those in Peru is that they were established previous to Spanish exploitation of the land rather than emerging from the use of the land. Generally speaking, Peruvian towns which were founded principally for this purpose, like Huanuco, never reached great importance in the colonial era or afterwards. Their static condition was to be expected since the agricultural land of Peru is found in relatively small and isolated patches. The resource imposed specific limitations on growth, and its profitability was weakened with the reduction of the Indian population in years to follow.

Administration of political jurisdiction. In this period travel was difficult, communications over long distances poor, and public morality, in part as a consequence, was very low. In order to govern successfully it was necessary for the government to have an enforcement arm within all settled regions. In fact, the founding of a city to govern a regional jurisdiction is a tautology since in Spanish governmental terminology the "city" included an urban area and its entire expanse of hinterland, all governed by a municipality. Its jurisdiction extended to the boundaries of the surrounding cities; the municipality was the exclusive unit of local government. Thus, every municipality had political privileges and responsibilities that extended over the full area of its resources. There was no form of local rural government, ex-

---

[20] José Varallamos, *Historia de Huánuco: estudio de vida social* (Buenos Aires: Imprenta Lopéz, 1959), p. 126.

cept in the form of minor powers, under close municipal control, delegated to villages within the municipality. Thus, urbanization was concomitant with administration.

The cities with the larger political roles became the major metropolises of the continent. Others had a stable economic activity derived from this role with an over-all growth pattern related to their other opportunities.

Exploitation of mineral resources. Although purposes for the founding of cities invariably overlap, the mining towns come closest to being single-purposed. Huancavelica and Potosi were settled by miners who went to these localities after the discovery of mercury and silver in them. They did not have the distinction of formal foundations as did the other towns, almost without exception. Their street plans show the lack of disciplined building of the town. Huancavelica did not have a municipality until the title of "city" was later conferred upon it by Viceroy Toledo after more than two decades of existence, and Potosi always remained a *villa*. Even with the largest urban population in the western hemisphere, its aspirations to higher rank were frustrated by the dominance of La Plata (Sucre), in whose jurisdiction it lay.

The mining towns often grew with unparalleled speed immediately after the discovery of ore. It is impossible to generalize about their long-term growth, however. Their populations and prosperity varied with the fortunes of their enterprise. They grew with the discovery of new veins of minerals and diminished with the exhaustion of them. Some experienced recovery with the introduction of new technical methods which enabled the exploitation of lower-grade ores. Most of them did not last long as important cities, but a few have remained significant industrial centers to the present time.

Port cities. The exploitative nature of the economy and the need for communication resulting from the strong centralization of administrative power in Spain necessitated provision for intercontinental travel of elaborate proportions. With all things favorable, a round trip between Peru and Madrid took about a year. The cities most characterized by the communication function were those at the main convergences of transport routes in the Caribbean area, but several Peruvian cities were also dominated by it. Lima was established primarily as a political capital, and its nature itself implied a need for easy communication with Spain and made its dependent port city of Callao the major port of Peru. Pizarro is known to have located the city to facilitate this function. Remoteness from a port was a principal complaint with the situation of the earlier capital at Jauja. Elsewhere on the coast, the town of Camana was founded as a port convenient for transportation of the silver which passed to the ocean through Cuzco and Arequipa from Potosi. There were many others.

Port cities which lacked political roles grew and declined with the minerals and other resources which were shipped from them. Close control over the movement of commodities by colonial authority in Spain and the dominance of Lima as port of entry effectively limited the long-term success of other port cities.

Way stations. As a result of Spanish domination of commodity movements, most of the cities in this category were on routes converging at Lima or extending from the mining towns to specialized mineral ports. Others were located for limited intracolonial trade to provide supply stations and defensive garrisons on the long dangerous roads between the principal cities. Huamanga (Ayacucho) was located on the road between Lima and Cuzco as a way station. Arequipa was founded by Pizarro for this purpose between Potosi and the port of Camana via Cuzco, as well as to provide landholdings for some of his followers.[21] La Paz grew as a small town to serve the same function between Potosi and Cuzco. Several of these towns found themselves in

[21] Ventura Travada y Córdova, *El suelo de Arequipa convertido en cielo* (1752) (Arequipa: Primer Festival del Libro Arequipeno, 1958), pp. 36–37; Jorge Basadre, *La multitud, la ciudad y el campo en la historia del Perú* (Lima: Editorial Huascarán, n.d.), p. 39.

fortunate positions with respect to other functions in their later histories, but those which never succeeded in expanding their activities did not grow to importance.

Means of personal advancement. The Crown and its colonial administrators made the founding of towns a profitable enterprise in order to encourage settlement. The privileges of land-ownership, appointment of political positions, and alleviation from taxes which were normally enjoyed by the founder made personal advancement an important motive. As one would expect, there were occasional efforts to establish towns outside the law or in contention with existing jurisdiction. The founding of Quito in such circumstances by Sebastián Benalcázar was typical. As was frequently the case, the foundation was approved and issued a *capitulación* by Pizarro in the name of Benalcázar when the venture was found to be profitable.[22] There were several others.

Means of income to those without livelihood. With immigrants arriving in large numbers, many destitute—with nothing but "their capes over their shoulders"—but convinced that the colonies offered great opportunity, there were large numbers of vagrants in the cities who constituted a drain on the economy and a potentially dangerous group in search of military and political involvement. The creation of new towns to entice these persons from the existing ones and cause them to be profitably engaged was an obvious remedy to the situation. This use is suggested in correspondence from the King to officials at Potosí.[23] Vargas Ugarte concludes that it was one of the central motives of the urbanization policy of Viceroy el Conde de Nieva (1551–1556) and cites several towns as examples.[24]

---

[22] *Libro de cabildos de la Ciudad de Quito*, José Rumazo Gonzáles and Jorge Garcés, eds. (30 vols.; Quito: Imprenta Municipal, 1934–1955), I, 45–47.

[23] Lewis Hanke, *The Imperial City of Potosí* (The Hague: Martinus Nijhoff, 1956), p. 34.

[24] Rubén Vargas Ugarte, S.J., *Historia del Perú: Virreinato (1551–1600)* (n.p., 1949), p. 128.

In addition to these objectives for the establishment of towns, there were others of less importance or later initiation. Most of the towns combined functions for service to the religious tradition, for military defense and control of the surrounding hinterland, for exploitation of the accessible agricultural lands and native populations, and for political administration of broad jurisdictions. In special cases they served the transportation channels of the empire or facilitated the extraction of precious ores. They provided opportunity to their founders and early settlers in the form of landownership, political position, and the opportunity for social prestige.

THE GROWTH OF URBAN POPULATIONS

Growth patterns of the colonial cities are hard to follow in detail since large portions of the population were omitted from the censuses. It is nevertheless useful to consider relative rates of growth among different types of towns, changing proportions among different types of city dwellers, and the proportion of the total regional population in the cities.

It is clear that most of the towns experienced continual growth throughout the period. The fastest growing were the mining towns, endowed with the minerals that made America a legendary place to European peoples. Second to them was Lima, seat of the Viceroy and the funnel through which all commodities and authority passed on its way between Spain and Peru. Next come the towns that had the greatest tributary Indian populations and the greatest expanses of the scarce agricultural land. The growth of Cuzco answers to this description. Probably the seats of *reales audiencias* also experienced unusual growth, as in the cases of Quito and Sucre. More generally, growth in the towns responded to the aggregated intensity of their several roles in colonial life. The most important city-building factors were: mining, political administration, availability of land and indigenous population, service to transportation routes, and military control. Generally, these factors are mentioned in order of im-

43

portance to the building of Peruvian cities, but only their intensity and the number of them in a particular city had made them determinants of growth.

The physical growth of the towns did not keep up with their growth in population. With the surrounding lands and positions of privilege in the towns rapidly being exhausted, newcomers were not afforded the same opportunities as the earlier inhabitants. The newcomers' limited participation in the life of the cities was physically evident in the beginning of the subdivision and crowding of house lots. There was reluctance to allow the city to spread physically in a manner commensurate with its growing population because the stature of its prestigious families would thus be reduced. A large proportion of the immigrants were Indians who were called as servants or who came in search of opportunity after being deprived of their lands. They had a limited impact on the physical city, but swelled its numbers and took part in its activity.

This is not to say that the amount of land occupied by the cities did not grow. Additional house lots were continually being distributed throughout the period, though in much more limited numbers toward the end. The municipality of Quito was warned late in the century that land between the existing houses should be allotted before further lands at the margins of the city be assigned to new immigrants. Garcilazo de la Vega (circa 1610) mentioned that a town near Cuzco he had once known as a small exurban settlement had during his lifetime been completely overcome by the expansion of the city. Toward the end of the century, Lima found it easy to utilize new land across the river in the district of San Lazaro when it was vacated by the Indians, who were forced to leave by administrative regulations.

The size of the preindustrial city, and particularly of the Peruvian city, was frequently overestimated or purposely exaggerated. This was to be expected in a situation when numbers were often used more to create an emotional effect than to serve as means of careful measurement and when long distances to remote places kept readers from checking the claim. Xeres reports that 100,000 Indians gathered daily in the market at Jauja, and early estimates of the populations of Cuzco and Tenochtitlan reach similarly preposterous numbers. There was also a tendency to count the populations of communities in the local hinterland with that of a central city.[25] Such communities surely account for some of the 160,000 inhabitants estimated for Potosi in 1650.[26] There was also a noticeable tendency to regard a city as large because it was, for some reason, important. Care must be taken, however, not to err on the low side. Urban populations of this period were subject to great temporary increases because of institutional patterns, such as the need for Indians to bring their tribute to landholders in the major cities, and because of crises such as war, which caused large numbers of people to seek safety in cities they did not normally inhabit.

Official sources often contain lower estimates than unofficial ones. They may have been more realistic, or they may have represented attempts of local officials to minimize tax demands from higher authorities.

Scarcity and incompleteness of censuses in the sixteenth century are to be expected and suggest important characteristics of the society. This was a period when the structure of authority did not rest upon the consent of the people at large, and when the latter were not a matter of concern to the upper classes. They were of little consequence even in wartime, since only a limited number of them could be equipped and supported in the field; and they contributed to the income of the landholding class through the products of the land they occupied rather than as individuals. The ruling class had no need to take notice of the desires of the masses of people or to count their meager assets. Since the administrators were seldom interested in planning the

[25] Gideon Sjoberg, *The Preindustrial City, Past and Present* (Glencoe, Ill.: The Free Press, 1960), p. 81.

[26] Personal interview with Ingo. Giullermo Obando-Sanz, Universidad Tomás Frías, Potosi, September, 1961.

revision of the social or economic order, there was little use for objective description on that account.[27] Further, since the urban area was not a consequential jurisdiction, little information about urban populations was collected. This issue too is often confusing, however, since "city" to a nonofficial observer sometimes meant the urban area alone.

The important city dweller to authorities who would count their resources was the *vecino*. He was the citizen-landholder, who had the use of land and Indians granted him by the municipality, had the right to hold office, bore most of the (direct) financial responsibilities to the municipality, and had the right to bear arms and the obligation of military service to the city and Viceroyalty in time of need. As a measure of the level of urban activity in a broader sense, however, *vecinos* do not suffice, since they were just a fraction of the economically active city dwellers and represent only those in particular sectors of urban activity.

Counts of *vecinos* in the towns were much more frequently made than complete censuses, but *vecinos* were not distributed among the total population in any uniform manner. William Prescott and many historians after him have assumed a ratio of one *vecino* to five residents in cities,[28] possibly based on a belief that all heads of families held the title. Such, however, was not the case. At the founding of a town all the socially qualified members of the group who were disposed to remain at the site received allotments of land and became *vecinos*. If the town did not develop rapidly thereafter, as in the case of many isolated towns of the interior which had little industry or commerce, the *vecinos* remained a major percentage of the total number of male inhabitants. On the other hand, in the more prosperous cities, and particularly those which attracted people for reasons

[27] Sjoberg, *op. cit.*, p. 308.

[28] For example, Victor Manuel Albórnoz, *Acotaciones a las relaciones geográficas de Indias concernientes a la gobernación de Cuenca* (Cuenca, 1951), p. 97.

other than landownership, the *vecinos* became a proportionally small, aristocratic, and privileged group.

These remarks are substantiated by the tabulations in Table 1

Table 1. Urban population of principal municipalities in the Viceroyalty of Peru.

Municipality	Vecinos	Moradores*	Vecinos
	(1569)	(1569)	(1581)
Lima	32	2,500	57
Cuzco	80	500	125
Arequipa	35	400	33
La Plata	32	300	29
Huamanga (Ayacucho)	20	250	33
Piura	35	200	29
La Paz	30	200	41
Potosi	0	800	0
Quito	50	250	31
Trujillo	35	300	34

* Resident adult Spanish males.

of municipal populations at the time of Viceroy Toledo's arrival in America in 1569.[29] Additional counts taken during the travels of Toledo in 1581 are included in the table.[30] Since the Spanish population was almost exclusively concentrated in the cities, these can be regarded as urban populations.

The appearance of relatively numerous *vecinos* in Cuzco and Quito reflects the heavy Indian populations, and therefore numerous landholdings, in those localities. Potosi had none because its informal settlement did not entitle it to a municipality which could confer the title. It is reasonable that Lima had the most *moradores*, but many of the wealthy *vecinos* of other cities in the Viceroyalty customarily lived there, so the count is probably a very low estimate of the current habitation. By converse use

[29] Constantino Bayle, *Los cabildos seculares en la América Española* (Madrid: Sapientia, 1952), p. 66.

[30] Silvio A. Zavala, *La encomienda indiana* (Madrid: Centro de Estudios Históricos, 1935), p. 325.

of the same reasoning, the count of resident *vecinos* in many of the other cities is probably too high. More rapid growth was soon to follow for Lima, which allegedly had a population of 14,000 by the end of the century and of 26,000 by 1626.[31] This agrees with Gideon Sjoberg's claim that among preindustrial cities, societal capitals are the foci of growth.

Though the figures for *moradores* in Table 1 are obviously loose approximations, being rounded off to hundreds and half-hundreds, they agree in order of magnitude with most parallel sources. In 1561 a report of Pedro de Avendano, Secretary of the *Audiencia* in Lima, mentioned that the Viceroyalty contained seventeen "towns of Spaniards" and 427 *vecinos*.[32]

The difference between the populations of towns and of hinterlands is revealed by contrasting the figures in Table 1 with those reported by Avendano (Table 2), showing the total popu-

Table 2. Total population of principal municipalities in the Viceroyalty of Peru, 1561.

Municipality	Persons of all ages
Lima	99,600
Cuzco	267,000
Arequipa	201,830
La Plata	232,800
Huamanga	112,520
Piura	16,617
La Paz	150,655
Potosi	—
Quito	240,670
Trujillo	215,000

lation for 1561 of all ages and races in the jurisdictions of the same municipalities.[33]

Figures of urban population unquestionably require a great

[31] Ricardo Tizón y Bueno, "El plano de Lima," *Monografías históricas sobre la Ciudad de Lima* (2 vols.; Lima: Consejo Provincial de Lima, Gil, 1935).

[32] Zavala, *op. cit.*, pp. 323–324.

[33] *Ibid.*, p. 324.

deal of qualification. Even if reasonably accurate for the time they were taken, they were subject to rapid change. The Indian populations migrated and were rapidly reduced by contact with Spanish culture, the demands made on them, and the frequent wars. Some were to be found in the cities as unofficial dwellers and personal servants. The figures suggest that the city was a diminutive part of the demographic structure of its region, a minute cluster of people amid the heavily populated agricultural lands of its jurisdiction. Yet its unique social and economic organization gave it a power that dominated colonial society.

THE MORPHOLOGY OF CITY GROWTH

The growth of towns during the sixteenth century caused changes of various kinds in their physical and social character, particularly since persons who came after development was under way necessarily took different roles in the towns than those who had arrived in time to occupy more favored positions. In some respects expansion of towns was more easily achieved in this period than it was later because of the inherent flexibilities in the relatively simple physical structure.

The provisional physical nature of the towns made rebuilding for internal change easier than it would otherwise have been. A key to the lack of great concern for the physical plant of the towns during the early years is the fact that their locations were often moved within the localities they dominated. A large proportion of the towns was moved at least once, and several of them were moved three or four times before their final locations were established. This mobility is particularly interesting in view of the fact that as political and social entities the towns were remarkably permanent; the few failures of towns in the region include only the abandonment of Jauja, the decimation of Sana by flood and pirates, and a few small towns overrun during the early Indian uprisings. The readiness with which towns were moved to new locations, even several years after their founding, suggests that the resources put into buildings at the vacated site could be easily expended. Debates about the propriety of changing location, found in the journals of a few of the cities' councils, refer to no regret in leaving the buildings erected at the first site. The adjustments for change in functions of the physical plant must have been correspondingly simple.

The universal grid pattern of town layout was another characteristic that offered flexibility. In many cases, room for considerable expansion was anticipated at the time of founding. Pizarro, for example, laid out 117 blocks for the development of Lima (which, in fact, used up the 9 by 13 rectangle before expanding), a larger space than was to be occupied for some years following the initial founding. The grid was easily expanded by extending the straight streets and adding more identical blocks. There were no buildings with specific functions, or other impediments, at the periphery of the city; no walls, markets, or storehouses as in other traditions. The colonial city had only a single focus: its central plaza.

Another element of flexibility in the physical structure was the fairly low initial population densities in the towns. Since law required that land be enclosed by walls shortly after receipt by the townsman, the effective building density remained high and generally constant. The large size of the lots caused more than one chronicler to mention that the early cities of Peru seemed much larger than they actually were. Subdivision of lots occurred as pressures for space grew, and in later periods many of them were cut by additional streets, parallel to and halfway between the streets originally bordering the lot.

Changes in the use of buildings during periods of city growth were facilitated by the relative lack of differentiation between buildings erected for different purposes; also the use of land was not as specialized, of course, as it became in subsequent periods. But particularly in this tradition the same building type was used for residence, commerce, artisanal activity, and even public functions: a simple series of rooms arranged around a rectangle, opening onto a central patio. Though the buildings varied in size and detail according to their use and wealth of the owners, there is substantial basis for claiming that only two building types were used: ecclesiastical and nonecclesiastical. Thus, as artisans had to expand their urban enclaves or as ambulant merchants of the central plaza began renting nearby stores, they had merely to secure occupancy of an adjacent building to have an accommodation which was similar to ones they had already used for the same purpose.

Actually, the movement and enlargement of commercial establishments in the city only slightly altered its physical structure because urban commercial activity had low prestige. Commerce was considered a necessary evil, dangerous to the soul, and merchants were socially marginal people. Since their prices and profits were unilaterally controlled by the municipality, most of them were men of very modest means whose business was transacted at stalls in the plaza or under awnings by the surrounding buildings. Thus, commerce consumed relatively little space.

There was, however, an invasion of surrounding buildings by commercial establishments. They first entered the buildings immediately surrounding the plaza. (Contrary to the assumption of many authors, there was no Crown law requiring that the surrounding lots be reserved for this purpose until 1573, after most of the important colonial towns were well established.) They then extended down the adjacent streets. Concolorcorvo, in the eighteenth century, commented on Cuzco that "the houses on the plaza are the worst in the city, *as happens almost everywhere,* because the . . . owners of those places threw them to profit by permitting them to serve the merchants, who pay the highest rent." [34]

The main alteration in the balance of land allocation during the century occurred as a result of the increasing holdings of the Church. Religious orders received limited urban lots and supporting agricultural lands shortly after the establishment of

[34] Calixto Bustamante Carlos Inca [Concolorcorvo, pseud.], *El lazarillo de ciegos caminantes* (Paris: Desclee de Brouwer, 1938), p. 221.

the cities, but their proportion of the total land space increased rapidly for two reasons. Land was often bequeathed to them by citizens of the city, which meant permanent removal of the land from secular uses because canon law prohibited the sale or disposal by any means of Church property; secondly, religious orders were extraordinarily successful in obtaining additional land by request from the town councils, even under circumstances which clearly violated the principles stated by the Crown for the distribution of land. This is a matter difficult to investigate in detail, but apparently political linkage in these years between the Crown and the newly nationalized Church, as well as its social dominance, made church land policy difficult for the laity to control. They probably found it not only embarrassing but politically and spiritually dangerous to refuse favors to the religious orders. According to responsible contemporary observers[35] and impressions from cartographic evidence, ecclesiastical ownership in the cities may have included more than a quarter of the land area by the last decades of the century— though no reliable figures are available. Some of it was in secular use, rented for annuities.

Counteracting the physical characteristics amenable to growth and expansion, there were social and administrative factors which tended to impede growth. Perhaps the foremost of these were conditions related to the dominance of society, politics, and economy in the towns by a landholding class. As a basic problem, one could not hold citizenship in a town without being a landholder. This meant that the exhaustion of agricultural land accessible to the city effectively discouraged the immigration of ambitious people of the land-oriented tradition. Those who held proper status to become citizens, but who arrived after the exhaustion of landed property in the towns, comprised a residual

[35] *Colección de documentos inéditos relativos al descubrimiento, conquista y organización de las posesiones españolas de América y Oceania sacados de los Archivos del Reino y muy especialmente del de Indias* (42 vols.; Madrid: Imprenta de Manuel G. Hernandez, 1864–1884), IV, 440–462.

group called "soldiers." The word came to have the bad connotation of members of the idle privileged class with no visible means of support.[36] A survey of Peru was made by the Viceroy in the late 1550's to discover the reasons for frequent anarchy and violence in the province. He found that of the eight thousand Spaniards in the Viceroyalty at that time three thousand were "soldiers" by profession.[37] Local officials frequently complained that shortage of land often made it impossible to give arriving colonists their proper opportunities.

The landholdings generally remained in the hands of the same families for long periods of time (notwithstanding Crown rulings to the contrary in order to prevent permanent vesting of interest). Further, the holdings could not be forfeited in lieu of debt; to permit this was considered dangerous to the welfare and defense of the city.[38] Finally, it was illegal to leave a city in which one held land or for anyone to obtain land who had holdings in another jurisdiction—an effort to curb exploitation of land. Although these regulations seem to have been frequently violated, particularly by the more powerful personalities of the era, and expropriations were not unheard of, they no doubt effectively rooted most landholders to the localities of their first interests and rigidly stabilized the tenure patterns.

In order to fortify the intent of these regulations, it was also made illegal to sell land under most circumstances. This was reinforced by a vestigial medieval disinclination to sell land—it was regarded as social and economic capital, and its disposal for liquid funds was to incur social and financial ruin. Urban land, as opposed to agricultural land, was sold more readily,[39] and even more generally rented by private parties, the government,

[36] Bayle, *op. cit.*, p. 58.

[37] Victor Manuel Albórnoz, *Historial de la fundación de la Ciudad de Cuenca* (Quito: Editorial Fray Jodoco Ricks, 1957), p. 41.

[38] Bayle, *op. cit.*, p. 70.

[39] "Protócolo de escrituras públicas hechas ante el escribano Diego Gutiérrez" (March–May 1545), MS, Lima, Sala Investigaciones, A 31, 1545.

and the Church. Here also townsmen were theoretically bound to inhabit their lots permanently, beginning a short time after receipt.[40] This requirement, however, seems to have been more generally violated, no doubt because social prestige and livelihood were not dependent upon it.

THE BEGINNINGS OF SCARCITY

These comments on the development of towns have thrown into relief certain basic scarcities, both natural and institutionally determined, of growth-related resources. For western South America, the limitations of many natural resources were immediately apparent. Shortages of timber over most of the area, of water in the coastal regions, and most especially of farmland over most of the Viceroyalty combined with the often unreliable availability of the tributary Indian population to put natural strictures on growth. Exhaustibility of minerals within the grasp of contemporary mining technology limited the potentialities of some cities; strict controls on intercolonial trade and the Crown monopolies on intercontinental goods movement minimized the opportunities of other cities.

The severe shortage of arable land was the greatest limitation, and consciousness of it was apparently first and foremost. Shortly after the close of the initial conquest (1539) Pizarro ordered the founding of Huanuco with the rank of "city," but the citizens of Lima (200 kilometers away over the mountains) insisted that this title infringed on their rights to hinterland, so he was forced to revoke it and reduce Huanuco to a "town," [41] which had only subsidiary territorial powers. Potosi was prevented from ever achieving the rank of city—even when its mines had made it the

[40] Raúl Porras Barrenechea, *Colección de documentos inéditos para la historia del Perú* (2 vols.; Lima: Departamento de Relaciones Culturales, 1944), I, 166.

[41] Antonio de Herrera, *Historia general de los hechos de los castellanos en las islas, y tierra-firme de el Mar Oceano* (Asunción: Editorial Guaranía, 1944–1955)

largest urban place on the continent—by pressures from the city of Sucre, in whose jurisdiction it was located. Late in the century a viceregal order to locate a city that would have removed part of the land under the jurisdiction of Quito was fought bitterly by the citizens of that city.[42] There were a number of similar cases, and the limited capacity of the hinterland to support urban populations was occasionally specifically argued.

Unlike the more naturally developed town, which emerges from an agriculturally developed countryside, the colonial cities were planted as full political systems with their tributary hinterland specified as part of their structure. Thus, there was little incremental expansion; the resources were quickly accounted for. Further, the landholding leadership was necessarily conservative in nature, since the source of its power was a finite and totally committed resource. This was leadership of a very different nature from that which would have been produced by merchant domination, calculating its fortunes on the basis of expandable markets.

Finally, poverty of financial resources, particularly in the case of municipal government, was a constant strain. The condition is reflected in the very slow acquisition by towns in this period of the municipal appurtenances considered most basic: town halls, slaughter houses, jails, and so forth. In some cases town councils were unable even to provide wooden chests for the storage of records or to supply paper to record actions. The councils existed primarily on rents, the collection of fines, and the licensing of tradesmen; and these sources of income, particularly the second, were very inefficiently administered. The councils were constantly close to bankruptcy and depended on a system of special assessment for most improvements. Late in the century, when a ship arrived in the port near Lima loaded with oriental silks and other finery, the Lima council, aware of the poverty of their surroundings, decided it was better to conserve the money of the people by having the contents of the

[42] *Libro de cabildos de la Ciudad de Quito*, XIII, 365–366.

ship removed to the docks and burned.[43] Destitution led the councils to rent and eventually to sell the public lands originally allocated to the use of the people at large—particularly the municipal pastures. Similar exigencies led the Crown to sell to the cities much of the land allocated to its use.

These problems identified or created in the early decades of Spanish urbanization in America were long to afflict the efforts of the cities to enlarge and to improve their welfare. The cities were founded by men who were very much aware of their role in urbanizing an entire new continent. They laid out great plazas in the presence of small founding parties in expectation of a great future, surveyed ambitious areas of urban land for the homes of those to come later, and showed limitless enthusiasm for the supposed wealth of the continent. Their ingenuity was not unusual, but the strength of their determination was monumental. Yet the moment a city was created its defensive posture was established as a result of both external pressures and conflicting internal interests. The cities were launched into a long history with expectations of abundance and expansion, but with attitudes conditioned to scarcity and conservation.

Editor's Summary and Elaboration

Latin America has been called "a continent in the process of modernizing." Only too often, however, the description of conditions leads to the conclusion that, far from suffering from modernization, its countries are still wrestling with the conditions of colonialism. This does not mean stagnation or that no progress has been made since the sixteenth century. It does, however, indicate that the obstacles to modernization faced by these countries are not new but are rather solidly entrenched and not likely to disappear of their own accord.

[43] *Libros de cabildos de Lima*, Bertram Lee, ed. (13 vols.; Lima: Consejo Provincial de Lima, 1935), XIII, 267.

More than other Western regions, Latin America seems to be a "captive of its history." Hoselitz's survey of five thousand years of history indicates that in western Europe cities developed out of the countryside in response to economic needs and became focal points which, in turn, supported the countryside. Significant characteristics of early Western cities were: (1) the generally uncommitted nature of their populations to any past influence and their freedom to pursue their own interests; (2) the development of trade and commerce; (3) the development of self-sufficiency to the extent that a large surrounding state was not necessary; and (4) changes in the size of cities, in both area and population, in relation to their technology and function. Because of their strong position as focal points and their economic and political significance, these Western cities were in a position to become industrial and economic centers for national growth after the industrial revolution.

STAGES OF URBANIZATION IN LATIN AMERICA

Jorge E. Hardoy described six stages of urbanization in Latin America, which may be used as the point of departure for more detailed discussion.

The first stage, of course, is the precolonial urban culture of the Aztecs and Incas, which occupied about 5 per cent of the total area in central Mexico, the Andean highlands, and along the Peruvian coastline. These were not urban centers as we know them, in the sense of being economic units and exchange points for trade and the infusion of new ideas and culture. Rather, they were strongholds of the traditional culture, frequently religious centers or centers from which traditional power and authority were exercised. They functioned as cities, however, in the sense of bringing people together and providing them with some form of occupation away from the land. For their time and place they can be considered urban, and their existence might be said to have made the second stage easier to establish. The second stage was the determination by the Spanish of the territorial pattern of foundation, on the basis of the regional and urban infra-structure of the indigenous culture and the distribution of the Indian population.

During the third stage, the Spanish and Portuguese established the essential settlement pattern of Latin America. Taking into account the earlier foundations, the location of resources, and the need to maintain direct contacts with the sponsoring country, regional and local ports, mining and colonizing centers, forts, and settlements for other purposes were established. Physically, the Spanish cities were well planned, in accordance with the ideas of Charles V and Philip II. In the seventy years prior to 1576 the Spanish founded most of the important cities on the Latin American continent, all in accordance with legislation that in 1576 was collected into the *Real Cedula*. This legislation specified sites near rivers on unoccupied land (or land freely given), with cities to be laid out in a way that permitted expansion. Details of the city planning of Philip II could be read with profit by some of today's city planners: orientation of streets in relation to the sun, width of streets, orientation of location to take account of prevailing winds, sizes of the squares, selection of places for public buildings—everything from a technical viewpoint was fairly completely covered. The Mediterranean pattern of colonizing cities was followed; the plaza replaced the Greek agora that faced the sea, but the cities looked toward Spain rather than inward toward the continent.

This pattern was practically completed by 1580. Sixteen of the twenty largest cities of today had been founded by that time. In addition, the establishment of these and other cities which are no longer important stimulated the development of subordinate centers which, in turn, determined the development of secondary regions.

This stage has several important aspects for the present situation in Latin America. The settlement pattern had well-defined boundaries. In Mexico and southern South America, where topography permitted, the urbanization pattern included most of the territory. But the heart of South America, in spite of its great natural resources, received no attention from the colonial administration. Cities were planted on the countryside rather than growing out of it. The functions of the city were assigned; so also was its authority, rather than developing from within as response to the course of events. No allowance was made for expansion—all resources (some scarce at best) were allocated at the beginning. The population was committed to following the edicts and wishes of the royal families of Spain and Portugal, at least if it wished to prosper. The early assignation of resources meant the concentration of sources of wealth, whether minerals, land, or control of the Indians, in a relatively few hands, and concentration was favored by royal authority. The boundaries of each city extended to the boundaries of the next city; there were no villages or small cities. Isolation was imposed, with unfortunate consequences today.

Numerous restrictions prevented the cities from functioning as western European cities did, even after trade and commerce developed: "Colonial Venezuelan production originated on the plantations, flowed to the mercantile cities connected with the foreign market, and [its profits] returned to the plantations without changing the economic conditions which prevailed there." [44]

Trade between cities was not encouraged, so that local cultivation of resources through exchange of products was restricted, as was the development of a community of common interests that might have promoted a feeling of nationalism.

As in other areas, cities were founded for a number of reasons and grew or declined as their *raisons d'être* waxed or waned. Cities with political functions sometimes were favored at the expense of cities that developed in response to resource utilization.

[44] Federico Brito Figueroa, *La estructura económica de Venezuela colonial* (Caracas, 1963), pp. 271, 275, quoted in Richard M. Morse, "Recent Research on Latin American Urbanization: A Selective Survey with Commentary," *Latin American Research Review*, I, 1 (Fall, 1965), 40.

Thus, as Gakenheimer mentioned, Potosi remained a *villa*, although it was larger than Sucre, the seat of administration. The economic sources of wealth lay in the countryside, and the economic base of most cities made them financially dependent. Whether political or economic reasons can be identified as the chief reason for founding colonial cities, it was during this period that the foundation was laid for rural dominance.

The fourth stage was a period of consolidating colonial institutions and establishing the structure of colonial society. This stage covers about two hundred years, during which no deep change disturbed the general pattern. The pattern of urbanization that would persist until the advent of the railroad or the highway was completed. The principal centers from which the colonies were administered were consolidated. Only a few centers acquired importance and presented some urban aspect, chiefly those in which commercial activities and religious, administrative, military, and cultural institutions were concentrated. Thus, the continental importance of Lima, Mexico City, and Bahia, and the regional importance of Havana, Rio de Janeiro, Buenos Aires, Caracas, Santiago, Bogota, and other centers, were defined.

There was little or no change in the Latin American social and economic structure after independence. Perhaps the most significant development was emphasizing the importance of the established centers, helped by their location, by their dominating political influence, and by the concentration of economic and other activities in them. "The greater international exposure of Latin American cities after independence made them more provincial rather than more metropolitan." They were subjected to different influences of a colonial nature and were "imitative, derivative, and merely typical" rather than unique and exemplary.[45] The geographic vastness and the lack of transportation,

[45] George A. Kubler, "Cities and Culture in the Colonial Period in Latin America," *Diogenes*, XLVII (Fall, 1964), 53–62, quoted in Morse, "Recent Research on Latin American Urbanization," p. 42.

the rivalry between the capital cities of new nations, exposed to limited contacts with Europe and the United States, and with the interior, shaped the social, political, and economic structures of each country.

Consequently, in spite of the same general plan and pattern of settlement throughout the region, Latin America did not become a unit. The countries fall into several geographical and cultural groupings. Nor are the cities all alike. The differences among them were accentuated during the fifth stage, when immigration from Europe was the chief factor of change. This stage, according to Hardoy, did not take place simultaneously in all the countries:

It had its beginning in Argentina, Uruguay, and Brazil. To its ports and in a lesser degree, to its fields, arrived, from 1880, waves of immigrants. The European immigrants not only strengthened the priority of some cities with their effort, commercial capacity, and even with capital, but brought about the formation of new institutions, in order to protect their work and interests, and also a different political structure. The European immigration reached afterwards Chile and Cuba, and later Venezuela, Colombia, Mexico, and other countries. Those decades coincided, at least in the most favored countries, with the opening of new territories; with the development and beginning of technology in agriculture; with the creation of the first urban industries, with the construction of railroad lines, ports, and roads, and with the appearance of a new professional class and a bureaucracy not known until then.

Latin American cities that grew during this period, according to one viewpoint, were those in a position to profit from the prevailing economic advantages of the nineteenth and early twentieth centuries. Buenos Aires, for example, grew because it was outward-looking, European, dynamic, and economically active. Valparaiso became the leading Chilean city in the nineteenth century, according to Tom E. Davis, surpassed only by Santiago around 1880 or 1890, after the development of the central valley regions of Chile.

In a last stage, Hardoy continued, "the one we are living in, the long delayed incorporation of rural groups has sent these groups to the cities. There have grown, faster than before, the few industrial centers of each country, and in a lesser degree, the provincial capitals. The population of the rural towns and areas has decreased."

CHARACTERISTICS OF URBAN GROWTH IN LATIN AMERICA

Three aspects of the process of urbanization are important, according to Hardoy:

First, until very recently it took place within the broad territorial boundaries that had been more or less established in 1580, and moved around the same cities that for almost four centuries have been national or at least regional centers. Next, the gravitation to the principal city in each country, with the exception of Brazil and Colombia for historical and geographical reasons, is proportionally much stronger today than a hundred or more years ago. At that time, around each secondary regional center had developed a sort of self-sufficient regional economy, while today all the regional centers increasingly move around the main metropolis of each country, even for insignificant details of their administrative, economic, and cultural life. Finally, in each country the lack of direct transportation and communication between regional centers with a complementary production, and their absolute dependence on the national capital, prevents the beginning of the regionalization that is usually enunciated as an urgent need to reach economic maturity.

The force of traditionalism remains strong for a number of reasons, Hardoy continued:

A hundred and fifty years of politically independent life have not brought the structural changes that some members of the independentist movements expected. Quite possibly the reason is that the truly revolutionary leaders soon lost control of the direction of the liberating movements which, in a short time, were polarized in various personalist attempts without a national sense. The general population was kept out of these movements. It is true that the people participated in great numbers in external and internal wars, but they did it without clearly understanding their true significance, deluded by the structural changes and the justice that the new constitutions promised them.

Another contributing factor to the lack of basic change may be the flexibility shown by the traditional structure, which over the centuries has been able to modernize many of its elements without effecting modernization. This process continues. The modern Latin American city is less an "urban society in change" (that is, concerned with "revolution, self-transcendence, obliteration of the past") than a society in which the trappings of Western industrial civilization are being fitted onto a traditional way of life.[46]

According to one viewpoint, set forth by James R. Scobie, the city in Latin America has grown like an "exotic flower" with little relation to the rest of the country. It has expressed the values of dominant minority groups, but not those of integrated and national societies. Its role, therefore, must be reoriented before it can become a vehicle for modernization.

Political considerations and motivations, rather than economic or social, have historically controlled urbanization in Latin America. The city has, therefore, often emerged as an imposition, an appendage, tacked onto a relatively underdeveloped agricultural countryside—the military centers of the Aztecs, the political centers of the Incas, the political towns of the Spaniards, the political capitals of the nineteenth century republican cities of Latin America. Not only has the city not grown out of the economic needs or in relation to the socioeconomic development of its surrounding area; it has until very recently been totally divorced from the national reality. Take any major Latin American city of the pre-World War II period and can we honestly say it reflected its surroundings? Most indeed were luxuriant, exotic replicas of European cities: a Lima, little related to its Andean and Indian land; a Buenos Aires which faced Europe, not the Argentine provinces; a Caracas, a Santiago, a Rio.

[46] Morse, "Recent Research on Latin American Urbanization," p. 41.

In most areas these same political considerations have led to cities based on bureaucracy and service populations, and the last really important 150 years—or perhaps more fairly for Latin America, the last seventy-eighty years—have been ones in which the industrial sector has been a very weak contributor, often located only with a view to the largest consumer public possible. The political orientation has also determined the well-known phenomenon of the Goliath's head, the over-sized capital city, so marked in many Latin American nations, inhibiting development of other urban centers and forcing unhealthy centralization in the nations' industrial and economic development.

The city, nevertheless, has become in Latin America not only the symbol but also the practical means of national integration and the main hope for national economic and social development. But the pouring of rural masses into the cities since World War II places the generalization that the over-all benefits to the majority of people far outweigh the disadvantages in serious doubt. Historically, there can be little optimism that the city in Latin America, a political creature in its origins, one little related to the economic and social realities of its surrounding area, can respond to the crushing contemporary problems without drastic reorientations of its role.

Let me move in conclusion to the microview of an investigator working on a particular city in a relatively short time span. Buenos Aires in the period 1870–1920 obviously supports some of the above generalizations.

(1) Political determination of Buenos Aires' development is so marked as to require no commentary. Few cities historically have been located more unfortunately for their commercial and general economic growth, and yet Buenos Aires has become the megalopolis of Argentina and southern South America.

(2) Buenos Aires in its gilded era at the turn of the century was the Paris of South America—exactly that exotic flower which flattered the upper and middle classes but provided no stimulus to national economic expansion. Here the immigrant waves could be absorbed and controlled by an oligarchy, here nationalism of sorts could be fostered, here the appearances of economic progress could be unveiled to dazzle all observers. But here, likewise, we find no encouragement for industrial development, no transport system to

link the nation together, no stimulus to other cities to supplement or compete with Buenos Aires' domination.

(3) The contrast of the optimistic and proud Buenos Aires of 1910 with the doubts and problems of the 1960's is evident to all. The historian, such as myself, may be able to conclude that the questions of the 1960's have their roots in Buenos Aires' gilded era.[47]

FUNCTIONS OF LATIN AMERICAN CITIES

The cities of Latin America perform certain definite functions, which were described by Aldo Solari in the following terms:

In Latin America, national integration, to the extent that it exists, is a consequence of the cities, and especially of the leading cities. This is an important function of leading cities, because if, in most countries, there is only one large city, there are at the same time several rural societies and local groups that strongly resist national projects designed for change. Because of the nature of the process by which Latin American nations originated, the development of a national consciousness has been very slow—as slow as the effective realization of state power and law in the whole territory. Thus, many of the rural social groups are marginal to the national society. Frequently, for example, punishment for crimes that lie within the jurisdiction of state authority is meted out by local leaders, who may decide to give punishment or to reprieve. The real growth of a national state has been, to a great extent, the process of expansion

[47] *Ed. note.* There was some agreement with the thesis that Latin American cities grew for political reasons, but the conference, in general, leaned toward economic reasons for urban growth. Eduardo Neira Alva expressed the latter point of view: "It is doubtful that it is entirely accurate to say that only political considerations determined the establishment and location of cities in Latin America. Spanish colonization had a well-defined economic motivation and communication centers were needed between Spain and the colonies. For this reason, the most important towns and nearly all the capital cities, except Mexico City and a few others, were established on the coastal fringes. It should be made clear that the political reasons for establishing colonial towns were strongly backed by economic reasons, and possibly economic reasons predominated—an important conclusion from history useful for the future."

65

of the power of the leading city. National integration has been, and is, a goal of urbanization in Latin America.

Cities represent the country in international affairs.

Another goal which cities lead to is innovation, and Latin American cities have performed this function.

Another function of cities, though more or less latent at present, is the distribution of social and political power, and the changes such distribution brings with it.

The results of their functioning are, unfortunately, ambiguous:

Pressures against national integration are applied by the numerous rural societies against the city. The effects of economic, social, and cultural dependence hamper the city in acting as the intermediary between its nation and foreign nations. Extensive ambiguity is found in the introduction of innovations: the products of industrialist society are accepted, but the attitudes of industrialist society are rejected. The majority of the middle class resist innovations that may imply the adoption of the values of industrialist society. Both right-wing and left-wing groups maintain the values of traditional and aristocratic society. They can accept only the values that do not menace their position in a still traditional or semiaristocratic society. Consequently, in the cities cosmopolitan patterns similar to those in cities of the United States and Europe coexist with attitudes toward efficiency, education, and so forth, that are based on traditional values. The middle-class urban groups that adopt the upper-class values resist many transformations that are typical of the industrial society. Examples are the occupation prestige scale, the place of science and technology, and so forth. The rightist groups preserve the maintenance of an aristocratic and idealistic conception of society, and are supported by a large proportion of the leftist groups in the determination of accepted values.

Nor can the city operate to redistribute power, according to Solari.

There are several balances or imbalances in the distribution of social and political power in the different countries between those whose source of wealth is land and those whose source is industry or service. But all of them have one feature in common (Cuba excepted) in that the power of the landowner has not been broken. Theoretically, it is held that agricultural improvement is achievable with *latifundia*, but experience in Latin America shows that no improvement has been obtained with this structure. More important, no national development can exist without improving strongly productivity in agriculture. This has been the great failure of urban groups. They have not been able to push a real modernization in the primary sector. Because of this failure, the cities have slums, *favelas, villas miserias, tugurios,* and so forth. The nation has not been able to improve agriculture and to make wealth distribution in the countryside more equitable, and thus the primary sector is not able to support and finance the growth of cities. In the poverty of the cities can be seen, simply enough, the real face of the countries.

A more subtle insight into the problem possibly is that in all Latin American countries there is an agreement, implicit but changing: rural society, to a point, finances the city, provided that the urban groups do not operate in an effective way against the establishment. The rural dominant groups can hold some of the strategic positions in global society if structural transformations in land tenure do not take place. This transformation does not take place because strategic urban groups do not attack profoundly the bases of the power of the dominant rural groups, so long as the latter admit some distribution of power in their favor.

The fault of this ambiguity is not some evil that pertains to the city. It lies, rather, in the structure of the society. If cities are ugly, they are merely the reflection of ugly countries.

In Latin American cities, few, if any, of the factors associated with economic development and industrial growth function as they do in cities of other Western countries. Thus, the development of urban trade and commerce did not bring economic growth, since the city was bypassed. The middle class, traditionally the stable element in industrial society, allies itself with the elite and does not bring about economic development, social mobility, or political stability. The professional group, trained in modern techniques, is frequently barred from the decision-making process or becomes so involved politically that it cannot perform its normal function of breaking the political system, thus contributing further to political immobility. There is a good chance that the urban working class as well aligns itself in support of the established order rather than with the migrant job-seekers.

CAUSES OF MALFUNCTIONING

There is good reason to ask if the key elements of city growth in the West (as analyzed by Hoselitz), that is, the agricultural revolution and the industrial revolution, have taken place in Latin America. The rural population has declined in proportion to the urban population, but there is no decline in its absolute numbers. This indicates that no major transformation has taken place. Industrialization lags behind urbanization, indicating that rural unemployment is being transferred to the cities.[48] The proportion of urban population employed in industry, for example, ranges from 7 per cent to 12 per cent, compared with 30 per cent to 40 per cent and more in the highly developed countries. Unemployment, as the term is used in western countries, is not a serious problem in Latin American cities, but an overconcentration of employment is to be found in unnecessary and low-paying service occupations that do not contribute to either urban or national productivity. Investments are concentrated in a few regions; more important, they do not stimulate to any great extent the growth of other industries. Rural tensions and conflicts resulting from class polarization are pushed into the cities. Political activity does not engage large masses of the urban population, and the majority of the rural population remains outside the political process. In short, instead of integration, a situation of

[48] This point is discussed in depth in Chapter IV. See also "Demographic Aspects of Urbanization in Latin America," pp. 91–117, and "Creation of Employment Opportunities in Relation to Labour Supply," pp. 118–148, in Philip M. Hauser, ed., *Urbanization in Latin America* (New York: International Documents Service, Columbia University Press, 1961).

social, economic, and political duality exists, with sharp, abrupt breaks between rich and poor, urban and rural, traditional and modern.

The situation is the diametric opposite of the conditions usually considered necessary for modernization. These may be summarized briefly from the papers in the succeeding chapters as: (1) industrialization sufficiently developed to absorb the major proportion of the unemployed, and agricultural productivity sufficiently advanced to support the industrial urban population, with a simultaneous gradual decline in agriculture's share of the employed and of total productivity; (2) integration of the population into modern society by means of upward occupational mobility and access to a greater abundance of consumer goods; and (3) sufficient power and political independence in the cities to bring about change through reform rather than make violent, abrupt breaks through revolution.

An important factor for change in the second half of the twentieth century is the rural migration to urban centers. The city is a growing entity. The question is how to cope with this growth? Should Latin America utilize the experience of the developed countries? Can Latin America afford to pay the cost of development and redevelopment that advanced countries are now paying? Can a per capita income of $5,000 or $6,000 a year be compared with the per capita income of $300, or the eighty pesos, a year of Latin American countries? Or should planners, as social scientists and responsible individuals, find ways and means to set up national policies to guide the processes of urbanization?

Urbanization has to be guided. The question is how? What are the most important problems and bottlenecks to be dealt with? There is competence in the fields of urban design and physical planning but weakness in the administrative structure. Consequently, César Garcés-Vernaza indicated, planners must decide to take the step of creating urban environments that will foster the development of modern social and economic patterns for the nations. This action, in turn, will stimulate the initiation of constructive work on the urgent problem of guiding urbanization.

The following chapters explore the demographic situation and consider in turn the potential of the urbanization process for economic, social, and political modernization, together with some major problems related to turning this process to advantage under existing conditions in Latin America.

III | The Demography
of the City

Urbanization and Modernization in Latin America:
The Demographic Perspective

HARLEY L. BROWNING

Fundamental demographic variables as they apply to urban concentrations play positive roles in the process of modernization in Latin America.[1] To identify these roles the process of urbanization as demographically defined must be considered together with the implications of some aspects of the urban hierarchy. On the city level, population size and density must be investigated, and finally, the components of population change—mortality, fertility, and migration—as they apply to cities in Latin America have to be followed.

Modernization is a key concept in this paper. Rather than delve into the problems implicit in its definition, I want to use modernization in its broadest sense to mean the fundamental social and economic transformation of societies. (And, of course, I accept modernization as a desirable goal.) In this regard, the tempo of modernization is an important consideration, as is the

[1] Because of the general nature of this paper and the restrictions on length, statistical and bibliographical data have not been included to support the author's arguments. The most recent and best documented discussion of the subject is by Richard M. Morse, "Recent Research on Latin American Urbanization: A Selective Survey with Commentary," *Latin American Research Review*, I, 1 (Fall, 1965), 35–74.

distinction between the short-term and long-term consequences of existing conditions or proposed policies.

URBANIZATION AS A PROCESS

Everyone is well aware of the rapid rate of urbanization in most Latin American countries, but there are certain misconceptions about the nature of urbanization and urbanism, as the latter term was defined by Louis Wirth in his classic essay, "Urbanism as a Way of Life." Urbanization, in the sense I will be using it, has quite a restricted meaning. It means, simply, an increase in the proportion of the total population of a country or area living in relatively permanent points of concentration of high density. Urbanism, on the other hand, is a much more expansive and therefore elusive concept because it attempts to identify the consequences, both social and personal, of life in urban environments. At present there is little consensus as to the distinctive features of urbanism, especially when it is viewed cross-culturally.

Confusion also exists between urbanization and the growth of individual cities. Urbanization, properly understood, is a quality of a country or some large region and is not applicable to any individual city or group of cities. Since urbanization is a characteristic of a country, it follows that the rural population inevitably must be included in any index of urbanization. It is entirely possible—although the phenomenon is seldom encountered—that the growth of the urban population of a country may proceed without changing the level of urbanization because the rural population is growing at exactly the same rate as the urban population. The distinction between urbanization and the growth of individual cities is quite important in terms of its implications for policy. As I shall attempt to show, one may support a continuation of the process of urbanization while at the same time recommending the slowing down of growth of individual cities or groups of cities.

Any general discussion of urbanization in Latin American

countries is a hazardous undertaking because of the great variations of levels and rates of urbanization. Nonetheless, compared with other world regions, Latin America has been urbanizing at a comparatively rapid rate for at least the past two decades and there is no indication that the pace is slowing down at the present time. In a recent study, the Centro Latinoamericano de Demografía (CELADE) estimated that 51 per cent of the population of Latin America is found in urban places, and that for 1975 an estimated 56.5 per cent will be urban.

Without question, most Latin American countries are now in the most dynamic and critical stage of the urbanization process. We are all witness to a period, almost within the compass of our own lifetime, in which Latin America will be transformed from a primarily rural to a primarily urban continent. It must be kept in mind that in the life span of societies this period of especially rapid urbanization occupies only a short interval. The period of time required for this basic transformation has been continuously reduced throughout world history. Western Europe and the United States took more time for this vital transition than Latin America is taking and therefore had more opportunities to adapt themselves gradually to changing conditions. Any leisurely accommodation to the process of urbanization in the Latin American countries is not possible.

If the historical record is any guide, once the urbanization process is well under way, a point of no return is reached, after which this basic trend can be reversed only by a major catastrophe involving at least partial breakdown of the social order. What I am suggesting is that urbanization develops a sort of momentum of its own which, to a certain extent, may vary independently of other fundamental changes, principally economic, within the society. Thus urbanization may exactly parallel, lag behind, or move ahead of the industrialization—narrowly defined—of the country. There are few historical instances of urbanization lagging behind industrialization but in several contemporary instances urbanization is apparently moving ahead of it. This is the condition several writers have termed "overurban- ization," by which they mean that the growth of the urban population outruns the employment opportunities in cities. I believe much of the discussion on this subject is misguided, not because those who talk of overurbanization necessarily have their facts in error, but that rather their interpretation is questionable. Basically, the confusion lies in the tendency to compartmentalize the urban sector of society and to treat it independently of the country as a whole. Yet, as already noted, we cannot define ur- banization without taking into account the rural sector. It has been pointed out that any society suffering from overurbaniza- tion is one certain to be suffering from over-ruralization as well, for the root difficulty of both is insufficient utilization of labor. In fact, because of the direction of rural-urban migration, if one wishes to find *the* cause for overurbanization, it is a better bet to seek it in the rural rather than the urban environment.

The rapid tempo of urbanization in Latin America frequently leads to suggestions to the effect that it should be slowed down substantially, and that to attain this objective much of the gov- ernment's attention and investment should be directed to rural rather than urban areas. If rural areas can be made more attrac- tive, so the argument goes, people will be less likely to abandon them for city life. I am very skeptical of such a policy on a num- ber of grounds. I think discussions as to what should be the proper rate of urbanization in particular countries, and whether the current rate should be slowed down, held constant, or even increased, border on the presumptuous, because I find little evidence in either the past or the present to indicate that *any* society has been at all effective in regulating or controlling its rate of urbanization. It is not well appreciated that to do so im- plies the existence of mechanisms for the management of societal change that have not been developed, even in totalitarian so- cieties. Given such limitations, would it not be more strategic to accept the existence of long-run trends in urbanization and to try to work effectively within them rather than against them?

Perhaps some of the alarm over the current rates of urbanization in Latin America reflects, at least in part, an ancient distrust of cities, a posture which causes considerable mischief, and one which hampers our efforts to understand clearly what is actually going on. I have suggested that urbanization tends to develop a momentum and force difficult to check and almost impossible to reverse. Instead of viewing this process from a negative point of view we should recognize that it is, in effect, a built-in stimulus or challenge to social change (one to be considered in the same way that Hirschman has discussed for the process of economic development). One can convincingly argue, on a short-run basis, that it would be better to slow the rate of urbanization so as to make living conditions more tolerable in the rapidly growing urban areas, but this simply delays the necessary and inevitable transformation. Indeed, affording some temporary amelioration may make the final adjustment more rather than less difficult.

I can hardly defend the position that all changes induced by rapid urbanization are beneficial for the societies undergoing the process. Clearly, they are not. But urbanization, at least potentially, helps to ensure the continuation of the process of modernization of these societies. Fundamentally, the matter boils down to a very simple question: Is the process of modernization best carried out in urban or in rural areas?

There are many weaknesses to the choice of rural areas, but I will only mention one of a demographic nature. Villages as a mode of social organization evolved in times during which population growth was extremely slow, at times nearly stopped. These settlements also initially developed in areas where unused land was available for expansion. In most of the developing countries of the world today neither of these conditions now holds to the same degree. Current population growth, even in the most backward rural areas, is sufficient to double the population within a period of twenty-five to thirty years. This means, eventually, that the village will grow beyond the size limits most suitable for its type of social organization. Nor is the formation of new villages, in cell-division fashion, a realistic alternative, for another consequence of sustained population growth is lack of suitable land, especially in the immediate vicinity of villages. Consequently, the growing pressure of population upon local resources manifests itself in many areas. To lessen the pressure on the agricultural sector by having a substantial portion of the village labor force engage in handicraft production is generally unrealistic because of organizational and marketing difficulties.

I am not advocating, I must emphasize, that rural areas should be neglected. On the contrary, I think improvements in agricultural productivity are absolutely essential for sustained urbanization. What I believe to be ill-advised are those plans of "community development" that assume the village to be a viable unit in the process of modernization. This skepticism is based on the knowledge that traditional peasant societies generally are quite resistant to the change required in the modernization process. To break the cake of custom in such environments is exceedingly difficult, and it is questionable that the rewards are worth the effort. It is true that villages can be modernized to some degree with the introduction of modern technology, but I am arguing that the successful introduction of new tools and techniques in a village environment implies a population at least moderately well educated and receptive to innovation. Moreover, at least in the beginning stages, villages must be helped from outside sources not only in terms of material goods but also by a corps of trained experts and demonstrators. The high cost of such efforts has not often been appreciated, partly because the demonstrations have always been limited to a few pilot or test situations. It is difficult to believe this approach is practicable when applied to a whole rural population.

Let us return to the initial question as to whether urban or rural environments are best suited for the carrying out of modernization. This process is a difficult one in any setting, but urban areas have inherent advantages that serve to facilitate the transformation. To ignore this point in formulating policy is to jeopardize the whole process of modernization.

If I am convinced that urbanization is not only inevitable but also essential for successful modernization, I do not want to give the impression that I advocate a complete laissez-faire approach to problems of urban planning. What I am suggesting is that urban planning be tailored to the fundamental trends we observe in Latin American societies; here the distinction between urbanization and the growth of cities becomes relevant. Urban policy, instead of trying to change the urbanization process as such, might best be directed toward facilitating or retarding, as the case may be, the growth of individual cities. In particular, large-scale regional development plans need to give a more prominent place to urban factors than has been customary in the past. Many river-basin developments have focused their energies and funds on agriculture and the infrastructure, with little attention to or understanding of the importance of cities as focal points in regional development. More and more countries are attempting to stimulate the development of their lagging regions by development programs. Since lagging regions are almost invariably characterized by a low level of urbanization, the opportunities to influence the urban pattern of these regions is considerable. It should be, therefore, the office of urban experts to see to it that the most suitable city, from the locational standpoint, be made the focus of attention and investment.

The most spectacular example we have in Latin America of a conscious effort to use city-building for the development of a region is Brasilia. Whether Brasilia can be judged a success or a failure is subject to the same qualifications about short- versus long-term consequences referred to earlier. By the end of the next two decades we probably will be able to say with more assurance whether this audacious and much maligned experiment was warranted. What we can say now is that such experiments are feasible only on a very limited basis. Completely new cities planned from the ground up are not realistic solutions to the over-all problem of urban development in any country, especially in Latin America. They simply are too costly, both absolutely and because urban development does not effectively utilize existing urban centers.

Problems involved in planning for individual cities and their place in the urban hierarchy are most acutely demonstrated in the matter of high primacy. With few exceptions, Latin American countries are characterized by the dominance of the largest city over the other urban centers of the country. Indeed, several of the smaller Latin American countries have only one real city. Not only demographically, but also economically, politically, and culturally, the first city in a high-primacy country reveals a typically high degree of centralization. While the condition of high primacy has been long recognized, both its causes and its consequences have been generally misunderstood. In particular, criticisms (such as that the primate city[2] is "parasitic") have been founded more often on emotional rather than factual bases.

It is quite dangerous to generalize about high primacy because its consequences will vary according to the population size of the country as well as the country's stage of development. It must be recalled that Latin America is characterized by a substantial number of relatively small countries, both in area and in population. Twelve have less than five million inhabitants. For most of these countries there is no reason why they should *not* be represented by high primacy. In such circumstances one large city can be more effective than several medium-sized cities. Spatially and organizationally, the primate city is the metropolis and the rest of the country is, in effect, its metropolitan region.

[2] The term "primate city" has come into quite general use by scholars concerned with urbanization and the developing countries. For a definition of "primate city," see *ibid.*, pp. 47–48. For general discussion, see Mark Jefferson, "The Law of the Primate City," *Geographical Review*, XXIX, 2 (April, 1939), 226–232.

The scarce resources of these countries can be more effectively mobilized within the boundaries of one rather than several urban centers. If for no other reason than the requirements for successful functioning within the world community of nations, every country must have some urban center of sufficient size and diversity in which to exercise the many activities representative of the modern state. My point is that every country needs a city that is modern in the universal sense, in order to accommodate the technology and innovations which characteristically are introduced into a country through the primate city. We do not, unfortunately, have any empirical studies to tell us what the minimum size of such a city should be, but it is probable that the size requirement will vary from country to country depending upon the level of development. I would hazard a guess at this time that the less developed the country, the larger the population must be to meet the minimum requirement. Therefore, at the risk of bringing Mumfordian wrath down upon my head, my conclusion is that a number of countries in Latin America need at least one city considerably larger than any now in existence. In a country with a population of five million, for example, a capital city with a population of one million would not be undesirable, even though it were ten times the size of the next largest city.

For the larger countries in Latin America, where conditions are different, the same reasoning does not hold. To evaluate the size of primate cities and the effects of primacy on modernization, short-run versus long-run considerations once again become relevant. Even in the largest countries it is probable that during the initial stages of industrialization and modernization the country will benefit more than it suffers from high-primacy situations. Rather than the few skilled personnel and capital resources being scattered out in several urban areas, the concentration of them in the capital city helps to accelerate, rather than to curb, economic growth. The processes which lead to high primacy through the concentration of activities in the primate city, however, tend to have a sort of snowball effect which, once it develops sufficient momentum, is exceedingly difficult either to slow down or to alter.

Over the long run, under such conditions, high primacy becomes increasingly a negative factor for several reasons. For one thing, the centralization it represents may serve to handicap the development of other regions of the country. And the development of skilled personnel and facilities in the primate city may actually reach the point of excess supply, while at the same time serious deficiencies continue to exist in other areas. In addition, assuming continued high rates of in-migration, it is only a matter of time before the capital cities of large countries become extremely large. To take the case of Mexico, for example, Mexico City first reached the one-million mark about 1930. Thirty-five years later it now has about six million inhabitants with good prospects that by 1980 the population of the metropolitan area will be very close to ten million. At the beginning of this period certain economic advantages undoubtedly accrued to a city of one million as a result of size, but they are much less evident in an agglomeration of ten million people. The disadvantages of such a concentration tend increasingly to outweigh the advantages.

The problem is that such large cities rarely stop growing, so we have to think of the population of Mexico City not just in terms of ten million, but in the more distant future of fifteen million or more. In these terms, there can be little doubt that such a gigantic concentration poses grave problems. While we may agree that such cities should be limited in growth, there is little basis for optimism about our present ability to control them. France, England, the U.S.S.R., and China have developed plans for managing the growth of their primate cities and all have had, at best, rather indifferent success. In China, for example, Shanghai, viewed as a symbol of the worst manifestations of imperialism, was for a time destined by the rulers of the state to undergo a substantial absolute decline in population. But even in that regimented society, with instruments of control like food-ration cards, this plan had to be dropped because of the difficulties in carrying it out. Large cities seem to develop surprising resiliency in the face of unfavorable conditions.

Whether or not the capital cities in several of the larger countries will attain the great size their current rates of growth seem to indicate depends upon what is done now or in the next few years to conceive and execute a program designed to make other urban areas relatively more attractive. Fundamentally, the problem must be one of the orderly decentralization of activities, and the success of this operation is basically contingent upon the willingness of the government to give wholehearted cooperation. Not only must policies be formulated to encourage manufacturing industries to locate outside the capital city; they must also be designed to move out noneconomic activities, such as governmental operations, as well. Urban planning for changes in the urban hierarchy has been generally unsuccessful in the past not only because of insufficient knowledge of the workings of the urban hierarchy, but also because of the unwillingness of power groups, including the government itself, to subordinate their own ends to that of the country.

THE POSITIVE IMPLICATIONS OF CITY SIZE AND DENSITY

From the demographic point of view, the most salient difference between urban and rural areas is size of locality. Related to size is density, for there tends to be a fairly close association in cities between change in size and increase in density. In this section I am interested in exploring some consequences of differences in size and density in urban areas when compared with rural areas. In doing so, I must depart from the tradition common in sociology and exemplified in the article by Wirth, referred to earlier. In sociological terms the orientation toward the city has been quite negative, mainly because of the influence of the rural-urban dichotomy, which has appeared again and again, although in various guises, throughout the history of this discipline. Interestingly enough, the identification of what is distinctively urban has not been generally attempted. Instead, the urban component is defined almost wholly in terms of what the folk or communal society is not. Social cohesion, for example, is seen as a characteristic of the small traditional community. It follows that the urban community necessarily lacks social cohesion. There is at last a growing realization that such dichotomies do justice to neither rural nor urban communities, but only in recent years has there been a sustained attack on this mode of thought.

Another tradition that has encumbered the urban sociologist's ability to appreciate the positive aspects of city existence has been that generated by the very influential Chicago school of urban sociology which flourished during the 1920's and 1930's. Much of the work of this school has an enduring value because its representatives were among the first to investigate empirically the phenomena they were studying. They tended, however, to concentrate their attention on pathological aspects of life in Chicago, such as delinquency, gangs, mental illness, and homeless men. As a result, perhaps without intending to do so, they produced an image of the city which emphasized the negative aspects of urban existence.

Still another factor accounts for the comparative neglect of the positive aspects of the city. Sociologists have tended to see the city in terms of its impact on the individual or his family, often in psychological terms. This emphasis upon the individual rather than upon organizations and facilities has deflected attention from important aspects of urban existence.

It is precisely on the organizational level that the advantage of the city over the rural community is most striking. Cities allow for the division of labor on a scale impossible in rural areas. The resulting specialization permits a greater variety of institutions and facilities, by no means limited to economic activities. Let me illustrate this point with several examples. Consider the problem of education. In virtually all Latin American countries the level of educational attainment of persons living in urban areas is higher than that of those in rural areas, and often the difference is very great. There are many reasons for this situation, among which are the inappropriateness of much educational training in the traditional rural environment, the reluctance of parents in rural areas to dispense with the labor of their children, and the unwillingness of teachers trained in urban areas to take up jobs in isolated rural areas. Aside from these considerations, however, it is indisputably difficult to provide education, particularly above primary grades, in rural areas comparable to education in urban areas. In countries like the United States the problem of the dispersal of the school population has been fairly well resolved by the device of transporting pupils, often for considerable distances, to schools located in urban areas. In most Latin American countries this alternative is not feasible, nor will it be for many years because of the lack of a good secondary road system, to say nothing of the high expense. One may conclude that, other things being equal, if a country wishes to push its educational program forward as rapidly and effectively as possible, a high level of urbanization, and even a high rate of urbanization, will help rather than hinder attainment of this goal. This is not to say that the problem of providing adequate educational facilities is ever an easy one, particularly in urban communities with extremely high growth rates. But it is far easier to assemble in cities the pupils, their teachers, and the facilities for education, at least beyond the primary level. In addition, students in urban areas should be able to gain a better understanding of the value of education and a greater incentive to develop their educational skills, for the rewards of such effort are more apparent in the urban than in the rural environment.

Another way in which the city operates to facilitate the modernization process is observed in the changing role of women. Evidence supports the assertion that a society which is modernizing is also one in which the general position and status of women are being improved. Specifically, one index of this change of status is an increase in the participation of females in the labor force. In rural areas very few employment opportunities exist for women outside the family context. Work within the family does not increase generally her independent position. Lack of work opportunities is one stimulus to the stream of female migrants, especially young girls, from rural areas into the cities. As a group, Latin American cities probably have the lowest ratio of females to males in the active working population (ages 15 to 64) of any world region. While it is true that many of the migrant females work as domestics and therefore have relatively little opportunity to advance either in their work or their social status, an important part of the recent increase of women in the urban labor force has been in activities other than domestic service, principally in clerical and sales positions. Work outside the home is one of the most effective ways of breaking down the so-called "cloister" pattern of upbringing; even though a girl may work for only a few years before her marriage, they can have an effect on her throughout her lifetime.

The mobilization of people, for whatever purpose, is much easier in urban places than in rural areas. Such assemblage may work in two ways. On the one hand it permits the ready organization of riots and other political activity detrimental to political stability and orderly processes. On the other hand the greater accessibility of large numbers of people to one another in urban environments facilitates growth of and participation in voluntary associations of all kinds. As political sociologists have come to recognize, one of the fundamental reasons for the continued instability typical of many Latin American countries has been the relative absence of organizations that intervene between the individual and the state. Under modern conditions, this argument goes, a genuinely democratic society must offer the individual a variety of choice in group affiliation and participation, for it is only on this organizational level that democratic processes can take place. While such organization is not impossible in rural environments, it is the cities that offer the greatest potentialities for it.

MORTALITY, FERTILITY, AND MIGRATION

There still remain the specific demographic components of change—mortality, fertility, and migration—as they apply to urban centers in Latin America, and their link to the process of modernization. In doing so, I must treat the cities in very general terms, a procedure subject to considerable danger. Latin American cities, according to both country and size of place within the country, display wide variations with respect to all three of the demographic components. Consequently, the generalizations to be offered here are subject to exceptions. In the main, my discussion will keep the larger urban centers in mind, in order to reduce somewhat the variations.

Of the three demographic variables, mortality is least subject to variation among cities. As late as a generation or so ago most urban areas in Latin American countries had higher mortality rates than rural areas, largely because of the greater risk of exposure to communicable diseases. The great advances in the control of such diseases, so that they no longer pose much of a threat, has radically changed the situation in the last several decades. It is true that the official data on mortality for a number of Latin American countries seem to show mortality to be higher in urban than in rural areas. These figures, however, do not make adjustments for age differences, for the practice in many countries of reporting deaths by place of occurrence rather than place of residence, and for the fact that more deaths are unreported in rural areas. When all these factors are taken into account, I believe few, if any, urban areas in Latin America would be found with mortality at a higher level than in the rural areas as a whole.

If, then, it may be concluded that mortality is lower in urban environments, albeit in several situations by rather narrow margins, the advantage of urban over rural areas is much greater upon consideration of morbidity and preventive medical care. The reasons for this are evident, although little systematic investigation has been made of the subject. Only in the larger cities can one find the full complement of modern medical care in terms of specialists, hospitals, clinics, special equipment, and the like. In most rural areas in Latin America there is a severe shortage of doctors, whereas in the largest cities there is often an excess.

Medical services of all types are becoming more readily available to a larger part of the urban population as a result of the expansion of social-welfare programs. Social security coverage, and its accompanying medical-care service, still are relatively rare in rural areas and are confined largely to urban centers. A number of reasons account for this differential coverage, but certainly an important factor is simply the difficulty of reaching the dispersed population in rural areas. Government-sponsored medical care means a healthier, more vigorous urban population compared with rural areas where malaria, intestinal disorders, and other energy-sapping illnesses are still a major factor in reducing the effectiveness of a greater part of the population. The superiority of urban areas over rural areas is not likely to be appreciably reduced during the coming decades.

In turning to fertility, we are faced with one of the most problematic aspects of demographic change in Latin America. This is surprising, for as recently as a decade ago most scholars considered urban fertility as very definitely a positive force in the modernization process. Urban fertility rates, from the available evidence, were demonstratively lower than fertility rates in rural areas. There was also the comfortable expectation that as countries became more urbanized national fertility rates would decline because of the increasing weight of the urban sector. A declining birth rate would mean a lower rate of natural increase, which in turn would lead to a lessening of the pressure of population growth on the process of modernization. Since

evidence indicated that this sequence occurred in the development of Europe and the United States, there seemed little reason
to doubt that the same process would repeat itself in Latin
America. Recently, however, this assumption has been called
into question, by Robinson among others. Although the trend
is not universal in Latin America and the data for recent years
are still incomplete, an unexpected pattern seems to be emerging.
Fertility has not been low and declining in urban areas; on the
contrary, it has been rising. While urban fertility rates still remain lower than those in rural areas, the difference between
urban and rural rates is being narrowed, but in such a manner
that urban rates are rising toward the rural rates rather than the
reverse or anticipated movement.

Our present difficulty in interpreting this phenomenon stems
from our lack of adequate knowledge about the demographic
factors that account for the increase. One interpretation explains
the rise as a consequence of the fertility behavior of migrants
from rural areas to cities. Their attitudes conducive to high
fertility are unchanged in urban areas, with the result that their
completed fertility differs little from what it would have been had
they remained in rural areas. This argument is not wholly convincing in explaining the recent rise in urban fertility because the
proportion of the population that is migrant in many of the larger
Latin American cities has tended to decline rather than increase,
as would have been suggested by the foregoing interpretation.
Fortunately, within a few years we should have the complete
results of the CELADE-Cornell comparative studies of fertility
in a number of the capital cities of Latin America, and our understanding of the specific factors at work will be much better.

If we accept the apparent fact that urban fertility in a number
of countries in Latin America is rising to a relatively high level,
the crucial question becomes: Does this change represent a temporary phenomenon or is it likely to persist indefinitely? If the
latter is true, we must conclude that urban fertility will have
a negative rather than a positive effect upon modernization;

it would imply that the prospects for a substantial lowering of fertility in this part of the world are relatively remote. I do not accept this conclusion, although I must admit I have little evidence at this time to repudiate it. I believe the rise in urban fertility is a temporary phenomenon, and I predict that fertility rates in urban areas will decline appreciably within the next several decades. I also believe that fertility will decline in rural areas as well, although not as rapidly as in the urban areas. My main reason for this belief is a conviction that the practice of birth control will become increasingly common in Latin America, with either private or public sponsorship, or with both as is more likely. In this event, urban areas will doubtless offer superior opportunities to learn about the existence of contraceptive devices, to have better access to them, and, very important, to develop the motivation to use them effectively. I also believe that if and when birth-control clinics are established, they will first be concentrated in urban areas.

The third demographic factor bearing on population change is migration. It is also the most important one because it accounts for most of the variation in growth rates between urban and rural areas. Migration may be divided into movement into the country from abroad, or immigration, and the movement within the country, or internal migration. Quantitatively, immigration is presently at a low level in Latin America and is likely to continue so throughout the foreseeable future. From a qualitative standpoint, however, immigrants are important because they are quite a selective group, with better education and a higher order of skills than the native population possesses. These foreign migrants characteristically concentrate strongly in urban areas, especially in the largest cities. To this extent they provide urban areas with an important advantage, and their skills make them a positive force in the process of modernization.

Internal migration, specifically rural-urban migration, presents a more complex and difficult situation. There is also considerable disagreement as to whether rural-urban migration, at least under present conditions, is beneficial to the development of Latin American countries. The argument that migration has harmful effects breaks down into three parts. First, the sheer volume of migration to cities, particularly the larger cities, is judged to be too high. The flood of migrants, it is argued, makes it very difficult to provide housing and other essential urban services, thus reducing the effectiveness of the cities themselves. Second, it is believed that the social characteristics of the migrants are such as to have negative implications for proper development. Many of the migrants are peasants with little or no formal education and few skills useful in the urban environment. Even assuming full employment conditions in the city, which is not often the case, it is difficult to incorporate the migrants into the labor force because of their lack of training. To the extent that they are fish out of water, it is argued, they are a drag on the development of the city and of the country. Third, it has often been suggested that rural migrants have great difficulties in making the social and psychological adjustments necessary for life in urban areas. To the extent that they are poorly assimilated in this sense, they impede proper development.

Although sometimes only implied, these three arguments suggest that rural-urban migration is too high, and that conditions would improve if a large part of the potential rural migrants were to remain in their community of origin. Unquestionably, all these arguments have merit, but I think they have been exaggerated to the point of distorting reality. They also fail to consider the long-run implications of rural-urban migration.

Consider the matter of volume of internal migration, which is unquestionably great, involving millions of people. In the last decade or so for all but a few countries in Latin America the growth of the urban population has been much greater than that of the rural population. In the two largest countries, Brazil and Mexico, the rural rate was approximately one quarter that of the urban. Actually, it should be mentioned that urban growth rates tend to be overstated and rural growth rates understated.

This is an artifact of the classification scheme, which means that in nearly all cases a change of definition of an area means a 100 per cent loss for the rural category and a 100 per cent gain for the urban category.

It must be pointed out that, with the exception of those in Chile, rural areas have not been losing absolutely in recent years, despite the rapid urban growth. Population is continuing to pile up even though the economic opportunities, particularly those in agriculture, are quite restricted. In Mexico, for example, between 1950 and 1960 the growth rate per annum of rural areas was 1.5 per cent, but the growth rate in agricultural employment was much higher, 2.8 per cent. It is apparent that changes in the rural population are not always a good indicator of changes in agricultural employment. I would even venture to say that it is not the date at which a country becomes officially more urban than rural that signals a major transformation or turning point in a country's economic development, it is rather the time when the agricultural labor force undergoes an absolute rather than a relative decline. Until this point is reached, it is likely that the reservoir of potential migrants to urban areas will continue to rise because an increase in the modernization of agriculture must increase rather than reduce the amount of redundant labor, a proportion that is at least one third of the labor force in agriculture. Whatever the limitations of cities and their current ability to absorb migrants, it can hardly be denied that, over the long run, expansion in employment opportunities is inherently greater in urban than rural areas.

The second basic criticism of the migration process in Latin America states that, because of their lack of training, migrants would be unable to compete effectively with the native born in urban centers. Much comment has been made about the miserable living and working circumstances of migrants in the large Latin American cities. But even this seldom challenged argument can be subjected to contrary evidence. At the University of Texas we have been doing some preliminary work with a sample of the 1960 Mexican census of the Distrito Federal, the metropolitan equivalent to Mexico City. Contrary to expectation, migrants, those born outside the Distrito Federal, do *not* differ greatly in most respects from the native population in some socioeconomic characteristics. The major exception is education, in which the migrants, especially workers, are much inferior to the natives. This does not seem to have much effect, surprisingly, when it comes to occupational and income differences. Natives are superior but the difference is not large. And when standard of living indicators are taken from the census data (availability of running water in households, sewage facilities, separate bathrooms, ownership of radio and TV) there is virtually no difference between the two groups. These findings are, it must be stressed, tentative and limited to one place, but they do lend support to the argument that the status of the migrant vis-à-vis the native is not as great as has been assumed. It is fairer to say that *both* groups are lower in relation to these socioeconomic characteristics than is desirable.

The third criticism relating to the difficulties of social and psychological adjustment on the part of migrants to urban areas is also one that has more often been assumed than demonstrated. Oscar Lewis was one of the first to challenge this assumption and he provided some evidence to indicate that many migrants from village origins do in fact make very satisfactory adjustments to their urban surroundings. The problems of psychological adjustment probably have been overrated. Some migrants to cities, in fact, have reported a greater feeling of personal freedom and emotional satisfaction in cities when compared with life in rural areas. It is evident that we will need more field research on this matter before any conclusions can be drawn.

Migration, as has been indicated, is a very complex affair, and it is difficult to conclude that its consequences are either wholly positive or wholly negative. If, however, one accepts the necessity for the transformation from an essentially rural to an essentially urban society, then the current high rates of migration, although they create many difficult problems, do place people in an environment in which they can potentially make their greatest contribution to the modernization process.

Editor's Summary and Elaboration

DEMOGRAPHIC FACTORS AND THE URBAN EXPLOSION

Because Latin America is a continent undergoing modernization, it is also a continent experiencing an extraordinary trend toward urbanization. Probably the soundest empirical evidence of urbanization rests in demographic factors—factors relating to the population increase in cities. Much of the discussion that follows relates to the particular demographic factor of migration simply because individuals and families newly entering urban areas—at the rates they are entering—create problems greater than those resulting from normal population increase within cities. Migration, however, cannot be considered in isolation. Any discussion related to it immediately takes one into the closely related problems which it causes: for example, the need to have industrialization accompany urbanization if migrants are to find work in their new locations.

Migration, admittedly, is the key matter of concern, but of course other demographic factors are causing our cities to increase in population. The high birth rates typical in Latin American countries also have contributed to the increase in urban population, and problems derive from this factor as well.

The rate of migration plus the natural increase in the rate of population growth, then—at the high levels at which they are occurring in Latin American cities—are most directly responsible for the urban explosion on this continent.

URBANIZATION AND MIGRATION

Some figures showing the trend in urban growth were cited by Hoselitz in Chapter II. Morse has provided additional details. From 1950 to 1960 urban growth in Latin America increased from 39 per cent of the population to 46 per cent in cities with populations of 2,000 or over. Cities grew at an annual rate of 4.5 per cent, compared with a rate of rural growth of 1.4 per cent. In 1960 four countries had more than 60 per cent of their population living in cities, and by 1975 this number is expected to increase to eleven countries, while the number with less than 40 per cent urban population will decrease from twelve to two. In 1960 ten cities in Latin America had populations of over a million (compared with only one in 1930), and by 1980 this number is predicted to increase to twenty-six.[3]

Population in the largest cities in Latin America has in general been growing faster than that of the next largest cities and faster than the population of the countries. "Rates of growth for cities of 20,000 plus inhabitants are, with few exceptions, very high. Average annual increases above 4 or 5 per cent are frequent. In Venezuela, for example, the rate of increase for the period 1941–50 averaged 7 per cent *per annum*. In this and some of the other countries . . . there is even evidence of an acceleration of urbanization."[4] Much of this increment is in larger cities. Present estimates indicate that from 1950 to 1960 population in cities of 20,000 or more inhabitants increased approximately two thirds, or at an average annual growth rate of 5 per cent. According to provisional figures, the average urban population in those larger cities in Latin America increased from 25 per cent of total population in 1950 to 32 per cent by 1960. This was the largest percentage increase in urban growth of any major world region except Oceania, which, interestingly, is the most highly urbanized region in the world.[5]

[3] *Ibid.*, pp. 42–43.

[4] United Nations, Bureau of Social Affairs, Population Branch, "Demographic Aspects of Urbanization in Latin America," in Philip M. Hauser, ed., *Urbanization in Latin America* (New York: International Documents Service, Columbia University Press, 1961), p. 100.

[5] John D. Durand and César A. Peláez, "Patterns of Urbanization in Latin America," *The Milbank Memorial Fund Quarterly*, XLIII, 4 (October, 1965), Part 2, 177.

A few of the observations concerning the urban growth rate in Latin America made during the conference are worth citing. To quote Garcés-Vernaza:

In Colombia the population growth rate is 3.43 per cent a year. Consequently, the population doubles every eighteen years. The nine million now living in cities will be eighteen million by 1985, and close to thirty or forty million by 2000. The reason for this growth seems to be mainly that the development of technology in agriculture is limiting the number of people who can gainfully live from agriculture.

Sánchez Baylón stated:

The urban growth rate in Mexico increased from 5.93 per cent between 1940 and 1950 to 6.12 per cent between 1950 and 1960, while the rural growth rate changed only from 1.60 per cent to 1.63 per cent. All the cities are growing explosively: 7 per cent a year is the urban growth rate, and in the northern states some cities have growth rates from 15 to 26 per cent annually.

Wingo said:

Recently I made some simple projections to determine how long it would be before, at the present rate of growth, the urban and rural sectors in Latin America would converge to the point where they replicated the proportions in developed countries. Projections on basis of the growth between 1950 and 1960 indicated that this point would be in fifty years time for Mexico, sixty years for Brazil, and only twenty-five for Venezuela. With the population growing at some 3 per cent a year, when these populations converge, around the year 2000, the population of Latin America is likely to be three times what it is today.

Data reflecting the significantly higher increases of urban over rural population are shown in Table 3. On basis of the estimates shown in the table, the rate of increase in urban population jumped to 61 per cent in 1940–1950 and has increased in 1950–1960. Rural population, meanwhile, remained stationary, show-

Table 3. Decennial increases in urban and rural population in Latin America, 1920–1960 (rough estimates by per cent).

	1920–1930	1930–1940	1940–1950	1950–1960
Urban*	40	39	61	67
Rural and small-town	17	17	16	19

Source. United Nations, Bureau of Social Affairs, Population Division, *World Urbanization Trends, 1920–1960, An Interim Report on Work in Progress,* Working Paper No. 6, Inter-Regional Seminar on Development Policies and Planning in Relation to Urbanization, held at the University of Pittsburgh, October 24 to November 7, 1966. Data from Tables 5 and 6, p. 16.

* Cities of 20,000 or more inhabitants.

ing only a small increase in rate of growth during the decade from 1950 to 1960.

Table 4 shows the trend toward urbanization in selected Latin American countries where census data are available. The trend is especially marked in Brazil, Chile, Mexico, and Venezuela, but in all the countries the urban population has increased over the years.

It is generally believed by students of the demographic situation in Latin America that approximately half of the urban growth, if not more, in several countries stems from rural-urban migration.[6] A United Nations study of ten Latin American countries for the years preceding 1950 indicated that rural-urban migration accounted for between 40 and 70 per cent of urban growth.[7] A study of in-migration in San Salvador (1960) and in Santiago (1962) indicated that 42 per cent of the population of the former city and 34 per cent of the population of the latter were made up of migration into the city. Of these percentages, foreign immigration accounted for only 4 and 6 per cent, respectively.[8] The proportions vary among the countries. From calculations based on probable urban and rural proportions with-

[6] See the authorities cited in Morse, *op. cit.*, p. 68, n. 31.

[7] "Demographic Aspects of Urbanization in Latin America," p. 110.

[8] Carmen A. Miró, "The Population of Latin America," *Demography,* I, 1 (1964), 27.

Table 4. Urbanization trends in selected Latin American countries.

Country and census year	Per cent of total population	
	Urban	Rural
Argentina		
1895	37.4	62.6
1914	52.7	47.3
1947	62.5	37.5
Brazil		
1940	31.2	68.8
1950	36.2	63.8
1960	45.1	54.9
Chile		
1920	46.4	53.6
1930	49.4	50.6
1940	52.4	47.6
1952	60.2	39.8
1960	67.2	32.8
Colombia		
1938	29.1	70.9
1951	38.0	62.0
Costa Rica		
1927	18.8	81.2
1950	33.5	66.5
Ecuador		
1950	28.5	71.5
1962	34.8	65.2
Mexico		
1930	33.5	66.5
1940	35.1	64.9
1950	42.6	57.4
1960	50.7	49.3
Panama		
1930	30.1	69.9
1940	33.8	66.2
1950	36.0	64.0
1960	41.5	58.5
Paraguay		
1950	34.6	65.4
1962	35.4	64.6
Peru		
1940	35.4	64.6
1956*	43.6	56.4
1961**	47.1	52.9
Venezuela		
1936	34.8	65.2
1941	39.3	60.7
1950	53.8	46.2
1961	67.5	32.5

Source. United Nations, Department of Economic and Social Affairs, *Demographic Yearbooks*, New York: United Nations (various years).
Note. See also Table 15.   * Estimated.   ** Provisional.

out migration, Ducoff indicates a range of from 7 or 8 per cent of the gain in urban population in the highly rural countries of Costa Rica and Paraguay to 50 per cent in Brazil and Venezuela.[9]

It can be seen, then, that migration is a powerful force. Careful analysis of its causes and its impact on the cities is basic to the determination of the future size and quality of urban areas in Latin America. One should not view it in too narrow a context, however. As Wilson Garcés remarked:

The demographic process is difficult to isolate from the economic and social forces that are shaping it. What is actually creating the problem is the way in which the process is taking place and where it is going on: urban growth is not a deliberate action but rather is independent action taken without regard to interactions and interrelationships. The problem would not be so intense in Latin America if it were to take place in a more evenly distributed way; that is, if enough alternative potential centers for development could grow up.

Causes of urbanization. There is no solid body of tested quantitative data describing the reasons for such a large-scale movement toward the cities. Theories of causes center around two points, the advantages of the city for a better life and the disorganization of rural areas.

Among the advantages of the city (the "pull" factors) are: opportunities for economic and social achievement and mobility, the possibility of educational advantages, at least for one's children, better facilities for health care, and, in general, the hope for a better way of life. The disadvantages of rural life (the "push" factors) are the lack of opportunities for achievement, education, and health welfare, and the intensification of poor living conditions as a result of increasing mechanization of farms, soil exhaustion, and lack of incentives for farming, such as, among other things, credit facilities and good transportation.

[9] Louis J. Ducoff, "The Role of Migration in the Demographic Development of Latin America," *The Milbank Memorial Fund Quarterly,* XLIII, 4 (October, 1965), Part 2, 203.

The rural-urban migration, Juan B. Astica pointed out, whether in response to push or pull factors, is not entirely made by exercising freedom of choice. Important values frequently are sacrificed. So long as this migration is to escape poverty, to search for jobs, or to find at least a slightly better access to opportunity for better living, it most likely can be expected to remain a drift toward the centers that seem to offer these.

At the same time, it is generally speculated that this migration is selective, with the more dynamic members of the rural population going to the cities. Existing conditions of rural poverty prevent those who remain from benefiting by the out-migration and make programs of rural integration and land reform difficult to carry out. In the cities, this potentially usable talent is wasted in uneconomically rewarding jobs and struggling with the problems of slum life. Great potential is being lost to both rural and urban areas.

Development of high primacy. Urbanization universally takes place in response to various economic and sociocultural factors. It may result in a network of urban areas throughout a nation, an increase in growth in certain cities only, or in concentration in one or two large cities, usually the capitals. The latter is the case in most of Latin America.

Urbanization in this region is characterized by the concentration of the urban population in the big cities, usually the largest city in the country. A partial explanation for this phenomenon may be the multifarious functions of major cities in the region: the largest city in each country usually serves as the political capital, the centre of commerce and industry and the seat of culture, education and entertainment.[10]

A connection does exist, though, between the present distribution of population in a few large cities and the course of past economic development, as Neira stated. Several characteristics of this course that affected the growth of cities developed

[10] "Demographic Aspects of Urbanization in Latin America," p. 95.

during the period when economic development was directed mainly to foreign markets, that is, *crecimiento hacia afuera* (outer-directed growth): (1) agriculture or development of resources for export rather than intensive subsistence farming; (2) a railroad system that linked the economic centers with ports rather than with the interior; (3) subordination of budgetary policies in taxation and exchange to the dictates of the great world powers; (4) isolation of cities; (5) irregular or slight development of the continental interior. Development in the 1930's and after was chiefly in the nature of manufacturing substitutes for imports of consumer goods, that is, *crecimiento hacia adentro* (inner-directed growth), and was a step toward greater economic self-sufficiency. It did little, however, to counteract the deficiencies of earlier development. Manufacturing tended to concentrate in the large cities, where there were markets and a labor supply. Much of the development was sponsored by the governments, which further reinforced the factors that were leading to accelerated growth of a few cities.

During the period of prosperity after World War II, the cities did seem to hold out the promise of a higher standard of living. Unfortunately, this prosperity resulted less from economic policies than from circumstances that were largely fortuitous so far as the several countries were concerned. These were "(1) the favorable terms of trade enjoyed by many Latin American countries during and following World War II, and (2) the substantial exchange reserves that many Latin American countries had accumulated during World War II." [11] Meanwhile, agricultural development lagged, production for overseas rather than domestic markets was encouraged, and industrial development remained "urban" (or concentrated in a few areas) rather than becoming national in scope. But during the relatively short period of postwar prosperity people had been given a glimpse of what prosperity meant, and they continued to look to the

[11] Harry Stark, *Social and Economic Frontiers in Latin America* (2d ed.; Dubuque, Iowa: William C. Brown, 1963), p. 206.

cities for fulfillment even after the pace of economic development slowed down.

The general lack of opportunity outside the cities is one factor, Hardoy stated in his remarks, in the development of high primacy:

The growth of the population and of the economy has concentrated population in a small number of the cities in each country and has stressed the regional differences of opportunity between centers with very different scales, areas of influence, and functions. During the last two decades all the provincial capitals of Argentina grew, even in those provinces that had lost population. I think that the situation is similar in countries with a small territory and only one important center, such as Uruguay, and no doubt it must be similar in the rest of Latin America. This does not mean that the possible orientation of internal migrations will continue to be polarized to all the existing urban centers of each country. The selection that the rural population makes when beginning its migration is made not only because of the choices that each center offers the migrant but also because of the effort that the process demands from them. The big city, with its greater opportunities for other than hand work, its more complex labor structure and greater social mobility, no doubt is the great attraction. Only the poor systems of transportation and communication and the illusion of a partial eradication seem to have helped in some way the provincial capitals and smaller towns in spite of the few opportunities concentrated in them. The opportunities to rise in the social, educational, and labor scales are still the privilege of a very few cities in each country.

High primacy and the migrants' urban environment. The most visible effect of migration to the city is the deterioration of the urban environment. Hardoy discusses this in his remarks.

It is paradoxical that political leaders, technicians, scientists, and labor, business, and industrial leaders are conscious of the effects of the process of urbanization, but do not try to find deep solutions. An immediate and quite visible consequence of the intense contemporary process of urbanization has been, then, the deterioration of the urban environment, and the load that urban utilities and services in general have had to support. Together with the slow and insufficient expansion of the sources of work in relation to the new demands for employment, this constitutes the most direct and immediate image that the rural migrant has of the large cities of Latin America at the present moment.

Overloaded facilities, congested streets, and transportation difficulties all are less apparent, and less spectacular, than the growth of the "mushroom colonies" that provide shelter for the migrants. "In Brazil it is called *favela;* in Argentina, *banda de miseria;* in Peru, *barriada.* In Colombia it is *tugurio.* But whatever the name, its characteristics are the same: It is the rudest kind of slum, clustering like a dirty beehive around the edges of any principal city in Latin America." [12]

The principal concern with these settlements is their rapid growth rate, though there is some national variation in it. For all of Latin America a growth rate of the urban marginal population from 1965 to 1975 of 2.9 per cent per year has been predicted. A few examples may be cited. In Lima, the *barriada* population increased from 10 per cent of the city population in 1958 to 20 per cent in 1964; in Rio de Janeiro, the *favela* population increased from 8.5 per cent of city population in 1950 to about 16 per cent in 1964. In other countries, the marginal population apparently did not increase: in Greater Santiago, the number of *callampa* dwellings showed a slight decline between 1952 and 1961, partly because of government action to eradicate them and partly because the smaller and more provisional nature of later *callampas* kept them from being counted. In Caracas, "superblock" apartment houses were built as a means of eliminating the *ranchos*, though in 1958, after construction had stopped, 30 per cent of the city population was living in *ranchos*. In Greater Buenos Aires, the period of rapid growth is considered at an end: some 10 per cent still living in the *villas* are without resources, 30 per cent have good prospects of moving out

[12] Sam Schulman, "Latin-American Shantytown," New York *Times Magazine,* January 16, 1966, p. 30.

within the next five years, and the remainder are at varying points between these extremes. In Mexico City, 1952 figures indicate that 11 per cent of the city's population live in *jacales* (squatters' shacks), "14 per cent in *colonias proletarias* (low-density, relatively substantial squatters' huts without urban services), and 34 per cent in *tugurios* (traditional slums)."[13]

A number of significant differences exist among the types of *barrios*. In Santiago, no less than fifteen varieties of dwellings or communities of the lower economic class have been identified. The basic structures may be grouped in three categories that can be considered typical of other countries as well:

(1) *Conventillo* type:[14] located in older districts of the city center; access to public utilities; traditional "slum" dwelling for urban proletariat; rental occupancy; structures built as *conventillos* disappearing, being replaced by conversion of houses to multi-family use. Corresponds elsewhere to *vecindad, cortico, callejón*. (2) *Callampa* type: segregated urban nucleus; illegal land occupation; waste material used for construction; generally single-room dwelling without sanitary facilities; generally peripheral location with constant displacement by growth of city. . . . Corresponds elsewhere to *favela, villa miseria, rancho, barriada, jacales*. (3) Suburban settlement: semisegregated urban nucleus; land titles acquired through settlers' initiative or by government intervention; heterogeneous building materials; construction by settlers, government or private firms; generally peripheral location; varying access to public utilities.[15]

The sheer volume of the migration and the lack of useful skills among the migrants pose, particularly for countries with low capital resources, serious problems of investment in housing

[13] Morse, *op. cit.*, pp. 50–51.

[14] *Conventillos* are multifamily dwellings, with one room for each family and common sanitary facilities.

[15] Guillermo Rosenblüth López, "La participación de las poblaciones urbanas en el crecimiento urbano," MS (January, 1965), quoted in Morse, *op. cit.*, pp. 52–53.

and services that drain resources from other investments considered more directly related to economic development. Luis Dorich Torres spoke on this point as follows:

Probably one of the main questions to be posed for cities in Latin America today is the matter of differences in earnings of the population. Are cities where average earnings are $100 to $200 per capita able to supply all the urban facilities needed—housing and other structures, schools, and so forth? Aid from North America and Europe has been available for some of this, and this aid may obscure the recognition that perhaps Latin American cities cannot afford to pay for all the things they need to be efficient.

The transfer of unemployment from the countryside has produced the typical slum areas at the outskirts of cities. It has produced shortages of houses, schools, and community facilities. Public services are not sufficient for the demand and, worse, most of the demand comes from the slums, from people who do not have the means to pay for them even when costs have been kept low through special legislation—so low that the corporations involved cannot raise the capital needed for expansion and improvement of installations and equipment. The only public services installed have been sanitary ones—mainly water supplies. For housing we are receiving foreign loans, but for the rest, the situation, with possibly one or two exceptions, each day becomes worse.

At the same time, the resources of our cities do not grow. The question is, in general terms, how are we going to find the money to invest in the infrastructure of our cities?

Rapid urbanization, under some circumstances, may supply a stimulus to higher capital investment in consumer goods for an expanding market as urban living increases needs and furnishes cash income. It has not worked out this way in Latin America, according to the UN Economic Commission for Latin America, because the low and uncertain urban incomes are scarcely sufficient to cover costs of the basic necessities of food, clothing, and shelter. Relatively few urban workers attain occupational stability and most of them are unable to progress to higher stages in what is considered the normal pattern of demand: housing stability, purchase of some durable goods, improvement of housing and "extension of comforts" through purchase of a wide range of durable consumer goods, education for children, followed by accumulation of savings in order to protect the standard of living attained. Institutional savings are lowered by overstaffing in an attempt to create employment. Less money is available for direct investment in productive activities because more has to be spent to provide for the marginal urban population.[16]

The employment opportunities generally available to migrants are a mixture of traditional and modern, sometimes to the extent that it is difficult to determine the scope of real industrial employment. Construction work absorbs a high proportion of them, and the fluctuations typical of construction work are sharper in countries where capital for investment evolves from the external market. In other fields, labor-intensive industries are found in juxtaposition with productive, modern, capital-intensive industries. "The survival, in Latin America, in some branches of industrial production, in towns and even in some capital cities, of a large number of artisan and homecraft establishments . . . side by side with small and large factories, is a clear illustration of the phenomenon, which . . . inflates over-all figures of industrial employment." [17]

Hardoy described the situation and its background:

We are aware that in Latin America urbanization is ahead of industrialization; that is evident in the primacy of the principal city in each country, with the possible exception of Colombia and Brazil; that along with the process of urbanization there has been an even faster expansion of tertiary activities; that public employment has become one of the main sources of absorption of the excess of urban laborers; that there are deep differences in what we could call "the quality of urban life" and "the opportunities of socialization" be-

[16] United Nations, Economic Commission for Latin America, Secretariat, "Creation of Employment Opportunities in Relation to Labour Supply," in Hauser, *op. cit.*, pp. 132–136.
[17] *Ibid.*, pp. 142–143.

tween the capital city and, in a few cases, the two or three important cities in each country, in relation to provincial capitals and other urban centers in general; that the process has already had important effects in electoral patterns, and in the same way with other similar examples.

The concentration on commercial investments, though profitable to the entrepreneurs, not being accompanied "by a parallel expansion in the volume of industrial and agricultural goods produced and distributed by the urban commercial system," amounts, in effect, to a redistribution of existing resources, either in the urban system or between urban and rural areas. It has operated to accelerate migration, since it places an undue hardship on rural areas, which must pay more for services and at the same time receive fewer industrial goods. For increased productivity of both capital and labor, what is needed are investments that lead to the development or increase of resources through technological change.[18]

Various other conditions work against the migrant's bringing about a real change in his situation by moving to the city. Hardoy mentioned some of them:

Without education, without capital, without specialization, without contacts or only with contacts with people in a situation similar to theirs, the alternatives offered to the migrants are, in everyday life, very few. The rural migrant does not have, besides, the experience of a minimum political participation. He does not know the way the institutions of modern society work. His experiences about the role of the government in relation to the governed have been, in general, established according to the values of a traditional society. His attitude is one of total passivity, or it obeys impulses, but with considerable lack of knowledge of his rights and duties.

Alternatives to high primacy. If the growth of primate cities has resulted from a lack of opportunity elsewhere in the countries, one facet of a new orientation for urbanization could be

[18] *Ibid.,* p. 145

to stimulate the widespread production of opportunities throughout more areas. "Will people," Hardoy inquired, "come to the present cities or will there be new cities to absorb them? The problems of large cities are increasing. There are two alternatives: to anticipate the growth of cities (even poorly located ones) or to promote the development of new cities."

In his paper, Browning makes the distinction between urbanization and the growth of individual cities. Urbanization, he recommended, should be linked to the underlying trends in a country in order to avoid the overgrowth of only a few large cities.

Current economic trends in Latin America, by their nature, will influence the course of urbanization in the future, according to Davis, and steps should be taken now to prepare for their impact:

What are the new economic considerations? The period of development based on export for European and North American markets is largely a thing of the past. If economic integration will play an important role in Latin American development, this would seem to have major import for the location of future populations and future urban population in Latin America. The impetus will be to develop cities in the interior. Mendoza, for example, possibly could, on basis of the trade between Argentina and Chile, become the area of most rapid expansion in the next fifty years, if economic integration assumes the same role that development *hacia afuera* played earlier. The historical record to examine is not the one that rationalizes nineteenth-century and early twentieth-century growth of Buenos Aires on political grounds but the one that interprets the economic significance of Buenos Aires in that period. Then the current distribution of population can be looked at in terms of the major factors likely to be significant for the remainder of the twentieth century and for the twenty-first.

On both national and international scales, the economic trends in Latin America today are designed to correct the imbalances of past development and urbanization. One trend is toward a greater emphasis on large-scale heavy industry. One reason for the lack of industrialization in the past has been that markets were too small to attract much investment. This objection is expected to be overcome by a second trend, the economic integration of the Latin American countries. This is a revival of the idea of supranational integration that began with Bolivar and has never been entirely forgotten in Latin America. Besides attracting both domestic and foreign investment in industrialization, integration is looked to as a means of avoiding present disparities of growth between the several Latin American countries. Allied with these trends, to some extent, is development of the interiors of some of the countries. Criticisms of the trends relate mainly to scarcity of some resources in Latin America, deficient information on the industrial or agricultural potential of some areas, and general lack of transportation and power facilities. There is little disagreement, however, with the objectives of balanced growth and modernization.

The background of the economic trends was touched on briefly by several members of the conference. The economic crisis of the 1960's in Latin America, Hélio Jaguaribe stated, stemmed from the fact that industrial expansion along the lines of import substitution had about reached its limit. It was, then, necessary to change to capital-intensive industries if the countries were to go on to a higher level of development. Economic integration of the Latin American continent held great promise for the future development of the region, in economic welfare, balanced growth, and social integration; to Hardoy, for Latin America to reach economic maturity depended on this integration. Development of the continental interiors is considered to be scarcely less necessary. Gabriel Andrade Lleras, among others, spoke about this:

Two experiences in Latin America are impressive. One is Brasilia and the other is the marginal highway. Both are cases of long-range planning, and more action like this will be necessary if future population is to be as large as predicted. How can we keep on with cities like Buenos Aires, Mexico City, Bogota, or others, either medium or large, if only the lesser parts of our countries are open?

Latin America needs to be colonized in the interior. A very large part of it is not being used. This problem does not exist in Europe and the United States. Consequently, people who have studied the European and North American situations do not have solutions for the problem. One example is an engineering firm that studied the construction of a highway in the Amazon region that would link all the South American countries together by an inland route. Their report was that such a highway was not economically feasible. Obviously, such a highway was not economically sound for a developed country, the kind the firm was familiar with. It did not link existing market areas or production and consumption areas. But it is necessary, in order to open up the land for the future expansion of Latin America. Also, Brasilia may not be economically or sociologically sound today, but the usefulness of such a project has to be judged from the viewpoint of the year 2000.

This statement of Andrade's points out some of the unique characteristics of Latin America which have a linkage to the urbanization process and which may, in fact, have some impact on that process.

Developing the interior involves resource-development programs, land reform, the opening of new land for agriculture, resettlement schemes, and other plans. An over-all objective of all such plans may be defined as improvement of rural areas, including their agricultural development. In some countries, rural improvement programs are looked on as part of a program to halt the large-scale migration to the cities, or, at the least, to lessen its selectivity, by providing more opportunity in the countryside. Resettlement schemes are open to criticism, according to some observers, on the basis of lack of information about soil fertility in some regions, distance to existing markets, and an expansion of agriculture at a time when already too many people are trying to make a living from the land. Such schemes will, as Browning suggested, need urban centers for their success. Among others, accessibility to markets is judged to be a key factor in the success of interior colonization, and towns and cities are needed to absorb the surplus agricultural population as improved agricultural technology releases more people from the land.

There is, it was pointed out several times, an interrelation between urban and rural development that has to be taken into account. The urbanization process should be directed in such a way as to bring about a better balance between development in rural and in urban areas. Solari, taking a position quite different from that described by Scobie (Chapter II), stated that rather than being "exotic flowers" Latin American cities now are true products of the countryside:

Cities do not exist alone but are part of the social, economic, and cultural structure of the country. In all the Latin American countries, the type of city, and of city growth, and of city composition, is an important part and function of the economic structure of the countryside, and the problems of the cities cannot be discussed independently of the problems of the countryside. With certain types of rural economy, cities grow. And that explains the variations in city growth, because there are many types of groups and many types of rural country behind the cities.

What should be recognized, according to Kempton E. Webb, is that

we are dealing with one geographic reality, and that the rural areas are one phenomenon and cities are another, and both are the product of specific sets of processes. If we take as our objective a viable society in Latin America, including a viable economy, a viable nation, I would say that what is necessary is productivity— productivity per unit area, per producing unit, and per person. This problem of raising productivity can be attacked both in the rural areas and in the cities.

Some ways in which the backwardness of rural areas affects urban communities were touched on during the conference. One effect is that, with the migrants, rural areas export their unemployment, traditional attitudes, and tensions to the city. Another is the increase in urban costs, especially of food, which prevents higher urban wages from bringing a higher standard of living. Still another is that the undeveloped rural areas do not provide a market for urban goods and thus do not stimulate greater productivity in the industrial sector that would attract more investment and create more jobs. Any steps taken to improve rural conditions and agricultural productivity, obviously, would benefit urban areas, not only in lower costs and consumer markets but also in bringing in-migrants trained to a high enough level of skills to meet the technological demands of modern industry. Therefore, as stated several times during the conference, urban problems should be viewed as part of a national problem and not merely from the "urbanistic point of view."

Earlier orientation to the urbanization process in Latin America, several members of the conference pointed out, had been directed only toward its quantitative aspects: how to halt it altogether, slow it down, or divert it into regions, mainly rural, away from the capital city area. Considerable emphasis has been placed on rural development, ran one explanation, because the prospective migrants had no direct channel through which to express their wishes. What was planned for them, consequently, was based on interpretations of what they were looking for in the city, with a view to providing it for them outside the large urban complexes. Meanwhile, the people "voted with their feet," as Thomas A. Reiner put it, and continued to move to the large cities.

Programs directed toward rural improvement and economic growth of lagging regions are essential. They should not, however, be carried out in isolation. Desperately needed were both a higher standard of living in operation throughout each country and an integrated society: "*urban* integration," Renato Poblete observed, "of the *barrios marginales* with the rest of the city; *national* integration, of rural with urban sections; and, ultimately, or possibly concomitantly, *intracontinental* integration, of Latin American countries with one another."

It is a question of emphasizing the potential of the city for modernization, not urban development at the expense of rural development. "Rural and urban cannot be separated in policy considerations," Browning stated.

They can be separated in terms of relative density and differences in environment, with different consequences of activities carried on in them. Studies of productivity are interesting, but the city inherently has greater variety, greater potentiality, for raising productivity in general, and this is the reason for focusing more attention, more investment, on the city instead of solving the problem within the rural environment. Large cities have to be recognized as having vitality and resilience and endurance, and they should be accepted and planning should take place within them.

Therefore, Anatole A. Solow remarked, there should be less searching for alternatives to urban growth, particularly in rural areas, and more attention to the qualitative aspects of urbanization: (1) the socioeconomic status of the people in the city and how to raise it; (2) how to increase their productivity and mobilize it; (3) the moral, ethical, and value systems of the emerging urban society as reflected in its social and political institutions.

NATURAL POPULATION INCREASE

Latin America has one of the highest, if not the highest, rates of natural increase of any major world region. Population increased throughout the area by about a third during the decade from 1950 to 1960 (from 155.6 million to 204.9 million).[19] The high average annual rate of population growth, around 3 per cent for Latin America as a whole, is expected to be maintained, or possibly to increase. There are, of course, variations among

[19] Ducoff, *op. cit.*, pp. 198–199, Tables 1 and 2.

the countries, but the general trend is toward a higher rate of acceleration. Miró observes:

Around 1935, 12 countries comprising 39 per cent of the Latin American population had annual rates of growth under 2 per cent. It is estimated that only 2 countries and 10 per cent of the population of the region will be growing at that rate by 1975. On the other hand, while only 1 country with 1 per cent of the population grew in 1935 at a rate over 3 per cent, it is estimated that 10 countries comprising 67 per cent of the population will increase at this pace by 1975.[20]

The serious problems that will result from the prospect of over half the population living in cities by 1975, therefore, will have their origin in the expanded growth from natural population increase as well as from rural-urban migration.

In Latin America, as in other modernizing areas, mortality rates have declined earlier than fertility rates. The UN Economic Commission for Latin America has compiled figures indicating that mortality rates in all the countries have been reduced substantially, although they vary. Three countries, for example, have crude death rates over 20 per 1,000 population; Argentina and Uruguay have a low rate of about 8 per 1,000 population, and other countries have rates from 10 to 20 per 1,000.[21] At the same time, the fertility level remains high. Although this level varied in response to different economic and national situations prior to World War II, and, of course, varies among the countries, it has remained at about 41 to 43 per 1,000 population for Latin America as a whole since about 1945.[22]

Studies in Latin America indicate that the urban birth rate may be lower than the birth rate in rural areas. On the basis of preliminary findings from a study organized by CELADE, some

[20] Miró, *op. cit.*, p. 17.

[21] Cited in Miró, *op. cit.*, pp. 38–39; see also Table 18, p. 39.

[22] Robert O. Carleton, "Fertility Trends and Differentials in Latin America," *The Milbank Memorial Fund Quarterly*, XLIII, 4 (October, 1965), Part 2, 15.

variables correlated with lower fertility have been isolated: higher education, higher social status, urban origin, higher occupational level of husband, and women working outside the home.[23] The effect of education is particularly striking, as Table 5 shows.

Table 5. Average number of live births by educational level of women interviewed in three Latin American cities.

Educational level	Panama City	Rio de Janeiro	San José
All women	*2.74*	*2.25*	*2.98*
No education	4.00	3.33	3.89
1 to 3 years of primary education	4.18	2.93	3.73
4 or more years of primary education	3.73	2.46	3.74
Completed primary education	3.14	2.17	2.83
1 to 3 years of secondary education	2.67	1.63	2.26
4 or more years of secondary education	2.14	1.43	1.91
Completed secondary education	1.65	1.38	2.00
Less than 5 years of university education	1.09	1.05	1.59
5 or more years of university education	1.22	1.21	1.18
Not specified	3.00	2.00	—

Source. Carmen A. Miró and Ferdinand Rath, "Preliminary Findings of Comparative Fertility Surveys in Three Latin American Cities," in *The Milbank Memorial Fund Quarterly*, XLIII, 4 (October, 1965), Part 2, 51.

While lower fertility rates are related to living in cities, up to the present there has been no substantial decline in over-all fertility, even though the urban population has increased. The reasons for this strange phenomenon are presently under investigation. One of the factors explaining it may be the differences between structures of urban and rural age groups. It is possible,

[23] Carmen A. Miró and Ferdinand Rath, "Preliminary Findings of Comparative Fertility Surveys in Three Latin American Cities," *The Milbank Memorial Fund Quarterly*, XLIII, 4 (October, 1965), Part 2, 44–56.

however, that the explanation may lie in such factors as incomplete information on births (under-reporting in rural areas), or other limitations of the data.[24]

Critical elements in the natural population increase, therefore, are birth control and family planning. It has been pointed out that there is no magic in urbanization *per se* that will lower the birth rate. Such a change will come about mainly through a change in attitude toward birth control practices. Until very recently, the attitude toward population control was one of indifference.

This attitude is changing very gradually toward the positive as a result of the rapid expansion of population (and abortion figures), reconsideration by the Catholic church of its attitude, rural-urban migration, growing reliance on economic planning, and increased monetary and technical assistance from United States universities and other organizations.[25]

It remains, however, a highly controversial subject. More is involved than merely disseminating information on birth control or leaving the matter to personal choice, sanctioned by public approval. The whole question of birth control represents a clash between ideologies and penetrates not only the entire social structure but national and international political relations as well.

Concerning ideological and political implications of fertility trends, birth control, and family planning in Latin America, J. Mayone Stycos commented as follows:

In any future Latin American birth control and family planning programs, or discussion on fertility trends, ideological and political implications can become priority number one. Thus, a great po-

[24] See J. Mayone Stycos, "Needed Research on Latin American Fertility," *The Milbank Memorial Fund Quarterly*, XLIII, 4 (October, 1965), Part 2, 299–315, in which he discusses the possible effects of the recency of urbanization and other factors.

[25] J. Mayone Stycos, "Opinions of Latin-American Intellectuals on Population Problems and Birth Control," *The Annals of the American Academy of Political and Social Science*, CCCLX (July, 1965), 11, 17.

tential danger exists today for the non-Latin American scientist or politician in lacking understanding of the significance and rationale of these programs.

Latin American intelligentsia and powerful nationalistic political élite (left and right) could easily and emotionally exploit strong cultural and religious forces against "imperialist" (U.S.A.) and native economic feudal power sectors for keeping the masses of the population poor and exploited, and also for a "criminal attempt to prevent life and interfering with the most precious evolutionary biological process of the human race." Many Latin American intellectuals, following Marx's ideological attack on Malthus, view population growth as a problem of the social and economic structure, rather than as a biological phenomenon.

Most of the present family planning programs in Latin America are the result of the initiative of the members of the medical profession, who tend toward political conservatism. Moreover, health services are heavily concentrated in the rich urban areas and are almost nonexistent in the poor rural areas.

Since rapid, ideological regrouping is constantly in motion in Latin America, it is naturally confusing and difficult to understand and forecast the confrontation of the political and ideological forces *vis-à-vis* birth control and family planning. The new powerful left intelligentsia may well assume a more and more vocal and militant position against family planning as a result of: (a) the Catholic Church's change from opposition to neutral, but *de facto*, favorable attitude toward family planning, and (b) upper and middle class support to family planning under the leadership of the right and of conservative members of the medical profession.

A realistic appraisal of the ideological and political implication of family planning in Latin America will consider, as the only successful strategy, its total or complete subordination and integration with social and economic developmental structural programs for democratic and radical change. An alternative strategy of independent, isolated, or exclusive family planning programs, which appears to be the present pattern, will not only end without the support of the people, but will offer a powerful and explosive ideological and political weapon, to be used principally against the U.S.A. and its potential friends in Latin America.

While these matters remain controversial, it is fortunate that in Latin America we have reached a promising level of maturity in discussing them. Only first steps have been taken on this highly delicate social, religious, and cultural problem but those steps are in the right direction. As more knowledge is gained, from the kinds of solid studies being undertaken, it seems probable that some control of the population explosion may result.

In conclusion, rural-urban migration and the associated urban problems of high primacy, growth of slums, transfer of under-employment, to mention only a few, are the most conspicuous features in the rapid growth of urban areas in Latin America. Consequently, this aspect of urbanization has received the most attention so far as measures and proposals to retard it, or, at the least, to hold it back from the largest cities, are concerned. The principal discussion on demography, consequently, focused strongly on how to cope with this particular manifestation of urban growth. The high rate of natural increase in population makes it essential, however, that urban problems be attacked along this front also.

IV | *The City and Economic Development*

Urbanization, Industrialization,
  and Economic Development   BENJAMIN HIGGINS

In its Report on Social Development in Latin America, for the May, 1963, meeting of the Economic Commission for Latin America, the ECLA Secretariat stated:

The most striking aspect of the social structure of the majority of the Latin American countries is the rapidity of their urbanization process—a seemingly hopeful circumstance, in apparent contradiction with the agricultural bottleneck. . . . Is it not precisely the big city, that is, figuratively speaking, the vehicle of modernity?

Urbanization is, of course, not confined to Latin America, nor to recent decades. On the contrary, urbanization and economic development have been closely related ever since the industrial revolution of the seventeenth and eighteenth centuries. As shown in Table 6, between 1800 and 1950, the share of the world population living in cities of 5,000 and more increased from 3 to 29.8 per cent. The proportion of the population in cities over 20,000 in the same period rose from 2.4 to 20.9 per cent and the percentage of the population in cities of 100,000 and more grew from 1.7 to 13.1 per cent.

If one accepts the 20,000-inhabitant size as the lower limit of "urban," the urban population in 1850 was 2.3 times that of the population in 1800, the 1900 urban population was 2.9 times as large as that of 1850, and the 1950 urban population 3.4 times

Table 6.   World's urban population compared to world's total population, 1800–1950.

Year	World population (millions)	Cities of 5,000 and over		Cities of 20,000 and over		Cities of 100,000 and over	
		Population (millions)	Per cent of world population	Population (millions)	Per cent of world population	Population (millions)	Per cent of world population
1800	906	27.2	3.0	21.7	2.4	15.6	1.7
1850	1,171	74.9	6.4	50.4	4.3	27.5	2.3
1900	1,608	218.7	13.6	147.9	9.2	88.6	5.5
1950	2,400	716.7	29.8	502.2	20.9	313.7	13.1

Source. United Nations, Economic and Social Council, Economic Commission for Latin America, *Preliminary Study of the Demographic Situation in Latin America*, E/CN.12/604 (New York: United Nations, April 23, 1961), p. 31.

as large as that of 1900. On the other hand, says the Economic Commission for Latin America, "the striking fact remains that growth in the world's rural population has changed little in the course of time despite marked acceleration in the growth of the world's total population." [1]

As mentioned in earlier discussions, Latin America is more urbanized than the world as a whole. The proportion of the urban population (here defined, as above, as people living in localities of more than 2,000) was 39 per cent in 1950 and 46 per cent in 1960. During the 1950's the absolute increase in Latin America's urban population seems to have been about double the increase in the rural population. In some Latin American countries the urban population is concentrated in one or two large cities, the next towns in size usually being much smaller. In countries like Canada, the Netherlands, and Sweden, ECLA points out, the population in each of four size-groups of cities (5,000–20,000; 20,000–100,000; 100,000–500,000; and 500,000 or more) is much the same. In India and Turkey, on the other hand, more people live in small towns than in the big cities. In

[1] United Nations, Economic Commission for Latin America, *Preliminary Study of the Demographic Situation in Latin America*, E/CN.12/604 (New York: United Nations, 1961), p. 31.

Latin America, however, and particularly in Argentina, Brazil, and Chile, considerably more people live in large cities than in the next size class of cities. Moreover, the large towns are growing faster than the small ones. Thus the urban population structure in Latin America is "top-heavy" and tending to become more so.

Is this pattern of urban growth to be welcomed or deplored? One can find strongly voiced opinions on both sides of this question. We know, of course, that industrialization, economic development, and urbanization have gone together in the past. Is there really an inseparable link among these three trends, or could a more astute policy give us economic development without industrialization, or industrialization without urbanization—assuming that such a pattern of growth would somehow be preferable to what is now observed in Latin America? By "economic development" I mean a broadly diffused rise in per capita income throughout the population. Since figures of income distribution are seldom available, it is often necessary to use some such composite index as the "level of living" index proposed by the statistical division of the United Nations. This index includes such variables as levels of health, nutrition, education, newspaper circulation, and so forth, which are essentially "proxy" variables for the distribution of income and the level of public services.

By "industrialization" I mean merely the relatively rapid growth of the nonagricultural sectors of the economy. For countries as advanced as the United States, it might be worthwhile to make a distinction between growth of the secondary (industrial) sector and growth of the tertiary (services) sector. For developing countries, however, the cross-correlation between relative decline of the primary sector and relative growth of both the secondary and tertiary sectors is so high that one can ignore the distinction between the secondary and tertiary sectors as a first approximation. Thus, when Leo F. Schnore, for example, writes that "empirically, massing in cities can just as readily be attributed to technological progress—in the sense of expansion of the energy base, improvements in transportation and communication, and so forth—or to a whole host of other variables," as to industrialization, he is making a false distinction. Technological progress and other variables in his matrix are in fact a part of the general process of industrialization as here defined.

INDUSTRIALIZATION AND ECONOMIC DEVELOPMENT

As may be observed from Table 7, the statistical relation between rising per capita income and a declining proportion of the labor force in agriculture is very close indeed. Professor L. J. Zimmerman of the Institute of Social Studies in The Hague found a relation in the form $\log y = 0.0202 x + 1.3235$, with a regression coefficient of 0.92, "y" standing for per capita income and "x" for the percentage of employment outside the agricultural sector.[2] Indeed no country can be considered advanced with more than one third of its national income produced in the agricultural sector, or more than 40 per cent of its labor force engaged in that sector.

I have sometimes said that, if compelled to summarize the problem of underdevelopment in three words, I would reply "too many peasants." Economic development in the past has consisted very largely of transferring population from low productivity agriculture to much higher productivity industrial occupations, thus at the same time reducing population pressure on the land and permitting agricultural improvement in the form of conversion to large-scale mechanized agriculture. We have learned recently that even regional differences in productivity and income within the same country are largely a reflection of differences in the occupational structure among regions, and particularly of differences in the share of the labor force engaged in agriculture. The well-known convergence of per capita income among major regions in the United States is a

[2] L. J. Zimmerman, *Poor Lands, Rich Lands: The Widening Gap* (New York: Random House, 1965), p. 47.

Table 7.   Population engaged in agricultural occupations in specified countries.

Continent and countries	Percentage		Per capita GNP 1961 (US $)
	1930–1944	1945–1962	
	(average)		
Europe			
Great Britain	6	5	1,345
France	36	26	1,203
Italy	48	26	623
Ireland	49	40	570
Yugoslavia	—	—	306
North America			
United States	19	7	2,790
Canada	26	11	2,040
Latin America			
Venezuela	50	32	644
Argentina	—	20	533
Uruguay	—	14	449
Chile	35	28	348
Colombia	72	54	287
Mexico	65	54	297
Costa Rica	63	55	278
Brazil	67	58	268
El Salvador	75	60	191
Guatemala	71	68	184
Paraguay	—	54	129
Asia			
Ceylon	—	53	123
China, Taiwan	—	50	116
India	66	70	70
Indonesia	66	72	99
Israel (Jewish pop.)	—	13	733
Japan	48	40	383
Malaya, Federation of	61	58	368
Philippines	73	58	188
Africa			
Rhodesia	—	77	161
Nyasaland	—	92	161
Egypt (UAR)	71	57	150
Congo	—	84	103
Oceania			
Australia	19	13	1,475
New Zealand	23	14	1,470

Source. FAO Statistical Yearbook: Rosenstein-Rodan, *Review of Economics and Statistics*, XLIII (1961), 107–138.

direct result of a convergence of occupational structure; there remains no truly agricultural region in the United States. By the same token, the failure to produce convergence of productivity and income among regions of countries like Brazil, Colombia, and Mexico reflects failure to produce convergence of occupational structure. Indeed, now that this kind of development is nearing its end in the United States—a country where comparative advantage is most clearly marked precisely in the agricultural sector—we cannot move very many more farmers into industry. Fears have been expressed to the effect that maintaining high rates of growth in the future may prove extraordinarily difficult.

All this is not to say that increases in agricultural productivity are unimportant in the process. On the contrary, increasing concern is being expressed among development economists regarding the "agricultural lag." This lag is particularly striking in Latin America. Agricultural productivity is low in all developing countries, almost by definition; but in some countries the low output per man-year reflects overcrowding on the land, a phenomenon which is still relatively rare in Latin America. In Latin America more than any developing region, perhaps, the gap between actual and potential agricultural productivity, with existing population densities in agriculture, seems needlessly large. Moving large numbers of people from rural to urban occupations requires an increase in the supply of foodstuffs and agricultural raw materials to the industrial, urban sector. If these increased requirements for food and agricultural raw materials are not met by increased domestic production, they must be met by imports, increasing the burden on the industrial sector. Any country that ignores agricultural improvement in the course of economic development does so to its peril, as one socialist country after another has learned. In short, industrialization and agricultural improvement are not alternative roads to economic development, but are necessarily complementary.

Almost from the beginning of the renewed interest in economic development (or from the time of the classical economists, especially Malthus) it has been recognized that the key to economic development lies somewhere in the interactions between the agricultural and industrial sectors, which can also be expressed as a relation between the traditional and modern sectors, between rich and poor regions. Efforts to produce a general theory of underdevelopment have produced a variety of two-sector models, including one of my own.[3] The main lesson to be derived from such models is that economic development may be inhibited either by failure of investment in the industrial sector to expand fast enough to absorb an increasing share of the labor force into that sector, or through failure of agricultural productivity to rise enough to produce the necessary agricultural surpluses. There is indeed a need for a kind of "balance" between agricultural improvement and industrial expansion; but the kind of "balance" which effectively raises levels of living is one involving a progressively shrinking share of agriculture, both in total output and in total employment. In short, economic development without industrialization is unthinkable.

INDUSTRIALIZATION WITHOUT URBANIZATION?

Once the close relation between industrialization and economic development is established again the next question to be asked is whether an equally close relation between industrialization and urbanization exists. Once again we face a problem of definition, this time complicated by differences in statistical practices among various countries, even those within Latin America. "Urban" is variously defined to include centers of more than 2,000, more than 5,000, or more than 20,000. From a sociocultural point of view, perhaps even the lowest of these figures is too high. A Balinese village like Ubud with its palace, its market,

[3] See especially Benjamin Higgins, *Economic Development: Principles, Problems, and Policies* (New York: W. W. Norton, 1959), pp. 416–430, 548–551; and his review of Ranis and Fei, *Development of the Labor Surplus Economy*, in *Economic Development and Cultural Change*, XIV, 2 (January, 1966), 237–243.

its temples, its art school, and its performances of dance, theater, and music, is in some ways very urbane indeed. Gino Germani's distinction between "urbanization" and "urbanism" is worth bearing in mind. Where possible and convenient, however, we shall use the term "urban" to mean centers of more than 20,000 population.

It might be well to clear away one misunderstanding at the outset. A connection between industrialization and urbanization does not require that industries be established in cities. It could happen (although it is fairly rare) that the actual factories are built in a countryside, with the services connected with them concentrated in the cities; but even then, industrialization and urbanization will proceed side by side. Thus when Bert Hoselitz says that "although industrialization and urbanization go usually hand in hand, there is no necessary connection between the two processes. Industries can be and have been established in rural districts, and cities have grown up without large industrial plants," [4] he is evading the issue.

The same is true of Heberle when he says "industrialization and urbanization should not be considered as identical processes . . . cities have been in existence before industrialization and not all cities are highly industrialized." [5]

Why should we expect urbanization and industrialization to go together? I believe it unnecessary for me to belabor this question here. The tendency toward agglomeration of services in cities, the economies of scale involved in urban growth, and the external economies created for other activities by each new enterprise or service established in one town are too well known to need repetition. A point which is perhaps too little stressed in the literature on the subject, however, is that highly trained people of the kind needed for middle and high positions in either

[4] "The City, The Factory, and Economic Growth," *The American Economic Review*, XLV, 2 (May, 1955), 166–184.
[5] Quoted in Leo F. Schnore, "Urbanization and Economic Development," extended version of a paper read to the American Sociological Society, September 3, 1959.

the public or the private sector like to live in or near cities. In short, the kind of people needed to launch and maintain a process of industrialization have urbane tastes. The ludicrous spectacle of cabinet members in Brazil solemnly boarding their planes on Tuesday morning to fly to Brasilia for a cabinet meeting, and flying joyously back to Rio de Janeiro on Tuesday evening, is evidence enough of the difficulties involved in moving such people even from large cities to small ones. The painfully slow growth of Canberra since its establishment in 1920 provides further support for this argument.

The ECLA has provided some data on urbanization and industrialization in Latin American and European countries (see Tables 8 and 9). Urbanization is defined as cities of more than

Table 8. Indices of urbanization and industrialization for selected Latin American countries, latest census year.

Country	Census year	Indices	
		Urbaniza-tion*	Industri-alization**
Argentina	1947	48.3	26.9
Chile	1952	42.8	24.2
Ecuador	1950	17.8	17.8
Venezuela	1950	31.0	15.6
Paraguay	1950	15.2	15.5
Bolivia	1950	19.7	15.4
Colombia	1951	22.3	14.6
Peru	1940	13.9	13.2
Brazil	1950	20.2	12.6

Source. Official census data.
* Percentage of total population in places of 20,000 or more inhabitants.
** Percentage of economically active males engaged in manufacturing, construction, gas and electricity production.

20,000 inhabitants. Industrialization is defined alternatively as the proportion of the active male labor force engaged in manufacturing, construction, gas and electricity production, and as a percentage of the total labor force working as salaried employees or

Table 9. Urbanization and structure of employment.

Country	Census year	Urbaniza- tion index*	Industrial employment**	Second index as a percent- age of the first
Latin American Countries				
Argentina	1947	48.3	17.3 (1)	36
Venezuela	1950	31.0	7.1 (5)	23
Mexico	1950	24.0	8.4 (3)	35
Puerto Rico	1950	27.1	16.2 (2)	60
Bolivia	1950	14.0	3.8 (6)	27
Costa Rica	1950	10.9	8.2 (4)	75
Haiti	1950	5.4	2.0 (7)	37
European Countries				
Great Britain	1951	67.7	38.6 (1)	56
Western Germany	1950	45.3	27.6 (4)	61
Austria	1951	39.8	21.5 (5)	54
Sweden	1950	34.5	28.7 (3)	83
France	1946	31.4	18.9 (6)	60
Switzerland	1950	31.2	33.4 (2)	107
Finland	1950	24.0	18.4 (7)	77

Source. Adapted from Table 16, United Nations, Economic and Social Council, Economic Commission for Latin America, *Preliminary Study of the Demographic Situation in Latin America*, E/CN.12/604 (New York: United Nations, 1961), p. 55.

* Percentage of total population in places of 20,000 or more inhabitants.

** Percentage of total active labor force working as salaried employees or wage earners in manufacturing.

wage earners in manufacturing alone. It is therefore a narrower definition of industrialization than the one I have suggested. A glance at the tables shows that the rank correlation is fairly high, although the ratio of the industrialization index to the urbanization index varies a good deal. The number of cases here (particularly the number of cases in Latin America itself) is too small to provide a rank correlation of any high degree of reliability. Broadening the definition of "industrialization" would no doubt improve the correlations.

Leo Schnore, in a statistical analysis of sixty-nine countries, finds a rank correlation coefficient for the relation between urbanization and employment in nonextractive industry of .77 and between metropolitanization and nonextractive industry of .87 (Table 10). There are similarly high correlations between ur-

Table 10. Spearman rank-correlation coefficients for correlations of two measures of urbanization with ten indicators of economic development, *ca.* 1950–1955.*

| Indicators of economic development | Correlation of indicators of economic development with: | | | |
| | Urbanization | | Metropolitanization** | |
	r	N	r	N
Technological factors				
Energy consumption	+.84	72	+.83	73
Motor vehicles	+.74	67	+.80	67
Newspaper circulation	+.82	73	+.82	74
Organizational factors				
Nonextractive industry	+.77	69	+.87	69
International trade	+.55	65	+.63	64
Income per capita	+.69	54	+.74	54
Physicians per capita	+.78	68	+.81	69
Literacy level	+.73	73	+.76	73
Demographic factors				
Population growth	−.21	67	−.24	67
Age composition	+.56	62	+.52	63

Source. Leo F. Schnore, "Urbanization and Economic Development," extended version of a paper read to the American Sociological Society, September 3, 1959.

* Computed according to the formula $r = 1 - \dfrac{6 \sum D^2}{N(N^2 - 1)}$ where D = difference in ranks.

** Rank-correlation coefficient, metropolitanization and urbanization = +.89.

banization and other indices of economic development (Table 11).[6] These lead Schnore to maintain:

[6] In any case, too much weight should not be attached to rank correlations for countries which vary so much in size and importance as those in Schnore's list.

The major conclusion to be drawn from these materials, however, is that the usual linkage assumed between industrialization and urbanization—valid though it may be in a gross way—represents an overly simplistic view. In point of fact there are a number of variables that show equivalent degrees of association with urbanization. This is not a denial of the possibility that many of these other indices are themselves consequences or concomitants of industrialization. It is a plea, however, for the recognition of the many facets of the topic that are likely to be overlooked by focusing exclusive attention upon industrialization in a limited sense of industrial structure.

Table 11. Correlation matrix: Spearman rank-correlation coefficients, twelve measures of urbanization and economic development, *ca.* 1950–1955.*

Variable	(1)	(2)	(3)	(4)	(5)	(6)	(7)	(8)	(9)	(10)	(11)	(12)
(1) Energy consumption		.85	.92	.80	.66	.78	.82	.84	−.45	.64	.84	.83
(2) Motor vehicles	65		.78	.81	.81	.79	.70	.69	−.41	.41	.74	.80
(3) Newspaper circulation	74	68		.74	.69	.76	.84	.91	−.45	.60	.82	.82
(4) Nonextractive industry	70	64	70		.64	.71	.72	.73	−.39	.68	.77	.87
(5) International trade	64	64	65	60		.76	.53	.62	−.36	.32	.55	.63
(6) Income per capita	55	51	55	55	50		.74	.67	−.07	.60	.69	.74
(7) Physicians per capita	70	65	70	65	62	53		.85	−.38	.66	.78	.81
(8) Literacy level	73	68	74	69	65	54	70		−.45	.68	.73	.76
(9) Population growth	67	62	68	64	60	53	65	68		−.27	−.21	−.24
(10) Age composition	63	61	63	62	57	51	60	63	60		.56	.52
(11) Urbanization	72	67	73	69	65	54	68	73	67	62		.89
(12) Metropolitanization	73	67	74	69	64	54	69	73	67	63	72	

Source. Leo F. Schnore, "Urbanization and Economic Development," extended version of a paper read to the American Sociological Society, September 3, 1959.

* Above the diagonal, Spearman rank-correlation coefficient (defined in note to Table 10); below the diagonal, the number of cases upon which the correlation in question is based.

As one may judge from this paper, sociologists do not seem to have learned, as economists have, that when everything is going up everything will correlate with everything. In this situation, merely running hosts of regressions is of little use. What is necessary is first to specify logically consistent theoretical models, and then to test each of these against the facts. Clearly, the close relation between urbanization and industrialization does not mean that urbanization "causes" industrialization, or even that industrialization "causes" urbanization. It means only that in the past industrialization and urbanization have been found together—along with a lot of other things.

Schnore himself seems appalled by the possibility that all the major variables in the economic development process must move together. He quotes Jaffe Stewart as saying that "all the factors discussed in our matrix must change significantly, and also simultaneously, or at least with a minimum time lag." He then laments:

If the situation is indeed as complex and ramified as this passage suggests, both theoretical and practical goals may indefinitely elude attainment. The theoretician is unable to enter the closed system, and the planner has no real chance of breaking the vicious circle. Faced with the intertwined image of a whole host of variables changing simultaneously, and in complex interaction, either may be led into desperate stratagems.

Unfortunately, the more we learn about the economic development process, the more certain we become that it is indeed "as complex and ramified as this passage suggests." Economists, however, do not feel that the inevitable conclusion is that "the theoretician is unable to enter the closed system," and that "the planner has no real chance of breaking the vicious circle." One cannot help but feel that when Schnore refers here to the "theoretician," he really means the statistician. True, if we have a multivariable system, with high correlations among all variables, we cannot isolate the strategic causal factors by regression analysis alone. But why should we do so? There are other methods of arriving at causal relationship, including field studies, controlled experiments, and use of psychological and engineering data. The high correlation between birth rates in Sweden and the immigration of storks does not mean that we cannot exclude the possibility that the storks bring the babies (or that the babies bring the storks). We have other evidence that enables us to exclude this possibility without question. (Nor is this correlation a "nonsense" correlation; as in other Western countries, girls in Sweden like to be married in June, and the storks return to

Sweden in April.) The question is not whether the high regression coefficients reflect causal connections or not; the question is whether these connections could be broken, if it seemed desirable to do so, by active policy. Alternatively, if it is desired to retain all the interactions, the question is, if one wants to stimulate the process of growth, which are the most strategic variables on which to act. These questions are clearly open to research, and we do not need to rely on statistical analysis alone.

In the present context, the question to ask—assuming that industrialization is desired as an inevitable concomitant of economic development, but that urbanization for some reason or other is not desired—is whether an act of policy could retard the rate of urbanization without retarding the rate of industrialization and thus of economic development? Alternative versions of this question might be, "What is the optimal size of city from the standpoint of economic development?" or, "Could we have economic development based on small industries located in small towns?"

I have not myself done research on the optimal size of city. All I could do would be to repeat what I said some years ago in an article somewhat pompously entitled "Towards a Science of Community Planning":

Urban centers grow up largely because people want to be "close to" a variety of facilities—business and professional contacts, educational institutions, recreation and cultural facilities requiring participation of large numbers of people, specialized shops—and to other people with similar tastes. "Close to" is obviously not a matter of mere distance but of travel time. Three miles of congested city streets may remove people farther from the points they want to reach than ten miles of open highway. Thus one of the major objectives of city planning must be minimum travel time. The city planner must try to provide effective proximity to places of work, recreation, education, and residence. If such proximity cannot be provided the city ceases to function as a city and becomes an inconveniently arranged collection of specialized communities. (The

Standard-Vacuum Company's move from the Wall Street area to Westchester County and back to mid-Manhattan is an illustration of the frustrations that arise when a city ceases to perform its functions effectively.) A city of "optimal size" must be big enough to be urbane in its range of activities and small enough to provide effective proximity to these activities for its residents, with the available techniques of city planning and transportation.[7]

With respect to decentralization of industrial activities through reliance on small industries which can be grouped together in correspondingly small towns, more can be said. As the evidence comes in, it becomes clear that over a very wide range of industrial activity, small enterprises cannot be afforded by developing countries, because they are too expensive in terms of capital. Small industries, with relatively low capital:labor ratios frequently turn out to have high capital:output ratios. At first blush, it would seem that underdeveloped countries, where capital is scarce and unskilled labor redundant, can keep the aggregate capital:output ratio down, without undue loss of efficiency, more easily through choice of product-mix than through choice of technology. If it is difficult to produce a wide range of commodities efficiently with labor-intensive methods, cannot developing countries specialize in production in which efficiency is possible with a relatively high labor:capital ratio? The answer, unfortunately, is "not always." The country's resource pattern may be such that its comparative advantage in international trade may lie in industries that require relatively capital-intensive techniques—oil, tin, bauxite, copper, and plantation agriculture, for example. The balance of payments situation may be one strongly favoring the development of import-replacing industries of a capital-intensive nature. The subtle factor of "linkage"—stimulation of investment in other fields by initial investment in one field—may be higher for heavy, large-scale, capital-intensive industries than for light, small-scale, or

[7] Benjamin Higgins, "Towards a Science of Community Planning," *Journal of the American Institute of Planners*, XV, 3 (Fall, 1949), 9.

labor-intensive industries. Acquisition of fundamental technical and managerial skills, "technology-mindedness" and "development-mindedness," may be more closely associated with modern technology of a capital-intensive nature than with old-fashioned technology of a labor-intensive type.

Very little research has been done on choice of technology for particular undertakings. The complexity of the analysis that must be undertaken before one can be sure which technique is best has been admirably set forth by the Indian economist A. K. Sen.[8] In addition to the capital:output ratios for the whole range of available techniques, one needs to have information regarding labor costs at present and probable future wage rates; working capital requirements; quality and price of the product with different techniques; managerial costs; surplus available for reinvestment; impact on the balance of payments; linkage effects; and even—since the time-pattern of expansion of output will be different for different techniques—communal time-preference functions.[9] Applying his analytical framework as best he could with the data available, Sen came to the conclusion that "the case for hand looms or for power looms is much less straightforward than the Hand Loom Board of India on the one hand and the Millowners' Association of Bombay on the other seem to suggest."[10] His calculations show that the Benares hand loom has the higher output:capital ratio; but the rate of surplus is so much higher with the nonautomatic power loom that, with reinvestment of the surplus, total output with the power loom will surpass that of the hand loom within six years. Dr. Sen is much more definite regarding the Ambar Charkha spinning wheel: "As a technological possibility, the Ambar Charkha seems to offer very little."[11] The failure of China's backyard foundries is another case in point.

[8] A. K. Sen, *Choice of Techniques* (New York: International Publications Service, 1960), *passim.*

[9] *Ibid.*

[10] *Ibid.*, p. 114.

[11] *Ibid.*, p. 119.

Dhar and Lydall present Indian data which suggest a general tendency for output:capital ratios to rise with size of factory. The Netherlands Economics Institute has gathered statistics for several manufacturing industries in the United States, Mexico, Colombia, and India which indicate a wide range of possible capital:labor ratios in these industries, but, except for cotton textiles and bakery products, the capital cost per job is high in all countries—above $2,000. A United Nations study for France, India, Poland, and the U.S.S.R. shows a relatively narrow range of capital:output ratios, with a much wider range of capital:labor ratios, resulting in almost equal costs per cubic meter-kilometer for a combined operation of excavation, transport, and compaction.[12]

Thus a country like the United States can afford small industries, but one like Brazil cannot. This fact is at least part of the explanation of the "Leontiev paradox." The United States turns out to be a net importer of capital and a net exporter of labor through its pattern of international trade, exporting labor-intensive products and importing capital-intensive ones. Efforts such as the Chinese program for backyard foundries, or the Indian program for use of home spinning wheels and hand looms, almost always turn out to be dismal failures. If we are to think of reducing the rate of urbanization by decentralizing industry, therefore, we must think in terms of the minimal size of town necessary to support the efficient operation of large-scale, capital-intensive industries.

On the other hand, large-scale industries do not necessarily require large cities. Any country wishing to do so could probably achieve some decentralization by moving industry and related services from large cities (like Rio and Melbourne) to middle-sized cities (like Brasilia and Canberra). We have not yet asked the question, "Why should anyone wish to do so?"

[12] These data are all reproduced in the International Labour Office Report, *Employment Objectives in Economic Development*, Appendix III (Geneva, 1961).

THE URBAN EXPLOSION IN LATIN AMERICA

URBANIZATION WITHOUT INDUSTRIALIZATION

While it would appear that significant industrialization is not possible without some accompanying urbanization (although metropolitanization may not be absolutely necessary), it is less clear that urbanization is impossible without industrialization. There is substantial evidence that during recent decades the pace of urbanization has been faster than the corresponding rate of industrialization would require, especially in Latin America. This imbalance takes the form of urban unemployment, urban under-employment, and urban low-productivity employment. Through the process of urbanization, in Latin America as in Asia and the Middle East, there has been a transfer of these three aspects of underdevelopment from the countryside to the city.

Raymond Firth tells the story of some Trobriand islanders who, observing the high standard of living among American soldiers occupying their island, rearranged their villages with a rectangular street pattern, threw away their ceremonial regalia, and marched up and down the streets with sticks looking like rifles, hoping thereby to achieve economic development. There is nothing about the fact or form of growth of cities which guarantees rising levels of income. The 1957 United Nations *Report on the World Social Situation* made this observation:

Open unemployment is not a serious problem in most of the Latin American countries, either among the permanent city population or the migrants. (Cuba and Puerto Rico, in which a high proportion of the labour force depends on seasonal plantation work, are the known exceptions.) However . . . with the probable exceptions of Argentina and southern Brazil, the growth of the cities "has multiplied considerably the unsalaried sector of the urban lower class; poor artisans, shopkeepers on a small scale or with semi-permanent places of business, ambulatory pedlars and workers many of whom have occupations that constitute incredibly poorly paid forms of under-employment." As in other less-developed regions, there has been a transfer of rural underemployment to the cities, where it may be statistically concealed under "services" or "activities not defined." [13]

The comparison of the figures for Latin America and Europe in Table 9 (and particularly the ratio of industrialization to urbanization) leads the ECLA to state: "Not only are Latin American countries less industrialized than European countries are, or were, at similar levels of urbanization, but the increase in Latin America's urbanization—as distinct from Europe, North America, or the Soviet Union—was not accompanied by commensurate increase in industrialization." The Commission adds: "Unfortunately, as is well known, services that are unsolicited or are only in small demand are being performed in Latin America by a low class of urban workers so numerous that their earnings are not far superior to those of beggars." [14] The Commission concluded, accordingly, that in Latin America urbanization has outrun employment opportunities outside the agricultural sector. Measures were recommended to improve conditions in the rural areas, including providing rural employment, increasing rural productivity and purchasing power, improving education, housing, and health in rural societies, and creating a wider dispersal of industries.

The conditions noted in the late 1950's have since become aggravated. The *Report on Social Development*, presented to the Tenth Session of the Economic Commission for Latin America at Mar del Plata, Argentina, in May, 1963, after pointing to the continuing rapid urbanization in Latin America, makes the following comment:

[13] "Urbanization in Latin America," in United Nations, Department of Economic and Social Affairs, *Report on the World Social Situation*, E/CN.5/324/Rev.1; ST/SOA/33 (New York: United Nations, 1957), p. 181. The quotation included in this passage is from José E. Iturriaga, *La estructura social y cultural de México* (Mexico City: Fondo de Cultura Economica, 1951), p. 40.

[14] *Preliminary Study of the Demographic Situation in Latin America*, p. 56.

A rapid urbanization process should imply the presence of conditions similar to conditions found elsewhere. In other words, there should presumably be that continuum between the urban and rural sectors which is typical of the great industrial countries of our time. In Latin America, however, no such continuum exists, but a complete rupture. No smooth, straight-forward transmission line—where distances are naturally a bridge—but the ragged series of abrupt switch-overs, jumps and hiatuses. May there not be a flaw in the prevailing theory with respect to the urbanization process? How is it possible to account for the steady expansion of the larger towns alongside a stationary agricultural productivity?

Dualism may even be increasingly aggravated in Latin America because of the increasing discrepancy between urban and rural development. The old type of organization of work known as the *hacienda*, says the Commission, holds out against the rationalization and modernization called for today. It is a survival of the past that hinders quick and easy adaptation to the demands of modern industry. Thus the rapidity of urbanization in Latin America reflects the "expulsion" of the agricultural population (Table 11) as much as the attractions of job opportunities in the cities. One would think, says the Commission, that the "rapid expansion of the larger towns is attributable to the concurrent establishment of thriving industrial activities in the urban areas concerned. But the correlation is so tenuous—quite irrespective of its probable causal links—that it has become a matter of controversy." The Commission is careful to add, however, that "the suggestion in the preceding paragraph is not that there has been no widespread modernizing effort—the rationalization process has been an effective operation as everywhere—but that the degree of modernization achieved has not been sufficient."

In short, the solution may not be to retard the movement to the cities by making conditions more attractive in the countryside—a policy which is in itself anti-developmental—but rather to accelerate the rate of industrialization and consequently the rate of employment-creation outside the agricultural sector. As pointed out by the Bureau of Social Affairs of the United Nations on another occasion, in presenting their paper to the Joint Conference with UNESCO, ILO, the OAS, on urbanization problems in Latin America: "This paper takes it for granted that the cities will continue to grow, and that a policy of *preventing* further urbanization would not be realistic." But the Bureau adds: "Such an outlook, however, does not imply disregard of the numerous warnings that have been made on the over-rapid and unbalanced character of Latin American city growth at present. It may well be desirable to slow down the rate of urbanization and to divert from the capital cities to provincial towns as much as possible of the stream of internal migrants." [15]

URBANIZATION AND TECHNOLOGICAL AND REGIONAL DUALISM

Perhaps no feature of underdeveloped countries is more general or more striking than technological and regional dualism. The relation between over-all underdevelopment and wide gaps between productivity and incomes of major regions of a country has become a familiar part of the theory of underdevelopment. The recent stress on "balanced growth" in developing countries has included emphasis on the importance of narrowing these gaps. The development programs of a good many such countries include special measures to accelerate growth of their poor and lagging regions. Professor Gunnar Myrdal, examining the European experience, was perhaps the first to suggest that underdeveloped countries are characterized by large and increasing gaps in productivity and income among major regions, advanced countries by small and diminishing ones. The correlation between the degree of regional integration and maturity of the occupational structure, and between both of these and per capita income, is indeed very high. Even small underdeveloped coun-

[15] United Nations, Bureau of Social Affairs, "Some Policy Implications of Urbanization," in Philip M. Hauser, ed., *Urbanization in Latin America* (New York: International Documents Service, Columbia University Press, 1961), pp. 294–295.

tries like Ceylon, Guatemala, and Greece have sharply defined rich and poor, leading and lagging regions; while in larger countries like Brazil, Chile, Indonesia, Italy, and Mexico the regional contrasts are dramatic. One might even be tempted to define underdevelopment in these terms: an underdeveloped country is one with large and increasing differences in per capita income among major regions, and with a large proportion of the population living in the poor and lagging regions; an advanced country has small and diminishing gaps among regions, and only a small proportion of the labor force is employed in the poorer and relatively lagging regions.

Economic growth in any country involves leading and lagging sectors, frequently identified with leading and lagging regions. Healthy growth, however, seems to require that the lagging sectors and regions be converted into leading ones before too much time has passed. Otherwise the agglomerative pull of the leading sectors may become so strong that lagging sectors are converted into poor ones, like the Italian or Mexican south or the Brazilian northeast. The problems seem to be especially acute when sectors and regions overlap, as they do in many underdeveloped countries. At best, identification of lagging and leading sectors with lagging and leading regions aggravates the problem of reallocation of resources. In many cases the leading sector is identified not merely with a region but with a few cities. Latin American countries are already substantially urbanized and are rapidly becoming more so. Asian cities have grown fantastically since 1940. The agglomerative pull of the capital cities is particularly strong, but some commercial, financial, and industrial centers (such as São Paulo, Medellin, and Bombay), in addition to the capital city, show rapid rates of growth.

TECHNOLOGICAL DUALISM

The sharp division of underdeveloped countries into two distinct and contrasting sectors, frequently identified with two distinct regions, has been labeled "technological dualism." The general theory of technological dualism and the population explosion has been presented in some detail elsewhere.[16] A very short summary of it must suffice here.

In most underdeveloped countries investment has been concentrated in the "modern" sector: plantations, mines, oil fields, and the financing, transport, and processing operations associated with these. Because of the highly capital-intensive nature of this investment, it has provided less increase in employment than in output and exports. Yet it was accompanied by a "population explosion" because industrialization brought public health measures, law and order, and improved transport, which reduced the dangers of famine. Thus the process of industrial investment meant rapid growth of the number of people who had to be employed in the other main sector: peasant agriculture and the small or cottage industries, plus the finance, transport, and processing connected with these—together labeled the "rural" sector.

While good land was abundant, the rural sector could absorb increased numbers without either unemployment or a fall in per capita income. But as good land gave out, diminishing returns to labor on the land, work-spreading devices, underemployment, and disguised unemployment appeared in the rural sector. Technological progress was increasingly confined to the industrial sector, where *skilled* labor was scarce and labor-saving innovations worthwhile. In the rural sector, where labor was redundant, there was no incentive for introduction of labor-saving devices. Productivity and incomes in the two sectors grew increasingly farther apart. The level of investment in the industrial sector was frequently sufficient to create inflationary pressure in markets where monetary transactions predominate, without reducing unemployment in the rural sector.

Under conditions of technological dualism it is possible to have very substantial investment in the modern sector and quite satisfactory increases in per capita income in that sector, without

[16] Higgins, *Economic Development,* Ch. 2.

making any dent in the problem of poverty in the traditional sector and region. That is precisely the situation in Brazil, Italy, and Mexico today. Impressive though it is, the investment taking place in the modern sector does not provide new employment opportunities at a rate high enough to permit the significant decline in the rate of population growth in the traditional sector and region which may prove necessary for a solution to the problem of poverty in that region. In Greece, on the other hand, thanks to large-scale emigration from the country as a whole, even the absolute level of population in some poorer areas is declining.

In the worst cases the lagging sectors and regions are associated with less highly developed social groups as well. In these cases, moving people from low-productivity occupations to more highly productive ones is not only a matter of moving them from one part of the country to another; it is also a matter of moving them from one sociocultural framework to another.

For a Brazilian peasant in the northeast or a Mexican peasant in the south both the geographic and cultural distances he must move to obtain a job in the progressing sector of the society may be very great indeed. Once both technological and sociological dualism set in together, a "feedback" mechanism tends to appear, for the simple reason that the pattern of emigration tends to dilute the quality of the population—without sufficiently reducing its quantity. The best-educated, best-trained, most progressive, most ambitious men and women—those with the highest level of "need-achievement," in McClelland's terminology—will be the ones to leave the lagging region for the progressive one. Thus the lagging region is denuded of the very qualities needed to reconstruct it and reverse the trend, and launch a process that will narrow the gaps in productivity and income. Meanwhile, at the other end of the migratory route, underdeveloped countries suffer from urban congestion, slums, urban underemployment, and urban parasitism.

AREAS AND REGIONS

If an underdeveloped country is one where the lagging region absorbs a large share of the population and where the index of dispersion is rising, is a lagging region one in which a large proportion of the population lives in "depressed areas," and in which the index of dispersion between depressed areas and growing points in the region is rising? Certainly some recent programs and legislation seem to rest on the assumption that it is. The "trial and demonstration zones" of the European Productivity Agency were at least implicitly based on the assumption that lagging or poor regions are haphazard collections of depressed areas. The Area Redevelopment Act in the United States provides for technical and capital assistance from the federal government to designated "development areas," defined mainly in terms of chronic unemployment. The Canadian legislation concerning the Area Redevelopment Agency is similar in tone. The underlying rationale of such legislation is that the unemployment problem consists primarily of a collection of rather small areas with peculiar employment problems, and that the solution is to create job opportunities in precisely those areas.

It is clear that the phenomena of technological dualism and regional dualism are closely related to the urbanization process. Much of the modern sector tends to be concentrated in cities, although it would be a mistake to identify the modern sector with urban areas completely. The modern sector includes capital-intensive, large-scale, mechanized agriculture and modern mining. What is true, however, is that growth of the modern sector and of the urban sector are closely correlated. In small countries like those of Central America, the modern sector and leading region tend to consist of the capital city and its hinterland. Even in larger countries, one finds technological and regional dualism *within* both the rich and poor regions. Thus within the Brazilian northeast and Amazonia much of such modern sector as there is can be found in the large cities of Recife and Belem. The solution, however, is not to delay urbanization but to accelerate it, and so to empty the countryside of low-productivity farmers.

"EVILS" OF URBANIZATION?

We have mentioned above two undesirable by-products of the urbanization process in Latin America: first, the transfer of unemployment, underemployment, and low-productivity employment from farm to city; and second, the frustration of the main purpose of urban concentration (being "near to" a variety of activities) through the increasing difficulties of traffic circulation in the very large cities. The solution to the first problem is accelerated economic growth; the solution to the second is improved city planning, perhaps combined with an improved "national urban policy" which might involve a higher degree of decentralization of the industrialization process.

There is a tendency on the part of the general public, and even on the part of some social scientists, to associate urbanization with other undesirable by-products as well: crime, juvenile delinquency, broken families, slums, disease, and the like. Bert Hoselitz quotes Motwani as describing cities as "huge mausoleums of coal, smoke, iron and steel, dirt and squalor, over-crowding, coolie-lines, long hours, low wages, bad housing, woman and child labor, prostitution, gambling, dance halls—etc." [17]

It is extremely doubtful whether in fact cities are any worse than the countryside in terms of such social evils. With a national urban policy combined with effective city planning, competent social welfare organizations, and more rapid economic development, there is no reason for the experiences of the early phase of the industrial revolution of Europe to be repeated in other countries. As I have pointed out on another occasion:

Perhaps the earliest association of social factors with economic development was concern over the "evil consequences" of industrializa-

[17] Hoselitz, *op. cit.*, pp. 166–167.

tion in Europe. In the late nineteenth century, the United Nations Bureau of Social Affairs points out, "the goal of social policy was to protect the weak and the poor against further exploitation or to achieve a radical redistribution of wealth in the name of social justice." With this approach, "industrialization was widely seen as a negative or retrogressive influence from a social welfare point of view. Deep concern arose over social ills that were observed in rapidly growing industrial and urban centres—unhealthy working conditions, starvation wages, child labour, disruption of family life, overcrowding, filth and sordidness in slums, delinquency and corruption of youth." Some of these attitudes still prevail. The Bureau considers them anachronistic, for today social scientists no longer believe that "such social ills are a necessary consequence of industrialization. Many of them simply represent evils of urban poverty and overcrowding that appear quite independently of growth; they often result from a transfer through migrants of rural destitution to an urban setting where it becomes more conspicuous. What is needed in these cases is not less industrialization but more industrialization." [18]

There can be no doubt that the levels of education are higher in the cities than in the rural areas. Indeed, so difficult is the problem, as Browning stated, of bringing universal primary school education to the remoter rural regions that the Ministry of Education in Brazil, for example, has simply despaired of meeting the targets of the "Charter of Santiago." [19]

It is also clear that health conditions are, on balance, superior in the cities, because of the better availability of medical services and the greater ease of controlling epidemic diseases. The effects on fertility are less clear, as indicated in an earlier conference discussion. At the Santiago Conference on Urbanization, the

[18] "An Economist's View," in *Social Aspects of Economic Development in Latin America*, II, by José Medina Echavarría and Benjamin Higgins (Paris: UNESCO, 1963), 182–183.

[19] See J. Roberto Moreira, "Education and Development in Latin America," in *Social Aspects of Economic Development in Latin America*, I, Egbert De Vries and José Medina Echavarría, eds. (Paris: UNESCO, 1963), 308–344.

United Nations Bureau of Social Affairs said in its basic paper: "Perhaps the most striking feature of the data is the absence of any systematic relationship between degree of urbanization and level of fertility, although the most urbanized country—Argentina—has the lowest fertility." The report goes on, however, to speculate about the fertility ratio in terms of children of zero to four years of age per 1,000 women of child-bearing age and probable differences between the single and nonsingle fertility ratios. This speculation leads the Bureau to say: "In general, therefore, it may be said that, within the limitations of the data, in this region the fertility of the urban population is uniformly below that of the total population." [20] On the other hand, an analysis of the census and of the national sample survey in India "failed to show any significant rural-urban differentials in fertility," [21] and, while Indian experience obviously cannot be projected to Latin America, the data in this case were certainly better than are available for most Latin American countries.

A more recent statement of the United Nations Bureau of Social Affairs also casts doubt on the relation between urbanization and fertility. Among countries with gross reproduction rates higher than 2.0, the Bureau says, "little consistent association can be found between the levels of these rates and indices of the degree of urbanization. . . ." On the whole, no conclusive evidence shows that urbanization is bringing with it high hopes for early curtailment of the population explosion. In this respect, at least, the experience of Europe during the industrial revolution is not yet being repeated in Latin America. The Bureau adds that "the implication of these findings is that fertility levels in the developing countries are determined to a large extent by cultural

[20] United Nations, Bureau of Social Affairs, Population Branch, "Demographic Aspects of Urbanization in Latin America," in Hauser, *op. cit.*, pp. 103, 104.

[21] United Nations, Economic Commission for Asia and the Far East, Secretariat, *Economic Bulletin for Asia and the Far East*, X, 1 (June, 1959), 8.

traits that have not been greatly affected by the social and economic changes of the modern era." [22]

Of particular interest in Schnore's computations is the negative correlation between urbanization and metropolitanization and population growth. At first thought one might have expected that more rapid population growth would lead to even more rapid crowding into cities. This negative correlation, however, is a clear reflection of technological and regional dualism. Those countries that have experienced the most violent population explosion have been least able to bring about a significant transfer of the growing labor force into the industrial, urban, modern sector. Where population growth is high, capital requirements merely to meet the basic needs of a growing population within the existing occupational structure are also high, and insufficient capital is left over to bring about the fundamental structural change which is the essence of economic development.

HOUSING AND PHYSICAL PLANNING

Perhaps the most obvious drain on development potential through urbanization—and especially through urbanization in excess of industrialization—is the increased requirement for housing and the complication of physical planning. When people move from village to city they do not bring their houses with them, and in an urban environment the construction of satisfactory housing through traditional "mutual help" methods is a great deal more difficult. The difference in housing standards between *favelas, jacales, villas miserias* and the villages can be exaggerated; and the concern over the urban slums may reflect nothing more basic than that they are a good deal more visible to high-income persons and foreigners than the villages are. Yet in some basic sense housing is without doubt less far below ac-

[22] United Nations, Department of Economic and Social Affairs, *1963 Report on the World Social Situation* (New York: United Nations, 1963), p. 17.

ceptable standards in the villages of many developing countries than it is for the lowest income groups in the cities. Certainly the movement from farm to city has aggravated the housing shortage in underdeveloped countries and perhaps in Latin American countries in particular.

HOUSING AND ECONOMIC DEVELOPMENT

One of the most difficult problems confronting the development planner is to determine the appropriate standards for housing. When I was attached to the U.S. Housing Authority I was prepared to argue, along with other specialists, that improved housing raised productivity, reduced incidence of disease, crime, and juvenile delinquency, and made people Live Right, Think Right, and Vote Right. The simple truth is, however, that the evidence for this kind of argument is awfully thin. It is true that average incomes of slum dwellers went up after they moved into public housing projects—but the move took place during the recovery from the great Depression, when incomes of those remaining in the slums went up, too. It does appear that in the United States the provision of family housing has some tendency to reduce labor turnover. But just how good must housing be in each country to hold a labor force where it is needed? The difficulty is that high-standard urban housing has a higher incremental capital: output ratio than almost any other major investment sector—higher even than petroleum, railroads, or iron and steel. The opportunity costs of providing such housing are accordingly very high.

The Economic Commission for Asia and the Far East, in grappling with this problem, suggests as a general principle that "in the lowest-income countries, the case for higher investment priority to housing and urban services is greater than in higher-income countries. The lowest-income countries are those which lack the satisfactory requirements or the fundamental minimum in housing and related services." [23] Unfortunately, the same state-

[23] United Nations, Economic Commission for Asia and the Far East,

ment applies to education, health, transport, power, nutrition, and every other item in the gross national income. ECAFE goes on to list eight requirements for investment programs in housing and urban services: objective housing needs must be ascertained; economical but satisfactory housing standards must be adopted; nonmonetary resources in labor and materials should be mobilized; personal monetary savings should be mobilized for homes; the efficiency of the building industry should be improved; investment in housing and urban services should be controlled to serve sound social and economic objectives; a clear, properly defined statement of national housing policy and program should be articulated; and housing and urban services should be adequately staffed. Fair enough; but most of these "requirements" apply equally well to any other sector of an over-all economic and social development program.

The basic difficulty in programming housing and related urban services as part of economic development is the same as in the field of education: housing is both a capital and a consumers' good. Some quantity and quality of housing (and related services) are necessary to maximize productivity of the labor force; or better, there is an "optimal" supply of housing where the marginal cost of more or better housing is equal to the marginal returns in increased output. But, in addition, housing is an important component of personal income and so of individual welfare. One cannot determine appropriate housing standards by effects on productivity alone, any more than one can determine appropriate standards of public health or education in this manner.

One can, however, say that the minimal requirement for housing and urban services is that the "optimum" equating marginal costs with marginal output should be reached. Beyond that, unless a clear decision is made to redistribute income from rich to poor *in the form of housing* (which means in effect

Economic Bulletin for Asia and the Far East, XIV, 2 (September, 1963), 59.

that the planners and politicians do not trust people to decide for themselves how they should spend an increased income or what they should sacrifice when their income is reduced by public policy), housing should be as good as people are willing to pay for at cost. The "cost" is, however, subject to control by public policy to some extent; if labor and materials are allocated to other uses, housing costs will rise. One might, for example, leave housing to the market after determining what is the minimal use of strategic materials consistent with health and safety—which is more or less what we did in the War Production Board during World War II.

The difficult questions are: "Should housing standards be higher than that, even if other programs have to be cut down to provide materials and skilled labor to the housing industry?" "Should lower income groups be provided with housing below cost?" Answering "yes" to the second question, let us note once again, means making the decision that planners and politicians are wiser than other people, and that the latter must be prevented from spending on something else increased income that "ought" to be spent for housing. If there are opportunities for cost reduction through public housing, these could be seized, and the units rented at cost, the lower income groups receiving a generalized subsidy in the form of family allowances, for example. The U.S. Housing Authority really made housing cheaper by making available to tenants the low rates of interest and long terms at which the federal government was then able to borrow. It was "subsidized" only in relation to the unnecessarily high financing costs of private housing.

In our latest economics jargon we could say that programming housing requires putting a "shadow-price" on it as a consumers' good, for various income groups, and adding the shadow-price to the increase in other output produced by more and better housing, and comparing the sum with costs of providing more and better housing. The problem is statistical rather than conceptual, and a great deal more empirical research is needed as a foundation for such policy decisions.

Meanwhile, looking at Table 12, we can see that the Latin American countries included are for the most part spending a smaller proportion of national income on housing than countries in other regions in the same income category, even though the rate of population growth is lower in those other countries than it is in Latin America. For what they are worth these figures suggest that Latin America may be spending too little on housing; but more study is needed for a firm conclusion.

Table 12. Dwelling construction as percentage of gross domestic product.

Gross domestic product per capita	Annual average rate of population increase, 1953–1959					
	under 1 per cent		1 to 2 per cent		over 2 per cent	
$1,000 or more	Denmark	2.8	United States	4.5	——	
	Norway	4.2				
	United Kingdom	2.7				
$300–$1,000	Greece	5.1	Argentina	4.1	Chile	3.3
	Italy	6.1	Jamaica	3.0	Mauritius	3.5
	Malta	4.2	Netherlands	5.0	Venezuela	3.2
			Puerto Rico	5.0		
Under $300	Portugal	3.2	Japan	2.0	British	
			Kenya	3.5	Guiana	3.5
			Korea,		China	
			Republic of	1.8	(Taiwan)	1.8
			Nigeria	4.6	Colombia	2.7
			Tanganyika	4.7	Ecuador	2.2
					Honduras	3.9
					Mexico	2.4

Source. United Nations, Economic Commission for Asia and the Far East, *Economic Bulletin for Asia and the Far East*, XIV, 2 (September, 1963), 60.

INTEGRATION OF ECONOMIC AND PHYSICAL PLANNING

Both economic and physical planning are needed at all levels of government, and integration of "land-use planning" with "capital-use planning" is essential. The neglect until very recently of the spatial aspects of economic development is all the more unfortunate because it is gradually being realized that spatial relations are the very core of the development problem. There are almost no "underdeveloped countries." There are only underdeveloped areas, and an underdeveloped country is one in which the underdeveloped areas are a large proportion of the total economy.

On the other side of the coin, the addition of economic development planning to the responsibilities of government makes it all the more essential for physical planners to know exactly what it is they are doing that is different from what any other government officials or advisers are doing and which requires special training geared to that activity. In the Western democracies in which physical planning grew up, there was for a long time little conflict arising from the growing scope of physical planning, since no other planning was being undertaken. In many underdeveloped countries, on the other hand, the central government has assumed wide responsibilities for promoting economic development. There can be no doubt that location of industry, land-use patterns, and rural-urban relations are essential parts of a national development plan. Indeed the rural-urban pattern is the very core of the economic development problem. Consequently, in countries where both physical planning and development planning is carried on, the overlap between the current concept of physical planning in the West and the new task of development planners is readily apparent.

Frequently the two major sectors in dualistic economies appear in a contrast between one or a few large and growing cities and the surrounding countryside—Djakarta and Surabaya in contrast to all Indonesia; Delhi and Calcutta in India; Manila in the Philippines; San Juan in Puerto Rico; Harcourt in Nigeria; Mexico City and Monterrey in Mexico; Tripoli in Libya—examples can be given for virtually every underdeveloped country.

Economic development means eliminating the lagging sectors

and taking full advantage of the leading sectors or "growing points," maximizing the "spread effects" of growth where it occurs and overcoming the tendency for productivity of "leading" and "lagging" sectors to pull ever farther apart. An economic development plan must be defined in terms of intersectoral relations. In short, a development plan is concerned with interspatial relations and must be cast in terms of urban-rural relations.

It is clear that there must be a two-way street between city and regional planners and national development planners. Draft city and regional plans should be among the data studied by national development planners. The national development plans should then be submitted in draft to city and regional planners for analysis of the impact on the city or region of execution of the national plan. The analysis of the city and regional planners should in turn be made available to the national planners, and utilized in revising the draft national plan in preparation of the final one. National development plans, once in final form, should be immediately available to city and regional planners, so that they in turn can make their final plans accordingly. The whole process is one of solving a set of simultaneous equations through successive approximations, and planning at one level cannot be really complete until it is complete at all other levels as well.

SOME PROBLEMS OVER THE LONGER RUN

Such administrative devices can help to meet the immediate problem of determining national urban policies, as a minimal basis for integrating national development plans with city and regional plans. The real problem of integration, however, is so deep-seated that in the long run it is doubtful whether mere exchange of views and information among planners and planning authorities at different levels of government will produce truly integrated planning. There must also be greater uniformity of approach and methodology than now exists in the fields of physical planning and national development planning.

National development planning is generally considered to be one facet of economic policy. It is designed primarily to maximize per capita income over the perspective planning period within the limits imposed by other goals of economic policy. Economic development planning tends to be "market-oriented" to a large degree. A development plan calls for direct government intervention where the market does not work and cannot be made to work. The first job of the development planner is to find out, by empirical and theoretical analysis, how the market is operating and the places and ways in which it is yielding unsatisfactory results. Next, the possibilities of making the market work better through monetary, fiscal, foreign exchange, and similar policies (perhaps including antimonopoly legislation) should be fully explored. If important aspects of the economic development process still remain to be taken care of, the economic planner may suggest direct controls over the private sector or expansion of the public investment sector.

The over-all approach to development planning is "economic," in the sense that the market process and ways of influencing it are the core of the planning process. Engineering, sociological, and other data are fed into the analytical machinery, but the analytical tools are essentially those of the economist.

It is true that economic development requires discontinuous and large-scale change in the structure of the economy, as distinct from comparison of marginal returns on isolated investment decisions. It is also true that economic theory as it now exists does not provide a reliable guide for decisions where such discontinuous jumps are needed. Nevertheless, even in socialist countries, development planning is still largely a matter of "patching the market," however big the patches may be.

Perhaps the chief contribution of economics to general knowledge has been the construction of a method for testing social policies by objective and quantitative means. The broad goals of city and regional planning, however, are usually stated in some such terms as "an efficient and harmonious environment."

As stated, such goals are subjective and unmeasurable. Could "thermometers" be developed to measure—indirectly—"efficiency and harmony" in the environment? If so, it would be possible to use in physical planning a method that would make integration with national policy a good deal easier and more effective. It would then be possible to analyze the market process, isolating its defects in terms of these quantitative indicators of efficiency and harmony. Next the planner could decide, on the basis of empirical and theoretical analysis, what might be done to remove these defects by indirect policies (taxation, credit policy, and so forth). Finally, analysis could be undertaken to isolate those remaining defects in the market operation which could be best removed by public investment in unprofitable impulse sectors, and which ones could best be handled by direct controls of private investment, such as zoning, licensing, legal master plans, and the like. All this analysis should be conducted in terms of quantifiable functional relations, the derivatives of which would be unequivocally related to the *direction* of change in degree of "harmony and efficiency."

In other words, the first requirement for the development of a national urban policy, as a guide to inclusion of land-use aspects of development in the development plans, is an analysis of what is happening now. Most underdeveloped countries show a disturbing tendency toward agglomeration, conurbation, and the like. Why have these trends appeared since World War II? Is it a healthy or an unhealthy development? What objections are there to permitting the pattern of land use to develop "naturally"? These questions deserve much more study than they have yet obtained. Conditions seem to vary from one country to another. UNESCO studies, for example, suggest that in India people move from partial employment in rural areas to total unemployment in the cities. In Indonesia, on the other hand, it seems that unemployment among in-migrants is lower in the capital city of Djakarta than it was in the rural areas whence they came.

At the same time, national development planning must pay much more attention to spatial aspects of development than it has done to date. A national development plan should include a map as well as an investment budget—as a city plan should include a budget as well as a map. Most development planners are not trained to think in land-use or spatial terms. It is not merely a matter of analyzing location of industry, but also of taking account of the physical interrelations of the projects included in a development plan.

TRAINING PLANNERS

What all this means with respect to training depends on how much teamwork can be expected at the national and local level. If we could be sure that every city planning organization would include professional economists, public-opinion-poll specialists, engineers, sociologists, and architects, as well as city planners, and if national development teams would include all these disciplines and also agriculturalists, geologists, and so forth, then city and regional planners could be trained primarily to test proposed plans in terms of their physical balance—their contribution to "harmony and efficiency in the environment" as indicated by quantitative analysis. But such teamwork is probably more than we can hope for in every case. Accordingly, it would seem safer to make sure that city planners are capable of conducting economic analysis and that development planners can conduct physical analysis. If we accept these capabilities as part of our training goal, the organization of courses in both city planning and in development planning will need substantial revision.

ROLE OF EDUCATION

A gigantic international effort is currently being made to improve economic and social conditions throughout the world. Major universities are expected to play an increasingly active role in this effort.

As governments and international organizations assume new

national and international responsibilities, they require university graduates with new kinds of training. In particular, training in "planning" can no longer be confined to city planning of the traditional sort. There is also need for training in regional planning (including planning for distressed areas), national development planning, social development planning, and possibly military strategic planning and private enterprise planning. Even in the United States more professionally trained people are engaged in types of planning other than city planning. In other countries, and particularly in underdeveloped countries, city and regional planning have become essentially branches of national development planning. Even in city planning the pure design aspects are diminishing in importance, and in other types of planning design plays a minor role. University programs for training in planning should reflect this changed situation.

The key characteristic of planning is that it is a process of decision-making. For the most part the decisions relate to public policy, but many of the techniques of decision-making are also useful for private enterprise, especially in such matters as choice of location for new industries, choice of technology, design of training programs, and the like. The relative importance of the design aspect of planning, which has played so important a role in the field of city planning, clearly varies a great deal from one type of planning to another. Accordingly, it is not possible to force all planners into the same procrustean bed; training programs must be to some degree tailor-made for specific purposes. To deal effectively with problems of urbanization and economic development, our schools of planning must themselves be redesigned.

Editor's Summary and Elaboration

A major issue relating to the broad theme of the city and economic development is whether the present concentration of population in a few large cities is better for national development or whether the population should be diverted into more cities spread over a wider area. The problems involve how to slow down urbanization by redistributing population and how to regulate urbanization so that cities can function as cities. "The main point," according to a statement made by Andrade, "is not whether it is desirable for people to come to the cities, since they can be expected to do that, whether cities are large or small: the major problem is how to cope with the enormous population increase predicted for the next forty years, when there will be many more people living in both urban and rural areas, even though the rural population has declined in relative terms."

One implication for urbanization of economic policies is "whether future economic development will continue indefinitely to inflate the tertiary sector with disguised unemployment and mendicancy." [24] A second implication for urbanization of economic policies is the integration of backward and modern regions, "geographic integration." [25] The function of the city in this respect apparently does not depend strictly on its size, though a certain size may be necessary, but on the interaction of economic and social factors within the city.

An investment program to stimulate economic growth will stimulate urbanization. The continuation of urbanization in response to pull and push factors, rather than in response to increased agricultural and industrial productivity, can be expected to increase unemployment in the cities, and add to all the other urban problems.

Concurrent with development trends, schemes to promote a better distribution of population in Latin America are gradually

[24] Richard M. Morse, "Recent Research on Latin American Urbanization: A Selective Survey with Commentary," *Latin American Research Review*, I, 1 (Fall, 1965), 56.

[25] See Germani's section of Chapter V for a summary of the arguments favoring geographic integration.

evolving. In general, the issue is whether the city itself should be strengthened or whether the elements that generate modernism should be moved closer to the nonmodern regions. Policies under consideration are: (1) strengthening the small and medium-sized urban areas; (2) concentrating public investment in selected urban centers; and (3) establishing new towns, in connection with the development of natural resources.[26]

It is conceded to be possible, whether desirable or not, to distribute industry over a wide area and thus encourage a wider dispersion of cities. As expressed by Higgins: "We don't know whether economic development requires increased concentration in large cities; this needs research, but we suspect that a country looking for economic development may divert future industries from large to medium or small cities."

REGIONAL DEVELOPMENT

The effects of present trends in economic development on urbanization can, of course, only be estimated, since programs toward their full-scale realization are just being implemented in some countries, only at the planning stage in others, and, in still others, merely ideas. Their influence on urbanization, however, is apparent in a number of ways. One is a shift in emphasis from localized planning for urban and rural areas separately to integrated planning of rural development with industrial development in urban areas and supranational economic integration. Planners, according to Wilson Garcés, "have looked for alternatives to urbanization in order to help the depressed areas, but now urbanization is being recognized as an important process whose positive aspects should be taken advantage of in order to bring about development."

Unfortunately, as Garcés-Vernaza observed, "The process of urban growth has brought disorder, imbalances in the social and

[26] John P. Powelson and Anatole A. Solow, "Urban and Rural Development in Latin America," *The Annals of the American Academy of Political and Social Science*, CCCLX (July, 1965), 53,

economic order, and may hamper the attainment of cities desirable to live in." Two principal difficulties are the overconcentration of population in a few large cities and the poor economic condition of the migrants entering the cities.

Regional development is intended to be based primarily on a dispersion of industrial development.[27] The premise is that locating new industries in the lagging regions will transfer modernizing elements to them that will hasten their transformation into modern sectors.[28] Industries may be, and have been, enticed to decentralize through special incentives such as improvement of electrical power supplies and transportation; selective tax exemptions; provision of factory buildings at low rental; help in recruiting, housing, and training labor; advisory services to help prospective investors decide where to locate. Other facilities also may be decentralized: universities, hospitals, and research institutes, for example. Some governmental functions may be relegated to provincial or local governments, thus reducing the attraction for industries of the capital city as the source of political favors. The principal difficulties with plans such as these are how to avoid a scattering of institutions that prevent them from attaining first-class status in their fields, and the dangers of overprotecting unproductive industries and of continuing to concentrate governmental authority in the capital.[29]

Several conditions in Latin America seem to favor regional distribution of cities. One is the present "high primacy" and the general lack of a series of cities of different sizes. "It is also generally considered that urban growth should be more evenly distributed than it is at present, preferably within the framework of regional plans, and thus that part of the flow of migrants to

[27] There is very little evidence, if any, in Latin America of considering revival of traditional rural patterns. As Higgins said, "Any concept of economic development based on the idea of preserving the traditional village is sheer romanticism."

[28] Higgins, "An Economist's View," p. 204.

[29] "Some Policy Implications of Urbanization," pp. 305–307.

huge 'primate' cities should be diverted to provincial towns." [30]

The large city, with its concentrated investments, may be operating against modernization, in the absence of a supporting set of smaller cities, as remarked by Ricardo Jordán and Neira: "Economic development does not start from one focal point and spread out through a country. If this were so, big metropolitan centers would be no problem. But it is not so. One characteristic of economic development is that it tends to concentrate geographically and socially, and this has to be changed or the gap between underdeveloped and developed regions and countries will grow wider."

Overcentralization in the few large cities of Latin America has brought serious present problems, which will be followed by graver ones in the future. The chief concern, Salvador M. Padilla said, is the cost of investment in housing and services and whether the countries have the resources to make these investments, especially as larger cities will require increasingly higher levels of service. Therefore, "we need to ask whether it is not better to have a system of cities of different sizes on the theory that costs of investment will be less."

In fact, it is considered that, for some countries, if the influence of the city does not depend solely on its size, regional development is the only solution. Luis Ortiz de Zevallos cited Peru as an example:

Cities are a tool for modernization, but not only large cities; medium-size cities and even villages also operate in this fashion. Conditions differ in each country. In Peru, geographic barriers of deserts and mountains make little cities important. The Incas and Spaniards both used them. Also, Peru has only a small amount of arable land—about the same as Puerto Rico, though it is a much larger country. For growth, Peru seems to have only two possibilities. One is to open the other side of the Andes, which is now being done, and the second is to plan regions in which cities or villages will be the levers or tools of modernization of the country.

[30] *Ibid.*, p. 305.

In several countries, because of their size, high primacy may be acting as a brake on future growth. (See Browning's paper in Chapter III.)

Various examples of regional development have emerged on the Latin American scene. Probably the most spectacular is Brasilia, which was created to stimulate development of the interior. Social and economic integration through urbanization is, however, expensive. Completely new cities like Brasilia are not a solution many countries could afford, nor are they necessarily the best or only answer to development and integration.

The utilization of existing small (in comparison with capital) cities is favored in some countries. In fact, the attention given to the question of population concentration in a few large cities frequently obscures the fact that, in some of the countries, other urban centers, though considerably smaller, are growing in response to various economic stimuli. In Venezuela, for example, Tomás José Sanabria stated, though Caracas has one third of the population, small and medium-sized cities such as Valencia, Barquisimeto, and Maracaibo, and others in the Guianas also are growing, and some of this growth is the result of planned development. Brazil has a number of large cities, as does Chile and Colombia. Several cities are developing along the west coast of Peru, in response to development of the fishing industry. "The growth of large cities does not make it impossible to have other smaller cities," Félix Sánchez Baylón added, and continued:

Mexico, for example, has both centralization in cities and dispersion in regional areas. Some of the latter are almost industrialized and others are becoming so as a result of regional planning. Conditions in Mexico favor this combination, with its mixture of cultures and variety of climates. In this country, a number of urban centers are growing rapidly. This growth is not spontaneous, but rather is the result of planning, for social, cultural, and economic goals, accompanied by the development of transportation, irrigation, electrification, industries, and so forth.

Guatemala and El Salvador also have or are planning to have programs of this nature. Puerto Rico is working toward the same end with programs designed to attract industry to other areas of the island and away from San Juan. Various "administrative-financial institutions, such as national municipal development banks, are assisting the development of small municipalities away from the large urban centers." [31]

Some incentive to locate industry elsewhere may arise from the situation existing in the large cities: "Because of inadequate urban services and profiteering in urban real estate, Paulista industry is not necessarily attracted to the city and its outskirts. A broad dispersal pattern has already developed which is eroding the urban-rural polarity." [32]

The basic problems of such planned decentralized schemes are much the same as those related to centralization—low income levels, low educational levels, marginality, provision of housing and services, and the like. They can be attacked as part of long-range planning. Mexico, for example, Sánchez Baylón stated, has a program that includes existing large cities and rural areas:

In Mexico the urban population is 52 per cent, but the urban housing need is four times that of the rural areas. About 240,000 houses a year will have to be produced, and this should be increased annually, while at present only 10 per cent of that is being produced. Water, pavements, services, parks, schools, clinics also have to be provided. Urban programs for renewal, rehabilitation of the accumulated deficit or of the slums, will require long-term plans. Education is under an eleven-year plan designed to abolish illiteracy.

A number of other factors make decentralization difficult for some countries, as a study of urbanization in Peru indicates. One is the participation of the central government in urban planning and in the provision of urban services, when that government

[31] Powelson and Solow, *op. cit.*, p. 53.
[32] Luiz Saia, "Notas para a teorização de São Paulo," *Acrópole*, XXV, 295–296 (June, 1963), 209–221, as summarized in Morse, *op. cit.*, p. 64.

favors centralization. Another is showing effective results in regional plans or in regionalization that has already developed, for a variety of reasons: lack of municipal financing or municipal autonomy, duplication of effort among agencies doing the planning, lack of central government support, and general public unawareness of the aims and objectives of such plans. One successful area program is in northern Peru, where homes and urban services have been provided by oil companies. The important iron and steel development in Chimbote, however, grew without planning and "undoubtedly constitutes the most acute problem facing Peruvian town-planners today." [33]

Meanwhile, the capital is favored in the competition since it has at least some of the facilities that attract industry and population—services, transportation, and buildings. Investments in existing urban centers may show immediate results as against only future possibilities from investments in the newer sections. In fact, one argument used against small towns in Latin America is that they "have had industries for many years, but these industries have usually remained stunted and unprogressive, whether for lack of entrepreneurial talent, cheap power, or adequate markets." [34]

Cost is a major barrier to regional dispersion of cities. Not only do the necessary urban services (and perhaps some of the amenities) have to be provided but investment also has to be made in connecting transportation links, power, and other infrastructure to remedy their present deficiencies. Many smaller cities do not have a large enough economic base to be self-sustaining with respect to provision and maintenance of the services associated with urban living.

As indicated earlier, lack of organized planning for smaller cities in the past also adds to present-day costs and problems. Some small cities grew because of a temporary "boom" in some

[33] Luis Dorich Torres, "Urbanization and Physical Planning in Peru," in Hauser, *op. cit.*, pp. 280–286.

[34] "Some Policy Implications of Urbanization," pp. 306–307.

economic resource, which for one or another reason was not sustained. The period of decline left them with a larger population and the typical urban problems of larger cities. Some of these cities may have other economic potential which will lead to future growth, but first the slum problem has to be faced and at least a minimum of services provided.[35]

A large amount of scarce resources will have to be invested to develop a set of secondary cities fairly evenly distributed over a country. Some plans to this end have been modified, as in Puerto Rico, where plans now are to concentrate investment in only a few urban centers outside San Juan. The conclusion reached by one study of Central America is that the "overhead public investment to make secondary cities attractive would be out of proportion with present resources." [36]

One of the most pressing needs for successful regionalization probably is the adoption of an over-all policy for area programs that would provide a firm basis for the effective improvement of family incomes.

EXISTING CITIES

The decentralized form of development has been criticized in recent years on the ground that "there has been loose thinking and remarkably little actual research on this important matter." [37]

Utilizing the present large cities to bring about economic and social development has been winning support from two sides: first, active support from those who believe that the large city has inherent, and hitherto unsuspected, advantages for stimulating development, and second, reluctant support from those who

[35] Gonzalo Rubio Orbe, Reinaldo Torres Caicedo, and Alfredo Costales, "Problems Confronting the City-Planner and Administrator in the Town of Esmeraldas, Ecuador," in Hauser, *op. cit.*, pp. 278–279.

[36] Powelson and Solow, *op. cit.*, p. 54.

[37] Harley L. Browning, "Recent Trends in Latin American Urbanization," *The Annals of the American Academy of Political and Social Science*, CCCXVI (March, 1958), 116, quoted in "Some Policy Implications of Urbanization," in Hauser, *op. cit.*, p. 305n.

have come to look upon regional development under present conditions in Latin America as too costly in scarce resources and too delayed in benefits.

Active supporters of the first group argue that (1) scarce resources should be concentrated, not dispersed, and the large city permits this; (2) the large city is a dynamic center of education and of technological innovation; (3) the concentration of population to and beyond the point of overurbanization may act to hasten economic development and industrialization; (4) differences in degrees of development among geographic regions may be a positive factor in stimulating the transition to industrial society.

The existing cities represent an investment that the countries can ill afford not to utilize:

The size and density of urban populations should be viewed as economic assets in a condition of a favourable urban-rural balance. They signify the availability of labour supply, markets and a wide variety of public services which encourage industrial and business enterprise and make possible efficient business operation by minimizing the frictions of transport and communications. It would be wasteful, not fully to utilize the economic potential of existent urban populations, before developing new urban centres.[38]

As Browning remarked, the concentration of urban services also may be "a valuable economy for a capital-poor nation."

For some countries, high primacy may serve an integrating function. One authority claims that "all of Uruguay forms part of Montevideo's metropolitan area," and that the whole country is becoming absorbed in "a rural-urban environment, that is, a way of life which participates in an urbanized society even though the population centers do not strictly constitute cities." [39] There is also a political aspect to consider. Solari stated: "Since

[38] In Hauser, *op. cit.*, p. 78.
[39] Carlos M. Rama, "De la singularidad de la urbanización en el Uruguay," *Revista de Ciencias Sociales*, VI, 2 (June, 1962), 177–186, quoted in Morse, *op. cit.*, p. 48.

the leading cities have been the main force in the growth of national design, it should be considered whether the country in question can afford to develop small cities without reinforcing peripheral pressures against a national design."

Some question exists as to the effectiveness of plans to redistribute population. Smaller cities may serve only as stepping stones to persons whose ultimate goal is to live in the metropolis, and hence they may be a wasteful and ineffective way to slow down migration. Further, transportation routes built to service the smaller cities also may serve as highways to increase migration to the large urban centers. The question, as raised by Irving L. Horowitz during the discussion, is: "If people don't want to move into the tertiary centers but would rather go directly to the big centers, should effort and resources be spent on devising a way to get them into the tertiary centers?"

Some cities have grown despite governmental steps to prevent their growth. Santiago is an example. This city grew "from roughly 800,000 in 1930 to nearly 2,500,000 today," though "not . . . as fast as some Latin American capitals":

It is not true that Santiago represents something artificial. It developed spontaneously, against the will of the government itself. . . .

The government had done what it could to hold back Santiago. It has established no important industry in the capital and has located them as far off as possible.

Urban construction . . . was stimulated by inflation, which diverted domestic capital from economic production into urban real estate. But even if one sharply limits this sort of abuse . . . Santiago will keep on expanding, and we should entertain no illusions about being able to hold back that growth.[40]

The growth of Mexico City, on the other hand, has been encouraged by the government:

[40] Carlos Keller R. in "Seminario del Gran Santiago," *Boletín Informativo* (Universidad de Chile), VIII, 34 (October, 1958), 197–198, quoted in Morse, *op. cit.*, pp. 47–48.

Food products, fuel oil, electricity and natural gas have all been subsidized to hold back living costs and to attract industry. There is evidence that freight rates have been managed to encourage shipment of raw materials rather than finished goods to the metropolitan market. While approving any reduction in the amount of sheer political favoritism enjoyed by the capital, Richard Bird warns against egalitarian regionalism for its own sake: ". . . one can make the strong argument that the growing urban center is the leading 'growth pole' in a developing country and should be encouraged, not hampered."[41]

The positive aspects of overurbanization are perhaps best summarized from Andrade's remarks at the conference:

Latin American countries are very different from one another, and what might work in one country, say Argentina, would not necessarily be good in another, say Colombia. The expansion and acceleration of urbanization would not mean that Colombia, for instance, would have cities the size of, say, ten million, because Colombia does not have large cities like Buenos Aires and Mexico City. Bogota, the largest, with 2,000,000, and other smaller cities (around half a million), are about the size of medium-sized towns in the United States. So Colombia is not likely to develop a megalopolis.

It is a matter of strategy. Acknowledge the problem, know what we have to work with, how we can use it, and the most beneficial way to use it. In Colombia, for example, we have an investment in cities; this can be an element of growth if we open markets for consumption. This means that investment should go into other fields besides industrial manufacturing, into fields where people can be brought from rural areas and employed right away. The development of other areas is merely postponed. After a while, investment can be diverted in a different direction. The government will have to direct this, through a program of industrial development for cities that do not now have capital investment, such as Manizales and Bucaramanga, and start their economic growth.

[41] Richard Bird, "The Economy of the Mexican Federal District," *Inter-American Economic Affairs*, XVII, 2 (Autumn, 1963), 50–51, quoted in Morse, *op. cit.*, p. 48.

The danger of investing in areas that do not now have some capital investments is that much of the resources may be wasted or underutilized. This is the present situation. Attention is given to specific needs, as, for instance, so many houses, sewers, and water-supply systems for so many people. Money is put into housing developments destined to remain unoccupied because they are in towns where sewerage and water supplies are nonexistent. Projects such as these serve only to persuade people that something is being done for them, and are politically inspired, but they do not hold much promise for real development.

Is dispersal less expensive than concentration? There are many different kinds of cost. Social cost is one. Comparison of costs should be made. How much do you have to spend to provide a job, housing, and public services in urban areas compared with the costs of agrarian reform? In Colombia, just expropriating land and providing a peasant with a house—without any other benefits—were much more expensive than a project to bring one family to an urban area. This does not mean that we should not have agrarian reform, but it is now a cliché to support the idea of agrarian reform and agrarian reform programs, for political reasons, personal reasons, and, perhaps, professional reasons. This support should not make us turn our backs on the real problem of economic development.

From the more reluctant supporters come some equally strong arguments. Santiago Agurto Calvo stated: "The large city is a fact of existence and it should be possible to take advantage of its existence. Perhaps such cities are a kind of *mal necessario*, at least for the conditions in Latin America."

Neira, though favoring the dispersion of cities, added:

In planning for the maximization of national income, there is no alternative to using the cost-benefit criteria to select your investments and these will show a definite preference for large towns, because that is where the external economy is already located and thus they have some existing factors that decrease the cost for the same level of production. This need to increase the net national income makes it almost unavoidable that new industries be located near the place where large external economies are already located. That is an economic force that is difficult to change, and it will be easier to gain more political support for progress in this direction.

On the other hand, existing cities have not been notably successful in exercising leadership to create a higher standard of living. Rather, they have been at the mercy of expensive problems that are beyond their resources. At the same time, urban wages, though high in comparison with those in rural areas, are low in relation to the cost of urban living. The cost of providing urban services is high. Some of this high cost is artificially created, through land speculation, inflation, uneconomically high standards, and the like. But the principal difficulties are, first, that the resources and productive capacity of the urban community are not great enough to subsidize the difference between available resources and needed urban services, and, second, that the productive base of the city does not expand as the population of the city grows.[42]

In short, the fundamental issue with respect to centralization—just as with decentralization or rural improvement programs—is that its potential for development depends on how effectively it can be utilized to provide a better distribution of income and meaningful opportunities for employment.

URBANIZATION AND MODERNIZATION

It becomes obvious from this discussion that the point under debate is not the size or location of the city but the larger question of the best means to utilize scarce capital, resources, and technology. What is the best investment pattern that will (1) accelerate the process of urbanization and (2) speed up the development of an industrial base for the Latin American countries?

Latin America is an area of great diversity, which is reflected by the separate nations in their economies, cultures, and other ways. It is also obvious, though frequently lost sight of, that one

[42] Powelson and Solow, *op. cit.*, p. 51.

over-all plan of development is not likely to be best for all the countries. None of them, however, can afford to neglect urbanization or to exclude it from their development plans:

Urbanization cannot be isolated from general economic development policy, since balanced urban growth must be based on a well-balanced growth of the whole economy and of all the different regions within a country. This implies a reasonable amount of industrialization together with the agricultural development of individual areas, through the application of measures to ensure a distribution of urban centres of various sizes best suited to the proposed development of productive activities in each area.[43]

Solow pointed out:

Urbanization, change, and growth by themselves are not bad. What makes them good or bad is the policy orientation given to them.

The city is an artifact; it represents the utmost control over his environment by man; it implies a complete change in the ecological balance between man and environment. If this change is guided toward goals, urbanization can be a challenge and an opportunity, but when it is the result of uncontrolled forces, as at present, it can be a disaster. It has no built-in safety valve—men and society have to develop the control and guiding system. With modern technology and science, even capital-poor countries can mobilize their resources to this end.

Latin American cities have concentrations of a tremendous latent human resource, and the guided process of urbanization could be an instrument to mobilize this human resource toward productive ends. The productive value of absorbing submarginal urban population into submarginal clerical occupations is doubtful.

The key to accomplishing social goals through urbanization is to raise the productivity of people in Latin American cities and to create the will and motivation for the people to raise productivity themselves. How to mobilize the human resources through urban institutions and within the limitations of capital resources is the main

[43] United Nations, Economic Commission for Latin America, Secretariat, "Creation of Employment Opportunities in Relation to Labour Supply," in Hauser, *op. cit.*, pp. 145–146.

question. The future of urbanization and the future development of a country depend on what kind of institutional tools can be used and developed and what policy of urban development is adopted, and when it is adopted.

Both concentration and dispersion are different parts of the larger problem of economic development. Both long-range and short-range objectives have a part in this comprehensive goal. What is involved is deciding on a level of investment and the type of investment that will promote growth, without concern as to whether or not people migrate to the largest cities.

Jordán stated: "Economic development means that productivity should rise in the countryside. This means urbanization, but not necessarily in a few large cities."

The criteria for investments will have a decided influence on the location of cities, Garcés-Vernaza stated:

The discussion about redistribution of population must stem from a sense that the present distribution is inadequate and that the mobility of the population requires new capital investment to cope with individual, family, and social needs. At the same time, we have to cope with the problems of investing not just to increase economic development but to keep what we already have. Our countries have signed agreements with other countries and organizations and the International Monetary Fund that require us to stay within a certain type of economic organization for other countries. This requires that the Latin American countries guide their policy in terms of balance of payments and investments, and similar factors.

Political aspects may be the deciding factors in the development of regions. One such aspect is a general lack of municipal autonomy. Another is the possible centralizing influence of direct government participation and investment in economic development. The latter, of course, will be operative or not on the basis of the type of investment selected. If, for example, the trend toward heavy manufacturing is sustained, growth of other cities and regions can be predicted, particularly as basic natural-resource development will be part of this. Much of the regional development in Venezuela, for example, has come about from this emphasis.

Several panel members pointed out that regional development and the growth of small cities can be expected where economic opportunities develop. Sometimes this growth has been sufficient to capture the functions of the large city, which has led to a larger growth of the smaller urban center. Highways operate as a factor in changing the arrangement of cities; by making smaller cities more accessible, highways permit them to take some functions away from large cities—and thus change their size.

Central America provides examples of the relation between the type of economy and the location of cities. Jordán pointed out:

Until recently, these countries had a *hacia afuera* type of growth based on the external market, with the market based on one or two products. The pattern of urbanization was one large city in each country, and not always a port city. With integration, diversification of their economies has begun, and secondary cities have begun to grow in all the countries. This illustrates the importance of strategy for economic development in distributing the population of a country and how by manipulating strategy the distribution of population can be changed.

Since economic considerations have been an important element in the present pattern of distribution of Latin American cities, Neira suggested that "a study of how the past processes of development led to the present distribution, and what changes took place as the economy changed, would provide a model that would be related to Latin American conditions, which, in turn, would be a useful tool for planning in the future."

According to Browning, "A system of studies on patterns of urban growth is difficult to make successfully, and such studies so far have been mainly on a descriptive level. Lack of information on this point is a barrier to a satisfactory arrangement of city growth in terms of urban hierarchy."

Given the relation between past industrialization and urbanization, a different type of urban pattern may be desirable, Neira suggested:

Now, it appears, is the time for another type of pattern. This could be called a radial one. Entering the third stage of development is perhaps the time to create secondary nuclei centers to bring economic growth to a few regions and at the same time incorporate them into the national economy—a sort of multinuclei pattern, that, in fact, seems to be developing in the more advanced countries of Latin America. Then, after population accumulates, mass consumption comes into being, and transportation is developed, because of the rising standard of living and rising incomes, perhaps a kind of grid pattern can be produced that will organize these center patterns. This should provide a good place for research and possibly provide us with a more certain base for a policy on population distribution as to whether large towns or small towns are better.[44]

The potential of the entire metropolitan area for modernization, Jorge R. Riba suggested, should be given consideration:

We have generalized too much from the concept of cities and overlooked the fact that from a demographic point of view the wider area the city covers is becoming more and more important. This area is nonrural but not yet urban, and it is on this area that the city has its major effects as a modernizing force. The process of modernization is faster in this larger area than in the city. In this sense, the city may be considered the central place of a much wider area, or there may be various centers or cities within areas that are becoming larger, in physical terms and in the degree of urbanization taking place.

We have to consider the future effects of rearranging demographic growth in the context of areas larger than cities. With or without integration of countries, it can be predicted that there will be a rearrangement of city patterns as the functions of the city change.

[44] In his reply to the panelists, Higgins commented that experiments on the nuclei pattern are being undertaken in Canada, using focal points of growth, in the hope of creating small and large cities to divert industrialization from Montreal and Quebec.

If, for example, the Central American countries were to develop without national boundaries, there is no question but what a rearrangement of city patterns would take place. Of course, integration is not general, but transportation patterns will have the effect of *hacia afuera* for geographic reasons. The freedom of movement of people and capital between countries also enters in.

Metropolitan areas in some countries are growing fast, Dorich agreed. For example, the population of Rio de Janeiro and of the Estado de Guanabara is growing at 3.3 per cent annually, while the population of the Rio metropolitan area is growing at 4.4 per cent a year, with some communities in the area growing at 9 per cent a year.

Another consideration is that rural areas should be included in over-all urban development plans. Dorich, for example, stated: "The Pan American Health Organization feels its sanitation improvements in rural areas of Latin America will be wasted unless living conditions are improved. Our concern should be to find realistic solutions that could be applied to all our cities, large and small, and those solutions should be for Latin American conditions."

The point is worth emphasizing: in any country urban problems seldom have only local causes. Local conditions may aggravate the situation but, in the main, urban problems are manifestations of disturbances elsewhere in a country. Alleviating them is not merely correcting a local situation; it is part of integrated national development. Removing the effects of the past from the city and the causes of the problems from the countryside are both essential to establishing a reciprocal relation between urban and rural, modern and traditional, new and old. Astica commented on this:

City planning in Latin America cannot be practiced locally but has to be referred to the national environment. Chile, for example, is now abandoning local emphasis and trying to establish a network of cities within the framework of national economic and social planning. This is not a plan to limit migration; it will probably release more people to migrate, because freedom to migrate comes only after minimum standards have been distributed over the country. Latin American countries should not be regarded as a whole but should be separated into different groups. This is not to speak against economic integration, which is desirable, but the urban problems of each country are related to the economic, social, and political life of the country and this main structure has to be considered first before considering urban problems.

V The City as an Integrating Mechanism

The Concept of Social Integration

GINO GERMANI

Under certain conditions the city may be considered an integrating mechanism for the rise of a modern, well-developed national society. Within the general process of transition, it is convenient to distinguish two main groups of processes: modernization and economic development. Within each of the two main groups, several partial processes may also be distinguished. Although all of them are correlated, the correlation is not very strict. One of the major problems to be investigated is that of the different sequences which characterize the partial processes. Variation in the sequences may be considered an important factor in explaining the variety in the forms of transition and in types of industrial societies.

Consideration of the role of the city as an integrating mechanism includes two different aspects: (1) "geographical" integration of the national society, which may be defined as the "balanced" or equilibrated modernization and economic development of its component regions and their equal or proportional participation in the economic, cultural, and political life of the nation; and (2) "social integration," the integration of individuals, social groups, or categories into the various institutions of the modern national society.

Only a brief mention will be made of the first aspect. What

we have called "geographical integration" is certainly a problem of great importance in the process of modernization and economic development in Latin America. The usual pattern has been the growth of urban concentration (especially of primate cities), linked with the rise of an economy dependent on international trade, that is, the export of a few primary commodities, accompanied by a transportation system whose main purpose was precisely to serve such trade, using the cities—usually primate cities—as a connecting point between sea and land transportation. The central question here is to determine under which conditions this type of urbanization may be considered a factor of national integration, or, vice versa, will make difficult the equilibrated development and modernization of the various regions within the country. Most of the analysts consider that urban concentration originated mainly as a result of the needs of a "dependent" economy and has not been favorable to national integration. The primate city, with its high concentration of wealth, modern culture, and economic expansion, has been—according to these views—a negative factor in the development of other regions and of the nation as a whole. Material and human resources have been disproportionately concentrated in such areas, to the detriment of other regions within the nation. The upsurge of the great rural-urban migration has also created new problems, insofar as it was not originated by growth or industrial demand, but by push factors from the countryside. The creation of a "pseudo-tertiary" is an expression of the transfer of unemployment or underemployment from the rural areas to the cities.

Other observers do not share this pessimistic view. The notion of "overurbanization" itself has been challenged; the concentration of scarce resources in a few urban centers may be more efficient than if they were spread over a large territory; the positive function of the city as a dynamic center for education and technical and social innovation may well compensate the costs—economic and social—of "overurbanization." "Overurbanization" itself in underdeveloped regions may be a factor for economic development and industrialization. In any case, the function of the city in presently developing societies is rather different from its historical role in the early industrialized countries.

The desirability of an integrated development and modernization has been questioned. It might be possible that the conditions under which both processes occur make it impossible to reach such integration. Or perhaps, internal geographical discontinuities may be a positive factor in certain stages of the transition.

As indicated earlier, we are concerned with integration into modern societies. Integrating mechanisms in this sense are those which facilitate the *effective* and *legitimate* (in terms of the predominant norms) *participation* into the various partial structures of a "modern society," within a modern social structure. Two difficulties must be mentioned here. In the first place, we need a definition of "modern society," but the variety of forms of the "modern," and the different types of industrial societies, have introduced considerable uncertainties in this respect. In the second place, it is well known that traditional structures may be integrated into modern societies (may turn out to be functionally compatible, that is, with the other modern structures in the same society). Perhaps such archaic structures are playing the role of transitional adaptative mechanisms, which in time will disappear or be "modernized," or, perhaps, our conception of "modern" should be changed. Finally, we must distinguish between *integration* and *adjustment*. The latter refers to the ability of the individual to perform his role without excessive or unbearable psychological stress or without personal disorganization. The main emphasis is on the individual *qua* individual, that is, on personal adjustment. The concept of integration refers to the nature of the participation of individuals and social groups into the different institutions and partial structures of the society. While personal adjustment may be an aspect of integration—at least a certain minimum degree of adjustment is required for it—

adjustment may occur without integration (into the structures under consideration).

Integrative mechanisms must be considered in connection with particular institutions or partial structures. Integration does not occur simultaneously in all aspects of life, for the same group or category of individuals, or even for the same individual. A person or a group may be integrated in the sphere of work, and not integrated in the political sphere, and so forth.

URBAN RESEARCH

While in the last ten years urban research on Latin America has developed considerably, it is still insufficient as a basis to formulate valid generalizations. The great variety of historical and sociocultural situations, and the uneven degree of modernization and socioeconomic development of the different countries, would require a great number of local studies. Such variety is certainly very stimulating for the undertaking of comparative studies, but they are lacking at present. Most of the research has been devoted to the assimilation of internal rural migrants and has tended to emphasize the "social problems" of rapid urbanization. Another approach is provided by studies concerning the adaptation of rural migrants to their industrial milieu, the working situation, the formation of a new urban proletariat and its integration into the political life of the country. Social integration, however, is an aspect of a process of change which affects not only the newcomers, but also the "older" sectors of the population, in its low, middle, and high strata, and the analysis would require a theoretical and empirical approach which is not usually provided by presently available studies.

The classical tradition in urban sociology was concerned more with disintegration than with integration. Both the "Chicago School" and its European background emphasized the anomic aspects of urban life. Research conducted both in Western advanced societies and in developing countries introduced many doubts on the validity of earlier generalizations. It was recognized that the usual dichotomic typologies of a rural-urban continuum needed a revision or complementation and that a new theoretical approach should be formulated.

Although urban research in Latin American countries is rather recent, one may observe the same reaction. In fact, part of the empirical data which stimulated the criticism of the prevailing theories and hypotheses was based precisely on Latin American material. "Urbanization without breakdown," to take the title of one well-known contribution to this subject, may be considered as determined by several factors: (1) transference from the rural areas of institutions, values, and behavioral patterns and their persistence or adaptation to the specific requirements of the urban setting; (2) character of the rural society and especially high degree of integration; (3) small or relatively small cultural distance between rural and urban areas in terms of degree of modernization. Kinship groups, extended family relationships, the *compadrazgo* system, combined in certain cases with voluntary association (as in Lima), or with particular conditions offered by the type of neighborhood, seem to be powerful means of maintaining integration. Under different circumstances, marginal groups of recent migrant origin have shown a high degree of disorganization, while reorganization did take place, according to the urban pattern, through change of neighborhood, social mobility, and increased social participation.

It may be noted that the above-mentioned mechanisms, which facilitate the adjustment of the migrant to the city, do not involve their assimilation to the urban culture. In fact, they may perpetuate quasi-rural patterns, not only in the migrants, but in their descendants as well. The adaptation arising in such conditions maintains the marginality of this sector of the population. It originates a subculture peculiar to the most deprived groups. The notion of a "culture of poverty," as formulated by Oscar Lewis,[1] certainly provides a most useful approach to the study of

[1] See "The Culture of Poverty," *Scientific American*, CCXV, 4 (October, 1966), 19–25, which discusses this concept and its implications for

the persisting marginality of large sectors of the urban population in several Latin American cities. The questions regarding their integration into modern urban culture, however, remain unanswered: Is this a transitional adaptation, which in time will facilitate the rise of a modern industrial proletariat? Or could it persist as a barrier, even under the impact of economic development?

ECONOMIC DEVELOPMENT AND SOCIAL INTEGRATION

The relation between economic development and social integration of the large marginal sectors of the population into the national society and modern culture is very complex. Social integration required a very long time and is still occurring in advanced Western countries. It took place gradually and tended to follow and not to precede economic development. In fact, social integration reached an advanced stage (both regarding its extension to the great majority of the population and to the range of behavioral patterns and affected institutions) after (or simultaneously with) mass consumption. Certain aspects of modernization, however, were required as precondition of the process of economic development or, at least, had to begin and to expand at the same time. As regards the lower strata, their incorporation into the modern sector of the economy required the adaptation to new occupational roles and the attainment of the educational level required by the state of technology. But in most areas of behavior integration into the modern culture and participation in the national society were delayed in comparison with the advance of the economy.

On the basis of this experience one could say that economic development provides the main mechanisms for social integration. But this statement oversimplifies. On the one hand, integration takes place at different rates in different areas of social life; on the other hand, other aspects of integration (in addition

---

the continuance of marginality even under conditions of general prosperity in a society.

to work and education) may precede economic development. In fact, one of the main differences between the experience of Western countries and the developing ones is precisely the contrast in the type of sequences among the various partial processes of mobilization, social integration, and economic development. Finally, other factors such as ethnic barriers may intervene.

The basic mechanisms through which economic development creates the conditions for social integration are the modification of the occupational structure and changes in the quantity and composition of consumption of goods and services. Both involve well-known changes in the stratification system: (1) higher occupational differentiation; (2) a general trend toward occupational upgrading (in terms of skill, education, and status); (3) as a consequence, the enlargement of the middle strata; (4) finally, the expansion of consumption allows growing access of the lower strata to goods and services which in the immediate past were typical of higher classes. These changes involve considerable social mobility in its various forms; the expansion of the middle sectors and the occupational upgrading creates structural mobility; the increase in the proportion of statuses based on achievement (especially through education) increases the fluidity of the system (and exchange mobility); expansion of consumption originates a continuous transference of status symbols from top to bottom, that is, a kind of psychological upward mobility. When the types of mobility tend to affect the majority of the population, that is, when the process acquires the nature of a mass process, it is likely to originate important changes both at the psychosocial and the cultural levels. Attitudes will change, new types of relations, new values and norms will replace the old ones. Perhaps structural changes must affect a considerable proportion of the population to produce such impact. A minimum size and concentration may be required in order to create the conditions for the rise of new attitudes and values. The old problem as to the real nature of the middle classes in Latin America could be analyzed from this approach. Intermediate sectors, occupationally incorporated into modern activities, will acquire middle-class self-identity and cultural patterns when they attain a given absolute size. For instance, such size may condition the existence of a market for middle-class consumption. Analogous considerations could be applied to the formation of modern lower strata.

The cities, the largest metropolises, are the loci of such structural change. In Latin America, the contrast between the stratification profiles of urban and rural areas is striking. As Hoselitz observes with regard to Asia, the urban occupational structure resembles the Western pattern. It is true that the "pseudo-tertiary" introduces an important bias in census statistics, but even taking into account this fact, in several Latin American countries the urban population occupationally incorporated into the modern economy sector seems large enough to create the conditions favorable to the rise of the corresponding values and attitudes. This can be seen from Table 13, where an attempt has been made to distinguish the quasi-traditional "pseudo-tertiary" from the the middle strata. Even in the less advanced countries, the table indicates, the proportion of the urban middle strata of the total working population is quite large (and several times larger than in the rural areas). The process and its outcome will be affected by local historical and cultural conditions. Other factors such as ethnic barriers, persistence of archaic patterns imported from the rural areas, types of neighborhood and housing may delay the integration. Traditional patterns may become fused or adapted to the modern structures. The structural changes induced by economic development, however, should provide in the long run the basic mechanisms for the participation of an increasing proportion of the population in the modern pattern. The "model" for such pattern, that is, the type of emerging "modernity," will be shaped not only by local structural change, but to a considerable extent by the effect of demonstration from advanced countries, especially from the United States.

Table 13.   Urban and rural stratification profiles, *ca.* 1950.

Countries	Urban			Rural		
	Secondary and tertiary activities			Primary activities		
	Middle class*	Lower class		Middle class*	Lower class	
		self-employed	employees		self-employed	employees
Argentina	41.4	5.5	53.1	32.1	4.7	63.2
Chile	29.4	10.6	60.0	2.3	28.3	69.4
Costa Rica	31.0	9.8	59.2	15.0	25.6	59.4
Cuba	35.9	12.4	51.7	1.4	36.1	62.5
Venezuela	26.8	17.5	55.7	4.8	58.2	37.0
Colombia	28.1	16.6	55.3	17.0	39.9	43.1
Brazil	35.2	13.3	51.5	3.2	62.5	34.3
Panama	31.9	14.1	54.0	1.1	89.6	9.3
Paraguay	26.8	24.4	48.8	3.8	86.0	10.2
Ecuador	20.1	19.1	60.8	1.5	58.5	40.0
Salvador	24.2	18.3	57.5	2.9	47.6	49.5
Guatemala	16.2	41.9	41.9	2.7	64.8	32.5
Bolivia	25.6	24.4	50.0	1.0	59.8	39.2
Haiti	12.6	46.2	41.2	1.3	92.2	6.5

* Includes higher stratum.

At this point, in order to avoid misunderstandings with regard to the causal primacy of structural changes originated by economic development, it is convenient to formulate two observations: (1) In the first place, the beginning of economic change and its maintenance requires an explanation in terms of the total sociocultural context. In this paper, description of the causal chain has been interrupted arbitrarily in order to limit the analysis to the process of extension of integration of the majority of the population. For this reason we are not concerned with the role of the modernizing élites, the conditions of their formation, rise of rationality, new attitudes, and the other preconditions usually mentioned in this respect. (2) In the second place, changes in the occupational structure may occur to an extent out of proportion with the degree of economic development (as measured by this proportion in advanced countries). This is especially true in Latin America with regard to the growth of bureaucracy. Such growth may produce the same impact on the stratification system, and stimulate the other psychosocial and cultural consequences as well. (This is the distinction made by Latin American social scientists between economic development and economic expansion.) Finally, we must mention that white-collar personnel are not included in the "pseudo-tertiary," which is composed mainly of manual workers, self-employed ("own account"), and servants.

INTEGRATION AND SOCIAL MOBILITY

In the long run, the rate of social integration of the majority of the population will depend mainly on their absorption into modern occupational roles and on the progressive extension of modern forms of consumption. The process may be considered a continuous flow, from top to bottom, strongest in the largest cities. During the transition, rural-urban differences are likely to increase. Duality will be accentuated, and only in the more advanced stages of economic development will the process affect directly the rural areas and duality be reduced. Until then, the first stage of integration will be rural-urban migration. Even if urban conditions and insufficient occupational absorption will maintain the marginality of a large proportion of the urban population, the precondition for integration will be the physical transfer to the city. It is true that education and mass media may irradiate directly in rural areas and in smaller urban centers, inducing important changes. In this case, we should speak of *mobilization* more than *integration*. The term *mobilization* is used here to indicate *release* from the traditional structure and *disposition* or aspiration to participate in the new roles, or to obtain access to new forms of consumption, while integration involves effective participation. Moreover, one may distinguish between *integrated participation,* when participation is legitimized and accepted in terms of dominant norms in the society and *nonintegrated participation* when legitimization and acceptance are lacking. (This distinction is important for the analysis of political and ethnic integration.)

Mobilization, like integration, does not occur at the same time in all aspects of behavior. Release from the traditional pattern may take place in certain areas and not in others. In this sense we may say that migration to the city, especially to large cities, usually involves a higher degree of mobilization (in comparison with rural areas or small towns) even for the urban marginal population. The persistence of traditional traits—especially with regard to family and other primary relations—and their relative segregation from urban life do not preclude a higher exposure to mass media and higher chances of participation, particularly in politics. In fact, the concentration of large marginal sectors in the city has been considered one of the bases of populism.

Integration through the mechanism of social mobility (in one of its forms) may be illustrated with recent research in Argentina and Brazil. While mobility affects migrants and the city-born differently, it seems sufficiently high in all sectors to produce widespread psychological impact. This statement is hypothetical since we do not have verified data on the psychosocial meaning of mobility, and such interpretation is even more difficult with regard to shifts from rural to urban occupations. But some indirect evidence is available.

The research mentioned confirms the well-known pattern of occupational upgrading of the city-born and their replacement in the less favored positions by newcomers. In Buenos Aires nearly one half (47 per cent) of the city-born, sons of manual laborers, had reached nonmanual positions, while this rate was much lower for the migrants. The lowest upward manual to nonmanual rate was found among the third-generation Argentinians born in the less developed regions (23.3 per cent), and an intermediate position was held by Argentine migrants, sons of foreign parents, born in more developed areas (38.4 per cent). Similar differences were observed by Hutchinson in Brazil. But if we consider mobility within the manual stratum it can be seen that even the less favored migrants experienced "mass" mobilization: 72 per cent of third-generation Argentines born for the most part in less developed regions and children of un-skilled workers had reached skilled occupations or higher positions. This rate was even higher for the city-born (87 per cent). It is true that migration does not necessarily involve upward mobility: in Buenos Aires some 60 per cent of the migrants of nonmanual background had descended to manual occupations. Most of these persons, however, were born in families of artisans, small shopkeepers, small rural landowners or tenants; that is, from lower "own account" occupations.

The majority of migrants going to industrial cities in Argentina and Brazil seem to consider the migration as beneficial; in Buenos Aires, among the most deprived group, some 80 per cent were satisfied with the decision to migrate. Gláucio Dillon Soares and others report similar reactions in Brazil. The criterion for comparison for the recent migrant is his previous situation at the place of origin and, given the extremely low standard predominating there, migration to the city is experienced as a change for the better. Other important factors frequently mentioned as operating in the same way among migrants are the better educational and occupational possibilities for their children.

These illustrations have been taken from large cities among the higher industrialized ones in the region. But, as indicated above, the rate of occupational absorption must maintain an equilibrium with the rate of mobilization and immigration. The persistence of large marginal sectors, both rural and urban, is immediately related to the problem of economic development. Given the rate of population growth, the size of marginal population may increase, if not in proportion, at least in absolute size. The observations made by Gonzalez Casanova concerning marginality in Mexico—where the rate of economic growth was higher compared with the rest of Latin America—could be extended to other Latin American nations. ECLA has indicated that "between 1945 and 1962 when the active population increased at an annual rate of 2.6 per cent, and employment in production and transport of goods absorbed manpower at the rate of 1.9 per cent, employment in services increased at the high annual rate of 5 per cent." According to the same source, the real need in the services sector could be roughly estimated at an annual rate of 2.6 per cent, so that the "excess" in the tertiary sector was nearly one half. Also we must remember that economic marginality is not related exclusively to services: a considerable proportion of the increase of the urban active population was absorbed in small or artisanal industries, with very low productivity and a type of organization more traditional than modern. From the point of view of social integration, this excess tertiary may be considered the occupational aspect of marginality and it would be important to establish how much they effectively coincide. It must be mentioned, however, as indicated above, that the growth of white-collar personnel and other non-manual employees of middle-class status, even if in excess of the needs of the economy, stimulates mobility and expands the sector of the integrated and participating population. It remains to be seen what the political and other consequences of this process are.

An analysis of marginality and its possible consequences would require more systematic research and better analytical tools than are at hand. There are many types and different degrees of marginality. Rural marginality cannot be considered the same as urban marginality, even if a number of common cultural traits may be found in both, as Lewis suggests. In the city urban marginality is not confined to the population living in shanty-towns, *favelas, villas miserias, callampas, jacales,* and so forth. Inhabitants of these are an extreme case, and other types may be less severe. Marginality, we have seen, may be associated with organization, that is, it may be *integrated* but *segregated* from the urban (and the national) society. Or it may be affected by considerable disorganization (that is, have a conflictual relation with urban and national society). The emphasis on the peculiar adjustment of marginal population to urban life in certain countries and cities does not eliminate the fact that urban disorganization exists. In Buenos Aires (and probably in Montevideo as well), extreme marginality (in the *villas miserias*) is associated with high disorganization. And the most important condition in the maintenance of both disorganization and marginality seems to be the type of neighborhood, the "normal" urban slum being more integrative both in the sense of a lower degree of anomie and higher participation in modern society. With regard to the degree of personal adjustment and anomie, observations made in Lima seem to indicate considerable differences between the "*barriada* marginal," begun in a planned invasion and highly organized through the adaptation of imported rural patterns, and the ordinary slum, characterized by a high degree of maladjustment.

The degree of a city's modernization may be another important factor in determining the stability of marginal population on the basis of quasi-rural patterns modified to meet the requirements of urban life. The less heterogeneity between place of origin and the city, the easier to adapt original traits to the urban situation. The absolute size and the ecological concentration of the urban marginals may well affect the stability of the marginal subculture. Finally, it has been observed that urban groups and institutions may develop mechanisms of adjustment to the marginal sector, an arrangement which is likely to contribute to its persistence.

Persistent urban marginality may be the origin of politically important cleavages within the working class: an "old," more urbanized, more participatory "modern" sector, and a "new," less urbanized, more archaic sector. The former would be politically integrated through leftist parties—moderate or radical; the latter would be either passive, that is, nonparticipatory, or mobilized through national-popular movements. It is worth while to note that this type of "temporal" stratification based on different "ages" of formation is not limited to the lower strata. The middle class usually has also been formed at successive stages, and the differences in historical conditions prevailing at the time of their formation are likely to exercise a deep influence on their political attitude and its organized expression. But the specific impact of marginality is relevant only for the lower strata, and not for the intermediate sectors.

The urban marginal sector may remain politically nonparticipatory for a long time. Or its political mobilization and integration into organized movements may occur through its absorption into more modern occupational roles. As shown by several studies in Brazil and elsewhere, even in this case politicalization is likely to take place in different stages and will depend considerably on the degree of modernization of its place of origin. But under particular circumstances political participation may occur without occupational changes. The urban marginal sector may become politically relevant without losing its cultural and economic marginality, and this may turn out to be a very important consequence of urbanization.

Editor's Summary and Elaboration

USING THE CITY AS AN INTEGRATING MECHANISM

The process of urbanization has to be accepted as irreversible. Consequently, the issue becomes one of using it most fruitfully in order to further economic and social development.

Andrade spoke on this point as follows:

We are going through the process of urbanization in Latin America but are not taking advantage of it. If we can use the process of urbanization to hasten economic development, it may be the answer to the problems of the cities and of raising the standard of living in Latin America. Our resources for economic development are scarce. The city can be used as a turning point to accelerate economic growth.

Most general plans for development ignore the problems of urbanization, and hence are wasting a large capital investment that could work for the benefit of Latin America. If we can bring people who are now unemployed in agriculture into the cities and put them into more productive work, and have the gross national product increase just by this one step alone, it is possible that in a short period of time we can accelerate the process of development in Latin America.

Concentration, besides its advantages for social integration and for mobility, also allows a better use of small economic resources. In Colombia, for example, we have a capital investment in five cities and in private enterprise that can be enlarged. If we enlarge the market for manufacturing products in the cities, the gross national product will increase, while at present we are merely surviving.

Admittedly, this is a new and untried theory. Also, it has political implications that may keep it from being tried, especially as there is general unawareness of how the cities promote social integration.

PRESENT CITIES AS MODERNIZING AGENTS

Under general consideration of using the city to promote modernization, a major topic was the extent to which Latin American cities could be considered modern. Three questions were raised. Are the Latin American cities modern in their economic and social structures and their facilities? Is there a modern open society in Latin America or are the characteristics of the traditional stratification still dominant? Under the conditions that exist, what becomes of the migrants when they place themselves in the city and begin the process of integration?

Under existing conditions in Latin America, as Solari remarked, urbanization is not synonymous with modernization:

Urbanization cannot be considered the same thing as modernization. There are differences between the two processes. Montevideo can be used as an example to show the ambiguity of urbanization. On the basis of indicators of urbanization, such as proportion of population in the city (almost half), small number living in slums (less than 4 per cent), number employed in industry (30 per cent), Montevideo is an example of urbanization at its best. The composition of the labor force, however, shows a percentage in domestic service the same as in the United States a hundred years ago. The consumption of electricity and gas is the same as in the United States fifty years ago. And the same with other indicators—social and cultural indicators all show the same ambiguity.

Neira also questioned whether the cities might not be maintaining traditionalism rather than promoting modernism:

The problem of cultural dualism is important—the coexistence of two different societies in Latin America, one for which the residences and institutions were designed and the other hidden and ignored. Now mobility is bringing these two societies together physically, with one group living in one area and the other marginal and living in another area, not sharing in urban life. This dramatic confrontation of two different societies makes it doubtful that cities presently are promoting integration. Figures indicate that the percentage of population living in places of 20,000 or more in a few countries, such as Venezuela, Brazil, Argentina, puts those countries in the same urbanization range as countries like Sweden, Canada, France, and so on. In the latter countries, however, and in other Western countries, the rate of industrial employment is 20 or 30 per cent and more, while in Latin American countries it is between 7 and 12 per cent. Also, on the index of electricity generated, the figures for the individual countries show higher use among more advanced countries. And so with other indicators. Employment is not keeping pace with geographic urbanization. Under these circumstances, perhaps cities are maintaining traditionalism rather than promoting modernism.

Poblete pictured the urban environment into which the migrant moved as follows:

The requisites of development must imply the total social reality and may be defined as a constructive process which tends to satisfy the material and spiritual needs of the members of the society. Therefore, a developed society is one that offers opportunities for the full realization of the individual who is a person and who is an individual member of the community, and at the same time creates the necessary mechanism that allows him to generate his proper dynamism.

But the real picture of Latin America is quite different. A lack of dynamism and social integration, a lack of internal forces and creativity make impossible the participation of all the sectors. The diagnosis of the continent shows a lack of continuity in the social structure, a poor distribution of goods and services, and a lack of internal organization that make it impossible for the lower strata to participate in the common good. The main value system which prevails is the personal relation, the strong family ties, and paternalism, that in one way or another are mingled with all the social aspects under the dominion of the traditional élite.

The society, as well as the cities, lacks modernization. According to Hardoy:

The incorporation of the Latin American nations into the groups of modern states is either very recent or has not been carried out yet. Even in those countries where it is possible to notice promising indications of that modernization, there still prevails, regionally, a colonial and even semifeudal trait in human relations and in the social and economic structures.

Other evidences of lingering traditionalism also were cited by Hardoy:

The true, responsible incorporation of the scientific, technical, and popular groups into the decision-making organisms of these nations has scarcely begun. And where this incorporation has taken place, frequently it was not based on conscious meditation but was led by the adoption of emotional positions. In those countries where the inevitable process of leveling is being carried out, the incorporation of these groups is still far from clear. And in those in which the process of leveling has not started yet or is scarcely hinted at, those groups are still kept ignorant of the position they might have in modern society.

The techniques usually used in agriculture are irrational and even primitive, and there still prevail, in some areas, systems and tools of cultivation that date back to precolonial times. Industrialization has not made, so far, as effective use of science, technology, and modern administrative techniques as might be expected. Many enterprises survive as a result of expensive measures of protection. Higher and technical education has not been modernized, is scarcely experimental, and still is practically inaccessible to the children of workers and low-income groups.

Latin America, Hardoy felt, has not achieved that level of development that facilitates social integration:

In the planned expansion of education, and in the absorption of skilled workers into new occupations, lies the possibility of increasing production, improving standards, and introducing large groups to conscious participation in national life. The correct use of the scientific and technical discoveries of our times is, then, essential to modify substantially the way and the level of life in our countries.

The general picture of Latin America in these aspects is disheartening despite some evident progress during the last decade, and criticism must equally be shared by private as well as public enterprise.

A potent factor in maintaining traditionalism is the class structure and the alignment of classes in urban society. Whether or not universally true, the middle class in Latin America is generally regarded as aligned with the upper class, particularly in values and attitudes. The politics of scarcity still prevails. Morse may be cited on this point:

It still appears to be a silent premise of Latin American life that individual or group advancement is more likely to occur through a change in distribution of resources than through dramatic increase in total resources available. . . . Maximum economic growth can scarcely be expected in economies where private choice is still important, where conspicuous consumption motivates the upper class, and where redistribution rather than augmentation of the social dividend motivates the middle.[2]

[2] Richard M. Morse, "Recent Research on Latin American Urbanization: A Selective Survey with Commentary," *Latin American Research Review*, I, 1 (Fall, 1965), 58.

One reason why the emerging middle class created no social disturbance is that its course of development was strategically diverted by the upper class. Sánchez in Chapter I pointed out that the class was intended to serve as a "buffer." Jaguaribe briefly summarized its development:

From 1900 to 1930, the urban middle class developed outside the economic process. The countries were two-class societies, of peasants and landlords, and the middle class was superfluous and potentially aggressive toward the established order. This middle class was co-opted by the upper class by being given useless jobs, in order that it support the establishment and maintain an equilibrium. Consequently, the middle class supports the upper class. The middle class is the class that developed a capacity for sudden change in the 1940's and 1950's. As is well known, this change came about through employment opportunities related to the development of import substitutes. The bottleneck which was created when this development reached its limit has created a social crisis as well as an economic one.[3]

As Germani states, "The urban population occupationally integrated seems large enough to create the conditions favoring the rise of the corresponding attitudes and values." Many countries of Latin America have sizable middle classes. "Yet the cities almost *function* as two-class societies—in the sense that 'middle classes' tend to look for accommodation within upper-class clientage systems, or else, under certain pressures, they endorse and even formulate lower-class demands for social justice." [4]

The middle class has not remained static, of course. It has grown through the entrance of new groups. One is the professional class, many of whom are from élite families. Another is the group of white-collar industrial workers. The amount of social mobility is relatively small in most of the Latin American countries, however, since slow economic growth curtails the economic opportunities that make it possible. Consequently, the

[3] See also Solari's comments on the middle class in Chapter II.
[4] Morse, *op. cit.*, p. 63.

middle class is not, apparently, as yet either large or integrated enough to act as a dynamic force in changing the traditional social order into a modern one.

THE MARGINAL MAN AND THE GLASS CURTAIN

There is in most of the countries, a percentage of the total population that, as Solari remarked, "is marginal to the social system, both in the countryside and in the city. This percentage is very high in some countries—Brazil, for instance—and very low in others—Argentina and Uruguay."

Solari defined this marginal population as those "who do not receive the minimum of gratifications from the social system (food, houses, shoes, education, and the like) and also do not have active participation in the determination of the goals of the society. They do not vote, for example, because illiterates are not allowed to vote, or because real elections do not exist; in either case, political decisions are taken by the traditional groups in power."

Consideration of this marginal mass, Solari continued, is necessary to explain any problem which affects the structure of society.

For instance, in cities, where the urban proletariat is very important, its members probably have developed against the marginal masses attitudes of fear which make the proletariat support the groups who are interested in maintaining the status quo. The manual worker in the cities, in other words, has against the marginal groups attitudes similar to those which in more integrated countries the middle class holds against the working class.

The relatively small and new urban group of industrial workers, according to one hypothesis, may be an élite that sees itself threatened by the influx of migration.[5]

The marginal population, Poblete contended, encounters *only* lack of opportunity in the cities and lives behind a "glass curtain":

[5] *Ibid.*, p. 59.

One of the main aspects of the urbanization of Latin America is the growth of the marginal population. The urban phenomenon could be a failure in view of the discrepancy between the general aspiration of the people to participate in the benefits the great urban centers could offer and the real possibility to participate in that benefit. In every one of the large cities of our continent we can observe that a great part of the population has no participation whatsoever in the distribution of the goods and services the city can supply nor in the total decisions that make the development of life worthwhile in a modern world.

The cities are offering modern opportunities for social, economic, and cultural development, but their growth juxtaposes an enormous difference between the living conditions of the marginal population and of the city dwellers. The marginal lacks security and a minimum health standard for his family. He is alienated from culture, he is generally illiterate, and lives with a minimum of food, in an extremely uncomfortable condition, threatened also by unemployment. He sees himself rejected by the rural areas and not accepted in the social structure.

This growth of the marginal population shows the tremendous lack of integration in Latin America. In the city itself there is an iron curtain which in this case we may better call a "glass curtain." Through it, the marginal people can see the enormous differences between their life and the life of the others, this contrast being observed in kinds of housing, health, education, food, and so forth.

Less visible is the lack of participation of the marginal man in the active life of society and its institutions. These men cannot participate in the decisions affecting their own future or that of their families. They have no organization that enables them to incorporate themselves in the social structure. They do not take part in the making of the goals, plans, or other strategies that society may follow for development. Briefly, marginal men have no role in the urban life in which they are living, except just to be there. They see themselves as completely limited in their most essential right, that is, self-determination, which is basic for any freedom.

The marginal man may be defined as the one who has been rejected from the rural areas or the one who, although he lives in the city, has no access to the structure and social mechanism of the city. He feels the impulse to be integrated into the life of the city, he wishes to have more culture, a more permanent work that will allow him to obtain a better level of income as a means to fulfill his aspirations.

The farmer who comes to the city after having been trained in solitude among the distances of the rural world has generally a great sense of individualism and self-sufficiency that makes him suspicious, without trust in the others and the group. It is only through a constant effort to conquer the adverse world, when he finds himself in a worse condition than his previous life, that he feels the need for unity and solidarity in his efforts to overcome his difficulties. Nevertheless, the immense target does not allow him to have even the adequate organization which will permit him to be assimilated into society. This lack of means to overcome difficulties tends to diminish his effort and to increase his state of hopelessness.

This may develop into a general passive attitude, with no interest for other things—a sense of fatalism that sooner or later will be observed in the community and in his work. There is also another danger, increased by the attitude taken by the people of organized society, whose help sometimes is shown in works of charity or in a philanthropic way, with the sole result of adding to his conscience the sense of a passive man, the one who has to receive everything.

To recapitulate, the migrant moves from the country to a city that, by all accounts, is as ill-prepared to receive him as the countryside was to retain him. His chances of finding a job in industry are unlikely; he will not be surrounded by modern appurtenances; his opportunities for access to urban goods and services are so limited as to be practically nonexistent. He will be exposed to co-optation by the upper class for its own purposes, ignored by the middle class, and viewed with suspicion by the lower class. What becomes of him in the city?

SITUATION OF THE MIGRANT

Several available studies[6] give information about the economic

[6] See J. Matos Mar, "Migration and Urbanization—The 'barriadas' of Lima: An Example of Integration into Urban Life," pp. 170–190; Andrew Pearse, "Some Characteristics of Urbanization in the City of Rio de Ja-

and social life of the migrants and their living conditions. Some of the highlights of these studies are given below.

Opportunities for mobility. Most of the migrants have been able to find jobs of a sort, and the large majority have found full-time work, usually, as indicated earlier, in services, construction, transport, and similar fields. There is considerable difference of opinion as to whether jobs of this nature have any economic value. Some experts believe that any form of urban unemployment, "open or disguised, is more onerous than rural because the minimum resources for survival are fewer in the city, and that it is more 'dangerous' because social tensions are more explosive there." Others feel that no real distinction exists between types of employment and that urban employment of any kind aids in obtaining the best degree of employment possible.[7] One advantage is that families are forced to change to a money economy, and to that extent at least move toward a modern society. An economic disadvantage frequently cited is that the continual renewal of the supply of unskilled labor reduces the incentive to develop industrial technology.

The attitude of the migrant toward work is, of course, important with respect to the degree of change it makes in his traditional attitudes and practices. It is frequently pointed out that the migrant brings with him a traditional attitude toward the rural *patrao*, which he seeks to transfer to the urban boss, and that his attitude toward work does not reflect the values of a modern society. Studies of migrants at work have found that they tend to look upon the urban boss as a patron who will help

---

neiro," pp. 191–205; Gino Germani, "Inquiry into the Social Effects of Urbanization in a Working-Class Sector of Greater Buenos Aires," pp. 206–233; Juarez Rubens Brandão Lopes, "Aspects of the Adjustment of Rural Migrants to Urban-Industrial Conditions in São Paulo, Brazil," pp. 234–248; and H. Rotondo, "Psychological and Mental Health Problems of Urbanization Based on Case Studies in Peru," pp. 249–257; all in Philip M. Hauser, ed., *Urbanization in Latin America* (New York: International Documents Service, Columbia University Press, 1961).

[7] Morse, *op. cit.*, p. 46.

them with their personal problems, that some of them change jobs frequently, that there is a strong desire to own their own business. This latter operates also toward greater turnover, in order to obtain severance pay, which can be used to finance the undertaking. The city, according to one viewpoint, is the place where it is desirable to live. A job is valued, not for itself, but because it makes urban living possible.[8]

On the other side, the structure of much industrial activity in Latin America is considered to fail to provide mobility for those who obtain industrial jobs. In an earlier study, Germani pointed out that the requisite for occupational mobility is rational selection of employees based on the requirements of the job to be filled. If selection is made on the basis of "optimum efficiency," the occupational structures in any field should serve as channels of social mobility. Mobility, which should bring about "optimum distribution and exploitation of the society's available manpower assets," depends on (1) institutions based on "rational norms," (2) acceptance of values and attitudes conducive to the rise of people through efficiency and achievement, and (3) social motivation for individuals to aspire toward upward mobility. "Irrational" selection of employees on the basis of kinship or other irrelevant factors remains a practice in Latin American industry, according to various reports, and hence operates to block occupational mobility.[9]

A high birth rate also tends to block upward social mobility. There is no opportunity for those on a lower level to move upward into "vacancies" when these are filled from within each level.[10]

Institutional influences. The *barriadas* of Lima, in which the migrants group themselves along traditional community lines into

[8] *Ibid.*, p. 59.

[9] Gino Germani, "The Strategy of Fostering Social Mobility," in *Social Aspects of Economic Development in Latin America*, I, Egbert De Vries and José Medina Echavarría, eds. (Paris: UNESCO, 1963), 212–214.

[10] *Ibid.*, p. 214.

organizations that operate toward obtaining improved living conditions for the group as a whole, have received considerable attention. *Barriadas,* however, are not typical of urban marginal communities. The kin group provides assistance for most migrants in obtaining a place to live, helping to build a house, providing temporary shelter, finding a job, or helping with finances. For most migrants, the kin group represents the only approved source of sociability and close friendships. Families often are not intimate with their neighbors, except to help in times of illness. Associations outside the kin group are not approved often, except with other select groups, as, for example, church associations. There appears to be little neighborhood sentiment.

The importance of relatives is not confined to recent migrants but continues among earlier migrants and the city-born, as Germani points out in his Buenos Aires study. In this study, the recent migrants, who were from small and large cities, some of which were predominantly rural in occupational structure, were at a disadvantage in having fewer relatives in the city than the earlier migrants. Sometimes friends, that is, persons to be trusted or approached for help in case of need, were as important as relatives. These friends may have lived in the same quarter, and some such friendships were formed at work. The nuclear family was the typical group, augmented by relatives who were trying to establish themselves in the city. The family represented "the greatest source of security." One reason for this, it is held, is that in Latin America the family performs different functions from the ones it performs in more developed countries. In Latin America, the family provides "for society the stability" which in other countries is provided by other institutional forms.[11]

Though the family continues to be the main socializing force, various modifications seem to take place within it as residence in the city lengthens. Germani's study in Buenos Aires indicates

[11] William F. Whyte and A. R. Holmberg, *Human Problems of U.S. Enterprise in Latin America* (Ithaca, N.Y.: Cornell University, New York State School of Industrial and Labor Relations, 1957), p. 5.

"a remarkably regular pattern in the progressive tendency to accept the cultural pattern of legal marriage" in accordance with length of residence, facilitated sometimes by a greater contact with urban culture, as, for example, not living in a *villa miseria*. Migrants sufficiently urbanized to have affiliated themselves with formal organizations in general also tended to be legally married. Germani states: "The acquisition of this trait can thus be regarded as a sign of integration into urban society; and the same can be said of legal marriage, which becomes a symbol of respectability once we take as reference group . . . the urban society, which . . . considers it essential." Other family characteristics tend to modify with length of residence. Recent migrants, for example, tended to have more children than did those who had been born in the city. Also, those born in the city displayed a tendency to be more businesslike in the handling of family money than were the recent migrants. Authoritarianism also declined under the impact of urban living, with reliance on mutual aid taking its place. This was helped possibly by removal from the *villas* to better living conditions.

The stable family apparently operates as a strong integrative force. In the studies, family instability, resulting from omission of legal marriage or other causes, was credited with the blame for much of the disorganization. (The family is the only organization that could be blamed—no others existed.) Poor neighborhoods were another factor; children left alone (of necessity, as all family members worked) were exposed to vagrancy and vice. Also, some parents neglected to take advantage of opportunities offered by the city. Truancy and failure to attend school, for example, were frequent occurrences, and children of recent migrants tended to leave school at an earlier age than other children.

There are indications that migration sometimes worsens existing problems or brings about new ones. Economic pressures mount in the city: frequently among families exhibiting disorganized behavior, one or the other parent has ceased to assume responsibility for the family. Jobs are seldom secure. Alcoholism provides an escape from the problems of everyday urban life. Poor housing and insecure tenure contribute to the difficulties of maintaining an organized and protective family environment. In fact, the Buenos Aires group of recent migrants considered housing and dangers to children from their environment among their most serious problems.

Villas (or other slums) frequently are situated near areas where illegal activities are prevalent. Normal controls of kinship bonds which have been influential in the provinces frequently are broken by the move, and have not been replaced by any similar structure in the *villas*. In other words, the family with high standards has no social reinforcement of them.

Some of the studies also inquired into exposure to mass media and the extent of formal or informal organizations among the migrants. Newspapers were read regularly by most of the inhabitants and, Germani points out, the daily newspaper "has the greatest (in fact universal) impact; the frequency of use is smaller for all other media, including radio." According to one study, the migrants did not view the city as an open society which they could enter, but the theme of their popular pastimes could be interpreted to express their desires to do so. The most popular radio programs and newspaper articles, for example, emphasized support of the poor and chastisement of their persecutors. The popularity of figures in sports and the entertainment world emphasized the success of individuals who had risen through merit rather than through birth or wealth. Games of chance, providing everyone with a chance of winning, regardless of his social status, were popular.

A "feature common to all the working-class population of Buenos Aires, though in varying degrees, is the local voluntary association," mainly "devoted to sports or providing entertainment." Some of these associations, most of which had been organized spontaneously, have, through the efforts of the members, grown into clubs. Other organizations with which marginal persons have contact are trade unions and mutual benefit societies. Recent migrants showed less participation in these informal associations than the better established groups, but they did avail themselves of the opportunity to some extent: 40 per cent did not belong to any available association and others belonged to only one. Some belonged to trade unions or mutual aid societies but did not participate actively.

REINFORCING THE INTEGRATIVE MECHANISMS OF THE CITY

It seems apparent that most of the conditions which the migrant encounters support the continuation of marginality, provided that his situation does not deteriorate. Certain aspects of the city, Hardoy stated, should be considered in order to increase its efficiency for the modernization of Latin America.

Education. Hardoy, among others, thought that the principal socializing agent after the city is education. Until recently, education has been handicapped by overemphasis on preserving the status quo and by not paying enough attention to the needs of development.

Education, because of its influence on the occupational position of the individual, and the city, especially in countries of great urban-rural contrasts, because it exposes its inhabitants to the means of mass communication, set up the indispensable frame of socialization. Unfortunately, very rarely does education proceed according to plans that take into consideration national needs and realities, just as the respective processes of urbanization have not been led so that they will become instruments of the regionalization that is expected to incorporate important groups of the population and bring the resources of vast territories into the national and supranational efforts of industrial production.

The output of Latin American universities is limited and, to make things worse, the deficit is greater in those fields that we might call strategic for development. Their graduates have limited specialization as a result of traditional academic systems of teaching (as mentioned earlier in this discussion) which are still used in an overwhelming majority of schools and departments. Further, they have little or no contact with research and practical experience.

Over the long term, education is expected to be the most effective means of accomplishing the transition from traditional society to modern society. Only in recent years has the educational system in Latin America begun to break away from its traditional moorings. In addition to formal instruction, it can be expected to exercise indirect influence in a number of ways. It offers an atmosphere in which achievement through ability is possible and rewards for success are reasonably equal, regardless of other considerations. It can be important in fostering the desire for achievement and for upward mobility, as well as for the use of talent and intelligence in the process. It encourages the attitude of rational approach to problem-solving rather than acceptance of things as they are. For education to be effective, changes in attitudes are necessary. Not only must changes be accomplished through education in the individual, but changes in social attitude must be sought that will accept the new viewpoint fostered by education and permit new ideas, new methods, and new solutions to be given a fair trial.[12]

No Latin American country denies the value of education. Available resources, augmented by outside aid, limit the investments in it that can be made. In 1964, six countries spent at least 20 per cent of their national income on education. Most of this was allocated to operating expenses, and there was a dearth of funds for new construction. Because of the recognized need for technical skills, a tremendous effort is being made to develop them. Higher education received the most emphasis and the highest proportion of available funds, with high proportions going into such fields as agricultural sciences, basic sciences, train-

[12] Wilbert E. Moore, "The Strategy of Fostering Performance and Responsibility," in De Vries and Medina Echavarría, *op. cit.*, pp. 238–239.

ing of professors, and education, social sciences, and applied sciences.[13] A ten-year educational crusade has been linked to general development plans. Its goals are to give every school-age child access to at least six years of schooling and to expand and modernize the training facilities for vocational and technical training and higher education. Modernization of the educational system is recognized as necessary in economic development, as part of this crusade.

Several members of the conference pointed out that the better educational facilities available in urban areas was one of the few advantages of the city over the countryside for the migrants, if not the only one. Partly the superiority of the city in this respect comes from the high cost of education, as Browning pointed out, and it is less expensive and considerably easier to provide facilities in the city than to provide them for the scattered rural population. Even in the city, however, the educational situation tends to follow the economic status of the community. Where city populations are made up of fully employed, partially employed, and unemployed groups, the school situation is likely to show some groups fully enrolled in schools while other groups are only poorly educated or receive no education.[14]

Clubs and organizations. The migrants, and even groups who were settled but who were not adequately assimilated, should be shown how the city and the urban society function.

Some urban social organizations now exist, although in general very few attempts have been made to provide any special services in the cities for the migrants. A number of cities, recognizing that many of their needy are migrants, are attempting with limited resources to adapt their services to migrant needs. Some of the more obvious assistance needed by migrants is recognized, such

[13] "Facts and Figures of the Americas: Expenditures for Education," *Américas*, XVIII, 3 (March, 1966), 46.
[14] J. Roberto Moreira, "Education and Development in Latin America," in De Vries and Medina Echavarría, *op. cit.*, p. 318.

as reception centers, temporary living quarters, help in caring for children between the minimum age for leaving school and the minimum age for employment, or prolonged schooling during this period, vocational training, and organized youth activities. All of these are means of lessening delinquency or keeping children from illegal employment in low-paying service occupations.[15]

Opportunity to participate in groups and associations and in this way take part in urban life is frequently cited as an advantage of cities, but the migrant often does not have free access to such associations. All too often the groups with which the migrant comes into contact are not designed to help him individually. Some labor unions were cited at the conference as an example.

The city itself, Poblete suggested, is too large to help the individual effectively. The government might fortify or create agencies in the city that will help to take migrants into city life. One way is to help them organize by themselves: slum dwellers' organizations, meeting centers, or other agencies formed for community development. A study of other agencies probably would reveal that they, too, had tremendous potential for integration. Sometimes schools would be important vehicles; sometimes churches, especially neighborhood churches. Experience with Puerto Rican groups in New York City has shown that small units, such as neighborhood churches, can be effective in integrating people into city life and preventing anomie. Very little attention has so far been given to agencies of this type in Latin America.

Once the migrant becomes accustomed to urban ways, however, Agurto suggested, only the city offers the specific advantages for social and political participation in labor unions, professional and trade associations, universities, and organized political parties. The better educational facilities will at least offer

[15] United Nations, Bureau of Social Affairs, "Some Policy Implications of Urbanization," in Hauser, *op. cit.*, pp. 308–311.

the best hope for social integration of the migrant's children, according to Neira.

One suggestion was that reception committees to bring migrants together might be formed. These would provide for the dissemination of information on job opportunities as well as serve social functions. More purely social clubs, similar to the *Quintas Vecinales* and *Clubs Culturales* now functioning in Peru and among Puerto Rican immigrants in New York City, also might be useful.

Information about the migrant and his relation to the city is lacking. What is needed, Reiner suggested, is to recognize that the values of the migrant are not the same as those of the "establishment," including planners. Aspects of the urban environment that are unfavorable to the migrant himself have to be kept in mind. For example, conditions of density and congestion probably do not bother him to the extent that they do planners, and, in spite of their poor living conditions, many migrants seem to feel that they are better off in the city.

Also, Andrade suggested, it is important to know which persons come to the city, what characteristics they have, what type of jobs they need, what kind of work they are going to do, what services they will need, and so on. Census figures in Colombia, for example, indicate that older people tend to stay in the rural areas. It would be helpful to have more specific knowledge, in order to plan for the houses, services, and schools that will be needed for young people in the cities.

The question arose as to whether or not the migrant should be better prepared before he leaves for the city, at least to the extent of being told that his hopes for a higher standard of living are not likely to be fulfilled. Orientation courses have been suggested for those who plan to move to the city. There is some opposition to this plan in official circles, on the ground that it might stimulate more people to move to the cities. An informal system of information (for example, through relatives and friends) operates now between the cities and the countryside, and it is believed that few migrants come to the city without some information about conditions and the job situation.[16] If urbanization were accepted as an inevitable process, more specific information could be given to the migrant, about skills needed for urban jobs, educational requirements, types of work that pay good wages, higher urban prices, and so forth.

Housing and type of neighborhood. Obviously, housing and urban services are among the most serious needs of migrants, both of those who are newly arrived and of those who are living in the slums. Investment in housing has been overshadowed by the need to invest in what are usually considered more productive industries. Housing has a high capital:output ratio, and, as Sánchez Baylón pointed out, until recently, "Latin American economists have tended to regard housing and social services and even education as luxuries that could be afforded only after some measure of industrial and economic development has been achieved." Without sustained economic development, incomes of the groups most seriously in need of housing have not increased. Apart from this, there are other factors: a building industry geared to the requirements of well-to-do classes; high standards for housing; high urban land costs; lack of credit facilities and savings institutions—in short, a general deficiency of all the institutional supports needed by a housing program. As a result, the situation has continued to deteriorate, and forbiddingly high investments are needed to remedy it. "According to United Nations estimates 1.5 million urban dwellings are needed a year for thirty years to overcome present deficits and meet population growth. At $2,000 per unit the cost would be $3,000 million annually. If to this were added all the other essential urban and community facilities, utilities, and services, the investment required could easily be doubled." [17] Or, as stated at the confer-

[16] *Ibid.*, pp. 307–308.
[17] John P. Powelson and Anatole A. Solow, "Urban and Rural Development in Latin America," *The Annals of the American Academy of Political and Social Science*, Vol. 360 (July, 1965), 52.

ence, "the investment required for housing alone is more than the total resources of some of the countries."

Recently, with international financial aid, measures are being taken to improve the situation. The need for a building industry and housing as part of programs for economic development is becoming recognized. "Housing," Sánchez Baylón pointed out, "is being considered as a productive investment, too. It can regulate other types of investment and works toward social-political stability." "The Economic Commission for Latin America program in education," Higgins stated, "most probably will be followed by programs in housing, public health, and other fields of social development." All, or practically all, the Latin American countries have housing programs in effect, with emphasis on different needs. A large investment is being made in housing and related facilities, in spite of a lack of consensus on whether or not it might be more productively used elsewhere. Various efforts are being made to bring down the cost of housing, such as the development of indigenous materials, utilization of self-help, and lowering standards for houses to more realistic levels, though at the same time maintaining a higher standard than presently found in rural areas.[18] Also, economies of agglomeration in housing and services are possible in the urban

[18] Turner has suggested that, if more attention is given to the priority of needs of families based on their socioeconomic level, it would be possible to solve much of the "housing problem" with available resources. He feels that while higher socioeconomic classes demand modern standards in their shelter, the poor, immigrant family is far less interested in the quality of its shelter. Emphasis for these families should be placed on the provision of land and community facilities. See John C. Turner, "A New View of the Housing Deficit," in Charles A. Frankenhoff, ed., *Housing Policy for a Developing Latin Economy* (Rio Piedras, Puerto Rico: University of Puerto Rico, November, 1966); and "Uncontrolled Urban Settlement: Problems and Policies," Working Paper No. 11, Inter-Regional Seminar on Development Policies and Planning in Relation to Urbanization, University of Pittsburgh, October 24 to November 7, 1966. Prepared for the United Nations Centre for Housing, Building and Planning, n.d.

areas and should be utilized. Recommendations include the improvement of existing housing and environmental conditions as a way to benefit more people without additional cost. There is some feeling also that housing should be built by the private sector rather than directly by the government. Savings and loan companies are being founded to encourage savings for housing and have met with a good response where they have been tried.

With the deficit already accumulated, which increases each year, results of housing programs will become apparent only slowly. Also, the largest proportion of the investment has to be made for the masses of population who live in the *favelas*. They are not in a position to help themselves, nor are they likely to be for some time to come. Although Latin Americans are determined that "the slums must go," remedying the housing situation is likely to be a long-term proposition. Even countries like Puerto Rico and Mexico, where housing programs have been in effect for a period of years, have not been able to eliminate their *ranchos* and *jacales*.

Urban development, Horowitz points out in his paper (Chapter VI), is as necessary as industrial development, if a modern society is to result from the "well-nigh universal ferment of change" Latin America is now undergoing. The existence of the *barriadas* merely indicates that the cities are growing at the same low standard of living as most of the rest of each country. The problems are not confined to economics. Many slums have television, refrigerators, and other modern conveniences. The situation of the inhabitants does not always change when the straw houses have been replaced by adobe, or even by brick. The problems are social and cultural as well as economic.

GEOGRAPHIC INTEGRATION

While measures to help the migrant before or after coming to the city were recognized as desirable, they were also recognized as minor steps in view of the scope of investment needed to provide better jobs, educational facilities, better environmental conditions, and other urban facilities for effective integration. With continuing urbanization, it could safely be predicted that the situation would become worse rapidly; in fact, it had already outrun measures taken to alleviate it. The questions thus became whether urbanization should be encouraged and whether some of the flow of migrants should be diverted to other areas.

Though the city provides greater exposure to modernizing influences, Sanabria pointed out that merely living in the cities does not automatically bring about social integration. Cities in developed countries had absorbed the rural population as industrialization spread. To reverse the process by first collecting people in cities was, in a way, to "put the cart before the horse."

The problem was, however, according to Reiner, that urbanization, with or without encouragement, was going on. It was a matter of how best to utilize it.

The problem, Andrade agreed, was not getting people into the cities—they can be expected to come even if measures were taken to prevent it. The problem is how to obtain economic benefits from their coming.

In Colombia, for example, under Operation Colombia, a desirable population increase for Bogota was considered to be about 550,000. The recent census figures (1965) indicate that this increase has already taken place, but it was not accompanied by an increase in terms of the economy. During this same period, Colombia had a billion-dollar loan from the Alliance for Progress but showed only the same economic progress that it had in the years just preceding the loan.

With respect to geographic integration, Padilla made the following remarks:

Geographic integration is important, as this is where our major problems arise in terms of urban-policy decisions. There is a tremendous difference between cities of different sizes, and the problems of small and medium-size cities have not received the same attention as given to the problems of large cities.

We have to consider the economic cost of urbanization programs for social integration. Urbanization is being taken for granted as good in itself, especially urbanization through large cities. But it requires a tremendous investment in housing, community facilities, streets, sewers, aqueducts, hospitals, and so forth. It is doubtful if countries can afford the investment that is needed in the existing large cities. It should be considered whether such an infrastructure could be better and more cheaply provided in cities of different sizes. Smaller cities, it appears, can be just as effective nurseries of social change as large ones.

Further, Padilla continued, some things are lost in the too-large city:

Community development and self-help programs are important for development, especially political development, and it is doubtful whether community development can be as effective in large cities as it has been and can be in smaller communities. Its value is not recognized in large cities.

The question arises as to whether we are not separating classes too much, by the type of urban facilities and urban areas we are developing; that is, whether we are not making social integration more difficult. Are we paying sufficient attention to analyzing how best to organize the cities so that social needs could be met better?

Most conferees agreed that urbanization is not a process that can be stopped, nor is it desirable to stop it. "There is, though," Sánchez Baylón suggested, "considerable difference between encouraging urban growth in a big metropolitan area and encouraging it in middle-sized towns and cities. A balanced policy between the two would be best. If the magnetic attraction of the big city cannot be stopped, the creation of magnets in other areas could be encouraged."

The possibilities for social mobility in cities of different sizes are not known, Francis Violich pointed out, and little attention has been paid to the smaller cities already in existence in Latin America. There is, he felt, some danger in oversimplifying and overgeneralizing the urban problem by emphasizing its manifestations in the large cities.

We need to know more about the potential for participation and for establishing a sense of identity in the smaller cities. For policy-making, we need to explore how these smaller cities, in the range of 50,000 to 100,000 population, might be exploited, not necessarily to drain off the population from the big complexes but to anticipate ways of guiding more population in the future, as the total population situation becomes even more complex.

There is considerable variation among small and middle-sized cities in Latin America with respect to industrialization, modernism, and other factors effective for integration. Social structure, especially in countries with strongly developed old cultures such as Peru, according to Ortiz, is complex and not easy to understand, with much of it interrelated and some of it responding to change. Even in the relatively undifferentiated rural society, there are several levels within classes, and changes are taking place in them. Not all the middle-sized cities, Violich pointed out, have a relatively low grade of industrialization and an undifferentiated class system. Some small cities have retained traditional social structures that are not designed to accommodate newcomers easily. Others have responded to economic pressures and have a fluid social system.[19] Some smaller cities, regardless of a population figure that classifies them as urban, are rural in structure and economy.

[19] See Andrew H. Whiteford, *Two Cities of Latin America: A Comparative Description of Social Classes* (Garden City, N.Y.: Doubleday, 1964). This comparative study contrasts social classes as found in one city, Popayan, Colombia, that has retained traditional class structures, with social classes in another city, Queretaro, Mexico, where the traditional social structure is succumbing to economic changes and pressures.

Although less attention has been paid to the smaller cities of Latin America, some of them have been found to have urban problems that mirror those of the larger cities. Some of these problems are the result of unplanned growth; some come from a prosperity-depression cycle following resource exploitation; and a large part of them are the result of a lack of local resources to cope with growth. It is possible that in many of the small and medium-sized cities the same problems and obstacles would be encountered as in the primate cities.[20]

To develop new cities or old ones, small cities or large, Poblete emphasized, it was necessary first to look at the marginal areas:

They are neuralgic points of social disintegration and social unrest. We cannot look at the city as the center for economic development without first doing something with the marginal people. We need, first, to change the cultural values; second, to insist more on education for all; third, to have housing developments that will be more human. Nor can we wait until we have the best solution: we need action now, even if we are not giving the most adequate things according to United States standards.

What is the answer? There is certainly no simple one. Certain elements of the situation must be accepted while others may be changed. We know, for example, that mobility cannot be stopped. We also know that today there probably is no great improvement in living standards when migrants move from rural areas to the city. We know that social integration cannot occur by itself; there must also be economic and probably political integration. But one answer suggests itself: there must be more attention given to social planning in Latin American cities than we have seen heretofore.

[20] See Gonzalo Rubio Orbe, Reinaldo Torres Caicedo, and Alfredo Costales, "Problems Confronting the City Planner and Administrator in the Town of Esmeraldas, Ecuador," in Hauser, *op. cit.*, pp. 258–279.

The City as a Crucible
for Political Action

Electoral Politics, Urbanization, and Social Development in Latin America   IRVING LOUIS HOROWITZ

Electoral politics is the implementation of major decisions by noncoercive means. The two most important facts to recognize about the enormous land mass stretching from the Rio Bravo to Tierra del Fuego are the degree to which such political power is located in the big cities of the coastal regions or high plains, and the concentration of this power among the economic classes of the upper social stratum. Electoral politics is restricted to specific types of positions and professions linked to the money economy. Acknowledgment of the polarization of political life into electoral and pressure groups is central to an understanding of Latin American political culture. The faith in electoral politics, in its turn, is fused to the universalistic criteria and achievement values found in urban life.[1]

The following remarks are acknowledged to be tentative. Indeed, given the state of reliability of data on Latin America, it is hard to speak in any but a cautious way.[2] There are, nonethe-

---

[1] See Seymour M. Lipset, "Some Social Requisites of Democracy, Economic Development and Political Legitimacy," *American Political Science Review*, LIII, 1 (March, 1959), 69–105.

[2] An exploration like this comes up against problems of data reliability, data comparability, and the simple fact that the measures we now have are often of a crude sort, and hence unsuitable for specialized cross-cultural or comparative international purposes. For an excellent summary of

less, enough pieces of information—of an ethnographic as well as an economic nature—to posit a set of hypotheses which at least warrant further investigation.

RIFT BETWEEN URBAN "CLASSES" AND RURAL "MASSES"

The division between city and country dwellers is more point-edly a rift between "classes" that inhabit the cities and "masses" of disenfranchised peasants and rural laborers who live in the countryside.

The power structures of Latin American countries are typically oligarchical. In his work on Brazilian careers and social structure, Anthony Leeds,[3] elaborating upon the model developed by A. S. Teixeira,[4] has pointed out that the Brazilian power structure (with reference to political pressure groups) shapes up as a cupola in which classes alone engage in politics. The masses are simply not included by these classes in basic calculations concerning the distribution of power and wealth. Hence the advanced cities rise on a precarious and asynchronous social structure. Enveloping this structure is a combination of fixed bureaucracy and the Church.[5] The power structure itself is divided in relatively even proportions: coffee interests, military and civil servants, social security personnel, railway and port workers, maritime personnel, highway and road builders, heavy

---

present needs and dilemmas, see Roger Messy and Hans Pederson, "Statistics for Economic Development with Special Reference to National Accounts and Related Tables," in Werner Baer and Isaac Kerstenetzky, eds., *Inflation and Growth in Latin America* (Homewood, Ill.: Richard D. Irwin Co., 1964), pp. 112–142.

[3] Anthony Leeds, "Brazilian Careers and Social Structure: A Case History and Model," in Dwight B. Heath and Richard N. Adams, eds., *Contemporary Cultures and Societies of Latin America* (New York: Random House, 1965), pp. 379–404.

[4] Anisio S. Teixeira, *Educação nao e privilégio* (Rio de Janeiro: José Olympio, 1952).

[5] That this model with respect to the Church at least requires serious modification in the light of recent events is made clear by David Mutchler, "Roman Catholicism in Brazil," *Studies in Comparative International Development*, I, 8 (1965), 103–117.

and light industrial interests, and bank workers. Even though such an equilibrium model does not account for the circulation of élites, it does help to illustrate the continued gap between class and mass and, of equal weight, the instability of élite sectors.

Without too much effort, a parallel design can be worked out for Mexico, which shares with Brazil the distinction of rapid urbanization combined with an enormous agricultural sector. They both exhibit a higher rate of urbanization, which may be considered the *style* of modernization, than of industrialization, which may be considered the *substance* of modernization. Of particular importance in the Mexican case is the politicalization of the bureaucracy, which is not set up to accommodate the majority of mass groups. Despite differences in formal parliamentary arrangements, Mexico and Brazil are both politically inelastic systems. Undue growth of any one interest sector causes profound and immediate disequilibrium in the precariously built edifice. In both countries there is incessant political maneuvering to modify and even stifle regional development at the expense of proscribed nuclear centers.

Given the nature of competing and conflicting elements within a modern class system, added to continuing traditional factionalisms, democratic "Falangism," in which the national State becomes the exclusive lever of growth, itself becomes a source of instability. This is the case even for the more highly developed Latin American societies. In Mexico not simply the State but the Central Executive Committee of the ruling party (PRI) harnesses nearly all forms of national authority,[6] while in Brazil the creation of a ruling party (ARENA) has had the same effect—without the benevolence of the Mexican system.

Summarizing a mass of data, Pablo González Casanova has recently shown that even in a nation like Mexico, where eco-

---

[6] See Robert E. Scott, *The Mexican Government in Transition* (Urbana: University of Illinois Press, 1959). For a verification of one-party domination, see William V. D'Antonio and Richard Suter, "Primary Elections in a Mexican Municipio: New Trends in Mexico's Struggle Toward Democracy," 1965 (mimeographed).

nomic growth rates and political stability indices are quite high, the urban-rural dichotomy with respect to electoral politics remains fully intact. Because of their significance, his findings are worth quoting at some length:

(a) The agricultural population, and particularly the rural working class that is far poorer than the economically active population as a whole, is that which has a lesser proportion of members who belong to worker organizations. (b) The political parties, which in all parts of the world are predominantly urban organizations, in Mexico, as far as can be determined, do not have either the characteristics or the dimensions of citizen organizations in highly developed countries. The citizens, and particularly those who live in the countryside, are marginal to the parties—passive instruments of their leadership. (c) The rural population, that is to say, the poorest, are those who vote least; it is the general tendency of this sector to be most marginal to the voting process. (d) The illiterate population is connected with the lowest voting process. (e) The rural population that does not vote displays the least opposition (to the official party in power) of any group. (f) The poorest states are those where the least electoral opposition is registered.[7]

The prima facie situation is clear: the gap between the political and the apolitical at the same time represents and symbolizes the rupture between urban and rural life.

The actual depth of the urban-class-versus-rural-mass schism would seem mitigated by the fact that the landed aristocracy forms an essential *class* ingredient in the power structure of Brazil. In fact, however, the landed aristocracy has changed its function—from a feudal aristocracy tied to local interests to a supplier of primary goods for national and international markets. It has also exchanged its characteristic traditionalist *Gemeinschaft* orientation for a highly refined, modernist *Gesellschaft* outlook.[8] Directly put, the source of traditional *wealth* may still be

[7] Pablo González Casanova, *La democracia en México* (Mexico City: Ediciones Era, 1965), p. 107 and *passim*.

[8] See Aldo E. Solari, *Sociología rural latinoamericana* (Buenos Aires: Editorial Universitaria de Buenos Aires, 1963).

the land, but the sources of *power* are clearly in the urban centers. And no class in Latin America knows this better than the often besieged but rarely beaten landed aristocracy. The "struggle" between city and country from the perspective of the landed aristocracy has therefore become largely mythic and nostalgic. This newly retooled sector is, properly speaking, a landed capitalist class neatly absorbed in and defined by the larger urban political apparatus.

What mediates intensive class competition is the safety-valve aspect of internal migration. The movement of the peasantry from the rural areas to urban centers in countries such as Brazil, Mexico, and Peru has clearly served to reduce revolutionary discontent in these nations. This is, however, by no means a universal high road to decreasing class antagonism in Latin America. In Argentina, for example, the movement from rural regions to urban centers provided a revolutionary base to the Peronist movement. Only when cities do in fact relieve social and economic sources of discontent by enlarging upon industrial opportunities do the mass forces of revolution become shriveled. And this withering away of the revolutionary impulse is not so much a function of ecological motility as it is of industrial mobility.[9]

In Latin America the problem of local versus national types of political participation is less important than in the United States. The felicitous phrase of Scott Greer, "metropolitics," implies the sort of local politics vis-à-vis national politics found in the United

[9] Urgently needed to test the effects of both internal migration and foreign immigration on the urban-industrial complex are studies of specific cities. Some efforts in this connection are contained in Hector Ferreire Loria, *Evolução industrial de São Paulo* (São Paulo: Livraria Martins Editoria, 1954); Fernando Henrique Cardoso, "The Structure and Evolution of Industry in São Paulo: 1930–1960," *Studies in Comparative International Development*, I, 5 (1965); Irving L. Horowitz, "The Jewish Community of Buenos Aires," *International Review of Community Development*, 9 (Summer, 1962), 187–213; Tulio Halperín Donghi, "La expansión Granadera en la Campaña de Buenos Aires," *Desarrollo Económico*, III, No. 1–2, pp. 57–110.

States, where there is a high division of political labor based on a constant strain between local and national politics. Local and national élites compete for control of the "metropolity," that is, of metropolitan activities.[10] But in Latin America the division is rather between urbanism as the style and locale of electoral politics in contrast to ruralism as the style and locale of pressure politics. This is one reason why, in the industrially backward nations of Latin America (such as Paraguay and Haiti), there seems to be no noticeable upward movement of politicians from a local to national level. The more backward the national economy, the more strictly a national politician is beholden to a class sector. Class interest, being national, cuts across regional interests and local issues. But for this very reason the "cosmopolitan" political style is a source of weakness, since a politician cannot rely on a local or regional voting base to protect him in times of major crisis and upheaval.

DISPROPORTIONATE URBAN AND RURAL GROWTH RATES

Throughout Latin America the population of the cities is growing faster than that of the countryside. The disproportionate rate of growth signifies a deep transformation in power relations and power balances, as urbanization and politicalization are intimately associated.

Even highly developed nations are captives to their history, no less than makers of it. Latin America is certainly no exception to this general rule. First, history bequeathed it Spanish and Portuguese conquerors who were more concerned with extracting wealth than with establishing permanent settlements. Cities were built in coastal areas, the better to ship goods and grain. Needless to add, such cities were often built without much concern for the Indian inheritance, or for regional social characteristics. These neo-European centers were often more in touch with the needs of Old Spain than with those of New Spain. As

[10] Scott Greer, *Metropolitics: A Study of Political Culture* (New York: John Wiley, 1963).

such, the urban process raised *social* aspiration levels without relieving *economic* pressures.

Second, nature bequeathed a series of fine, easy-to-settle coastal regions. In marked contrast, the interior of Latin America is characterized by climatic extremes and severe topological obstacles. Thick jungles rise up to meet steep and youthful mountains. Nature combined with society in contributing to uneven regional development. Thus, the rural sectors, where agricultural production is dominant, are seriously limited by factors of topology and general geography. The economic differences between rural and urban politics should not prevent an appreciation of the geographic contiguity between these two main sectors.

Third, there is a Latin life style which values immediate gratification more highly than postponed or future reward. This cultural style stifled internal national development—first, because of the "pot of gold" orientation and second, because of the constant emphasis on spending rather than on investing. The drive of internal migration and exploration characteristic of the westward expansion in North America gave way to the drift toward coastal comfort in Latin America. Cultural factors conspired with nature and with history to create in Latin America an asymmetry of rural and urban development which remains intact to this day.[11]

This series of imbalances is reflected in current statistics showing the ratio of city dwellings to national population figures. As Table 14 illustrates, and as has been discussed in previous sessions, Latin American nations tend to suffer from "the problem of Goliath's head"—a situation in which a giant urban head rests on a demographically minute rural body. Blanksten has noted that "there is no Latin American country in which there has been a trend away from urbanization; everywhere the im-

[11] For an acute examination of this imbalance, see Kingsley Davis, "The Urbanization of the Human Population," in *Cities* ("A Scientific American Book"; New York: Alfred A. Knopf, 1965), pp. 3–24.

Table 14. Centralization of Latin American population.

Country	Population of largest metro-politan area*	Metropol-itan area as per cent of nation	National population*	Census year
Uruguay	1,204	46.5	2,592	1963
Argentina	9,334**	44.5	20,959	1960
Brazil	29,685***	41.8	70,967	1960
Costa Rica	499	36.4	1,370	1963
Bolivia	1,170	33.2	3,520	1964
Chile	2,430	32.9	7,374	1960
Cuba	1,998	28.0	7,134	1963
Panama	273	25.4	1,076	1960
Venezuela	1,757***	23.4	7,524	1961
Nicaragua	275	17.3	1,593	1964
Peru	1,875	17.3	10,857	1961
Paraguay	305	16.8	1,817	1962
Dominican Rep.	529**	15.3	3,452	1964
Colombia	2,221**	14.7	15,908	1963
Mexico	5,520	14.4	38,400	1963
Guatemala	573	13.4	4,278	1964
Ecuador	506	11.0	4,585	1962
El Salvador	256	10.2	2,511	1961
Honduras	154	7.7	2,008	1963
Haiti	250	6.3	4,000	1961

Source. Data drawn from S. H. Steinberg, ed., *The Statesman's Yearbook; Statistical and Historical Annual for the Year 1965–1966,* New York: St. Martin's Press, 1965; and Economic Commission for Latin America, "Geographic Distribution of the Population of Latin America and Regional Development Priorities," *Economic Bulletin for Latin America,* VIII, 1 (March, 1963).

* In thousands.

** Includes suburban and non-nuclear regions in the totals, i.e., they are "megalopolis" figures rather than central city figures.

*** Includes population of the *two* largest metropolitan areas.

pressive fact has been the movement toward the city, the swelling of urban populations." [12] This fact, firmly established in the available data, indicates that the base of political power has shifted to the urban regions.

A further indication of the growth of this tendency toward

[12] George I. Blanksten, "The Politics of Latin America," in Gabriel A. Almond and James S. Coleman, eds., *The Politics of the Developing Areas* (Princeton: Princeton University Press, 1960), p. 470.

urban concentration emerges from a consideration of Table 15. It provides a conservative estimate of population expansion in the urban sectors in relation to the nation as a whole. Here one can immediately see that the countryside, far from enveloping the urban regions, is being rapidly abandoned in favor of the cities. While this table offers no information about the numbers of people, or percentage increase, for the capital city in relation to the smaller urban centers, present trends indicate a greater concentration in the large cities than that which presently exists. The rate of urbanization is especially higher in such rapidly industrializing societies as those of Brazil, Chile, Colombia, Mexico, and Venezuela. Indeed, on an average, these countries exhibit a rate of urbanization more in keeping with geometric population bursts than with the currently modest rates of industrialization.

Table 15. Urbanization of Latin American population.

Country	Total urban population, 1965*	Urban regions as per cent of nation	Total urban population, 1970*	Urban regions as per cent of national population	Percentage increase in urban population
Argentina	16,000	74.1	17,600	74.3	0.2
Bolivia	1,300	35.0	1,400	35.0	—
Brazil	40,590	49.3	52,850	55.1	5.8
Chile	5,962	68.7	7,115	72.6	3.9
Colombia	9,611	53.1	12,274	57.9	4.8
Costa Rica	509	34.8	628	34.9	0.1
Dominican Rep.	1,185	33.3	1,530	36.1	2.8
Ecuador	1,834	38.2	2,264	38.7	0.5
El Salvador	1,102	39.3	1,304	40.4	1.1
Guatemala	1,521	34.3	1,946	37.6	3.3
Haiti	730	15.9	810	16.2	0.3
Honduras	518	23.2	645	25.0	1.8
Mexico	22,300	54.7	27,900	62.6	7.9
Nicaragua	683	41.7	836	44.3	2.6
Panama	504	40.9	577	40.1	−0.8
Paraguay	694	35.6	797	35.6	—
Peru	5,250	46.6	6,520	50.1	3.5
Uruguay	1,971	72.5	2,095	72.5	—
Venezuela	6,005	67.4	7,913	72.9	5.5

Source. Data drawn from Inter-American Development Bank, *Social Progress Trust Fund* (Fifth Annual Report) (Washington, D.C., 1965).
* In thousands (estimated).

Whether this drive toward the city is due to "push" factors (difficulties in rural life) or "pull" factors (attractions of urban life) is difficult to ascertain. The tendency in Latin American studies is to emphasize push factors: the lack of opportunity for change in status; the displacement of functions by rapid farm mechanization; the high degree of soil exhaustion in many areas; the ineffective administration, marketing, and servicing facilities in rural areas.[13] On the other hand, the fact that the flow to large cities is significantly greater than actual opportunities for stable employment or adequate housing indicates the existence of large-scale pull factors. The attraction of the city cannot be attributed to industrial growth alone, since the rate of urbanization is much higher than (often double) the rate of industrialization. This "lure" is undoubtedly linked to achievement drives, to the desire to give children the advantages of education, health welfare, general culture, and the like, associated with city life throughout the world.[14]

The essential sociological undertaking begins with this "chicken and egg" problem. First, what is the nature of the mix between push and pull factors? Second, why do some families or family heads migrate to the cities, while others of like background and training do not? Third, why do those who migrate often appear more stable and more rational than their offspring —as one notes in the case of Oscar Lewis's ethnographic studies?[15] Fourth, why do some of those who make a relatively satisfactory adjustment to urban patterns leave their positions and return to the agricultural settlement from whence they

[13] See, for example, Gino Germani, *Política y sociedad en una época de transición: de la sociedad tradicional a la sociedad de masas* (Buenos Aires: Editorial Paidós, 1962).

[14] See Philip M. Hauser, ed., *Urbanization in Latin America* (New York: International Documents Service, Columbia University Press, 1961). This work emphasizes the pull factors in the urbanization process.

[15] *The Children of Sánchez* (New York: Random House, 1961); and *La Vida: A Puerto Rican Family in the Culture of Poverty* (New York: Random House, 1966).

came? These unresolved questions indicate the extent to which social-psychological factors in migration to the cities have yet to be correlated to basic economic and political data.[16]

The political officials of Latin America, by virtue of their urban focus—their attentiveness to the needs of union officials, petty bureaucrats, urban-centered militarists, export-import middlemen, and businessmen—are compelled to give short shrift and second place to rural reform. Insistence of political leaders on agrarian reform, whether through expropriation or through some more cautious device such as high taxation, has often been a primary cause for the toppling of regimes. The political demise of João Goulart was in large part due to his insistence on reform, both economic and electoral, in rural Brazil. Similar experiences have been frequent in Central America. In Mexico, even after the revolution had been consolidated in 1917, politicians showed a profound reticence to engage in the politics of agrarian reform. Partial land reform finally took place in the mid-thirties under the rule of Lázaro Cárdenas. As one commentator recently observed: "Widespread distribution did not begin until twenty-five years after the first blood was spilled and almost twenty years after the constitution was amended."[17] Where thoroughgoing agrarian reform was enacted in the wake of revolutionary ferment, as in Cuba in 1960, this very simultaneity almost brought down the government. Castro's strategy of total land redistribution led to many economic and political complications with the middle sectors who at first encouraged the revolu-

[16] Significant work in this direction has recently been undertaken by Joseph A. Kahl, "A Study of Career Values in Brazil and Mexico," 1965 (mimeographed); and from a psychological perspective, see John F. Santos, "A Psychologist Reflects on Brazil and Brazilians," in Eric N. Baklanoff, ed., *New Perspectives of Brazil* (Nashville: Vanderbilt University Press, 1966), pp. 233–263; and Rogelio Díaz-Guerrero, "Neurosis and the Mexican Structure," *American Journal of Psychiatry*, CXII (1955), 411–417.

[17] See John P. Powelson and Anatole A. Solow, "Urban and Rural Development in Latin America," *The Annals of the American Academy of Political and Social Science*, CCCLX (July, 1965), 60.

tionary regime, and he continued his program only at the cost of losing their support. Thus, because of the political risks involved, a serious alteration of the land tenure system seems to entail revolution rather than reform. The Latin American record thus far would indicate that a solution to this land problem in "reform-mongering" terms has been largely unsuccessful.

But our main concern is how the tremendous shift of the population from rural-agricultural to urban-industrial pursuits has restructured basic power loci. First, political machinery can serve to displace direct revolutionary action by absorbing the goals without using the methods of revolutionary movements. To the extent that urbanization takes place in such a way as to further the growth of an electoral party apparatus, direct revolutionary solutions become difficult to initiate. At the same time, and despite its ideological propensities, urban politicalization often makes exceedingly difficult the landholding class's traditional recourse to illegality, terror, and intimidation.[18]

Second, the traditional classes are faced with the need to engage in coalition politics for the first time. Isolated, they are no longer capable of exercising effective or exclusive political power, either directly or through appointed "*gorila*" military personnel. The more closely these rural landholding interests are linked to the international economy, the more they become enmeshed in big city life and its bureaucratic-industrial norms. The rural mass–urban class dichotomy is therefore actually sharpened by the emergence of the *latifundista* as an additional oppressive urban class factor.

Third, control of the leading city (or cities) in nearly every nation of Latin America now signifies effective political control of the nation. The country-based, nineteenth-century type of *caudillo* can rarely frighten a city into obedience. Sarmiento's

---

[18] See Gláucio Dillon Soares, "The Political Sociology of Uneven Development in Brazil," in Irving L. Horowitz, ed., *Revolution in Brazil: Politics and Society in a Developing Nation* (New York: E. P. Dutton, 1964), pp. 164–195

great fear of the rural "barbarians" overrunning urban "civilization" has become historically interesting rather than socially relevant.[19] Indeed, the more likely situation is for the city-based political-military cadre to stamp out significant military threats in the countryside. Sometimes, when rural strength is unbroken, as in the case of Colombia, the urban political regime arranges a compromise solution between contending factions. This solution is made possible not only by the strength of the urban region, but by the nonideological, patrimonial character of many rural struggles in Latin America.

Fourth, the city provides a great deal of personal stability in contrast to the rural regions. The legal bases of city life are far less problematic than those of rural life. This assertion may seem contradicted by the large number of *golpes* and *manifestaciones* in the cities, but in fact such events only redistribute power among the holders of power, and do not shatter the structure of power as such. These *golpes* and *manifestaciones*, however dramatic, are momentary in their effect.

Fifth, the violent characteristics of life in the backlands, the very absence of any regulative machinery, make politics a more openly violent encounter between forces and hence tend to eliminate the role of the political mediator. The fact that agrarian disputes are often jurisdictional, concerning who has the rights to what lands at what time and in what proportion, further weakens the possibilities of leadership emerging from the agricultural sector because it divides the potential holders of rural power among themselves. Relative to the urban sector, however, these agrarian upper-class interests are increasingly losing ground as they become (1) merged with commercial activities

[19] D. F. Sarmiento's account reflected the traditional liberal fear of *caudillos* like Rosas and Quiroga, rather than any dislike of rural values as such. See his classic statement in *Facundo: civilización y barbarie* (1845) (New York: Doubleday, Colección Hispánica, 1961); also see his more visionary statement, *Argirópolis: capital de los estados confederados*, Vol. XIII of the *Obras de D. F. Sarmiento* (Buenos Aires: [Publicado bajo los auspicios del gobierno argentino], 1896).

in the cities; (2) engaged in combat with radical or revolutionary forces; and (3) lose their indispensability to the structure of the national economy.

Above all, urbanization—whether linked to industrialization or not—enfranchises large numbers of people by bringing them into contact with political organizations. Whether political eligibility is a consequence or a cause of the urban division of labor is less important than its having taken place in the cities. This drastically affects the structure and distribution of State power. The redistribution of power is not necessarily more democratic because it is based in cities; but it must be more facile and opportunistic (that is, responsive to the "will of the people") to survive.[20]

THE URBANIZATION PROCESS AND POLITICAL INTEGRATION

As the urban process matures, and as the rural sector shrinks in importance, political rights tend to be uniformly diffused throughout the nation. The mobilization and integration of the masses in Latin America thus tend to be funneled through the urbanization process.

In Latin America the extent of the division of labor, or at least the degree to which differentiated social classes can be identified, varies from city to city and region to region. In Buenos Aires and Montevideo one can tell the difference between a middle-class white-collar worker and a blue-collar factory worker by the color and cut of their clothes. These class divisions can be noticed only in circumstances of relatively advanced industrialization, and in large cities. The middle-sized cities of Latin America tend to have a relatively low degree of industrial rationalization and a correspondingly undifferentiated

[20] See Francisco C. Weffort, "State and Mass in Brazil," *Studies in Comparative International Development*, II, 12 (1966), 187–196; and for an empirical account of this process, see Orlando M. Carvalho, *Política do município* (Rio de Janeiro: Agir Editores, 1946).

class system.[21] They remain suppliers of raw materials, where perhaps the first stages of processing may take place. One study notes that for one middle-sized Mexican city, "a rule of thumb" for lower class membership is simply "any person who earns his living by working with his hands." [22] In other words, the main distinction is still between "hand" work and "head" work, rather than more sophisticated indicators of urbanization.

Inevitably, because political decisions in Latin America are desperate pragmatic choices to stave off chaos and the choices are made by the classes to the exclusion of the masses, the fusion politics of urban Latin America has been from its inception highly unstable. Of the thirteen multiparty systems listed as unstable in a recent factor analytic survey, nine are in Latin America: Argentina, Brazil, Dominican Republic, Ecuador, El Salvador, Guatemala, Panama, Peru, and Venezuela.[23] These nine countries are also those in Latin America (with two exceptions, Argentina and Venezuela) with the largest agricultural sectors. In each case, the rural sector exceeds half of the total population, which is another way of saying that the majority of their citizens are nonparticipants in the electoral political process. It is instructive to note that in a nation such as Mexico, with high urban concentration, there is a correspondingly high political participation even in the rural regions.[24]

The relation between population and politics must now be placed in focus. In another connection, but quite relevant to our

[21] What is meant here by low degree of industrial rationalization is simply the absence of diversification, not necessarily the quality of goods manufactured.

[22] Andrew H. Whiteford, *Two Cities of Latin America: A Comparative Description of Social Classes* (Garden City, N. Y.: Doubleday, 1964), pp. 136–138. The same situation seems to be the case for Brazil. See Charles Wagley, *Amazon Town: A Study of Man in the Tropics* (New York: Macmillan, 1953).

[23] See Arthur S. Banks and Robert B. Textor, *A Cross-Polity Survey* (Cambridge, Mass.: The M.I.T. Press, 1963), sections 152–155.

[24] Pablo González Casanova, *op. cit.*, pp. 239–245.

investigation, Kornhauser has pointed out that: "Non-participation results in lack of exposure to information and indoctrination concerning democratic values, and in the lack of habits of discussion, debate, negotiation, and compromise—modes of conduct indispensable to democratic politics." He goes on to indicate that, in critical times, mass movements and revolutionary parties recruit precisely from such nonparticipants: "Within all strata, people divorced from community, occupation, and association are first and foremost among the supporters of extremism. The decisive social process in mass society is the *atomization* of social relations; even though this process is accentuated in the lower strata, it operates throughout the society." [25]

Tables 16 and 17, taken together, provide solid evidence that the structure of political parties is most advanced where indicators of high urban development are clear-cut. Urbanism does not necessarily yield democratic politics; rather, it makes possible the kind of mass participation which is a necessary if not a sufficient cause for democratic politics. The degree of class stratification, the literacy of a population, the number of university students, the number of voters in the society, and the degree of unionization are sound indicators of urban growth. The decisive issue now (one we shall later deal with in a separate point) is whether this urbanization process is far enough developed to make possible further social change through the reform-mongering impulses of the cities, or whether social change will be effected by the revolutionary impulses of the countryside.

The countries that are consistent for the stated measures of social stratification and mobilization fall at the opposite poles of development. Consistency (herein defined as parallel rankings on four out of five measures given) is shown for Argentina, Uruguay, Chile, Mexico, and Brazil at the highly urbanized pole;

[25] William Kornhauser, *The Politics of Mass Society* (Glencoe, Ill.: The Free Press, 1959), p. 73; for a more recent study directed toward developing regions, see David E. Apter, *The Politics of Modernization* (Chicago: The University of Chicago Press, 1965), esp. pp. 453–458.

and for Honduras, Haiti, Nicaragua, and El Salvador among the least urbanized nations.[26]

It is noteworthy that the level of expenditures for education is the only radically asymmetrical feature of Mexico and Brazil. It is also the case that the urbanization rate is disproportionately higher than other developmental measures for at least half of the nations of Latin America. Only Cuba reveals a lower rate of urbanization than its norm on the other indicators. This gives quantitative substance to the primacy of pull factors in urbanization. Thus it can be hypothesized that rapid development tends to be symmetrical, whereas uneven development tends to be asymmetrical.

The symmetry in economic development does not carry over into political development. The uneven characteristics of political mobilization can be gathered from Table 17. Taking proportions of voters and union membership as central, one finds that only eight nations (Uruguay, Chile, Mexico, Peru, Brazil, Paraguay, Bolivia, and Honduras), when ranked in quartiles, reveal themselves to be either in the same quartile for the two items or apart by only one quartile. It may be significant that high stability in the political culture (whether of a democratic variety as in Chile or an undemocratic variety as in Paraguay) does tend to reveal a correlation between these two variables. The greatest discrepancies appear in Central America, where a high degree of formal legal-parliamentary rules obtain, but a low degree of mass mobilization and integration. As in so many other instances, the Argentine case seems exceptional. Its mobilization, as evidenced by the degree of unionization and voting measures, is

[26] Irregularities tend to maximize where the level and rate of economic development, as evidenced by the industrialization process, occupies some middle ground. For example, the proportion of the population engaged in secondary and tertiary activities in Panama, Paraguay, Peru, and Ecuador is too high for the kind of stratification and mobility systems exhibited in these countries—all of medium development. On the other hand, the number of university-trained personnel is disproportionately low for such nations as Colombia and Venezuela.

Table 16. Types of social stratification in Latin America, *ca.* 1950.

Country	Per cent in middle and upper brackets of population	Per cent engaged in secondary and tertiary activity	Per cent of literate population	No. of university students per 1,000 population	Annual rate of urbanization
Argentina	36	75	87	7.7	17
Uruguay	—	82	95	5.2	14
Chile	22	65	80	3.9	16
Costa Rica	22	43(−)	80	3.9	16

(*a*) Middle strata: 20 per cent or more; (*b*) cultural existence: psychology of a middle class; (*c*) ethnic homogeneity and cultural homogeneity: national identification and considerable level of participation in various sectors; (*d*) urban-rural differentiation and geographical discontinuity: exists but to a lesser degree than in other countries in Latin America

Cuba	22	56	78	3.9	9(−)
Venezuela	18	56	52(−)	1.3(−)	29(+)
Colombia	22	42	63	1.0(−)	17

(*a*) Middle strata: 15 to 20 per cent approximately; (*b*) emerging middle class (but degree of self-identification questionable); (*c*) ethnic and cultural heterogeneity: sharp unbalance in degree of participation in national society and other aspects; (*d*) marked discontinuity between rural and urban areas, and considerable regional differences

Mexico	20	44	59	0.9(−)	17
Brazil	15	38	49	1.2(−)	13

(*a*) Middle strata: between 15 and 20 per cent approximately; (*b*) cultural, psychological, and political existence of middle class (but see (*d*) above); (*c*) ethnic and cultural heterogeneity: marked differences in degree of urbanization and industrialization in certain areas; and (*d*) predominance of rural life in the major part of the country

Panama	15	45(+)	70(+)	2.6	15(+)
Paraguay	14	46(+)	66(+)	1.3	12
Peru	—	40(+)	42	1.8	11
Ecuador	10	49(+)	56(+)	1.4	12(+)
El Salvador	10	36	40	0.3	9
Bolivia	8	37	12	2.0(+)	8
Guatemala	8	25	29	0.1	10(+)
Nicaragua	—	29	38	0.7	8
Dominican Republic	—	30	43(+)	1.2	10(+)
Honduras	4	24	35	0.7	10(+)
Haiti	3	23	11	—	5

(*a*) Middle strata: less than 15 per cent; emerging middle strata in some countries, but clear persistence in varying degrees of traditional patterns; (*b*) ethnic and cultural heterogeneity: in almost all; (*c*) vast sectors of population still marginal; (*d*) rural pattern: predominant, but with regional differences

Source. Data drawn from Gino Germani, "Estrategia para estimular la movilidad social," in J. A. Kahl, ed., *La industrialización en América Latina* (Mexico City and Buenos Aires: Fondo de Cultura Económica, 1965), pp. 294–295.

Note. Symbols (−) too low and (+) too high for quartile ranking.

Table 17. Types of political mobilization in Latin America, *ca.* 1950.

| Country | Basic nature of the political system | Political mobilization | | | |
		Per cent of voters in adult population	Sequence and quartile rank	Per cent of workers affiliated with unions	Sequence and quartile rank
Argentina	U mp A	61.8	6	48.4	2
Uruguay	S mp D	58.3	7	24.5	10
Costa Rica	S mp D	57.6	8	4.4	15
Chile	S mp D	37.4	12	31.7	5
Venezuela	S mp A	83.8	2	30.8	6
Cuba	U sp T	69.1	4	80.4	1
Colombia	S mp A	40.2	11	18.4	11
Mexico	S sp D	34.6	14	44.6	3
Brazil	U mp A	34.4	15	26.0	8
Panama	S mp D	56.2	9	1.3	19
Paraguay	S sp T	29.1	17	26.5	7
Peru	U mp A	39.2	12	7.4	14
Ecuador	U mp A	28.4	18	10.4	12
El Salvador	U mp A	29.3	16	3.0	18
Bolivia	U sp A	51.4	10	34.1	4
Guatemala	U mp A	27.5	19	1.1	20
Nicaragua	S sp T	92.7	1	4.1	16
Dominican Rep.	U mp T	63.6	5	25.5	9
Honduras	S sp T	36.5	13	9.7	13
Haiti	S sp T	74.2	3	3.6	17

Code: U: unstable, S: stable
mp: multiparty, sp: single party
D: democratic, A: authoritarian, T: totalitarian

extremely high, yet the sort of national integration found in other nations where such measures are consistently high simply does not obtain.

The data appear to indicate that totalitarianism is consonant with both ends of the rank order. Where there is a very high electoral participation there seems to be a strong correlation with stable and totalitarian systems; where there is a very low electoral participation there appear to be unstable and authoritarian systems. Venezuela is the exception to this rule. At the other end, where there is a clustering at the median (40 to 60 per cent) range, there is a tendency toward stability of either a democratic or authoritarian sort. Again, Chile is an exception, with its relatively low level of electoral participation and highly democratic political system.

Strong unionism is generally correlated with this middle range electoral participation. It serves as a useful, if crude, measure of democratic tendencies. But here, too, the data inspire caution. Paraguay has an extremely totalitarian system, but government intervention has organized a large number in union participation. On the other hand, Costa Rica has an exceptionally low level of unionization, which is atypical for a democratic polity.

Finally, items like voting patterns for socialist and communist parties, religious parties and secular parties, present such a mixed mosaic that the search for meaning is at the level of biological explanations of Brownian movement. Ethnographic and qualitative information is vital for making sense of the quantitative data. For example, although the Christian Democrats in Chile have a nominal "clerical" ideology, it is far to the Left of many secular political parties in Chile, and even more Left than "secular" parties in nations like Argentina, El Salvador, Panama, and Paraguay.[27]

The "moral" of the data presented in Table 17 is to avoid any equation of electoral analysis with political analysis.

In a matrix of correlations in which the items in Table 17 were considered (nature of the political system, per cent of voters, and per cent unionized) and selected items from Table 16 (per cent of literacy, and urbanization rate), it becomes clear that the strongest measure is an inverse relation between totalitarianism and literacy (−0.661734). No other measure tested shows anywhere near the same relational strength, either positive or negative. Several qualifying aspects, however, should be listed. First, the scale of democratic, authoritarian, and totalitarian

[27] See Bruce M. Russett and Associates, *World Handbook of Political and Social Indicators* (New Haven and London: Yale University Press, 1964), pp. 82–96.

systems is itself unstable. Guatemala had a revolution in the control year (1950), while the growth of repressive mechanisms in Venezuela and Paraguay was becoming evident in this period. Second, any general characterization of political systems into three categories is itself subject to considerable debate. Thus, whether in the long run literacy is related to high democratic values remains difficult to ascertain. What does emerge from the data analysis is the extent to which high educational norms are connected to urban processes.

Rather direct evidence that education in general is connected to urbanization is provided by Harbison and Myers. The information in Table 18 indicates the extent to which a high agri-

Table 18. Urbanization and education in Latin America.

| Country | Per cent of pop-ulation in agriculture | Rank* | High-level manpower (10,000) | | |
			Teachers at primary and secondary levels	Physicians and dentists	Expenditures on education as per cent of national income
Argentina	25	(01)	88.1	17.5	2.5
Chile	30	(02)	na	7.5	2.4
Uruguay	37	(03)	na	13.0	na
Venezuela	41	(04)	59.4	6.5	4.1
Cuba	42	(05)	36.6	13.0	3.4
Ecuador	53	(06)	40.8	3.0	1.7
Colombia	54	(07.5)	41.1	5.0	2.1
Paraguay	54	(07.5)	78.3	6.0	1.7
Costa Rica	55	(09)	77.5	4.5	4.0
Dominican Rep.	56	(10)	24.2	2.5	1.6
Mexico	58	(11.5)	36.0	4.5	1.4
Brazil	58	(11.5)	48.9	5.0	2.6
Peru	62	(13)	44.4	3.0	2.9
Guatemala	71	(14)	34.9	1.2	2.4
Bolivia	72	(15)	28.3	3.5	na
Haiti	83	(16)	20.3	1.0	na

Source. Data drawn from Frederick Harbison and Charles A. Myers, *Education, Manpower and Economic Growth* (New York: McGraw-Hill, 1964), pp. 45–48.

* Nations are ranked in terms of per cent of population in agriculture. It will be noted that the percentages for the size of the agricultural population vary from the previous tables. This variation is not statistically or qualitatively significant. The difference simply reflects the use of various census reports and population estimates.

cultural population is inversely related to high-level technical manpower such as teachers and professionals. While expenditures on education seem inconclusively related to levels of development, such expenditures may be indicative of rates of development.

One significant feature not represented in the data is the phenomenon of miseducation.[28] Nations like Argentina, Uruguay, and Brazil have a relatively decent supply of high-level manpower. Such proficient manpower, however, is poorly distributed throughout the nation. In fact, cities like Buenos Aires, Rio de Janeiro, and Caracas have an overabundance of high-level personnel with respect to the short supply available for the nation as a whole. This may help to explain why, even when a nation in Latin America has a large number of technically competent personnel, economic development tends to be dramatically inconsistent in output and equally irregular in ecology.

The interconnection of social stratification and political mobilization is further enhanced by the fact that even small and predominantly agricultural nations, such as the Central American republics, boast of potent urban centers, in which both social and political development is largely concentrated. The technically competent personnel often find themselves involved in one form of government machinery or another. The size of the urban bureaucracy further contributes to the structural imbalances mentioned, by fusing the trained and highly skilled work force not just to the urban center but to the national political apparatus concentrated in that center.

In this fashion, the one social sector which, in theory, would be capable of breaking through the yin and yang of a proletarianized bourgeoisie and a bourgeoisified proletariat is itself linked to

[28] For two interesting essays on miseducation, see William S. Stokes, "The *Pensadores* of Latin America," in George B. de Huszar, ed., *The Intellectuals* (Glencoe, Ill.: The Free Press, 1960), pp. 422–429; and David Nasatir, "Student Action in Latin America," *Trans-Action*, II, 3 (March–April, 1965), pp. 8–11.

the stratification system that creates a large politically aware bureaucracy, but one decisively removed from the national interests as a whole.

In examining Table 19—describing the economically active population of Latin American nations in terms of occupations—several important, albeit tentative, conclusions can be reached.

Table 19. Urban-rural dichotomy and occupational distribution, *ca.* 1950 (per cent per 100 active population).

	Urban sector			Rural sector		
Country	Urban middle strata	Urban workers	Combined urban	Landowners and medium-income farming entrepreneurs	"Peons" and other rural workers	Combined rural
Argentina	28	45	73	8	19	27
Chile	21	50	71	1	28	29
Venezuela	16	45	61	2	37	39
Cuba	21	38	59	—	41	41
Ecuador	10	38	48	1	51	52
Panama	15	31	46	1	53	54
Costa Rica	14	31	45	8	47	55
Paraguay	12	33	45	2	53	55
Colombia	12	32	44	10	46	56
Brazil	13	24	37	2	61	63
Guatemala	6	31	37	2	61	63
Bolivia	7	20	27	1	72	73
El Salvador	9	27	36	2	62	64
Honduras	4	12	16	—	84	84
Haiti	2	12	14	1	85	86

Source. Adapted from Gino Germani, "Estrategia para estimular la movilidad social," in J. A. Kahl, ed., *La industrialización en América Latina* (Mexico City and Buenos Aires: Fondo de Cultura Económica, 1965).

Note. "Urban middle strata" includes (*a*) entrepreneurs in business, industry, and service occupations, that is, persons performing these activities with the aid of dependent personnel; (*b*) the professions; (*c*) technicians and managerial personnel; (*d*) white-collar workers, both public and private. "Urban workers" includes all persons working in the secondary and tertiary activity branches and not covered by the preceding categories (mainly persons who are in dependent situations, but also including persons doing manual work for their own account, without dependents). "Landowners and entrepreneurs" includes only those persons using wage labor. "Peons and other rural workers" includes farm wage labor and all those working the land as lessees, owners, or on a similar basis, but without having employees working for them.

Where the combined rural working classes and landholding classes are less than 30 per cent, as is the case in Argentina, Venezuela, and Chile, the political system tends to be multiparty and under urban "liberal" domination. In addition, socialist politics in Latin America tends to be city-based, coalitional, and reformist in outlook. Where the rural classes are 40 per cent or higher, as is the case in most of Latin America, including Cuba and Brazil, the political system tends to be more exclusively concerned with the class interests of the urban sectors. But these are, furthermore, the regions where peasant-based revolutionary movements tend to be more violent and more successful, as was the case in Cuba, Bolivia, Guatemala, and Brazil, at one time or other during the postwar era. That such regimes have often been unstable and/or overthrown only accentuates the correlation of urbanism generating political reform and ruralism generating political reaction and revolution.

The statistical evidence unquestionably points to the decisive role which urbanization has played in the political culture of Latin America. Approximately 90 per cent of the variance is accounted for when urbanization measures are combined with industrialization measures.[29] Perhaps the most interesting finding, if for no other reason than that it is unexpected, is the significance of educational-literacy measures in the determination of the types of political culture found throughout Latin America. It is important to find out that the only other strong correlation also involves education—as a factor in unionization. Whether this is an indirect consequence of the work habitat in the industrial plant, or a direct relation, is less important than the recognition of the intimate connection of education with vertical social mobility, no less than with political mobilization.[30]

[29] See Neuma Aguiar Walker, "A Quantitative Study of Mobilization in Brazil" (unpublished paper, mimeographed).

[30] See on this Robert J. Havighurst, "Education and Social Mobility in Four Societies," in A. H. Halsey, J. Floud, and C. A. Anderson, eds., *Education, Economy and Society* (New York: The Free Press of Glencoe, 1961), pp. 105–120.

THE CITY AS A CRUCIBLE FOR POLITICAL ACTION

URBAN COMPLEX A CENTER OF POLITICS OF REFORM

The Latin American urban complex is a center of reform because it contains the bulk of reform-minded social sectors. The Latin American rural complex is the center of both reaction and revolution because class polarization and class disenfranchisement are relatively complete, and because the class variable is not moderated by other factors.

Before examination of the urban political structure, some commentary on traditional decision-making procedures is in order. A predominantly ascriptive and caste system of relations has tended to reduplicate itself throughout the social system. The primary context of social relations has not been that of rights and privileges of equal citizens interacting with one another, but that of superordination and subordination based upon lineage, race, and inherited status. Within this hierarchy, the rural sectors comprised of Indians, mestizos, Negroes, and mulatto elements have tended to occupy the bottom rung. These same elements have relied more on personalism than upon politics to get their way.

The appeals of the *caudillo* to personalist impulses of the rural mass are not unlike a Latin variation upon a Tammany Hall politician. While heaping great contempt upon these rural masses, the *caudillo* at the same time undoubtedly knows their problems and is willing to act on their needs—for a price. What this indicates is a process of co-optation of the lower classes of society by the élite elements for use in military forays, organized civil wars, and even stuffing the ballot boxes in elections. Such co-optation was accomplished through a traditional chain of command involving the authority figures of the various ruling castes. The polarization of political interests provoking such co-optation in the last century was a function of the internecine conflicts of the élite and required no particular understanding of the true nature of these class interests on the part of the co-opted elements. Political conflict could be characterized as vertical polarizations of a society in which competing groups symbolically acted out the demands of various descendant or ascendant élites. Rural politics in Latin America is thus another way of describing the tightly knit élites that have been largely drawn from the agricultural sector. This includes not only landowners but also a heavy percentage of the military leadership. The rural populace as a mass has been marginal to the political process except as its incidental victims and willing or unwilling instruments.

One indication of how this rural *caudillo* style insinuates itself into urban life is provided by Carlos Medina's description of political campaigning among the *favelados* of Rio de Janeiro.

While the great topics are being discussed, each voter looks for a personal benefaction and each *politico* strives to guarantee his constituency. This is where the most important figure in Brazilian elections appears: the *cabo eleitoral;* . . . He fills the gap between what the candidates proclaim and what they will perform. Politics is thus imbued with a highly demagogic content. The candidate presents the voter with a program of action, but to the individual he promises his personal intervention. It is this which counts.[31]

Just as it might be said that urban politics is simply politics, there is another sense in which the "personal approach" acts to prevent any meaningful urban reform: by rigorously avoiding specific issues related to urban life such as slum dwellings, sanitation and sewage systems, fire alarm units, garbage disposal trucks, protection against false weights and measures, and so forth. Indeed, the only exception to civic disinterest is the police corps—and that because the police of many large Latin American cities function more as military reserves than as local law enforcement agents.

---

[31] Carlos Alberto de Medina, *A favela e o demogogo* (São Paulo, 1964), pp. 97–98, as quoted in Richard M. Morse, "Recent Research on Latin American Urbanization: A Selective Survey with Commentary," *Latin American Research Review*, I, 1 (Fall, 1965), 57; also see Andrew Gunder Frank, "Urban Poverty in Latin America," *Studies in Comparative International Development*, II, 5 (1966), 75–84.

Industrialization, bureaucratization, and modernization placed very great strains on this traditional style of unpolitics. It created the need for symbolic representation of stratified, developed, and highly ambitious class forces, all of which crystallized in the urban sector. The rise of a multiparty system was in effect a response to the impossibility of any further continuance of the *anti-politique* of violence. It was not a national decision or an intellectual commitment to make the political order democratic, but an exhaustion of the rural classes, and an exhibition of urban pre-eminence.

Table 20 indicates, with the notable exceptions of Argentina and Cuba, a significant correlation between deaths from mass violence and numbers of people engaged in farming activities.

Table 20. The rural-urban dichotomy and group violence.

Country*	Number of deaths from group violence, 1950–1962	Rank**	Per cent of population in farming	Rank**	Per cent of population in cities over 20,000	Rank**
Cuba	2,900	1	42	65.5	36.5	26
Bolivia	663	4	72	16.5	19.4	57
Colombia	316	6	55	49.0	22.4	52
Argentina	217	8	25	80.5	48.5	14
Honduras	111	10.5	66	32.0	11.5	80
Venezuela	111	10.5	42	65.5	47.2	15
Paraguay	60	12	55	49.0	15.2	70
Guatemala	57	13	68	28.0	11.2	82
Dominican Rep.	31	19	56	47.0	12.2	78
Peru	26	20	60	40.0	13.9	72.5
Panama	25	21	54	51.0	33.1	30
Costa Rica	24	22	55	49.0	15.4	67.5
Ecuador	18	25	53	52.5	17.8	64
Haiti	16	27	83	7.0	5.1	101.5
Nicaragua	16	27	68	28.0	20.1	55

Source. Adapted from Bruce M. Russett, *et al.*, *World Handbook of Political and Social Indicators* (New Haven and London: Yale University Press, 1964).

* The nations listed cover only the first four deciles, or those nations for which there is a significant number of deaths due to group violence.

** The rankings have not been recomputed for Latin America alone, since an indication of where this region ranks with respect to the rest of the world can be ascertained better from the figures shown.

Such highly urbanized nations as Uruguay, Brazil, and Mexico show little "unsponsored" violence. At the same time an inverse correlation exists between the urbanization process and these causes of death. The emergent parliamentary style in urban politics successfully ordered and centralized its machinery as a first task, but did little to ameliorate or control rural politics. For the first time in the twentieth century this choice in politics pervades Latin America. Constitutional reform occurs in the cities and at those junctures in each of the Latin American countries when the choice between centralized state law and rural terror had to be made.

As Table 20 shows, while there is evidence for correlating high violence and low urbanization, there is also evidence of high violence coinciding with high urbanization. Perhaps what is involved is violence of different types at different levels of economic development. Before we dismiss the relation of violence to urbanization, several points should be noted. In each of the three nations that exhibit a correspondence of high violence and high urbanization, major revolutions have occurred during the periods covered: Castro in Cuba (a Left-wing revolution), Perón in Argentina (a Right-wing revolution), and Betancourt in Venezuela (a Centrist revolution). Where there have been coups d'état, or revolutions from above, violence continues to be high, despite the relative backwardness of the societies involved. The Mexican revolution was undoubtedly costly and violent, but the relatively high stability which has obtained since 1920 indicates that once a revolution consolidates and institutionalizes itself, violence sharply declines.[32]

It should be noted that Table 20 covers the period between 1950 and 1962. This means that it does not cover the present "guerrilla phase" of violence. It may well be that rural violence will expand, despite the institutionalization of the political sys-

[32] See Harry Eckstein, *Internal War: Problems and Approaches* (New York: The Free Press of Glencoe, 1964), pp. 1-32.

tem in the urban zones. If my main hypothesis is correct, we can expect to find an increase in violence even in relatively advanced nations of Latin America, but such violence will increasingly be ecologically confined to the rural areas of the advanced nations. Thus, guerrilla violence has already been widely reported in Peru, Brazil, Argentina, and to a lesser degree, even in Mexico. Such violence does not take place in Lima, Rio de Janeiro, Buenos Aires, or Mexico City, but in the rural zones. Leadership for such violent groups may be drawn from the political marginals or "modernizing intellectuals" of the big cities, but the popular masses must be willing and able to engage in combat.

The landed aristocracy is still in a position to command the loyalties of the tradition-bound peasant masses. Instead of having politics as a symbolic recognition of different class interests, the landed interests, through their feudal paternalism, compel the development of politics by other means, that is, by force of arms.[33] This brings the situation to a full circle. The urban-rural dichotomy in Latin America is one in which the old aristocratic ruling classes have at their disposal a mass base of relatively loyal peasants while the new middle classes have at their disposal the urban working classes who feel they have a vested interest in the going social system. The dichotomization between urban and rural regions begins to develop an autonomous character, and instead of the classical Marxist or European pattern of a struggle between classes, a struggle between class and mass takes place, with the landed aristocracy becoming increasingly "marginal" in the political struggle.

What this means in political terms is that the city becomes the reforming area and the countryside becomes the revolutionary area. The Latin American city is now the center of reform. It is the clear representation of middle-class needs and ambitions. But such liberalism is not to be confused with revolutionary sentiments.

[33] Cf. Gláucio Dillon Soares, *op. cit.*, pp. 164–195.

When an agrarian revolution succeeds, the likelihood is that the urban reform elements will pay a premium price. The Cuban revolution is a classic example. First, the trade union movement became politicized under unified leadership. Second, the urban working class was tithed 4 per cent (in some cases 5 per cent) of their salary. Third, the urban workers were required to take a "voluntary" cut in wages to stabilize the economy. Fourth, and finally, the essential tasks of the urban proletariat were redefined away from class interests and toward firm cooperation with government planning agencies. Those who protested this natural history of the revolution were severely castigated. Castro, in 1960, made a violent attack on the electricity workers and other urban unions, saying that they "had sold the right of primogeniture of the working class, its right to rule and direct the country, for the miserable pottage of special economic privileges." [34] Clearly then, one function of agrarian revolutions is to treat the urban proletariat as one more special interest group, and not just as the "vanguard" of the revolution. This mass versus class phenomenon is characteristic of most revolutionary movements in the Latin American sphere. The urban working classes are part of the liberal center, and their voting patterns reveal precisely such tendencies.

The countryside remains the polarized expression of reaction and revolution—of total solutions to total problems. In the absence of an adequate growth of middle-sized cities, or of mass colonization of the hinterlands by the "developed" sectors, this condition is likely to remain unchanged. A few ethnographic illustrations of this should suffice.

In his study of *caudillismo*, Raymond E. Crist long ago pointed out:

The destiny of the revolutionary cause in Venezuela was decided on the Llanos, for there the patriots enjoyed natural advantages.

[34] For this and other statements by revolutionary leaders in Cuba, see Boris Goldenberg, *The Cuban Revolution and Latin America* (New York: Frederick A. Praeger, 1965), esp. pp. 193–213.

Climate was, for example, a major ally for Páez [José Antonio Páez, guerrilla leader of Venezuela who was born near the village of Acarigua in 1709]; the rainy season was as disastrous for Spanish troops as winter was for Napoleon's Grand Army in Russia. As a guerrilla leader, a caudillo, Páez was himself a product of the grasslands; . . . The common people will continue to see in him a reflection of themselves because he was one of them and they will, therefore, assign to him the virtues which they themselves would like to possess. He was flesh of their flesh and blood of their blood; he did not look down on them from Olympian heights as did Bolívar, the intellectual. Páez was certainly among the greatest caudillos, although he was nothing but a guerrilla leader. He had learned nothing about military tactics from books, but he knew his country and he knew his people.[35]

The appeal made by Juan Perón to the memory of Manuel Rosas was an attempt to rekindle mass against class sentiments: Argentine nationalism against the cosmopolitanism of Buenos Aires. Rosas's rule of the whip, his pose as a "white gaucho" and bearing the holy crusade against enlightenment, against unitarians, against positivists, against Freemasons meant nothing or next to nothing to the rural masses. The lesson of Rosas was not lost on Perón, for no matter how politically authoritarian Perón was, and despite the certain disaster to which his economic policies were leading, he could claim with pride and justification that a *social* revolution had been carried out. And even though this urban *caudillo* (Perón) distinguished himself from the rural *caudillo* (Rosas) in many ways, the rhetoric of nostalgic nationalism, of the rural regions against the urban sectors, received an enormous response. Perón, too, was anti-officialist; he was a populist. The contents of this populism, however, remain as cloudy today, ten years after the collapse of Peronism, as ever. If anything is needed to show that reaction and revolution are

[35] Raymond E. Crist, "Geography and Caudillismo: A Case Study" (1937), in Hugh M. Hamill, Jr., ed., *Dictatorship in Spanish America* (New York: Alfred A. Knopf, 1965), pp. 84–85.

245

closer to each other than either is to reform, the history of Argentina should readily demonstrate the case.[36]

This concept of the city as essentially a liberalizing rather than radicalizing environment is reinforced by the interesting observations of Oscar Lewis:

The population of Mexico City has very close ties with the rural hinterlands. Mexico City is essentially conservative in tradition. In Mexico most of the revolutions have begun in the country. The city has been the refuge for the well-to-do rural families whose local positions were threatened. Mexico City is not as highly industrialized as many American cities and does not present the same conditions of life. Mexican farmers live in well-organized villages that are more like cities and towns than like the open-country settlement pattern of American farmers. Finally, Tepoztlán is close to Mexico City, not only geographically but also culturally. The similarities between the value systems of working-class and lower-middle-class families in Mexico City and those of Tepoztecans are probably much greater than those between, let us say, families from the hill country of Arkansas and working- and middle-class families from St. Louis or Detroit.[37]

At a different level, and as a result of the migration of the masses to the cities, there has been a reinforcement of the reform impulses of city life. The concerns of the city are absorption of the peasantry, making them an industrious group and providing them with an effective political franchise which would help in transforming the urban center from a colonial possession into an industrial base with minimal friction. Germani indicates that this is the case in Argentina:

[36] On the history of Buenos Aires, see Julio Rinaldini, "Buenos Aires," in Germán Arciniegas, ed., *The Green Continent* (New York: Alfred A. Knopf, 1954), pp. 382–400; and for some marvelous vignettes, see Roberto Arlt, *Nuevas aguafuertes porteñas* (Buenos Aires: Librería Hachette, 1960).

[37] "Urbanization Without Breakdown: A Case Study," in Heath and Adams, *op. cit.*, esp. p. 435.

Urbanization gained an unusual impetus with the massive migration to the cities from the interior of the country. During the decade 1936–47 the proportion of *argentinos* born in the provinces who moved to the metropolitan zone of Buenos Aires was equal to almost 40 percent of the natural increase of these same provinces. It was an exodus en masse, by which vast layers of people from the under-developed zones—masses until this moment completely outside the bounds of the political life of the country—were established in the large cities and particularly in Buenos Aires.[38]

There are three great differences in migration patterns from the early twentieth century to now, according to Germani. First, the rhythm of the earlier was much slower, since the urban population growth lasted over at least three decades; second, the masses that exerted political pressure and led toward effective universal suffrage were not immigrants themselves (who, being foreigners, were participating only indirectly and with difficulty in political processes), but their offspring; and lastly, above all, it was a matter of a rise of the newly formed middle class, leaving a nascent urban proletariat in a subordinate situation. These large masses, transplanted in short order to the cities, transformed suddenly from rural *peones*, artisans, or persons with hardships into industrial workers, acquired political significance without at the same time finding the institutional channels necessary for integrating themselves into the normal functioning of the democracy.

Strong evidence is provided by Johnson that this combination of working-class mobilization *without* any corresponding class integration, far from adding to social unrest, gave great support to the middle classes. The working classes not only changed the social morphology of city life but provided precisely that sort of battering-ram for the bourgeois parties which in Europe was channelized into socialist parties. "When the middle sectors

[38] "The Transition to a Mass Democracy in Argentina," in *ibid.*, pp. 468–469.

struck out on their own and began to provide the urban laborers with direction, their intractability was converted into a political asset. Everywhere the industrial workers contributed significantly to the initial victories of the middle sector leadership." [39] The "bourgeoisification" of the workers thus proceeded through the general urbanization process.

The country-based *caudillo* gives the masses their reflection in a charismatic personalistic leader able to register their frustrations through his will. Thus the *caudillo* is everywhere celebrated among those masses who were often most exploited by the military clique. This is because while the *caudillo* saw his role as redeemer of national unity by converting the city into an arm of the State—in other words a Right-wing image of national restoration—the peasantry saw in him the means of their liberation from the oppressiveness of politics as such.

The residue of strength which the new-style *caudillo* retains among marginal groups—especially transitional groups in the process of moving from rural to urban centers—cannot be ignored in weighing this "populist-officialist" dichotomy. The *caudillo*, in his personalist appeals and in his public display of gifts and goods to the very poor, is an exemplar of the "doer" (military man) over and against the "talker" (political man). The strength of General Manuel Odría in the *barriadas* of Lima and of Juan Perón in the *villas miseria* of Buenos Aires indicates the continued identification with authority figures of a large portion of the unabsorbed spillover into semiurban life.[40]

Hirschman's analysis of reform and revolution in terms of gaming analogies offers some cogent arguments as to why tradi-

[39] John J. Johnson, *Political Change in Latin America: The Emergence of the Middle Sectors* (Stanford: Stanford University Press, 1958), pp. 41–42.

[40] François Bourricaud, "Structure and Function of the Peruvian Oligarchy," *Studies in Comparative International Development*, II, 2 (1966), 17–31; and Irving L. Horowitz, "Modern Argentina: The Politics of Power," *The Political Quarterly*, XXX, 4 (October–December, 1959), 400–410.

tional classes *should*, if they were rational and in control of the political system, adopt "reform-mongering" tactics. Yet, as Hirschman himself indicates, there is "only a remote chance that the maneuver will work." But he urges that this chance be taken, or face the specter of revolution, "the last of our possible outcomes." [41] This, however, is not the last outcome. Revolutions are neither ultimate nor irrevocable. One may follow another. Reaction, or in economic terms, stagnation, is the ultimate outcome.

Hirschman's analysis would probably be more appropriate for factory owners in urban regions than for landholders in rural regions. Indeed, factory owners have often, although with some reluctance, accepted unionization on precisely the grounds that the alternatives would be mass proletarian uprisings. The same approach seems to fall on deaf ears among the traditional classes. Several reasons, structural rather than strategic, suggest themselves for this capacity of the urban regions to accept and absorb reform-mongering, and the incapacity of the rural regions to do likewise. First, the notion of traditionalism implies a fixed relation of superordination and subordination—which, when threatened, threatens the entire social system based on the patron-laborer relation. Second, it is far easier to divide money into "equal shares" than land. Land tenure and landownership lead to total change. It is not something which landlords and peons are able to divide into equal shares. Third, the function of the factory owner is to provide investment capital, incentive, organizational skills, and so forth, all of which make him relatively

---

[41] Albert O. Hirschman, *Journeys Toward Progress: Studies of Economic Policy-Making in Latin America* (New York: The Twentieth Century Fund, 1963), pp. 251–297. It is interesting to note that although Hirschman dedicates his book (in part) to Celso Furtado—calling him a "master reformmonger"—Furtado never so designates himself. Indeed, his own analysis of "the revolutionary process in the Northeast" stands in sharp contradiction to the Hirschman strategic approach. See Celso Furtado, *Dialética do desenvolvimento* (Rio de Janeiro: Editora Fundo de Cultura, 1964), pp. 137–155.

understandable to the factory worker. But when the landholder loses his authority he can rarely, if ever, replace it with real offerings. Fourth, the rise of universalistic criteria tends to depersonalize relations, hence it "impersonalizes" solutions. These, at any rate, provide some explanation for why industrialization tends to yield reform rather than revolution, and why the opposite is the case in the rural areas of Latin America. The question, nonetheless, persists as to why reform-mongering has not dominated political styles to a greater extent.

Scott indicates that for Mexico, at least, there is a direct correlation between social class and political socialization. "The 10 or so percent who share participant political culture norms are found primarily in the upper and in the stable middle-middle class; of these no more than 1 or 2 percent could be characterized as viewing politics from the perspective of the more nearly democratic 'civic culture' of Almond and Verba." [42] Scott goes on to cite factors, primarily of a psychological type, that may account for this lag in mass politicalization. He cites the authoritarian values inculcated by the Church, the traditionalist *machismo* inculcated by the primary socializing agents of family and friends, the mistrust of collective action bred by poor work relations, the stubbornness of rural values that tend to carry over perhaps more in Mexico than elsewhere—given the traditionalistic aspects of Mexico City. Whatever the causes of this lag in politicalization, the consequences are clear enough: the homogenization of the power structure and its tendency to become a bureaucratic élite. This process tends to confirm the stereotyped visions of politics in Latin America among Latin Americans. Thus, if the politics of reform is well-nigh impossible in the rural regions, it becomes difficult even in urban areas because the interest parties have never been able to succeed, and ideological

[42] See Robert E. Scott, "Mexico: The Established Revolution," in Lucien W. Pye and Sidney Verba, eds., *Political Culture and Political Development* (Princeton: Princeton University Press, 1965), pp. 330–395.

parties have never been required to meet the pragmatic test of success.

The strategy of urban development is just as necessary to determine the future course of politics in Latin America as the strategy of industrial development. Urbanism can be viewed as coincidental and parallel with the growth of industrialization, rather than as a "stage" on the road to industrialization.

According to figures compiled by the United Nations, in those Latin American nations considered most developed (Argentina, Chile, Venezuela, and Brazil), the level of urbanization is approximately twice the level of industrialization. Whereas in those nations often thought to be the less developed (Bolivia, Ecuador, Paraguay, and Peru), the percentages of urbanization and industrialization are in an almost exact one-to-one ratio. Thus, we either thoroughly redefine the notion of development or, what is more rational and simple, appreciate the fact that while urbanization is a necessary condition for industrial growth, it is also true that urbanization is consonant with a relatively low degree of industrialization. Such cities as Recife in Brazil and Puebla in Mexico attest to this. Thus, it would be short-sighted and intellectually risky to assume that urbanism is but a stage on the road to industrialism. Herbert Blumer has indicated this:

Early industrialization is neutral with regard to each of the four basic conditions which set the character of the classes of early industrial workers. Industrialization does not account for the differences in the composition of these classes, it does not account for the differences in the industrial milieux, it does not account for the differences in outside conditions of life, and it does not account for the definitions used to interpret experience and to organize action. We have to look elsewhere for explanations of the make-up, the experiences, and the conduct of the working classes that come into existence.[43]

Single-causation theories of industrialism as the leading factor in revolutionary discontent may be useful, but it must be recognized that, to the extent a society is rapidly industrialized with a minimum of transitional fissures, the city, the cradle of such industrial enterprises, tends to promote reform movements in contrast to revolutionary movements. Industrial classes develop organizational solidarity, a sense of upward mobility within the larger monied portions of the society, and a firm conviction that their specific class needs can be met by a "fair share" and fair distribution theory rather than by revolutionary activities as such. This seems to be indicated by the ideologies of the Mexican, Argentinian, and Brazilian labor movements.[44] It would further be reinforced by the close, almost paternalistic, ties of the trade unions with the dominant political forces in each country.

The supreme importance of the question of urban politics in Latin America is its direct political implications for the current situation. For the difference between urban and rural attitudes may be seen not just in contrasting attitudes toward change, but in a mode of life where change is institutionalized (the city complexes) in contrast to a mode of life where change is apocalyptic and sporadic (the rural regions).[45]

Three essential strategies of change are now current: the United States strategy of concentrating on developing a national politics of a multiclass variety, the Soviet model of developing a politics of an industrial class variety, and a Chinese model of

[43] "Early Industrialization and the Laboring Class," *The Sociological Quarterly*, I, 1 (January, 1960), 13.

[44] Michael Everett, "The Political Role of Trade Unions in Mexico" (mimeographed); Neuma Aguiar Walker, "The Organization and Ideology of Brazilian Labor," in Horowitz, *op. cit.*, pp. 242–256; Torcuato S. Di Tella, *El sistema político argentino y la clase obrera* (Buenos Aires: Editorial Universitaria de Buenos Aires, 1964).

[45] See Nels Anderson, "The Urban Way of Life," *International Journal of Comparative Sociology*, III, 2 (December, 1962), 186–187.

developing politics on the basis of mass peasant movements. What is involved is nothing short of the choice between reform and revolution on one side and between two strategies for making revolution on the other. While it may well be, indeed is even likely, that Latin America will create its own political mixtures (as it has until now), it is worth at least listing the choices as they are seen from the main political and ideological centers of the world.

If the United States model is to become successfully integrated in Latin America, it will be necessary for the class-mass dichotomy to be eliminated, and for a genuine national politics to emerge. The difficulty thus far for achieving the requisite conditions has been the remarkable ineptitude and even corruption of the middle sectors. For the Soviet model to emerge as successful, the industrial class within the cities would have to see itself as linked to the peasant mass in the countryside, and see its own role in politicalization as the essential agent of revolution. In this orthodox Soviet view, the group that controls the cities controls the nation. The aspirations of the working class, however, have moved closer to the middle sectors than to the peasant masses in most instances. The third model, the Chinese strategy, is the reverse. In the Maoist view, the peasant mass surrounds the urban centers and overwhelms all the minority classes. According to this doctrine, in the initial phase of revolution at least, he who controls the countryside controls the nation. The supreme difficulty with this approach for Latin America is the heavy concentration of the population in the coastal regions— and the increased reliance upon migration rather than recourse to revolution to secure mass goals.

It has been said that "the cities of Latin America are laboratories for the examination and analysis of emerging social classes, for the exploration into the social effects of industrialization, and for studies of social change." [46] They certainly play this role for North American social scientists. But it must equally, if indeed

[46] Whiteford, *op. cit.*, p. 255.

not more emphatically, be kept in mind that the cities of Latin America for their inhabitants are labyrinths of sharp class differentiation, examples of industrial distortions produced by centuries of both external and internal colonialism. These cities are essential proving grounds for social change based on social reform, and when that fails, for change based on social revolution.

Editor's Summary and Elaboration

The basic political difficulty in Latin America is the rift between classes (urban) and masses (rural). Power has been transferred to the city as a result of urbanization. Political mobility, however, requires industrial mobility, and in the absence of an industrial base that provides this, large groups in the cities remain outside the political process.

The mobility made possible through past industrialization has been sufficient to make the traditional revolutionary means of exercising power inoperable and to require the development of coalition politics. Such is apparently the current situation in Latin America, brought about by a combination of historical forces and developed political institutions. In a sense, the city has the same function to perform for political development as for economic development: to integrate the backward political masses with the modern urban classes.

Since urban political development is incomplete, the city does not bring about political integration. Political integration apparently does not take place until the economy is sufficiently modernized to bring about a diversity of jobs. The urban environment also has to develop, however, since industrialization by itself does not operate to produce sufficient differences between workers. The concentration of political activity in the city means, under present circumstances in Latin America, that attention is focused on national interests. Neither urban problems nor rural ones receive attention. Large cities with an industrial base, supported by smaller cities and development of the interior, are one answer. Decentralization, however, needs to be supported by economic development if rural isolation is to be overcome; otherwise, no real change will take place. Migration acts as a safety valve by drawing off tension from rural areas, but the migrants themselves remain outside the political process in the cities, except insofar as they are mobilized by political leaders along traditional lines.

LACK OF NATIONAL POLITICAL INTEGRATION

It can be said, as Poblete stated at the conference, that "there is so much variation in any of the political indexes (whether of political stability or other) and so much importance attached to the different pressure groups, such as the army, economic pressures, or ideological pressures from Russia, Cuba, or the United States, or some other Latin American country, that it is almost impossible to make a political generalization about any problem in Latin America."

Latin American countries do, however, have certain characteristics in common. One is similar political histories. The *hacienda* over a long period of time was the basic structure through which political control was exercised, and it continued to be an effective force in social, economic, and political affairs even after the development of commercial and industrial activities. Different groups exercised power under the system at different times. The sequence, as traced by Ortiz in his discussion, was, first, the conquistadors and their sons; second, the administrators sent from Spain to govern from the province of Peru; third, the rich merchants who were given titles; fourth, the middle classes who led the countries to independence, and fifth, in the present century, the leaders—the politicians, the president, and the new middle class—who came into the political orbit through economic forces. As each new group appeared, it was adopted into the existing power structure that had developed under the *hacienda* system. As trade, industry, and commerce became important, political control was taken over by urban leadership groups, in the form of a system of two or more parties. Government was rule by a minority, but its capabilities must be acknowledged: "The fact that, broadly speaking, these ruling minorities lacked the feeling for a well-timed exit to leave the stage clear for new actors, and thereby justified the subsequent attack on their 'oligarchic domination', ought not to preclude acknowledgement of their economic achievements and their sometimes undeniable political capacity." [47]

Many present-day attitudes, such as authoritarianism and the appeal of the personal leader, toward the functions of government can be traced to the *hacienda* influence. One viewpoint is that difficulties of governments have come about because the formerly effective political systems proved unadaptable to the demands of the changes the society is undergoing. However, since the institutions that supported the past political development still remain, the influence of the past continues. The two most important factors are considered to be the hold of the *hacienda* system on the rural areas and the influence of the international frame of reference on urban decision-making.

The unbalanced political development makes it possible for the system to perpetuate itself, as Hardoy pointed out:

The mentality of the Latin American people identifies itself with noble purposes and thoughts. When given an opportunity, the people have shown their vocation for a real representative democracy. Their violent and sometimes even cruel reactions are but natural if we consider that for centuries they have been left out of the great decisions that affected their welfare and freedom. They have been traditionally used, confused, and postponed, because, thanks to that confusion and ignorance, it was possible to maintain

[47] José Medina Echavarría, "A Theoretical Model of Development Applicable to Latin America," in *Social Aspects of Economic Development in Latin America*, I, Egbert De Vries and José Medina Echavarría, eds. (Paris: UNESCO, 1963), 48.

the weak social structures supported by the opportunist political parties that plague our constitutional history.

At the same time, this unbalanced political development also prevents the functioning of an urban style of politics. Most political systems in Latin America were adopted from more advanced countries. Jacques Lambert has indicated that political democracy worked well enough for the advanced sectors of the society but "no regulations can be effectively applied at one and the same time to two such different types of culture as those into which the general run of Latin American societies are divided." Lambert also states:

But the survival of outdated structures, resulting from the system of large estates, causes an imbalance between the effects expected from the desired forms of government and those actually produced. When applied to the traditional rural social structure, representative democracy leads to the representation of the interests of small local groups or small family cliques and this type of representation does nothing either to help public opinion to crystallize in relation to the problems of national development, or to encourage the representatives to regard the solution of these problems as their main mission. It then becomes difficult to avoid some violation of the legal processes of democracy; the power of the President tends to become too great and the risk of dictatorship and *coups d'état* appears.[48]

Urban and rural groups are isolated from each other, as Lambert explains:

From the legal point of view, the Latin American countries make only limited provision for local self-government, but this does not mean that many of them are not in actual fact highly decentralized, far more so than the United States of America. Distance, difficulties of communication—in short, isolation—are very effective agents of decentralization. Between the State and the individual intervenes the *de facto* authority of the large estates, small communities which

[48] "Requirements for Rapid Economic and Social Development," in *ibid.*, pp. 61, 62.

can take no notice of the law because, being closed societies, they can disregard both the law and the civil service.[49]

In federalist states like Argentina, Hardoy pointed out, the existence of provincial governments reinforces the isolation. One of the problems in such countries is that each province duplicates the structure of the national government.

Each one is an image of the national government, with many of its defects and few of its advantages. Formosa in northern Argentina is an example: this province has 50,000 square kilometers and a population of some 130,000, 95 per cent of whom live on 5 to 10 per cent of the territory, the remainder of which is unexplored. This province not only has ministries of education, government, and economics, which might be considered necessary, but also departments of transportation, agriculture, statistics, on through all the national bureaus. Because of its organization and of the impact of this structure on national politics, the political machinery of the province rarely has a consciousness of the problems of the country as a whole and very rarely will it support a regional approach to problem-solving.

The situations in rural areas vary among the countries, but only a few exhibit politically integrative forces actively operating. According to Jaguaribe, Latin America has at least three different types of rural society. One is relatively modern and is being incorporated into the social order. Argentina is an example of this. In the second type, the rural society is not modern, but there is a special facility for migration, which provides a way of escape for the pressures that accumulate in the countryside. Mexico and Brazil are examples of this type. In the third type, the rural society is extremely backward and, in addition, there is no facility for migration, as, for example, in Peru, Colombia, and Guatemala, although Guatemala is also affected by its small size. In the first type, there is a good chance for the peaceful and gradual development of a model basically semicapitalistic and democratic, if allowance is made for the larger role the

[49] *Ibid.*, pp. 62–63.

government will play in any country of Latin America than it does in the United States or in European countries. In the second type, where there is some capacity for absorbing the semi-employed or unemployed rural class, countries now are being dominated by right-wing forces that are trying to keep the migrants from the cities. Jaguaribe continues:

They are becoming apartheid countries and, under the guise of democracy and modern principles, a confederation of cities is trying to keep the peasants in their present destitute condition because the cities cannot hold any more. Largely because of the excess marginal working class, some of these countries are, willingly, letting themselves be maneuvered into the third category. Strong and immediate reform measures are needed, if they are to be stopped. In countries in the third category, revolutions are likely whenever the contradictions generated by the authoritarian traditional patterns make such a decision necessary. In these countries, the rural sector has enough influence to freeze the process of change and reform, the polarization of classes is becoming worse, and the future course of events is uncertain.

The social structure does not permit representation in government or social participation on an effective level. Under these circumstances, ideologies—not necessarily political ones but any ideologies that influence thinking—assume importance when they support the status quo. In this connection, Solari stated:

For instance, there is the political significance of maintaining a rural ideology, found in even the most advanced countries, that the soul of the nation lies in its rural areas and that the rural areas are the main support of the nation. Even in Argentina, industrialists have not been able to develop an ideology of their own to combat this rural one. The problem in Latin America is that only the rural upper class benefits from this ideology. Unfortunately, it is taught in the elementary schools and is reinforcing the wealthy landowners in maintaining power.

There are, Horowitz replied, in actuality two rural ideologies, one for the aristocrats and one for the lower class. The *caudillo* ideology is not the same as that of the rural upper class but is peculiar and unique and enables the masses to identify with that particular strain of ruralism and not with the aristocratic strain. The *caudillo* attitude comes to the city with the migrants and sometimes is transformed into support of any ideology, whether or not politically inspired, that promises strong leadership, redress, and manipulation of political structures to obtain special benefits for particular groups.

SOCIAL CHANGE AND URBAN POLITICAL DEVELOPMENT

Nevertheless, the way is being paved for urban political leadership. Deep social change took place under the traditional class rule. In at least the most important group of Latin American countries, there have appeared new social strata with a strong upward impetus, which in some cases are only awaiting the necessary political framework for their complete incorporation into national life. Waldemiro Bazzanella elaborates:

It seems obvious that the power structure based on the country landowners, on tradition, is losing influence. However, the vacuum left by the comparative loss of influence by the country landowners is not being filled concurrently by the action of other groups. The result is a hiatus in political leadership, where the mass of the electorate vacillates at the whim of circumstances in contradictory movements of opinion that seem to be paradoxical and incoherent. It is a characteristic of Brazil that it is precisely in the areas most highly developed industrially, where the loss of influence by the traditional powers has accordingly been greatest, that party allegiances are least firm.[50]

The power vacuum is being filled by various expedients, including agreements among various groups, the army, or a contemporary version of the "man on horseback."

With most of the Latin American economies dependent on

[50] "Priority Areas for Social Research in Latin America," in De Vries and Medina Echavarría, *op. cit.*, p. 375.

foreign trade in a narrow range of primary products for which markets are unstable, external forces can still call the turn on the urban political scene. Riba's statement is pertinent:

How much of our present-day urban politics in Latin America is determined by political decisions made by external, extracontinental powers? Panama, where all the major decisions that affect the life of Panama have been made outside Panama from the time of the Spanish on down, is an extreme example of the direct and important relation between decisions made outside the country and local urban politics. In many of the Latin American countries, the price of commodities or the price of major products is made by external forces.

The changes in class structure that have been taking place have not been, in general, accompanied by an equivalent growth of opportunity to attain a higher standard of living. A middle class of professional people (teachers, journalists, government employees, and so forth) has grown up. The interests of this group differ from those of the older oligarchy, that is, the large landowners, merchants, capitalists, and army and church officials. Dissatisfaction exists among the new group because opportunities for employment have not expanded fast enough to absorb trained men and women. As a group, they have political awareness as a result of their education, and a strong desire for economic development to accelerate. Much of the urban political conflict is assigned to the differences between the new and older strata. It is, however, less a conflict between one group opposed to economic development and another committed to it as it is a conflict over the course of development to be sponsored and the group to have power at a particular time. The newer strata are not large enough in most of the countries, or strong enough, or—possibly—politically active enough, to be able to retain political power, even where they achieve it, without the support of other groups. And given the nature of programs needed for economic development in Latin America, such as accumulation of capital for investment, measures to increase agricultural productivity, and so forth, by which one or another group may find its interests imperiled, such coalitions rest on uneasy foundations.

Hardoy contributed several observations on the Latin American political picture. One was the tendency of political leaders to confine themselves to a narrow range of problems.

With alarming frequency the republics of Latin America have been led by men who lacked foresight and who were more interested in maintaining an unstable political and social balance that would secure their survival for a certain period of time than in the search for new ideas and the fulfillment of new solutions. They were men who could be capable and honest administrators to determine short-run programs, but who generally lacked the political imagination and generosity to consider problems clearly and in advance, to make decisions in advance.

These men have formed and integrated the traditional political parties and have chosen themes on which they based their political platforms before elections, but very rarely have they begun something new in depth.

Another observation is that groups who are active in politics and occupy relatively strong positions have mainly parochial interests and work for the enhancement of their own groups. One result of this is a lack of continuity in government programs:

The inflexibility of the Church, of the labor unions, of the professionals and students, of the agrarian associations, of the commercial and industrial groups, and of the military lodges constitute, with different shades, an extended and sad phase of our history and our present. Too often those groups force the prevalence of their privileges without seeking the participation of other groups, except in cases of extreme common interest. And frequently, they lack the foresight and the sense of collaboration and of mutual respect that are essential to reach national unification and back the process of modernization that will make possible the effective integration of our countries. Logically, in this situation, the necessity for structural changes is denied or delayed by those groups who wish to keep privileged positions or is insisted upon by those who lack a clear and guiding idea that will enable them to put in order those changes and give them priority. As a consequence, instead of guidance toward new goals, there is the sudden destruction of public advising councils, on any level of the government, of research institutions, and of excellent professional and technical groups, without a knowledge of how those men and their activities will be replaced.

Finally, Hardoy mentioned the continuing tendency to exclude professionals in various disciplines from planning and decision-making:

The reality is that traditionally the professional politician of Latin America has done without the advice of technicians and scientists and has preferred to sacrifice the eventual effects of long-run national policies to the immediate advantages of programs based on their own intuition or convenience. Examples of technicians and scientists participating with their knowledge, support, and foresight in the elaboration of political plans have been neither frequent nor lasting. In this way we lost opportunities that now, seen with the perspective that history gives us, might have changed the course of our development and the vitality of our institutions.

Consequently, where governments are stable, they are more likely to reflect the current strength of a particular group or party than to mean the attainment of political maturity where government represents the entire population. Further, given continuance of the rural situation, reinforced by economic dependence on forces outside the control of a country, the stability of the government might be said to be incidental, since it rests on inherently unstable conditions—conditions that can be changed only by decisions within Latin America itself.

POLITICAL ASPECTS OF MARGINALITY

Added to the urban forces that impinge on the power structure, whether traditional or coalitionist, is the rapidly growing marginal population, whose expectations from a new economic order are becoming increasingly vocalized. Still not accepted as fully responsible national citizens, they are appealed to by skillful manipulators of traditional politics, with a local political figure taking the place of the rural *padrone*.

Urban political leadership is being expressed more by the "influence of charismatic leaders having their political basis in the towns" than by group action in accordance with definite ideologies.

At the same time that millions of "marginal" Latin Americans are straining for access to urban security and opportunity, their allegiance is being courted by a new stripe of "populist" political leader. Populism is a tricky term. Some define it as politics for a mass society: demagogic, paternalistic, nationalistic, non-ideological— a kind of Bonapartism or democratic Caesarism. Pearse, while accepting this framework, Latin-Americanizes the term by stressing the "informal and non-institutionalized" structures of clientage upon which populist politics rest. This clarifies the distinction between the urban "mass society" of a northern industrial nation and a Latin American urban society which resists "the organization of common interest groups or co-operative groups." Populism is the surrogate for such organization, bridging the gap between city life and "a tradition of rural dependence." [51]

Much of this manipulation is made possible by lack of knowledge on the part of the marginals as to how the political process operates and also from lack of interest in or experience with group action based on personal initiative and responsibility.

As Germani states in Chapter V, a number of consequences may derive from the persistence of urban marginality. One of them is that political cleavages may develop between different parts of the low-income groups. The migrants who find work, for instance, particularly outside the service occupations, tend to identify their interests with those of the middle class. Or the marginal population may remain politically nonparticipatory

[51] F. C. Weffort, "Política de massas," in Octavio Ianni, *et al.*, *Política e revolução social no Brasil* (Rio de Janeiro, 1965), pp. 159–198; and Andrew Pearse, "Some Characteristics of Urbanization in the City of Rio de Janeiro," in Hauser, *op. cit.*, pp. 191–205, summarized in Morse, *op. cit.*, p. 43.

even after they are integrated in other ways. Whether this results from a lack of channels or other cause, it fosters, by default, the continuation of traditional political maneuvers. Still another result may be that the marginals become politically participant while still culturally and economically marginal. According to Solari, the population that considers itself marginal to the system may explain the evolution of two such different political systems as those of Argentina and Uruguay—countries that in many other ways are alike.

A study of the Lima *barriadas,* which are usually cited as examples of political activity directed toward achieving citizens' goals, discusses some of the implications of the situation:

Bourricaud has studied how conventional party politics become inserted into the Lima *barriadas.* In explaining the strength of rightist General Odría among the "marginal" population in 1962 and 1963 he stresses the ideological apathy of the *barriadas.* He then describes the political machines, which were: (a) set in motion by transactions between the candidates' agents and the local political leaders who can deliver the votes of clienteles of friends and kin, and (b) lubricated by handouts of food, clothing and other necessities. Such a system is precarious. Charity tends to reach only the disinherited and least integrated elements. It creates indifference among local leaders, who wish to show their power by delivering precisely those *community* improvements . . . which the highest authorities reserve for allocation by themselves. The key question is whether the local leaders' policy of prudence, ideological indifference and calculated horse-trading will continue; or whether "it will give way, suddenly or gradually, to acute radicalization and to a sharp revolutionary sensibility." [52]

At the least, urban marginality represents a latent political force from which deep change may be expected. The condition lacking in most Latin American politics is social integration or consensus within a given social system. Germani pointed out that

[52] François Bourricaud, "La place de Lima dans la vie politique péruvienne," *Caravelle,* III (1964), 138–146, quoted in Morse, *op. cit.,* pp. 56–57.

the transfer from rural to urban areas, that is, the process of urbanization, is a condition that originates such an integration and consensus. Conflicts of interest are not avoided entirely, but the conflicts are integrated. Reform takes place, but not a radical change in the revolutionary sense. A combination of isolated, highly mobilized masses and a deprived élite favors extreme action of one kind or another. In Latin America, the masses are not mobilized, nor are they always isolated. The rural élite is not deprived, nor does it feel displaced "nor ready to anti-status quo anything." Economic development, and concomitant urbanization, operates to overcome the isolation and to integrate the masses into the social and political orders.

The city sometimes, Poblete added, can be the origin of a social revolution, that is, a revolution in the positive sense. The term "revolution" has another connotation besides violence and is being used to describe the peaceful revolution going on in Latin America. Hence, it represents a positive sign of development, even of political development, because more and more people become involved in politics and greater political participation increases the chances of bringing about change through reform.

Marginality may operate as a force that can break down the existing political exclusiveness within the urban political framework. In fact, Horowitz remarked, a high degree of marginality may be necessary in order for the political system to become fluid and "unfreeze" the rigid pattern of social relationships.

In Chile, the government utilized existing *callampa* organizations for better political stability among the marginal population.

A primary research target is the elaboration of strategies for avoiding the disintegration of urban society, for countering overcentralization by creating and/or giving legal status to grass-roots structures for community initiative and action. It has been decided that the strongest mechanisms for reform and reconstruction will be the *comités* and *juntas de vecinos* now so widespread among urban *pob-*

laciones; . . . The specific aim of such mechanisms is to stimulate a change of outlook by which citizens in a marginal situation . . . can, through new organizational structures, integrate to the values of the contemporary world.[53]

Along these same lines, Sánchez Baylón cited as an example, the *paracaidistas* (paratroopers), a movement among the marginal population in Mexico that began thirty years ago and is now organized in Mexico City and in most of the other important Mexican cities. This development arose spontaneously among the marginal population without stimulus from the government, but has been encouraged by political forces to bring out more voters and more participation in voting.

URBANIZATION AND POLITICAL DEVELOPMENT

A few factors pertaining to the city as the central political arena seem clear. One is that the city is the principal agency for political integration. This may be less from its being the place of political activity than from certain qualities that the city has. Rose K. Goldsen remarked:

According to Horowitz, the city is a center of social differentiation and provides an exposure to culturating influences, and as a result of this, it is possible for a politics of compromise to arise. The city, that is, provides an *infrastructure* for a politics of coalition or compromise or "reform-mongering." In other words, there is the possibility that the organic qualities of the city itself may be growth factors rather than the urban factor.

There is a growing belief that the factors that now are perceived as unstabilizing can be made to yield to planned economic development. The reasoning is that economic development requires a policy based on agreement among groups, or at least the approval of the majority. Differences between groups that now keep them apart might be expected to yield in the face

[53] Comisión Promoción Popular, "Informe," Santiago, 1964 (mimeographed), quoted in Morse, *op. cit.,* p. 57.

267

of common agreement on a major objective. In the light of trends toward integrated national development, the traditional power groups, it is predicted, will not regain their former hold on the political machinery. Urban industrial growth tends to realign the sources of economic power, with the strength of urban-based groups growing as the economic base expands.[54]

In some countries, there is "a growing distaste for dictatorship and a spreading demand for representative, honest, and efficient government." The present conception of the form such a government would take involves giving considerable latitude to the government in economic programs, which would take in both private and public sectors, "with the private sector subject to a good deal of public management."[55]

The problem, or part of it, as seen by Hardoy, is to define what political institutions are available in the countries, how they may best be utilized, and what changes should be made in them in order to foster economic development.

Theoretically, the problem is, which is the best and most convenient political administrative organization in a country for a particular stage of development? What is the strategy of allocating not only various scarce financial resources but also human resources, especially scientific and technical ones?

This is a field where little research has been done in Latin America. More thought should be given to what institutions we have at the national, provincial, and local level that have effectiveness in the process of developing our countries. Historians and scholars concerned with the problem of government can play a large role in tracing the development of Latin American institutions. The way

[54] For elaboration of these points, see José Medina Echavarría, "A Sociologist's View," in *Social Aspects of Economic Development in Latin America*, II, by José Medina Echavarría and Benjamin Higgins (Paris: UNESCO, 1963), 118–122; and John P. Powelson, *Latin America: Today's Economic and Social Revolution* (New York: McGraw-Hill, 1964), p. 82.

[55] Benjamin Higgins, "Requirements for Rapid Economic Development in Latin America," in De Vries and Medina Echavarría, *op. cit.*, pp. 165–166.

out is to give full use to those institutions that still have a chance of being effective for integration in each country and for the integration of all Latin America, then to create those institutions which we need—this has to be done because the political administrative organization of our countries still has not had a chance to become fully developed.

Evidence in countries that have achieved economic development indicates that it is possible under more than one form of government, Higgins remarked. Consideration, even if information on the best government for different stages of growth were available, must also be given to how changes in an existing government could be accomplished:

High rates of economic growth have been achieved under a wide range of political systems. There is quite a diversity among the star performers since World War II: Japan is, of course, at the top of the list, but Yugoslavia and the U.S.S.R. are close behind. Yugoslavia and the U.S.S.R. have very different planning systems and economic organizations, although both are nominally socialist. Then you have a group consisting of most of the other Soviet bloc countries, plus West Germany, Greece, and Italy. Then you move to countries like Venezuela, which is up with the leaders. Then you have the medium or moderately good performers like Brazil and Mexico, and at the bottom you have advanced countries like Canada, the United States, Australia, Belgium, and some Latin American countries, like Chile. Thus, there is no obvious correlation between political framework and higher rates of economic growth.

Political theorists have been negligent in not providing us with analyses of the kind of political framework which, given the general social and cultural background, would be most conducive to economic development in a particular country at a particular time. Such a search would be amusing. Whether, confronted with irrefutable evidence that the economic and political system installed in a country was unfavorable for economic development, the politician in power would step aside is a moot point. There is a step between the acquisition of the knowledge of what would be the optimum political framework and its achievement—a step that sometimes resists a century of revolution.

It would be unrealistic to expect that commitment to economic development, or any other national policy, would necessarily bring with it complete agreement among all factions. Assuming majority agreement on the course of development, as the effects of industrialization become apparent on attitudes, the social structure, the family institutions, and so on, further sources of conflict may be predicted. If the full potential of the city as a crucible for political action can be realized, much of this conflict will be resolved through reform tactics. The city, as Violich pointed out, has more than one level from which it is operating toward political integration: the national or international frame of reference, the city itself, and the *barrios*. Recognizing and developing the urban political potential on each level would clear away much of the confusion on national issues, inaction on urban problems, and lack of interchange between rural and urban politics.

Urban politics should recognize, Violich continued, the decision process with reference to the physical city and its related geographic hinterland, and its quality should, therefore, grow out of the pressing problems which exist city by city and region by region around Latin America. Politics implies primarily national politics or an international frame of reference, though the theater for this debate happens to be urban areas, which have always ruled Latin America. National and international issues are somewhat removed from issues relating to the modernization needs of Latin American cities. Violich explained:

There are three possible scales of urban politics which need to be explored and which show certain differentiating elements. The first is the national or international scale already discussed.

The second is the city itself, where political decisions and policies having to do with development are intimately related and where perhaps the most dynamic forces are to be found because of the specific problems of the city. In spite of an élite dominated by the capital, it is an overgeneralization to ignore the fact that lively patterns of politics exist within cities themselves, in the secondary range of cities below the capital level, which often center around the issues of betterment and economic development of the regions. Urban politics in Maracaibo, for example, is quite different from urban politics in Caracas. Also, urban politics in Monterrey or Guadalajara is quite different from that in Mexico City; those in Medellin, Cali, and Barranquilla differ from that in Bogota; those in Concepcion and Valdivia differ from that in Santiago; Mendoza and Tucuman from Buenos Aires, and Recife, Bahia, and Porto Alegre and a whole chain of other Brazilian cities from Rio de Janeiro or Brasilia. Then there is the city in the 20,000–50,000 category, which makes up a whole series of smaller strategic focal points having to do with resource development and in which there are political life and vitality with regard to modernization needs. Examples of these are Arica, Manizales, Popayan, Buenaventura, Ciudad Bolivar. There is potential political force in the system of such tertiary cities that should be understood. The force is latent at present; in fact, another name for Latin America is Latent America.

The third urban level is the *barrio*, in which we have a potential political force, and, through the techniques of community development being practiced in Venezuela, Colombia, Peru, and Chile, there have been demonstrations that indicate that these are, indeed, tiny crucibles for political action which could become grass roots of major urban reform. Local government is one objective of community development.

Latin American cities may be described as crucibles in which important political action toward modernization may be brewing; the reverse also can be said, that political processes in Latin America may well serve as a crucible to force the rebuilding of Latin American cities and the development of more rational patterns of urbanization on a regional and intergovernmental level, to accommodate the increasing population. The process, however, is not a one-way street from the top down. The forces of the élite are being countered by forces from the bottom up that draw their stimulus from the need for modernization. If these forces can be understood better in their relation to each other and to the potential for guiding development policy, then a practical way may be found for solving some of the problems.

As Browning stated in Chapter III, "Any leisurely accommodation to the process of urbanization in the Latin American countries is not possible." Three forces might be said to conspire to make urgent the prompt resolution of political conflicts in Latin America. One is the "survival of liberal aspirations" from the days of the early republics more or less unchanged, in spite of the "unhappy reality of dictatorships and military coups." This ideology conflicts with the traditional oligarchy over the contemporary trend of economic development. Another is the need for Latin America to adapt rapidly to conditions in the outside world, in which change also has speeded up. "Given the continuance of its life in an historical void, with plenty of time ahead, Latin America could 'now' bring to maturity the liberal society of the old type. But in the age of 'collectivity,' and in face of the need for rapid adaptation entailed by the speed of world processes, the old textbook prescriptions sound like ineffective patter." [56] The third force is the desire for economic integration with other Latin American countries at the same time that "the national integration of many of its countries is only just beginning to be completed and perfected." [57]

From Horowitz's formal remarks and the discussion, it can be seen that the source of Latin American political difficulties lies in its condition of urbanization without industrialization. Urbanization provides the means by which all the city's groups may be integrated into a unified whole that resolves its difficulties through institutions and compromise rather than through upheaval. What seems to be lacking at present for political devel-

[56] José Medina Echavarría, "A Theoretical Model of Development Applicable to Latin America," in *ibid.*, pp. 47–48.
[57] *Ibid.*, p. 49.

opment in Latin America is the occupational mobility fostered by industrialization that would provide a channel for integration of aspiring groups, including the marginals, and at the same time modify the existing structures that now prevent their assimilation.

VII | *The Goals of* | *Urbanization*

Suggested Goals of Urbanization
Related to Modernization   Jorge E. Hardoy

ACHIEVEMENT OF NATIONAL INTEGRATION

Many efforts have been made in past years in the search for an operating system that would allow us to enlarge our markets and to strengthen a regional bloc, but there has not been a similar interest in bringing about and directing the structural changes that would back a steady growth. We seem to have definitively overcome the stage of discussion on the disadvantages of isolation and the advantages of commercial integration. But success of the latter will be doubtful and its unity will be difficult to maintain if the countries that form it do not reach basic national unification. So far, in the majority of cases, the existence of that indispensable unity, to make possible a common national effort so far as essential objectives are concerned, is still fictitious.

I think that as a rule we have lacked an idea that will prove the importance and necessity of a national common effort and then a realistic program that, backed by the indispensable administrative system and institutions, will set each nation in movement. When I analyze our past I feel that very often only power, used so frequently in the history of each of our countries, has avoided a greater dismemberment. But power will never be a solution over a long period, and the people, sometimes instinctively, try to find in balance and order the road that will allow them to reassert their free determination.

The absence of a national ideal, as a consequence of the frequent lack of direction and coordination and of well-defined objectives on all levels of government, has left our nations during long periods in such a state of confusion that political and administrative discontinuity is accepted without alarm by many groups. Nobody should be surprised, therefore, when fundamental institutions are concerned exclusively with their own interests even when they assume publicly and absolutely their identification with the destiny of the nation to which they belong.

What could the urgency be to advance toward unexplored and unexploited territories? How long will Brazil, Venezuela, Peru, Bolivia, Ecuador, and Paraguay be able to do without their interiors? How long will Argentina and Chile be able to do without Patagonia, Mexico without Chiapas, Yucatan, and Campeche; Guatemala without Peten, and so on? What alternative is there in each case? What would be the common benefit for Latin America of a coordinated effort directed to works of continental interest? Even simpler, what is there in those regions and how can they affect regional and even balanced continental growth?

Undoubtedly these are questions that require an integrated analysis. In many cases, its fulfillment is beyond the scope of the isolated effort of most of the nations involved. The integrating function and the symbolic value of Brasilia for Brazil, the geopolitical impact of the highway in the eastern regions of Peru, the great roads that connect the interior of Paraguay and Bolivia with the Brazilian and Argentine ports, the Panamerican highway, the big hydroelectric projects everywhere, Venezuela's regional conception establishing the enforcement of a great new pole of development in its Guiana, show that Latin America is advancing toward its own boundaries. And new centers of life, and a pattern of urbanization complementary to the existing one, no doubt will emerge as an expression of a new Latin America no longer tied to the limits of the past and seeking in the idea of integration the expression of its modernization.

I understand that the modernization of our countries cannot reach only limited areas and a reduced group of the population. There is a latent anxiety too powerful for decisions to be postponed. In one way or another, modernization must advance rapidly to the areas and to the groups that have been traditionally isolated. And the services and opportunities that at present are offered to very limited groups, and in very few cities, will have to reach the rural areas, too. There is an urgency for order that will enable our institutions to advance; there is a need for foresight so that development will come about steadily; there is a need for a broad national sense so that progress will reach all the regions of our countries; and, essentially, there is a need for a new spirit, a spirit of confidence in our men, in the riches of our territories, and in our common effort.

EFFECTIVE USE OF THE MATERIALS AT HAND

In many of our countries we need new ideas and a modern system of government that will be in charge of enforcing them. For that, a different attitude on the part of a generation that will express its convictions freely and without fear is necessary. It is not by attacking and destroying but by supporting and building that the modernization of Latin America will be accomplished. It is not simply by fighting the ideas of others but by expressing our own with firmness and clearness that it will be possible to understand how our countries, and Latin America as a whole, function. Because this knowledge and understanding of how each of our countries, and how Latin America, functions is one of the main tasks that lie before us. It is only by knowledge and understanding of our history and our culture, of our potentials and limitations, and of our human and institutional relations that we will be in a position to act and to reach lasting results.

We attending this symposium are linked by a common interest in urban development. We believe in the importance of an efficient urban life for the development of our countries. Our time is devoted to research, teaching, the spreading of knowledge, and, in some cases, to a direct action that, in different ways, influences the development of our cities. Our experiences are inevitably different but without doubt they represent contributions to the enlightenment of problems in our respective countries. This joins us together. Some of us have known one another for years and have even worked together in this union of interests. But I think that what has brought us closer is the understanding we share of the situation in our countries, of the weariness and frustration of some groups, and of the terrible poverty in which other groups live.

In the face of such experience, is it not, then, the moment to seek and make indispensable the dialogue and the collaboration among political leaders and technical and scientific groups? As urban, social, or economic planners, but essentially as people interested in the theory of our own disciplines, we understand the need for the political leader to reach practical results that will make an impact on our communities. It is not by judging others that we will develop the image of Latin America that each of us has, but by listening, respecting, and finding channels of continuous action. It is not by blindly adopting the solutions used in countries with a different psychology and an organization very different from ours that we should direct our institutions, but by analyzing and understanding the way of applying other strategic disciplines to our economic and social development, or by creating these disciplines when they do not exist, so as to set to work integrated plans for the development of each of our nations.

The second half of the twentieth century began in Latin America with the inevitable restlessness that originates in societies kept from the decisions that mold their lives. Recent changes have been caused mostly by the growing consciousness, on the part of the most numerous groups in the population, of their rights and of their possible mission in a new Latin America. The deep, unavoidable changes of the coming years will point out this epoch as a key period in the development of the ideas and institutions of Latin America, and will point out this generation as the one responsible for giving sense to those ideas and shape to those institutions. For in this dynamic, impatient world, increasingly conscious of the tools available to it, each generation has to examine and readapt its institutions and lawful tools and plan new goals. Each generation has the responsibility of finding its political orientation and of making it possible by applying the best scientific and technical knowledge at its disposal.

We lack national plans for higher education or plans for each university, just as we lack national plans and coordinated efforts that will guide scientific and technical research. Often it is said that one of the signs of maturity in a nation is the way in which its government uses its best scientists and technicians. But almost all Latin American nations, due to various circumstances, have experienced long periods during which the forced or self-imposed exile of some of their most talented people has been common.

The evolution of higher education in Latin America has been delayed by the lack of economic resources. But that is not, as is sometimes claimed, the main problem, which is, above all, a problem of orientation and of government, and then a problem of coordination and priorities. Except for a few isolated cases, in its present state, even a massive channelization of economic resources would only serve to extend the quantitative development of unnecessary careers with little benefit for the strategic ones. That is not the road that will lead us to bring the university structures up to the needs of a society in transition.

The same situation occurs in scientific and technical orientation. Scientific and technical research affects such a varied number of sectors that national governments should not disregard them but should rather promote their planification. Ideally, it would be convenient to promote basic and applied research in the most varied fields of knowledge, but for the time being, this is beyond the possibilities of each Latin American nation by itself. Perhaps it will be possible to coordinate a common action among institutions of different nations, and in this way originate an organization that will have not only coordinating functions but also will be a center of training, research, and documentation, projecting its action on those sectors in most urgent need. But for the time being, each country should establish its priority in higher education and research, taking into consideration the balance between needs and available resources.

My conviction is that the first and most urgent need is the study of our own problems. Greatest deficiency, overwhelmingly so, is in this field. Possibly, in countries like ours, some branches of medicine, physics, chemistry, and similar fields could wait. But the knowledge of the social and economic factors and of the human and natural resources, in the correct use of which lies the potential of our countries; of the institutional and legal organizations—in other words, of the factors that explain how each of our countries functions—that knowledge has a degree of urgency that cannot be postponed. Such knowledge cannot be carried across political boundaries. In each country and situation it acquires its own characteristics, which should be analyzed and understood in order to begin a policy of development with some probability of success.

Before the alternatives of dispersal or concentration, I consider that the obvious decision is to concentrate our efforts not only upon those fields of higher education and those branches of scientific and technical research which are essential because of their relation to the knowledge of our problems, but also to choose among them those that will make the greatest impact on our development and that could be used in programs with the best possibilities of success.

FREEDOM AND DEMOCRACY IN LATIN AMERICA

Personally I do not agree with those groups which seize the word freedom and accuse others of making the mistakes that they themselves have not been interested in avoiding or denouncing. In the same way I am not enthusiastic about those who talk of democracy but lack the energy to proclaim their own ideals and to back the institutions in which they believe. Freedom and democracy have almost always had, in Latin America, a doubtful sense and unfortunately appear to be the possession of those who have prostituted them the most. This tergiversation of values which should be of fundamental importance to our people, as to any people, is mainly the consequence of the isolation historically imposed in one way or another by those who have ruled our countries and who delayed the development of essential institutions. It is the consequence of the ignorance in which the most numerous groups have lived, thus postponing a knowledge of themselves and the possibility of an effective national and international integration. And, it is the consequence of the dependence, shown in many different ways and favored by corrupt governments, for generations, that has caused doubts and hesitations, to such an extent that even in our own countries there are groups who deny our own capacity to solve our own problems.

One of the greatest deficiencies of the present time in Latin America, as in the whole world, is our ignorance of regional and national processes of urbanization and of contemporary urban life. This is hard to understand, not only because of the importance of urban life in the patterns of distribution of income and in the potential social relations of groups disconnected so far, but also because of the crushing effect that having only one or a very limited number of cities has on the political, economic, and cultural activities.

THE GOALS OF URBANIZATION

I will try to show briefly how, in my opinion, the city and urban life could be effective in the modernization of Latin America. I think that the degree of effectiveness could be measured according to two scales. A *regional* scale, that will take into consideration the integration of large geographic and economic spaces into national and international settlement patterns, and an *urban* or urban-region scale that will produce elective occupational patterns, that will make institutional the changes of attitude, and that will make the rules and values of an industrial society meaningful to important groups of the population.

The positive contribution of the first scale has been scarcely hinted at. The contribution of the second scale is right now in full force, and the attraction of some of the large cities even goes beyond international boundaries. Both processes are being carried out spontaneously and possible alternatives have not been analyzed, much less introduced in the context of regional and national plans. In other words, in each Latin American nation the characteristics of its process of urbanization shows with a certain clarity its stage of development, but that process has never been submitted to policies of investment and social progress that would guide and improve it. And in the face of the efforts toward integration reflected by the discussions of a plan for regional investment for all Latin America, so far no analysis has been made of the impact that those investments will have on the future settlement pattern of the continent or of the functions that each of the principal centers in such a pattern will have to fulfill, or of other multiple derivations.

Of the two scales I have mentioned, it is the regional one, because of its continental implication, that will have the most lasting effects. But inevitably its effects will have to be awaited a long time. One of the missions of this generation is, then, to prepare the attitudes, to create and strengthen the political, scientific, and technical institutions so that the inevitable structural changes at a regional level will be made with balance, freedom, and order and with the urgency that the situation of the Latin American countries requires. It can be achieved through the conscientious national effort of each country, coordinated in the search for international goals, helped by the technical and financial resources that other powers might provide for those goals, on the basis of equality and not of a relation that involves the concept of developed-undeveloped. The common architectural, urban, and institutional tradition of the Spanish-American nations—Brazil is a different case—creates, superficially, great similarities in Latin American cities. But in their inner life, in the psychology of their inhabitants, and in their cultural heritage, Buenos Aires is as different from Lima as Mexico City is from Caracas, and Rosario from Guayaquil as Maracaibo from Monterrey. It is in smaller examples—in Popayan and Salta, in Potosi and Tunja, in Cajamarca and Corrientes—where there are still common points, such as the concentration of the wealth and economic power of the region in the hands of the aristocracy, and the stiffness of the social structure, all of them characteristic of a traditional society. These contrasts represent the coexistence in almost all of the countries, of industrial societies or societies in a stage of transition with others in which many of the values and structures of the colony still prevail.

I am not sure what the best territorial scheme of urbanization for Argentina, the country I know best, would be. I am sure it is not easy to determine, and I do not think, either, that it is easy in the countries where you live. Simply, I think we do not know enough. But the urgency of implementing solutions is so great that I am convinced of the possibility of making decisions that, within a short time, will improve aspects such as the ones I have mentioned as well as others. The goal is to develop a better type of urban life and a more efficient integration of the functions that should be assigned to each center in the national and regional plans. National plans, however, very rarely take the problem into account despite the traditional system of centralized decision-making existing in our countries.

I am worried, then, about how to improve the role of the city in this inevitable and irreversible process of urbanization which will continue, at least for some decades. It is evident, on the one hand, that our countries are not, and will not be for a long time, in an economic condition to face simultaneously the creation of necessary sources of work, to build houses and provide services, and to encourage the key institutions. Also it is evident that to encourage only some cities would mean to draw migration to them. The solution must be dealt with according to the two scales, and must take into consideration in both scales the possible deviations in the regional economies caused by future commercial agreements leading to an integration of Latin America. Accepting the necessity of reorganization in each country in order to balance the economic and financial situation of some regions with respect to others, one cannot expect that all regions in a country will get the same priority. But those that receive first priority will have to determine urgently the territorial and functional scheme of their urban centers. Even so, there will be, outside these regions with priority, urban centers with strategic value for national development, as, for example, the centers of the oil, steel, petrochemical, and other basic industries, the principal ports and centers of transportation, and the leading administrative and cultural centers. Because of their functions they are natural centers of in-migration and all efforts would have to be concentrated in them.

Some measures could be adopted nationwide and be used in an urban scale or an urban-region scale to establish the basis for better functioning: to control the land market, to build up basic utilities, and to develop public transportation; but, essentially, to embark on a massive program of technical, professional, and scientific education that will prevent possible strangling of economic development, to create new sources of work, and to encourage the formation of institutions and elements that will facilitate the integration of the different urban groups.

Planning

GLENN H. BEYER

A laissez-faire policy of urbanization has handicapped the city in performing its integrative functions. Other problems stem from the distorted economic development which may have over-emphasized the importance of a few large cities, and from the survival of outmoded political and economic institutions and attitudes which have tended to support the status quo rather than act as forerunners of change. The results are apparent in high primacy, deterioration of the urban environment, and the living and other conditions in the city from which the migrants have to extricate themselves, usually without help. As Neira suggested, the values that came out of this system are mostly negative and operate against development:

Most of the historical values are not favorable for development. The historical and traditional values work against development; they are negative values that pose important obstacles for development. Paternalism, conformism, endurance of injustice, caste systems, do not have positive values for development. All these values should be taken into consideration when economic development is considered as a means of social change. Historical and traditional values are negative values for development and it is our duty to overcome such obstacles.

Historically, both the Spanish and Incas used the city to further the progress of the country, according to Morse:

The elaborate ordinances for planning colonial towns emanated from a broad social and political philosophy to organize the settlement of a hemisphere. Far from being static design, the urban chessboard was a radiating center of energy—visible symbol of an adaptive social structure, an intricate system of acculturation, and a regulated process of territorial appropriation and economic development.[1]

For the present-day city to play a leading role in the modernization of Latin America, planning directed toward well-defined goals is held to be a basic requirement. This subject, as might be expected, received marked attention throughout the conference.

NATIONAL PLANNING

The chief criticisms leveled against planning as it had been conducted until recently in Latin America related to its lack of results in economic development, social integration, and in achieving stability in the political realm. The benefits of economic development had not been spread throughout the national societies, and social change had been left to occur more or less as a by-product. With a few exceptions, much of the planning had given attention to local issues only and the interrelation between rural and urban issues and problems had, to a large extent, been neglected. Rather than being used to improve the countries, the cities themselves were in a critical state—and, in some areas, no plans existed to counteract their steadily worsening situation.

Some of the trouble was believed to lie in the structure of planning. In general, physical planning in Latin America has been characterized by: a concentration of planning programs in larger cities, and in capital cities in particular; serious deficiencies and bottlenecks in basic urban facilities in the metropolitan areas; urban plans not integrated with regional or national plans for either economic or social improvement; and planning beset by problems of "rural-urban balance, equitable distribution of limited urban services to various sectors of urban population, long-run versus short-run considerations, and priorities to be assigned

[1] Richard M. Morse, "Recent Research on Latin American Urbanization: A Selective Survey with Commentary," *Latin American Research Review*, I, 1 (Fall, 1965), 61.

to the many pressing needs." Further, planners are hampered by "low income levels, rapid population growth, ill-conceived housing criteria, monetary devaluation and rent controls." [2]

Though the situation and problems differ from country to country, the general situation was considered to stem from a failure to analyze the economic potential of a country or an area and to use the urbanization process to further it—with a resultant waste of effort and resources. "Obviously," Andrade stated, "we have not been investing in the right things." "What is needed," another participant added, "is an urban policy that will increase productivity, by the use of urban institutions and within our limited capital resources."

The ideology of planning for development in Latin America comprises acceptance of active participation by national governments in the planning process, with plans to be implemented by both private and public investment.[3] National planning by governments is necessary in order to allocate resources in such a way as to bring about rapid economic growth. One reason is that a fully free-market system has not developed in several Latin American countries. Another is that the free-market system cannot, of itself, be relied on to make the investments required for *rapid* and *balanced* economic development with relatively scarce capital. "The assertion that Latin American progress depends on government planning is based on sound economic theory. Rapid development in underdeveloped countries cannot occur unless there is balanced development . . . progress in a

[2] Philip M. Hauser, ed., *Urbanization in Latin America* (New York: International Documents Service, Columbia University Press, 1961), pp. 61, 79–80.

[3] Under the terms of the Charter of Punta del Este for the Alliance for Progress, Latin American governments are committed to preparing comprehensive national plans for social and economic development. The active participation of the private sector is to be encouraged, and guided under the national plans in such a way that "new perspectives for the benefit of the community" will be opened. For discussion, see John P. Powelson, *Latin America: Today's Economic and Social Revolution* (New York: McGraw-Hill, 1964), p. 254.

variety of industries is needed even to create the market on which the development of any individual industry depends." [4]

As pointed out frequently during the conference, Latin America has to plan in order to avoid repeating the mistakes of the developed countries, where development took place more slowly than is desired for Latin America. The present state of undeveloped resources in Latin America is not considered to permit the waste that accompanied the haphazard development, for example, in the nineteenth century:

If development is slow, as it was in the United States in the nineteenth century, the errors of such individualism are minimized, for the external conditions on which the entrepreneur bases his decisions are not much changed for many years. If growth is fast, as is contemplated for Latin America, an entrepreneur who bases his calculations on what he sees about him at the moment is apt to be fooled some years hence. . . . But if his enterprise fits into the framework of a national plan, those entrusted with the overall direction of the economy will already have taken these factors into account.[5]

The broad program of social and economic development envisioned for Latin America requires the support of the governments. Private investment is not attracted to the large social investment needed in transportation, communications, power, and the like, that still have to be supplied for future economic growth, nor, at least through direct investment, in the educational, health, and other social facilities that will be needed to supply a skilled and trained labor force for industrial growth.

Development also entails deciding between alternatives, which should be done by the governments. "It is clear," Astica stated, "that the deep differences between the two alternatives of growth poles and compacting development is related to the economic and social structure of a country and what it is considered desirable to do with that structure."

[4] William Withers, *The Economic Crisis in Latin America* (New York: The Free Press of Glencoe, 1964), p. 79.
[5] Powelson, *op. cit.*, p. 9.

Only integrated planning can provide and direct the efforts needed to change the conditions that are creating, or contributing to, urban problems.

Arguments against governmental participation in development, briefly touched on during the conference, center chiefly around the issues of (1) direct state investment in enterprises and (2) neglect in carrying out the usual governmental functions of protection of property, collection of taxes, and the like. Government investment in an enterprise that does not succeed spreads a loss throughout the whole economy rather than confining it to a few entrepreneurs, it is argued. Also, if governments carried out their normal obligations, more private investment might be attracted into fields that now are shunned.[6] There was, however, little quarrel with the thesis that national planning required active support and participation by national governments.

INTEGRATION OF SOCIAL AND ECONOMIC OBJECTIVES IN PLANNING

Experience with economic development in Latin America to date has made it apparent that under today's social and economic conditions some social factor can operate to nullify the results expected from even the most carefully drawn plans. Realization of this has led to emphasis among Latin American countries on including certain social goals in economic development plans. In another source, the several objectives that should be included in social policy have been summarized as follows:

Since economic development would cause some sharp alterations in social patterns it should be accompanied by measures of alleviation to relieve the social costs resulting from economic change. Structural modifications were required in the agrarian systems, even at the cost of a short-term decline in productivity, and economic, social,

---

[6] For a statement of arguments similar to these, see George Jackson Eder, "Urban Concentration, Agriculture, and Agrarian Reform," *The Annals of the American Academy of Political and Social Science*, CCCLX (July, 1965), 27–42.

and cultural inequality between rural and urban areas should be reduced even at the expense of the current urban position in large cities. The support of the people should be sought for development policies, and social mobility as well as occupational and physical mobility should be encouraged to aid development. The juridical systems of various countries should also be reviewed from the standpoint of increasing social stability and developing a spirit of confidence and equity. In the field of political organization it was thought that the representative character of the political process should be widened, and the scope of political participation by the population at large be extended, and the formation of a stable and responsible middle class should be a major objective of economic as well as social policy.[7]

Introducing social aspects into economic development plans, however, is a phase of planning as yet practically unexplored. As Reiner remarked, "The problem as stated is how to harness the energies urbanization releases and channel them into a population distribution that is good—politically, economically, and socially. Except that no one knows for sure how to do this."

"Social planning must be given more emphasis in Latin America," Padilla observed, "and Latin America may have to pioneer in development techniques in order to do this." There are very few guidelines. In an earlier analysis of the problem, Higgins suggested that the search for a theory generally applicable to all countries undergoing development be abandoned in favor of concentrating on the "development process as it occurs in particular countries—or at least particular regions, such as Latin America—at the present time." Economists could subject "theories cast in terms of traditional variables" to "further empirical testing in a variety of environments," and could construct new models of development "in which sociological, psychological, and political variables are added to traditional economic variables

[7] H. M. Phillips, "Conclusion," in *Social Aspects of Economic Development in Latin America*, II, by José Medina Echavarría and Benjamin Higgins (Paris: UNESCO, 1963), 255–256.

289

as part of a single theoretical system," which later could be "econometrically tested." [8]

It seems clear, at any rate, that two of the most important aspects in the initial stages are the selection of the social goals that should be included in the development plans and the assignment of values to the social measures. Considerable differences among Latin American countries can be expected at this stage, in view of their different resources, levels of development, and particular problems.

One recommendation is that the social measures selected for emphasis be keyed to the two principal objectives of economic development:

In most of the Latin American countries, there can be no satisfactory solution to the major urban problems without a considerable rise in income levels and in productivity, and it is clear that the priorities given to different social measures should depend to a large extent on the contribution they can make to progress toward this goal. Attempts to apply advanced social policies under present conditions of mass poverty and limited public funds are likely to lead to types of action that are wasteful and almost irrelevant to the real needs: (a) small-scale "show-piece" projects that meet high standards but serve only a small and relatively well-off group of people; (b) the creation of elaborate administrative apparatuses that cannot carry out their ambitious terms of reference because their funds are barely sufficient to pay their own personnel; (c) systems of financing social services by taxing the poor who are to benefit from them and that may take more from the poor than is returned in services.[9]

The values assigned by any society to social goals, are, Higgins stated at the conference, included in the concept of per capita income:

Per capita income is merely a convenient summary of all the factors that are of importance to people in any society. The purpose of

[8] Benjamin Higgins, "An Economist's View," in *ibid.*, pp. 247–248.
[9] United Nations, Bureau of Social Affairs, "Some Policy Implications of Urbanization," in Hauser, *op. cit.*, pp. 295–296.

economic development is to improve allocation of resources so as to give people what they want, and it is important to know where the market price structure does not reflect accurately the relative values people place on various things. This is one of the most difficult aspects of development planning, to recognize where market prices are inadequate and decide what other values should be attached to a particular thing. This requires an interplay between the professional planner and the politician who has to make the ultimate decision. Probably it is necessary to think in terms of phases of development, provided that development is given a broad enough definition, that is, everything of importance to the people of a country has to go into the definition of development. Before starting planning, ideally it would be desirable to have a decision, objective, or practice that would set forth clearly all the objectives of the government concerned, with respect to income and employment, and to the balance of payments and the redistribution of income from one region to another and from one group to another. If such things as national security and national prestige, and the retention of traditional cultural values are important, those, too, have to go into the definition—they are part of the national income. We cannot evaluate any development policy without knowing what the people of the country really wanted from it. One of the secrets of planning in conjunction with politicians is to find out the relative weight of these objectives. There is danger in thinking in terms of phasing and priorities and time; danger, for example, in neglecting housing and education, unless you are well aware of the value of such sectors in terms of their contribution to productivity for other services and also in terms of their direct contribution to welfare.

IMPLEMENTATION OF PLANS

To state the obvious, neither economic nor social goals of planning, however carefully defined and provided for, can be attained until, and unless, the plans can be implemented. Comments on the political aspects of planning made at the conference may be summarized as follows: There is sufficient professional talent available in Latin America for rational planning. The question is not planning, but, rather, how to implement the plans, who will implement them, and who has the political power required to implement them. Politicians as a group (with several individual exceptions) are unaware of the importance of social integration along with economic planning. Their solutions to problems usually have been more or less impromptu devisings intended to please either as many people as possible or the most clamorous groups. The city is a severe test of political action for both planners and politicians, and many technicians in urban planning have suffered from adverse decisions made for political reasons.

The situation, of course, is not peculiar to Latin America. Some of it arises from the nature of politics. Uneasy partnerships are formed, that depend on devising a mutually advantageous course of action. The situation, perhaps, is made worse in Latin America because of the need for economic development, which requires attitudes and practices at odds with the traditional political attitudes and practices in the countries:

Under an economic development programme, specific requests, or pressure on behalf of solutions to the liking of those concerned, have to be met as impersonal principles decree, and, consequently, no political or economic capital can be made out of the action taken by the authorities. Again, the Latin American leader must shrink from the idea of a long and arduous process of persuasion and negotiation such as would be entailed in securing the voluntary acceptance of an economic development programme by all, or the most important, of the sectors, public and private, which it might affect. And he may well find even less to attract him in the prospect of having to force it on an unwilling minority.[10]

Other factors are the insecurity of the groups holding political power, as discussed in Chapter VI, the survival of rural paternalistic attitudes in urban groups, and the absence of political

[10] Daniel Cosío Villegas, "Programmed Economic Development and Political Organization," in *Social Aspects of Economic Development in Latin America*, I, Egbert De Vries and José Medina Echavarría, eds. (Paris: UNESCO, 1963), 252.

power and leadership among the urban middle classes who stand to gain the most, economically and socially, from development planning. Coupled with these is the highly centralized planning structure, usually in urban areas, with its immediate focus on the inescapable urban problems, responsibility for project plans scattered through a number of governmental bureaus, and a lack of coordination or of "the institutional framework . . . to induce or to compel joint planning and execution." [11] Padilla summarized the difficulties: "Planning in all urban areas should be institutionalized. Most governments are weak and should be provided with better technicians and better financing, and, above all, with a planning system properly staffed, to work through all levels of government."

Some of the structural impediments are being attacked, under the direction of the Economic Commission for Latin America and with the help of professional public administrators.[12] During the conference, some feeling was expressed that planners should take the initiative themselves for planning and for implementing the plans. Jordán expressed this sentiment: "In the absence of political leadership or interest, planners should take the initiative themselves to plan. It is no longer enough for them to continue to say that they are outside the decision-making process or have suffered from political decisions."

Indeed, Violich suggested, instead of comparing Latin America with an ideal (which may not exist anywhere), greater optimism for the future of planning could be generated by comparing it with its situation in the recent past:

In the past twenty years, the potential for making policy has changed greatly. At one time, decisions were made entirely by the international market, which brought about the concentrations of population. Even up to recently there was no field of economics or urban sociology. So Latin American countries have come a long way

[11] Herbert Emmerich, "Administrative Roadblocks to Co-ordinated Development," in *ibid.*, p. 350.
[12] *Ibid.*

technically in understanding the nature of the problem. Also, they have come a long way in government: in most countries there is some agency attempting to find ways of looking at the problems of development as a whole. The whole field of economic development was brought to life virtually out of nothing in Latin America in the past decade or so, even though lack of coordination, instability of some governments, and bureaucracy at national and international levels remain.

Planners thus can expect to find it more and more possible to work within the system. They might, Violich went on to suggest, find it advantageous to put themselves in a position where they influence political action by pointing out alternative courses of action:

The resources for implementing policy are good, and more and more technical work is going into decision-making. National budgets are being made up every year. So choices between various expenditures can be pointed out. Money could be spent, for example, in building houses in Lima, but the same money could also be spent to build a highway on the other side of the Andes, by means of which a whole chain of small cities could be built. Another example would be the probable impact of economic integration on the present Spanish pattern of urbanization in Latin America, cities with undeveloped interiors, that is, on the hollow shell.

This is how we need to think: be prepared to point out all the possible alternatives. In order to change the urbanization pattern of Latin America during the remainder of this century, we need to look over the available resources and have the highest priority given to projects that appear to have the most desirable pattern.

RECOMMENDATIONS FOR FUTURE PLANNING

Considerable discussion centered around methods by which planners could meet the obligation of coordinated, integrated, and national planning. Reiner spoke on the development of coordination between regional and national planning, and offered a comment on attaining social objectives:

The conference has not given much consideration to the desirable degree of decentralization of planning—this issue is important now in national economic planning. What can urban planners learn from national planners in terms of development? Three things: (1) The economic (national) planner has a theoretical discipline in the conceptualizing of planning problems; he identifies objectives, constraints, and relations, and the instruments he can control, and identifies desirable levels of performance for these. Urban planners should do likewise. (2) The economic planner knows the importance of working with a limited set of instruments and controls and of mixing incentives, free-market operations, planned and unplanned sectors in order to achieve goals. He recognizes that he cannot control everything. The urban planner seeks complete control and management—which is time-wasting. (3) The national planner expresses plans in terms of fairly precise indices of performance; the urban planner does not. Consequently, it is more difficult to evaluate urban plans, either in making a choice between alternative plans or in assessing a plan's effectiveness after it has been put into operation.

The urban planner needs (1) a change of approach and (2) guidelines and information. Two of the latter can be furnished by the national planner: a policy on urbanization and a policy on regional allocation of investment clearly related to the urbanization policy. At present, allocation decisions, if made by planners, relate to sectors without much reference to location; the regional allocation criteria have political overtones, and also have considerable impact on urbanization in various regions.

The national planner can learn from the urban planner: (1) the specific physical and resource restrictions of areas; (2) an understanding of working with nonlinear facets of planning, that is, with agglomeration economies and diseconomies; and (3) verification of certain components of a national policy, for example, the effects of plant location sites on local employment, which is essential in understanding interregional mechanisms and studying feedback effects.

One direction that could be called social planning is the technical analysis of societal objectives: to identify compossible objectives for a society and study the consequences of pursuing them. This would provide other values and goals for the economy and society besides maximum system output.

To some extent, planners should be better prepared for the environment in which they expect to practice, through better training methods in colleges and universities. More comprehensive training is necessary than is presently being received. Higgins in Chapter IV makes a number of positive and significant suggestions concerning planning.

It was felt by some that the emphasis being placed on national planning should not override urban planning to the detriment of the latter, and that attention to urban physical planning might help in solving some of the larger problems. In this connection, Wilson Garcés stated: "We have discussed the economic problem, the social problem, and even have had a highly sophisticated discussion of politics, but we have not said anything about the morphology of the city, a subject architects know most about since they have been trained in design and in how to manipulate and change the spatial order. Design may help solve some of the problems of urbanization."

"One of the great strengths in Latin America," Burnham Kelly stated, "is the way in which form and design are used, and this strength represents an important asset of its cities. There are aesthetic values in urbanization that have not been mentioned specifically, possibly because architects take them for granted."

Latin America might have to look to the future for inspiration in its urban planning, in view of the results of the general lack of foresight in city planning that are evident in most large cities today throughout the world. Not only in Latin America, but in all countries, the cities of tomorrow can be expected to be different from the cities of today, though their form and services and functions are scarcely imagined at the present moment.

Planners also should be careful not to confuse the separate objectives of short-range and long-range planning. Neira remarked that two separate criteria were applicable, depending upon whether long-range goals were sought or only short-range targets. The two, he commented, were incompatible "on economic terms, as they might require action in opposite directions." Sánchez Baylón suggested that when short-range and long-range planning were undertaken simultaneously, the concepts outlined by Higgins in Chapter IV should be followed; that is, a budget prepared and a time schedule set up at the same time the plan is made.

SOME RESEARCH SUGGESTIONS

Throughout the conference it was frequently mentioned that one of the most serious handicaps for all types of plans was the lack of sound facts on which to base decisions. Of necessity, much of the discussion at the conference revolved around generally accepted statements that had not been tested. Lowdon Wingo, Jr., addressed himself to the situation and made some suggestions for research.

Growth and development are urgent, he emphasized, and we should accept them as facts of life. But there are vast areas of ignorance about the processes involved. Migration is an outstanding example: whether or not we can actually do anything to curtail it. In delineating some general areas of inadequate information, Wingo referred back to Higgins's paper. Higgins, he recalled, focused attention on the crucial economic processes at work creating the problems being considered. Rural-urban migration, for example, is one dimension of the changes in labor-force mobility taking place in developing countries. Around the year 2000, the Latin American population probably will be three times as large as it is today. It is, Wingo pointed out, hard to fully appreciate or deal with figures like that.

Given this rate of population growth and the need to change from an agricultural to an industrial society, the problem of migration is easily lost in the larger issues. The real question is how we react to dimensions of this size. Probably never before have policy makers been confronted with this kind of numbers, and with the kind of resources they have to work with.

Higgins also analyzed, Wingo continued, the problem and aspects of the dimensions of developmental dualism.

A characteristic phenomenon of developing countries, Higgins pointed out, is the coincidence of high primacy with developmental dualism. We have decided that high primacy is here, though we do not know what we are going to do about it. We have some ideas about trying to find patterns that are not high-primacy patterns. While it is useful, perhaps, to talk about the minimal size of cities in terms of being large enough to support large-scale industries, and so forth, this reflects an attempt to reach a point of view that large primate cities are an ill, and this we do not know.

Therefore, a useful contribution of a conference of this type is to suggest in a general way an agenda for research that will include the urgency of planners and the interests of social scientists. Elements that should go into such an agenda, according to Wingo, are the following:

1. Examination of the problems of migration within the broad concept of national labor-market analysis over a long period of time is necessary. We have some tools and theory to begin with this; we have suggestions that relative incomes make a difference in the rates and characteristics of migration flows among parts of the country; we have a framework of intervening opportunity, which seems to work pretty well in some contexts, that determines the destinations of migrants.

2. Studies of the economies or advantages of agglomeration and urbanization in large-scale cities are needed. There is no present body of substantiated knowledge on this. On the point concerning the general feeling that management people like to live in cities—we may, for example, find that such people are metropolitan-minded, not just urban-minded.

3. Another issue is to determine the actual cost picture of various sizes of cities and various organizations of the urban

sectors. There is no body of knowledge on this. We have been arguing about whether big cities are more costly than small cities, but cost minimization is not the real policy issue; if it were, we would only have to find the cheapest kind of city and build it everywhere. Developmental strategy, however, should be keyed to the size and scale of the city that is most productive in terms of its contribution to the gross national product and the rate of growth of the economy. Such a scale of the city and such conclusions likely will depend on the industrial mix or industrial composition of the country; on the scale or kind of technology used; and on many variables that have not been mentioned here. A number of suggestions were listed for consideration. Urban services, for example, are not of the same character —some, like education, are expensive in small cities, and some, like water supply, are expensive in large ones. We have to define the services being talked about before generalizing on differences in cost in cities of different sizes. We have a choice in the quality of services and in the scale and level of services to be provided. We have imported North American viewpoints on what these standards should be, and when they are priced in the context of what developing countries can afford, they become unattainable. U.S. standards cannot be afforded in Latin America.

4. Studies are needed on the institutional aspects of dualism in developing countries. Research in North America is only loosely related to this. We have been able to see the institutional mechanisms that operated to permit our regions to converge over a period of time in terms of per capita income. The real question is: What happened to these similar mechanisms in Latin America or what are the imperfections that created dualism? We need to know more about the way capital flows take place between parts of the country in job-producing enterprises, and for this we should observe many things outside the experience of the U.S.; for example, the way in which industrial location processes take place in developing countries. (We have one process that applies in the United States, but probably we cannot do the same

thing in Latin America. There we must relate the theory to the institutional framework existing in Latin America and introduce Latin American parameters in the variables.)

5. We need to know how the public economy functions in developing countries. There has been discussion about levels and costs of public services. We could view the government as an enterprise-producing public service within a quasi-market context and ask how it functions within this market. What kind of relation does it have to the consumer? What kind of parameters regulate the output or quality of public services to consumer needs? We do not know much about this in developing countries, but we continue to make decisions about levels of public services and kinds of social organization and urban organization as though we had perfect knowledge.

To Wingo's list, Reiner added the necessity to study population flow: a system of panel samples of the population, to be followed through their migrations and through their changing positions in the economic and social systems. Probably the most challenging basic question raised by the conference is: What is the nature of the cityward flow, what is its magnitude, and what are its prospects?

Little is known about the effect of the physical context to which migrants and the industry come and the influence it has on their interaction. Strongly recommended, therefore, is a solid study of (1) the physical structure and growth of Latin American urban areas and (2) the relations of this structure and growth to the social-economic-political phenomena of urban areas.

There was considerable feeling at the conference that planners should immediately become more involved in decision-making processes. The present situation calls for action. Current problems will not wait for the ideal solution. Sanabria's paper, in the Appendix, includes some significant remarks pertinent here. Several participants expressed the thought that it is the duty of planners to take part in the development process, to guide it, if possible, but at the least to be active members of their societies. Quoting Hardoy:

When I analyze the most urgent obligations and responsibilities of this generation, my generation, I can find but one answer, very simple yet truly complex: to act. And to act means to participate openly, with frankness, conscious of the great probability of making mistakes, even of confusing the means and the ends, but showing with actions and words each one's position whenever necessary. Not hiding, but exposing constructively, the realities of my country and of others, with the conviction that solutions to our problems will only come when we participate in the creation of a more worthy and just society.

None of this meant, however, that a great deal more knowledge is not needed. Research of the type mentioned above (which admittedly represents a highly inadequate listing) should be undertaken to solve some of these problems, and Wingo even suggested that "research has to be undertaken now in order to know what should be done for the year 2000 in Latin America."

VIII | *Résumé*

Themes and Issues

GLENN H. BEYER

Today the city in Latin America faces the challenge of rapid growth. The problems this growth is bringing are so great and solution of them is so urgent that they tended constantly to divert the deliberations of a conference which had as its objective to focus on the positive aspects of the city in the process of modernization. On the other hand, the outstanding issues discussed and the themes delineated were not of the conventional "problem" character.

STRUCTURE AND ECOLOGY OF LATIN AMERICAN CITIES

The structure and growth patterns of Latin American cities are important since they define the physical environment within which social and economic interactions, which were the primary focus of the conference, take place. Because the differences among the cities resulting from their individual histories, functions, hinterlands, and other factors are sometimes great, generalizations are unsafe, and there are many exceptions to any one pattern. Nevertheless, a brief summary of a growth pattern rather common to many Latin American cities is being made at the outset of this chapter in order to provide some general information on the physical surroundings and their effect on the urban area.

In general, the principal cities of Latin America were established as points of contact between the mother country and the resources of the continent. Their sites were therefore selected, insofar as possible, on the basis of this objective. Aside from considerations of defense, other factors, such as a topography favorable for physical growth, received little attention. A few cities, of which Caracas is the best example, have serious topographical drawbacks to physical expansion on the scale required by their present development.

The Spanish settlements were urban from the beginning, and the cities were political as well as economic units. The area of jurisdiction of one city often stretched out to the area governed by another. The city was the center of government, economic activity, and culture. Actual power, however, lay in the ownership of land, minerals, and control of the Indian populations. A base of limited resource development thus was rooted in rural control, though such control was exercised in the cities. Trade with Spain was a principal function, if not the only function, of the colonial cities. Trade among continental cities themselves was restricted. Cities grew more or less in isolation from one another, and all looked to Spain as the main sponsor of their wealth and power.

Essentially, this situation continued after independence, the chief difference being a wider range of trade with other countries. With the land all allocated at the beginning of the settlement, with retention of landownership by the same families (encouraged by political and social sanction), and with such competition as might arise absorbed by the dominant group, it is not surprising that there was little actual change throughout Latin America for several centuries. The conditions of trade—the chief source of income—supported the situation. The principal cities, usually the capitals, grew, but urban growth in most countries was limited for centuries to one or two large cities.

In all countries, cities are often the point of contact with the outside world, the central source of political power, the place where social change occurs, the reservoir of skills and professional talents, and, usually, the place where investments are concentrated. In Latin America, cities generally serve these same functions, but they are more handicapped in a number of ways than in other Western countries. They are the chief support of national integration, to the extent that it exists in opposition to pressures against it. Economic, social, and cultural dependence, however, hampers the effectiveness of Latin American cities as a medium of social interchange. Some innovations have been accepted by the society; others have been rejected. More important, however, is the fact that the attitudes and values that accompany the innovations imported from industrial countries have been strongly resisted. Thus, the occupational prestige scale of the industrialized countries has not been fully accepted, science and technology have had difficulty in gaining footholds, and, in general, only the values that support an established way of life have been sanctioned. So long as wealth and power have been based on landownership rather than on commerce and industry, cities cannot operate to redistribute political, economic, and social power widely throughout the countries. Social change is apparent in most of the cities, but access to sources of mobility is still a limited privilege. One result is that investments and skills have remained highly concentrated in a few large centers. The relative importance of various urban functions and of various urban groups is clearly reflected in the pattern of city growth.

We have seen that an urban pattern for the Spanish cities of Latin America was carefully devised by the Spanish rulers and set forth in the *Law of the Indies*. (To a large extent, the patterns and growth of Brazilian cities have developed along lines similar to those of the Spanish cities, and in response to the same cultural forces and attitudes.) With surprisingly few modifications, the same pattern was used throughout the continent. A *plaza mayor* (central plaza) was laid out, around which the important government and religious offices were housed, with surrounding lots assigned to the founders. Streets were laid out from the main square in a gridiron pattern, which facilitated the distribution of lots and provided for future expansion. As cities grew, and more streets were occupied, frequently space was set aside for squares and open spaces along them. The main square was a social meeting place, a promenade, and an entertainment center, where games and sports were played, besides being the economic and political center. The desirability of residence was in relation to its closeness to the main square of the central city. The scope of desirability was limited to being within walking distance, for obvious reasons, or about a radius of a mile from the plaza. Selling land was discouraged and not socially sanctioned, a condition that led, as the open spaces filled in, to extensive new subdivision to provide for the later settlers. The Indian population was assigned to a *cercado*, usually outside the city walls, from which it had access to both the city and the mountains or agricultural regions. With growth, in most cities, *barrios* replaced the *cercados*, beginning within a mile of the central plaza. Each *barrio* usually had its own plaza, church, shops, and also its own governing council, and sometimes an indigenous language.[1] The *barrios* were separate and distinct from one another and their relations were conflictual and competitive rather than cooperative. None had access to the urban facilities and amenities of the *plaza mayor*, which was reserved exclusively for the upper classes. There were, of course, variations on this main pattern, which developed in response to various environmental factors. Lima is typical of the planned city, with relatively slow and stable growth. La Paz, on the other hand, grew rapidly, in response to economic forces—expansion of silver mining, and so on—and without much direction, a dynamic but haphazardly developed city that absorbed more and more functions, including, finally, the function of government. In Mexico City, the Spanish plan was laid out over the remains of an indigenous city, with narrow, winding streets as well as a gridiron.

[1] Asael T. Hansen, "The Ecology of a Latin American City," in E. B. Reuter, ed., *Race and Culture Contacts* (New York, 1934), pp. 124–142; quoted in Richard M. Morse, "Recent Research on Latin American Urbanization: A Selective Survey with Commentary," *Latin American Research Review*, I, 1 (Fall, 1965), 49.

In spite of minor variations from the Spanish plan, however, segregation by residence was a characteristic feature of practically all the more important cities. Since basically the structure of the economy and the sources of wealth did not change after the colonies became republics, a pattern of residential segregation continued as cities expanded. High-status residences were near the center of the city, less desirable residences farther out, and the least desirable around the periphery. Each residential area remained more or less self-contained, with its own privileges, rights, and activity centers.

To a large extent, this colonial pattern continues today, though with some changes and modifications and on a considerably more extensive scale. The rise of new wealth after independence and the industrial and commercial expansion in the nineteenth and twentieth centuries created a new wealthy class. This new class built suburbs in desirable locations farther out from the city—near beaches, on hills, or near and around other desirable, and usually exclusive, topographical features. Practically every major city has such developments of beautiful residential areas, several of which were cited in Chapter I. Whether in all cases suburban development resulted from scarcity of land in the central city or as imitation of suburban developments around other major Western cities is not entirely clear. A combination of factors undoubtedly operated. In any case, the social distance between the highly segregated groups remained glaringly evident. As might be expected, urban services tended to be provided for the central areas and wealthier residential areas first, and sometimes for them alone over a period of years.

A comparison between the usual course of development followed by other Western cities and the development of those in Latin America serves to point up some contrasting features. Though no one city fits into the model perfectly, it is generally accepted as typical.

Whatever theory of urban growth is followed, in general it may be said that the evolution of most Western cities shows a concentration of land uses and of population. This depends on several factors: availability of transportation, access to transportation, the economic ability to move; a centralization of functions focused around pivotal points of activity, to the extent that one activity is dominant; a decentralization of activities as population, commerce, and industry move and compete for choice land space; a segregation into like population units; and a specialization or concentration of like nonpopulation units. The process takes place through invasion, that is, the penetration of one area of use by another use, usually climaxed by succession, in which the invading use becomes dominant.[2]

In short, most Western industrialized cities have shown important changes in land use and concentrations of population, and their growth has been rapid. The pattern—regardless of whether in concentric circles around a focal point, along transportation lines radiating out from the city, or around several centers situated independently throughout the city—begins with a center of the city devoted to retail merchandising, amusements, finances, clubs, cultural centers, and similar activities, close to which is a wholesale light manufacturing district. This is followed by residences, the poorest being closest in and the highest quality being farthest out. Heavy manufacturing is ordinarily on the outskirts of major industrial cities, with a business district nearby, followed by residential and industrial suburbs and commuters' zones. Not all cities have all these elements, but, in general, as cities grow and their functions expand, segregation by land use tends to take place. Commercial, residential, and manufacturing operations become segregated in response to competition for choice sites and the tendency for like units to group together, for economic, social, and sometimes aesthetic advantage. There is a distinct separation between residential use and other uses, fortified in many United States and northern European cities by zoning controls. Invasion, with further expansion,

[2] Gerald Breese, *Urbanization in Newly Developing Countries* (Englewood Cliffs, N. J.: Prentice-Hall, 1966), pp. 108–114.

continues, and between most areas transitional zones are found, which have a high mix of land use and nonsegregated residential use. Areas of blight and poor housing frequently result in transitional or other zones when high land value is combined with a "low" use. Slums, clustered in the central cities, are conspicuous examples of this.

While not many Latin American cities have been studied in depth, available data indicate that only a few of the most highly developed ones show development that resembles the pattern described above. Over a long period of time, Latin American cities were characterized by a relatively stable population and economic growth, in the sense, at least, of not being subject to waves of high population influx in response to rapid industrial development. Because the manufacturing and industrial operations were of the light variety, such as processing raw materials, they fitted easily into urban locations. When "being in trade" became a means of increasing prosperity, many of the more important activities were taken over by the upper class, though, as stated earlier, a sizable group of "new" wealthy also grew up. Another factor is the manner in which competition was limited, made possible, in part, because the control of financing rested in the hands of the already wealthy. The centering of social life around the family made it convenient to continue to live within walking distance of both home and place of work. The high degree of segregation by residence, inherited from the colonial pattern, as well as the strong tendency to keep land within the family, also was a factor. Several cities, in addition, had a planned growth, with developments guided in directions that allowed for the greatest expansion. Some cities were partially destroyed by earthquakes, and the necessary rebuilding, or sometimes relocation, has played a part in keeping down urban deterioration. At the least, the possibility of such disruptions has had considerable influence on architecture in the cities affected, in keeping down building heights and keeping the central areas as much suited for residential as for other use.

Clearly, the pattern of landownership has a strong influence on the pattern of urban growth. Historically, in Latin America especially, landownership has been the source of political power, economic sustenance, and social prestige. In part, this emphasized trait was inherited from Spain, but it has been further strengthened by a general lack of other investment opportunities for capital. The early disinclination to sell land has continued, and much land, in some cities, is leased or converted to other use rather than sold. Often where land is sold, titles have not been recorded. In the absence of recorded sales of property or title registry (which are now being required in some Latin American cities), a study of property values in the urban areas is, of course, difficult. There are some indications, however, that the same relations operate with respect to land values as in other Western countries, that is, land use, its location, and historical or other associations related to it are considered. For example, downtown land and land in choice residential locations have high values, and land prices vary with other locations and use. Land speculation is conspicuous, especially in the more rapidly developing cities, since new developments and investments may increase the value of particular sites enormously. In many cities, the municipalities own large parcels of land, which aids them in controlling development. Idle land, however, whether publicly or privately owned, has served as a source of attraction for migrant settlers and contributed further to haphazard development.

Zoning as it is known in North America has taken only slight hold. A stigma which might be expected to result from the close association among residential, industrial, and commercial land uses frequently does not exist. Wealthy landowners in the nineteenth century sometimes used part of their houses in the central city for commerce and other activities without suffering loss of prestige or a decline in property values. The centering of family and social activities around inner patios has caused an indifference to the existence of nearby commercial and even manufacturing activities. Conditions of extreme crowding are known to exist along with this haphazard pattern of land use, particularly in many slum areas. Unfortunately, population and housing statistics in Latin American cities do not yet provide sufficient data on urban densities on any broad scale.

A large proportion of Latin American cities today exhibit characteristics that, in general, may be summarized as follows: (1) peripheral slums of squatter housing, as more and more migrants come to the cities and settle on the most available land; (2) greater "permanent" growth in central areas than in the outskirts; (3) a weakness of commercial concentration; (4) some upper-class residences near the center of the city; (5) absence of blight in connection with succession in land use; (6) stability of commercial enterprise and related activities; and (7) a concentration of professional skills and services in capital cities.[3] Land use throughout the cities shows a high mix with manufacturing and commerce and professional and other services scattered more or less haphazardly, and with little segregation of exclusive residential areas from other activities. In the absence of concentrated and specialized use, there is a comparative lack of intensive competition for choice land use. Consequently, invasion does not take place, no one use dominates an area, and there is little evidence of clear-cut succession of land use.

One result of the pattern is a serious damper on urban functioning in carrying out routine daily activities, as, for example, movement of people and goods. Streets are crowded downtown and at other points throughout the city. Daily movements of people to and from work, shopping, and the like, are carried out under enormous difficulty, and traffic is heavy throughout the day. Most cities have public transportation in the form of buses, but transportation systems designed to carry large numbers of people at one time have not, in general, been developed.

[3] See Theodore Caplow, "The Social Ecology of Guatemala City," in George A. Theodorson, ed., *Studies in Human Ecology* (Evanston, Ill.: Row, Peterson, 1961), pp. 331–348. This study also includes summaries of ecological studies made of other Latin American cities.

Much travel is on foot or by bicycle as well as by bus, and the extremely high proportion of travel that has to be done by privately-owned automobiles adds to the congestion. Some countries have limited the numbers of automobiles that may be brought in. The situation is further complicated by the presence of street vendors and of other commercial activities carried on along the streets.

There are signs, however, that the cities now are tending to develop the growth patterns of North American cities and to exhibit some of their problems, in response to twentieth-century pressures. For one thing, urban population growth no longer occurs at a rate that allows for easy absorption. The cities, in addition to their relatively high rates of natural increase, are being subjected to an intensive immigration from the rural areas. Economic progress, a developing society, and a more favorable attitude toward technological innovation also are having an effect on the pattern of city growth. Developments in transportation facilities and the extension of other urban services and amenities are important factors that make possible outward expansion. In some cities, while a few of the traditionally wealthy have retained residences near the central square, others have moved out to high-status residential suburbs. Latin American cities have not yet experienced the heavy rate of construction of high-rise luxury apartments witnessed in so many North American cities. High-rise public and private office buildings, however, with a concomitant specialization of functions, have become prominent features in downtown areas of several cities. Some cities have rebuilt their central areas, widened streets, and constructed broad boulevards, along which high-class residential areas may be found, more or less segregated from industry and commerce.

These responses to orderly and, frequently, planned growth have been in recent years rudely interrupted by the "onslaught of the land and the people against the city" expressed in the "phenomenon of the *barriada*." The key characteristic in the recent growth and present structure of Latin American cities is thus the overwhelming proportion of poor quality shelter—substandard "permanent" dwellings in the central city and "temporary" squatter housing on the periphery. This phenomenon has not lent itself to orderly and relatively slow absorption or to equally leisurely expression of it in the physical environment of the city. It is a determined invasion of enormous size and has exhibited a stubborn resistance to efforts to halt it, slow it down, or divert it elsewhere. To a large extent, when judged in the light of a world-wide trend toward urbanization, it may be looked upon as inevitable. In a number of ways, some subtle and some dramatic, its impact on urban culture is being felt.

POSITIVE FUNCTIONS OF THE CITY IN MODERNIZATION

Modernization may be defined as a fundamental social and economic transformation of a society. Urbanization is considered the process of population increase in cities, a process that eventually reaches the stage where it is irreversible and difficult to control. The positive aspects of the city, when compared with rural areas, arise from the city's larger population and greater density. These two characteristics make possible the organizations and facilities that give the city one of its striking advantages over the rural community. Greater division of labor is possible than in rural areas. The resulting higher specialization of labor, in turn, makes possible a greater variety of institutions and facilities. Not all of these are economic. Educational facilities, for example, are usually better and are more easily provided in urban areas than in rural ones, although they are difficult to provide at all. The educational level of urbanites usually is high compared with that of country dwellers. The city also provides the stimulus to attain a level of education high enough to meet the needs of the technology. Health levels are better in the city. Women find more opportunity for employment outside the home, and this helps to break down their tradition-bound training. People are more easily mobilized; hence, the growth of and participation in voluntary associations is easily facilitated, which has obvious advantages for political as well as social development.

For social integration, that is, the integration of individuals and social groups or categories into the various institutions of the modern national society, the city is a positive and vital force. The conditions for social integration are created by economic development through modifications in the occupational structure and changes in the quantity and composition of consumption patterns. Such modifications change the stratification system and involve mobility. There is greater occupational differentiation and a trend toward occupational upgrading through higher levels of education (structural mobility), enlargement of the middle strata (exchange mobility or increased fluidity in the stratification system), and access to goods and services by the lower strata ("psychological mobility" through the transfer of status symbols). When the majority of the population becomes affected, important changes take place in attitudes, relations, values, and norms. A minimum size and concentration of population are needed before this last step takes place; the intermediate sectors, for example, may become middle class when they reach a size sufficient to support a market for middle-class consumption. A similar transformation takes place in the lower strata when a certain size is reached.

Social integration occurs in the cities. Under any circumstances, all aspects of integration do not take place simultaneously. Social integration may lag behind occupational integration. Political integration may be delayed, or it may occur before the individual or group is integrated occupationally or socially.

The economic advantages of urbanization lie in the agglomeration of services found in urban areas, economies of scale made possible by concentration, external economies created for other activities by each new enterprise or service in the same city, and the urban atmosphere that attracts and retains managerial and entrepreneurial talent.

The significance of the city for political modernization, as compared with that of rural areas, is the creation of a need for coalition politics in place of *personalismo* and "total solutions for total problems." Because of the diversity of its groups and objectives and lack of concentrated power in any one group, the city encourages the exercise of power through political machinery and provides greater personal stability for its inhabitants; since they are enfranchised, city dwellers can participate in politics at least to that extent.

The negative aspects of the city relate more to the process of urbanization as it is taking place under existing urban conditions. The high fertility rate of the urban population in some instances is viewed as a negative factor in the modernization process. The causes of the rising urban rate of fertility have not been isolated; one explanation offered—that it is a transfer of rural attitudes and practices to the city—is open to question. Of itself, it seems clear that urbanization does little to change fertility rates, until attitudes toward birth control and large families have been modified. In this connection, it should be pointed out that the urban birth rate in all classes is currently fairly high. Countries with the highest population growth rates seem to be the ones that have least been able to transfer the labor force to urban-modern pursuits. The higher rate of population growth makes necessary a diversion of capital and resources from directly productive investment into urban and other services, housing, and facilities needed to take care of the population. It is a factor that contributes to regional dualism.

Less clear-cut is the question of whether rural migration to cities is a negative factor. The aspects that are usually considered negative for development are: (1) the volume of the migration, which inundates the cities and reduces their effectiveness; (2) the social characteristics of the migrants themselves, such as illiteracy, lack of skills, training, and experience; (3) the difficulties migrants are considered to experience in adjusting socially and psychologically to urban life. These factors are considered negative in that the urbanization taking place runs ahead of employment opportunities, adds to urban problems, and fosters traditionalism rather than modernism in the city. The type of housing and neighborhoods in which the migrants are forced to remain, because of a lack of anything better that they can afford, hampers the functioning of the socially integrative mechanism of the city. Class polarization persists with marginality. Marginal persons are not secure enough to challenge power groups; they are manipulated by one power group or another with promises of temporary alleviation of their situation.

There is no denial that all these deleterious effects exist. Some of the more highly publicized ones, however, are not inherent in city living, as reported. Upon close examination, the argument that the migrant is unable to adjust to the urban working environment does not seem valid. One preliminary study found few differences between the city-born and the migrants, except for the lower educational level of the latter group. This lower level did not make much difference between the two groups in income or occupational level, and on various standard-of-living indicators there was practically no difference. On a tentative basis, it may be stated that both the city-born and the migrant are undesirably low on several socioeconomic characteristics.

On the basis of available studies, the assumption that all migrants experience difficulties in adjusting to urban life is being re-examined. The general conclusion is that, while disorganization, anomie, delinquency, and other undesirable social characteristics are found among migrants, in many cases these result from a transfer of similar characteristics from the countryside heightened and reinforced by characteristics more or less peculiar to the urban neighborhood in which the migrants lived. Considerable evidence shows that many migrants find the city a more desirable place than their previous rural abode. In the political realm some analyses indicate that, where the migrants become industrial workers, the lack of class integration does not always cause unrest but rather leads the working class to support the middle classes in their early struggles for political leadership.

In the long run, migration can be considered a positive factor in the modernization process. The city has greater potential and greater variety for modernization than rural areas. Improvement in rural conditions is needed, and agricultural improvement is as essential for economic development as industrialization. But agricultural development means greater productivity from fewer people. The transformation of a society from rural to urban takes place only after the agricultural labor force undergoes an absolute rather than a relative decline. Migration is a necessary first step toward modernization at the present level of development in Latin America. Rural areas are not affected significantly by the integrative mechanisms of the city until a relatively advanced stage of modernization is reached, though they may be "mobilized" for integration through education and communications.

The first stage, then, is rural migration to cities, where migrants are exposed to mass media and prepared for participation, and, ultimately, integration. Urbanization makes possible the mass participation necessary for democratic politics. Rather than leading to social unrest, rapid industrialization with a minimum of transitional fissures tends to promote reform movements. Industrial classes tend to develop organizational solidarity, a sense of upward mobility, and to accept the tenet that specific class needs can be met under the theory of fair share and fair distribution. Industrialization provides the mechanisms for integration, but it is the city that provides the locale in which they can function.

URBANIZATION AND INDUSTRIALIZATION

Another negative aspect of the urbanization process in Latin America is that it has taken place without sufficient industrialization to support it. The cure for this lies in investments to accelerate the rate of industrialization (and, by implication, the rate of urbanization) rather than in investments to retard urbanization.

RÉSUMÉ

There is a growing conviction that industrial investment should be in large-scale, capital-intensive industry, since this has particular relevance for underdeveloped countries with respect to diffusion of technology, creation of jobs, linkage, and other factors that form the basis of an industrialized society.

Industrial employment facilitates social integration. One condition necessary for social integration is balance between the rate of occupational absorption and the rate of mobilization. Employment in white-collar jobs out of proportion to the degree of economic development does seem to originate the same psychological and social results as employment in industry. Excess employment in the pseudo-tertiary, however, does not originate much deep-seated change in the situation or attitudes of the migrants. Hence, marginality persists after the arrival of the migrant in urban areas. Other factors related to the persistence of marginality are type of neighborhood, a low level of modernization in the city, the size and concentration of marginals, and adjustment of urban groups to the marginal population.

Industrial employment is essential for political integration as well. Work differentiation arising from the division of labor weakens the class polarization of political power. Rural-urban migration tends to remove political tensions from the countryside, under some circumstances. It may, however, operate also to transfer revolutionary tendencies to the city. Industrial mobility, that is, a move from rural-agricultural to urban-industrial pursuits, is a more reliable means of reducing the social and economic sources of discontent that support revolutionary tendencies than is geographic mobility alone.

Large-scale industrialization does not necessarily mean large-scale cities. The urbanization process can be manipulated through directed and coordinated planning to avoid some of its present negative aspects. The growth of individual cities can be facilitated or retarded by urban policy. Investment and attention should be concentrated on the most suitable city or cities for the situation in each country. The establishment of urban centers can be encouraged as integral parts of resettlement schemes. The agglomerative pull of the leading regions and the concurrent regression of the lagging regions can be overcome to some extent by investment in the lagging regions. Hence, the creation or stimulation of urban-industrial cities in lagging regions should be part of such investment plans.

The ultimate objective is a distribution of population that is best from the economic, social, and political standpoints. In some countries, depending on size, resources available, and level of development, this could mean encouraging the growth of the primate city. Other countries may have reached the stage of development where the growth of secondary and smaller cities should be encouraged. In either case, and particularly for smaller cities, an industrial base is all-important for the economic, social, and political benefits of urbanization to materialize. The growth of smaller cities should be linked to investment plans that include industries that will stimulate growth and technological development rather than small-scale industries, established for the purpose of absorbing excess labor, managed along traditional lines, and outside the mainstream of economic development.

ALTERNATIVES TO URBAN GROWTH

The overconcentration of migrants in a few large cities generally has been viewed as a negative aspect of urbanization. The central issue here is how to encourage urbanization without at the same time encouraging the growth of the large primate cities.

The primate city. Under what conditions may the primate city be considered a factor of national integration or when will it make difficult the equilibrated development and modernization of the various regions of the country?

On the positive side, the primate city has a concentration of scarce resources that, depending upon the size and resources of the country, can act as a greater stimulant to economic development than their dispersion among several cities; the position of such cities as centers of educational, technological, and social innovation may compensate for the costs of "overurbanization"; overdevelopment of a few cities may, of itself, bring pressure to hasten economic development, and the lack of balanced urban development also may be a positive factor in certain stages of the transition from traditional to modern.

On the negative side, the primate city with its high concentration of wealth, modern culture, and economic expansion is considered to have prevented the development of other regions and of the nation as a whole. Resources, both material and human, have been disproportionately concentrated in such areas; and migration has transferred conditions of unemployment and underemployment into the city.

Possibly the positive aspects of the primate city might receive more favorable attention if the deficiencies resulting from its spectacular growth were not so glaringly apparent and so well known. As it is, however, the negative aspects of high primacy receive considerably more attention than its positive aspects. Primate cities, it is held, are faced with problems beyond their capacities to solve, and these problems are not only housing, education, welfare, and other urban services, although these are serious enough in terms of cost. The primate city represents unwieldy agglomerations of population that will grow larger, absorb more resources, and continue to contribute to unbalanced development. While they grow, the development of other cities will be stifled.

Some of the difficulties of high primacy result from past neglect and lack of planning, or planning on too local a scale. More, however, come from the nature of past economic development. The cities are handicapped by economic ties to external economies and a general lack of industrial growth, which, in turn, results in lack of employment opportunities, little development of occupational diversity, poor distribution of income throughout the economy, and little incentive for the manufacture of consumer goods or the development of consumer markets. In the absence of other growth centers, rehabilitating the environment in the primate city is largely wasted effort, since subsequent migration will continue to undo any good that might obtain.

Much of the trouble lies in the factors that have brought on urban growth rather than in the size of the city per se. A deteriorating agriculture, uneven economic development, and economies dependent on trade in primary products for which markets are unstable would be likely, it is considered, to create urban problems regardless of the size of the city. In fact, with fewer resources, smaller cities might develop the problems faster and in more aggravated form. Conversely, if measures are adopted to industrialize the economies and to increase agricultural productivity, would the primate city be less likely than other size cities to benefit?

Optimum city size for development has not been and possibly cannot be definitively determined. Urban mechanisms for modernization, however, seem to require a certain concentration of population in order to function, and cities have to be large enough to support the large-scale industries needed for future economic development. Since economic opportunities are not the only attractions of the cities, they also have to be large enough to sustain the educational, recreational, cultural, and aesthetic ingredients that make up the intangible urban atmosphere that attracts and holds the skills and talents needed for development. Investments in smaller cities, without regard for noneconomic considerations, are likely merely to hasten migration to the larger centers.

Another point with regard to size is that several of the primate cities in Latin America, in spite of their rapid growth, are not yet excessively large. Their population is similar to that of middle-sized North American cities. Thus, their growth could be encouraged without serious danger of megalopolities developing. The size of the country also has important implications for high primacy. Where the national population is only five million to ten million, one large city may be sufficient, since the remainder of the country forms the hinterland for this metropolitan region. Such countries might easily have primate cities considerably larger than any of them now have.

On the all-important question of cost, the primate city represents an investment of resources that has already been made. In the current state of scarce capital and scarce resources, the existing cities, if only by default, already have the mechanisms for modernization. What is needed is to make operation of the mechanisms possible, by investments in development and in recruiting and training talent and skills, and in institutions that will be effective carriers of modernism. Attention and resources devoted to the national aspects of urban problems can do much to alleviate urban difficulties and make the city an efficient instrument.

Physical planning also enters into the process of making the primate city more livable. City growth can be expected in terms of metropolitan regions rather than of central cities, and this should be anticipated and planned for.

Dispersion of cities. A strong case can be made on its own merits for the dispersion of cities on a regional basis, regardless of whether or not dispersion effectively offsets the negative aspects of the primate city. The major economic trends in Latin America today—heavy industrialization, supranational economic integration, and resettlement programs to develop the interiors of the countries—indicate that secondary and smaller cities will be established and that those in existence, where favorably located, will grow. The trend toward heavy industrialization means resource development and the location of industries and cities near resources, transportation lines, and power sources. Favorably situated cities already are growing in response to the growth of trade and markets and development of resources in connection with economic integration and large-scale industrialization, and more can reasonably be expected for the future. As the functions of the cities change, some will grow and others will decline. The concern here is to direct investment insofar as possible to the localities where other growth will be stimulated, or where growth should be stimulated in order to hasten the integration of lagging regions. Enough of the secondary and tertiary cities should be encouraged to grow so that none will acquire a position dominant enough to inhibit the growth of other cities.

Encouraging the establishment or growth of small cities, particularly in remote regions, is open to the criticism that such cities will require considerable investment, where local resources have not been developed, and might be likely to stimulate migration to the larger centers. Against this is posed the strong argument that the functioning of the primate city in the modernization of Latin America has been severely handicapped by the absence of supporting sets of cities of smaller size. Modernizing influences, it is held, move more quickly and encounter less resistance when they reach rural areas, or other outposts of tradition, through cities of various sizes than when they must make a sharp descent from modern-urban directly to rural-traditional. Also, balanced growth requires the integration of leading and lagging sectors. The development of existing small cities, or the creation of new urban centers, is an integral part of this. Utilizing the small city as a means of integrating rural areas has been largely neglected, probably because of the emphasis placed on improving rural and urban regions as separate entities. Continuing such an emphasis might easily widen the gap between city and countryside and possibly lay the groundwork for future urban problems which Latin America can ill afford.

Further support for the dispersion of cities comes in the form of arguments based on size of country. Many of the cities that have suffered the most malfunctioning because of overurbanization are in the larger and more developed countries. These countries have possibly reached a stage of development where high primacy is acting as a brake on future balanced growth. Investments in the export trade and in import substitution had created and encouraged the growth of the chain of coastal cities. Nuclei centers could now be developed that would act as check-dams to keep the migrants from the primate cities. The growth of these centers would stimulate the development of the whole sur-rounding area, and ultimately could be developed into a grid pattern that would cover the whole country.

In contrast to the primate city, dispersed cities suffer on the question of cost. Though urban dispersion might not be as costly as resettlement schemes and other rural-improvement programs, it nevertheless is costly. Further, neither its benefits nor its problems can be predicted accurately in Latin America. Of necessity, regional dispersion of cities, it is considered, should be part of a long-range program. Some countries are encourag-ing the growth of both types, as is, for example, Mexico. Brazil has created a completely new city that "faces inward," as an investment in future growth. The effectiveness of dispersed cities in checking migration to the primate city remains to be tested. Relatively few Latin American countries have any large number of functioning secondary or tertiary cities. All of the countries, however, seem to have high primacy, and the capital or other large center continues to increase in size even when efforts at industrial dispersion and more widespread investments have had governmental support and encouragement.

It is strongly believed by the supporters both of the primate city and of dispersion of cities that as development proceeds growth of urban centers will occur throughout most of the countries. Such growth, consequently, should be foreseen and planned for, and directed as much as possible, in order to avoid the problems of haphazard development.

RELATION OF PEOPLE TO THE ECONOMY AND OF THE ECONOMY TO URBAN PROBLEMS

One of the worst features of the urbanization now taking place is that no actual improvement usually occurs in the circumstances of the migrant after he reaches the city. One reason for the present situation seems to be that the social benefits of economic development have been ignored. Basic to remedying the situation, it is considered, is accepting migration as a fact and considering how this urbanization process can further the process of transforming a traditionally rural society into a modern urban one.

The approach to remedying the social situation should emphasize less doing something for the migrant and stress more making possible the development of a modern society, of which the migrant would be part. Integration brings about changes in all classes, rather than in the marginal group alone, and sets the stage for the development of a modern society.

Much of the discussion on the location of cities revolves around the issues of improving the social order and of improving the migrant's standard of living. The mechanisms for modernization, it is contended, would operate more effectively in smaller cities than in the overgrown primate city, and the integration of the migrant into urban culture would be effectuated more quickly in smaller cities. Against this is the consideration as to whether an urban culture that will offset the attraction of the larger city can be created in a smaller city. There is the additional question of whether or not small urban centers can supply the necessary employment opportunities and job diversification. Also, the primate cities usually have more educational and recreational facilities.

Urbanization and concentration both should be encouraged, according to another point of view, first in existing cities, until they are functioning as modernizing agents, and then in other cities, where the same process would be repeated. Against this is the argument that economic development has not spread out but, rather, has tended to concentrate. Constant emphasis on the primate city could continue to exclude large masses from the integrative process.

The major question is: Would the factors that are now blocking or delaying social integration in the primate and other large cities also be operative in cities of smaller size or if more smaller cities were available?

RÉSUMÉ

In Latin America, the occupational incorporation of the urban labor force into industrial employment is already great enough to create the conditions necessary for the rise of the corresponding attitudes and values. Integration, however, may be temporarily blocked by a number of factors, such as ethnic barriers, transfer of traditional attitudes and practices, and types of neighborhood and housing. There is a tendency, in countries with a high Indian population, for groups to live together in the same neighborhoods and to continue their traditional way of life. Studies have shown that among the new migrants the family is usually the only social institution on which they can depend for support and help. These situations, and also the high urban fertility rate, are not, in general, confined to the migrants, but reflect to some extent the practices and attitudes of the upper classes.

It has been suggested that integration in Latin America does not necessarily mean taking people into an existing social order. What is needed, it is felt, is a new social order. The path has to be cleared so that a new order would emerge along with economic development. The lack of continuity in the existing social structure presents a serious drawback to integration. Poorly distributed goods and services and a lack of organizations keep the lower strata from benefiting by urbanization. As a result, they have to depend on the family and other traditional institutions. What is needed is change in cultural values, more widespread education, and housing developments in line with the needs and incomes of the migrants. Even if it means adopting lower standards, immediate action along these lines should be taken.

With respect to specific measures to help the integration of the migrants and, incidentally, improve the city, two considerations receive attention. One is measures designed to improve the rural areas; the other is to improve the migrant's situation in the city.

There is not much support for the thesis that urbanization

should not be encouraged at all. The village is most effective only under conditions of slow population growth and when there is a large amount of good land near it. There is considerable difficulty in transferring modern technology to areas where the inhabitants do not have a fairly high level of education or a strong motivation for change. Community development programs can be extremely costly if they are applied on a basis large enough to reach a majority of the rural population. There was, however, at the conference considerable endorsement by several Latin American participants of community development programs and the development of financial and other institutions as effective means of improving the rural situation and, eventually, improving the cities as well, in a higher quality of migrants, better skills, and the like. In low-income countries, it was held, community development is about the only way open to help the *pobladores* toward modern technology and institutions. One argument against the primate city is that the merits of community development are not appreciated and thus are not used to help *callampa* residents.

In general, however, it is accepted that the cities offer a wider variety of institutions for integration. The problem is to bring the migrant into contact with them. At present, the migrant is left to his own devices so far as social institutions and channels of communication with other groups are concerned. Groups, such as labor unions, which have the closest contact with the migrants, it is felt, should be encouraged to help the migrant take part in urban living. Neighborhood school and church groups are other channels of communication that should be developed.

With respect to improving urban living conditions, the question arises as to whether the migrant should not be advised before coming to the city about its conditions and the costs of urban living. The cost of food, for example, absorbs a large proportion of urban wages, due mainly to the inadequate agricultural structure, which continues to be geared to the requirements of the export trade. Even the migrants who obtain industrial employment and have steady wages find it difficult to go on to a higher standard of living because of the high costs of housing and, in some areas, a lack of better housing. In what was until recently a two-class society, with marked income disparity between them, institutions, and the building industry, among other manufacturers, have designed their products and services for the upper group where wealth is concentrated. Because the migrant does not have a large income, his possible ability to pay some of the costs, particularly at a lower standard, of his needs is largely ignored. Existing housing can be improved, as often recommended, but this does not solve the problem of the additional housing needed as migrants keep on coming into the city. The choice may be said to lie between redistributing income to the lower strata in the form of housing (with the state, in effect, deciding how additional income should be spent) or making investments in job-creating industries that will give the migrant more income, then encouraging him to spend it on better housing by making credit and financing easier. The latter choice is recommended. There is, however, strong feeling among Latin Americans that "the slums must go." This is not only because they are so apparent; it is also considered a matter of social justice—sharing scarce resources in the form of housing is one way of ensuring income redistribution. Programs of slum clearance and public housing to date have, however, absorbed and continue to absorb large amounts of capital, and have made relatively little progress. Further growth of already large cities should be inhibited, it is frequently argued, until their facilities can be improved and extended.

Improving the urban environment represents a long drawn-out process, and deterioration is to some extent self-perpetuating as more and more migrants come to the city. There is a relation between urban problems and the economy. If past economic development set up the situation that created overconcentration, the effects of future economic development should not be left to chance. Investments in economic growth will encourage urbanization; so also will improvements in agricultural productivity. Much past planning has been based on what somebody else thought people wanted. Urban growth (since measures to control or retard it have been unsuccessful) thus should be guided in accordance with a predetermined goal. If the goal of a modern society is set, then investments should be viewed in the light of this objective rather than from the narrow standpoint of economic benefit alone. Investments for economic and social improvement are not necessarily competitive—both are essential parts of economic development. Economic investments that lead to the creation of employment opportunities and job diversification as well as income redistribution throughout the population represent social investments. They permit the mechanisms of social and political development to operate and to bring about not only improved standards of living for the migrants but changes and modifications in the whole social order. Too much emphasis has been placed on the manifestations of underdevelopment and not enough on changing the conditions that create them. Where such investments should be made is, in a sense, less important than that they should be made in a manner that turns the national society toward modernism instead of, as until recently, prolonging traditionalism.

The migrant meanwhile should not be left to struggle alone. Efforts to help him should be made from the standpoint of his incipient role as a member of a modern society rather than in the form of palliatives to keep him bound to traditionalism.

It is possible, once they are recognized as important, to include all these values on the balance sheets of economic development plans under the item of per capita income—all the goods and services that are valued and held desirable by a society. Recognition of the importance of social improvement throughout the social structure is crucial—recognition, for instance, that the full effects of economic development now under way are being crippled by the continuance of traditional behavior and values, not only among the marginal population but throughout the social order.

ESTABLISHING NATIONAL GUIDELINES

Though there are differences of opinion on how best to utilize urbanization to further economic, social, and political modernization in Latin America, there seems to be general agreement that obtaining such modernization depends on establishing national guidelines directed toward that end. The problems caused by urbanization and its negative aspects have to be recognized as stemming from national conditions rather than being creations of the city. Consequently, the problems have to be dealt with on a national basis. Past efforts to solve urban problems have suffered from regarding rural and urban as separate and distinct entities. Too much emphasis on purely local aspects has, it is contended, caused past plans to fail.

Only through national plans can the social aspects of development receive the attention and be accorded the position they should have in the scale of wants. Too much planning in the past seems to have focused narrowly on economic objectives alone; these, too, have been "sound failures." Economic objectives alone do not take into account the situation in Latin America where social change is as essential to economic development as economic change. Social objectives should be a part of economic development planning. This is simple social justice—not to move forward at the expense of the most needy groups—and also economic sense—not to set up future problems that might be more difficult to cope with than present ones. The lack of social development has been a hampering force on economic development in the past: illiteracy, continuation of traditional values, lack of skilled labor, scarcity of entrepreneurs, an educational system that emphasized the attitudes of traditional society rather than fostered the development of attitudes best suited to modernism, the continuation of enclaves or groups easily manipulated to support the status quo in one form or another; institutions, housing, facilities, and consumer goods geared to an upper class and out of the reach of emerging groups from the lower strata; as well as numerous other manifestations of duality. Some of this situation is considered to stem from the narrow focus on the purely economic results expected from development plans. Economic development, however, is only part of the larger goal of modernization of Latin American societies.

Regional and national planning should be integrated. Both national and regional planners can exchange information and techniques that will result in coordinated national plans directed toward national goals that, at the same time, recognize the local implications of suggested programs. The spatial aspects of economic development have been neglected, and thus the heart of the development problem has not been reached. Planning in underdeveloped societies is different from that in developed societies in view of governmental participation in the former in the direct promotion of economic development. Current situations of agglomeration, urban sprawl, and the like deserve more study than has been given to them.

Planners also should take the initiative in implementation of plans. They should not continue to claim that political decisions have been unfavorable. Their professional training qualifies them to take the responsibility for making definite recommendations that would lead to development of the positive aspects of urbanization. Political situations vary among the countries, as do the planning facilities. Most of the countries, however, are committed to economic development and most of them have some institutions for economic planning. Planners can accomplish much by putting themselves in a position to recommend alternatives to proposed investment schemes. An investment, for example, applicable to a local condition only might, if made in another area, stimulate greater growth and ultimately result in an improved local situation.

Planners need a working knowledge of various fields. Planning schools can contribute to better planning by provding comprehensive training that includes familiarity with the various fields—sociology, economics, geology, physical science, and others—that enter into national planning.

There is, unfortunately, a serious lack of basic information on which decisions can be made. With respect to the question of the primate city, for example, as compared with secondary and smaller cities, there is not enough factual information on which sensible decisions can be based. Also, not much is known about the institutional aspects of dualism—in terms of knowing why the mechanisms that brought about integration in developed countries have not operated in Latin America. A research program covering these areas is recommended.

The rapidity with which urbanization is taking place in Latin America and the vast numbers of people involved in the process call for immediate action, as has been stressed. There is little possibility that Latin America can accommodate itself leisurely to the process. Within a relatively short period, there will be more people living in cities than are living in rural areas. And, with the continuing high rural birth rate and the agricultural development needed to accompany industrial development, the rate of urbanization can be expected to remain high for some time to come. National guidelines need to be established that will divert the flow into channels for growth rather than into the backwaters of stagnation.

ROLE OF THE CITY IN THE FUTURE

The richness and quality of today's knowledge in the field of urban planning make it possible to anticipate some of the basic future trends for the next fifteen to twenty years. A few are suggested:[4]

1. The quality of social research in Latin America today, plus

[4] Excerpt from remarks by Glenn H. Beyer at the Seminario sobre Saneamiento Ambiental en la Planeacion Urbana, Mexico City, Mexico, November 7–12, 1966, sponsored by the Asociacion Fronteriza Mexicana-Estadounidense de Salubridad.

the large number of first-class Latin American social scientists, has already had an influence in a broad dissemination of information and culture within the continent. In the near future, we must devise new methods of communication and coordination and more cooperative research between Latin American and North American urban specialists. The European research specialist will also be important in this new form of international cooperation, which will without any doubt increase at a significant rate.

2. The old-fashioned classifications of rural and urban will be replaced by a new concept, which will integrate both views around the more dynamic reality of today's increased mobility, a concept typified by terms such as "transience" or "temporariness." The rural Latin American *campesino*, with his Japanese transistor radio on his horse, mule, or city-purchased bicycle, has outmoded the old sociological or anthropological image of the traditional isolated rural man. Long-lasting relations between man and his environment are today replaced by short temporary relations. Mobility, "temporariness," and "transience" today add a totally new quality to urban life which needs a more scientific study by urban specialists.

3. The accelerated rate of change in Latin American urban life styles, as well as in all of the world's large urban centers of more than a million population, is producing a mental shock affecting almost every sector of the population with a new modern illness, called "urbanitis." Research has advanced sufficiently to make possible a massive attack on this front. A high priority should be given to the study of social class structure and the effects of mobility on this structure and on personality. A sociologist at Massachusetts Institute of Technology has said:

The standard findings regarding the personality characteristics of socially mobile individuals and the impact of mobility on personality may be seriously incomplete. It may turn out that insofar as mobility is oriented toward occupations or social groups whose status and style are importantly rooted in traditional values (which remains true of most middle- and upper-status occupations in urban

Latin America), mobility, far from impelling change, serves to re-inforce tradition.[5]

This realistic assessment of the impact of mobility in Latin America opens to us new perspectives to understand better some of the social problems created by the "urban shock."

4. The Number One urban environmental problem in Latin America may well be how to control the growth of new large squatter areas and shantytowns. The realistic recent predictions of the Inter-American Development Bank,[6] that vast urban areas in Latin America will be converted into gigantic slums and shantytowns, have stimulated both a redefinition of this tremendous problem and more coordinated research on it. Turner has proposed new strategies for the United Nations Housing, Planning, and Building Centre to use in attacking the problem. His proposals give only second priority to the question of shelter in the marginal areas but first priority to more realistic, comprehensive environmental total planning. Housing development plans, for example, will be implemented by first resolving the questions of land subdivision and the provision of water supply and community services before the more strictly housing questions are considered. Naturally, the implementation of these strategies will require long-term planning policies, for periods of ten to twenty years at a minimum.[7]

5. A new environmental urban planning field, in which we may advance rapidly, is in the area of family planning and

[5] Frank Bonilla, "The Urban Worker," in John J. Johnson, ed., *Continuity and Change in Latin America* (Stanford: Stanford University Press, 1964), p. 190.

[6] Banco Interamericano de Desarrollo, Reunion sobre Financiamiento Municipal en Latinoamerica, Washington, D. C., 23–26 de Enero de 1966, Doc. 36, 22 de Enero 1966; *El desarrollo urbano de America Latina*, pp. 2–3.

[7] John C. Turner, "Uncontrolled Urban Settlement: Problems and Policies," Working Paper No. 11, Inter-Regional Seminar on Development Policies and Planning in Relation to Urbanization. University of Pittsburgh, October 24 to November 7, 1966. Prepared for the United Nations Centre for Housing, Building and Planning, n.d.

fertility studies. In Latin America a promising level of maturity has been reached in tackling this highly delicate social, religious, and cultural problem. Under the leadership of a group of Latin American and North American demographers, the future knowledge and control of the population explosion seems more realistically possible as the result of a better interdisciplinary approach. We have only taken the first steps, but we are moving in the right direction.

6. The last two years' evaluation of United Nations strategies for ten-year planning, through the "Development Decade," and the realistic appraisals of the Alliance for Progress ten-year planning, prove clearly that the future global trends in economic, social, and environmental planning will be projected for larger units of time: twenty, thirty, and fifty years. Long-range urban planning in Latin America will require closer cooperation and more dynamic and flexible programming than at present. Another authority has suggested that "while in 1962 there were from 1.4 to 1.5 million full-time research workers in the world, 35 years from now we may expect between 10 and 20 million of them." [8]

A question raised often during the conference discussions concerned the relevance of the past for the future of Latin America. Too often in the past, the course of events has overrun even well-devised urban development schemes and made them useless. The answer would seem to be that urban planning in Latin America—as elsewhere—has to be "future-oriented." A prominent writer has recently pointed out that the historic jumps we have taken in the twentieth century—air travel and space flight, television, the development of nuclear energy, the invention of the computer, to name only a few—represent not a continuation of "normal" progress but rather a sharp break with historic continuity:

For what is occurring now is a transformation that is, in all likelihood, bigger, deeper, and more important than the industrial revolu-

[8] Steven Dedijer, "The Science of Science: A Programme and a Plea," *Minerva*, IV, 4 (Summer, 1966), 491.

tion. In fact, there is a growing body of reputable opinion that the period we are now living through represents nothing less than the second great divide in human history, comparable in magnitude only with that first great break in historic continuity, the shift from barbarism to civilization.[9]

Is it possible, amidst the violence and rapidity of future change, for the life of the individual to remain untouched? "The answer is that the mood, the pace, the very 'feel' of existence, as well as one's underlying notions of time, beauty, space, and social relations will all be shaken." [10]

This provides the challenge to Latin America and the world, not only for our cities but, in fact, for our total living environment.

The characteristics of current urban development in Latin America signify that the continuing rise of shantytown developments, *barriadas, favelas, ranchos,* or the like, is a force that will have to be reckoned with in any future plans for the city. It seems scarcely necessary to say that such a reckoning requires more than the provision of housing and urban services. Rather, it means that the city has to absorb these presently disruptive elements and provide an environment that favors utilizing their capacities effectively. Obviously, as these and other integrative mechanisms of the city function successfully, significant changes can be expected to take place in its physical pattern.

It is not essential that the city in Latin America follow a growth pattern identical with the growth patterns of other Western cities. In fact, much of the charm and appeal of the South American cities could be lost if the aura of history which so many of them now have is ignored under the impact of development. It is essential, though, that as they grow they take on the same qualities that have made cities a dynamic force throughout world history.

[9] Alvin Toffler, "The Future as a Way of Life," *Horizon,* VII, 3 (Summer, 1965), 110.
[10] *Ibid.,* p. 111.

Appendix

Urbanization on an Ad Hoc Basis:
A Case Study of Caracas TOMÁS JOSÉ SANABRIA

Cities, seen as organisms, can be compared to living beings. If living beings can be classified according to their idiosyncrasies, so may cities.

The case of Caracas (a city of over a million and a half inhabitants) can be compared to a human being who is young and full of vitality, anticipating the future, but who because of indolence is currently suffering a serious illness that blocks his basic functions. Clear evidence of this, in the case of Caracas, is given in manifestations such as lack of free spaces, poor transportation in general, and the invasion of *ranchos*. This last point is what I intend to analyze because I consider it intimately bound to the central theme of this conference: the role of the city in the modernization of Latin America.

Today's *rancho* is in Venezuela what *villa miseria* is in Argentina, *favela* in Brazil, *poblaciones callampas* in Chile, and *jacale* in Mexico. These words usually describe spaces that are enclosed by four wall surfaces for which various materials that would otherwise be leftovers are used, such as packing-box wood, tin plate, soft board, and paper, with a roof of the same materials; that is, the most primitive form of human refuge one can think of, where a number of people live in a state of overcrowding. In them they cook, eat, rest, and sleep, thereby emphasizing the problems caused by overcrowding. Their floor is the plain earth. They have neither sewers nor water service.

I do not pretend to view this phenomenon as a housing problem since that is not the real problem, although it functions basically as such. It is more like what we call in Spanish *un lastre urbano*, which is characteristic of Latin American cities, and it is the product of collective indifference. The indifference, together with the incapacitation of the responsible authorities, has generated for more than thirty-five years the type of problem we have been talking about. The problem becomes increasingly accentuated and aggravated as time passes.

HISPANIC VALUES

I would like to analyze briefly some of the influences that have worked directly or indirectly on the city of Caracas since the time of its founding.

In about a year and a half, Caracas will celebrate its *Cuatrocentenario*. It was founded in 1567 according to standards already established by the *Leyes de Indias*, in a healthful valley, near a small river, and outlined by creeks that served as defenses for the town. Judging from documents of that time, one of the reasons why the city was founded there was that the valley was supposed to be rich in gold, which could be found in the creeks. The town's life was continually altered by constant attacks from the Indians who lived in that region, and it was almost totally destroyed by an invasion of pirates who had come into the town hunting for treasure.

Until 1600 the city consisted of a series of blocks divided into four equal parts. The main square (*Plaza Mayor*), which served as a site for common defense purposes, was protected by a thick wooden fence. In that main square feasts, horse shows, and public celebrations took place. The church was at the front, and the government houses were between it and the main square, placed in such a manner that in an emergency the inhabitants could help one another. The city of that time had but very primitive buildings, since there was no desire to improve them so long as the danger of attacks remained. What was built was solely for the purpose of defense.

Aside from the fact that the valley was rich in gold, it is quite difficult to understand why the Spaniards built Caracas in it, especially if we compare this selection with the sense of urbanistic vision that they had used in the founding of other cities throughout Venezuela ten years earlier—near lakes, near the seashore, or by large rivers such as the Orinoco. There is no question about the extraordinary natural beauty of the valley of Caracas. The mountains that delimit it are of majestic proportions, and the climate is a very agreeable one. Unfortunately, its natural resources are not sufficient, or its physical surroundings ample enough, to allow a logical expansion.

Once the region became safe from attack the city began to grow and to develop normally. Both its climate and its natural beauty enticed thousands of families to settle in Caracas. The Venezuelan architecture of that time, which we usually call its colonial period, is characterized by its great simplicity, the use of plain materials, and ingenious, unpretentious forms. There was, undoubtedly, a marked Spanish influence on it, since it was based on concepts brought from Spain. If there is an outstanding characteristic in our colonial architecture, it is in the continuity of the original concepts. The same construction systems and ways of living, for example, were being carried on in the nineteenth century as two centuries before. Blocks that were originally divided into four sections underwent gradual subdivision as the price of land rose, and houses began to undergo alterations to the point where a very deep house with only 26 feet of frontage became the main characteristic of the city.

The city never had significant urban spaces that would reveal an intention to improve it or indicate any vision toward the future. There existed only "plazas" (green spaces) in every parish, on each of which a church was situated. There was not the slightest conception of what a promenade was, or a boulevard, or a park. Each parcel of land was used to the maximum, and this became a system, that, like an atavistic formula, went on repeating itself until our own time. Other countries of Latin America that had been colonized had urban spaces, parks, squares, monuments, and the like that served as an inspiration to new generations, gave faith to a culture, and established a tradition which, as time passed, still influences the attainment of new artistic expressions of local character.

THE PRESENT SITUATION

The city has continued to develop and has experienced very rapid growth in the last twenty years (370 per cent, approximately). That which usually takes place in countries where the industrialization process is delayed also occurred in Caracas: an all too rapid process of urbanization. If we add to this other factors of a political nature that helped to increase the peasant exodus toward the city, we shall understand the magnitude of this problem.

In 1830 the city was only a series of little population centers that had been formed down the valley and along its principal road. By 1900 *ranchos* existed, but these were only the shelters that poor people used because they had to work in the city. They could never be compared with the *ranchos* of today. On the contrary, dwellers kept them very clean even though they did not have complete sanitary services. At that time, lack of sanitary services was not only a problem of the *ranchos* but also a problem of the city as a whole. As a result epidemics ravaged Caracas on various occasions. Materials used in the construction of those *ranchos* were practically the same as the ones used for construction throughout the city. The main difference was that the *ranchos* were built on mountain slopes which did not have any urbanistic value at that time, while the city continued to develop in the flat zones.

By 1930 Caracas was already taking the form of a city, and new areas that would be occupied by residential developments began to open. The *rancho* zone had expanded, since there was increasing demand for domestic services, public jobs, and small industries that consequently caused the growth of living zones for the poor. In regard to this problem, however, they were considered to have aesthetic value when seen from certain points of Caracas from which the hills full of bright colored *ranchos* could be viewed. No one thought of the problem they would create a few years later. This lack of vision toward the future, this urbanistic myopia, continued to characterize the development of the city. Any modern urban planner would have been alarmed if faced with such a situation. The methods of building and the materials used had begun to decrease in quality, and the problem had reached such proportions that action was badly needed.

By 1950 the problem had become immense. The *ranchos* of twenty years back could not be compared with the current dwellings, which could no longer be viewed as picturesque from afar. They presented, rather, a tragic panorama where only the products of overcrowding and promiscuity could be found: juvenile delinquency, vagrancy, vice, and all the other social shames that prosper in this type of environment.

In 1961 the year of the latest Venezuelan national census, Caracas had not only filled the total capacity of the valley, but it had also invaded its mountain zone, where it occupied an area almost equal to the valley area. According to this census, the population of the Metropolitan Area was 1,330,000 inhabitants, of which 21 per cent lived in *ranchos*. This figure has obviously grown since then.

It is timely here to remind ourselves that the unsanitary conditions in *rancho* zones are deplorable. A great number of the shacks do not have windows, and access to them is only through tortuous paths, which are narrow and steep. Garbage collection is made only in places of relatively easy access to vehicles. In general, garbage is thrown down the hills, which stimulates the proliferation of flies and disease. At the same time, in the Metropolitan Area only about 3 per cent of the dwellings lack electricity for lighting. Most *ranchos* have refrigerators, television, and other modern appliances. This incongruity becomes even more incredible if we add to it the fact that a high percentage of *rancho* inhabitants own cars.

Such conditions make us feel how tragic and disturbing this matter is. And I repeat once again, it is not a problem of housing —it will never be solved by taking measures of sanitation for the surroundings, by regulating densities, or by applying blindly the techniques of international classical urbanism. It is a very different problem. A new approach is necessary, as are emergency measures that are intelligent and, above all, carried out in accord with a modern criterion that grows out of our own environment.

Our cities are in a state of emergency, not only Caracas but those of most of Latin America, the only difference being that in some, because of topography, the squatter towns are more exposed than in others. In Caracas and Rio de Janeiro, for instance, we could not walk long before seeing the ever-present *ranchos* on the hills. On the other hand, some areas of *ranchos* in Bogota, Mexico City, and Buenos Aires would have to be purposefully sought out in order to be found.

In the case of cities that are developed on flat zones, an apparent solution to the problem seems to be offered, since the topography implies the elaboration of a study, more or less complex, on how to incorporate the *rancho* zones into the structure of the city. But in cities that are developed on hilly grounds, it is impossible to provide the basic services. At least, this is the case in Caracas.

Now then, assuming for the moment that both solutions were hypothetically feasible, what would happen if we were instead to tackle the problem from a social point of view?

The majority of the rural people have come into towns without knowing why; they feel lost. They do not know what to do, so they settle themselves in *rancho* zones. Could these people be considered citizens? They are more like refugees. Yet we must ask of them what we ask of any citizen. If we let them take aid for granted, there will come a moment when they will accept this situation as just. It will simply repeat the circumstances to which they were accustomed in the countryside.

GENERAL CONDITIONS

Today we are not certain whether it would be more convenient to create incentives outside the urban areas, that is, in the countryside, in order to assure that those who remain in the city can be useful citizens as well as active members of its social structure, or whether we should be prepared to accept the migration to the urban centers as normal, by solving the problems derived from social mobility. About 50 per cent of the population of Latin America lives in cities, and the urban population continues to grow at a rate approximately twice as high as in rural areas. According to ECLA, it is calculated that between 1960 and 1975 Venezuela's urban population will double.

Latin America promises a great future—all of the trends in social and economic betterment indicate this. That future is in our hands, and there is a great responsibility placed upon us. If we study population graphs for any Latin American city arranged by group, age, and sex, we realize the lack of proportion that exists in the structure of the cities. They have the characteristic triangular form of new or developing nations. If we specifically look at the one for the urban area of Caracas, we learn the following in regard to the three most significant groups of inhabitants: 1. The ones from new-born to nineteen years of age represent 46 per cent of the total; 2. those between twenty and thirty-four years old represent 30 per cent; 3. those between thirty-five and sixty years old represent 21 per cent. Such proportions emphasize the fact that the last age group of experienced adults is very small, and they have to face the immense task of solving problems created by youth in the violent and continuous process of growth. If, for instance, we take in Caracas a sample of one hundred inhabitants, we will find that, of the 21 per cent who are between thirty-five and sixty years of age, only two will be professionals and just a fraction of one of them (0.2 per cent) will be technically prepared to work for the betterment of the city. Therefore, we must keep alert not to fall into improvisation—which is a manifestation that easily occurs under these circumstances.

FINAL PROPOSITION

It is essential that, aware of such a reality, we act together when facing common problems, as inhabitants of the same continent, not only as Venezuelans or as Latin Americans but as Americans.

When I say this, I implicitly include the U.S.A. and Canada. It is essential to leave aside the traditional division of North, Central, and South America. Such division does not fit the subject that we are discussing, because even developed countries, with a balanced social structure, are not necessarily lacking in significant problems similar to those we have considered at this conference.

The population of the U.S.A. increased by 48 million between 1940 and 1960. By 1970 at the present rate of increase, it will have 215 million, and by the year 2000, around 385 million inhabitants. Our countries in Latin America will expand even more and at a much greater rate. Latin America will have by that time about 600 million inhabitants. By then we may have several cities like New York, or even larger. Let us not forget what Malthus said in 1798: "The world population will soon outrun its food supply," and the result could be "war, crime, poverty, vice and general human misery."

Growth of cities does not necessarily imply their betterment unless we work in an orderly and disciplined way toward common objectives. Let us study, then, how to attain our common objectives without falling into the error of creating organizations that parallel those already existing and, above all, by knowing how to act as *modern professionals*. The present means of communication places us in a very advantageous position compared with the past and, more importantly, since we can participate simultaneously in world happenings while they are occurring, places *all our countries equally* in the present time.

Convinced that we are inhabitants of the same continent, we must plan our cities to be oriented by the same "philosophical goal" in order to achieve a faultless physical, economic, and social development.

Conference Participants

Fernando Aguirre Tupper, Ing.
Presidente, Sociedad Interamericana de Planificación
Santiago, Chile

Santiago Agurto Calvo, Arq.
Rector elect, National University of Engineering
School of Architecture
Lima, Peru

Gabriel Andrade Lleras, Arq.
Decano, Facultad de Arquitectura
Fundación Universidad de América
Bogota, Colombia

Juan B. Astica
Professor, Instituto de Planificación Fisica
Universidad Católica
Santiago, Chile

Glenn H. Beyer, *Conference Director*
Director, Center for Housing and Environmental Studies
Professor, Housing and Design
Cornell University
Ithaca, New York

Harley L. Browning
Director, Population Research Center
Professor, Department of Sociology
University of Texas
Austin, Texas

Tom E. Davis
Director, Latin American Program
Professor, Department of Economics
Cornell University
Ithaca, New York

Martin E. Dominguez
Professor, College of Architecture
Cornell University
Ithaca, New York

Luis Dorich Torres, Ing.
Instituto Latinoamericano de Planificación Económica y Social
Comisión Económica para América Latina
Naciones Unidas
Santiago, Chile

Ralph A. Gakenheimer
Editor, *Journal of the American Institute of Planners*
Professor, Department of City and Regional Planning
University of North Carolina
Chapel Hill, North Carolina

César Garcés-Vernaza, Arq.
Executive Director, Corporación Autónoma Regional de la Sabana de Bogota y los Valles de Ubate y Chiquinquira
Bogota, Colombia

Wilson Garcés
Chief, Planning and Urbanization Section
Centre for Housing, Building and Planning
Bureau of Social Affairs
United Nations
New York, New York

Gino Germani
Monroe Gutman Professor of Latin American Affairs
Department of Social Relations
Harvard University
Cambridge, Massachusetts

Rose K. Goldsen
Professor, Department of Sociology
Cornell University
Ithaca, New York

Jorge E. Hardoy, Arq.
Director, Center for Urban and Regional Studies
Instituto Torcuato Di Tella
Buenos Aires, Argentina

Walter Harris
Chairman, Department of City Planning
Yale University
New Haven, Connecticut

Benjamin Higgins
Ashbel Smith Professor of Economics
Department of Economics
University of Texas
Austin, Texas

Irving Louis Horowitz
Director, Studies in Comparative International Development
Professor, Department of Sociology-Anthropology
Washington University
St. Louis, Missouri

Bert F. Hoselitz
Director, Research Center in Economic Development and Cultural Change
Professor, Economics and Social Science
Department of Economics
University of Chicago
Chicago, Illinois

Philip Huber
Senior Specialist, Housing and Urban Development Program
Department of Social Affairs
Organization of American States
Pan American Union
Washington, D.C.

Octavio Ianni
Faculdade de Filosofía, Ciências e Letras
Universidade de São Paulo
São Paulo, Brazil

Hélio Jaguaribe
Department of Government
Littauer Center
Harvard University
Cambridge, Massachusetts

Ricardo Jordán, Arq.
Asesor Regional, Programación y Políticas de Vivienda y De-
sarrollo Urbano y Regional
Comisión Económica para América Latina
Mexico City, Mexico

Burnham Kelly
Dean, College of Architecture
Cornell University
Ithaca, New York

Thomas W. Mackesey
Vice Provost, Cornell University
Ithaca, New York

William Mangin
Department of Anthropology
Syracuse University
Syracuse, New York

James A. Moore
Director, Division of International Affairs
United States Department of Housing and Urban Development
Washington, D.C.

Eduardo Neira Alva, Arq.
Consultant, Inter-American Development Bank
Professor of CENDES
Universidad Central de Venezuela
Caracas, Venezuela

Luis Ortiz de Zevallos, Arq.
Director, Instituto de Planeamiento de Lima
Universidad Nacional de Ingeniería
Lima, Peru

Salvador M. Padilla
Vice Presidente, Sociedad Inter-Americana de Planificación
Director, Programa Graduado de Planificación
Universidad de Puerto Rico
Rio Piedras, Puerto Rico

Renato Poblete, S.J.
Centro de Investigación y Acción Social
Centro Bellarmino
Santiago, Chile

Thomas A. Reiner
Department of Regional Science
Wharton School of Finance and Commerce
University of Pennsylvania
Philadelphia, Pennsylvania

Jorge R. Riba, Arq.
Director General, Instituto de Vivienda y Urbanismo
Panama, Republica de Panama

Harold Robinson
Deputy Director for Plans and Programming, Housing and
Urban Development Division
Bureau for Latin America
Agency for International Development
Washington, D.C.

Tomás José Sanabria, Arq.
Professor, Architecture and Urbanism
Universidad Central de Venezuela
Caracas, Venezuela

Luis Alberto Sánchez
Senator of the Republic of Peru
Rector, Universidad Nacional Mayor de San Marcos de Lima
Lima, Peru

Félix Sánchez Baylón, Arq.
Professor of Planning and Urban Design, School of Architecture
National University of Mexico
Mexico City, Mexico

James R. Scobie
Professor, Department of History
Latin American Studies
Indiana University
Bloomington, Indiana

Aldo E. Solari
División de Asuntos Sociales
Comisión Económica para América Latina
Naciones Unidas
Santiago, Chile

Anatole A. Solow
Professor, Graduate School of Public and International Affairs
University of Pittsburgh
Pittsburgh, Pennsylvania

Stuart W. Stein
Professor, Department of City and Regional Planning
Cornell University
Ithaca, New York

J. Mayone Stycos
Chairman, Department of Sociology
Director, International Population Program
Cornell University
Ithaca, New York

Francis Violich
Professor, Department of City and Regional Planning
College of Environmental Design
University of California
Berkeley, California

Kempton E. Webb
Professor, Institute of Latin American Studies
Columbia University
New York, New York

Lowdon Wingo, Jr.
Program of Urban and Regional Studies
Resources for the Future, Inc.
Washington, D.C.

Index

Agriculture:
  early centers of, 3, 36, 39
  lack of opportunity in, 97, 108–109,
    192
  per cent of population in, 90, 121,
    235, 238, 241
  political implications of, 229, 238,
    241–243, 263
  productivity of, 61, 67, 76, 77, 99,
    120–123, 136, 141, 316, 328
Anomie, see Social disorganization

Barriadas, 8, 9, 12, 101, 102, 188, 199,
    200, 210, 248, 265, 311, 335
  see also Slums
Barrios, 4, 102, 270, 271, 305
  see also Slums
Birth control, 2, 88, 116, 314, 333
  political implications of, 114–115
  see also Fertility
Birth rate, 112
  see also Fertility
Brasilia, 7, 14, 77, 107, 108, 133, 160,
    271, 275, 323

Callampas, 8, 101, 102, 187, 266, 337
  see also Slums
Capital city, see City and Primate city
Caudillo, 226, 239, 240, 244–246, 248,
    259, 260
Charter of Punta del Este, 286n.
City:
  center of integrative mechanisms,
    182, 246, 321
  centralization of activities in, 18,
    60–61, 78, 98, 99, 100, 141, 159,
    176, 181, 190, 304
  and the future, 331–335
  influence of colonial, 49, 55, 56
  optimal size of, 130–131, 156, 320
  problems of, 130–131, 142, 310–311

  see also Primate city, Urban popu-
    lation, and Urbanization
City, functions of, 65–66, 177, 303–
    304
  ambiguity in, 66–67
  and city growth, 63–64, 65n., 170–
    173, 283, 321
  colonial city, 36–43, 59–60
  reorientation toward, 64
City planning, 58, 130–131, 142, 173,
    296, 321
  in colonial cities, 284–285
  see also National planning and Plan-
    ning
City structure and ecology:
  of colonial cities, 3–7, 33–35, 44, 49–
    54, 58, 304–305
  growth of suburbs, 12, 306, 311
  growth patterns, 302–312, 335, 339–
    341
  land use, 153, 306–310
  physical characteristics, 40, 310–311,
    338
  planning problems of, 4–7, 296, 300
Climate and geography, 159, 160, 221,
    303, 308, 338, 339
Colonial influence, 56, 60–61, 246, 254,
    282
  see also History
Community development, 76, 326
  in cities, 206, 212, 266–267
Community services, 10, 82–84, 100–
    101, 102, 119
  in national planning, 161, 162, 164
  problems of providing, 89, 103, 146–
    147, 159, 168, 208, 212, 214, 240,
    299, 314, 320, 342
  in slum-elimination programs, 209n.,
    333
  see also Education and Housing

355